AF251222

The Philosophical Challenge from China

The Philosophical Challenge from China

edited by Brian Bruya

The MIT Press
Cambridge, Massachusetts
London, England

© 2015 Massachusetts Institute of Technology

MIT Press books may be purchased at special quantity discounts for business or sales promotional use. For information, please email special_sales@mitpress.mit.edu.

Set in Stone Sans and Stone Serif by Toppan Best-set Premedia Limited. Printed and bound in the United States of America.

Library of Congress Cataloging-in-Publication Data

The philosophical challenge from China / edited by Brian Bruya.
  pages cm
Includes bibliographical references and index.
ISBN 978-0-262-02843-1 (hardcover : alk. paper)
1. Philosophy, Chinese. I. Bruya, Brian, 1966–
B5230.P45 2015
181'.11—dc23
2014025223

10 9 8 7 6 5 4 3 2 1

for Roger Ames, Eliot Deutsch, and Arindam Chakrabarti, in appreciation of their guidance, instruction, and lived examples in the field of comparative philosophy

Contents

Acknowledgments

Thanks, first, to all of the contributors to this volume for agreeing to be part of this project and tailoring their work to fit. I especially appreciate David Wong's encouragement. Thanks, as well, to Philip Laughlin at the MIT Press, who saw the value in this project from the start. Funding for the time I spent on this project was provided by Eastern Michigan University and by the Fulbright Program of the U.S. Bureau of Educational and Cultural Affairs. I'd like to thank the libraries of Eastern Michigan University, the University of Michigan, and National Taiwan University for their immense resources. Special thanks to my graduate students at National Taiwan University who read many of the chapters with me in class and provided useful feedback. Finally, tender thanks to Giorgio and Yuling for their love and support.

Pronunciation Guide

Chinese words in Roman transcription are often easy to pronounce simply by sounding them out, but some idiosyncratic uses of letters in transcription make some pronunciations less obvious. The guide below is designed to give a rough estimate of the proper pronunciation of sounds in contemporary Mandarin Chinese. (Pronunciations of the same terms in pre-modern times would have differed significantly.)

A number of the Mandarin sounds have no exact equivalents in English, and so the guide below is not technically precise. For technical precision one would use the International Phonetic Alphabet, but few people are proficient in it. (That includes the editor of this volume.) The guide below is intended to give "good enough" approximations. For example, we see j as the English pronunciation of the Chinese "zh," but we also see the letter j in the spellings of some Chinese words (e.g., *junzi*). There are two distinct sounds in Mandarin similar to the English j sound, one pronounced with the tongue toward the front of the mouth and the other with the tongue toward the back of the mouth. For the English j, the tongue falls between these two positions and is the closest we come to both Chinese sounds.

a   absent a subsequent vowel, read as the short o (ä) sound; e.g., *zhuang* is pronounced jwong and *fa* as in father

ai   like the pronoun I; e.g., *wai* rhymes with high

c   ts, as in sits; e.g., *ce* is pronounced tsuh

e   short u sound (e.g., *ren* is run, *ben* is bun), except after i and u, when it is pronounced as a short e (e.g., the e in *yue* is pronounced like the e in bet)

ei   ay; e.g., *wei* is pronounced way

i   appearing after ch, sh, or zh, pronounced ir (as in sir; e.g., *zhi* is pronounced jir); otherwise pronounced ee (e.g., *qi* is pronounced chee), except after c, s, and z, when it is silent (e.g., *ci* is pronounced ts) o   appearing alone between consonants, read as a long o; e.g., the o of *song* is pronounced like the o of so

ou   long o; e.g., *mou* is pronounced like the English mow

q   ch; e.g., *qi* is pronounced chee

ü   ew as in few; e.g., *lü* is pronounced lew, with the ew the same as in few

x   sh; e.g., *xiao* is pronounced shyow (rhymes with how)

z   dz; e.g., the *zi* appearing in *Laozi* and *Zhuangzi* is pronounced dz

zh   j; e.g., *zhi* is pronounced jir, and *zhou* is pronounced joe

Introduction: Chinese Philosophy as a Resource for Problems in Contemporary Philosophy

Brian Bruya

Genesis of the Book

Many years ago, as a graduate student attending a professional philosophy conference, I sat chatting with the chair of a philosophy department who said he was trying to build a "top ten" PhD program. Coming from a thoroughly comparative program that had multiple experts in Asian traditions, and in my youthful naiveté, I assumed that this prospective "top ten" department would surely include a Chinese specialist and asked him whom his department had hired in that field. He did his best to suppress a chuckle. With apparently genuine sincerity, he asked me how Chinese philosophy could help solve the problems that occupy current philosophers. I wasn't sure that philosophy was best understood as a problem-solving discipline, but it seemed obvious to me at the time (and still does today) that Chinese philosophy had plenty to say about problems that occupy current philosophers.

At just about the same time (1999), after a series of conferences spanning five years and engaging philosophers, sociologists, political scientists, and activists, Joanne Bauer and Daniel Bell published *The East Asian Challenge for Human Rights*, the first book that forcefully challenged Western assumptions from the strength of East Asian theoretical arguments on an issue of widely recognized philosophical importance. As a result, it is difficult now for rights theorists to engage the topic without recognizing the importance of non-Western viewpoints. I could have recommended that book to the above-mentioned department chair as one that explicitly brought Chinese theory to bear on a current problem in philosophy.

A few years later—in 2003—Thomas Metzinger published a landmark book, *Being No One*, in which he marshaled analytical argument and cognitive scientific evidence for his claim that there is no such thing as a persistent self. This book also would speak to the chair's question, not from a specifically Chinese perspective but from a broadly Buddhist perspective; and not because it explicitly brought Buddhist theory to bear on current problems in philosophy but because it did so implicitly.[1]

The two books I have mentioned represent the extremes of a new movement in which non-Western viewpoints and theories are gradually infiltrating current controversies in philosophy. In Bauer and Bell's book, rationales are explicitly announced as originating from East Asian contexts; in Metzinger's, a traditional Asian position is propounded but Asian influence is not announced. What is common to both cases is that the immense resources of non-Western philosophy are being brought to bear on current problems in philosophy.[2]

Over the last decade a number of monographs and articles have appeared that marshal specifically Chinese resources and apply them, entirely or in part, to current problems in philosophy. Stephen Angle's *Sagehood* and Karyn Lai's *Learning from Chinese Philosophies* stand out for their comprehensive approach to clarifying issues in Chinese philosophy and then applying them to issues that have been raised by prominent contemporary philosophers. Journal articles by David Wong, Julia Tao, and others expound Chinese or Chinese-influenced positions to advance issues in political and moral philosophy.[3] What is most encouraging is that mainstream publishers and journals are increasingly open to the possibility of publishing such works. See, for instance, Hagop Sarkissian's article "Minor Tweaks and Major Payoffs" in *Philosopher's Imprint* (a major online journal published by the University of Michigan) and Edward Slingerland's recent article in *Ethics*, "The Situationist Critique and Early Confucian Virtue Ethics."

However, there is still an enormous gap between what the Chinese tradition can offer and what is actually present in mainstream philosophical literature. Some recent books have begun to address this gap, among them Kam-por Yu, Julia Tao, and Philip Ivanhoe's *Taking Confucian Ethics Seriously*, Bo Mou's anthologies on analytic philosophy and Chinese philosophy, and Joel Kupperman's *Learning from Asian Philosophy*. Yet no book has focused exclusively on the expansive Chinese tradition with the intention of applying exclusively Chinese arguments and concepts to current issues in philosophy. *The Philosophical Challenge from China* is intended to highlight and foster this movement of the East-to-West flow of philosophical insights, focusing on Chinese contributions to current issues in philosophy.

The Crisis

Just a few years ago, the American Philosophical Association's *Newsletter on Asian and Asian-American Philosophy* published a densely printed 21-page red alert about the deplorable lack of Chinese philosophy in American graduate programs in philosophy.[4] In the report, Stephen Angle addresses the loss of Chinese philosophy from the philosophy departments of Stanford University, the University of California at Berkeley, and the University of Michigan.[5] Roger Ames notes the contrary growth in openings in Chinese philosophy in undergraduate philosophy programs.[6] Bryan Van

Norden traces the lack of sinology in philosophy PhD programs to ignorance, inertia, and "chauvinistic ethnocentrism" in the programs.[7] Justin Tiwald goes on to make a case for Chinese philosophy in the larger discipline. He notes that, statistically, a minor Western philosopher such as Anselm garners more attention in PhD programs than the entire Chinese tradition combined, though he concedes that perhaps "we could do more to make our research accessible to others."[8] Manyul Im notes the departure of several major Chinese philosophers to Hong Kong.[9] Donald Munro emphasizes that sinological philosophers must address large humanistic concerns and not focus only on narrow controversies.[10] "Genuine consolidated change will take place," David Wong concludes, "when philosophy departments recognize the value of Chinese philosophy and directly seek positions in that field without the aid of joint appointments. Realistically, this will come about when some of those who do Chinese philosophy can do so in a manner that speaks to Anglophone philosophy … and when Anglophone philosophy reciprocally widens its receptiveness to different approaches."[11]

The rationale for the present volume is consistent with the above observations. There is a scandalous dearth of sinology in mainstream philosophy. For some 2,500 years, China's best minds have been engaged in studying the human condition, and yet their results are almost entirely ignored by mainstream philosophers and philosophy programs. This volume is intended to take a step toward remedying that situation by directing sinological resources to current controversies in analytic philosophy, or, as Wong puts it, to do Chinese philosophy in a manner that speaks to Anglophone philosophy.

The Model

Contributions to this volume were solicited with a particular model in mind: a contribution appropriate to this volume would, first of all, treat a topic that would be recognizable to a philosopher working in one of the many subfields of analytic philosophy. Second, it would be a model of clarity and precision, clearly defining terms, locating positions in current and/or historic literature (Eastern and/or Western), and articulating well-drawn arguments without engaging in unfounded speculation. Third, it would advance the current discussion—something that could be accomplished in a number of ways, among them supporting a minority view with a persuasive new argument, contradicting a prominent position, and problematizing a position or an issue and thereby demonstrating that the issue has a significant dimension that has been neglected or that a distinction is not as clear-cut as has generally been assumed.

This model for contributions to the volume does not require explicit reference to Chinese sources, even though the main ideas must include the Chinese tradition at minimum as an inspirational resource. The purpose of the volume is not to persuade current philosophers to take up study of the Classical Chinese language. Rather, it is to show that serious engagement with Chinese philosophy can yield insights that can contribute to advances for current controversies in philosophy. Similarly, the model does not value Chinese philosophy over any other tradition. Although the title of the volume is *The Philosophical Challenge from China*, the intention is not to demonstrate that Chinese philosophy is superior to current analytic philosophy; rather, it is to demonstrate that, without insights from Chinese philosophy, analytic philosophy is significantly impoverished.

Finally, according to the model for contributions, the general direction of the transfer of philosophical insight is from East to West. For many decades now, philosophically concerned sinologists have been injecting the wealth of Western philosophical insights into Chinese philosophy. This volume is intended to reverse the flow, injecting Chinese insights into current analytic philosophy.

Consistent with this model, the chapters in this volume generally have three main characteristics: targeting an untenable position in current or traditional Western philosophy, taking the Chinese tradition as an intellectual resource, and considering the prospects of the issue in light of what the Chinese tradition brings to bear on it. Some of the chapters focus more, and some less, on these characteristics individually.

The Fundamentalist

A committed proponent of Chinese philosophy may take exception to the arrangement of this volume's table of contents, in which chapters are grouped by traditional Western philosophical categories—after all, should not the hegemony of these categories be challenged as well? In an ideal world, yes. I don't, however, have a missionary's fundamentalist zeal. In this particular circumstance, the categories in the table of contents serve two purposes: they set the stage in a way that will be familiar to mainstream philosophers while also demonstrating the range of topics in the volume. They could also have been arranged by the time period of the Chinese resources from which they draw or by Chinese sub-tradition.

But a Chinese fundamentalist may take the criticism a step further and attack the book as an exercise in the assimilation of Chinese philosophy to Western concerns. Further, lifting ideas out of their original contexts and using them as resources in foreign controversies may be viewed as either bastardization or intellectual colonization of the Chinese tradition. In response, first let it be said that the book is a reflection of an existing trend, not a manifesto. Second, my view of philosophy is that it is a joint enterprise that crosses boundaries of time and tradition. We are working on human issues, not Western or Chinese issues. Thus, where we get our ideas should not matter as much as how we put them to use. It is true that, insofar as the topics are resonant with current analytic tradition, they are Western; however, it should be noticed that many, if not all, of the chapters attempt to shift the direction of the conversation rather than simply take a step in some predetermined direction.

Precedents

It is a legitimate worry that some important elements of the Chinese tradition may be lost if they are taken out of context. This is a perennial problem in comparative philosophy. What is new in this volume is that the contributors generally attempt to play down the contextual origins of the ideas. That is not the same as ignoring the original contexts. The contributors explain the ideas to the extent necessary to make their point, and refer the reader to other literature for more complete treatments. Thus, the ideas are not handled in a context-free way; they are simply handled in a way that exploits the inherent plasticity of all ideas. To argue from analogy, traditional Chinese hauling practices differed from traditional European hauling practices, in particular with reference to the conveyances and the kinds of things hauled. However, when efficient horse harnesses made their way from China to Europe,[12] it is safe to say that no one objected that they should not be used on the ground that they had come from a different context. The same goes for the many other Chinese inventions—the seed drill,[13] the printing press,[14] the fishing reel, playing cards,[15] the compass, gunpowder, porcelain, the metal stirrup, and so on.[16] Chinese ideas were adapted to their new contexts. Just as these ideas changed the course of European history, there is no reason that more abstract ideas cannot also make contributions. Some already have.

Consider paper money, which is more an idea than a material good. The idea is that a bank, issuing a note, proclaims that it is worth a certain amount in exchange, and that amount then becomes the initial standard for that note. No coins or precious metals need exchange hands; the note represents worth, but only among those who accept its representation of worth. This idea originated in China around the beginning of the ninth century, and the first true bank notes were issued by a government currency reserve bank in 1023. In the thirteenth century, European travelers transmitted the idea to Europe, and today paper money is an indispensible part of life.[17]

Now consider another fundamental economic concept. It is well documented that the idea of laissez-faire economic practices, so strongly associated with Adam Smith's idea of the invisible hand of the market, originated to a significant degree in Smith's time in France, when he was exposed to the predominant economic theories of the French Physiocrats. Less well known is that the leading Physiocrat, Francois Quesnay, as part of the Enlightenment trend that glorified the Chinese model of governing, was inspired by Europeans travelers' writings on China. Such works described an enormous agrarian country—as big as all the countries of Europe combined—that was governed by a single leader in a remote corner of the country. The Chinese emperor's effectiveness was attributed to his hands-off approach, in which laws were created and then let work on their own, without continuous governmental interference. Quesnay, known as the "Confucius of Europe," found inspiration not only in the writings of travelers but also in the early philosophical texts of the Chinese tradition.[18] *Laissez-faire* is a French translation of the Chinese term *wu wei* 無為, and it was Quesnay who coined the phrase *laissez-faire, laissez passer*.[19]

And consider another fundamentally modern concept, not exactly economic but inseparable from modern economics. It was in the time of Quesnay that another term was coined, meant pejoratively, by one of Quesnay's followers: *bureaucratie*.[20] Anticipating arguments still in circulation today, the Physiocrats saw a natural tension between a free market and the intrusion of government bureaucrats (those who govern from their desks). What the Physiocrats didn't realize (or accept), while other Europeans did, was that the relatively smooth functioning of imperial China was due to its far-reaching and deeply entrenched system of civil service.[21] As the idea of a meritocratic system of civil servants gradually infiltrated European states, the awarding of government offices shifted from patronage and hereditary arrangements to systems of competence. The notion of meritocratic government advancement can be traced all the back to the time of Confucius (551?–479? BCE). Over many centuries, a stable system of professional bureaucrats—mandarins—was created and developed. Thus, it is safe to say that two of the signal achievements of current Western society—free-market economics and professional bureaucracies—are not entirely Western, and owe their genesis in part to ideas transmitted from China.

One doesn't want to exaggerate the influence of China on the West (related ideas were not unknown in earlier Western periods) or romanticize China's own achievements (its government and its economic system were far from perfect), but it cannot be denied that significant inspiration for the great intellectual ferment of the Enlightenment can be traced to the Chinese philosophical tradition. Further, paper money, laissez-faire, and a meritocratic civil service are examples of ideas from China that have found a home in our contemporary intellectual milieu. But they are not the only worthwhile ideas to have come from the Chinese confrontation with the human condition. This book attempts to bring to light several more ideas from that vast tradition that are relevant to current philosophical conversations.

The Chapters

Moral Psychology

Moral psychology, a popular subfield of contemporary philosophy, requires not only a background in moral and ethical theory but also a command of the relevant literatures of psychology and cognitive science. We begin with Confucius, who flourished about 500 BCE. Hagop Sarkissian considers arguments for and against giving the benefit of the doubt. He finds in Confucius a highly contextualized account of human behavior—an account that steers us away from immediately attributing blame to an individual for moral missteps and toward looking closely at possible contributing factors. One of the contributing factors may be one's own role in the situation. From multiple examples of subtle behavioral interactions in the *Analects* of Confucius, Sarkissian moves on to relevant psychological literature, demonstrating a deep-seated asymmetry between how we explain our own behavior and how we explain the behavior of others. We tend to excuse ourselves on the basis of external exigencies and to see others as possessing personal defects. Sarkissian proceeds to consider winning strategies in the Prisoners' Dilemma game, one of which is to forgive the initial missteps of others. Drawing on the results of psychological studies and game theory that he uses to support Confucian theory, Sarkissian concludes that we generally (but not always) have good reason to give the benefit of the doubt in ambiguous situations of normative transgression and that this conclusion can be assimilated into one's own behavior through self-reflection.

A strength of the Chinese tradition becomes obvious when we notice that the Chinese did not posit a false dichotomy between the body and the mind. David Wong capitalizes on Chinese mind-body unity in his chapter, exploring the interrelationship of reflection, emotion, and motivation in moral development. Wong analyzes the notion of compassion in Mencius (fourth century BCE), noting three major components—cognitive, emotional, and motivational—and then, not content to take Mencius' word for it, supports his analysis of compassion using studies from current psychological literature. With an accurate descriptive assessment of the basic aspects of compassion, Wong goes on to examine how these aspects may be developed over a person's life span, again exploiting Mencian theory buttressed by psychological literature. Finally, Wong considers the limitations of Mencius' theory and suggests how it may be amended. Like the other authors in part I, Wong has particular strengths in working with the current philosophical and psychological literature, and he draws inspiration from ancient Chinese texts.

A growing body of evidence from cognitive psychology shows that theory of mind has distinct cognitive and affective aspects. Bongrae Seok, in his chapter, also takes us into Mencius' theory of developmental psychology, this time for a close examination of the Confucian ethic of care. Seok analyzes Mencius' implicit theory of the incipient nature of empathy, an emotion that is fundamental to a mature ethic of care. According to Seok's analysis, Mencius' notion of proto-empathy includes a sense of affective concern for the other but not necessarily a social cognitive theory of mind with regard to the other. To demonstrate that such a distinction is empirically feasible, Seok guides us through recent psychological literature on autism, theory of mind, and empathetic judgment. He concludes that passages in Mencius along with empirical studies enable us to conceive of empathy as possessing two dissociable components: an affective embodied component and a social cognitive component. Lacking the social component, one can still have an incipient form of empathy that, according to Mencius, acts as a developmental basis for ethical conduct.

Political Philosophy and Ethics

Tongdong Bai takes direct aim at liberal democracy, which is central to present-day Western political structures. Drawing on a wealth of statistical data, he demonstrates that liberal democracy's actual manifestations do not live up to its ideals. Jumping off from John Rawls' argument that liberal peoples must tolerate nonliberal but otherwise decent peoples, Bai constructs from Confucian political theory a more realistic political utopia that matches the practical ideals of liberal democracy better than current liberal democracies, despite jettisoning the foundational liberal principle of one person, one vote. The basis of Bai's Confucian alternative depends on the idea of meritocratic advancement—that is, the idea that those making decisions in the government should be those with demonstrated capacities to do so effectively.

Donald Munro, in his chapter, attacks another foundational belief of current theory: the widely accepted credo of equal human worth. After looking at its historical foundations, he exposes some of its deep flaws, one of which is the failure to take into account the common implicit belief that those closest to us deserve our attention more than others do. Drawing from Confucian theory, Munro builds an explicit theory on this implicit belief, articulating a rationale for the strong tendency to look after those closest to oneself. At the same time, Munro doesn't lose sight of the need for objectivity at the socio-political level and so posits a two-tiered system of norms. The idea that Munro imports from the Chinese tradition has two sides. On one side is the understanding, or acknowledgment, that humans are of limited malleability and have overriding tendencies of partiality toward kin and close acquaintances. The flip side of this limitation is that these tendencies can be cultivated and exploited in pro-social ways (as we also see in David Wong's chapter). Munro calls his synthetic view *two-level consequentialism*.

Stephen Angle focuses on the tension between acting according to general laws of the socio-political realm and particular norms of the ethical sphere. We see this tension in various recent interpretations of Aristotle, some of which claim that he took politics as primary and some of which claim that he took ethics as primary. By drawing on the work of Mou Zongsan, a major twentieth-century Chinese philosopher, Angle introduces the idea of self-restriction into the conversation. Self-restriction, he says, becomes a requirement when we realize that the political realm is a necessary extension of the ethical, and that the only way to eventually attain the ultimate ethical ideal of extending our ethical actions over the broadest domain possible is to restrict ourselves to the limits of the law. Insofar as this tension persists in the virtue ethics of both Aristotle and Hume and extends to their present-day heirs, Mou Zongsan's ideal of self-restriction can begin a conversation that may lead toward a theoretical reconciliation between the demands of the two conflicting realms.

In his chapter, Kwong-loi Shun moves from ethical self-restriction to ethical self-commitment, an idea that Shun synthesizes from a web of related concepts in the long Confucian tradition. Ethical self-commitment, on Shun's account, is an agent's devotion to ethical standards despite personal interest to the contrary, the falling below which would amount to a kind of ethical (as opposed to social) disgrace. That there is the potential to fall to a level of low regard in terms of one's ethical agency implies that one begins from a level of relatively high regard for one's ethical agency. Ethical self-commitment thus implies ethical self-esteem, or self-respect, which Shun ties into current discussions around self-respect as it relates to ethical/moral agency. According to Shun, the distinctive way in which Confucians articulate the concepts of ethical self-commitment relies on the ability of an ethical agent to transcend one's immediate circumstances to attain a state of reflective equanimity. While one is thoroughly engaged in the vagaries of the ethical life, one is able to ignore counterproductive influences by maintaining an awareness of one's commitment to the ethical path. The imperative to accomplish reflective equanimity implies not just a rational commitment to the ethical path broadly but also a rational commitment to the active cultivation of one's own inner sphere—to developing "purity of the mind." However, to bring the focus of one's ethical endeavors back to one's own well-being is to risk becoming mired in self-indulgence. Shun engages the current literature on the topic of moral self-indulgence, concluding that the Confucian view of ethical self-commitment side-steps objections of self-indulgence in the sense that self-reflection plays a constraining role in one's ethical path rather than a motivating role. This distinctive way of construing ethical agency has many implications for other theories in current literature about the limits of ethical or moral agency and the possibility of overcoming some of those limits.

Owen Flanagan and Steven Geisz shift our attention away from explicit ethical theory to its meta-ethical foundations in China and in the West. In their chapter, they ask the reader to consider the fundamental sources of morality and the fundamental rationales for it. Flanagan and Geisz conclude that the traditional Chinese sources and rationales are more favorable to harmonious social order than the traditional Judeo-Christian sources and rationales. And those who wish to move beyond a religious, Abrahamic worldview need not move beyond Confucianism, owing to its naturalistic tendencies. In contrast to the monotheistic pitfalls of heresy, blasphemy, and apostasy in the face of an all-powerful spirit-being, the basis of moral decision making in the Confucian tradition lies with the agent who is bound up closely with other moral agents and who, via a web of ritual and ceremonial acts and activities, works toward a harmonious community rather than a netherworld reward. Because there is no ultimate judge of ethical action, there is a practical imperative toward tolerance.

Metaphysics and Epistemology

Chinese philosophy is best known for its sophisticated ethical and socio-political theories. Less well known and less explored are its metaphysics and its epistemology. Oneness has become a topic of inquiry in the field of psychology with respect to the notion of altruism: do apparently altruistic acts actually involve a kind of self-centeredness in which the agent feels connected in a unifying way to the recipient of the act? And yet the concept of oneness has, itself, not received sufficient elucidation. In his chapter, Philip Ivanhoe, drawing substantially from the Neo-Confucian tradition (and its influences from Daoism and Buddhism), isolates five distinct varieties of oneness, settling on a complex Neo-Confucian type that, he argues, can function as a more robust alternative to the empathy-altruism hypothesis in current moral psychology. In this way, Ivanhoe helps us make better sense of the selfish/selfless dichotomy that altruism theory presents.

Taking a different approach to interconnectedness, Brook Ziporyn draws on the extensive literature of Chinese Buddhism in order to expose and explain an important limitation of a foundational presupposition in current and traditional Western philosophy: the law of non-contradiction. It is difficult, even in informal conversation, to communicate without taking the law of non-contradiction (LNC) as granted, but the very granting of it has important epistemological and metaphysical implications that are rarely considered. Drawing on the Tiantai school of Chinese Buddhism, Ziporyn demonstrates that the LNC ("the same proposition cannot be true and false in the same sense") implies a necessary commitment to an essentialist ontology that there are real, discrete things designated by discrete concepts or terms. Ziporyn sees a necessary circularity in any attempt to distinguish one "sense" from another when attempting to avoid a contradiction, the two processes (determining what is and is not contradictory and determining which senses we use to interpret terms) become mutually entailing. The best, but not the only, ontological position, he says, is the Tiantai one of viewing all things as interpenetrating and all meanings as intersubsumptive. With the LNC door thrown open, one thing is for sure: the epistemological distance between provisional truth and actual truth creates pathways for the development of novel ontologies and concomitant epistemologies.

Stephen Hetherington and Karyn Lai, in their chapter, look closely at the idea of implicit knowledge in early Chinese philosophy and find a distinction that helps us refine our understanding of the traditional dichotomy between *epistêmê* (knowledge that) and *technê* (knowledge how, know-how). By examining the arguments of an early Chinese text that attempts to integrate diverse ideas of the time, Hetherington and Lai discover an epistemic gap between know-how and its successful execution—which is to say that just because one knows how to do something in general does not mean that one has the knowledge to execute it in every specific situation, even if circumstances are conducive to its execution. Excluding both external and internal obstacles, Hetherington and Lai posit an epistemology of *know-to*, the transient and situation-specific ability to deploy know-how, identifying four particular items that contribute to knowing-to: anticipating outcomes, acting in a timely manner, attentiveness to relevant contextual cues, and understanding what is important. This enrichment of our epistemology of know-how is the beginning of a potentially much larger conversation.

Exploring the relationship between epistemology and metaphysics, Bo Mou, in his chapter, looks at the limits of Quine's naturalized epistemology. Mou builds on the work of the liberal naturalists to highlight the tension between Quine's explicit claim that "science is the highest path to truth" and his view that the nature of knowing is "utterly dependent on context." To reconcile these seemingly incompatible views, Mou adverts to the complex epistemology of the Daoist philosopher Zhuangzi (fourth century BCE), in concert with Mou's own novel theory of comparative philosophical interpretation. The solution, according to Mou, is to embrace a well-articulated perspectivism that allows for the preservation of a scientific point of view within a broader, comprehensive naturalist epistemology that embraces multiple forms of truth-pursuit. This new, "transcendental" naturalism is transcendent not in the sense of going beyond nature but in the sense of going beyond a single realm of inquiry, transcending limited perspectives and aiming toward a unifying naturalized epistemology.

Working with sources from contemporary psychology, Brian Bruya attempts to expand the discussion in action theory, shifting from the problematic of compatibilism (which strives to account for the feeling of free will in the face of a determined universe and by virtue of which precludes natural human action) toward a problematic of accounting for human action that is fundamentally unified with natural movement, independent of the vocabulary of "determinism" and "free will." Drawing implicit inspiration from Daoist accounts of action, Bruya moves away from a strictly deterministic framework to the well-documented notion of self-organization as an explanatory framework for motion in nature broadly. As self-organized systems, humans move, and this kind of movement is of the same order as many other forms of motion in nature. The goal, for Bruya, is to isolate a kind of human action that is an undeniable example of action while also exhibiting the hallmarks of self-organized motion—that is, absent any characteristics that would seem to easily separate it from nature, any sense of agency, such as intention, volition, or self-consciousness. Bruya finds his target in the psychological literature of autotelic experience. Like many of the other ideas in this volume, the very notion of action without agency challenges the boundaries of our usual philosophical vocabulary.

Advances

Let us return to our initial question: How can Chinese philosophy help solve some of the problems that occupy current philosophers? It would be presumptuous, even ludicrous, to suggest that Chinese philosophy is a panacea that can put to rest, once and for all, *any* current controversies in philosophy. What Chinese philosophy can do is give us new perspectives on long-standing and current concepts and issues in philosophy. To make this claim more concrete, we can distill a list of potentially insightful ideas from the above summaries (limiting ourselves to one idea from each chapter):

- compassion as a developmental virtue
- justification for giving the benefit of the doubt
- proto-empathy
- meritocratic Confucian democracy
- unequal human worth
- self-restriction
- ethical self-commitment
- meta-ethical naturalism
- the oneness hypothesis
- intersubsumptive epistemology
- know-to
- perspectivist naturalist epistemology
- action without agency

The chapters in this volume challenge positions current in the philosophical literature and offer well-argued alternatives that, implicitly or explicitly, are derived from the Chinese tradition. It will be up to the reader to judge how successful these arguments are. Even if we grant the limitations of any particular chapter, collectively the chapters demonstrate that the broader enterprise of philosophy will be better off when we open the conversation to contributions from the Chinese tradition.

And so, to the chair of that aspirational top-ten philosophy department, the chapters of this book are a sample of what Chinese philosophy has to say to the problems that occupy current philosophers.

Editorial Concerns

Editorially, a few further characteristics of this volume are worth noting. The first is that the contributions cover a vast span of time, from the very beginnings of the Chinese tradition right up to the twentieth century, and cover the three main strands of Chinese thought: Confucianism, Daoism, and Buddhism. We see reference to works in the early period (c. 500 BCE–220 CE), the medieval period (220–c. 960), and the

Neo-Confucian period (c. 960–c. 1919). No chapter requires of the reader a significant level of familiarity with or expertise in the historical or conceptual details of the Chinese tradition. The authors have taken pains to explain their ideas in as full a way as possible while keeping contextual details to a minimum.

The prospect of decontextualization brings us to a larger editorial question that also has a significant philosophical component: Exactly what is happening when the Chinese and Western traditions are brought together in this way? There has been a strong tendency in modern scholarship on Chinese philosophy to view Chinese philosophy through the lens of Western philosophy. Earlier in this introduction, I acknowledged the potential criticism that this book, by attempting to insert Chinese insights into current controversies, is assimilating the Chinese tradition to Western concerns. As I pointed out in the chapter summaries, however, the introduction of Chinese ideas to current discussions challenges the very conceptual boundaries that constrain and guide the dialogue. Thus, we can construe the process not as the assimilation of one tradition to another but as the mutual development and transformation of both.

Another possible criticism hinges on the very possibility of conceptual commensurability across traditions. How tractable, for instance, is the Confucian concept of *ren*, or the Daoist concept of *dao*, to analysis or deployment in a non-Sinitic semantic web? This question deserves serious consideration and should not be blithely minimized or ignored. The working assumption for this volume, and I believe for many scholars working in comparative philosophy, is that, just as understanding what Plato meant by *eidos* requires a significant level of scholarly acumen and hermeneutic care, understanding what Confucius meant by *ren* requires a similar level of acumen and care. For examples of how this process is carried out, I refer the reader to some of the major journals of comparative philosophy—for example, *Philosophy East and West* and *Dao: A Journal of Comparative Philosophy*. One can judge for oneself whether such work is generally successful. If one's conclusion is that it is not successful because it is simply not possible, then one must consider where we must draw the line. At what point does another person's conceptual framework become incompatible with our current framework? The demarcation of any such boundary would, of course, be arbitrary, because the frameworks do not have well-delineated boundaries. I may have as much difficulty understanding an argument made by a conservative politician from the American South, or by a teenager in my own household, as I have understanding one made by a Han-dynasty Confucian.

Thus, owing to many combined decades of practice in the field of comparative philosophy, this volume takes as granted the possibility of making sense of Chinese philosophical concepts and applying them to current issues in philosophy. Some of these concepts receive more explanation than others. Kwong-loi Shun, for example, takes great care not to inadvertently import Western concepts into his examination of Chinese ethics, elucidating each term from its Chinese context. To gain a complete understanding of his position one should read his full-length monographs, but it is possible to get a working understanding of his position by reading the abbreviated explanation in this volume. Much the same can be said for the other chapters.

The question of how to treat Chinese technical terminology in a volume such as this is not trivial. Like the Greek terms *logos* and *eidos*, there are a handful of Chinese terms that have no satisfactory approximation in present-day English. Furthermore, with so many authors working from so many different periods across different schools of thought, terms that may have distinct meanings in one work or period may mean something different in another. The best solution for these complex terms is to keep them in transliterated form (e.g., *ren* and *dao*) while allowing each contributor to express the most appropriate meaning in parenthetical translation for that context. In this way, one can access the particular usage of terms in context while remaining free to compare terminology outside the constraints of any single chapter.

When a Chinese term with a complex meaning appears more than once in a chapter, a parenthetic translation is given on its first appearance in each section until repetition makes it clear on its own. The following is a brief glossary of some of the terms in this volume that are left transliterated. Others are explained fully within individual chapters.

Dao 道. Generally understood as a cosmological or metaphysical term referring to the natural order of things. It is often rendered as "way" because in the early Confucian tradition it had salient moral overtones. Virtually all Chinese schools of thought, whether construing it morally or not, understood it as shorthand for the normatively best way of getting on in the world. Each school of thought had its own *dao*.

Li 禮. Ritual, propriety, or ceremony, and the behavior that originate in it. Chinese culture, from very early times, was highly organized and stratified, and both explicit and implicit standards of what behavior was proper to one's relational status proliferated. Some philosophical schools, especially Confucian ones, emphasized the necessity and relevance of *li* as a means for maintaining good order; other schools downplayed it or openly attacked it. At its best, it was understood as an efficient vehicle for channeling normal human emotion.

Li 理. A cosmological or metaphysical term denoting the inherent and dynamic patterns of the universe that allow human beings to comprehend all things (including human behavior) in a tractable way. This term comes to prominence in the Neo-Confucian period (after the florescence of Buddhism), in response to Buddhist metaphysics. It has moral overtones in the sense that nature was understood as inherently good, and it was the goal of later Confucian philosophers to plumb the depths of the *li* of all individual categories of things as a way of understanding them and then of acting in a way that accorded with the proper order of things. Often rendered stiffly as "principle," it can also be understood as "category," "pattern," or "coherence."

Qi 氣. Started out in very early times as a term that can be understood as loosely equivalent to the Greek *pneuma*—the breath of life—but by extension referred to any gaseous entity, including both air and spirits. Retaining a sense of vitality, it gradually came, still in the early period, to have dual meanings—a positive meaning in the realm of medicine as the vital circulatory force in people, and a neutral cosmological meaning as the underlying substance of all material things, with both material and energetic connotations. This cosmological sense later acquired negative normative connotations as Neo-Confucians construed it in contradistinction to *li* (principles/ patterns/coherences), and as such, it came to connote a heaviness or darkness that blocked or obscured *li* inherent in things (including in the human heart/mind).

Ren 仁. Behavior that exhibits kindness toward others. Confucians understood it as the highest form of behavior toward others, often with reference to hierarchical directedness from higher to lower. The closest English equivalent is probably "benevolent," as it is often rendered, but rather than just describing altruistic acts as distinct from selfish acts, it also denotes a feeling of affection and an achieved virtue. It is a term generally reserved for the accomplished moral exemplar, a level of moral conduct aspired to by all Confucians.

Tian 天. Originally an anthropomorphized understanding of the vastly creative and normatively good powers of the heavens, in contradistinction to an even earlier notion of an even more clearly anthropomorphized pre-eminent god (*Shang Di* 上帝). Only vaguely theorized, *tian* was understood as having intentions and the power to achieve them in indirect ways but few other human-like characteristics. Often paired with "earth (*di* 地)," it took on connotations of nature broadly speaking. Depending on the philosopher and text, the connotations can tend more toward the divine (e.g., Confucius) or toward the natural (e.g., Xunzi [third century BCE]), though more than likely it usually bears at least a little of both. It should never be confused with the highly anthropomorphized creator god found in the Abrahamic traditions, as one who stands separate from all of creation.

Xin 心. While this term is not necessarily left in transliteration, it is worth mentioning that whenever the terms "heart" and "mind" appear in this volume in reference to a Chinese philosophical context, the senses of both terms are implied. The Chinese term *xin* in its most basic sense refers to the corporeal heart, but since the heart was understood as the seat of both feeling and intellect, *xin* always implies both affective and cognitive properties. And, as more than one of the contributors to this volume explains, it also implies conative, or motivational, properties.

Yi 義. The right thing to do. Different emphases are applied to this term by different philosophers. For some, acting from *yi* is set opposite to acting from personal gain. For others, it has a more legalistic sense of acting according to established standards.

For yet others, it is closely associated with ritual behavior. It has often been rendered as "righteousness." It is one of the fundamental Confucian virtues, along with *ren* and *li* (ritual propriety).

Notes

1. Metzinger's basic thesis in *Being No One* is that "no such things as selves exist in the world" (626), a point that he ultimately characterizes as trivial. The more interesting idea, he says, and one that resonates with the struggles of Buddhist philosophers historically to come to terms with the basic thesis, involves "an attitude of research that integrates first-person and third-person approaches in a … way … that … appears to be strictly impossible and absolutely necessary at the same time … . [It involves] the serious and sustained theoretical effort of *thinking* the unthinkable but also the ideal of phenomenally *living* it" (626–627). This leads to his final thesis, that when one realizes that "there is no one *whose* illusion the conscious self could be, … a new dimension opens. At least in principle, one can wake up from one's biological history … elevating her self-conversation to a new level" (634). Although Metzinger does not advance explicitly Buddhist justifications, the Buddhist resonances are obvious, and one could make a case that his decades' long practice of an Eastern form of meditation strongly suggests the possibility of some such Eastern influence. He does refer explicitly to Buddhist enlightenment, rechristening it "system consciousness" (566) and uses language reminiscent of Buddhism. For instance, he says that normal phenomenal consciousness "is a special kind of darkness" (632) from which we must "wake up" (634) and that the next big project for humans is a kind of "emancipation" from the objective processes that created it (633). He exhorts us to go beyond what Mother Nature has left us and take "responsibility for the future development of our own conscious minds" (633). For more on Metzinger, mind, and meditation, see his *Ego Tunnel*, where he recommends meditation instruction in public schools as the new "neuropedagogy" so that we "introduce our children to those states of consciousness we believe to be valuable and teach them how to access and cultivate them at an early age" (332). See also Ronald Engert, "Meditation und Wissenschaft" and Stefan Klein, "Das rätselhafte Ich." For the earliest Buddhist arguments, see *Saṃyutta Nikāya* 22.59, 12.61, and 12.2; for a somewhat later version, see the *Milindapañha*. For a capsule of basic Buddhist texts and explanations of basic Buddhist ideas, see Rahula Walpola, *What the Buddha Taught*.

2. Because my expertise and interests are more aligned with analytic topics, style, orientations, and sources, and because there remains a fairly large gulf between these and the topics, style, orientations, and sources of Continental philosophy, I elected to focus this book on engaging the analytic tradition. I have no doubt that a similar book could also be addressed to current concerns in Continental philosophy.

3. See David Wong, *Natural Moralities*, "Emotion and the Cognition of Reasons in Moral Motivation," and "Moral Reasons: Internal and External." Also see Julia Tao, "The Chinese Moral Ethos and the Concept of Individual Rights," "Dignity in Long-Term Care for Older Persons: A Confucian Perspective," and "Beyond Proceduralism: A Chinese Perspective on *Cheng* (Sincerity) as a Political Virtue."

4. Amy Olberding, ed., *Newsletter on Asian and Asian-American Philosophers and Philosophies.*

5. Stephen C. Angle, "Does Michigan Matter?"

6. Roger T. Ames, "A State-of-the-Art Reflection on Chinese Philosophy."

7. Bryan W. Van Norden, "Three Questions about the Crisis in Chinese Philosophy," 4.

8. Justin Tiwald, "A Case for Chinese Philosophy," 7.

9. Manyul Im, "Taking Stock."

10. "Professor Donald Munro on the State of Chinese Philosophy."

11. David Wong, "The State of Chinese Philosophy in the U.S.," 13–14.

12. Colin A. Ronan, *The Shorter Science and Civilization in China*, volume 4, 201–219.

13. Francesca Bray, *Science and Civilization in China*, volume 6, part 2, 54–273.

14. Tsuen-hsuin Tsien, *Science and Civilization in China*, volume 5, part 1, 132–383.

15. John Temple, *The Genius of China*, 88–89 and 116–117.

16. Arnold Pacey, *Technology in World Civilization*, 21–22.

17. Niv Horesh, *Chinese Money in Global Context*, 44–56.

18. Christian Gerlach, *Wu-Wei in Europe.*

19. J. J. Clarke, *Oriental Enlightenment*, 50. Liana Vardi says that Nicolas Baudeau (one of Quesnay's main followers) coined the term and that Pierre Du Pont (another of Quesnay's main followers) popularized it (*The Physiocrats and the World of the Enlightenment*, 7, n. 10). See also Wei-Bin Zhang, *Adam Smith and Confucius.*

20. G. Duncan Mitchell, ed., *A New Dictionary of the Social Sciences*, s.v. "Bureaucracy."

21. This isn't to say that Quesnay did not appreciate meritocracy. In fact, he lauded China's meritocratic educational system.

Works Cited

Ames, Roger T. "A State-of-the-Art Reflection on Chinese Philosophy." *Newsletter on Asian and Asian-American Philosophers and Philosophies* 8, no. 1 (2008): 3.

Angle, Stephen C. "Does Michigan Matter?" *Newsletter on Asian and Asian-American Philosophers and Philosophies* 8, no. 1 (2008): 2–3.

Angle, Stephen C. *Sagehood: The Contemporary Significance of Neo-Confucian Philosophy*. Oxford University Press, 2009.

Bauer, Joanne R., and Daniel A. Bell. *The East Asian Challenge for Human Rights*. Cambridge University Press, 1999.

Bray, Francesca. *Science and Civilization in China*, volume 6, part 2: *Agriculture*. Cambridge University Press, 1984.

Clark, J. J. *Oriental Enlightenment: The Encounter between Asian and Western Thought*. Routledge, 1997.

Engert, Ronald. "Meditation und Wissenschaft." In Engert's Logbuch (http://ronaldengert.com/tag/prof-dr-thomas-metzinger).

Gerlach, Christian. *Wu-Wei in Europe: A Study of Eurasian Economic Thought*. Working Papers on the Global Economic History Network. Department of Economic History, London School of Economics and Political Science, 2005.

Horesh, Niv. *Chinese Money in a Global Context: Historic Junctures Between 600 BCE and 2012*. Stanford University Press, 2014.

Im, Manyul. "Taking Stock: A State-of-the-Field Impression." *Newsletter on Asian and Asian-American Philosophers and Philosophies* 8, no. 1 (2008): 8–9.

Klein, Stefan. "Das rätselhafte Ich." *Zeit Online*, September 6, 2011 (http://www.zeit.de/2011/37/Interview-Metzinger/komplettansicht).

Kupperman, Joel. *Learning from Asian Philosophy*. Oxford University Press, 1999.

Lai, Karyn. *Learning from Chinese Philosophies: Ethics of Interdependent and Contextualised Self*. Ashgate, 2006.

Metzinger, Thomas. *Being No One: The Self-Model Theory of Subjectivity*. MIT Press, 2003.

Metzinger, Thomas. *The Ego Tunnel: The Science of the Mind and the Myth of the Self*. Basic Books, 2009.

Mitchell, G. Duncan, ed. *A New Dictionary of the Social Sciences*. Routledge and Kegan Paul, 1979.

Mou, Bo, ed. *Searle's Philosophy and Chinese Philosophy: Constructive Engagement*. Brill, 2008.

Mou, Bo, ed. *Two Roads to Wisdom? Chinese and Analytic Philosophical Traditions*. Open Court, 2001.

Munro, Donald J. "Professor Donald Munro on the State of Chinese Philosophy: Interviews with Cheung Chan-fai and Liu Xiaogan." *Newsletter on Asian and Asian-American Philosophers and Philosophies* 8, no. 1 (2008): 9–13.

Olberding, Amy, ed. *Newsletter on Asian and Asian-American Philosophers and Philosophies* 8, no. 1 (2008).

Pacey, Arnold. *Technology in World Civilization: A Thousand-Year History*. MIT Press, 1991.

Ronan, Colin A., and Joseph Needham. *The Shorter Science and Civilization in China*, volume 4. Cambridge University Press, 1994.

Sarkissian, Hagop. "Minor Tweaks, Major Payoffs: The Problems and Promise of Situationism in Moral Philosophy." *Philosophers' Imprint* 10, no. 9 (2010): 1–15.

Slingerland, Edward. "The Situationist Critique and Early Confucian Virtue Ethics." *Ethics* 121, no. 2 (2011): 390–419.

Tao, Julia. "Beyond Proceduralism: A Chinese Perspective on *Cheng* (Sincerity) as a Political Virtue." *Philosophy East and West* 55, no. 1 (2005): 63–79.

Tao, Julia. "The Chinese Moral Ethos and the Concept of Individual Rights." *Journal of Applied Philosophy* 7, no. 2 (1990): 119–127.

Tao, Julia. "Dignity in Long-Term Care for Older Persons: A Confucian Perspective." *Journal of Medicine and Philosophy* 32, no. 5 (2007): 465–481.

Temple, John. *The Genius of China: 3,000 Years of Science, Discovery and Invention.* Touchstone, 1989.

Tiwald, Justin. "A Case for Chinese Philosophy." *Newsletter on Asian and Asian-American Philosophers and Philosophies* 8, no. 1 (2008): 6–7.

Tsien, Tsuen-hsuin. *Science and Civilization in China,* volume 5: *Chemistry and Chemical Technology,* part 1: *Paper and Printing.* Cambridge University Press, 1985.

Van Norden, Bryan W. "Three Questions about the Crisis in Chinese Philosophy." *Newsletter on Asian and Asian-American Philosophers and Philosophies* 8, no. 1 (2008): 3–6.

Vardi, Liana. *The Physiocrats and the World of the Enlightenment.* Cambridge University Press, 2012.

Walpola, Rahula. *What the Buddha Taught.* Oneworld, 2001.

Wong, David B. "Emotion and the Cognition of Reasons in Moral Motivation." *Philosophical Issues: A Supplement to Noûs* 19, no. 1 (2009): 343–367.

Wong, David B. *Natural Moralities: A Defense of Pluralistic Relativism.* Oxford University Press, 2009.

Wong, David B. "The State of Chinese Philosophy in the U.S." *Newsletter on Asian and Asian-American Philosophers and Philosophies* 8, no. 1 (2008): 13–14.

Yu, Kam-por, Julia Tao, and Philip J. Ivanhoe, eds. *Taking Confucian Ethics Seriously: Contemporary Theories and Applications.* State University of New York Press, 2010.

Zhang, Wei-Bin. *On Adam Smith and Confucius: The Theory of Sentiments and the Analects.* Nova, 2000.

I Moral Psychology

1 When You Think It's Bad, It's Worse Than You Think: Psychological Bias and the Ethics of Negative Character Assessments

Hagop Sarkissian

We often find ourselves making judgments in the absence of complete information. This happens across a range of domains, including judgments about persons. Is this person praiseworthy or blameworthy? Honest or deceitful? Trustworthy or suspect? In such times of uncertainty, where evidence might be interpreted one way or another, one might consider giving the person in question the benefit of the doubt—that is, to suspend negative judgments for the time being and assume that, in the fullness of time and with increasing evidence and familiarity, the more favorable judgment will prove the correct one. The admonition to give others the benefit of the doubt is most straightforwardly understood as asking that we look upon others favorably and extend them a kindness in the face of countervailing considerations. But how far should one go in complying with it?

In a much-discussed article, Susan Wolf argues that extending to others the benefit of the doubt is an unwavering disposition of the moral saint, who must "be patient, considerate, even-tempered, hospitable, charitable in thought as well as in deed" and "must have and cultivate those qualities which are apt to allow him to treat others as justly and kindly as possible."[1] However, having stated these qualities, Wolf claims there is a substantial tension between being a moral saint and having certain other qualities of character that we would otherwise consider part of an enjoyable, well-lived life. For example, "a cynical or sarcastic wit … requires that one take an attitude of resignation and pessimism toward the flaws and vices to be found in the world," which is an attitude the moral saint cannot adopt.[2] Instead, the moral saint will do "whatever is morally necessary to secure good outcomes." Indeed, the moral saint "will be very reluctant to make negative judgments of other people," even in the face of counter-vailing considerations.[3] Insofar as cynicism or sarcasm would be inimical to this goal, a moral saint would shun such qualities of character.

A moral saint … has reason to take an attitude in opposition to [cynicism and sarcasm]—he should try to look for the best in people, give them the benefit of the doubt as long as possible, try to improve regrettable situations as long as there is any hope of success … . A moral saint will have to be very, very nice.[4]

In sum, the moral saint is committed to doing "whatever is morally necessary" in order to make the world a better place. This will regularly require that the moral saint give others a pass, let bygones be bygones, and extend to them the benefit of the doubt—notwithstanding the fact that there might be apparent reason to judge them morally suspect.

The moral saint, so described, might seem naive or overly trusting. She might even seem to lack a basic sense of justice, oblivious to the fact that the world does contain bad actions and bad characters, that cynicism is warranted at times, and that sarcasm can be an appropriate reaction to social (even moral) transgressions. Refusing to make negative judgments of others and routinely giving them the benefit of the doubt for "as long as possible" might seem to many neither heroic nor laudable but instead silly or misguided, apt for misapplication or even exploitation. If this is what morality demands, one might reasonably conclude that it demands too much. Indeed, Wolf ends up concluding that such considerations speak to the importance of intuitions (as opposed to principles) in helping us strike a balance between the moral and the amoral in our personal value orientations.[5]

In this chapter, I will argue that one need not be committed to the saintly goal of securing favorable outcomes at any cost in order to have a standing commitment to give others the benefit of the doubt and refrain from negative character assessments. Moreover, one need not rely exclusively upon some form of intuitionism to guide one in this regard. Instead, there are compelling reasons to abide by these commitments once we focus on the nature of negative character judgments themselves, and the mechanisms that give rise to them. Are they reliable? What is their epistemic status? In what follows, I will outline a number of reasons that should weaken our confidence in our ability to accurately judge others and find them worthy of condemnation. And I believe that some of the most fruitful resources for thinking about these issues come from an entirely different moral tradition than the ones that Wolf assays, a tradition which has a distinct perspective on the prompts of human behavior (both good and bad) and, therefore, a distinct way of evaluating the nature of character judgments.

1 Reasons to Give the Benefit: The *Analects* of Confucius

My main resource for thinking about these issues is the *Analects*, a collection of conversations among Confucius (551?–479? BCE), his advisees, and his colleagues, collected over the decades (fifth to third centuries BCE) following Confucius' death. As with Wolf's discussion of moral saints, the *Analects* addresses such topics as whether one should be reluctant to make negative judgments of others, or whether one ought to give others the benefit of the doubt. However, it does so from a particular perspective—namely, one of a highly interconnected social world. According to this perspective, how any single person acts in any social occasion hinges greatly on the behavior of the other individuals at hand.[6] Hence, whenever one wishes to explain or understand another's behavior—that is, whenever one were to judge it in some way—one would look beyond a person's motivations, goals, or traits of character. These would not, in the first instance, be the focus of judgment. Instead, one would examine a range of other considerations that, while external to the person's private mental life, would nonetheless be part of the context of the behavior in question and hence part of the explanatory account.

For example, one might consider who else was present at the time, what was said and in what tone of voice, how the individuals were related to one another, what roles they were occupying, and what expectations apply to them in these roles. The early Confucians (most especially Confucius and the third-century-BCE thinker Xunzi) viewed behavior as highly interconnected, prompted and shaped by one's social and environmental contexts in subtle yet sure fashion. It would seldom be appropriate to discount or overlook such factors in accounting for the person's behavior, as they might carry great explanatory weight. Imagine, for example, judging why a person is quiet at the dinner table. One might advert to various personality traits to explain this particular bit of behavior. For example, one might conclude that the person is shy, introverted, or diffident. Such traits might, indeed, be appropriate explanations for the token behavior in question. By contrast, one might advert to various aspects of the person's situational context. For example, one might note that the person is a junior member of the family, and that such members are not expected to lead discussion at the dinner table. One might also note that the person is in the presence of a teacher or mentor, and similarly advert to conventions about speaking improperly or out of turn.

Many passages of the *Analects* are centrally occupied with how one might be affecting or influencing the behavior in question oneself. A running theme throughout the text is cultivating one's own moral influence on others (one's *de* 德, or effective moral influence). In order to do so, one must mind one's comportment and monitor its effect on others. The following passage reflects this preoccupation:

There are three things in our *dao* that a gentleman values most: by altering his own demeanor he avoids violence and arrogance; by rectifying his own countenance he welcomes trustworthiness; through his own words and tone of voice he avoids vulgarity and impropriety. (8.4)[7]

Here we see a direct connection between features of one's scrutable self and the behavior of others. The *Analects* maintains that the *junzi* 君子 (nobleman / exemplary person) can understand behavior in others by attending to aspects of his own comportment. Thus, when accounting for the behavior of others, one's own behavior would often be part of the explanatory context and hence part of the explanatory account. Searching for explanations of others' behavior without accounting for one's own influence on it would be incomplete at best, wholly misguided at worst.

A related point concerns how one ought to react when one comes across disagreeable personalities or behaviors. In such instances—when one has friction with others, or experiences frustration with them (or worse)—one is typically directed to look at oneself when trying to explain such troubles.

Master Zeng said, "Every day I examine myself on three counts: in my dealings with others, have I in any way failed to be dutiful? In my interactions with friends and associates, have I in any way failed to be trustworthy? Finally, have I in any way failed to repeatedly put into practice what I teach?" (1.4)

Master Zeng strives to become an exemplary moral person—a *junzi*, or person of noble bearing. When he inspects his behavior he does not simply compare it to certain prescribed rules of conduct. Rather, he attends to the way his own behavior may be affecting others. For Master Zeng, moral failure consists not in failing to mimic formal ritual ideals (an important motivation for early Confucian practitioners) but rather in failing to successfully influence his environments. Given these aims, focusing on others to explain why interactions with them are less than optimal would not only be inaccurate and incomplete; it would also be unproductive.

The Master said, "Do not be concerned that you lack an official position, but rather concern yourself with the means by which you might become established. Do not be concerned that no one has heard of you, but rather strive to become a person worthy of being known." (4.14; cf. 14.30)

The Master said, "When you see someone who is worthy, concentrate upon becoming his equal; when you see someone who is unworthy, use this as an opportunity to look within." (4.17)

The *junzi* is distressed by his own inability, rather than the failure of others to recognize him. (15.20)

Since individuals are loci of influence, affecting those with whom they interact, working on *oneself* is a way to influence how *others* behave.

Attacking your own bad qualities, not those of others—is this not the way to redress badness? (12.21)

There is a distinct pattern in these passages that concerns how the moral exemplar is supposed to react when dealing with recalcitrant, disagreeable, or otherwise bad individuals—that is, when one has reason and opportunity to make negative judgments of others. The pattern is one of caution and restraint.

Zigong was given to criticizing others. The Master said [sarcastically], "How worthy he is! As for myself, I hardly devote enough time to this." (14.29)

Zigong asked, "Does the *junzi* despise anyone?" The Master replied, "Yes. He despises those who pronounce the bad points of others." (17.24) [8]

Similar to the description of the moral saint above, here we also find that the *junzi* frowns upon voicing criticisms and making negative evaluations of others. Yet distinct from the moral saint's aim of trying to maximize the chance of things going well, the reasons given here are largely epistemic, and have to do with whether such judgments are accurate or well supported. Consider the following commentary from the *Record of the Three Kingdoms* (third century CE) on this general theme in the text.

Criticism and praise are the source of hatred and love, and the turning point of disaster and prosperity. Therefore the sage is very careful about them … . Even with the *de* of a sage, Confucius was reluctant to criticize others—how reluctant should someone of moderate *de* be to carelessly criticize and praise?[9]

Here we see a couple of reasons adduced for this reluctance to judge others (whether negative or positive). Part of the reason for caution stems from the possible fallout from such assessments. Insofar as one's own assessments might inform those of others, or shape those of others, one must be cautious in being loose with them. More important, perhaps, being quick to judge risks moral hubris. Focusing on others' bad qualities shields one from the more important task of self-scrutiny. Blaming others is easy; admitting one's own deficiencies is difficult. This finds poignant expression in a comment by Wu Kangzhai 吳康齋(1392–1469): "If I focus my attention on criticizing others, then my efforts with regard to examining myself will be lax. One cannot but be on guard against this fault!"[10] So long as one is preoccupied with pointing out the flaws in others, one avoids this more arduous task. It's as though we have natural tendencies that blind us to our own causal role in influencing unfavorable outcomes, and compel us to pin the blame on others and their shortcomings.

We find in these passages a commitment to one value of the moral saint—being very reluctant to pass negative judgments on others. Yet the reasons supporting this commitment go beyond that of trying as much as possible to make the world a better place. Apart from any such motivations, the *Analects* suggests that one take a broader perspective on the prompts of the behavior itself. It suggests that we shift our attention away from the person and instead look at the context of the behavior—including oneself insofar as one is part of that context. What is most remarkable about these injunctions to resist the impulse to blame others and instead look at oneself is that doing so goes against a well-documented tendency to do the contrary—a tendency that has been investigated for decades in experimental psychology.

2 Reasons for Giving the Benefit: Experimental Psychology

The actor/observer asymmetry has long enjoyed a status as one of the bedrock findings of social psychology, revealing something deep about our ways of explaining social behavior. As its name implies, the actor/observer asymmetry posits a difference between how actors explain their own behavior and how those observing them explain the very same behavior: actors invoke *situational* or *external* characteristics, whereas observers invoke *personal* or *internal* characteristics. One way to capture the difference between these types of explanation is to consider the following sets of questions one might ask to explain the behavior in question[11]:

Personal or *internal* questions (asked when observers explain others' behavior): A person's personality, character, attitude, mood, style, intentions, thoughts, desires, and so on—how important were these in causing the behavior in question? To what extent can the behavior be attributed to the person's abilities, intentions, and effort?

Situational or *external* questions (asked when actors explain their own behavior): Situational context, the effect of other persons, the nature of the task at hand, the demands of one's position, environmental factors—how important were these in causing the behavior in question? To what extent can the behavior be attributed to situational variables or just dumb luck?

On the face of it, the asymmetry in explanation seems plausible. After all, why shouldn't we expect actors and observers to explain one another's behavior differently? Yet a meta-analysis by Bertram Malle has revealed very little support for the asymmetry as a *general* pattern of explanation.[12] Indeed, it emerges only when a handful of variables are in play. The strongest among these is when the behavior has a certain obvious *valence*—i.e., when it is seen as positive (successes; skilled activity; generosity; other socially desirable behaviors) or negative (failures; mishaps; aggression; other socially undesirable behaviors).[13] In short, we explain others' *negative* behavior as arising from *personal* or *internal* variables, and others' *positive* behavior as resulting from *situational* or *external* variables. However, when we explain our own behavior, this pattern is reversed (table 1.1).

The asymmetry is obviously self-serving: we disown our own failures, yet refuse to allow others to do so; we take credit for our successes, yet pin others' successes on things external to them. Could this, in fact, be an accurate assessment of what causes good and bad behavior? On the face of it, the self-serving nature of this tendency should provide us some *prima facie* reason to doubt the veracity of our explanations of others' negative behavior. But before jumping to this conclusion, it might help to try to understand why we have such a marked asymmetry in the first place. Here, I'll focus on two different accounts.

The first one explains this tendency as a by-product of evolutionary pressures faced by our ancestors.[14] Our ancestors struggled in competitive environments with limited

Table 1.1

	Positive behavior	Negative behavior
Actor's explanation	Personal or internal	Situational or external
Observer's explanation	Situational or external	Personal or internal

resources, and faced many threats and dangers; mortality rates were much higher than today, and life expectancy shorter. In such environments, where one is not guaranteed access to resources necessary for survival, reacting quickly and decisively at signs of perceived threat would be advantageous and fitness-enhancing. Potential threats to one's survival (such as competitive conspecifics who might endanger one's well-being) have an urgency and must be addressed immediately lest one bear terrible consequences. Keeping track of such individuals and adopting an intentional stance toward them (that is, attributing their threats as personal or internal) would be one way to ensure preparation against any potentially threatening behavior. Put another way, threats against the self signal that quick and decisive action is necessary, so evolutionary advantages would accrue to those who assumed that potential threats were stable and not ephemeral, and to those who acted quickly and automatically in response to them.

This explanation is, of course, highly speculative. Even so, let's grant for the sake of discussion that such an explanation is plausible. Can it justify the present asymmetry? Notice that for a behavioral tendency to be fitness enhancing it need not track truth. That is, it need not have been the case that all potential threats in our evolutionary past were intentional (or otherwise products of a person's motives or desires) in order for a tendency to consider them so to enhance fitness. False positives—treating threats as intentional when they weren't—might prove costly in terms of lost opportunities at forging cooperative relationships, but these would likely be outweighed by the costs of false negatives—where failing to react to a *true* threat might risk the very survival of the individual. Put another way, a tendency to attach negative behavior to the intentions of persons and then to track such persons over time would prove fitness-enhancing even if the tendency would routinely misfire. More important, perhaps, our present environments do not resemble those of our ancestors. We are no longer in a Hobbesian state in which personal security can be assured only through personal diligence. We have the entire apparatus of the modern state and its various policing institutions to help secure our persons and ensure an environment of predictable social interactions. This changes the cost-benefit structure of false positives as opposed to false negatives, making it unclear whether, strictly from a selfish perspective, pinning others' negative behavior to their character traits is beneficial.

A second type of explanation suggests that this tendency is the product of a naive theory of social behavior that individuals tacitly maintain—a theory that need not be influenced by evolutionary pressures.[15] According to this naive folk theory, individuals are continuously compelled by others to behave in socially desirable ways—that is, to be helpful, accommodating, and cooperative. These pressures are sufficient to explain why most individuals behave in ways that are generally helpful or benign; they do so owing to the continual demands of social existence. Why, then, do individuals act

Table 1.2

	Negative behavior	Positive behavior
Good people	Not capable	Capable
Bad people	Capable	Capable

contrary to accepted social norms and practices? The naive theory of social behavior maintains that it must be because either (a) they have a standing intention, desire, or motive to do so (indicating a person's bad character) or (b) they are constituted in such a way that they are incapable of acting otherwise. Both of these latter explanations refer to a person's character: if someone acts badly or poorly, it must be because of who he or she is. After all, since there are obvious costs that accrue to an individual for acting in a negative fashion, no individual would do so without intending to. As a consequence, negative behavior occurs less frequently but is intentional, and therefore more diagnostic.[16] Put another way, most individuals have good reason to act in socially desirable ways, and this is sufficient to explain why both good individuals and bad individuals will exhibit socially desirable behavior. By contrast, negative behavior can only stem from disreputable characters. Hence, inferences from good behavior to good character traits will be risky, and inferences from bad behavior to good character traits will be erroneous. Bad behavior comes from bad individuals (table 1.2).

This type of explanation might also enjoy an initial degree of plausibility. After all, the social pressures invoked seem real enough, and it seems reasonable to think that people would want to avoid the costs they would incur from contravening widely held norms. However, the explanation doesn't withstand critical scrutiny. For example, many instances of norm transgression or negative behavior might be accidental or unintended. In fact, if individuals have a standing motivation to act in socially approved ways, it seems just as likely to infer that any deviation must be the result of accident as opposed to intent. (Of course, being prone to accidents may reveal something about a person's character, but the asymmetry is not limited to instances of repeated observation.) More important, moral life is not free of conflict, and good people will often have to choose between several competing moral demands that cannot all be practically met. Failing to meet *all* of one's moral demands may lead to norm violations in some areas, yet it would be unfair to conclude that someone has a bad character or acted from bad motives simply because he cannot satisfy all of his demands.[17] It seems that one ought, instead, to take into account the situational constraints that may be impinging on the behavior in question.

Difficulties accounting for bad behavior are compounded when we judge unfamiliar persons—when we take their poor behavior on any particular occasion as indicative of their character or their motivations generally—just because there is so little evidence to judge the person's character. People act differently when presented with different prompts and when placed within different contexts, and so drawing conclusions about someone's character in any situation on the basis of the previously observed behavior of others in similar situations is necessarily tenuous. Unfortunately, it is in our interactions with strangers that we are particularly vulnerable to making and maintaining such negative character evaluations, and injunctions to withhold judgment and give others the benefit of the doubt are particularly vital in such interactions.

When we meet others we form impressions of them, and those impressions tend to stick.[18] This tendency for first impressions to persevere motivates numerous social practices, such as grooming before a first date or rehearsing before an important presentation. It can be unfair, of course, to judge or evaluate persons on the basis of their behavior on any particular occasion, as the behavior may not be representative. Nonetheless, first impressions are easy to form and difficult to overcome.

Indeed, first impressions are remarkable predictors of the overall trajectory of interpersonal relationships. A study by Michael Sunnafrank and Artemio Ramirez suggests that we decide within minutes what sort of relationship we'll come to have with someone.[19] For the study, participants (college freshmen) were paired on the first day of class with another student, of the same sex, whom they didn't know. The participant was told to introduce himself or herself to the other individual and to talk to that person for either three, six, or ten minutes, then was asked to list the things the two individual had in common, to assess the overall quality of the interaction, and to estimate what sort of relationship was likely to develop: "nodding acquaintance," "casual acquaintance," "acquaintance," "close acquaintance," "friend," or "close friend." After nine weeks, the participants were contacted and asked to describe their current relationships with the partners. The best predictor of relationship status turned out to be how positive the initial interaction was (all things considered), which turned out to be far more important than common interests or likeability in predicting the relationship's trajectory. Although this highlights the importance of positive first impressions, it also gives us reason to discount negative ones, lest we close off the possibility of forging positive relationships in the future.

Alas, when it comes to initial impressions of others, we also find a pronounced asymmetry between negative impressions and positive impressions.[20] Negative impressions are taken as more diagnostic of individuals than positive information; negative behavior is taken as indicative of a person's character, whereas positive behavior is not.[21] Negative behavior is more easily remembered than positive behavior.[22] We remember negative behavior more accurately than positive behavior, and we are more confident about such memories.[23] Similarly, we take less time to arrive at negative judgments,[24] and we require considerably less evidence and information to ascribe negative traits to individuals than to ascribe positive traits; in fact, the less favorable the character trait, the less evidence we need to believe in it.[25]

This asymmetry is likely related to the greater certainty we feel about our negative assessments of others relative to our positive assessments.[26] When we experience uncertainty we tend to be more systematic and careful when processing any relevant information we encounter; conversely, when we have a sense of certainty in our judgments we tend to process information in a more superficial fashion. Hence, those judgments that we tend to be certain about—namely, judgments resulting from negative behavior—tend to coincide with very shallow information processing, whereas those judgments we tend to be uncertain about—namely, judgments resulting from positive behavior—tend to coincide with more rigorous information processing. Finally, we tend not to look for alternative explanations of negative behavior once we have concluded that the behavior in question is representative of a bad character trait.[27]

In view of all the asymmetrical tendencies noted above, we have reason—above and beyond the moral saint's desire that everything go well—to doubt the veracity of our negative assessments of others—especially people not familiar to us. The suggestion here is not that we should always suspect them, or that all our assessments are equally susceptible to bias in every instance. Nonetheless, owing to the tendency of negative information to be weighed more heavily, to persevere longer, to be taken as more representative, and to be shielded from disconfirmation, we have good reason to doubt the negative assessments we make of others.

The doubt has two inter-related components. The first stems from the factors just mentioned—the asymmetrical weighting, perseverance, representativeness, and obstinacy of negative assessments versus positive ones. Since there seems to be no good reason to accept these effects as tracking truth, we should be willing to doubt them. Relatedly, a second reason stems from our systematic failure to search for other explanations of the token behavior in question—explanations that don't emphasize a person's character but instead look to situational, contextual, or accidental features. We may not be in error if we include character explanations in our understanding, yet we will often be in error if we take them to be exhaustive. We should try to expand our perspectives as observers and to explain the behavior of others as we would explain our own—that is, from the observed person's own perspective. In other words, when thinking badly of others, we should consider that we might be falling victim to a psychological tendency that prevents us from seeing their behavior in a more complete and accurate light. In doing so, we can leave open possibilities for constructive engagement and cooperation where they would otherwise be cut off.

3 Reasons to Give the Benefit: Game Theory

An analogue to the strategy of giving the benefit of the doubt in order to open up possibilities for engagement and cooperation can be found in game theory. In Robert Axelrod's famous tournament, players were pitted against one another in repeated encounters based on the classic Prisoners' Dilemma, in which each player has an opportunity to either defect or cooperate with the other. If the players cooperate, each receives a modest payoff; if both of them defect, neither receives a payoff; if one defects but the other cooperates, the defector gets an even greater payoff than he would have gotten if he had cooperated, while the cooperator is assessed a penalty. In view of these outcomes, it is rational to defect no matter what your opponent does: at best you get the highest reward, at worst nothing, whereas cooperating for a modest payout risks a considerable penalty. But if everyone always defects, no person receives any payoffs. That's the dilemma.

In Axelrod's tournament, a very simple strategy called Tit for Tat emerged victorious in the face of far more sophisticated strategies. The Tit for Tat strategy had only two rules:

1. When you first meet another player, cooperate.
2. Thereafter, choose the response that the other player chose when last encountered.

This strategy proved remarkably effective, besting several more complicated strategies. However, it had a significant flaw; it had no tolerance for noise or error. When noise is added to an iterated Prisoners' Dilemma tournament in the form of errors or misunderstanding, Tit for Tat strategies can become trapped in a long string of retaliatory defections, thereby depressing their score. Such noise may come in one of two forms: a co-player might either send the wrong signal (also known as misimplementation or "trembling hand") or might send the right signal yet be misinterpreted by other players (misperception or "noisy channels"). "Faulty transmission of strategy choices (noise) severely undercuts the effectiveness of reciprocating strategies"[28] such as Tit for Tat. In one and the same tournament, Tit for Tat can go from the winning strategy to sixth place if strategies are randomly set to misfire 10 percent of the time (i.e., defecting where one would otherwise cooperate or vice versa).[29] The reason is easy enough to grasp: Upon encountering a defector, a Tit for Tat strategy will reciprocate with defection, which will result in an extended series of mutual obstructions (that is, both players defect). In such situations, Tit for Tat strategies must rely on the co-player to initiate a cooperative move; without such initiative from the co-player, the Tit for Tat player will continue to defect indefinitely, even if the original defection of the co-player was an unintended result of noise. Indeed, Tit for Tat is particularly vulnerable against *itself* in noisy environments—a single miscue can result in an extended mutual obstruction, and only another miscue will be capable of triggering a new series of cooperation.

The obvious way to break the vicious cycle of retaliation is to requite defection with cooperation from time to time—to let bygones be bygones. Such strategies are generally known as Generous Tit for Tat. Consider, for example, a variant called Tit for Two Tats, or Forgiving Tit for Tat, which will wait for two defections in a row before retaliating with defection. In a mixed environment in which there are many strategies at play, Tit for Two Tats works just as well as Tit for Tat, and in some instances outperforms it. Indeed, in biologically relevant evolutionary games interactions can be twisted away from defection and toward cooperation by the introduction of such strategies, which are more tolerant of noise. Adding Generous Tit for Tat "greatly increases the overall level of cooperation and can lead to prolonged periods of steady cooperation."[30]

Our own social environments most resemble "noisy" games. It is not uncommon to misinterpret others' signals or to fail to convey our own intentions clearly. Wires get crossed, identities are mistaken, and unwarranted assumptions are made. Sadly, such miscues are often taken to be highly diagnostic of character and purpose, weighted accordingly, and thus reciprocated by real-life "defection"—our tendency to have negative impressions harden into obstinate beliefs. The social/moral game (as it were) can be decided quickly and ruthlessly. Opportunities for negotiation and moral advancement can be nipped in the bud as a result of bad first moves. Yet if negative assessments should no more admit to personal or internal explanations than to positive ones, it is important to foster this habit of giving others the benefit of the doubt and allowing fruitful, constructive, and productive relationships to unfold.

4 Reasons to Withhold the Benefit: *Analects*

In the theory of games, as in real life, being forgiving has benefits and costs. For example, Tit for Two Tats is at a disadvantage when faced with very aggressive strategies, which exploit them not once but twice before being punished in turn. In environments where individuals routinely exploit forgiving natures, it would be imprudent to forgive others' transgressions. This underscores the importance of both giving the benefit of the doubt *and* drawing accurate assessments of others—even if they are unfavorable. Without the latter virtue, one can be exposed to moral vulnerability.

If I am correct in claiming that giving others the benefit of the doubt is an important theme in the *Analects*—that it contains injunctions to look beyond internal or personal characteristics when explaining behavior, that it enjoins us to see others as like ourselves—then it would be putting its adherents at risk of being exploited by morally unscrupulous individuals. Indeed, this issue is broached in a number of places in the text.

Zai Wo asked, "If someone were to lie to a *ren* 仁 [humane] person, saying "A man has just fallen into a well!"—would he go ahead and jump in after him [to try and save him]? The Master said, "Why would he do that? The *junzi* can be enticed but not trapped; he can be tricked but not duped." (6.26)

The Master said, "Is a man not superior who, without anticipating attempts at deception or presuming acts of bad faith, is nonetheless the first to perceive them?" (14.31)

Edward Slingerland's selection of commentary on this passage merits lengthy citation:

The gentleman is trusting of others, and expects the best of them. As *Dai's Record* says, "The gentleman does not anticipate badness from others, nor does he suspect others of untrustworthiness." Li Chong sees this open attitude as the key to the Gentleman's ability to educate others: "If you perceive an act of untrustworthiness in the beginning and then necessarily expect untrustworthiness in the future, this indicates an impairment of the merit of patient forbearance, and also blocks the road to repentance and change." Nonetheless, the gentleman is not a fool, and is the first to perceive when his trust has been misplaced.[31]

Being capable of properly judging others and of despising them when that is necessary would be important for anyone for whom being cooperative, deferential, mindful, and conscientious are important commitments. Those pursuing the Confucian *dao* 道 would be prone to exploitation when surrounded by individuals seeking power, position, fame, and wealth, as was the case in Warring States China (475–221 BCE). In such environments, it would be imperative to identify those truly worthy of hatred (even while erring on the side of false negatives). Indeed, as E. Bruce Brooks and A. Taeko Brooks note, despising (*wu* 惡) is a classic virtue, appearing in the earliest stratum of the *Analects*.[32]

Only the *ren* can truly love others, and truly despise them. (4.3)

The Master said, "I have not seen a person who loved *ren* or despised what was not *ren*. He who loved *ren* would esteem nothing above it. He who hated what is not *ren* would be *ren* himself, since he would not allow anything that is not *ren* to be associated with his person." (4.6)

Nonetheless, it remains true that the text recommends a general attitude of favorableness toward others. After all, if expecting the worst from others can make them act poorly,[33] then expecting well from them, thinking favorably of them, might do the opposite.

The Master said, "The *junzi* helps others fulfill their attractive qualities rather than their unappealing ones. The petty person does the opposite." (12.16)

Admittedly, it seems difficult to figure out just how the *junzi* will balance the injunction to be favorable to others and give them the benefit of the doubt with the equally important injunction to properly judge some of them as being morally despicable. Yet no matter how the *junzi* might balance these injunctions, we should keep in mind that fighting the tendency to blame or resent others is a losing proposition unless the person's behavior changes within a reasonable length of time. In other words, giving others the benefit of the doubt is a strategy with a limited shelf life; the cognitively demanding act of staving off blame and resentment can be expected to last only so long. The injunction to give others the benefit of the doubt is, after all, a strategy to redress a standing psychological bias, and will prove effective only when others provide evidence of the transitory or contingent nature of their initial disagreeable behavior.

We find much of this summarized in a noteworthy passage in the writings of Mencius, a Confucian thinker of the fourth century BCE:

Suppose someone were to be harsh in their treatment of me. A *junzi* would, in such a case, invariably examine himself, thinking "I wasn't benevolent; I lacked propriety. How else could such a thing have come about?" But if, after examining himself, he discovers he had been benevolent, he had acted with propriety, and yet the person *still* treats him harshly, then the *junzi* will again invariably examine himself, thinking "I must have lacked commitment." But if he discovers that he was, in fact, committed, and the person *still* treats him harshly, only then would the *junzi* say, "I suppose he is the incorrigible one."[34]

Here we find the epistemic considerations adduced above expressed most directly. The *junzi* has encountered disagreeable conduct directed toward him. His first impulse is to see how he might have engendered the conduct himself: Was he indiscrete or unkind? Did he lack patience or resolve? Here he is merely trying to come to a proper or complete understanding of what may have caused the person to act in such a fashion. Only after arriving at a more definite understanding of the prompts of the behavior—after concluding that it is unlikely to have been the result of some contingent prompt—is the *junzi* satisfied with blaming the person. (Here we find an analogue to the Tit for Two Tats strategy: Pause not once but twice before retaliating with a defection—in this case, with a negative character assessment.)

Conclusion

At the outset of the chapter, I noted Susan Wolf's argument that morality can demand too much, and that there may be personal, amoral ideals of character that have valid claims among our personal aspirations. On this view, moral perfection cannot be the sole or primary ideal that structures our lives; we have reason to aspire to ideals that are amoral. For Wolf, this means that "we have reason to want people to live lives that are not morally perfect," and that "any plausible moral theory must make use of some conception of supererogation" to mark off moral demands that are optional and discretionary from those that are obligatory.[35] Presumably, this would include marking off the moral demand to give others the benefit of the doubt. Although this demand can be motivated by a number of considerations, none of them point to its being a strict duty. Instead, one will need to consider the particular contexts of any token negative judgment to determine whether it is, all things considered, something one ought to give credence to or something one ought to doubt. There is room for discretion here, so one can take on board Wolf's suggestion that intuitions will be necessary to the process.

Nonetheless, and in contrast with other supererogatory acts, I have argued that giving others the benefit of the doubt is motivated by strong epistemic reasons, and that we should question the veracity of our negative assessments of others—especially when we are unfamiliar with the individuals involved. Hence, though this particular virtue may not be obligatory, it warrants standing concern beyond any desire to maximize the chances that things will go well. Instead, it can be motivated by a desire to treat others fairly, to be accurate in one's assessments, and to avoid the costs associated with closing others off because of cognitive processes that are likely to be biased or erroneous. And although experimental psychology provides evidence as to the biased nature of this particular range of judgments, it remains a discipline that trades largely in descriptive facts as opposed to prescriptive norms. For the latter, it is fruitful to look to a tradition—Confucianism—that has, from its outset, taken a perspective on social life that recognizes the precarious nature of drawing such judgments, and which has rich normative resources structured around this perspective.

Giving others the benefit of the doubt may not be easy. On any realistic assessment of moral life, we must admit that, as we navigate the social world, there will be endless opportunities for friction with others to arise. Even if one is conscientious about one's own behavior and mindful of being respectful of others, these will never safeguard one from finding others disagreeable or difficult. Moreover, doubting such judgments can require going against what others have said about an individual and flagging the information as tentative and needing confirmation, as the *Analects* is well aware.

The Master said, "It doesn't matter if the multitude hates someone; you must still examine the person and judge for yourself. It doesn't matter if the multitude loves someone; you must still examine the person and judge for yourself." (15.28)

At other times, it will require overcoming first-person observations and evidence. Yet adopting such a stance may be a winning strategy both in the theory of games and in the game of life. And though serious moral tolerance and accommodation may not always be in the offing, and though certain individuals may not seem to warrant the benefit of the doubt, a disposition to giving one can be propitious to (and sometimes necessary for) accommodation and cooperation to emerge as live options.

Acknowledgments

My thanks to Brian Bruya for helpful suggestions on previous drafts, and to Owen Flanagan and David Wong for helpful discussions.

Notes

1. Susan Wolf, "Moral Saints," 421.

2. Ibid., 422.

3. Ibid., 421.

4. Ibid., 422.

5. Ibid., 439.

6. For an argument justifying an interconnected perspective in current moral psychology, see Hagop Sarkissian, "Minor Tweaks, Major Payoffs." For an important elucidation of this theme in early Confucian thought more generally, incorporating insights from newly unearthed texts, see Mark Csikszentmihalyi, *Material Virtue*, especially 178–192.

7. All translations are my own, using the Chinese text in D. C. Lau, *Confucius: The Analects*.

8. The passage continues: "He despises those who remain below while criticizing those above; he despises those who are bold but lack courtesy, daring yet violent."

9. Edward G. Slingerland, *Confucius Analects*, 166.

10. Ibid.

11. Adapted from Bertram F. Malle, "The Actor-Observer Asymmetry in Attribution," 896.

12. Ibid.

13. In much of what follows, I focus on the moral dimensions.

14. See, for example, Felicia Pratto and Oliver P. John, "Automatic Vigilance."

15. Oscar Ybarra, "Naive Causal Understanding of Valenced Behaviors and Its Implications for Social Information Processing."

16. See, for example, Susan T. Fiske, "Attention and Weight in Person Perception."

17. For further discussion of how competing moral demands, as well as the agent's attitude toward any transgression she may have to commit in choosing between such demands, are taken into account in our folk psychology, see Mark Phelan and Hagop Sarkissian, "Is the 'Trade-Off Hypothesis' Worth Trading For?"

18. This section shares parallels with portions of Sarkissian, "Minor Tweaks, Major Payoffs."

19. Michael Sunnafrank and Artemio Ramirez Jr., "At First Sight."

20. Fiske, "Attention and Weight in Person Perception."

21. Glenn D. Reeder and Marilynn B. Brewer, "A Schematic Model of Dispositional Attribution in Interpersonal Perception."

22. Jeffrey W. Sherman and Leigh A. Frost, "On the Encoding of Stereotype-Relevant Information under Cognitive Load."

23. Donal E. Carlston, "The Recall and Use of Traits and Events in Social Inference Processes."

24. John H. Lingle and Thomas. M. Ostrom, "Retrieval Selectivity in Memory-Based Impression Judgments."

25. Myron Rothbart and Bernadette Park, "On the Confirmability and Disconfirmability of Trait Concepts."

26. Carlston, "The Recall and Use of Traits and Events in Social Inference Processes"; Vincent Y. Yzerbyt and Jacques-Philippe Leyens, "Requesting Information to Form an Impression."

27. Ybarra, "When First Impressions Don't Last."

28. Robert Axelrod and Douglas Dion, "The Further Evolution of Cooperation."

29. Christian Donninger, "Is It Always Efficient to Be Nice?"

30. Martin Nowak and Karl Sigmund, "Chaos and the Evolution of Cooperation."

31. Slingerland, *Confucius Analects*, 166.

32. E. Bruce Brooks and A. Taeko Brooks, *The Original Analects*.

33. See, for example, Mark Chen and John A. Bargh, "Nonconscious Behavioral Confirmation Processes."

34. *Mencius* 4B:28.

35. Wolf, "Moral Saints," 438.

Works Cited

Axelrod, Robert, and Douglas Dion. "The Further Evolution of Cooperation." *Science* 242, no. 4884 (1988): 1385–1390.

Brooks, E. Bruce, and A. Taeko Brooks. *The Original Analects: Sayings of Confucius and His Successors*. Columbia University Press, 1998.

Carlston, Donal E. "The Recall and Use of Traits and Events in Social Inference Processes." *Journal of Experimental Social Psychology* 16, no. 4 (1980): 303–328.

Chen, Mark, and John A. Bargh. "Nonconscious Behavioral Confirmation Processes: The Self-Fulfilling Consequences of Automatic Stereotype Activation." *Journal of Experimental Social Psychology* 33, no. 5 (1997): 541–560.

Csikszentmihalyi, Mark. *Material Virtue: Ethics and the Body in Early China*. Brill, 2004.

Donninger, Christian. "Is It Always Efficient to Be Nice? A Computer Simulation of Axelrod's Computer Tournament." In *Paradoxical Effects of Social Behavior: Essays in Honor of Anatol Rapoport*, ed. Andreas Diekmann and Peter Mitter. Physica-Verlag, 1986.

Fiske, Susan T. "Attention and Weight in Person Perception: The Impact of Negative and Extreme Behavior." *Journal of Personality and Social Psychology* 38, no. 6 (1980): 889–906.

Guglielmo, Steve, and Bertram F. Malle. "Can Unintended Side Effects Be Intentional? Resolving a Controversy over Intentionality and Morality." *Personality and Social Psychology Bulletin* 36, no. 12 (2008): 1635–1647.

Lau, D. C. *Confucius: The Analects*. Chinese University Press, 1992.

Lingle, John H., and Thomas. M. Ostrom. "Retrieval Selectivity in Memory-Based Impression Judgments." *Journal of Personality and Social Psychology* 37 (2) (1979): 180–194.

Malle, Bertram F. "The Actor-Observer Asymmetry in Attribution: A (Surprising) Meta-Analysis." *Psychological Bulletin* 132, no. 6 (2006): 895–919.

Nowak, Martin, and Karl Sigmund. "Chaos and the Evolution of Cooperation." *Proceedings of the National Academy of Sciences* 90, no. 11 (1993): 5091–5094.

Phelan, Mark, and Hagop Sarkissian. "Is the 'Trade-Off Hypothesis' Worth Trading For?" *Mind and Language* 24, no. 2 (2009): 164–180.

Pratto, Felicia, and Oliver P. John. "Automatic Vigilance: The Attention-Grabbing Power of Negative Social Information." *Journal of Personality and Social Psychology* 61, no. 3 (1991): 380–391.

Reeder, Glenn D., and Marilynn B. Brewer. "A Schematic Model of Dispositional Attribution in Interpersonal Perception." *Psychological Review* 86, no. 1 (1979): 61–79.

Rothbart, Myron, and Bernadette Park. "On the Confirmability and Disconfirmability of Trait Concepts." *Journal of Personality and Social Psychology* 50, no. 1 (1986): 131–142.

Sarkissian, Hagop. "Minor Tweaks, Major Payoffs: The Problems and Promise of Situationism in Moral Philosophy." *Philosophers' Imprint* 10, no. 9 (2010): 1–15.

Sherman, Jeffrey W., and Leigh A. Frost. "On the Encoding of Stereotype-Relevant Information under Cognitive Load." *Personality and Social Psychology Bulletin* 26, no. 1 (2000): 26–34.

Slingerland, Edward G. *Confucius Analects: With Selections from Traditional Commentaries*. Hackett, 2003.

Sunnafrank, Michael, and Artemio Ramirez Jr. "At First Sight: Persistent Relational Effects of Get-Acquainted Conversations." *Journal of Social and Personal Relationships* 21, no. 3 (2004): 361–379.

Wolf, Susan. "Moral Saints." *Journal of Philosophy* 79, no. 8 (1982): 419–439.

Ybarra, Oscar. "Naive Causal Understanding of Valenced Behaviors and Its Implications for Social Information Processing." *Psychological Bulletin* 128, no. 3 (2002): 421–441.

Ybarra, Oscar. "When First Impressions Don't Last: The Role of Isolation and Adaptation Processes in the Revision of Evaluative Impressions." *Social Cognition* 19, no. 5 (2001): 491–520.

Yzerbyt, Vincent Y., and Jacques-Philippe Leyens. "Requesting Information to Form an Impression: The Influence of Valence and Confirmatory Status." *Journal of Experimental Social Psychology* 27, no. 4 (1991): 337–356.

2 Growing Virtue: The Theory and Science of Developing Compassion from a Mencian Perspective

David B. Wong

1 A Concrete Basis for a Relationship among Reflection, Deliberation, Emotion, and Desire

In this chapter I shall reflect on the implications of Mencius' (fourth century BCE) conception of compassion for one of the most important problems that defines the Western philosophical tradition: the relationship between reason on the one hand and desire and emotion on the other, especially in the development of moral character. The mainstream of Western philosophy and psychology has assumed a split between reason on the one hand and emotion and desire on the other, along with the claim that one is or should be dominant over the other. It is difficult to underestimate the multiple and profound ramifications of this split. We have only to look at the way Kant and Hume shaped the Western philosophical tradition on the subjects of moral motivation and the development of character. The contemporary debate still shows the Kantian-Humean divide in those who give exclusive or primary emphasis to reason as the basis for moral knowledge and (morally appropriate) motivation[1] and in those who give exclusive or primary emphasis to emotion and desire (with reason playing the role of servant or slave, gathering information as to how to fulfill the ends set by emotion and/or desire).[2]

The debate has often proceeded as if there were only two possibilities. I have argued in the past[3] that Mencius' conception of the moral sprouts and their development into the ethical virtues bears on the Western problem. It helpfully undermines the categorical distinction between reason and emotion. To say more positively and more clearly what should replace that categorical distinction, however, is not so easy. Though I still stand behind much of what I have said, I have never been entirely satisfied with it. I return to the subject here and try to articulate more clearly and with more specificity what philosophers working within the Western tradition could learn from the *Mencius* text (fourth to third centuries BCE), drawing from some contemporary scientific studies to support my suggestions that this text provides fruitful directions of thought.[4] Relative to mainstream Western philosophy, contemporary psychology and neuroscience are opening up a richer set of possibilities for the relationship among reflection, deliberation, emotion, and desire in ways that resonate with early Confucian philosophy.

This surprising convergence has several causes. First, the early Confucians held themselves accountable to a broad range of pre-theoretical experience of the moral life. Second, they set themselves the task of specifying in fairly concrete terms *how* actual human beings could cultivate themselves so as to realize the ideal of the exemplary moral person (the *junzi* 君子).[5] This emphasis on the pre-theoretical and the practical led to insights that correspond to conclusions that contemporary psychologists and neuroscientists have drawn from an intriguing and increasingly rich array of experimental evidence on emotion and cognition in general and in the moral life in particular. Third, the early Confucians, as part of a more general tradition of early Chinese thought, tended to take a more relational approach in trying to understand something: they tend to highlight a thing's relationships to other things and to the environment, rather than looking purely to its internal structure. They tend to understand themselves and other human beings as organic systems taking sustenance from and depending on larger surrounding environmental systems, and insights stemming from this outlook resonate with contemporary scientific theorizing about the development of unlearned traits as an organism interacts with its environment. Fourth, because they were used to thinking of mind and body as continuous and not of radically different kinds, Chinese thinkers were able to see that thinking, feeling, and sensing with the body are intimately connected. Some of the most intriguing contemporary psychology and neuroscience points in the same direction.

From here on, I shall avoid talk of "reason" except for discussing the views of Western philosophers. This is to avoid the implication that there was widespread belief in Chinese philosophy in "reason" as a unified entity. I see little to recommend such an attribution. What we encounter are references to forms of reflection and reasoning that influence and are influenced by forms of desire and affective processes. Pointing to some discussions in the *Mencius* and relating them to some contemporary scientific study of cognition and emotion, I shall argue for taking a more particularized and differentiated approach to the phenomena that we tend to obscure by using the word "reason." By contrast, contemporary Western philosophers and many psychologists continue a tendency to construe reason, desire, and emotion in dichotomous and overgeneralized terms to this day. Though I shall use the words "desire" and "emotion" in discussing the Chinese texts (because there are corresponding Chinese terms that are sufficiently similar in meaning), I shall also argue that we need to take a more particularized and discriminating approach to the phenomena covered by these terms. At the end, I shall discuss what I believe are some limitations in Mencius' approach and then gesture to the ways that the *Analects* and the *Xunzi* indicate ways the early Confucian tradition pointed beyond Mencius' limitations.

2 Components of the Sprout of Compassion

Mencius is concerned to identify the inborn beginnings of morality in *ren xing* 人性, commonly translated as "human nature." I shall adopt that common translation here, with a nuanced gloss that Kwong-loi Shun has suggested: "certain characteristic features of human beings that are particularly conspicuous, pervasive, and difficult to alter, without necessarily having the connotation of what is essential as opposed to accidental."[6] I add the gloss because, with Roger Ames,[7] I believe that the Chinese tendency to see things in relational and dynamic terms is not congenial to thinking of things as having essential properties. Such a dynamic conception of human nature is illustrated below by the discussion of Mencius' sprout metaphor for the development of the moral virtues. The beginnings of the virtues in human nature are sprout-like in the sense that they take shape only if there is significant nurturing of them within the right sort of social environment and conditions of sufficient material security.

These beginnings are the *duan* 端, translatable as "beginnings," "germs," or "sprouts," and used in 2A6 to refer to the four *xin* 心 (hearts or feelings) that can develop into ethical virtues: compassion can develop into *ren* 仁 (human-heartedness); shame/dislike can develop into *yi* 義 (as a virtue of persons, translatable as "righteousness" but with some infelicity for conveying its meaning as the ability to grasp and act on rightness or appropriateness to the situation as a property of actions); deference can develop into *li* 禮 (observing ritual propriety); and approval/disapproval can develop into *zhi* 智 (wisdom). Three of these sprouts are or include emotions—compassion, dislike/shame, and deference. Most of the *Mencius'* most provocative discussion of the ways that reflection and emotion interact in moral development concerns compassion, so I will focus on that sprout.[8]

What is the sprout of compassion like? In this section, I have laid out some preliminary characterizations. Subsequent characterizations in the next sections will focus on individual components of the emotion. I shall then go on to discuss how the components change as compassion grows into the virtue of *ren*. In 2A6 it is the phrase *"ceyin zhi xin"* 惻隱之心 that is usually translated as the "heart" (or feeling) of compassion." Mencius uses this phrase, and another for compassion, *"bu ren ren zhi xin"* 不忍人之心 (in context, it can be translated as "the heart (or feeling) that is unable to bear the suffering of others"). Mencius supports his attribution of this sprout to all human beings by giving the example of the alarm and distress (*chuti ceyin zhi xin* 怵惕惻隱之心) that anyone would feel upon seeing a child about to fall into a well. He emphasizes that there is no ulterior motive for this reaction: not the desire to get in good with the child's parents, not the desire for good reputation among one's neighbors, and not dislike of the child's cries. Mencius' 2A6 example implies that compassion can be felt for any human being (the child need not be a relative), and it can be felt for animals.[9] Mencius also holds that unlearned concern for the welfare of one's family is and should be stronger than one's concern for non-related others[10] and that it has a foundational role in the development of *ren* as human-heartedness.[11]

The compassion in Mencius' example has four components: a cognitive component of recognizing that a child is about to befall harm; a bodily visceral response that might involve catching one's breath, one's heart rate quickening, and perhaps reflexive movement toward the child; a motivational component that consists of concern for the child or a desire that harm not befall her (the motivational component overlaps with the visceral response insofar as it is a response that prepares one to act); and the "feeling" of the emotion itself, the felt alarm and distress that in this case has a visceral tone to it in the way that fear for someone whose welfare one values can grip the body.

2.1 The Bodily Component: *Qi* and Mind-Body Unity

Antonio Damasio has suggested that subjective feeling is constituted by the mental states arising from the neural representation of various changes occurring within the chemical landscape of the body.[12] These changes are responses to a precipitating event or stimulus and include those that ready one for action. Mencius is in an excellent position to acknowledge that the subjective feeling of an emotion can be bodily feeling. A general understanding of Mencius' time is that the person is constituted by *qi* 氣, an animating and elemental energy-stuff with psycho-physical characteristics. As Alan Chan remarks, there is little reason not to believe that Mencius shared with his contemporaries this general understanding of the person.[13] *Qi* fills the body, and the heart-mind is an organ of the body.[14] The heart-mind has the function of thinking and feeling, and its workings are enabled by the person's *qi*. There is no Cartesian problem of explaining causal interaction between substances that have nothing in common with one another. The energy-stuff of *qi* is a *psycho-physical* stuff. Emotions arise from different kinds of *qi*.[15]

Given common views of human *qi* of Mencius' time, it is reasonable to attribute to him the view that liking (*hao* 好) and disliking (*wu* 惡) are the most basic forms of cognitive-affective tendencies that arise from a person's *qi*.[16] They are basic in that liking gives rise to pleasure, and disliking gives rise to sorrow or anger. Anger in fact was conceived as a kind of rising-up of a person's *qi* (perhaps awareness of this rising up was thought to be the feeling component), and the alarm and painful feeling that can accompany compassion is another kind of *qi* and our awareness of it.

The bodily nature of compassion receives some confirmation from recent investigations into the neuroscience of compassion. Mary Helen Immordino-Yang and her colleagues conducted brain imaging studies on subjects they had exposed to true stories.[17] Some stories were selected to evoke admiration of morally virtuous behavior or for morally neutral skill; others were selected to evoke compassion for someone suffering physical pain (sustained through physical injury) or for someone suffering psychological/social pain (e.g., grief, despair, social rejection). The results of the imaging studies indicated that regulatory neural mechanisms responsible for sensing and regulating body functions and known to be engaged in "basic" emotions such as fear, anger, and sadness are also engaged in the experience of admiration and compassion.

2.2 The Motivational Component: *Qi* as Motivational Energy

Consider the aspect of emotion that is readiness to act. *Qi* supplies a person with motivational energy. In 2A2, Mencius notes that the heart-mind is the commander of the *qi*. It forms aims (*zhi* 志), and when these are focused or concentrated (*yi* 壹),[18] the *qi* follows and manifests as movement of the body. However, Mencius goes on to note, the *qi* when concentrated can in turn move the heart-mind's aims. That is, the energy-stuff of *qi* can gather so as to influence the heart-mind in the aims or directions it takes. Thus, the conception of the person as constituted by *qi* underlies not only the feeling component but also the motivational component.

For Mencius, the *qi* of human beings tends to flow in certain directions. Some of these directions correspond to the motivational directions embedded in the sprouts. In 6A7, Mencius says that just as meat pleases (*yue* 悅) people's mouths, *li* 理 (pattern)[19] and *yi* (rightness/righteousness) pleases their heart-minds. The inborn motivational directionality in the sprout of compassion lies in concern for the suffering other. It involves dislike for the suffering of others. Mencius conceives this dislike of suffering with interesting nuance. In the 1A7 story of King Xuan and the ox, the king decides to spare an ox being led to ritual slaughter because the ox's fear reminded him of an *innocent* man going to execution. In 3A5, Mencius, in dialogue with the Mohist Yi Zhi, again returns to his example of a child about to fall into a well, and this time implies that a relevant feature of the appropriate response to it lies in its *innocence*: it is not the child's fault, he says, that it is about to fall into the well. Thus, the dislike that goes into the sprout of compassion is a dislike for the suffering of innocents, those who do not deserve to suffer.

It might appear that in incorporating a significant role for innocence in the matter of whose suffering prompts compassion, Mencius is reading way too much cognitive sophistication into the structure of what is supposed to be an unlearned emotional disposition in human nature, but we should rethink this reaction in light of studies conducted by the psychologist Paul Bloom and his colleagues on infants (three- to twelve-months old). They exposed their infant subjects to shows featuring pro-social or anti-social creatures (blocks with "googly eyes" who helped or hindered other blocks with eyes trying to get up a hill; puppets who performed helping or hindering actions toward other puppets, e.g., trying to open a box). In this age range the experimenters found preferences in the infants (as evidenced by looking longer at them or by reaching for them) for helpers of third parties unrelated to the infants.[20] Even more surprising, eight-month-old infants selectively prefer characters who act positively toward pro-social individuals and characters who act negatively toward antisocial individuals. Additionally, young toddlers direct positive behaviors toward pro-social others and negative behaviors toward antisocial others.[21] They did not have any of these differential preferences when shown similar scenarios but with "inanimate" individuals (blocks *without* googly eyes, for example).

Given the age of the subjects, of course, this is extremely suggestive of unlearned dispositions not only to like others who help others and to dislike those who hinder others, but to like those who reward helpers and those who punish hinderers. Could this reflect, then, not only the sprout of an urge to be concerned about others but also the sprout of being able to discriminate "guilty" anti-social actors from the "innocent"? There is no doubt that culture and individual learning experiences play an irreplaceable role in the ability of matured human beings to make the familiar nuanced moral judgments that form the grist for moral philosophy, but Bloom's studies of infants seem to suggest that we might be *biologically prepared* to develop in certain directions which support our ability to engage in the intricate interdependencies of human social life. Infants might even be prepared to make relatively sophisticated discriminations not only in service of approving helping actions and attitudes (they even seem capable of discriminating between those who try to help but fail and those who do not try at all), but also those who support helping actions and attitudes and those who do not.

One more point about the motivational nature of the sprout needs to be made. The motivational elements need not and typically do not dictate specific action tendencies. In Mencius' example of the reaction to the child in peril, the response is characterized only as the alarm and distress, not the actual act of trying to save the child. Emotions do not always result in overt actions, for one thing, because they can be overridden by other emotions or interests a person has. Furthermore, even if one wanted to act from an emotion, the specific nature of such action would depend on the circumstances. My first reaction to the child crawling toward the well may be to rush over and grab it, but I may be too far away to get there in time, and my best action may be to shout to others closer to the child.

It is not uncommon for the contemporary scientific literature to mention "action tendencies" as components of emotions, especially those "basic" emotions such as fear, anger, and sadness that appear to have a very substantial biological basis and look to be universal or nearly so. The behavioral component of fear, for example, is often characterized as "flight," and very often this is the behavioral response. But freezing is not an infrequent response. Furthermore, human beings can fear a wide variety of things, and some of these things simply don't elicit flight as an appropriate or expected response: consider fear of losing one's youthful vigor motivating a man to buy a shiny red sports car.[22] What is appropriate or likely as a response depends on the situation, the character of the object of the emotion, and what is at stake for the person who experiences the emotion.

At the same time that we recognize emotions as not necessarily including any specific action tendencies, we note that they do act as an impetus for action of some kind (even freezing in the face of fear is a kind of behavioral response). The role of emotion in the production of action is real and crucial, but it is typically more complicated than is often recognized. Because emotions often involve visceral bodily changes, they can ready us for action. Because we feel our emotions and because they do not dictate specific actions, we have the flexibility to shape what actions satisfy the relevant motivations according to the situation. Part of what culture does is to provide us scripts for satisfying these motivations given certain kinds of situations. But individual learning, personality, goals, and reflection and deliberation also go into shaping what specific actions emerge from our emotions.

2.3 The Cognitive Component: Recognizing Patterns of Suffering

Unlearned compassion involves the cognitive abilities to discriminate those who are suffering or in danger of suffering. And as just discussed, there is evidence of ways in which the motivational component of natural compassion involves the beginnings of sophisticated discriminations among the potential recipients of the emotion. The motivational structure intertwines with the cognitive component, since part of the latter just is the capacity to make discriminations. To be able to properly dislike suffering in others and to be able to properly like the sparing of suffering in others, or to be able to properly dislike those who hinder helpers and to be able to properly like those who help helpers, one must discriminate the corresponding *li* (patterns—in this case that constitute who is a helper and who is a hinderer and patterns that constitute who helps helpers and who hinders helpers).[23] The differential motivational responses that seem to be the beginnings of approach or avoidance depend on such discrimination of patterns.

The cognitive component need not deliver judgments or beliefs in any full-blooded sense. A child can feel alarm and distress over a favorite doll's broken arm. She may perceive the doll to be suffering; but does she believe it? Such phenomena indicate that the cognitive component can sometimes remain at the level of "seeing something x as if it were y" that precedes and often, but not always, turns into belief.[24] The phrase "x as if it were a y" is neutral as to whether x really is a y. This capacity to see something in terms of something else allows us to entertain possibilities without fully committing to their reality. The capacity to see in terms of analogy, to see something in terms of something else based on similarities between the two, is fundamental to human cognition.[25] It is used to understand one less intelligible or accessible realm of experience in terms of another more intelligible or accessible realm (consider the analogy of billiard balls in motion to explain molecular or atomic motion; or the analogy of the computer to explain the workings of the mind). It is used in persuasion and argument ("Afghanistan is no place for the United States to be; it's another Vietnam"). Because this sort of cognitive strategy for making sense of the world is so basic to human life, it is plausible that the wiring for such a capacity might be set up so that much of our seeing something as another thing is non-conscious and automatic, but could have been even more adaptive for this capacity to be able to take sophisticated and reflective forms, whereby one can deliberate over whether x is sufficiently similar to past instances of y's so as to justify turning the seeing of x as a y into a warranted judgment.

The "seeing as" character of the cognitive component relates to the possibility of emotions being warranted or unwarranted. We distinguish at least some of the major kinds of emotion on the basis of the kind of appraisals they involve: the "seeing as" of emotion typically involves seeing something as having evaluative significance for the perceiver. Fear involves seeing something as posing danger or anticipated harm either to oneself or to someone one identifies with or has concern for. Jealousy in love involves seeing another as a rival for the affections of one's beloved. One can certainly have the relevant perceptions without having sufficient warrant for them.

This is why, in development of compassion from its unlearned form, judgments can enter into the emotion. One might judge one's initial perception of someone as suffering or not suffering to be mistaken upon further inquiry into the situation. One comes to "reappraise" the situation consciously and reflectively, even if one's initial appraisal of the situation was automatic and non-conscious. Furthermore, the *kind* of suffering for which one can have compassion might make a difference as to the cognitive resources one needs to draw upon. Immordino-Yang and her colleagues[26] found that compassion for another's social and psychological pain corresponded to somewhat different processes in the brain than compassion for another's physical pain. The former involved high levels of activity in brain areas associated with introspection, reflection on the self, and taking the perspectives of others.[27] The processing of information also took longer in the case of compassion for social and psychological pain.[28] The implication is that seeing someone as suffering social or psychological pain takes considerable cognitive development and learning. More instances of compassion for such pain probably involve explicit judgment and inference, and give us more opportunities for conscious reappraisal of the situation.

How cognitive is the cognitive component? Some philosophers and psychologists will put up considerable resistance to calling an automatic and non-conscious ability to discriminate a "cognitive" ability. To say that someone has made a judgment is to imply some degree of conscious consideration. But there need be nothing consciously considered or deliberated about the alarm and distress one feels at seeing a child about to fall into a well. The alarm and distress simply happen to us and displays "automaticity," to use the contemporary psychological term that connotes lack of cognitive control. If one associates the cognitive with the higher processes of conscious reflection and deliberation, then one will reject the idea that there is anything cognitive about unlearned compassion.

To some extent, this is a matter of what people choose to call "cognitive." If one insists that the label applies only to that which is conscious, deliberated and subject to assessment and cognitive control (e.g., such that assessing the lack of evidence for it results in lack of belief in it), then of course the spontaneous and automatic expressions of unlearned compassion cannot be regarded as having a cognitive element. Alternatively, the label can be defined much more broadly to include whatever is represented in some way, not necessarily to conscious awareness, such that it bears an appraisal of the situation that has affective meaning for the person.[29] There need be no substantive disagreement as long as we agree on what is there in unlearned compassion, apart from what we choose to call it.

I opt for the more inclusive meaning of *cognitive*, because it correctly suggests an important *continuity* between the initial pre-belief, perceptual, non-conscious and automatic appraisals of a situation by an agent and subsequent cognitive reappraisals that occur within an emotion as it stretches out over time, when reflection on what one initially feels may bring initial appraisals under cognitive assessment and some degree of cognitive control. Much of the early scientific study of emotion focused only on initial emotional episodes of emotions such as fear and anger, in which the appraisals of something as dangerous or offensive could very well be fast, automatic, and non-conscious.[30] In fact, these approaches to emotion simply continue the Western tradition of cleaving it from various forms of reflection and deliberation.

But at least some psychologists[31] have come to recognize that what is amenable to controlled experiment may occlude some of the most important emotional phenomena, such as the fact that we can reappraise objects about which we have made automatic and non-conscious appraisals. Take an instance in which one flares with anger at being ignored by an acquaintance. This reaction makes emotional sense only in relation to goals or desires to be treated in certain ways, certain *likes* and *dislikes*. In the next moment, however, one can catch oneself reacting in this way, reflect and identify the cause, and wonder why one should care about being treated that way by the callow person one knows the other to be, and the anger subsides.

There is a deeper point to be made against the Western philosopher's cleavage between the non-conscious and automatic on the one hand and the controlled and reflective on the other hand, as if these were two separate realms that influence human action. The cleavage obscures the way that the controlled and reflective must inevitably be built upon our automatic and non-conscious discrimination of patterns in the environment. As has become increasingly clear, the limited size of our working memories requires that most of the information-processing done by the mind must be done at the non-conscious level. At the conscious level, we bring up (or at least try to) some of what we have processed at the lower level, "as needed" for reappraisal and more complex processing and weighing.

Moreover, a recent psychological study indicating causal influence of the slow and reflective over the automatic and non-conscious discrimination of patterns suggests that we should re-examine the very distinction between automatic and controlled processing. Lisa Barrett, Kevin Ochsner, and James Gross summarize the studies that break down the distinction into different dimensions of automaticity and control.[32] For example, much of the earlier work operationalized automaticity by reference to the subjective feeling of the agent that he lacked control over his emotional response to a stimulus. The subjective feeling of lacking control, however, can co-exist with the internally represented goal states of the agent influencing which aspects of a situation are attended to and processed. The goals of an agent may also motivate not only reappraisal of an emotional object but an initial fast and non-conscious appraisal. Goal-directed focusing of attention in appraisal or reappraisal is a very important kind of controlled process, even if the agent has no subjective feeling of controlling her attention in accordance with her goals. What this implies, in other words, is that there is bidirectional causal influence between automatic and non-conscious appraisals and controlled, reflective appraisals and goals that people consciously reflect on and adopt.[33]

One striking possible instance of reflective processes influencing automatic non-conscious appraisals and responses to events is the surprising finding that older adults have fewer negative emotions than younger adults. It is surprising in light of the fact that they have the end of life "in view" while younger adults typically see the end in the distant horizon. Mara Mather and Laura Carstensen survey relevant studies and conclude that the older adults focus more on emotional self-regulation as a goal.[34] They are less likely to react to upsetting interpersonal situations by shouting or name-calling, and experience negative affect for shorter periods of time. In terms of what they pay attention to in a situation, they pretty much live according to the Harold Arlen–Johnny Mercer song, accentuating the positive and eliminating the negative. The point here is that a kind of cognitive control of emotional processes can take place even if the control is not an object of reflective awareness at the time it is exercised.

It may be objected that there can be no cognitive *control* unless the relevant effects are in some way intended by the agent. There is something to this objection, but people can and do try to change the way they emotionally respond to situations even if they are not consciously striving for this goal on particular occasions of response. They proactively implement strategies that have their effect on such occasions. It may be precisely the sense that the end is in view (e.g., the sense that life is too short to get caught up in insignificant quarreling with others) that motivates older adults to adopt goals of regulating their emotional lives, to change the outlook they bring to interpersonal interactions without necessarily regulating each such interaction with conscious regard to such goals, and there may be a great deal of wisdom in doing so.

To sum up this discussion component, then, let us note that the Mencian sprout of compassion involves capacities to discriminate others who are suffering or in danger of it, and there may be even more subtle discrimination of those who do not "deserve" to suffer—innocents. We need not claim that unlearned compassion involves explicit and reflective judgments about who is innocent and who is not. But we could say that the motivational structure of unlearned compassion involves the kind of differential response that prepares the way for the more explicit cognitive discrimination. This latter kind of discrimination could come along as the sprout grows and as an agent develops a normative framework for making explicit judgments about who is innocent and who is not. As this cognitive ability to judge and explicitly reflect develops, it can become integrated into the sort of compassion a virtuous agent feels. I will later discuss ways in which early Confucians employed something like this idea in designing their programs for cultivation of desired emotional dispositions.

3 Growing Compassion

Given the components of the sprout of compassion, what are the conditions for its growth into *ren* (human-heartedness)? The text displays ambiguity on this question. Sometimes the *Mencius* portrays growth of the sprouts as something that will occur unless it is actively interfered with. In 6A2, Mencius compares the tendency of human nature toward the ethical to water flowing downward. One can make it flow upward by damming it up or striking it. In some places, the exemplary person of comprehensive moral excellence is characterized as preserving what distinguishes human beings from the animals.[35] In other places realizing moral excellence is described as a matter of not losing the four hearts or feelings or of seeking the lost heart.[36]

Other passages in the text portray the growth of the sprouts as needing proactive nurture and the realization of conditions that are highly contingent. Passage 6A7 implies that the *duan* are like sprouts that grow equally well if the soil they are planted in is the same, if nourished equally by rain and dew, and if the human effort invested is the same. What are conditions enabling moral growth for which fertile soil and water are metaphors? In this section, I lay out five such conditions derived from Mencius' theory of the development of compassion: nurturing unlearned virtue; knowing what others desire and aspire to; development of *quan* (weighing reasons); reflection on reasons (patterns and their recognition); and analogical reasoning (inference to the best application). These conditions contribute to a more robust contemporary theory of the development of virtue generally.

3.1 Nurturing Unlearned Virtue

In 1A7, Mencius explicitly holds the king responsible for providing material security to his subjects and in other places puts forward some fairly specific taxation, agricultural, and military policy proposals for accomplishing this.[37] Moreover, Mencius places responsibility on people to cultivate their own sprouts. One who nurtures the smaller part of the self becomes a small person, while one who nurtures the greater part of the self becomes a great person.[38] People who are always eating and drinking are considered by others to nurture what is small. Nurturing the greater part of oneself is accomplished when the heart-mind (*xin* 心; the seat of thinking, feeling and intending) reflects (*si* 思; think, reflect, focus attention, or turn over in one's mind).[39] Reflecting, says Mencius, the heart-mind will get it; not reflecting, the heart-mind will not get it.

6A7 suggests that *li* (pattern, order) and *yi* (rightness) please our hearts just as meat pleases our mouths. The pleasure we take in reflecting on order and righteousness, especially as we ponder them as realized in our own actions, may result in a feedback loop mechanism: as we act on our sprouts and reflect on what we have done, we take pleasure (*yue* 說), and this motivates further action to nurture the sprouts. This mechanism helps to explain why in 2A6 Mencius describes knowing how to fill out the sprouts as like a fire starting up or a spring breaking through a hole in the ground.

I have argued elsewhere that the aforementioned ambiguity in the conception of moral growth (between that which occurs in the absence of interference and that which occurs only with highly contingent, proactive nurture) is ultimately rooted in ambiguity in the *Mencius'* conception of how a trait (and specifically a virtue) can be part of our original nature.[40] Western notions of the innate share this ambiguity, and I have adopted the suggestion of some scientists and philosophers of science that it is better to adopt the notion of canalization to think about how virtues develop from their unlearned beginnings in human nature.[41] Highly canalized traits develop in many different environments such that the developmental pathways leading to such traits are like very deep trenches that strongly discourage but nevertheless allow in unusual circumstances deviation from those pathways. One way to think about the ambiguity in the *Mencius'* discussions of moral growth is that it displays a slide from thinking of the virtues as highly canalized traits that grow from their sprouts unless there is interference (this corresponds to thinking of innate traits as developmentally invariant or as unfolding under "normal" circumstances) to thinking of them as less canalized traits that grow only if they are proactively nurtured and other highly contingent environmental conditions (such as material security and ethical education) are set in place.

I shall not discuss this argument in detail here, but simply assume the conception of the virtues as less canalized traits that grow from the sprouts (though I also think we must make room for varying degrees of canalization among the different sprouts). I assume it because I think it is by far the more plausible conception. 1A7 correctly suggests certain conditions for moral growth. People do need a minimum of material security to have the mental space and psychic energy to consider others' welfare in the way that morality requires; they need education and reinforcement from others and from their culture to support the development of dispositions to focus on ethical *li*, *yi*, and knowledge of how to effectively act on them. None of these conditions are ensured as a matter of the normal course of things.

3.2 Knowing What Others Desire and Aspire To

To see what a proactive nurturing of unlearned compassion would have to look like, consider what the virtue of *ren* (human-heartedness) would have to look like. The motivational directions of the sprout would have to transform and change so that they become dispositions to respond in the right ways to those who are suffering or in danger of suffering. Development of the motivational component necessitates (but is not identical with) development of the cognitive component. As was discussed earlier, part of the latter's development involves gaining knowledge of others and of how they might suffer in ways less obvious than suffering from the pain of purely physical injury. Both the positive and negative versions of the Confucian "golden rule"—"Do not impose upon others what you yourself do not want"[42] and "*Ren* persons establish others in seeking to establish themselves, and promote others in seeking to get there themselves"—come to mind as relevant.[43] In Confucius' (551?–479? BCE) program, study of the *Book of Songs* (1,000–600 BCE) and accumulated experience in social interaction aid in learning the range of human desire and aspiration.

3.3 Development of *Quan*: Weighing Reasons

Knowing what others desire and aspire to, however, is just part of what needs to be acquired for dispositions to respond in the right ways to suffering others. One has to know what weight to accord to these desires and aspirations, especially if there is conflict among several others or with oneself. The fact that others will suffer is not always reason to try to spare them. It is well known that Confucians believed it was right to accord greater weight to the interests of their family than to non-family, but how to do this well and adequately protect the interests of non-family is often not an easily solved problem.[44] Developing compassion into a virtue, therefore, requires the development of good judgment, of *quan* 權, weighing or discretion.

Considerations for acting this way or that way are weighed by the exemplary person. Let us call these considerations "reasons."[45] For Mencius, reasons are not given by desires; they are features of situations that support acting one way or another. The suffering of another is such a reason. In a virtuous person, the reasons for feeling and acting from compassion are the welfare of the people for whom one is feeling compassion. The reason is not the fact that a virtuous person desires the welfare of these others, because then a person who fails to have that desire has no moral reason to spare others from suffering. For Mencius and the other early Confucians, one should be trying to shape oneself to become the sort of person who desires the welfare of others: one has a moral reason to shape oneself in that way.

Part of the explanation of why judgments about reasons enter at a developmental stage of the unlearned emotion is that they enter into the apparatus enabling a person to decide on a particular action. One might have an unlearned urge to help, but one has to learn partly from one's culture what avenues of helping there are, and one has to develop reasoning about how to identify which avenues are appropriate given the situation at hand. One must also be prepared to deal with complicated situations in which one must prioritize helping strangers versus helping one's family. To act out of developed compassion is to realize these more sophisticated cognitive abilities. If moral development goes well, a person becomes *ren*, and such a person will know how to care for others. She will be able to balance and identify the relevant priorities in cases of apparent conflict between reasons. As was noted earlier, Mencius seems to conceive of morally appropriate compassion as channeled toward the innocent—those who do not deserve to suffer. While the unlearned form of compassion need not involve judgments as to who is innocent, there may be motivational proclivities in this direction (e.g., inclinations to approach or to avoid), and these proclivities get steered later on as the agent acquires the apparatus for identifying and reflecting on reasons.

3.4 Reflection about Reasons: Patterns (*Li*) and Their Recognition

Mencius has a conception of how we can engage in reflection about reasons. Such reflection is based on the recognition of patterns, which, as already noted, goes into the basic structure of emotion in both its motivational and cognitive components. The kind of pattern recognition that is relevant to more complex inference and reasoning is recognition of patterns that recur over time. That is, we look for recurring patterns and seek to understand the present situation in terms of patterns we have recognized and found useful in the past.[46] Consider a recent call by political scientist Valerie Hudson to recognize that human beings effectively make complex decisions based on this kind of pattern recognition:

Pattern recognition is the ability of an individual to consider a complex set of inputs, often containing hundreds of features, and make a decision based on the comparison of some subset of those features to a situation which the individual has previously encountered or learned. ... For example, chess involves a well-defined, entirely deterministic system and should be solvable using purely logical reasoning. Chess-playing computers use this approach, but Chase and Simon (1973) found that human expert-level chess playing is done primarily by pattern recognition.[47]

When used to make arguments or arrive at decisions about what to do, analogies do not compel in the way that sound deductive arguments or inferences do. They are often used when we do not know which general principles could be used as major premises of a syllogism, for example, to get a conclusion that would address the problem at hand. Instead, we often have the thought that this present problematic situation looks somewhat like a past situation about which we have more familiarity. But because problematic situations are very complex and possess many characteristics, the resemblance to the past situation will always be partial, and the potentially relevant dissimilarities may give us pause in applying the lessons of the past to the present. As a consequence, analogical argument and inferences often need to be supported through considerable discussion. The threatening dissimilarities need to be dealt with. More similarities need to be marshaled in favor of the analogy. By the time a compelling case is made, the analogy has been considerably enriched and probably qualified. Consider what type of conversation and reflection could be started with the assertion, "Afghanistan is another Vietnam for the United States. It is futile, and we need to withdraw as soon as possible."

3.5 Analogical Reasoning: Inference to the Best Application

In addressing moral problems, analogy is usefully employed when the present situation bears resemblance to past situations in which one has made sound judgments about what to do or reacted in sound ways (of course, we don't always make reflective judgments about what to do—sometimes we just act without much thought and get it right). If the past and present are relevantly similar, or perhaps more realistically, similar enough, then we may think about how the judgment made in the past has some relevant analog in the present situation. Pattern matching can take both non-conscious and conscious forms. We often are not aware of having reacted to a situation based on its similarity to past situations we have encountered until we reflect on why we acted as we did. Or we can consciously try to apply useful and illuminating patterns we have used in the past to a problematic present situation. Another important point to note is that pattern matching need not be accomplished by consulting some general principle that identifies relevant similarities. Rather, we might directly compare the features of past and present situations and find the relevant features similar enough so that the kind of judgment made in the past is transferable in some way to the present situation. In fact, reflection on relevant patterns instantiated by past and present cases may prompt us to formulate generalizations from which we derive some guidelines or rules of thumb that we could go on to consciously apply in the future.

Intertwining of Motivational and Cognitive Components   These points can be illustrated by familiar cases in which one comes to see reason to spare the suffering of certain others. This reason is based on seeing that these others are not so different after all from people one already sees reason to care about. It is probably no accident that greater acceptance of gays and lesbians in the United States has followed depictions in popular televisions shows of sympathetic gay and lesbian characters. These characters could be a respected teacher, or uncle, or brother, or daughter, and that has prompted actual teachers, uncles, brothers, and daughters to come out, making it more difficult for those who care about them to think of that group as "them." Another example is the way many come to see reason to respond to the suffering of animals. Knowledge of how they suffer, and of our biological and psychological continuity with nonhuman animals, has persuaded many to acknowledge such a reason. These cases illustrate analogical inference from reasons to respond to suffering of family or of others one has come to love and respect to reasons to respond to the suffering of others, perhaps others that one has formerly despised or at least ignored. The inferences need not be made on a conscious level. They *may* be made consciously, and indeed agonized over, but they may be experienced as just emerging from oneself to one's own surprise. To make the analogical inference, moreover, is not necessarily to commit oneself to a general principle to the effect, for example, that we have reason to spare any human being suffering. Perhaps some may come to that conclusion based on the more concrete analogical inferences already made to extend the acknowledgment of reasons to such a general extent, but some, perhaps Mencius, may not want to extend that reason to people who are very far from innocence. The point is that one might be a lot more confident that one has made a sound inference from a particular case in the past to the present situation without knowing what general principle would enable one to make countless other inferences.[48]

As indicated earlier, the motivational and cognitive components of compassion are intertwined, such that discriminating those who suffer and being ready to respond in some way are tied together. The person who has developed compassion as a reflective agent and is on the way to developing it as a virtue will feel compassion while recognizing a reason to spare the suffering of others. Her feeling of readiness to respond will be integrated with acknowledgment of a reason to respond. The motivational and cognitive components will be intertwined in these more sophisticated and developed ways.

This more sophisticated intertwining is frequently not an easy thing to accomplish. One can recognize and accept a reason to spare the suffering of certain others, but not be emotionally moved to do so. Indeed, one might be in that position about gays and lesbians. One might acknowledge that one has reason to respond to their suffering in ways that are similar to the ways one has reason to respond to the suffering of people one cares about. One might care about the gays and lesbians who turn out to be one's teacher, uncle, brother, or daughter, but remain uncaring about gays and lesbians who are strangers or mere acquaintances. The same situation might hold for animals. One now sees that they can suffer in ways that are relevantly similar to the elemental suffering of human beings who experience abuse and torture. But one remains uncaring or caring only for one's pets. The cognitive component is unaccompanied by the motivational and feeling components. One might feel no readiness to act but actually recognize a reason to act.

It might be argued that analogical inference can lead to change in one's motivations given concern about cognitive dissonance.[49] There are some people who are very concerned about cognitive dissonance that arises among their beliefs and perceptions, and that may lead to their feeling compassion toward others for whom they have previous not felt it. But many of us are not necessarily concerned above all else to eliminate cognitive dissonance. Many times we put up with it or manage very well to avert our attention from it. Even if we are very concerned with cognitive dissonance, we might choose to go in the "wrong" direction of retracting the warrant for feeling compassion in the past situation (maybe one's teacher is not so respected after all, if he is gay). Furthermore, people can be quite ingenious in finding some difference between groups of people that becomes relevant and that justifies a differential reaction to their suffering. Freud's reference to the "narcissism of minor differences"[50] is relevant here. Whether one comes to extend compassion, then, can start with coming to see relevant similarities one hadn't seen before, but that is not a sufficient condition.

Intertwining of Motivational and Visceral Components Given the drawbacks of strategies that attempt to use analogical inference to persuade someone to be more compassionate out of the concern for consistency or rationality, we must ask whether analogical inference can play some other kind of role in promoting compassion as motivational or visceral component. At this point, let me discuss in detail the passage in the *Mencius* that is most relevant to this question: the 1A7 story of Mencius' conversation with King Xuan about the time he spared the ox from ritual slaughter. In the course of trying to persuade King Xuan that he could become a true king who could bring peace to his people, Mencius asks the king whether it was true that he had spared an ox being led to ritual slaughter. In recalling the event, the king professes some uncertainty as to what his motives were, but is persuaded by Mencius that he was moved by compassion for the ox. Its trembling reminded him, the king recalls, of an innocent man going to execution. Mencius concludes that the king fails to bring peace to his people not because of any inability to act but because of a simple failure to act. All that the king has to do, Mencius explains, is to take this mind of compassion he has applied to the ox and apply it to his own people.

There has been quite a bit of debate over the question of how Mencius might have thought about what he was trying to do with the king. The passage itself does not provide definitive evidence. When it is combined with other things Mencius says about moral development, however, the passage is greatly useful as a stimulus for articulating a psychologically realistic picture of moral growth that is in the Mencian spirit. The passage, after all, is a plausible description of how one might try to encourage someone to expand the scope of his compassion, especially if the context is the king just having asked whether he could be the kind of king Mencius is urging him to be: one who could draw people to him because of the way he treats them rather than one who forces their submission through inciting fear. It would make sense in that context to ask whether it was true that he had spared the ox. This is reminding the king of a capacity he has that would draw his people to him if he extends it to them.

In this passage, the analogies that Mencius presses on King Xuan appear crucial for what Mencius is trying to do, but it is not the obvious role we might expect. He is not trying to motivate the king out of a concern for consistency, or at least, this interpretation doesn't give Mencius a very promising strategy for persuading the king, precisely for the reasons outlined earlier. His primary aim is probably not even to get the king to recognize that he has a moral reason to spare his people suffering. The king probably already knew that, at least intellectually. The question is whether he cares about that, and that is probably the thrust of the king's initial question to Mencius of whether he can be a true king. Mencius' answer is not to persuade him of the descriptive claim that the king does in fact care about his people's welfare. He is trying to get him to care, and not by way of appeal to consistency.

To motivate another interpretation of what Mencius might be trying to do with the king, let me turn to a claim that Clore and Ortony make about two ways in which an object can acquire emotional meaning for a person.[51] One way is through "direct computation" of the meaning of the object. Direct computation is a frequently conscious process. For example, one overhears belittling remarks uttered by a work colleague about oneself. One reacts by thinking that one has done nothing to deserve these remarks and becomes angry and hurt. The other way that an object can acquire emotional meaning is "reinstatement." A work colleague physically resembles a merciless bully from one's childhood. One is frequently provoked by apparently innocent remarks by this colleague. Reinstatement is frequently non-conscious and is based on resemblance between features of the past situation that provoked the emotion and those of the present situation.[52] If the association between the two situations is non-conscious, this can be a serious barrier to self-understanding of why one is presently feeling a certain way, and if the evocative point of resemblance does not warrant the present feeling, we have a paradigm case of unwarranted emotion. For example, the fact that one's work colleague has curly red hair, as the bully in the past did, is not a good reason to feel the way one is feeling. Clore and Ortony emphasize the non-conscious and frequently unwarranted nature of reinstated emotion.

However, reacting to the present on the basis of resemblance to a past situation can be warranted and/or a conscious matter. Sometimes one finds oneself reacting to a present situation on grounds one is not conscious of, but it may turn out that those grounds are available to conscious awareness upon introspection, and they turn out to be good reasons for feeling the way one is feeling. One might feel uneasy and anxious in the presence of a stranger, and one is picking up on a non-conscious level the signs of untrustworthy motives one has encountered in the past. Sometimes such emotions are better detectors of highly relevant features of our environment than conscious surveillance. But the knowledge of that fact may prompt one to pay conscious attention to what such emotions might be detecting in the environment. Or to go back to the case of compassion, one might with surprise find oneself reacting with compassion to the suffering of a gay or lesbian person. But one's feelings of compassion might convey that one has come to see them in a different way, perhaps as having the same concerns and qualities as people with whom one has identified and felt compassion for in the past. The perception of relevant similarity and the other components of the emotion may come along before one becomes consciously aware of how one's views have changed and the way the change has affected one's emotional dispositions. Or one might first become consciously aware of the relevant similarity, and that may arouse the compassion. The fact that we can conceive of its going in either direction is a sign of the continuity of non-conscious and conscious reflective cognition.

King Xuan's reaction to the ox was, in Clore and Ortony's words, a "reinstated emotion." As he recalls at Mencius' prompting, he saw the ox's suffering as like the suffering of an innocent man going to execution. But the king also thought the ritual had to go on, and so substituted a sheep. Does this mean he was mistaken to have spared the ox? Was he mistaken in a way like reacting angrily to a work colleague because of an irrelevant resemblance to a bully of the past? Emily McRae asserts that this is the case in arguing that in some of my previous work on this passage I was mistaken in thinking that analogical inference plays a role in Mencius' attempt to get the king to feel compassion for his people.[53] Mencius is not, McRae argues, trying to get the king to go from one case of right to another, because in his view it was not right to spare the ox and that there is certainly, she thinks, an incongruity in sparing the ox while not sparing the people. Though I agree with much of what McRae goes on to say about extending the sprouts in Mencius, I think she is wrong on this point about sparing the ox.

It is significant that King Xuan was not sure what his motives were for sparing the ox. He might have been confused by his own actions of first sparing the ox and then substituting a sheep so that the ritual ceremony could go on. Mencius in effect supplies the king with an explanation: he could not bear the ox's suffering having seen it, but (as Mencius himself believes), the ritual takes precedence over the ox's suffering. And that is the reason why it was right to substitute the sheep. But once having accidentally seen the suffering of the ox, the king was right to spare it. This is what an exemplary person would do, says Mencius. And that is why the exemplary person stays away from the kitchen.[54]

The suggestion here is that an exemplary person nurtures his compassion, even when in general he should avoid engaging potential objects of his compassion when he has weightier reasons not to spare them. Thus, the king was right to feel compassion and to spare it once having accidentally seen the ox's suffering; he was also right to substitute the sheep, not having seen it, for the ceremony. Though coherent and justifiable given Mencius' position on the lesser importance of animals and the great importance of ritual, this might appear to contemporary eyes to be an awkward position with respect to the suffering of animals, but many of us to this day find ourselves in similar awkward positions—seeing their similarity to us in their vulnerability to suffering, but asserting the priority of legitimate human interests over those of animals.

The analogy from sparing the innocent man to sparing the ox is a sound one in Mencius' view, and so is the analogy from sparing the ox to sparing the people. In fact, the king has far greater reason to spare his people. But, as was noted earlier, the point of pressing this analogy was not to teach the king some new moral knowledge. He probably already knew that he had a moral reason to spare his people. The point was to start with a case in which the king had felt compassion for another being's suffering and to have him recall it and to relive it. Mencius is trying to get the king to consciously reinstate his emotion of compassion through reflection on the analogies from the suffering of the innocent man to the suffering of the ox to the suffering of the people. He is reflecting on and reliving what he felt for the innocent man and the ox, and Mencius is hoping to get that feeling, the bodily readiness to respond and the motivational inclination, to flow to the king's people.

Thus, rather trying to teach the king anything new in reminding him that he has a reason to spare his people, Mencius is trying to get the king to *feel* the reason to spare his people. I have emphasized that reasons are not based on what the agent desires. They are situational features that make it right and appropriate for an agent to do certain things. But even though reasons are not grounded in motivational inclinations, they do depend on these inclinations for their efficacy. Recall that the heart-mind itself is not a separate agential entity pulling the levers that control *qi* (like a Cartesian mind manipulating the pineal gland) but is composed of *qi* itself and therefore must draw from at least some of the unlearned motivational directions of *qi* in forming and executing its aims. This dependence is plausibly the lesson of the parable of the man from Song in 2A2, who tries to "help" his seedlings to grow by pulling on them. He harms them by trying to force their growth without regard to their internal readiness to grow. On the other hand, Mencius believes it is a grave mistake to neglect the sprouts and in particular not to weed among them. This connects with the 6A14 reference to the need to nurture the greater parts of the self rather than the smaller parts. One must nurture the ethical directions of *qi* that are embedded in the sprouts, and that means not only to feed them but to get them to grow further in those directions. Acknowledging what one has reason to do will help, but such acknowledgment will only help if it becomes married to the motivational force of *qi*.

The relevant kind of analogical inference does not just transmit sound judgment and response to past situations along the lines of relevant similarity to sound judgment and response in present situations. In the right circumstances, it can transmit the motivational force of *qi* along those lines of relevant similarity. Thus, the "base" cases of sound judgment in past situations from which sound analogies are drawn must also be cases in which one was moved appropriately by emotion.

Motivation through Gratification   The bodily readiness to respond, and in general the forms of liking (*hao*) and disliking (*wu*) that constitute the motivational component of emotion, can grow along analogical directions, along the lines of relevant similarity. When we have wanted something x, and if in satisfying that desire we gain satisfaction, we look for other things that are like x. To take the most primordial cases, when we seek something to quench our thirst and succeed in finding something that provides gratification, we look for things that are similar. When we seek food to satisfy hunger, and find something that gratifies the hunger, we look for similar things. This is one of our most basic and adaptive dispositions. It is so important that we have non-conscious and fast ways of detecting the relevant similarities, but our consciousness provides slower and reflective means of examining or re-considering relevant similarities.

A crucial part of this story is that we find gratification in the object that our desire leads us to pursue. This is not always the case. Sometimes we are profoundly disappointed in pursuing something that we think will gratify. If compassion has the possibility of growing along the lines I have suggested, then, the desire to spare others from suffering must be gratifying. We must have built into us a disposition to find gratification in the object that our compassionate concern leads us to pursue, such that we look for similar objects. Mencius was confident that we are so built, and this is what he meant when he said in 2A6 that acting on our sprouts on knowing how to fill out the sprouts was like a fire starting up or a spring breaking through a hole in the ground. Acting on them gives us pleasure, which in turn spurs us on to finding relevantly similar opportunities to do more.

Mencius might indeed have put his finger on something that contemporary neuroscience confirms. Moll and his colleagues found that anonymous charitable giving based on ethical beliefs corresponds to activation of reward systems in fronto-limbic brain networks that are also activated by food, sex, drugs, and money.[55] Such giving is also linked to networks that control the release of oxytocin and vasopressin, the neurohormones that are linked to human and some other mammalian attachment to offspring, and among monogamous mammals, linked to attachment between cohabiting sexual partners and same-sex conspecifics.[56] Other studies link these neurohormones to temporary attachment between strangers, increasing trust, reciprocity, and generosity.[57] We might indeed have built into us dispositions to want and to find pleasure in responding to the needs of others.

Mencius' insight into how desire expands and grows in its objects is extremely important and points to an alternative way to think about how reflection and emotion and desire interact so as to produce new motivation. The Kantian tradition only gives us a rather impoverished version of a reified entity of reason generating its own motivation apart from the inclinations that drive our lives as social animals. The Humean tradition has tended to promote an instrumental view of how desires change in their scope or how new desires get generated. Changing or new desires result from existing desires, with reason providing relevant information: sometimes we desire new things as means to satisfying desires we already have; sometimes new desires get generated as more specific forms of a more general desire, such as the desire for something fabulous to garner my neighbor's admiration leading to the desire for a Porsche or for a swimming pool.

The alternative Mencian conception of desire as growing along analogical lines is plausible in an evolutionary framework, but it is also plausible from observation of the human psychic economy. It is a familiar phenomenon that we often don't know what we want and that we must engage with the world to get more knowledge of that. We have basic desires and aversions, likes and dislikes for certain things, but if we are lucky these only ensure our immediate survival. To know what else we want, we must explore other things in the world, and one's adaptive mechanism for doing so is starting with what has gratified us in the past. It need not be exactly the same, but only relevantly similar. But we must go and seek these out.

In this Mencian conception of the moral growth of compassion, moral teaching and learning interact with the unlearned form of compassion. Analogical inference may play a role in generating new moral knowledge. But in addition, extension of the visceral and motivational components to cases where moral knowledge points it is not ensured. Mencius seemed to envision a strategy of teaching in which the learner is prompted to experience compassion again in conjunction with being presented with a new and appropriate object for the visceral and motivational components.

Moral knowledge can grow through analogical inference, and so can desire. The double role of analogy is appropriate to the foundational role of pattern recognition in human response to the world. The two kinds of analogical processes are parallel. However, they are not the same because desire does not grow from the necessity to be logically consistent but from what one wants and has found gratifying in the past to what is relevantly like what one wants. There is no compulsion from logic for desire to move in this way. Nevertheless the two processes both operate in the moral growth of compassion. The trick is to get analogical growth of the feeling, the visceral and motivational components to interact with analogical growth of the cognitive component.

There is a striking resonance with this Mencian picture from some recent psychological theorizing on empathy and ethical development. The psychologist Martin Hoffman has suggested that a child begins to internalize morality when she experiences empathic distress upon witnessing another person's distress.[58] The earliest modes of empathic arousal are primitive, automatic, and involuntary processes. Hoffman thinks that the most effective child rearing takes advantage of occasions when primitive empathy is aroused and used in moral teaching. A child hurts another, for example, and an adult might arouse empathy in the perpetrator by pointing out the effect on the victim, expressing disapproval, and suggesting apology or reparation. When such a sequence is repeated many times, "scripts" are created and encoded in memory so that they influence later decisions and behavior. It is important that the kind of induction that presents moral reasons to the child be given in an emotionally evocative situation so that the cognition of what the child is being taught can be made "hot" by the activation of affective and motivational proclivities and through the linking of the proclivities to the reasons.

In Mencian terms, the primal empathic proclivities to which Hoffman points are part of the sprout of compassion. The neurological bases of these proclivities may include the release of oxytocin and vasopressin, as mentioned earlier. The sort of teaching that parents do with their children in the context of activated empathy for another who is suffering corresponds to the sort of teaching Mencius was trying to do with the king. Mencius is trying to embed a conception of what a true king does for his people in the king's emotional proclivities for compassion, such that this conception becomes emotionally charged and gains motivational efficacy. At the same time, the compassion is appropriately enlarged through getting the king to use his heart to reflect on what is right and appropriate for him to do as a king.

The anthropologist Naomi Quinn identifies one cross-cultural universal of child rearing as the linking of moral lessons with emotional arousal, so as to make the lessons unmistakable, memorable, and motivating.[59] In her discussion of Chinese child rearing, for example, Quinn identifies the practice of shaming as an instrument for bringing home a moral lesson to a child while emotionally arousing him or her. There is even a hint of shaming when Mencius tells King Xuan in something of a scolding tone that for the king to say his kindness can reach to the birds and beasts but that he cannot bring benefits to his people is like saying he is strong enough to lift 500 pounds but not strong enough to lift a single feather.

4 How Moral Development Becomes Self-Cultivation in the *Mencius*

So far we see Mencius nudging King Xuan to relieve his compassion for the ox and to transfer it to his people. But the development of character in Confucianism must ultimately place someone like King Xuan at the center of efforts to improve his character. Self-cultivation is never cultivation by the self alone, but as Mencius makes clear in 6A14–15, a person must take personal responsibility for cultivating his sprouts by reflecting on their manifestations and on what he experiences when he acts on them. As was noted earlier, Mencius believes with good reason that we are built to take pleasure in such reflection and action. Both the *Analects* (fifth to third centuries BCE) and the *Mencius* seem to assume that the very ideal of an exemplary person has magnetic power, i.e., that people are drawn to, are influenced and inspired by this person. And this magnetism is a kind of motivation for taking on the sustained project of self-cultivation.

The Immordino-Yang study of people who are told stories designed to evoke their admiration and compassion provides some striking confirmation of this idea. The results connecting the experience of compassion and admiration with felt visceral changes in one's body have earlier been noted. Immordino-Yang and her colleagues interviewed experiment participants to get self-reports about what they were feeling and thinking as a result of being told true stories about other people that elicited admiration or compassion. From the content of the interviews and from the finding that there was a high level of brain activity in areas of the brain associated with a feeling of self and interoceptive information from visceral sensation and regulation, they speculated that their grappling with the import of the stories evoked strong visceral reactions, the felt experience of which then prompted them to reflect on the meaning of these stories for themselves and their own moral standing.

One person, who reacted to a story meant to induce compassion and involving a mother and young son who made sacrifices for each other, described a "balloon or something just under [his] sternum, inflating and moving up and out." This made the participant think about how he had not thanked his own parents enough for their sacrifices.[60] Another experiment participant reported her reaction to a story meant to induce admiration for moral virtue as becoming "more sensitive to the temperature inside you … a visceral reaction that feels like an emotional alertness" and making her want to spend a year or two dedicated to the story protagonist's cause.[61] Immordino-Yang suggests that the participants' responses to the stories prompted visceral reactions in one's body that prompt self-awareness and self-evaluation. In the Confucian program of self-cultivation, "true" stories about historical leaders of the past seemed to have served the same function as stimuli for self-reflection and self-evaluation. We may see the participants in Immordino-Yang's study as engaging in Mencian reflection on the manifestation of their sprouts, beginning with feeling their *qi* move in response.

5 Going Beyond Mencius

It must be said that Mencius did not succeed in his attempted interventions with King Xuan. He did not help set King Xuan on course to become a true king. Perhaps a good part of the explanation of his failure is lack of the kind of constancy that Quinn describes as another universal feature of child rearing: moral lessons are a pervasive and consistent feature of social life for a child, often not explicitly stated, but communicated in a glance, a gesture, a posture, even in what is not said, that is observed in adults by children. Quinn even suggests some neurological correlates to the effects of these universal features. The regularity of lesson-giving strengthens certain synaptic connections in the brain; and drawing from Joseph LeDoux's seminal work,[62] Quinn points out that hormones released during emotional arousal actually strengthen synaptic connections and organize and coordinate brain activity, crowding out all but the emotionally relevant experience out of consciousness. One might surmise that constancy of lesson-giving, woven into the fabric of everyday life, strengthens these synaptic connections even more.

In the *Analects*, what we see there is in fact a community where such constancy and reinforcement are supplied under the leadership of Confucius. One can well imagine how the slightest look and posture of the body from Confucius could bring home a lesson to his students,[63] much less to speak of the times when he erupts into frank and sometimes harsh and shaming criticism of his students' failings.[64] The special value of the *Analects* lies in the way it portrays self-cultivation as a project done with others. A project in which the participants are committed to realizing the same values is one that can provide great support and reinforcement for each individual. After all, one has committed oneself "publicly," in front of one's fellows to the realization of these values in oneself, and that in itself can provide a great deal of additional motivation. There is also the fact that one is collaborating in such a project with others who know one well and can provide support, encouragement and needed criticism that is especially apt for the particular person. *Analects* 11.22 illustrates this last point: Confucius gives apparently contradictory advice to Zilu and to Ran You because they are two different people who need to improve in very different ways.

The special relationship between Yan Hui and Confucius illustrates a relationship of mutual support that can occur between two people deeply committed to the same project. The two share a deep and abiding love of learning, and in the early Confucian tradition learning was widely construed to include study and practice that can transform the self.[65] Such love of learning ensures constancy of effort in the face of obstacles and is a crucial quality for a successful project of moral cultivation. The *Analects* makes clear in various places why strong and constant motivation is needed in the face of resistance not only from circumstances but also from the self. No wonder, then, that Confucius singles out Yan Hui among all his students for being able to go for three months without departing in his thoughts and feelings from *ren* (human-heartedness), the trait of the exemplary person sometimes associated with loving others,[66] but most often treated in the *Analects* (but not the *Mencius*) as the all-inclusive and comprehensive virtue that includes all the particular virtues.

The two had a kind of father-son relationship that becomes poignant when Yan Hui dies young and Confucius grieves with abandon and desires to bury him as he would his own son.[67] The father guided the son in his difficult journey to follow the father's teachings: "The Master is good at drawing me forward a step at a time; he broadens me with culture (*wen* 文) and disciplines my behavior through the observance of ritual propriety."[68] But the son serves as inspirational example for the father in his love of, and quickness in, learning, and in his ability to focus on *ren*. This relationship of teaching and learning, mutual support, example, and inspiration fits the definition of Aristotle's character friendship, the highest form of friendship, in which friends value the moral excellence of each other's character and desire each other's well-being for their friend's sake.[69]

However, there are three respects in which the portrait of Confucius and Yan Hui's relationship complements and goes beyond Aristotle's discussion of character friendship. First, it provides a vivid and concrete sense of how two character friends can appreciate each other's moral excellence. Secondly, their relationship illustrates how character friends mutually support and sustain one another in their projects of moral cultivation. It is no surprise that two people whose moral excellence is especially notable for love of learning should forge a deep bond of mutual commitment and support. When Confucius lost his beloved Yan Hui, he lost (to use Aristotle's felicitous characterization of character friendship) "another self."

The third respect in which the *Analects'* portrait of Confucius and Yan Hui's relationship goes beyond Aristotle's discussion of character friendship has to do with how these two men differ. Friends not only share deep affinities, but can also bring different strengths to their relationship, such that each can contribute to the other's moral excellence in ways the other could not have achieved without that friend. Amy Olberding has deployed François Jullien's notion of the bland to suggest that Yan Hui's dullness as a character—he has no dramatic and attention-capturing traits such as Zilu's bull-in-a-china-shop boldness, for example—is precisely one of his great strengths, in that it results from all one's qualities held in a kind of balance such that no one quality predominates. This balance or equanimity makes the bearer open to determination, ready to absorb the requirements of the situation and to respond accordingly.[70] Confucius' character is so different from Yan Hui's salutary blandness that one is tempted to call it spicy. As Christoph Harbsmeier has pointed out, Confucius often comes across in the *Analects* as earthy, often self-deprecating, impulsive, given to outbursts that are often harsh or sweeping criticisms of politicians and of his students, but possessed of a short memory of his negative feelings and who is capable of appreciation and fondness for the strengths of the same students he criticizes.[71]

Confucius' persona is most appropriate for the "Master," one who has not only the authority and charisma but also the temperament to direct frank and, if need be, harsh criticisms of those engaged in cultivation. At the same time, Confucius' humor, often self-deprecating, defuses what might otherwise be the alienating effects of his criticism of students. They know he is not only prepared to be criticized, but invites it through his own affectionate critique of Yan Hui as never disagreeing with him. Thus, the way in which Confucius takes joy in questing after *ren* is not the same as Yan Hui's, and it is not the same in a way that is suitable to his role as a teacher and father figure to Yan Hui.

To make my final point about the need to go beyond Mencius, let us note that in the *Analects* and the *Xunzi* (third to second? century BCE) especially, there is heavy emphasis on performing rituals that are designed to symbolize and convey ethically appropriate attitudes such as concern and respect for others (from reverent ways of burying one's family members, respectful ways of getting married, to respectful greeting of others and ways of eating meals with others). If one takes care to perform these rituals with the right attitudes, one hopes to make them part of one's psychological "muscle memory," and again to instill them so that they become spontaneous and integral to one's being in the world.[72] Setting aside Confucius himself, it was Xunzi (third century BCE) among all the early Confucians, who was most appreciative of the necessity for constant and assiduous cultivation of the emotions and desires, and of how it took the right supportive relationships and engagement with the right cultural practices. Much more than Mencius, I believe, Xunzi had a correct and keen appreciation for the way that an undue focus on the self stands in the way of cultivating the morally congenial emotions such as compassion. Recall the vein of thought in Mencius that original goodness is like water flowing downward. I suspect it is this vein of thought that influenced him to underemphasize the need to discipline the part of the self that is concerned only for itself.

Centuries later, Neo-Confucians such as Zhu Xi (1130–1200) and Wang Yangming (1472–1529) canonized Mencius over Xunzi, and this might in part have been because the side of Mencius that likened the goodness of human nature with water flowing downward was more compatible with Buddhism's similar conception of goodness as residing complete in human nature but obscured by desire. In my view, the more fruitful direction would have involved a synthesis of Mencius and Xunzi, but that is the occasion for another discussion.

Notes

1. E.g., Thomas Nagel, *The Possibility of Altruism*; Nagel, *The View from Nowhere*; and Thomas Scanlon, *What We Owe to Each Other*.

2. E.g., Simon Blackburn, *Ruling Passions* and Jesse Prinz, *The Emotional Construction of Morals*.

3. David B. Wong, "Is There a Distinction between Reason and Emotion in Mencius?" and Wong, "Reasons and Analogical Reasoning in Mengzi."

4. I have learned from criticisms of my earlier writings on this subject by Craig Ihara ("David Wong on Emotions In Mencius"), Philip Ivanhoe ("Confucian Self Cultivation and Mengzi's Notion of Extension"), and Emily McRae ("The Cultivation of Moral Feelings and Mengzi's Method of Extension"). While I can't say that I fully accept their criticisms or their suggested alternative interpretations of Mencius, reflecting on their criticisms has helped me to form an interpretation that I hope is more plausible both as an interpretation and as a view of how emotions, such as compassion, can become moral virtues.

5. I owe the "how" formulation of the Chinese interest in the practical to Kwong-loi Shun, who articulated it in a commentary on my lectures on Chinese Philosophy and the Development of Compassion, delivered as the Philomathia Lectures at the Chinese University of Hong Kong in May 2012 and to appear in revised form in the journal *Dao*.

6. Kwong-loi Shun, *Mencius and Early Chinese Thought*, 185.

7. Roger T. Ames, "The Mencian Conception of *Ren Xing*."

8. I do not intend what I say about compassion to apply necessarily to all the other sprouts. For one thing, it is not clear that the approval/disapproval that is the sprout of wisdom is necessarily an emotion or has an emotional component. For another thing, it is not clear that all the sprouts that are or involve emotions need to have the same character or relate to reflective processes in exactly the same way. For a discussion of the emotional content of *hao* and *wu*, see Bruya, "*Qing* 情 and Emotion in Early Chinese Thought."

9. *Mencius*, 1A7.

10. Ibid., 3A5, 6A4, 7A45.

11. Ibid., 4A27.

12. Antonio Damasio, *Descartes' Error*.

13. Alan K. L. Chan, "A Matter of Taste," 52.

14. Should anyone but an early Chinese person take the conception of *qi* seriously? Contemporary physics has dislodged the mechanistic conception of matter as inert substance pushed around by forces. We are now closer to viewing matter as a kind of condensed energy-stuff. My point is not that the early Chinese were exactly right about the equivalence between matter and energy, but rather that their view of *qi* is an interesting form of naturalistic materialism, where the "material" is not as lumpy and inert as we used to think it was. This picture of *qi*, I hope to show, has plausible consequences for understanding the relationship between thinking, feeling, and motivation.

15. For more on different kinds of *qi*, see Chan, "A Matter of Taste."

16. See ibid., 51.

17. Mary Helen Immordino-Yang et al., "Neural Correlates of Admiration and Compassion."

18. D. C. Lau translates 壹 as "blocked," so as to make the relevant line in the *Mencius* read "The will, when blocked, moves the *qi*" (Lau, *Mencius*, 32), but a much less misleading translation would focus on the related meaning used by Zhu Xi in his commentary on this passage, i.e., that of "convergence" or "concentration" of *qi*. See Chan, "A Matter of Taste," 47–48.

19. I would gloss *li* 理 in this context as a "normative order in things," but later on I will emphasize a more general human ability for recognition of the relevant similarities and dissimilarities between things and situations is crucial to the Mencian development of the sprouts.

20. J. Kiley Hamlin, Karen Wynn, and Paul Bloom, "Social Evaluation by Preverbal Infants"; Hamlin, Wynn, and Bloom, "Three-Month-Olds Show a Negativity Bias in their Social Evaluations"; Hamlin and Wynn, "Young Infants Prefer Prosocial to Antisocial Others."

21. Hamlin et al., "How Infants and Toddlers React to Antisocial Others."

22. For a survey of the recent experimental evidence undermining the assumption that "basic" emotions such as fear and anger are reliably accompanied by a stereotypical set of actions, see Lisa F. Barrett, Kevin N. Ochsner, and James J. Gross, "On the Automaticity of Emotion."

23. See note 19 above.

24. In first writing about this issue, I held that unlearned compassion had a cognitive component that was something like a judgment: that one has a reason to help someone who is suffering or to spare someone suffering (Wong, "Is There a Distinction between Reason and Emotion in Mencius?"). Craig Ihara responded quite justifiably that a person can feel compassion and yet make no judgments about reasons ("David Wong on Emotions in Mencius"). My initial response to this criticism was to suggest that our concept of compassion is a prototype concept, the application of which is governed by a paradigm or prototype. There are no necessary and sufficient conditions for an emotion's being compassion, but rather a set of features embodying the average or most typical instances of compassion. An emotion is a candidate for falling under the concept of compassion is more likely to qualify the more it resembles typical instances, but there is more than one way of coming close enough to the typical. I still think this response is

in principle true, but as a response to Ihara is inadequate. It now strikes me that unlearned compassion need not have the cognitive component of recognizing a reason to help in order to serve as a sprout from which the virtue of *ren* (human-heartedness) can grow. It does not indeed have to be a judgment of any kind. As indicated earlier, it does have a cognitive component, but one that is less cognitively sophisticated than a judgment, much less a judgment of recognizing that one has a reason. At some point, as the sprout is developing on the way to becoming a virtue, I do think that compassion incorporates the judgment that one has reason to help.

25. *Encyclopedia of Cognitive Science*, s.v. "Analogical Reasoning, Psychology of."

26. Immordino-Yang et al., "Neural Correlates of Admiration and Compassion."

27. Ibid., 8024.

28. The brain areas showing high levels of activity in compassion for social pain were the inferior/posterior PMC (posteromedial cortices) and the anterior middle cingulate, which are affiliated with interoceptive information; by contrast, emotions related to someone else's "physical" state, e.g., painful injury, may recruit the sector of PMC most connected with lateral parietal cortices, suggesting a connection to exteroception and musculoskeletal information.

29. See Gerald L. Clore and Andrew Ortony, "Cognition in Emotion," 42.

30. Jesse Prinz appears to build his theory of emotion, including moral emotion, on such a restricted basis (*The Emotional Construction of Morals*).

31. Such as Clore and Ortony.

32. Barrett, Ochsner, and Gross, "On the Automaticity of Emotion."

33. For possible neurobiological models incorporating psychological theories of emotion and neurobiology that are meant to capture multidirectional causality between the various components of emotion, see Marc D. Lewis, "Bridging Emotion Theory and Neurobiology through Dynamic Systems Modeling."

34. Mara Mather and Laura L. Carstensen, "Aging and Motivated Cognition."

35. *Mencius* 4B19, 4B28.

36. Ibid., 6A10, 6A11.

37. E.g., ibid., 2A5, 3A3.

38. Ibid., 6A14.

39. Ibid., 6A15.

40. Wong, Chinese Philosophy and the Development of Compassion (lectures).

41. Conrad H. Waddington, "Canalization of Development and the Inheritance of Acquired Characters"; David S. Moore, *The Dependent Gene*.

42. *Analects* 12.2. All translations are mine unless otherwise noted.

43. *Analects* 6.30, adapted from Roger T. Ames and Henry Rosemont Jr., *The Analects of Confucius*.

44. *Mencius* 7A35 presents Mencius' view of what Shun the sage-king would have done had his father murdered a man, and thus when Shun had to balance his duties not to interfere with the Minister of Justice against his duties as a son.

45. An issue I will not get into here is where Mencius thinks moral reasons ultimately come from. I think the ultimate source for Mencius is *tian* (heaven). I am inclined to believe that Mencius' conception of *tian* is such as to imply a strongly realist view of moral properties such as moral reasons or rightness as part of the normative order given by *tian*, but this is a contentious issue (for a conception of *tian* as a creative force that includes human creative powers to collectively and individually fashion values and practices, see Ames, "The Mencian Conception of *Ren Xing*" and "Mencius and a Process Notion of Human Nature"). If the realist interpretation is right, then presumably *tian* confers on human beings the ability to identify moral properties. But I will not argue the issue here. Xunzi provides an alternative conception of where the properties come from that are more palatable to those with a more naturalistic bent—i.e., that they are human inventions designed in the course of regulating human psychology so that people may cease coming into conflict with each other over the means to satisfy desire. Xunzi thinks that nothing other than a radical psychological transformation will be required for a productive and harmonious society. But he agrees with Mencius that reasons are not derived from desire but rather from those considerations that guide the shaping of human desire.

46. See Wong, "Reasons and Analogical Reasoning in Mengzi."

47. Valerie M. Hudson, Philip A. Schrodt, and Ray D. Whitmer, "A New Kind of Social Science."

48. For further discussion of this question, see Wong, "Reasons and Analogical Reasoning in Mengzi."

49. David Nivison interprets Mencius as making this sort of argument in 1A7 but is appropriately skeptical about the effectiveness of such an argument (Nivison, "Mencius and Motivation").

50. Sigmund Freud, *On Sexuality*, 272.

51. Clore and Ortony, "Cognition in Emotion."

52. Clore and Ortony go on to characterize these processes in ways I don't necessarily think are the most useful. They hold that direct computation of emotional meaning is "theory-based," i.e., rule-based computation of emotional meaning based on "underlying" aspects of the situation rather than "surface" features that are perceptually accessible. Reinstatement is "prototype"-based processing that goes on the similarity of perceptually accessible features (ibid., 37) possessed by a present situation to that of a past situation that has triggered an emotion, resulting in reinstatement of that emotion in the present. This categorization neglects the possibility that the similarity between situations that can reinstate an emotion need not be based on surface similarity. This possibility will be explored shortly.

53. Emily McRae, "The Cultivation of Moral Feelings and Mengzi's Method of Extension," 593; Wong, "Is There a Distinction between Reason and Emotion in Mencius?"

54. *Mencius* 7A45. The exemplary person loves animals but is not *ren* toward them.

55. Jorge Moll et al., "Human Fronto-Mesolimbic Networks Guide Decisions about Charitable Donation."

56. Paul J. Zak, "The Neuroeconomics of Trust."

57. Paul J. Zak, "Trust: a Temporary Human Attachment Facilitated by Oxytocin"; Paul J. Zak, Robert Kurzban, and William T. Matzner, "Oxytocin is Associated with Human Trustworthiness"; Morhenn et al., "Monetary Sacrifice among Strangers Is Mediated by Endogenous Oxytocin Release after Physical Contact."

58. Martin L. Hoffman, *Empathy and Moral Development*.

59. Naomi Quinn, "Universals of Child Rearing."

60. Immordino-Yang, "Me, My 'Self' and You," 313–314.

61. Ibid., 314.

62. Joseph E. LeDoux, *Synaptic Self*, 200–234.

63. For the very interesting connections between the Confucian emphasis on subtle details of personal style and the way an agent can influence others through such details, see Hagop Sarkissian, "Minor Tweaks, Major Payoffs."

64. E.g., the interactions with Zai Wo in *Analects* 5.10 and 17.21.

65. Ibid., 1.1, 7.19, 6.3, 6.11.

66. Ibid., 12.22.

67. Ibid., 11.10, 11.11.

68. Ibid., 9.11; Ames and Rosemont, *The Analects of Confucius*, 128.

69. Aristotle, *Nicomachean Ethics*, Books 8 and 9.

70. François Jullien, "The Chinese Notion of 'Blandness' as a Virtue"; Amy Olberding, "The Consummation of Sorrow."

71. Christoph Harbsmeier, "Confucius Ridens."

72. For illuminating development of these themes in relation to the problem of "situationism" for virtue ethics, see Edward Slingerland, "Toward an Empirically Responsible Ethics" and Slingerland, "The Situationist Critique and Early Confucian Virtue Ethics."

Works Cited

Ames, Roger T. "The Mencian Conception of *Ren Xing*: Does It Mean Human Nature?" In *Chinese Texts and Philosophical Contexts: Essays Dedicated to Angus C. Graham*, ed. Henry Rosemont Jr. Open Court, 1991.

Ames, Roger T. "Mencius and a Process Notion of Human Nature." In *Mencius: Contexts and Interpretations*, ed. Alan Kam-leung Chan. University of Hawai'i Press, 2002.

Ames, Roger T., and Henry Rosemont Jr.. *The Analects of Confucius: A Philosophical Translation*. Ballantine Books, 1998.

Barrett, Lisa Feldman, Kevin N. Ochsner, and James J. Gross. "On the Automaticity of Emotion." In *Social Psychology and the Unconscious: The Automaticity of Higher Mental Processes*, ed. John Bargh. Psychology Press, 2007.

Blackburn, Simon. *Ruling Passions: A Theory of Practical Reasoning*. Oxford University Press, 2001.

Bruya, Brian. "*Qing* 情 and Emotion in Early Chinese Thought." *Ming Qing Yanjiu* (2001): 151–176. Reprinted in *Chinese Philosophy and the Trends of the 21st Century Civilization*, ed. Fang Keli, 72–106. Beijing: *Shang wu yin shu guan* 商务印书馆, 2003.

Chan, Alan K. L. "A Matter of Taste: *Qi* (Vital Energy) and the Tending of the Heart (*Xin*) in *Mencius* 2A2." In *Mencius: Contexts and Interpretations*, ed. Alan Kam-leung Chan. University of Hawai'i Press, 2002.

Chase, William G., and Herbert A. Simon. "Perception in Chess." *Cognitive Psychology* 4, no. 1 (1973): 55–81.

Clore, Gerald L., and Andrew Ortony. "Cognition in Emotion: Always, Sometimes, or Never?" In *Cognitive Neuroscience of Emotion*, ed. Richard D. Lane and Lynn Nadel. Oxford University Press, 2000.

Damasio, Antonio R. *Descartes' Error: Emotion, Reason, and the Human Brain*. Putnam, 1994.

Freud, Sigmund. "On Sexuality." In *Penguin Freud Library*, volume 7, ed. James Strachey and Angela Richards. Penguin, 1991.

Hamlin, J. "Three-Month-Olds Show a Negativity Bias in Their Social Evaluations." *Developmental Science* 13, no. 6 (2010): 923–929.

Hamlin, J. Kiley, and Karen Wynn. "Young Infants Prefer Prosocial to Antisocial Others." *Cognitive Development* 26, no. 1 (2011): 30–39.

Hamlin, J. Kiley, Karen Wynn, and Paul Bloom. "Social Evaluation by Preverbal Infants." *Nature* 450 (22) (2007): 557–560.

Hamlin, J. Kiley, Karen Wynn, Paul Bloom, and Neha Mahajan. "How Infants and Toddlers React to Antisocial Others." *Proceedings of the National Academy of Sciences* 108, no. 50 (2011): 19931–19936.

Harbsmeier, Christoph. "Confucius Ridens: Humor in the *Analects*." *Harvard Journal of Asiatic Studies* 50, no. 1 (1990): 131–161.

Hoffman, Martin L. *Empathy and Moral Development: Implications for Caring and Justice*. Cambridge University Press, 2000.

Hudson, Valerie M., Philip A. Schrodt, and Ray D. Whitmer. "A New Kind of Social Science: Moving Ahead with Reverse Wolfram Models Applied to Event Data." Paper prepared for delivery at the Annual Meeting of the International Studies Association, Honolulu, March, 2004. Quoted in the weblog *Seeing Complexity: Visualizing Complex Data*, posting of 02/09/2011, "The Brain as Pattern Recognition Machine" (http://seeingcomplexity.wordpress.com/2011/02/09/the-brain-as -a-pattern-recognition-machine/).

Ihara, Craig K. "David Wong on Emotions in Mencius." *Philosophy East and West* 41, no. 1 (1991): 45–53.

Immordino-Yang, Mary Helen, Andrea McColl, Hanna Damasio, and Antonio Damasio. "Neural Correlates of Admiration and Compassion." *Proceedings of the National Academy of Sciences* 106 (29) (2009): 8021–8026.

Immordino-Yang, Mary Helen. "Me, My 'Self' and You: Neuropsychological Relations between Social Emotion, Self-Awareness, and Morality." *Emotion Review* 3, no. 3 (2011): 313–315.

Ivanhoe, Philip J. "Confucian Self Cultivation and Mengzi's Notion of Extension." In *Essays on the Moral Philosophy of Mengzi*, ed. Xiusheng Liu and Philip J. Ivanhoe. Hackett, 2002.

Jullien, François. "The Chinese Notion of 'Blandness' as a Virtue: A Preliminary Outline." Tr. Graham Parkes. *Philosophy East and West* 43, no. 1 (1993): 107–111.

Lau, D. C. *Mencius*. Penguin, 2005.

LeDoux, Joseph E. *Synaptic Self: How Our Brains Become Who We Are*. Viking, 2002.

Lewis, Marc D. "Bridging Emotion Theory and Neurobiology through Dynamic Systems Model-ing." *Behavioral and Brain Sciences* 28 (2) (2005): 169–245.

Mather, Mara, and Laura L. Carstensen. "Aging and Motivated Cognition: the Positivity Effect in Attention and Memory." *Trends in Cognitive Sciences* 9, no. 10 (2005): 496–502.

McRae, Emily. "The Cultivation of Moral Feelings and Mengzi's Method of Extension." *Philosophy East and West* 61, no. 4 (2011): 587–608.

Moll, Jorge, Frank Krueger, Roland Zahn, Matteo Pardini, Ricardo de Oliveira-Souza, and Jordan Grafman. "Human Fronto-Mesolimbic Networks Guide Decisions about Charitable Donation." *Proceedings of the National Academy of Sciences* 103, no. 42 (2006): 15623–15628.

Moore, David S. *The Dependent Gene: The Fallacy of "Nature vs. Nurture."* Henry Holt, 2003.

Morhenn, Vera B., Jang Woo Park, Elisabeth Piper, and Paul J. Zak. "Monetary Sacrifice among Strangers Is Mediated by Endogenous Oxytocin Release after Physical Contact." *Evolution and Human Behavior* 29, no. 6 (2008): 375–383.

Nadel, Lynn, ed. *Encyclopedia of Cognitive Science*. Nature Publishing Group, 2003.

Nagel, Thomas. *The Possibility of Altruism*. Princeton University Press, 1979.

Nagel, Thomas. *The View from Nowhere*. Oxford University Press, 1986.

Nivison, David S. "Mencius and Motivation." In *Studies in Classical Chinese Thought: Papers Presented at the Workshop on Classical Chinese Thought Held at Harvard University, August 1976*, ed. Henry Rosemont Jr. and Benjamin I. Schwartz. American Academy of Religion, 1979.

Olberding, Amy. "The Consummation of Sorrow: An Analysis of Confucius' Grief for Yan Hui." *Philosophy East and West* 54, no. 3 (2004): 279–301.

Prinz, Jesse. *The Emotional Construction of Morals*. Oxford University Press, 2008.

Quinn, Naomi. "Universals of Child Rearing." *Anthropological Theory* 5, no. 4 (2005): 477–516.

Sarkissian, Hagop. "Minor Tweaks, Major Payoffs: The Problems and Promise of Situationism in Moral Philosophy." *Philosophers' Imprint* 10, no. 9 (2010): 1–15.

Scanlon, Thomas. *What We Owe to Each Other*. Harvard University Press, 1998.

Shun, Kwong-loi. *Mencius and Early Chinese Thought*. Stanford University Press, 1997.

Slingerland, Edward. "The Situationist Critique and Early Confucian Virtue Ethics." *Ethics* 121 (2) (2011): 390–419.

Slingerland, Edward. "Toward an Empirically Responsible Ethics: Cognitive Science, Virtue Ethics, and Effortless Attention in Early Chinese Thought." In *Effortless Attention: A New Perspective in the Cognitive Science of Attention and Action*, ed. Brian Bruya. MIT Press, 2010.

Waddington, Conrad H. "Canalization of Development and the Inheritance of Acquired Characters." *Nature* 150, no. 3811 (1942): 563–565.

Wong, David B. Chinese Philosophy and the Development of Compassion, a series of three lectures. Philomathia Lectures. Chinese University of Hong Kong, 2012.

Wong, David B. "Is There a Distinction between Reason and Emotion in Mencius?" *Philosophy East and West* 41, no. 1 (1991): 31–44.

Wong, David B. "Reasons and Analogical Reasoning in Mengzi." In *Essays on the Moral Philosophy of Mengzi*, ed. Xiusheng Liu and Philip J. Ivanhoe. Hackett, 2002.

Wong, David B. "Response to Craig Ihara's discussion." Philosophy East and West 41, no. 1 (1991): 55–58.

Zak, Paul J. "The Neuroeconomics of Trust." In *Renaissance in Behavioral Economics: Essays in Honor of Harvey Leibenstein*, ed. Roger Frantz. Routledge, 2008.

Zak, Paul J. "Trust: A Temporary Human Attachment Facilitated by Oxytocin." *Behavioral and Brain Sciences* 28, no. 3 (2005): 368–369.

Zak, Paul J., Robert Kurzban, and William T. Matzner, "Oxytocin is Associated with Human Trustworthiness." *Hormones and Behavior* 48, no. 5 (2005): 522–527.

3 Proto-Empathy and Nociceptive Mirror Emotion: Mencius' Embodied Moral Psychology

Bongrae Seok

As is well known in many areas of comparative philosophy, a philosophical tradition is not easily translated or interpreted in a straightforward manner into another school of thought in a different intellectual environment. Sometimes, diverse dimensions, developments, and layers of an original tradition are ignored and only its global orientations are emphasized. Other times, only certain aspects of an original tradition are discussed and analyzed from a viewpoint of an existing or prevailing school of thought. The interpretation and analysis of Confucian moral philosophy is no exception. Major terms of Confucian philosophy such as *xue* 學 (learning), *li* 禮 (ritual propriety), *ren* 仁 (benevolence), and *dao* 道 (way) are often interpreted from the perspective of Western philosophy; however, because of their complex relations to other Confucian values and their rich cultural and historical contexts, their original meanings are not always captured by a simple process of translation or interpretation. In this chapter, instead of developing a comprehensive or global interpretation of Confucian moral philosophy based on a widely held Western school of thought, or focusing on a particular aspect of it from within the tradition, I will discuss a peculiar characteristic of Confucian moral philosophy that has been neglected in many comparative interpretations but can make an important contribution to contemporary philosophy. I will link Confucian moral philosophy, particularly that of Mencius, to current discussions of embodied cognition and the mirroring functions of the brain. Mencius' (fourth century BCE) version of Confucian moral philosophy provides an insightful understanding of our spontaneous, embodied, and other-regarding emotion toward others' pain and suffering. I will argue that several passages of the *Mencius* (fourth to third centuries BCE) can be interpreted from the perspective of embodied moral psychology and, as such, provide new insight into current philosophical discussions on the nature of the moral mind and the functional characteristics of moral cognition.

According to well-known moral theorists, there are three major approaches to the study of moral cognition (the study of moral reasoning, moral judgment, and moral development): Kantian, Humean, and Rawlsian approaches.[1] According to a Kantian, or rationalist, approach, the moral mind (that is, the ability to understand moral standards and moral violations, to reason and draw moral judgments, to develop and implement decisions and actions, and to initiate and sustain moral development) is understood from the perspective of a conscious, deliberate, and rational faculty of a moral agent. In this approach, moral reasoning is the inferential process of deriving conclusions in practical decisions; moral judgment is the process of justifying a decision under universal principles of morality; and moral development is the process of intellectual maturation that takes sequential or dialectic steps to develop higher and more comprehensive reasoning skills to identify universal moral principles and to apply them to solve moral conflicts and dilemmas.[2] Ultimately, a moral action is characterized by the rational commitment to develop, recognize, and follow universally justified rules or principles of human conduct applicable to all humanity.[3]

In contrast to this intellectual approach to moral cognition, a Humean, or sentimentalist, approach emphasizes the role emotion plays in our moral judgments and actions. In this approach, conscious and deliberate moral reasoning does not play any role in our moral judgments—they only play the role of post-hoc justification of judgments already made by our affective moral sense.[4] David Hume says that reason is the slave of the passions.[5] Reason serves our emotions *for* (sympathy, compassion, pity) and *against* (guilt, shame, sorrow) certain actions and dispositions. This approach to moral cognition focuses on our deeply rooted affective concern toward others' well-being—moral reasoning, moral judgments, and moral actions are explained by our other-regarding emotions and their affective reactions.[6] Moral development is no exception. It is not the process of intellectual maturation culminating in the recognition, acceptance, and internalization of universal principles of human conduct but the extension and refinement of emotions such as empathy (the feeling of others' inner states) and sympathy (the feeling for others' well-being).[7]

The third approach to moral cognition is a Rawlsian, or faculty, approach. According to this approach, moral actions and judgments derive from a specialized function of the mind (the moral faculty), whose operating principles are not consciously accessible. The moral faculty is comparable to the faculty of language that generates grammaticality judgments (intuitive judgments of whether given sentences are grammatical or not). As we judge the grammaticality of sentences or utterances, we also judge the morality of actions, decisions, and dispositions by following principles that guide our intuitive decisions. This approach is called Rawlsian because John Rawls developed the linguistic analogy of moral judgments.[8] According to him, our moral judgments, like our grammaticality judgments, derive from our intuitive sense of right and wrong on the basis of the formal principles of the moral faculty. By analyzing trolley problems (a set of decision scenarios where one should decide whether to sacrifice one person to save five people), for example, Marc Hauser develops a hypothesis that we intuitively or unconsciously rely on a formal principle to draw moral judgments about justifiable harm.[9] In this model, moral judgments are neither rational nor emotional—they are not based on conscious and deliberate reasoning or the feeling of compassion or aversion.[10] Rather, they are the results of specialized formal principles that are not consciously accessible to us but reside in a deeply rooted structure of the mind.[11]

None of the approaches discussed here seriously considers the role the body (the physical structure and function of a moral agent and their interaction with the environment) plays in our moral perception, judgment, and action; instead, these approaches provide "disembodied" models of how a moral agent sees, thinks, judges, and acts morally.[12] In their explanations, the disembodied models utilize particular forms of computation (typically sequential or hierarchical processes), representations (typically discrete and modality neutral representations), and moral emotions (typically sympathy, care, and concern), but the moral mind, whether it is characterized as Kantian reasoning, Humean emotion, or Rawlsian principle, is detached from the concrete, spontaneous, and physical sense and activity of a moral agent.[13] Perhaps because of peculiar computational biases, cognitive orientations, or the lack of appropriate understanding, the possibility of embodied moral cognition is not fully explored in most traditional and current approaches to moral cognition. However, recent philosophical and psychological studies show that some social and moral judgments are served by spontaneous, quick, minimally deliberate, embodied, and affective processes with non-sequential, non-hierarchical computation over modality-specific representations and embodied emotions. Antonio Damasio discusses neural pathways that essentially include embodied processes serving our decision-making functions.[14] Jonathan Haidt analyzes how emotion affects our social and moral judgments in an intuitive and reflexive way.[15] Paula Niedenthal and colleagues report and analyze how social cognition is systematically and consistently influenced by physical conditions of the body (body position, temperature, heart rate, and so on).[16] Shaun Nichols and Jesse Prinz develop convincing analyses of the role strong and spontaneous emotional reactions play in our understanding of moral violations and cognition.[17] In these studies, embodied emotions and spontaneous reactions are analyzed to emphasize the role the body plays in social and moral cognition. Perhaps our understanding of others' social and moral behaviors depends primarily on spontaneous, affective, and embodied processes of the mind. From this embodied and affective viewpoint, I will develop a moral psychology of the body, i.e., a moral psychology of embodied and other-regarding emotion. How does the body initiate, influence, and sustain moral judgments and decisions? How does it motivate compassionate actions and other-regarding behaviors? I will explore this relatively uncharted territory of embodied moral psychology from the perspective of Confucian philosophy. In particular, I will focus on Mencius' concept of *ceyin zhi xin* 惻隱之心 (the heartmind of pity and compassion) to discuss how Confucian moral philosophy offers the insight of embodied proto-empathy to current discussions in moral psychology.

Mencius' notion of *ceyin zhi xin* is often understood as an emotional state of empathy. In moral psychology, empathy is typically studied and analyzed as an other-regarding emotion that connects social cognition (identifying, categorizing, and understanding others' behaviors and their inner states) and moral cognition (reasoning, justifying, judging, and deciding moral issues). As one understands, feels, and shares the inner states of others (social cognition), one naturally feels for them and is motivated to act for their well-being (moral cognition). As many psychologists report, understanding or sensing others' inner mental states, particularly their affective states, motivates prosocial behaviors and caring actions.

The relationship between social cognition and moral cognition, however, is not always simple and straightforward. There are quite a few psychopaths who have a good understanding of others' inner mental states and still commit horrible crimes, and there are also some autistic individuals who do not have a decent ability of social cognition and yet are capable of affectionate and caring behavior. As the so-called Machiavellian (or social) intelligence hypothesis suggests, knowing what others believe and desire does not necessarily motivate caring affection or moral action.[18] At the foundation of the Confucian heartmind and the virtue of *ren*, Mencius provides an amazing insight regarding this puzzling relationship between the social mind and the moral mind. He discusses an empathetic state (*ceyin zhi xin*) of the mind as an essential foundation of our other-regarding emotions (such as care, concern, or compassion) and virtuous moral dispositions (such as *ren* 仁 [Confucian benevolence]). Yet, this empathetic state is so fundamental and essential to the moral mind that it does not even require full social cognitive ability. Without complete understanding of what others think and feel, our moral minds start to develop basic empathetic states to prompt other-regarding affections and caring actions. Mencius describes this unique empathetic state in his example of a man seeing an innocent child about to fall into a well.[19] The man experiences a basic state of empathy, i.e., sudden fear, stress, and affective reaction toward the child's pain and suffering, but he does not seem to, or need to, know about the inner mental states of the child in imminent danger. I call this sudden affective reaction to the (potentially) suffering child *proto-empathy* because of its other-regarding interest without full social cognition. This basic ability of empathy, however, is neither limited nor morally indiscriminate. It is an independent and important moral emotion in its own right that Mencius picks up as the foundation of the fully developed virtue of *ren*.

In this chapter, I will compare and contrast *ceyin zhi xin* with other empathetic states that typically require social cognitive abilities and analyze it as a unique, or at least important, characteristic of the Confucian moral mind. Recent studies in neuroscience demonstrate the existence of neural pathways that support other-regarding affection with minimal social cognitive functions. Specifically, the function of the anterior insula, in the process of nociception (pain perception), is reported to be correlated with levels of empathy (according to an empathy scale) but not necessarily with social cognitive abilities. Put together, Mencius' discussion of moral emotion (e.g., *ceyin zhi xin*) and the cognitively asocial but emotionally other-regarding functions of the anterior insula demonstrate the existence of an embodied emotion that serves as the foundation of fully developed moral dispositions. If this comparative and interdisciplinary interpretation is successful, it will open up new territory in the field of moral psychology. In contrast to Kantian, Humean, and Rawlsian moral minds, a Confucian moral mind, in which other-regarding and embodied emotions can work independently of their social cognitive functions, explains this basic but important aspect of moral cognition better.

To explain and analyze the uniqueness of this Confucian approach and the empathetic and embodied nature of Mencius' *ceyin zhi xin*, I will take two steps. First, I will analyze possible interpretations of *ceyin zhi xin*, focusing particularly on that of feminist care ethics, to demonstrate that *ceyin zhi xin* is different from care or other moral sentiments that presuppose a particular kind of social cognition in a moral agent. I will argue that *ceyin zhi xin* is an other-regarding emotion, but it does not require full social cognition like care or concern does. Second, I will discuss the embodied nature of *ceyin zhi xin* by analyzing three distinct mirroring functions of the brain recently discovered and discussed by neuroscientists. By comparing *ceyin zhi xin* and nociceptive mirror emotion (emotion that derives from the simulation of others' affective pain experience), I hypothesize that Confucian proto-empathy (such as *ceyin zhi xin* and *bu ren* 不忍 [inability to bear the suffering of others]) is instantiated by neural pathways (particularly those that include the anterior insula) where other-regarding, embodied, and affective processes of nociception take place. Specifically, both Mencius' *ceyin zhi xin* and the anterior insula serve embodied, receptive, and empathetic nociceptive processes that motivate prosocial behaviors with minimal involvement of social cognitive functions of the mind. Since *ceyin zhi xin* is the foundation of the central Confucian virtue (*ren*), my interpretation of *ceyin zhi xin* and my hypothesis regarding its neural correlate reveal an important orientation of Confucian moral philosophy that can provide a unique and viable moral psychological perspective. This new moral psychological approach, if successfully developed, will contribute to current philosophical studies on the nature of the moral mind and pave promising paths for further exploration.

1 Interpretations of Confucian Moral Philosophy and *Ceyin Zhi Xin*

Recently, Chinese comparative philosophy has seen a surge of discussions on the nature of moral mind and virtue. Confucian philosophy, particularly, is at the center of this movement to interpret and integrate Chinese philosophy with Western schools of moral and political thought. Some Chinese and American philosophers interpret

Confucian moral philosophy from the perspective of Western theories of ethics such as Kantian deontology (or rule ethics),[20] virtue ethics,[21] and utilitarian ethics.[22] Others have developed a new theoretical framework called role ethics to emphasize unique social and interpersonal characteristics of Confucian moral philosophy.[23]

In addition to these, a group of scholars discusses Confucian moral philosophy from the perspective of feminist care ethics[24] and sentimentalist ethics.[25] According to this group of scholars, Confucian moral philosophy is a type of care ethics, or sentimentalist ethics. Confucian virtues are characterized as the ability and the sensitivity of the moral mind. As such, they are other-regarding dispositions and naturally arising emotions that can be interpreted as special forms of moral sentiments such as care (with its other-regarding emotion and motivational orientation) or concern (with its affective sense of others' well-being). One of the passages that is commonly used to support this interpretation is the "child by the well" passage from the *Mencius* already mentioned above. The passage reads as follows:

All men have the heartmind that cannot bear to see the sufferings of others [*bu ren ren zhi xin* 不忍人之心]. Suppose a man suddenly sees a child about to fall into a well, he will invariably have feelings of alarm and distress as well as pity and compassion [*chuti ceyin zhi xin* 怵惕惻隱之心]. He feels this way not because he wants to get along well with the child's parents, not because he wants to get fame from his neighbors and friends, and not because he is bothered by the sound of the child's cries. Without the heartmind of pity and compassion [*ceyin zhi xin*], we are not even human beings.[26] (2A6)

Mencius calls this strong reactive emotion *ceyin zhi xin* (the heartmind of pity and compassion, or the heartmind of commiseration) and defines it as the first sprout of the mind toward *ren* (benevolence, or human heartedness), the central Confucian virtue.[27] This passage, in fact, is one of the most frequently cited and intensely analyzed passages of the *Mencius*.[28] From the perspectives of care ethics and sentimentalist ethics, *ceyin zhi xin* exemplifies the unique moral psychology that is different from, say, a utilitarian moral psychology of hedonism or a Kantian moral psychology of the good will toward universal moral rules. For example, Wee explicitly uses the terms "care" and "concern" in her discussion of this particular passage of the *Mencius*. She says that Mencius

famously points out that the natural response of a person who sees a child about to fall into a well is to feel compassion and distress—it is natural to care that the child does not come to harm. Mencius holds that the human being has an innate predisposition to feel care and concern for others. In his famous passage on the Four Beginnings [sprouts], Mencius points out that all humans have the "heart" of compassion which, when fully developed, becomes *jen* [*ren*].[29]

To these Confucian scholars, examples like Mencius' child by the well and emotions like *ceyin zhi xin* are good evidence to support an interpretation that takes Confucian moral philosophy, with its general emphases on particularistic human relations and other-regarding emotions, as a form of care ethics or sentimentalist ethics.

In their theories of feminist care ethics, philosophers such as Carol Gilligan, Nel Noddings, Annette Baier, and Virginia Held discuss other-regarding emotions and affectionate bonds among human beings in their personal relationships.[30] Care is one of these other-regarding emotions. It is generally characterized as our understanding of, emotion for, and altruistic stance toward others, with a feeling of connectedness and affective moral engagement. Its inner motive, intention, dedication, and affection are all closely linked to the promotion and maintenance of meaningful human relationships that are essentially based on our natural affection toward others. Typically, care ethicists contrast the affective and personal orientation of care with impersonal duties and the abstract principles of justice and autonomy. According to this emotional, relationship based, and particularistic approach to ethics, helping a person out of a dangerous situation, for instance, is a good deed, but if it is done out of *a sense of duty* to a rule or an abstract principle, it is not an action of care.

In Confucian moral philosophy, a similar emphasis on the caring heart and personal relations can be witnessed. In many passages of Confucian texts, particularistic and relationship based moral virtues are discussed and praised as distinctive Confucian values. For example, the story of Upright Gong in the *Analects* (fifth to third centuries BCE) tells of a situation involving a moral dilemma—should a son report or cover up his father's crime?

The Duke of She told Confucius, "In my country, there is an upright man named Kung [Gong]. When his father stole a sheep, he bore witness against him." Confucius said, "The upright men in my community are different from this. The father conceals the misconduct of the son and the son conceals the misconduct of the father. Uprightness is to be found in this." (13.18)[31]

Confucius defends the son's action of covering up his father's crime as an appropriate action of uprightness and filial piety against the impersonal and principle-based duty to justice and social order. As Carol Gilligan does in her analysis of the Heinz example (one of the dilemmas used by Lawrence Kohlberg where Heinz decides to steal an unreasonably expensive medicine to take care of his sick wife),[32] some Confucian scholars take the action of Upright Gong as an act of care that truly represents the value of personal relationship and the particularistic nature of Confucian *ren* (benevolence).

1.1 *Ceyin Zhi Xin* and Care

Despite the similar emphases on the particularistic, relational, affective, and empathetic nature of the moral mind, the Confucian heartmind, in its foundation, is distinct from care in feminist care ethics. As a way to understand the moral psychological nature of *ceyin zhi xin*, I will analyze care in feminist care ethics and compare and contrast it with *ceyin zhi xin*. As I suggest above, empathy, with its psychological processes of taking another's inner states in one's mind and promoting prosocial behavior, combines social cognition and moral cognition together. However, *ceyin zhi xin*, even with its seemingly empathetic features, does not necessarily require social cognition. The man in Mencius' example (2A6) does not have to know the inner states of the child in danger for him to feel and act morally. Perhaps a quick and vicarious sense of danger, a stressful awareness of imminent pain, and an affective reaction to a victim's suffering would be sufficient. I will develop an *asocial* interpretation of *ceyin zhi xin* (i.e., the possibility of moral cognition without social cognition) in the following section. Here I will compare *ceyin zhi xin* with a full empathetic state of care to avoid possible misunderstandings regarding the quasi-empathetic but asocial nature of *ceyin zhi xin*.

According to the well-known care ethicist Nel Noddings, when A cares for B, it is expected that

(1) A's consciousness is in receptive attention and motivational displacement,
(2) A performs some act in accordance with (1),

and

(3) B recognizes that A cares for B.[33]

Noddings' first condition specifies the kind of inner states necessary for care. A sense of duty or a dedication to an abstract principle of human conduct is not the kind of inner state necessary for a caring feeling or action. Then what is the difference between an action coming out of a duty and the same action coming out of genuine care? Noddings argues that an action of care should emerge from the appropriate affective states, e.g., feeling, desire, or intention for others' well-being. For the same reason, Carol Gilligan rejects the identification of care with the *duty* of benevolence. A friend, for instance, visiting her ailing friend out of a duty or a previous arrangement is not genuine care. That is, care in care ethics is not a state of the mind where an abstract moral principle is recognized, endorsed, and acted on. Rather, it is an affective state with genuine other-regarding interest that motivates prosocial behavior.[34]

Noddings also emphasizes, in condition 3 above, that one's caring intention should be recognized or understood by another. One's recognition and understanding of another's intention requires one's appropriate social cognition that can result in a sustained relationship, where care is not just caring emotion (condition 1) and caring action (condition 2) but also caring understanding of others' inner states (condition 3). With the caring heart toward others, one does not simply feel for and act for others; one's action and intention should be understood in the context of a meaningful relationship. In Noddings' analysis of care, therefore, caring understanding is as important as caring emotion and caring action, and, as a result, the moral mind is combined with the social mind in its affection toward others.

Considering Noddings' three criteria of care, one can come up with two reasons why Mencius' *ceyin zhi xin* can be interpreted as "care" and why the example is popular among Confucian care ethicists. First, in Mencius' example, the man's *receptive attention* is fully engaged; the man quickly reacts to the possible suffering of the child. The man seems to have the appropriate ability of empathy because he cannot just sit back and watch the child suffer. In other passages (for example, 1A7, 2A6, 3A5, and 7B31), Mencius uses the term *bu ren* 不忍 (the affective state of not being able to bear the pain and suffering of others) to describe this strong reactive state of the mind. Mencius says that

all men have some things which they cannot bear [*bu ren*]. Extend that feeling to what they can bear, and humanity [*ren* 仁] will be the result. (7B31)[35]

A person with *bu ren* cannot stand others to suffer because she almost reflexively senses the problems another person is facing and reacts to the situation as if the problems are hers. Considering that *bu ren* and *ceyin zhi xin* are both closely related to *ren*, the man in Mencius' example (2A6) of *ceyin zhi xin* could perhaps be in this type of reactive emotional state that prompts an immediate reaction toward the child's pain and suffering because he is fully consumed by the surrogate experience of the approaching danger with full receptive attention.

Second, the man is not distracted or confused. His *motivational displacement* is focused on the child and the child's well-being; the man feels this particular emotion and is motivated to save the child, not for his honor, nor for recognition, nor for self-comfort. Because of this motivational focus, the man quickly, effectively, and single-mindedly focuses on the child and is ready to act to save the child. Mencius clearly states that the man does this for no other reason than concern for the child's well-being. Noddings' second condition requires action, and even though Mencius does not complete the story and describe the rescue, it seems consistent with the description that an attempt would be made, and so we can consider Noddings' second condition plausibly satisfied, too.

It is not clear, however, whether the third condition (the recognition of care and the promotion of a future reciprocal relationship) is satisfied in Mencius' original example, and not just because the example stops at the scene of the danger and the man's strong feeling of pity and compassion. Perhaps it can be imagined that the child or the child's parents will recognize the person's good intention and, possibly, appreciate the prompt action to save the child in danger. This type of recognition or understanding, however, does not seem necessary for *ceyin zhi xin* to arise when the man sees the child approaching a well. The full satisfaction of the third condition requires further social cognitive abilities and the ability to form long term relationships, but these extra abilities are neither discussed nor implied in Mencius' example. I will analyze the third condition further in the following sections to show that *ceyin zhi xin* does not necessarily satisfy this condition of care.

1.2 *Ceyin Zhi Xin* and Social Cognition

Despite the seemingly convincing comparison between *ceyin zhi xin* and care, there are several limitations on the care-based interpretation of *ceyin zhi xin*. I will argue that Mencius' example does not support the interpretation that *ceyin zhi xin* is the full-fledged affective state of care as it is understood in feminist care ethics. We can think of a person who acts and even feels like the man in Mencius' example yet who does not necessarily *care* for the child in the way care is specified by Noddings or other care ethicists. That is, *ceyin zhi xin* and care can be separate moral emotions even though they can sometimes accompany or interact with each other. This seemingly non-intuitive interpretation of *ceyin zhi xin* derives from the moral psychological distinction between moral cognition and social cognition that I made earlier in this chapter—moral cognition and social cognition interact with and supplement each other but they sometimes work independently. Why is this distinction important and how is moral cognition possible with minimal social cognition?

To explain the relationship between moral cognition and social cognition and to explore the possibility of moral agency without full social cognition, I will discuss autistic moral agency where moral cognition can function independently of social cognition, and apply this psychological dissociation to analyze Mencius' examples of moral emotion toward others' pain (2A6), animal suffering (1A7), and morally inappropriate behaviors (3A5). The pattern of dissociation observed in these examples demonstrates the asocial nature of our *basic moral emotion* toward others' pain. As far as physical harm and suffering are concerned, moral emotion, even without the aid of social cognition, can independently serve moral cognition. Additionally, or perhaps more importantly, this type of *asocial* moral cognition is served by *embodied* emotions. That is, with one's body (with the sense of one's bodily changes) one can affectively sense others' pain and react to help them spontaneously without full understanding of what others believe and feel. Both Mencius' examples and moral behavior of autistic individuals show this amazing possibility of embodied moral cognition without social cognition. Ultimately, the possible dissociation of moral cognition and social cognition and the embodied nature of our basic moral emotions suggest that, at the foundation of our moral sense (such as *ceyin zhi xin* in its initial development or moral judgments of autistic individuals), the moral mind, with its affective and embodied processes, can function independently of the social mind.

Recent studies on autism provide convincing evidence that autistic individuals, despite the lack of their theory of mind ability (the ability to understand others' behaviors by identifying and understanding representational inner states, such as beliefs and desires), can feel for others and act to reduce their pain and suffering.[36] It is well known that autistic individuals have limited abilities of social cognition and interaction, in part because of their impaired theory of mind ability and other-regarding emotions—they are insensitive to others' thoughts and feelings, and their social behavior is usually observed as non-empathetic.[37] Several studies, however, show that autistic individuals can still engage in consistent, effective, and morally appropriate actions with their intact ability to sense and to react to others' actual and potential pain and suffering. If a person with a challenged ability of social cognition acts and feels like the man in Mencius' example, then Mencius' example of *ceyin zhi xin* is not necessarily that of full-fledged care; care requires well developed social cognition, but *ceyin zhi xin*, sticking strictly to Mencius' example, does not require the understanding of others' inner representational states, if the inner sense and the motivation similar to those of *ceyin zhi xin* are witnessed in autistic individuals.

In their study of autism, Alan Leslie, Ron Mallon, and Jennifer Dicorcia analyze moral judgment and behavior of their autistic subjects and ask if they have the basic sense and ability of morality. One way to test the moral judgment of autistic individuals is to use distress cues (images, situations, and sounds that depict pain and suffering of innocent human beings) and to see how these individuals react to them. For example, what would I do if I were to see a person crying for help? Probably I would pay attention to the person and provide help if circumstances allowed. Usually this type of prosocial behavior is a morally appropriate reaction, but sometimes the behavior can be generated reflexively without conscious understanding and deliberation. That is, my reaction can be a morally neutral or irrelevant behavior if it comes out of an automatic and non-deliberate reaction to an unusual event that requires a quick solution, like a reactive behavior to deal with a medical emergency or a natural disaster. Leslie, Mallon, and Dicorcia call this morally irrelevant, reflexive reaction a *knee-jerk* reaction. A knee-jerk reaction, in this context of the reaction to distress cues, refers to a behavior that derives from morally unspecific (i.e., morally neutral or irrelevant) and reflexive (quick and automatic) processes. The affective and embodied sense of morality (the kind of moral emotion observed in Mencius' example of *ceyin zhi xin* and the kind of moral ability observed in young children's behavior) does not derive from this type of indiscriminate and automatic behavior. As I will discuss shortly, the embodied moral emotion does not originate from a generic sense and response to the environment. It focuses on a particular pattern of human behavior (for example, physical pain and suffering resulting from unreasonable harm or injury). Nor is it a reflexive response to distress cues. It can be quick and spontaneous, but it does not derive from automatically conditioned or innately fixed processes because it includes basic moral evaluation and accommodates socially or culturally induced development and cultivation.[38]

To be genuinely moral, therefore, an action should not be simply a knee-jerk reaction that typically correlates with the sheer intensity of distress cues, but a moral reaction that correlates with the seriousness of related moral violations. To test whether their autistic subjects' reactions to distress cues are morally irrelevant automatic reactions (i.e., knee-jerk reactions), Leslie, Mallon, and Dicorcia used the following cry baby (morally neutral or irrelevant) scenarios.

James and Tammy each had a cookie. James did not want just to eat his own cookie, he wanted to eat Tammy's cookie too. Teacher says that anybody can eat their own cookie if they want to. Tammy eats up her own cookie, but this makes James very unhappy and he begins to cry.

A girl takes her turn on a swing but cries when a boy takes his own turn on the swing because she wants his turn too.

These scenarios of the cry baby condition are followed by questions (such as "Was it OK for Tammy to eat her own cookie?" and "Was it bad for Tammy to eat her own cookie?") to the participating children to measure their understanding of the scenarios and their moral relevance. Compare these scenarios with another scenario in the following moral condition. How would you react to the following situation?

A girl hit another girl, making her cry.

It turned out that the autistic children in this study, like their typically developing peers, reacted differently to the two conditions (i.e., they took morally irrelevant cry baby scenarios as more acceptable than moral scenarios where moral violations were described), even though the outward distress cue (i.e., crying) was the same. That is, the responses (i.e., the responses to questions regarding the acceptability of given actions) of the autistic children are not based on blind and automatic reaction to the distress cues but on their understanding of moral violations, the recognition of which requires discerning processes to recognize and evaluate morally relevant features of the presented scenarios. At some basic level, these autistic children seem to have the sense of wrongful suffering and react to others' distress appropriately. Leslie, Mallon, and Dicorcia summarize their study as follows:

Both normally developing and autistic children responded more positively [i.e., approvingly] to cry baby stories indicating that their judgments distinguish between the distress of a "cry baby" and the distress of a victim. Although both the moral and the cry baby stories featured a character who starts to cry following the actions of another person, only in the moral stories can that action remotely be deemed culpable rather than a mere cause. This in turn suggests that the reaction to distress cues in moral transgressions is not simply of the "knee jerk" type but involves moral reasoning.[39]

This is a surprising result, because many psychologists believe that autistic individuals, because of their limited ability to connect with others, are not responsive to others' pain, particularly to their wrongful suffering.

Mencius' example of *ceyin zhi xin* can be analyzed in the same context. The scene of a child about to fall into a well constitutes a distress cue to the man. The man feels disturbed, distressed, and probably motivated to act quickly, without much deliberation.[40] The sudden emotion and motivation, however, do not necessarily demonstrate that the man has genuine moral motivation. Does Mencius' example constitute another cry baby (morally irrelevant) scenario? *Ceyin zhi xin* can be understood as a morally unspecific emotion expressed in an automatic reaction to a distress cue if the affective reaction comes out of a quick and reflexive response that does not involve any cognitive process of recognizing and evaluating moral significance of pain and suffering. But it is not the intention of Mencius to discuss a morally neutral emotion or a reflexive behavior in the passage where he explains the sprouts (i.e., the foundations or origins) of major Confucian virtues. That is, the example is not given by Mencius as a morally neutral or irrelevant scenario that invites a knee-jerk reaction but as a scenario that reveals the basic moral ability of the human heartmind.

To this *seemingly* reflexive feeling of the man, Mencius provides further information to explain why the man's quick and strong feeling is not a knee-jerk reaction. First, the child is young and innocent, and therefore we can easily imagine that the child, by accident not by intention, comes close to a dangerous situation and is about to fall victim to wrongful suffering. Second, Mencius says the man feels disturbed and ready to save the child, "not because he wants to get along well with the child's parents, not because he wants to be honored in front of his neighbors and friends, and not because he is bothered by the sound of the child's cries" (2A6).[41] If the child is an innocent and unintentional victim and the man reacts to the child's danger not because of the annoying sound of crying (a distress cue that facilitates reflexive behaviors), we can easily infer that this distress cue situation does not constitute Leslie and colleagues' (morally irrelevant) cry baby condition. It is a situation of potential harm and danger that deserves to receive genuine moral attention and action. Therefore, it is reasonable to analyze Mencius' example as an instance of moral emotion and moral motivation, not as an instance of a reflexive reaction. That being the case, do this emotion and the intention to save the child constitute full-fledged care and concern for the child?

Seen from the perspective of genuine moral interest (not from the perspective of reflexive reaction to distress cues), the man's sudden feeling in Mencius' example can be compared with care, but there are two reasons against interpreting the former as the latter. First, *ceyin zhi xin* does not require the full range of social cognition that is critical to care. When person A "cares" for B, it is not only the case that A senses the possible or actual pain and suffering of B; it is also the case, as Noddings specified, that A and B have a *mutual understanding*—A knows and understands B's inner mental states, and B recognizes that A is concerned about B's well-being. As was stated above, care not only requires caring emotion and caring action; it also requires caring understanding of each other's inner states, particularly inner representational states such as beliefs and desires.[42] The autistic children in Leslie and colleagues' experiments, however, do not fully understand what others believe and desire, owing to their limited theory of mind ability. Their emotional reactions do not satisfy Noddings' third condition of care, even though they can feel and act appropriately to distress cues and distinguish morally neutral scenarios from morally relevant scenarios. In addition to Leslie, Mallon, and Dicorcia's report, this positive moral ability of autistic individuals is consistent with reports made by many psychologists regarding autistic children's relatively intact moral judgments and their affective reactions to others' wrongful suffering.[43] Particularly, some psychologists report that autistic individuals have a basic ability of empathy, i.e., basic affective arousal and reactive behavior to others' emotional expressions, even though they do not have theory of mind ability.[44] R. J. R. Blair reports that his autistic subjects who failed the so-called false belief task (a standard measurement of theory of mind ability) can still distinguish moral from non-moral violations by maintaining a normal range of affective reactions and behaviors (increased bodily arousal and inhibition of ongoing behaviors including aggression) to distress cues.[45] Considering the positive assessments of autistic moral abilities, specifically with regard to a distress cue (such as a child crying as a result of wrongful pain) that is parallel to the distress condition of the *ceyin zhi xin* example, the affective arousal and moral motivation (or attention) discussed in Mencius' example of *ceyin zhi xin* do not require the full understanding of the victim's inner mental states. From an autistic individual's intact emotional and behavioral reactions to morally relevant distress cues, it can be inferred that part of the moral mind, particularly moral sensitivity that comes out of embodied emotion, can function independently of the social mind (the ability to understand others inner representational states and to develop personal relationships).

If care in care ethics requires the ability to understand a victim's inner mental states, *ceyin zhi xin* is not necessarily care and does not require care because in a situation like Mencius', autistic individuals can feel and act like the man with *ceyin zhi xin* but are incapable of full-fledged care in Noddings' sense. Compared with care, *ceyin zhi xin* is a more basic (spontaneous, quick, yet morally specific) emotion that does not require a moral agent to understand others' inner mental states. This rather minimal but psychologically plausible interpretation of *ceyin zhi xin* fits well with Mencius' original emphasis of *ceyin zhi xin*, not as a fully developed virtue or affective ability such as care and concern, but as a sprout, a foundation, or a beginning (not the fully developed end point) of the central Confucian virtue (*ren*).[46] It is, after all, in the context of the four spouts (one of which is *ceyin zhi xin*) where Mencius discusses emotionally disturbed feelings and reactions of the man.

Second, the action and the motivation described in the example of *ceyin zhi xin* in the *Mencius* does not explicitly include mutual (reciprocal), entrusting, and sustaining personal relationships, which are critical to one's caring encounter with others. According to Noddings, caring is a relation involving dialogue and exchange—"Dialogue is such an essential part of caring that we could not model caring without engaging in it,"[47] and "as we try care, we are helped in our efforts by the feedback we get from the recipients of our care."[48] Dialogue, exchange, and feedback are not possible if a carer does not have a sufficient level of social cognition—i.e., theory of mind ability. How can person A have care and concern for person B if A does not know what B is really up to? Knowing others' inner representational states—i.e., understanding their mental states such as beliefs and desires—is necessary in developing these other-regarding states of mind and the resulting personal relations of care and trust. Noddings says:

When we confirm someone, we identify a better self and encourage its development. To do this we must know the other reasonably well. Otherwise we cannot see what the other is really striving for, what ideal he or she may long to make real. Formulas and slogans have no place in confirmation. We do not posit a single ideal for everyone and then announce "high expectations for all." Rather we recognize something admirable, or at least acceptable, struggling to emerge in each person we encounter.[49]

From Noddings' perspective of a caring relationship, it is obvious that individuals with a limited ability of social cognition cannot form and maintain meaningful relationships through the process of dialogue, exchange, feedback, and confirmation. Even though autistic individuals can be empathetic enough to be disturbed by a scene of wrongful pain and be motivated to relieve the suffering of a person in distress or danger, this type of *minimal* empathy is not sufficient to support long term human relations and, ultimately, care.

In sum, the affective sense shared by autistic individuals and the man in Mencius' example is a basic form of empathy. This *proto-empathy* can arise from one's perception of and reaction to others' stressful situations without the full employment of theory of mind ability. Nor does it require the full ability to understand or experience the sensory or motor states of others. It simply requires basic "connectedness" to others, in the sense that one (in her proto-empathy) *senses*, *detects*, and *evaluates* another's emotions and situations and *reacts* to them in an appropriate manner. I believe that this basic form of empathy (particularly an affective and reactive emotion to others' pain) is the key to understanding the moral ability of autistic individuals and ultimately the moral psychological nature of *ceyin zhi xin. Ceyin zhi xin*, therefore, is not care or concern as specified by care ethicists but a proto-empathy, a more basic form of moral emotion.

This asocial characterization of *ceyin zhi xin*, however, does not imply that social cognition is not necessary for moral cognition—many moral judgments and actions are supported by relevant social cognition and communication. Nor, does it imply that one has to be autistic to feel *ceyin zhi xin* toward others. Mencius simply discusses his examples to explain *minimal* conditions or incipient foundations of the moral

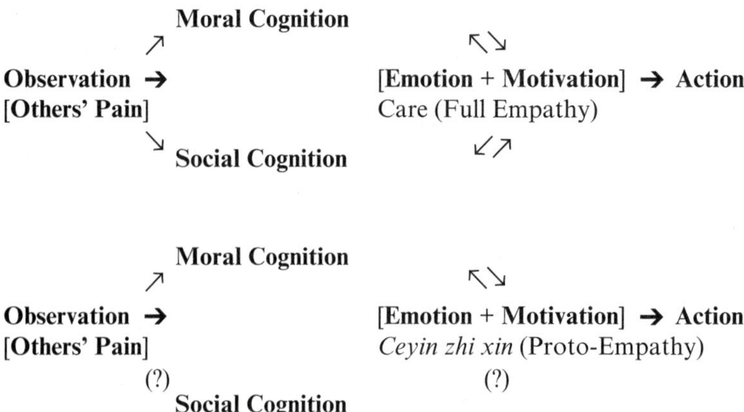

Figure 3.1
One's care or full empathy (top) and *ceyin zhi xin* or proto-empathy (bottom) in reaction to others' pain. In this figure, "moral cognition" means understanding others' negative experience regarding harm, injury, and danger, and "social cognition" means understanding others' pain behavior from the perspective of their inner representational states.

mind. According to him, the embodied moral emotion is a basic moral foundation of the mind that can either function independently or, if cultivated properly with its interaction with social cognition, can develop into fully mature Confucian virtues.

With this minimal but developmentally open interpretation of *ceyin zhi xin* in mind, I illustrate the roles social cognition plays in moral emotions in figure 3.1. The figure shows the important difference between care (full empathy) and *ceyin zhi xin* (proto-empathy), i.e., affective moral processes with or without social cognition.

1.3 *Ceyin Zhi Xin* and Mirror Emotion

Strong reactive emotions, such as *ceyin zhi xin*, are often observed in situations where people perceive, understand, and react to others' pain and suffering. When we observe another's pain, we often feel and react to it "as if" it is our own pain. It seems that our nociception (pain perception) is strongly driven by other-regarding emotions and other-directed reactions, and, as a result, our mind is often blind to the ownership of pain, not fully distinguishing one's own pain from another's pain. Recent brain imaging studies confirm the vicarious nature of pain perception: part of the human brain is active both when we experience pain and when we observe others in painful situations.[50] It seems that one's mind, in its understanding of others' pain, is mirroring others' pain as if it is one's own pain. Probably, this simulation process is an essential component of human nociception.

In general, there exist three different mirroring processes: mirror action (experience of others' motor behaviors, mostly their goal-oriented actions supported by mirror neurons), mirror sensation (surrogate pain sensation stimulated by the observation of others in painful situations), and mirror emotion (affective reaction to others' pain and suffering).[51] The third process, the process of nociceptive mirror emotion, is the main focus of my comparative analysis.[52] Mirror emotion is an affective mental state that arises from the observation of others in physically harmful and dangerous situations. Usually mirror emotion interacts with mirror sensation and mirror action to provide the full sense and understanding of others' pain, but it is distinct from them in two important ways: (1) it is involved primarily in affective, not sensorimotor, representation of others' pain processes of the brain—it supports more moral than social cognitive functions of the mind; (2) mirror emotion is associated with neural substrates, such as the anterior insula and the rostral cortex,[53] that are not directly involved with other mirroring functions of the brain.[54] Put together, mirror emotion is a unique state of nociception that motivates prosocial behaviors independently of social cognitive functions of the mind.

Several psychologists and neuroscientists point to the anterior insula as the major contributing neural substrate of nociceptive mirror emotion.[55] The anterior insula is involved in the basic but important regulatory function of supporting the stability of the body when the body goes through rapid or unexpected physical or biological changes. By sensing the changes of the bodily states (interoception), it controls and generates counterbalancing measures (such as changing heartbeat or blood pressure) to regain the balance and stability of the body. In this regulatory process, nociceptive mirror emotion emerges from the sensation of bodily change caused by the observation of others' pain. In several studies, subjects, when they see images of hands or other body parts being close to, being penetrated by, or being injected by sharp objects such as needles or knives, report disturbing sensations in their own bodies (mirror sensation) and strong reactive feelings and prosocial motivations (mirror emotion). At least for physical pain, this mirroring process of nociceptive simulation (taking others' pain into one's own body and sensing one's reaction to it) is probably the quickest and easiest way we feel, understand, and react to others' pain.[56] Without this type of direct mirroring process of the body, one (one's brain) has to spend more time and cognitive resources to understand and react to others' pain. The body, therefore, plays an essential role in this other-regarding or other-directed simulation process of nociception.

Considering its basic, embodied, yet other-regarding nature, nociceptive mirror emotion can be characterized as a basic moral, but not social, ability of the mind. In several psychological studies of empathy, the insula's interoceptive function is reported to be correlated with empathy scales[57] and prosocial behavior but is not related to social cognitive ability, i.e., theory of mind ability.[58] What social cognitive ability in general or theory of mind ability in particular does is to help us understand others' behavior by identifying their inner states, but the function of nociceptive mirror emotion served by the anterior insula is not involved in this type of social cognitive process. The anterior insula senses the changes of bodily states resulting from one's encounter with the improper, unfair, painful, and disgusting behaviors of others,[59] but doesn't necessarily identify or replicate others' inner representational states in one's own mind. From the pattern of dissociation between general conditions of social cognition and the embodied prosocial function of the anterior insula, it can be inferred that interoception based mirror emotion (the affective sense of one's own bodily changes, often resulting from the observation of others' behavior) does not require theory of mind ability. The latter is intrinsically related to social cognition while the former functions independently of social cognition. The two are functionally and neurologically different because they serve different psychological functions and use partially overlapping but distinct neural pathways. The function of mirror emotion, therefore, should be carefully distinguished from those of mirror sensation, mirror action, and other social cognitive functions of the mind. At the same time, empathy developed out of mirror emotion should be carefully distinguished from a group of other-regarding emotions such as sympathy, concern, and care typically served by psychological and neurological processes that include mirror sensation or mirror action.

This asocial interpretation of mirror emotion is strengthened by another piece of evidence. The affective mirroring function of the anterior insula is commonly and strongly observed in physical pain (for example, physical disturbance by bodily harm or injury) but rarely or weakly observed in social pain (for example, psychological stress resulting from social isolation or bullying),[60] because perception and reaction to social pain require social cognitive ability supported by neural regions or processes different from those of nociceptive mirror emotion. The findings of Masten and colleagues indicate that "neural regions supporting empathy for social pain may differ from those previously linked with empathy for physical pain."[61] Similarly, Immordino-Yang and colleagues report that "the activity in this region [anterior insula] peaked more quickly and for a shorter duration during CPP [compassion for physical pain] than during CSP [compassion for social/psychological pain]."[62] From these studies, we can infer that compared with our affective sense of others' social pain, our affective sense of others' physical pain comes "most efficiently and directly" out of the anterior insula, and mirror emotion coming out of the anterior insula is a basic moral emotion that can function independently of fully developed social cognition.

In sum, mirror emotion observed in human nociception is an other-regarding emotion that intrinsically relies on bodily sensation and reaction in a homeostatic process: it is specialized in sensing, feeling, and reacting to others' physical harm and danger, motivating prosocial and moral behavior, is correlated with self-evaluated empathy scales, but is independent of theory of mind ability that derives mostly from mirror action or mirror sensation. What these psychological and neurological characteristics of mirror emotion tell us is that our nociceptive mirror emotion (i.e., our quick and spontaneous emotion to others' physical pain) is a very special type of moral emotion. It is an embodied, other-regarding, and motivational state of the mind that promotes prosocial and moral behavior independently of social cognitive ability. The proto-empathetic state of *ceyin zhi xin* fits perfectly with these psychological characteristics of nociceptive mirror emotion. Since the functions of mirror emotion are served mostly by the anterior insula, perhaps *ceyin zhi xin* too is served by the anterior insula, with its intrinsically embodied and affective but asocial characteristics.

With the psychological functions of mirror emotion and the embodied neural processes of the anterior insula, Mencius' discussion of *ceyin zhi xin* receives a solid empirical interpretation: *ceyin zhi xin* is this embodied, other-regarding, asocial but proto-empathetic moral emotion that psychologists and neuroscientists discuss in their studies of affective nociception and our reactive affect toward others' pain. Perhaps, as Mencius characterized *ceyin zhi xin* as the beginning point of *ren* (Confucian benevolence), this proto-empathetic emotion can serve as a unique foundation of the moral mind, in addition to, or in replacement of, existing foundations such as principle based (Rawlsian) or reasoning based (Kantian) foundations of the moral mind. With regard to a Humean foundation, this embodied approach will refine it by way of a new dimension of moral mind, the dimension of asocial and embodied moral emotion.

2 Embodied Confucian Moral Psychology

To understand how this embodied and asocial mirror emotion relates to Mencius' spontaneous moral emotion, consider the following passage:

In great antiquity there were some who did not bury their parents. When their parents died, they took them up and threw them into a ditch. Later when they passed by them and saw foxes and wild cats eating them, and flies and gnats feeding on them, *their perspiration started out upon their foreheads, they looked askance and could not bear to look straight at them. Now the perspiration was not for the sake of other people. It was something at the bottom of their hearts that showed in their expressions.* They *immediately went* home and returned with baskets and spades and covered the bodies. If it was indeed right to cover them, then there must be certain moral principles which made filial [*xiao*] sons and men of humanity [*ren*] inter their parents. (3A5; emphasis added)[63]

In this passage, Mencius discusses the root and the foundation of *xiao* 孝 (reverence and obedience to older generations; filial piety) and *ren* from the perspective of embodied (sometimes unconscious) reactions to improper (i.e., lack of) burial practice. Mencius simply reports that people experience physical changes and discomfort in their bodies even before they are consciously aware of their negligence and misconduct. This is not an accidental reaction to inappropriate behavior. Mencius says that it comes out of their genuine moral interest: they have an embodied moral sense at the *bottom of their heartminds*. More important, Mencius uses this example to explain the foundational or developmental unity in our sense of moral appropriateness. If burying one's parents is right and that is what filial sons and people of *ren* do, then there must be something deep and important in sensing and following the direction to which the body points (i.e., burial of the dead parents' bodies). This other-regarding reaction of the body through its mirroring processes, therefore, is the developmental base of our mature moral actions and dispositions. Simply put, in Mencius' moral psychology, the body is not just a medium with which a moral agent feels and acts but the main, or at least a necessary, guiding foundation which we should follow and develop further.

The same type of direct, spontaneous, and embodied sense and reaction are observed in our nociceptive understanding of others' physical pain. As explained above, we do not understand others' physical pain (when we see their behaviors) through the sequential process of perception, categorization, reasoning, judgment, and resulting emotion and action. Instead, we take others' pain directly in our body, run embodied simulation (i.e., taking others pain as one's own pain and developing embodied affect), and react to others' pain. This intrinsically integrative, embodied, and other-regarding process is the one Mencius focuses on in his example of *ceyin zhi xin*, i.e., our natural reaction to others' suffering and the foundation of the Confucian heartmind.

The embodied and spontaneous moral sense is not limited to human pain and suffering. It can be observed in our reactive and empathetic experience of animal pain. When we see an animal in a painful situation, we naturally experience a strong reactive feeling, but some animals do not sense and feel pain as we do our pain. Their biology and psychology are different from ours: they have (to greater and lesser extents) different body forms with different sensory perceptual organs. For this reason, our social cognitive ability can barely identify their inner states and understand their behaviors. Can we easily understand what an anatomically different or phylogenetically distant animal (for example, an animal without a spinal cord or central nervous system) feels and desires? Surprisingly, despite our limited knowledge of animal minds, we often feel disturbed and empathetic toward animals in pain, whether they are biologically or psychologically close to us or not. This type of mirroring emotion of pain is possible not because we can identify and understand their inner representational states (i.e., what they think and desire), but because the perception or recognition of pain typically involves mirroring affective states in our body that can be readily extended to the behavior of non-human animals without full understanding of their internal states.[64]

If this affective arousal and the motivation to relieve others' pain can be regarded as a variety of empathy, it is a proto-empathetic state of mind that does not rely on our understanding of others' inner representational states. Perhaps one can think of projecting one's theory of mind ability to unfamiliar individuals or animals in order to sense and feel their pain as we often do to understand the behaviors of total strangers. Our reactive and empathetic emotion to animal pain, however, can hardly be described as a projection of our theory of mind ability. This special nociceptive emotion is direct and instant; it is too vivid and realistic to be called an imaginary projection of our theory of mind ability to unfamiliar animal species. Considering the quick and spontaneous nature of our emotion toward suffering animals, it is highly unlikely that our empathetic emotion to animal pain, particularly to that of animals whose biology and psychology are very different from ours, originates from social cognition of animal minds. Rather, this affective reaction comes out of an other-regarding emotion that is direct, spontaneous, and reliable across species but functions independently of social cognitive ability. Mencius tells a story of King Xuan's empathetic ability toward an animal:

The king was sitting up in his platform. There was an ox being led past by a man below the platform. The king asked, "Where is the ox going?" The man replied, "We are going to consecrate a bell with its blood." The King said, "Let it go. I cannot bear [*bu ren* 不忍] to see its frightened appearance, like an innocent person going to the execution ground." (1A7)

In this passage, King Xuan extends his compassion to an animal, even though the king does not have any (personal) relation to the animal and does not know or understand the inner states of the animal. If this type of compassion is the foundation of fully developed *ren* 仁, the underlying moral sensitivity of the Confucian heartmind is based on reactive and embodied emotion that functions independently of social cognitive ability. Later, Mencius recommends the king to develop this basic ability of empathy and extend it to his people for the full and balanced development of virtue and ideal leadership.[65] But even without the recommended development or refinement, this basic emotion is still an independently functioning, direct, spontaneous, embodied, and proto-empathetic moral emotion.

2.1 Embodied and Interactive Confucian Heartmind

From a historical viewpoint, this embodied characterization of moral emotions and dispositions is not an accidental or isolated development of Confucian tradition. It is a deeply rooted orientation of Confucian moral philosophy, not just Mencius' own interpretation of *ren* and the heartmind. In the Han period (206 BCE–220 CE), for example, Confucian virtues were often compared with and explained by functions of bodily organs and musical notes. Consider the following passage from the postscript of the "*Yue Shu* 樂書 (Treatise of Music)" chapter of the *Shi Ji* 史記 (*Records of the Historian*), where musical notes (*gong, shang, jiao, zhi*, and *yu*) and bodily organs (spleen, lungs, liver, heart, and kidneys) are correlated with the five Confucian virtues (*ren, yi, li, zhi*, and *sheng*).

Therefore *gong* moves the spleen and harmonizes it to correct sagacity [*sheng*], *shang* moves the lungs and harmonizes it to correct righteousness [*yi*], *jiao* moves the liver and harmonizes it to correct benevolence [*ren*], *zhi* moves the mind and harmonizes it to correct ritual propriety [*li*], and *yu* moves the kidneys and harmonizes them to correct wisdom [*zhi*].[66]

In this passage, Confucian virtues are linked to unlikely sets of physical entities and properties, i.e., five bodily organs and five musical notes. Surprisingly, this physical characterization of moral dispositions is a widely accepted style of explanation in the development of Confucian philosophy. According to Mark Csikszentmihalyi, this tendency to correlate and homologize diverse physical patterns (such as musical notes and internal organs) and Confucian virtues is one of the unique and important characteristics of Confucian philosophy, particularly in the Han dynasty.[67] Insofar as this physical characterization of Confucian virtues (that typically includes bodily organs and their functions) is not an analogy or a metaphorical image but a genuine belief regarding the nature of moral dispositions and their interactions in the physical universe, the passage demonstrates the deeply rooted orientation of embodiment in Confucian moral philosophy.

Xin 心 (Confucian heartmind) is another example where this peculiar but deeply engrained orientation of the embodiment of the moral mind can be witnessed in Confucian tradition. As was noted above, *xin* 心 is often translated as "heartmind" because it includes not only cognitive ability but also affective and conative abilities believed to be associated with the physical functions of the heart.[68] In addition to its association with a bodily organ, *xin* serves as the foundation of embodied processes of the moral mind. As I discussed above, the heartmind of *ceyin* (pity and compassion) is embodied, and, like other embodied processes, it combines sensation, perception, emotion, and motivation in an interactive fashion owing to the involvement of the body in these psychological functions.[69]

To understand the interactive and integrative involvement of the body in the heartmind, consider Wang Yangming's 王陽明 (1472–1529) discussion of the integration of knowledge and action, i.e., the integrative or interactive nature of the heartmind. He refers to a passage of the *Da Xue* 大學 (*Great Learning*; fifth century BCE?): "loving beautiful colors and hating bad odors." Following Wang, consider a situation where a person sees a beautiful color. How does she come to like it? Does she recognize its hue, judge its beauty, and then decide to like it because of her recognition and judgment? Or does she like it as soon as she sees it? What about smelling a bad odor? Does a person sense it, perceive it, categorize it, and then decide to turn away from it because her perceptual categorization and judgment tell her that it is a bad smell? The moment she senses it, her categorization, judgment, motivation, and action work together interactively. From a computational viewpoint, these perceptual processes are intrinsically interactive and holistic. Cognitive, affective, and motivational processes seem to be combined and integrated in our experience of beautiful colors and bad odors.

Confucian *xin*, as exemplified in *ceyin zhi xin*, has these characteristics. The moment the man sees the child near the well, he senses, feels, judges, and prepares to act to save the child. He does them together interactively in his sudden and spontaneous emotion of *ceyin zhi xin*. "*Xin*" in "*ceyin zhi xin*" refers to this interactive, integrative, and embodied process that combines intellect, affection, and motivation together to support spontaneous and intuitive moral sense and judgment.

To generalize, the Confucian heartmind is the interactive moral mind that reflects the affective, integrative, and embodied orientation of Confucian moral psychology. It represents a unique form of moral psychology that is different from rationalist and sentimentalist approaches of Western philosophy. As an alternative and viable conception of the moral mind, therefore, the heartmind should be analyzed further to provide insightful contributions to philosophical and psychological studies on the nature of moral emotion and moral disposition, particularly on the relation between the moral mind and the social mind exemplified, for instance, in the dissociation between a seemingly intact social mind and impaired moral emotion in the psychopathic population[70] and the early development of the moral mind through affective and embodied reaction to physical distress and harm.[71]

From a broad theoretical viewpoint, the *minimal* but *developmentally open* interpretation of *ceyin zhi xin* and the heartmind can explain and even support the insight of such moral psychological approaches as Haidt's social intuitionism where both the commonality of our deeply rooted affective moral dispositions and the particularity of culturally specific moral values are considered to explain human moral behavior.[72] By the same token, different interpretations of Confucian moral philosophy (as virtue ethics, care ethics, utilitarianism, and role ethics) can be understood as the theoretical attempts to explain diverse manifestations and developments of the proto-empathetic orientation of the Confucian moral mind. These interpretations can be compatible with my interpretation of *ceyin zhi xin* if they share the common understanding that the initiating foundation of the Confucian heartmind lies in its proto-empathetic and embodied moral affection. Ultimately, different interpretations of Confucian moral values, whether they are personal, communal, social, or political, can be developed on the basis of this developmentally open, spontaneous, and embodied moral affection.

3 Potential Objections and Responses

There are some potential concerns about my interpretation of Confucian moral philosophy as embodied moral psychology, speaking generally, and more specifically
about *ceyin zhi xin* as a kind of proto-empathy that comes out of nociceptive mirror
emotion supported by the functions of the anterior insula. Confucian moral philosophy is generally understood as a philosophical tradition of virtue and self-cultivation.
Often, it is interpreted from rationalist or sentimentalist perspectives that emphasize
fully developed moral dispositions or other-regarding emotions. Social cognition, in
these interpretations, is a very important component of Confucian virtues.[73] The virtue
of *shu* 恕, for example, is a moral disposition of sympathetic understanding that takes
others' beliefs, desires, needs, and intentions into consideration from their viewpoints.
But when it comes to basic emotional and moral orientations of Confucianism, there
exists an undeniable interest in the body and a clear emphasis on the concrete, situated, and embodied moral sensitivity that can exist and function independently
of detailed knowledge of others' inner representational states. Specifically, proto-
empathetic states like *ceyin zhi xin* and *bu ren* are the affective foundations of the
central Confucian virtue of *ren*.[74] They are embodied and reactive moral emotions that
can be explained without social cognitive functions of the mind but can hardly be
understood without affective bodily states, as recent studies of nociception and interoception demonstrate. As discussed above, bodily reactions (heartbeat, blood pressure,
perspiration, etc.) against morally inappropriate actions in the *Mencius* are not accidental byproducts of an embarrassing experience. Rather, as Mencius says, they come
out from the bottom of the heart (*zhong xin* 中心, or the core of the heartmind), i.e.,
from the center of the moral mind.[75] Therefore, the embodied and asocial nature of
our other-regarding emotions is an essential and unique foundation of Confucian
moral philosophy or, at least, of Mencius' moral philosophy.

Regarding the nature of proto-empathy and mirror emotion, one can challenge the
interpretation of *ceyin zhi xin* as a proto-empathetic mirror emotion. For instance, one
can argue that a proto-empathetic state and its associated mirroring function are not
really involved in *empathy* of others' pain but in the *detection* or *recognition* of their
pain.[76] One can also argue that nociceptive mirror emotion is a necessary but not a
sufficient condition of genuine empathy.[77] Since mirror emotion (with the underlying
functions of the anterior insula) plays a general role of detecting aversive stimulations
and estimating their obnoxiousness from the concomitant changes in the body, its
function is often described as reflexive and reactive, not specifically moral or genuinely
empathetic. I think this limited and misleading characterization of mirror emotion is
behind such potentially critical or skeptical arguments against the genuine moral
nature of embodied proto-empathy.

I believe that mirror emotion is a proto-empathy—a basic form of empathy and a moral emotion. It is an other-regarding moral emotion because it is directed to others' suffering and it motivates caring actions. It is a basic empathetic state because it takes others' pain as one's own. Its proto-empathetic and moral functions are supported by the anterior insula that is active with regard both to one's pain and that of others—its activity is correlated with intensity of and aversiveness to observed pain and, most important, with levels of empathy measured by an empathy scale.[78] Additionally, the anterior insula is reported to serve a basic evaluative function in the assessment of pleasant, obnoxious, and approachable features of stimulation and to support decisions for intentional actions.[79] If we put these empirical reports together, it is clear that mirror emotion and the underlying processes of the anterior insula serve a very distinct moral function that is independent of social cognition. Even though mirror emotion is only a basic form of empathy that reacts to a broad range of detestable or unbearable experiences, it is very reliable in evaluating physical and psychological conditions of suffering and very effective in motivating caring behaviors. Considering the morally distinct and motivationally effective nature of embodied proto-empathy, it is no wonder why this seemingly limited and underdeveloped mirror emotion is the foundation of our moral sense and affective reaction in Mencius' discussion of *ceyin zhi xin*.

Conclusion

In this chapter, I have argued that *ceyin zhi xin* is a spontaneous moral emotion that does not require social cognitive abilities. First, unlike the empathetic states of care and concern, it requires only the embodied mirroring process of taking others' pain as one's own and of generating reactive motivation for their well-being. Second, recent studies of autism and nociceptive mirror emotion demonstrate the existence of an other-regarding moral emotion that relies intrinsically on embodied and asocial functions of the anterior insula. By combining these two observations, I interpret *ceyin zhi xin* as a proto-empathetic state of the mind that is associated with or perhaps substantiated in the functions of the anterior insula in its embodied reaction to wrongful pain and unfair suffering without fully developed social cognitive abilities. The body is at the center of this spontaneous and proto-empathetic emotion that, according Mencius, serves as the foundation of the Confucian virtue of *ren*. Because of its basic and incipient nature, this foundational moral ability can be extended to non-human animals but, at the same time, can be developed into more mature moral dispositions in the human mind. In this sense, Confucian philosophy is a unique philosophical tradition that can provide a less explored but viable alternative to traditional approaches to moral cognition. The often neglected connection between moral cognition and the body and the partially misunderstood relationship between moral cognition and social cognition should be explored in future research of moral psychology. In particular, affective (the unique integration of sensation and reaction), embodied (the body's essential role in moral cognition), and integrative (interactive combination of perception, judgment, and motivation) features of the moral mind should be studied and analyzed further in the context of embodied moral psychology with insightful examples and discussions of Confucian philosophy.

Acknowledgments

This work was supported by the Faculty Excellence Grant of Alvernia University. The author wishes to thank the generous support of Dr. Thomas Flynn, Dr. Shirley Williams, and the development and research committee of Alvernia University. The author also wishes to express his sincere gratitude to Dr. Brian Bruya, the editor of the current volume, for his careful comments and insightful suggestions on this manuscript.

Notes

1. See, for example, Marc D. Hauser, *Moral Minds*; Greg Miller, "The Roots of Morality"; Steven Pinker, "The Moral Instinct." Whereas Hauser clearly argues for Rawlsian moral psychology, Miller and Pinker do not explicitly endorse any particular approach of moral psychology.

2. Lawrence Kohlberg, *Essays on Moral Development*; Jean Piaget, *The Moral Judgment of the Child*.

3. Immanuel Kant, *Foundations of the Metaphysics of Morals*.

4. Joshua D. Greene, "The Secret Joke of Kant's Soul"; Jonathan Haidt, "The Emotional Dog and Its Rational Tail."

5. David Hume, *A Treatise on Human Nature*.

6. Haidt, "The Emotional Dog and Its Rational Tail." An "other-regarding" mental state is an inner cognitive or affective state directed at others' inner states and their behaviors. As I will discuss in this chapter, they do not necessarily require full theory of mind ability.

7. Martin L. Hoffman, *Empathy and Moral Development*.

8. John Rawls, *A Theory of Justice*, 46–47.

9. Hauser, *Moral Minds*.

10. It is possible to develop hybrid models of moral cognition where Rawlsian moral intuition interacts with Humean emotion and Kantian reasoning (see, for example, Bryce Huebner, Susan Dwyer, and Marc Hauser, "The Role of Emotion in Moral Psychology"). In the pure approaches (Kantian, Humean, and Rawlsian approaches), however, emotion, deliberate reasoning, and

moral intuition are distinct and independently functioning abilities of the mind in the process of generating moral judgments.

11. John Mikhail, "Universal Moral Grammar"; John Mikhail, Cristina M. Sorrentino, and Elizabeth S. Spelke, "Toward a Universal Moral Grammar."

12. "Body" is potentially an ambiguous term. According to Shaun Gallagher, there are two different meanings of "body": body image and body schema. A body image is a represented image of the human body in the sensory and motor areas of the brain, but the body schema refers to physical, biological, or structural features and functions of the body (Gallagher, *How the Body Shapes the Mind*, 24). To this, I add another meaning of "body" that is closely related to my comparison of *ceyin zhi xin* and nociceptive mirror emotion: body sense. "Body sense" refers to the overall sense of bodily changes that is critical to nociceptive mirror emotion. It is not a particular body image represented in the brain. Nor is it a particular structural feature or function of the body (such as a particular sensory motor structure or function of the body). It is the holistic sense of physical changes in the body. Other than these general meanings, the term "body" (in the context of embodied cognition) refers to structural, functional, environmental, or historical features of a cognitive system under particular contexts or research methodologies. In this chapter, "body" is used inclusively to refer to structural (features of internal organs and skeletal structures) and functional (features of physiological and motor sensory functions) aspects of a human person. More specific meanings will be explained as necessary.

13. These are typical computational features of moral cognition characterized by the traditional (Kantian, Humean, and Rawlsian) approaches. For example, sequential processes refer to computational processes that follow linear and unidirectional algorithmic sequences from inputs to outputs. Hierarchical processes refer to formal information processing patterns where peripheral processes of modality-specific representations and central processes of modality-general rules and principles play different computational roles. In contrast to these computational features, embodied approaches to moral cognition focus on different sets of computational features (non-sequential, non-hierarchical, modality-specific, interactive, and parallel information processing patterns) that are essentially related to the functions and processes of the body. For further discussion, see the following sections and pp. 56–89 of Bongrae Seok, *Embodied Moral Psychology and Confucian Philosophy*.

14. Antonio Damasio, *Descartes' Error* and *The Feeling of What Happens*.

15. Haidt, "The Emotional Dog and Its Rational Tail" and "The Moral Emotions"; Haidt and Craig Joseph, "Intuitive Ethics."

16. Paula Niedenthal et al., "Embodiment in Attitudes, Social Perception, and Emotion."

17. Shaun Nichols, *Sentimental Rules*; Jesse Prinz, *Gut Reactions*.

18. Richard W. Byrne and Andrew Whiten, eds., *Machiavellian Intelligence*.

19. *Mencius*, 2A6.

20. Mou Zongsan 牟宗三, *Xin ti yu xing ti* 心體與性體.

21. Antonio S. Cua, *Encyclopedia of Chinese Philosophy*; May Sim, *Remastering Morals with Aristotle and Confucius*; Bryan W. Van Norden, *Virtue Ethics and Consequentialism in Early Chinese Philosophy*; Jiyuan Yu, *The Ethics of Confucius and Aristotle*.

22. Hoyt Cleveland Tillman, *Utilitarian Confucianism*.

23. Henry Rosemont Jr. and Roger T. Ames, *The Chinese Classic of Family Reverence*.

24. Chenyang Li, "The Confucian Concept of Jen and the Feminist Ethics of Care."

25. Joel J. Kupermann, "Feminism as Radical Confucianism"; Ann A. Pang-White, "Reconstructing Modern Ethics"; Michael Slote, *The Ethics of Care and Empathy*; Julia Po-Wah Tao, "Two Perspectives of Care"; Cecilia Wee, "Mencius, The Feminine Perspective and Impartiality."

26. All translations are mine unless otherwise noted.

27. Here the Confucian mind (*xin* 心) is translated as heartmind. *Xin* is typically translated as the mind but it is not necessarily the cognitive mind because it has extra dimensions of affective sense and motivational readiness. The translation "heartmind" emphasizes the integrative, interactive, and holistic engagement of the human person with the physical and social world. As Wang Yangming's (王陽明) example of hating bad odors shows, we do not sense, perceive, reason, analyze, categorize, and then act sequentially when we smell a bad odor. At the very moment we smell a bad odor, we instantly sense-feel-know-act interactively and holistically (Wang, *Chuan xi lu* 傳習錄, 1.5). See subsection 2.1 of this chapter for further discussion of this passage.

28. Li, "The Confucian Concept of Jen and the Feminist Ethics of Care"; Pang-White, "Reconstructing Modern Ethics," 216; Daniel Star, "Do Confucians Really Care?" 82–83; Wee, "Mencius, the Feminine Perspective and Impartiality," 5.

29. Ibid.

30. Carol Gilligan, *In a Different Voice*; Nel Noddings, *Philosophy of Education* and *Starting at Home*; Annette C. Baier, *Moral Prejudices*; and Virginia Held, *The Ethics of Care*.

31. Wing-Tsit Chan, *A Source Book in Chinese Philosophy*, 41.

32. Gilligan, *In a Different Voice*.

33. Noddings, *Starting at Home*, 19.

34. Gilligan, *In a Different Voice*.

35. Wing-Tsit Chan, *A Source Book in Chinese Philosophy*, 82. One should be careful not to confuse "*ren*" 仁 (benevolence) with the "*ren*" 忍 of "*bu ren*" 不忍. They are different characters and represent different states of the mind.

36. From a broad psychological perspective, "theory of mind" refers to our cognitive ability to understand others' behaviors by attributing inner states (such as beliefs and desires) to their minds. In this sense, it is equivalent to the cognitive ability of social cognition (understanding of others' social behaviors). Sometimes, however, it can refer to particular aspects of social cognition where behaviors of conspecifics are understood by utilizing general principles (such

as folk psychological platitudes or generalizations). There are at least three approaches to, or theoretical frameworks of, social cognition: theory theory, simulation, and interactionist approaches. In a simulation approach and an interactionist approach, for example, social cognition is not fully theory based: understanding of others' social behaviors (facial expressions, bodily movements) does not necessarily require theoretical generalizations. Technically, in these (simulation and interactionist) approaches, social cognition should not be equated with one's theoretical projection to others' behaviors. But, in general, these approaches are regarded as the approaches to theory of mind (as social cognition). In this chapter I will use the term "theory of mind" in a general sense, interchangeably with mind reading ability or social cognitive ability. If I need to distinguish different approaches or assumptions of social cognition, I will discuss the distinctive features and processes of social cognition. For more on the theory theory approach, see Susan Carey, *Conceptual Change in Childhood*; Alison Gopnik, "Conceptual and Semantic Development as Theory Change"; Henry M. Wellman, *The Child's Theory of Mind*. For the simulation approach, see Alvin I. Goldman, "Interpretation Psychologized"; Paul L. Harris, *Children and Emotion*. For the interactionist approach, see Shaun Gallagher, "The Practice of Mind"; Shaun Gallagher and Daniel D. Hutto, "Understanding Others through Primary Interaction and Narrative Practice."

37. Simon Baron-Cohen and Patrick Bolton, *Autism*; Uta Frith, *Autism*; Christopher L. Gillberg, "The Emanuel Miller Memorial Lecture 1991"; Francesca G. E. Happé, "Communicative Competence and Theory of Mind in Autism; Leo Kanner, "Autistic Disturbances of Affective Contact."

38. See Alan M. Leslie, Ron Mallon, and Jennifer A. Dicorcia, "Transgressors, Victims, and Cry Babies." In this study, typically developing children and autistic children are presented with short stories (scenarios) and asked whether the actions in the stories are good, bad, or OK. They are also asked about how good or bad the actions are and whether (and how much) the actions should be punished or rewarded. Numeric values are given to these responses and their overall values are compared under different conditions (conventional, moral, and cry baby conditions). The researchers observed no significant correlation between theory of mind ability (social cognition) and basic moral judgments (moral cognition) among autistic children.

39. Ibid., 279.

40. The rescue action is not mentioned in the original text but can be easily imagined.

41. There is no explicit indication that getting along with the child's parents, being honored in front of one's neighbors, and the child's cries are anticipated (non-occurrent) events, but as one can easily notice from the context, they are not physically presented to the man when he witnesses the child coming close to the well. In this case, mental representations of these anticipated events would be sufficient to initiate and sustain the man's emotion and reaction to the child in imminent danger. Van Norden discusses this aspect of *ceyin zhi xin*. "Benevolence," he says, "has as its object not just contemporary suffering, but can also be 'forward-looking': the child has not yet fallen into the well, but the prospect of this happening triggers the sprout of benevolence [*ren*]" (*Virtue Ethics and Consequentialism in Early Chinese Philosophy*, 248).

42. Noddings' third condition of care requires B's recognition of A's care, not their mutual understanding, but her elaboration clearly suggests that mutual understanding is an important condition of care. See *Philosophy of Education*, 19 and 190–191.

43. See, for example, R. James. R. Blair, "A Cognitive Developmental Approach to Morality" and "Brief Report: Morality in the Autistic Child"; Cathy Grant et al., "Moral Understanding in Children with Autism"; Shelly Steele, Robert M. Joseph, and Helen Tager-Flusberg, "Brief Report: Developmental Change in Theory of Mind Abilities in Children with Autism."

44. See Blair, "Brief Report: Morality in the Autistic Child," and "Psychopathological Responsiveness to the Distress of Others in Children with Autism"; Lisa Capps et al., "Parental Perception of Emotional Expressiveness in Children with Autism"; Marian Sigman and Lisa Capps, *Children with Autism*; Kimberley Rogers et al., "Who Cares?"; Nurit Yirmiya et al., "Empathy and Cognition in High-Functioning Children with Autism."

45. Blair, "Brief Report: Morality in the Autistic Child." From the perspective of understanding other minds, several psychologists argue that the ability of representing others' mental states is necessary for empathy to occur. (See, for example, Norma D. Feshbach, "Sex Differences in Empathy and Social Behavior in Children.") But other psychologists report that autistic individuals, like their typically developing or developed peers, are able to react to others' emotional expressions despite their lack of a full theory of mind ability. They still struggle to identify "what" others feel, but with their relatively intact reactive empathy, they can feel, at least to a certain extent, and react spontaneously to the distress and suffering of others. Probably they don't care for the victims of moral violations in the sense of full-fledged empathy, but at least they can attend and help them with their basic ability of reactive empathy, or proto-empathy.

46. Van Norden provides a very detailed discussion of the nature of our basic moral orientation and its developmental features, i.e., its (cognitive and affective) extension and (passive and active) cultivation in the context of Mencius' moral philosophy. He supports the interpretation that *ceyin zhi xin* as a *duan* 端 is the beginning, or the foundation, of mature moral dispositions of the mind. He says "We naturally have only incipient dispositions toward virtue, and ... these dispositions require cultivation in order to grow into mature virtues" (*Virtue Ethics and Consequentialism*, 217–218; see also 214–257).

47. Noddings, *Philosophy of Education*, 190.

48. Ibid., 191.

49. Ibid., 192.

50. Tania Singer et al., "Empathy for Pain Involves the Affective but not Sensory Components of Pain"; Philip P. Jackson, Andrew N. Meltzoff, and Jean Decety, "How Do We Perceive the Pain of Others?"; Matthew Botvinick et al., "Viewing Facial Expressions of Pain Engages Cortical areas Involved in the Direct Experience of Pain."

51. Many psychologists believe that these mirroring processes support social cognition (see Vittorio Gallese, Christian Keysers, and Giacomo Rizzolatti, "A Unifying View of the Basis of Cognition"; Marco Iacoboni and Mirella Dapretto, "The Mirror Neuron System and the

Consequences of Its Dysfunction"; Giacomo Rizzolatti and Maddalena Fabbri-Destro, "The Mirror System and Its Role in Social Cognition"). Some psychologists even argue that the lack of mirroring ability is the major cause of autism in the so-called "broken mirror" hypothesis (see Iacoboni and Dapretto, "The Mirror Neuron System and the Consequences of Its Dysfunction"; Lindsay M. Oberman et al., "EEG Evidence of Mirror Neuron Dysfunction in Autism Spectrum Disorder"; Lindsay M. Oberman and Vilayanur S. Ramachandran, "The Simulating Social Mind"; Giacomo Rizzolatti and Maddalena Fabbri-Destro, "The Mirror System and Its Role in Social Cognition"; J. H. G. Williams et al., "Imitation, Mirror Neurons, and Autism").

52. For detailed discussions of nociceptive mirror emotion and proto-empathy in the context of the heartmind and *ceyin zhi xin*, see Seok, *Embodied Moral Psychology and Confucian Philosophy*.

53. Keysers, Kaas, and Gazzola, "Somatosensation in Social Perception," 417.

54. "More recently, it has been suggested that brain areas involved in emotion processing, including the anterior insula and the rostral cingulate cortex (rCC), might perform an 'emotional simulation' of other individuals' experiences, showing activity not only when we experience positive and negative emotions but also when we witness those of others" (ibid.).

55. Xiaosi Gu et al., "Functional Dissociation of the Frontoinsular and Anterior Cingulate Cortices in Empathy for Pain"; Singer et al., "Empathy for Pain Involves the Affective but not Sensory Components of Pain."

56. Simulation, generally, refers to a process where a given phenomenon (usually its relevant features) is replicated to help us understand, explain, and sometimes even predict its behaviors. To run a successful simulation, theories and principles are often used. To simulate a trajectory of a hurricane, for example, laws of physics and atmospheric conditions need to be explicitly stated and calculated. In the embodied approach discussed in this chapter, however, simulations take a more direct form. Instead of explicitly formulating and applying general rules and theories to a given stimulus (typically a social or moral behavior), a simulator directly replicates or physically copies it to understand its social or moral significance. According to many psychologists, we usually understand others' facial expressions and bodily gestures not by categorizing and analyzing particular facial forms or bodily features with fully detailed algorithms or principles, but by physically mimicking them as they are simultaneously perceived and reacted to. Simulation is not the only way for us to understand others' behaviors, but it is often a common and effective strategy of social cognition where a cognitive agent has to deal with complex and constantly changing stimuli in a brief period of time. For further distinctions and examples of simulations in social and moral cognition, see Seok, *Embodied Moral Psychology and Confucian Philosophy*, 69–74.

57. Singer et al., "Empathy for Pain Involves the Affective but Not Sensory Components of Pain."

58. Carrie L. Masten, Sylvia A. Morelli, and Naomi I. Eisenberger, "An fMRI Investigation of Empathy for 'Social Pain' and Subsequent Prosocial Behavior."

59. Bruno Wicker et al., "Both of Us Disgusted in *My* Insula."

60. Mary Helen Immordino-Yang et al., "Neural Correlates of Admiration and Compassion"; Masten, Morelli, and Eisenberger, "An fMRI Investigation of Empathy for 'Social Pain' and Subsequent Prosocial Behavior."

61. Ibid., 386.

62. Immordino-Yang et al., 8024.

63. Chan, *Source Book*, 71.

64. The observed relationship between nociception and embodied affect, however, does not imply that all humans, actually and invariably, are affected and morally motivated by the scenes of others' (including animals') pain and suffering. Many psychologists report that some human beings (perhaps people with antisocial personality disorder, including psychopathy) do not properly sense and react to others' suffering. But this does not weaken the general line of argument for the embodied Confucian moral psychology. As Mencius says in his example of Ox mountain (*Mencius* 6A8), the proposed moral ability (asocial and embodied moral affection to other human beings and even animals) should be understood as a basic and common moral potential, even though, owing to non-moral or environmental contingencies, it may or may not be fully active. In this context, Mencius' bold statement that "without *ceyin zhi xin*, we are not even human beings" (2A6) can be properly understood not as a statement about the absolute nature of the human moral mind but as a statement about a moral potential that can be developed further by individuals in their environments. The appropriate environment, cultivation, and development, therefore, are necessary for this type of basic empathy to function properly.

65. *Mencius* 1A7.

66. Mark Csikszentmihalyi, *Material Virtue*, 221.

67. Csikszentmihalyi, *Material Virtue*.

68. The original meaning of *xin* is the heart as a physical organ, but its philosophical meaning (focal meaning or central meaning) used in the *Mencius* is the psychological faculty of thinking and feeling. Van Norden notes that "the *xin* combines cognitive and affective aspects. It knows and feels, perceives, and desires. We do not see here a sharp division between the cognitive and affective aspects of the mind" (*Virtue Ethics*, 216).

69. Unlike a sequential algorithmic process (typically run by conventional digital computers with von Neumann architecture), the Confucian heartmind does not compartmentalize the processes of sensation, perception, recognition, emotion, and motivation, and then put them in a *sequential cycle* or *hierarchical order* to generate appropriate feelings and actions. It combines them interactively and holistically to generate appropriate moral sense and emotion sufficient to motivate moral actions. Most important, the Confucian heartmind intrinsically includes the body with its sensorimotor activity and mirroring functions. Perhaps a computational system with the connectionist architecture (sometimes called parallel distributive processing architecture) may have a better chance to implement this type of embodied moral cognition because of its seemingly interactive and holistic information processing features, but embodied cognition

is not necessarily realized in all connectionist systems. Some connectionist systems are designed to incorporate embodied sensorimotor activities, but others are not designed that way. For further discussion, see Seok, *Embodied Moral Psychology and Confucian Philosophy*, 47.

70. Robert D. Hare, *The Hare Psychopathology Checklist*; James Blair, Derek Mitchell, and Karina Blair, *The Psychopath*.

71. Elliot Turiel, "Distinct Conceptual and Developmental Domains" and *The Development of Social Knowledge*.

72. Jonathan Haidt and Jesse Graham, "When Morality Opposes Justice."

73. The interest in others (i.e., their well-being, their inner thoughts and feelings, and even their virtues) is one of the key characteristics of Confucian virtue ethics. For example, Yong Huang, as he discusses the Confucian virtues of *zhong* 忠 and *shu* 恕, interprets the general orientation of Confucian virtue ethics from this perspective of strong other-regarding interest. "Confucius' virtue ethics," Yong Huang says, "clearly avoids the self-centeredness objection, as he makes it clear that a virtuous person ought to be concerned with the virtue of others" (*Confucius*, 55). In this interpretation, social cognition is necessary for Confucian moral virtues. But it is important to note, as I discuss in this chapter, that spontaneous and embodied moral sense with minimal social cognitive ability is an essential foundation of these other-regarding moral virtues.

74. *Mencius* 2A6 and 7B31.

75. *Mencius* 3A5.

76. India Morrison and Paul E. Downing discuss this hypothesis in their "Organization of Felt and Seen Pain Responses in Anterior Cingulate Cortex."

77. For example, Claus Lamm, C. Daniel Batson, and Jean Decety hypothesize that the activity of the anterior insula is not necessarily related to pain but to aversive or threatening situations in general. See their article "The Neural Substrate of Human Empathy."

78. Contrarily, the activity of the anterior insula is not related to location (the particular location of pain in the body), representation (how the pain is received, felt, or thought by a victim), or duration of observed pain. The identification of these nociceptive features is related to mirror sensation and, consequently, to social cognition.

79. Marcel Brass and Patrick Haggard, "The Hidden Side of Intentional Action: The Role of The Anterior Insular Cortex." The general hypothesis is that the anterior insula is involved in the somatic evaluation of intentional action-outcome.

Works Cited

Baier, Annette C. *Moral Prejudices: Essays on Ethics*. Harvard University Press, 1994.

Baron-Cohen, Simon, and Patrick Bolton. *Autism: The Facts*. Oxford University Press, 1993.

Blair, R. J. R. "Brief Report: Morality in the Autistic Child." *Journal of Autism and Developmental Disorders* 26, no. 5 (1996): 571–579.

Blair, R. J. R. "A Cognitive Developmental Approach to Morality: Investigating the Psychopath." *Cognition* 57, no. 1 (1995): 1–29.

Blair, R. J. R. "Psychophysiological Responsiveness to the Distress of Others in Children with Autism." *Personality and Individual Differences* 26, no. 3 (1999): 477–485.

Blair, James, Derek Mitchell, and Karina Blair. *The Psychopath: Emotion and the Brain*. Blackwell, 2005.

Botvinick, Matthew, Amishi P. Jha, Lauren M. Bylsma, Sara A. Fabian, Patricia E. Solomon, and Kenneth M. Prkachin. "Viewing Facial Expressions of Pain Engages Cortical Areas Involved in the Direct Experience of Pain." *NeuroImage* 25, no. 1 (2005): 312–319.

Brass, Marcel, and Patrick Haggard. "The Hidden Side of Intentional Action: The Role of The Anterior Insular Cortex." *Brain Structure and Function* 214, no. 5–6 (2010): 603–610.

Byrne, Richard W., and Andrew Whiten, eds. *Machiavellian Intelligence: Social Expertise and the Evolution of Intellect in Monkeys, Apes, and Humans*. Oxford University Press, 1988.

Capps, Lisa, Connie Kasari, Nurit Yirmiya, and Marian Sigman. "Parental Perception of Emotional Expressiveness in Children with Autism." *Journal of Consulting and Clinical Psychology* 61, no. 3 (1993): 475–484.

Carey, Susan. *Conceptual Change in Childhood*. MIT Press, 1985.

Chan, Wing-Tsit. *A Source Book in Chinese Philosophy*. Princeton University Press, 1963.

Craig, A. D. "How Do You Feel? Interoception: The Sense of the Physiological Condition of the Body." *Nature Reviews Neuroscience* 3, no. 8 (2002): 655–666.

Craig, A. D. "How Do You Feel—Now? The Anterior Insula and Human Awareness." *Nature Reviews Neuroscience* 10, no. 1 (2009): 59–70.

Critchley, Hugo D, Stefan Wiens, Pia Rotshtein, Arne Öhman, and J. Raymond Dolan. "Neural Systems Supporting Interoceptive Awareness." *Nature Neuroscience* 7, no. 2 (2004): 189–195.

Csikszentmihalyi, Mark. *Material Virtue: Ethics and the Body in Early China*. Brill, 2004.

Cua, Antonio S. *Encyclopedia of Chinese Philosophy*. Routledge, 2003.

Damasio, Antonio R. *Descartes' Error: Emotion, Reason, and the Human Brain*. Putnam, 1994.

Damasio, Antonio R. *The Feeling of What Happens: Body and Emotion in the Making of Consciousness*. Harcourt, 2000.

Feshbach, Norma D. "Sex Differences in Empathy and Social Behavior in Children." In *The Development of Prosocial Behavior*, ed. Nancy Eisenberg. Academic Press, 1982.

Frith, Uta. *Autism: Explaining the Enigma*. Blackwell, 1989.

Gallagher, Shaun. *How the Body Shapes the Mind*. Oxford University Press, 2005.

Gallagher, Shaun. "The Practice of Mind: Theory, Simulation, or Primary Interaction?" *Journal of Consciousness Studies* 8, no. 5–7 (2001): 83–108.

Gallagher, Shaun, and Daniel D. Hutto. "Understanding Others through Primary Interaction and Narrative Practice." In *The Shared Mind: Perspectives on Intersubjectivity*, ed. Jordan Zlatev, Timothy P. Racine, Christopher Sinha, and Esa Itkonen. John Benjamins, 2008.

Gallese, Vittorio, Christian Keysers, and Giacomo Rizzolatti. "A Unifying View of the Basis of Social Cognition." *Trends in Cognitive Sciences* 8, no. 9 (2004): 396–403.

Gillberg, Christopher L. "The Emanuel Miller Memorial Lecture 1991: Autism and Autistic-Like Conditions: Subclasses among Disorders of Empathy." *Journal of Child Psychology and Psychiatry, and Allied Disciplines* 33, no. 5 (1992): 813–842.

Gilligan, Carol. *In a Different Voice: Psychological Theory and Women's Development*. Harvard University Press, 1982.

Goldman, Alvin I. "Interpretation Psychologized." *Mind & Language* 4, no. 3 (1989): 161–185.

Gopnik, Alison. "Conceptual and Semantic Development as Theory Change: The Case of Object Permanence." *Mind & Language* 3, no. 3 (1988): 197–216.

Gordon, Robert M. "Folk Psychology as Simulation." *Mind & Language* 1, no. 2 (1986): 158–171.

Grant, Cathy M., Jill Boucher, Kevin J. Riggs, and Andrew Grayson. "Moral Understanding in Children with Autism." *Autism* 9, no. 3 (2005): 317–331.

Greene, Joshua D. "The Secret Joke of Kant's Soul." In *Moral Psychology*, volume 3: *The Neuroscience of Morality: Emotion, Brain Disorders, and Development*, ed. Walter Sinnott-Armstrong. MIT Press, 2008.

Gu, Xiaosi, Xun Liu, Kevin G. Guise, Thomas P. Naidich, Patrick R. Hof, and Jin Fan. "Functional Dissociation of the Frontoinsular and Anterior Cingulate Cortices in Empathy for Pain." *Journal of Neuroscience* 30, no. 10 (2010): 3739–3744.

Haidt, Jonathan. "The Emotional Dog and Its Rational Tail: A Social Intuitionist Approach to Moral Judgment." *Psychological Review* 108, no. 4 (2001): 814–834.

Haidt, Jonathan. "The Moral Emotions." In *Handbook of Affective Sciences*, ed. Richard J. Davidson, Klaus R. Scherer, and H. Hill Goldsmith. Oxford University Press, 2003.

Haidt, Jonathan, and Jesse Graham. "When Morality Opposes Justice: Conservatives Have Moral Intuitions that Liberals May Not Recognize." *Social Justice Research* 20, no. 1 (2007): 98–116.

Haidt, Jonathan, and Craig Joseph. "Intuitive Ethics: How Innately Prepared Intuitions Generate Culturally Variable Virtues." *Daedalus* 133, no. 4 (2004): 55–66.

Happé, Francesca G. E. "Communicative Competence and Theory of Mind in Autism: A Test of Relevance Theory." *Cognition* 48, no. 2 (1993): 101–119.

Hare, Robert. D. *The Hare Psychopathology Checklist—Revised*, second edition. Multi-Health Systems, 2003.

Harris, Paul L. *Children and Emotion: The Development of Psychological Understanding*. Blackwell, 1989.

Hauser, Marc D. *Moral Minds: How Nature Designed Our Universal Sense of Right and Wrong*. Ecco, 2006.

Held, Virginia. *The Ethics of Care: Personal, Political, and Global*. Oxford University Press, 2005.

Hoffman, Martin L. *Empathy and Moral Development: Implications for Caring and Justice*. Cambridge University Press, 2000.

Huang, Yong. *Confucius: A Guide for the Perplexed*. Bloomsbury, 2013.

Huebner, Bryce, Susan Dwyer, and Marc Hauser. "The Role of Emotion in Moral Psychology." *Trends in Cognitive Sciences* 13, no. 1 (2009): 1–6.

Hume, David. *A Treatise of Human Nature*. Oxford University Press, 1978.

Iacoboni, Marco, and Mirella Dapretto. "The Mirror Neuron System and the Consequences of Its Dysfunction." *Nature Reviews Neuroscience* 7, no. 12 (2006): 942–951.

Immordino-Yang, Mary Helen, Andrea McColl, Hanna Damasio, and Antonio Damasio. "Neural Correlates of Admiration and Compassion." *Proceedings of the National Academy of Sciences* 106, no. 19 (2009): 8021–8026.

Jackson, Philip L., Andrew N. Meltzoff, and Jean Decety. "How Do We Perceive the Pain of Others? A Window into the Neural Processes Involved in Empathy." *NeuroImage* 24, no. 3 (2005): 771–779.

Kanner, Leo. "Autistic Disturbances of Affective Contact." *Nervous Child* 2 (1943): 217–250.

Kant, Immanuel. *Foundations of the Metaphysics of Morals*. Tr. Lewis White Beck. Macmillan, 1959.

Keysers, Christian, Jon H. Kaas, and Valeria Gazzola. "Somatosensation in Social Perception." *Nature Reviews Neuroscience* 11, no. 6 (2010): 417–428.

Kohlberg, Lawrence. *Essays on Moral Development*, volume 1: *The Philosophy of Moral Development*. Harper & Row, 1981.

Kupperman, Joel J. "Feminism as Radical Confucianism: Self and Tradition." In *The Sage and the Second Sex: Confucianism, Ethics, and Gender*, ed. Chenyang Li. Open Court, 2000.

Lamm, Claus, C. Daniel Batson, and Jean Decety. "The Neural Substrate of Human Empathy: Effects of Perspective-Taking and Cognitive Appraisal." *Journal of Cognitive Neuroscience* 19, no. 1 (2007): 42–58.

Leslie, Alan M., Ron Mallon, and Jennifer A. Dicorcia. "Transgressors, Victims, and Cry Babies: Is Basic Moral Judgment Spared in Autism?" *Social Neuroscience* 1, no. 3–4 (2006): 270–283.

Li, Chenyang. "The Confucian Concept of Jen and the Feminist Ethics of Care: A Comparative Study." *Hypatia* 9, no. 1 (1994): 70–89.

Masten, Carrie L., Sylvia A. Morelli, and Naomi I. Eisenberger. "An fMRI Investigation of Empathy for 'Social Pain' and Subsequent Prosocial Behavior." *NeuroImage* 55, no. 1 (2011): 381–388.

Mikhail, John. "Universal Moral Grammar: Theory, Evidence and the Future." *Trends in Cognitive Sciences* 11, no. 4 (2007): 143–152.

Mikhail, John, Cristina M. Sorrentino, and Elizabeth S. Spelke. "Toward a Universal Moral Grammar." Poster abstract. In *Proceedings of the Twentieth Annual Conference of the Cognitive Science Society*, ed. Morton Ann Gernsbacher and Sharon J. Derry. Erlbaum, 1998.

Miller, Greg. "The Roots of Morality." *Science* 320, no. 5877 (2008): 734–737.

Moran, Joseph M., Liane L. Young, Rebecca Saxe, Su Mei Lee, Daniel O'Young, Penelope L. Mavros, and John D. Gabrieli. "Impaired Theory of Mind for Moral Judgment in High-Functioning Autism." *Proceedings of the National Academy of Sciences* 108, no. 7 (2011): 2688–2692.

Morrison, India, and Paul E. Downing. "Organization of Felt and Seen Pain Responses in Anterior Cingulate Cortex." *NeuroImage* 37, no. 2 (2007): 642–651.

Mou Zongsan 牟宗三. *Xin ti yu xing ti* 心體與性體. Taipei: *Zheng zhong shu ju* 正中書局, 1990.

Nichols, Shaun. *Sentimental Rules: On the Natural Foundations of Moral Judgment*. Oxford University Press, 2004.

Niedenthal, Paula M., Lawrence W. Barsalou, Piotr Winkielman, Silvia Krauth-Gruber, and François Ric. "Embodiment in Attitudes, Social Perception, and Emotion." *Personality and Social Psychology Review* 9, no. 3 (2005): 184–211.

Noddings, Nel. *Philosophy of Education*. Westview, 1998.

Noddings, Nel. *Starting at Home: Caring and Social Policy*. University of California Press, 2002.

Oberman, Lindsay M., and Vilayanur S. Ramachandran. "The Simulating Social Mind: The Role of the Mirror Neuron System and Simulation in the Social and Communicative Deficits of Autism Spectrum Disorders." *Psychological Bulletin* 133 (2) (2007): 310–327.

Oberman, Lindsay M., Edward M. Hubbard, Joseph P. McCleery, Eric L. Altschuler, Vilayanur S. Ramachandran, and Jaime A. Pineda. "EEG Evidence for Mirror Neuron Dysfunction in Autism Spectrum Disorders." *Cognitive Brain Research* 24 (2) (2005): 190–198.

Pang-White, Ann A. "Reconstructing Modern Ethics: Confucian Care Ethics." *Journal of Chinese Philosophy* 36 (2) (2009): 210–227.

Piaget, Jean. *The Moral Judgment of the Child*. Free Press, 1965.

Pinker, Steven. "The Moral Instinct." *New York Times*, January 13, 2008.

Prinz, Jesse. *Gut Reactions: A Perceptual Theory of Emotion*. Oxford University Press, 2004.

Rawls, John. *A Theory of Justice*. Harvard University Press, 1971.

Rizzolatti, Giacomo, and Maddalena Fabbri-Destro. "The Mirror System and Its Role in Social Cognition." *Current Opinion in Neurobiology* 18 (2) (2008): 179–184.

Rogers, Kimberley, Isabel Dziobek, Jason Hassenstab, Oliver T. Wolf, and Antonio Convit. "Who Cares? Revisiting Empathy in Asperger Syndrome." *Journal of Autism and Developmental Disorders* 37, no. 4 (2007): 709–715.

Rosemont, Henry Jr., and Roger T. Ames. *The Chinese Classic of Family Reverence: A Philosophical Translation of the Xiaojing*. University of Hawaii Press, 2009.

Rozzi, Stefano, Pier Francesco Ferrari, Luca Bonini, Giacomo Rizzolatti, and Leonardo Fogassi. "Functional Organization of Inferior Parietal Lobule Convexity in the Macaque Monkey: Electrophysiological Characterization of Motor, Sensory and Mirror Responses and Their Correlation with Cytoarchitectonic Areas." *European Journal of Neuroscience* 28, no. 8 (2008): 1569–1588.

Seok, Bongrae. *Embodied Moral Psychology and Confucian Philosophy*. Lexington Books, 2013.

Sigman, Marian, and Lisa Capps. *Children with Autism: A Developmental Perspective*. Harvard University Press, 1997.

Sim, May. *Remastering Morals with Aristotle and Confucius*. Cambridge University Press, 2007.

Singer, Tania, Ben Seymour, John O'Doherty, Holger Kaube, Raymond J. Dolan, and Chris D. Frith. "Empathy for Pain Involves the Affective but not Sensory Components of Pain." *Science* 303, no. 5661 (2004): 1157–1162.

Slote, Michael. *The Ethics of Care and Empathy*. Routledge, 2007.

Star, Daniel. "Do Confucians Really Care? A Defense of the Distinctiveness of Care Ethics: A Reply to Chenyang Li." *Hypatia* 17, no. 1 (2002): 77–106.

Steele, Shelly, Robert M. Joseph, and Helen Tager-Flusberg. "Brief Report: Developmental Change in Theory of Mind Abilities in Children with Autism." *Journal of Autism and Developmental Disorders* 33, no. 4 (2003): 461–467.

Tao, Julia Po-Wah Lai. "Two Perspectives of Care: Confucian *Ren* and Feminist Care." *Journal of Chinese Philosophy* 27, no. 2 (2000): 215–240.

Tillman, Hoyt Cleveland. *Utilitarian Confucianism: Ch'en Liang's Challenge to Chu Hsi*. Council on East Asian Studies, Harvard University, 1982.

Turiel, Elliot. *The Development of Social Knowledge: Morality and Convention*. Cambridge University Press, 1983.

Turiel, Elliot. "Distinct Conceptual and Developmental Domains: Social Convention and Morality." In *Nebraska Symposium on Motivation*, volume 25: *Social Cognitive Development*, ed. Herbert E. Howe Jr. and Charles Blake Keasey. University of Nebraska Press, 1977.

Van Norden, Bryan W. *Virtue Ethics and Consequentialism in Early Chinese Philosophy*. Cambridge University Press, 2007.

Wang Yangming 王陽明. *Chuan xi lu* 傳習錄. Taipei: *Zheng zhong shu ju* 正中書局, 1954.

Wee, Cecilia. "Mencius, the Feminine Perspective and Impartiality." *Asian Philosophy* 13, no. 1 (2003): 3–13.

Wellman, Henry M. *The Child's Theory of Mind*. MIT Press, 1990.

Wicker, Bruno, Christian Keysers, Jane Plailly, Jean-Pierre Royet, Vittorio Gallese, and Giacomo Rizzolatti. "Both of Us Disgusted in *My* Insula: The Common Neural Basis of Seeing and Feeling Disgust." *Neuron* 40, no. 3 (2003): 655–664.

Williams, J. H. G., A. Whiten, T. Suddendorf, and D. I. Perrett. "Imitation, Mirror Neurons and Autism." *Neuroscience and Biobehavioral Reviews* 25, no. 4 (2001): 287–295.

Yirmiya, Nurit, Marian D. Sigman, Connie Kasari, and Peter Mundy. "Empathy and Cognition in High-Functioning Children with Autism." *Child Development* 63, no. 1 (1992): 150–160.

Yu, Jiyuan. *The Ethics of Confucius and Aristotle: Mirrors of Virtue*. Routledge, 2007.

II Political Philosophy and Ethics

4 A Criticism of Later Rawls and a Defense of a Decent (Confucian) People

Tongdong Bai

1 The Inadequacy of Rawls' Discussion of the Decent Peoples in *The Law of Peoples*

In his discussion of the basic laws of international relations in *The Law of Peoples* (*LP*), Rawls suggests that a liberal people should tolerate and accept a certain kind of nonliberal people—dubbed by Rawls a "decent people."[1] The basic features of a liberal people are given in his *Political Liberalism* (*PL*). In particular, a liberal people or a liberal society is a plural and yet stable society in which even citizens with non-liberal political doctrines are respected, "provided that these doctrines are pursued in ways compatible with a reasonable political conception of justice and its public reason."[2] The call in *LP* for toleration of nonliberal but decent peoples internationally is, then, a natural extension of and analogous to such toleration on a domestic level.[3]

Not only are decent peoples tolerated, but they, together with the liberal peoples, belong to the "well-ordered peoples."[4] Only the well-ordered peoples adopt, obey, and enforce the law of peoples, a Rawlsian liberal, pluralistic, and stable international regime.

Not denying the possibility of other kinds of decent peoples, Rawls only discusses the decent "hierarchical people."[5] Different from the liberal people, the decent hier-archical people has a comprehensive—religious or secular—underlying doctrine. Two criteria make the decent people "decent" and a member of the well-ordered peoples. The first criterion requires that the people not be aggressive but rather respect other peoples. The second criterion has three parts. The first part is respect for human rights—that is,

the right to life (to the means of subsistence and security); to liberty (to freedom from slavery, serfdom, and forced occupation, and to a sufficient measure of liberty of conscience to ensure freedom of religion and thought); to property (personal property); and to formal equality as expressed by the rules of natural justice.[6]

The second part is the imposition of "*bona fide* moral duties and obligations (distinct from human rights) on all persons within the people's territory."[7] The third part is "a sincere and not unreasonable belief on the part of judges and other officials who administer the legal system that the law is indeed guided by a common good idea of justice."[8] The first two parts of the second criterion are also guided by this "common good idea of justice,"[9] which implies the following:

> Although all persons in a decent hierarchical society are not regarded as free and equal citizens, nor as separate individuals deserving equal representation (according to the maxim: one person, one vote), they are seen as decent and rational and as capable of moral learning as recognized in their society.[10]

In particular, in this society, different voices are heard, not in the form of equal participation and representation, but in the form of consultation with the voices of the groups—rather than individuals—and for the sake of the common good.[11] Thus, this society can be further called "a decent consultation hierarchy."[12] Compared with a liberal democracy, this society has an underlying comprehensive doctrine, and doesn't have full-fledged equality. This relative lack of equality is embodied by the lack of democratic participation—or, as many liberals would call it, a human right to democratic participation[13]—in the form of one person, one vote.

Are there any merits of the decent consultation hierarchy vis-à-vis liberal democracy? From the moral high ground that is political liberalism, Rawls focuses on showing how this regime, though not "as reasonable and just as a liberal society,"[14] should nevertheless be tolerated by liberal peoples.[15] His tone tends to be rather condescending, and he suggests, in a "diplomatic" way, that the decent consultation hierarchy is a regime to be perfected toward the ideal of liberal democracy. The only potential justification of this decent society in *LP* that implies some possible intrinsic merits of it, instead of merely showing that it is not so bad as not to be tolerated, is a Hegelian one:

> Whereas, so the [Hegelian] view goes, in a liberal society, where each citizen has one vote, citizens' interests tend to shrink and center on their private economic concerns to the detriment of the bonds of community, in a consultation hierarchy, when their group is so represented, the voting members of the various groups take into account the broader interests of political life.[16]

The example of a decent people Rawls offers is an imagined and idealized people, the people of "Kazanistan."[17] From the name of this people and from Rawls' own description, we can see that what he has in mind is an Islamic people that is tolerant and non-aggressive. A crucial sign of its nonliberal nature is the following set of requirements: "Islam is the favored religion, and only Muslims can hold the upper positions of political authority and influence in the government's main decisions and policies, including foreign affairs."[18] One might argue that the focus on this Islamic people and the problem of reconciliation and cooperation with this people reveals a possible America-centric or Euro-centric tendency in Rawls, as the religious and ideological conflicts between Christianity and Islam have been a focus for the Europeans and later Americans from the Crusades to the so-called War on Terror. But even if Rawls were guilty of this bias, it would not affect the soundness of his overall theory of the decent peoples. However, a much more serious problem with his discussion of the people of Kazanistan is that there seems to be no reasonable ground for the dominance of one religion in political affairs in this regime. The much more forceful Hegelian argument that Rawls mentioned earlier to justify the rejection of liberal democracy by the decent consultation hierarchy is mentioned only once, but is never exploited to justify the regime of Kazanistan. In general, throughout *LP*, Rawls largely ignores any positive merits of a decent society in comparison with a liberal society, which leaves his discussion of decent peoples inadequate.

To be clear, my criticism of the inadequacy in *LP* is not an internal criticism. That is, as was pointed out earlier in this section, *LP* clearly is written from the point of view of political liberalism, and the question of toleration is about what societies should be tolerated from this point of view. Thus, in *LP* Rawls is not directly concerned with the merits of other regimes from the point of view of these regimes. However, addressing this inadequacy may help to defend the validity of the political proposals of *LP*, for this book has been criticized by many for its call for toleration of decent peoples and related ideas.[19] Indeed, this call is even dubbed a "betrayal of liberalism."[20] After all, why should decent peoples be passively tolerated rather than be actively changed by liberal peoples, if the regimes of the former are considered inferior to those of the latter? Thus, if we can identify some potential internal merits of decent peoples, it may partly answer the challenge from the critics of the idea of toleration introduced in *LP*. (However, when all is said and done, this defense of liberalism in the form of fleshing out the merits of a decent people may end up as a direct assault on liberalism, though still, paradoxically, Rawlsian in spirit.)

As was pointed out earlier, a crucial difference between a liberal democracy and a decent hierarchy is that the latter lacks full-fledged equality and one person, one vote. In the following two sections, I will detail the problems of full-fledged equality and one person, one vote in liberal democracy. In the fourth section, I will offer an alternative model of a decent consultation hierarchy that may address the problems discussed in the previous two sections. Through the discussions in these three sections, I hope to show the positive merits of a decent consultation hierarchy in comparison with liberal democracy from the point of view of a decent people. In the last section, I will argue that, in spite of the differences between these two kinds of regimes or peoples in terms of democratic participation, the decent consultation hierarchy introduced in this chapter may share many ideals of Rawls' political liberalism, but may be a utopia that is more realistic than Rawls' in terms of realizing these ideals.

2 Rawls' Own Qualifications Regarding the Right to Vote

The aforementioned Hegelian criticism of liberalism is based on the idea that the right to vote comes with qualifications. That is, for voting to be justifiable, the voting entity has to consider the common good, rather than merely his, her, or its (in the case of a group's being the voting entity) own economic interests. Interestingly, an idea similar to this is supported by Rawls himself. Crucial to his understanding of liberal democracy in his later philosophy is the concept of being "reasonable," as well as the related concepts of public reason and reciprocity. On the concept of being "reasonable," Rawls writes the following:

Citizens are reasonable when, viewing one another as free and equal in a system of social cooperation over generations, they are prepared to offer one another fair terms of social cooperation … and they agree to act on those terms, even at the cost of their own interests in particular situations, provided that others also accept those terms.[21]

On the contrary, if one votes purely on the basis of one's comprehensive doctrine, and accepts the failure of pushing through his or her agenda by the majority of votes only as a convenient truce waiting to be broken, the stability achieved is a "modus vivendi" and is not stability for the right reasons.[22] In short, according to Rawls, to be a member of a liberal people means to vote not merely on the basis of private interests, including both material and doctrinal, but rather on the basis of a conception of the common good, although his conception may be much weaker than the Hegelian one.

Moreover, Rawls also thinks that, in a real—rather than formal—liberal democracy, citizens have to have their basic needs satisfied, to have education, and to be informed. For example, Rawls points out that "Hegel, Marxist, and socialist writers have been quite correct in making the objection" that "liberties taken alone" are "purely formal":

By themselves they are an impoverished form of liberalism, indeed not liberalism at all but libertarianism … . The latter does not combine liberty and equality in the way liberalism does; it lacks the criterion of reciprocity and allows excessive social economic inequalities as judged by that criterion.[23]

To ensure a plural liberal democracy that is stable for the right reasons, Rawls proposes the following institutions:

a. Public financing of elections and ways of assuring the availability of public information on matters of policy … .
b. A certain fair equality of opportunity, especially in education and training … .
c. A decent distribution of income and wealth meeting the third condition of liberalism: all citizens must be assured the all-purpose means necessary for them to take intelligent and effective advantage of their basic freedoms … .

He also proposes other means—among them society as employer of last resort and basic universal health care—that give citizens a sense of long-term security and of being a member of society.[24] Failing to establish these institutions, according to Rawls, will lead to the (American?) reality in which "congressional legislation is, in effect, written by lobbyists, and Congress becomes a bargaining chamber in which laws are bought and sold."[25]

It should become clear that, according to Rawls, the democratic element of liberal democracy is not simply one person, one vote. For one person, one vote to be an element of his liberal democracy, certain conditions have to be met first. That is, each person has to be properly educated and informed, and must understand that voting should not be based on private interests alone, be they material, religious, or ideological. This understanding of one person, one vote is related to the fact that, for Rawls, the desirable form of liberal democracy is a kind of deliberative democracy. In *LP* he expresses this idea explicitly: "Here I am concerned only with a well-ordered constitutional democracy ... understood also as a deliberative democracy."[26] Deliberative democracy, he writes, "recognizes that without widespread education in the basic aspects of constitutional democratic government for all citizens, and without a public informed about pressing problems, crucial political and social decisions simply cannot be made. Even should farsighted political leaders wish to make sound changes and reforms, they cannot convince a misinformed and cynical public to accept and follow them."[27]

3 The Sixth Fact of Modern Democracies, or the Failure of Democratic Participation

What if the political reality of an allegedly liberal democratic society is that many, or even the majority, of its citizens fail to meet the conditions for a person's vote to be counted meaningfully and equally? Indeed, as many observers—from both a more popular and anecdotal perspective and a more scholarly perspective—have pointed out, the appalling political ignorance of the (American) general public is a well-established fact over "the six decades of modern public opinion research."[28]

One source of this ignorance may be the social and economic inequality that leads to the lack of basic education of the public. As we see from the discussion in the previous section, this problem has been addressed repeatedly, if not adequately, by Rawls. Another problem is that, even if the populace is properly educated, many people may still not be informed about political matters if they are not offered adequate opportunities. For the public to be properly informed, freedom of speech is clearly needed. But more important, as Rawls points out, measures such as public financing of elections should be taken to ensure that public information on matters of policy is not distorted by the influence of money, and, in general, to ensure the availability of public information. Moreover, the public should be given an opportunity to digest information available. Otherwise, the availability of information becomes merely formal. For example, the political scientists Bruce Ackerman and James Fishkin propose that there should be a new national holiday, Deliberation Day, on which "registered voters would be called together in neighborhood meeting places … to discuss the central issues raised by the campaign" and "each deliberator would be paid $150 for the day's work of citizenship."[29] Clearly, the days when voters cast their votes should also be national or state holidays. Rawls doesn't deal with this issue extensively, but from his emphasis on making liberties real rather than formal, it is not difficult to imagine that he could have approved of this proposal.

However, what if the aforementioned measures—already drastic and radical against the political reality of today's democracies—are still not adequate? Liberal thinkers such as Rawls, Ackerman, and Fishkin have a vision of liberal democracy that is, at least in one aspect, fundamentally republican. That is, in their ideal form of democracy, citizens need to be well-informed and actively participatory. The ancient Greeks achieved this to some extent, but their achievement was made possible by slavery. That is, it was the use of slave labor that freed Greek citizens from daily labors and made it possible for them to fully participate in political matters. But even with this condition (the use of slaves), the adequacy of the political competence of Greek citizens was still challenged by classical writers such as Plato and Aristophanes. How likely, then, is it that the common people in a modern democracy, who need to work hard to maintain their basic living, can participate in politics to the extent of acquiring the political competence necessary for a desirable form of liberal and deliberative democracy? It is true that, through mass education, modern societies produce many more educated, white-collar professionals—scientists, engineers, doctors, financiers, teachers, and so on—than pre-modern societies did. But being consumed by their daily work and knowing little about public affairs or anything outside of their narrow specializations, they may justifiably be called "learned ignorami," as José Ortega y Gasset put it.[30]

Also crucial to the level of political participation in ancient Greece is the fact that Greek city-states were all small in size and in population relative to most present-day democratic countries. According to many political thinkers, on the issue of what kind of regime a state can adopt, "size matters." Montesquieu offers one of the most powerful arguments for this view. According to him, it is necessary that a democracy be small. No medium-size or large country can really be a democracy. The reasons he offers are the following:

In a large republic [whether democracy or aristocracy], there are large fortunes, and consequently little moderation in spirits: the depositories are too large to put in the hands of a citizen; interests become particularized; at first a man feels he can be happy, great, glorious without his homeland; and soon, that he can be great only on the ruins of his homeland.

In a large republic, the common good is sacrificed to a thousand considerations; it is subordinated to exceptions; it depends upon accidents. In a small one, the public good is better felt, better known, lies nearer to each citizen; abuses are less extensive there and consequently less protected.[31]

In short, for Montesquieu, a large republic leads to large fortunes. This corrupts the virtue necessary to a democracy. In particular, a person's interest becomes detached from, or even in opposition to, the common good. Moreover, the common good becomes too sophisticated for the citizens of this state to grasp.

One may argue that, for Montesquieu, a large state can be democratic in the form of the federal republic.[32] But what Montesquieu discusses is something similar to the federation of ancient Greek states, a federation much smaller than most of today's democracies. Also different from Montesquieu's understanding, the central government of today's democracies is directly elected, and has far greater power than what Montesquieu would allow.

One may also argue that the kind of democracy Montesquieu discusses is not the same as the liberal democracy Rawls and others discuss. This argument may be true, but this and the previous arguments do not affect the force of Montesquieu's challenge. Put in today's language, we can challenge the likelihood for citizens to be informed in a large state that does not allow the use of slave labor to free its citizens from their daily work by offering the following arguments. First, the overwhelming material wealth in a large state may tempt people away from the civil duty to be reasonable and informed citizens. This requirement of citizens to be reasonable and informed is much more limited than what Montesquieu considers the necessary virtue in a democracy,[33] but it is still very demanding. Second, corporations, especially in the age of globalization, develop interests separate from and even in conflict with the interest of their own states, be they democratic or otherwise. Third, the common good is beyond most people's willingness to comprehend, or simply beyond their comprehension, and the majority is doomed to be uninformed, however intelligent and well-educated and however willing to participate in political affairs each citizen is.

The journalist Robert Kaplan offers challenges to the viability of Western democracies similar to Montesquieu's,[34] and, interestingly, the solution Kaplan offers is a hybrid regime that combines democratic elements with paternalistic elements, similar to the decent consultation hierarchy I will discuss in the next section. More recently, the political scientist Russell Hardin discusses "three devastating theoretical claims" in postwar public choice theory, made by Kenneth Arrow, Anthony Downs, and Mancur Olson, that are "against the coherence of any democratic theory that is conceived as even minimally participatory, collectively consistent, and well-informed."[35] Hardin develops these claims by "relating them and, in particular, by subjecting them to an economic theory of knowledge."[36] Two of Hardin's crucial arguments are that each person's vote doesn't really matter and that to be informed is rather demanding (perhaps much more so than we usually think). If we put these two arguments together, the implication is that voters have—or should have if they are rational—very little interest in voting, let alone in getting informed. The first argument is partly a result of the fact that today's democracies—even on the scale of the state of New Hampshire, which has about a quarter of a million voters—are too large for one single vote to matter, "merely for practical reasons of the impossibility of counting votes accurately."[37] The second argument also has something to do with the fact of the size of today's democracies, as their large size (and concomitantly multifarious issues) makes the price of getting informed unbearably high. Thus, we can consider Hardin's thesis as yet another latter-day development of Montesquieu's. If all these thinkers are correct, then it is simply impossible for the majority of voters to even come close to meeting the preconditions for meaningful democratic participation.

Besides, the aforementioned Hegelian challenge—"in a liberal society, where each citizen has one vote, citizens' interests tend to shrink and center on their private economic concerns to the detriment of the bonds of community"[38]—can be considered yet another challenge to the possibility of meaningful participation in a liberal democracy. On a more sympathetic note, all the previous problems aside, some citizens may prefer other obligations and interests—such as family obligations or scientific or artistic pursuits—to a time-consuming involvement in politics. These citizens may choose to remain politically indifferent. This choice becomes increasingly sensible when the political matters become too complicated owing to the size of the state and the fact that modern citizens don't enjoy the guilty luxury of the ancient Greeks who forced slaves to do their daily chores. Unlike the ancient republican form of democracy, a present-day liberal democracy should let these voluntarily nonparticipating citizens be. However, there should also be a mechanism that prevents the indifferent citizens from having too much of a voice in political matters.

In *PL*, Rawls points out five facts about democratic society that lead to his consideration of the central problem: how a plural yet stable liberal democracy is possible.[39] To these five we can add a sixth fact about modern democracy: the failure of democratic participation (FDP). FDP has several parts. First, human beings have a tendency to fall back on their own self-interest, which is encouraged by one person, one vote; second, some citizens choose to remain politically indifferent; third, modern democratic states are in general so large that it makes it impossible for the majority of the citizenry to be adequately informed, however hard both the government and the individuals try, and this problem is worsened by the overbearing burden—due to the size of the state and the noble rejection of slavery—on citizens' intelligence, education, and willingness to be informed, by the insignificance of one vote, and by the material wealth and the power of big corporations running free and wild. The sixth fact or FDP seems to suggest that the Rawlsian liberal and deliberative democracy, or liberal and deliberative democracy in general, in which every citizen participates in an equal manner and in the form of one person, one vote, is impossible in the modern world, where each state is simply too large.

I hope I have shown that there are theoretical and practical shortcomings of liberal democracy caused by the sixth fact. In the next section, I will construct a decent society that tries to mitigate the sixth fact, thus showing its merits vis-à-vis a purely democratic regime.

4 Another Decent Consultation Hierarchy: Confu-China

In this section, I will give an outline of the regime of another hypothetical decent consultation hierarchy: Confu-China, an imagined and idealized society whose political system has certain Confucian characteristics. I have argued elsewhere that these characteristics are indeed Confucian, and I won't repeat that argument in this chapter.[40] The "China" part of this name is modeled after, and alludes to, Rawls' "Kazanistan." There were, after all Confucian features in traditional Chinese regimes, even if none of them embodied this idealized regime fully. In might be added that the political structure of present-day China is not intended as an example of Confu-China, nor is Confu-China an implicit support of the so-called China Model, if there is really such a model.

In Confu-China, the rule of law is established and followed, although the contents of laws may have features that differ from the contents of laws in a Western democracy (for example, the unit of certain rights is the family rather than the individual, and adult children have the legal duty to provide for their retired and aging parents). Many basic liberties are also recognized, although, again, they might be interpreted differently from the common Western interpretation of these liberties. For example, the right not to be tortured is interpreted as a demandable (legally enforceable) obligation of the lawful citizens and prosecutors to a suspect or a criminal rather than the latter's right. Freedom of speech is recognized on a utilitarian ground: it is needed to promote rational and reasonable discourse in political matters. Other than some exceptional cases, these differences don't lead to different treatments of citizens between Confu-China and a Western liberal democracy.[41]

Slightly more different from a liberal people are some of the following arrangements and ideas of the people of Confu-China. In Confu-China, the government is considered responsible for the material and moral well-being of the people. It is responsible for making it possible for the average citizen to have his or her basic material needs met, for ensuring that every citizen has access to education, and for containing economic inequality, following Rawls' own "Difference Principle."[42] It is also responsible for offering the following moral and civic education to every citizen:

• The role of the government is to maintain the material and moral well-being of the people.

- Each citizen should have compassion for those close to him or her and maintain proper relationships to them.
- The politicians in the government should be those who are morally and intellectually superior—morally superior in the sense that they are willing to extend their compassion to all the people who are within their power to help.
- If the politicians are indeed morally and intellectually superior, they should be respected by the common people.
- The right to participate in a certain political matter is inseparable from one's willingness to consider the common good and one's competence at making sound decisions on the matter.

In addition to educating every citizen, the government should offer all means necessary—for example, the aforementioned national holidays for deliberation and voting—for interested citizens to be informed about political matters and to participate in them. In short, through economic and educational arrangements, Confu-China tries to make its citizens informed and moral, which echoes Rawls' own requirements for voting to be meaningful.

An even more radical difference between the people of Confu-China and a liberal people is with regard to elections. As an attempt to deal with FDP, the regime of Confu-China makes the following arrangement. As already mentioned, the citizens are taught that the right to vote is competence-based. So, when a citizen considers himself or herself incompetent on certain matters and cannot improve his or her competence before the relevant election, he or she should willingly stay away from the decision procedure on these matters. More institutional arrangements help prevent incompetent citizens from having too much of a voice. In view of the sixth fact and the fact that it is more likely for people to be informed about matters limited to a small community, the reliance on popular participation alone is restricted to local and communal matters. At any higher level, various arrangements may be introduced to limit the power of popular elections. For example, at each higher level, each voter has to take a class and a test specially designed for this level before he or she can be allowed to vote. Different weights may be given to their votes on the basis of their test scores. Or, more practically, at a higher level, the popularly elected branch is still preserved. But in addition to it, there can be other branches of the legislature. Members of one such branch can be those "elders" who have local or lower-level administrative experience, who have done a good job at this level, and who are no longer exposed to popular elections and the sway of the local or lower-level interests.[43] This branch or another branch may also include the so-called Confucians—people who have been selected, through a series of exams, to attend "magnet schools" at different levels of education and eventually to be members of this branch. They have studied the classics and other subjects of liberal arts. They may have an expertise relevant to the political matters of the level of legislature they serve. In order to prevent them from being merely book-smart, they have also gone through practical training. Generally, in order to prevent these branches that are not popularly elected from forming a small circle and serving their own narrow self-interest, each branch has to have a significant number of members, and there can be elections held among their members at different levels. In addition, the popularly elected branch will also serve as a balance to these branches. How to distribute tasks and weights of their votes between the popularly elected branch and the "upper house(s)"—the way in which the tasks and weights are distributed between the American house and the senate is an example of a possible distribution between the popularly elected branch and the upper house(s) in Confu-China—can differ from one Confu-China to another.[44]

De facto, these arrangements of different branches of the legislature reduce popular will to the role of consultation and give more power to the relatively knowledgeable and compassionate. It is a government for the people, but not purely by the people; rather, it is only partly by the people and partly by the competent people. Its protection of liberties and rule of law, its effort to maintain economic equality and satisfy basic material needs of common people, and its promise not to be aggressive in international affairs make this people decent. Thus, it is a decent consultation hierarchy that combines democratic elements with paternalistic ones.

In contrast with Rawls' account of decent peoples, this decent people doesn't have a clear underlying comprehensive doctrine. The regime is based on some considerations of FDP, but these considerations are political rather than doctrinal. If this people is a good example of the decent people, we can say that Rawls' account of decent peoples, especially his description that such peoples have an underlying comprehensive doctrine, is limited by his implicit Western-centric obsession with the Islamic world.

A few criticisms can be raised against this version of a decent consultation hierarchy. The words "hierarchy" and "paternalism" sound derogatory in the ears of democratic people. John Stuart Mill, among others, warns of the danger of paternalism in his criticism of the idea that "if a good despot could be ensured, despotic monarchy would be the best form of government."[45] According to Mill, even if this good despot could take care of everything for the people, his paternalistic actions would chain up the free agency of his subjects and thus perpetuate their incompetence. In contrast, popular participation offers the best civic education of the people.[46] From the discussion of FDP, we should already see that Mill's praise of the educational function of popular elections may have been overly optimistic. Without certain arrangements, the voting public may retreat to their narrow and often misguided private interests.

On Mill's critical note, I should first point out that Rawls offers a similar argument. In *A Theory of Justice* (*TJ*), Rawls argues that, if we assume that the political liberties are subordinate to the other freedoms that define the intrinsic good of the people, plural voting—i.e., that "persons with greater intelligence and education should have extra votes" (an idea, interestingly enough, introduced by Mill)—is perfectly just.[47] But he then points out that the participation of all citizens "lays the foundations for civic friendship and shapes the ethos of political culture" and "enhance[s] the self-esteem and the sense of political competence of the average citizen."[48]

In response, we can see that in Confu-China popular elections are still preserved to some extent. In line with Mill's and Rawls' ideas, Confu-China may emphasize the civilizing role of mass participation. Indeed, Confu-China may even recognize the practical and psychological benefit of making people feel involved through mass participation in the age of democracy. But, owing to the considerations of FDP, it also restricts the real political power of popular elections. Moreover, in Confu-China, exams and experience are introduced as the basis for voting rights in the case of certain political matters and for the membership of certain branches of the legislature, but these exams are open to the public. The government has the responsibility to offer any means necessary to get citizens to participate in education and civil services. Even if people fail to pass the exams or choose not to take them, the door will always be open when they change their mind or improve their knowledge. That is, the hierarchy is not fixed; it encourages upward mobility. This mobility may also dispel possible resentment of the disenfranchised against the powerful elite. Clearly, the rule of law has to be enforced independently so that there is no perceived unfairness in the mobile hierarchy.

Another sensible objection is that learned and experienced people don't always make good decisions. This may well be true, but, as we see, their power is balanced by the popularly elected branch. More important, the existence of the branches of the experienced and the learned can be taken as a civic lesson to the citizens about the idea that participation comes with competence. Mill and Rawls are correct to say that participation offers the opportunity of civic education. But when participating, common people are also helped by looking up to the exemplary people and institutions. In short, the branches of the experienced and the learned also play a role in civic education.

There can be other very sensible objections to the political arrangements of Confu-China. For example, a concern based on the sixth fact is that common people are easily misled. However, one may worry that it is even easier to bribe or mislead a limited number of the elite in branches that are not popularly elected.[49] I would happily acknowledge that the jury may be still out on the relative superiority between Confu-China and liberal democracy. But the acknowledgment that the jury is still out, or at least the acknowledgment that there are sensible justifications for the preference of some decent society (over a liberal society) that Rawls fails to address in *LP*, is all I wish to argue in this chapter.

5 Confu-China: A More Realistic Rawlsian Utopia?

In his discussion of the decent consultation hierarchy, Rawls seems to believe that one person, one vote is an essential element to liberal democracy.[50] After all, according to Rawls, reasonable citizens in a liberal democracy should view one another as free and equal. However, his exclusion of the "right" to equal political participation from the basic human rights listed in *LP*—an exclusion criticized by many[51]—suggests that this right is not as important as what he considers basic rights. In fact, as we see from his discussion of plural voting in *TJ*, Rawls doesn't seem to think that the violation of one person, one vote is in conflict with liberal democracy.

Moreover, if we follow the rationale of Rawls' difference principle in *TJ* that economic inequality can be accepted if the least advantaged are benefited,[52] why can't we have a difference principle in politics (I will call it the political difference principle): political or electoral inequality (in terms of voting power) can be accepted if the least advantaged are benefited? One may object to this line of reasoning by arguing that the first principle of justice is the principle of equality, and some of the arrangements in Confu-China violate equality. However, according to Rawls, the first principle reads, "each person is to have an equal right to the most extensive basic liberty compatible with a similar liberty of others,"[53] and political liberty, one of the basic liberties, means "the right to vote [but not the right for each vote to be counted equally—my note] and to be eligible for public office."[54] As we see, in Confu-China, the democratic branch is still preserved, and the selection for the branch(es) of the "elders" and the Confucians is also open to the public (but not in the form of direct election). Indeed, the government is responsible for promoting the upward mobility of common citizens to participate in politics and in the activities of the "non-democratic" branch(es). Besides, other aspects of equality are well preserved in Confu-China. In short, the political difference principle embodied by some arrangements in Confu-China conflict only in a minor way, if at all, with Rawls' requirement of equality that is expressed in the first principle of justice.

It is undeniable that Confu-China is hierarchical. But, as I discussed in the previous section, there is no underlying comprehensive doctrine in Confu-China, and the hierarchy is not based on such a doctrine, in contrast to the hierarchy of Kazanistan. It is true that the political considerations underlying the civic education and the hierarchy may be "thicker" than what is political in Rawls' later theory, but they are not moral considerations based on one comprehensive doctrine. Thus, Confu-China can be a pluralistic society, as pluralistic as Rawlsian liberal democracy, that embraces some form of political liberalism.

More important, the regime of Confu-China shares Rawls' understanding that political participation presupposes that citizens should be properly educated and informed, and the former differs from the latter only in the former's belief that it offers a more realistic way to satisfy the presupposition.

Another way to look at this problem is that, as is implied by the third fact of democratic society,[55] Rawls' version of liberal democracy presupposes that at least a substantial majority of citizens have to be reasonable, but Rawls doesn't discuss how to deal with the situation in which the unreasonable people may constitute the majority or a substantial minority in a society. He has a good reason to make this presupposition. That is, we have to first solve the problem of stability in the ideal situation in which the majority of a society consists of reasonable people who nevertheless hold conflicting and irreconcilable comprehensive doctrines. Then and only then can we deal with the problem in a more realistic situation.[56] However, if we accept the fact that no real-world liberal democracy has a majority of reasonable and informed citizens, then liberal peoples as Rawls understands them simply don't exist. In contrast, Confu-China deals with the problem about the relations between reasonable and informed citizens and unreasonable, uninformed, or indifferent people. To be clear, my focus is not about Rawls' alleged failure to offer a proof of the desirability of liberal democracy, as may concern some people. On this alleged failure by Rawls, I share Burton Dreben's view, expressed in a response he offered to someone who asked a question about the justification for liberal democracy.[57] Rather, my concern is this: If, owing to the sixth fact, this ideal of liberal democracy is too utopian, can we have a regime that deals with this fact that is nevertheless in line with many of Rawls' ideals? I argue in this chapter that Confu-China might fit the bill.

There is yet another way to see the relation between Confu-China and the Rawlsian liberal democracy. If we follow Rawls' idea that there is an analogy between domestic political dynamics within a people and international political dynamics among different peoples, we see that this analogy breaks down in Rawls' own later philosophy.[58] That is, in his theory, domestically, a liberal people consists of free and equal citizens and its majority is reasonable; internationally, however, peoples who are not well-ordered are not reasonable, and the well-ordered peoples actually possess a higher position in a de facto hierarchy of peoples. The regime of Confu-China carries out the analogy much more nicely. Its domestic hierarchy corresponds to the hierarchy of peoples, although the percentage of incompetent citizens over all the citizens of a state might be higher than the percentage of non-well-ordered societies over the totality of all societies: the informed and compassionate play a justifiably larger role in domestic politics, just as the well-ordered peoples play a justifiably larger role in international politics. Many cosmopolitan liberal thinkers criticize Rawls for not being able to carry over his approach in *TJ* that deals with the domestic case to the international case, and argue for a consistent approach to both the domestic case and the international case that is based on his handling of the domestic case.[59] I, however, argue for a consistent approach in the opposite direction: to carry his approach to the international case over to the treatment of the domestic case. Where would we put Rawls' liberal people in my reverse analogy? The liberal people and its corresponding international society of liberal peoples can be taken as a domestic ideal and an international ideal.

To be clear, as I pointed out, Confu-China is an imagined and idealized people. It shares many Rawlsian concerns and insights, but it continues from where Rawls has left off, i.e., how to handle the more realistic situation of today's world. If this is the case and if we think that Confu-China does a good job at handling this situation (two big "ifs" indeed), we can call Confu-China a realistic Rawlsian utopia, more realistic than the realistic utopia described in Rawls' *LP* and in his *PL*.

Acknowledgment

I would like to thank the *New Perspective Quarterly* for allowing portions of a previous article to be reprinted here.

Notes

1. Rawls, *The Law of Peoples*, 60. For the distinction between a people and a state, see pp. 23–30. For a criticism of Rawls' distinction between state and people (as well as society), see Buchanan, "Rawls' Law of Peoples," 698–700.

2. Rawls, *The Law of Peoples*, 59. "Reasonable" and "public reason" are crucial to understanding Rawls' idea of a plural and stable liberal democracy in *Political Liberalism* and some later works. Confusion and objections may have resulted from the failure to understand these two concepts. I will discuss his concept of "reasonable" briefly in the next section.

3. Ibid.

4. Ibid., 63.

5. Ibid., 62–67.

6. Ibid., 65.

7. Ibid., 65–66.

8. Ibid., 66.

9. Ibid., 71.

10. Ibid.

11. Ibid., 72.

12. Ibid.

13. See James W. Nickel, "Are Human Rights Mainly Implemented by Intervention?" and Alyssa R. Bernstein, "A Human Right to Democracy? Legitimacy and Intervention."

14. Rawls, *The Law of Peoples*, 83.

15. On p. 676 of "Rawls' Law of Peoples," Charles Beitz points out that Rawls' justification for which society is to be tolerated is based on the point of view of liberal peoples.

16. Rawls, *The Law of Peoples*, 73.

17. Ibid., 75–78.

18. Ibid., 75.

19. See, for example, Charles R. Beitz, "Rawls's Law of Peoples"; Allen Buchanan, "Rawls's Law of Peoples"; Kok-chor Tan, "Liberal Toleration in Rawls's Law of Peoples" and "The Problem of Decent People"; and Nickel, "Are Human Rights Mainly Implemented by Intervention?" For a defense of Rawls' position, see Bernstein, "A Human Right to Democracy? Legitimacy and Intervention" and Charles Larmore, review of *The Law of Peoples*. See also Rex Martin and David A. Reidy, "Introduction: Reading Rawls's *The Law of Peoples*" for a review of various responses to the main themes of *LP*.

20. Buchanan, "Rawls's Law of Peoples," 697.

21. Rawls, *Political Liberalism*, xliv. An almost identical passage can be found in Rawls, *The Law of Peoples*, 136, and a similar passage can be found in Rawls, *Political Liberalism*, 49. See also Rawls, *The Law of Peoples*, 86–88 and 177–178.

22. See Rawls, *Political Liberalism*, xxxix–xliii and 150. See also Rawls, *The Law of Peoples*, 149–150 and 168–169.

23. Rawls, *Political Liberalism*, lviii; also see Rawls, *The Law of Peoples*, 49–50.

24. Rawls, *Political Liberalism*, lviii–lix.

25. Rawls, *The Law of Peoples*, 24, n. 19.

26. Ibid., 138.

27. Ibid., 139–140.

28. Bruce Ackerman and James Fishkin, "Righting the Ship of Democracy," 34. For a more detailed account, see Ackerman and Fishkin, *Deliberation Day*. There are also numerous popular accounts of the lack of basic political knowledge among Americans. For a recent one, see Nicholas D. Kristof, "'With a Few More Brains …'."

29. Ackerman and Fishkin, "Righting the Ship of Democracy," 34.

30. Ortega, *The Revolt of the Masses*, 108–112.

31. Montesquieu, *The Spirit of the Laws*, 124. Rousseau agrees with Montesquieu on this issue, and offers similar arguments; see his dedication "To The Republic of Geneva" in his *Discourse On the Origin and Foundations of Inequality among Men* in *The First and Second Discourses* and chapters 3 and 4 in book 3 of *On the Social Contract*.

32. Montesquieu, *The Spirit of the Laws*, 131–132.

33. Ibid., 22–26.

34. Kaplan, "Was Democracy Just a Moment?"

35. Hardin, "Street-Level Epistemology and Democratic Participation," 212.

36. Ibid., 213.

37. Ibid., 220. This impossibility may be a mathematical impossibility: the statistical error of counting a large number of votes is too great for a one-vote difference to be considered meaningful in determining the outcome.

38. Rawls, *The Law of Peoples*, 73.

39. Rawls, *Political Liberalism*, xxvii, 36–38, and 58. See also Rawls, "The Domain of the Political and Overlapping Consensus," 474–478.

40. Bai, "A Mencian Version of Limited Democracy." See also Daniel Bell, *Beyond Liberal Democracy*, in which Bell offers an East Asian version of democracy and points out many interesting differences between his version and the Western version.

41. For a detailed discussion of these rights in Confu-China, see Bai, "The Price of Serving Meat: On Confucius's and Mencius's Views of Human and Animal Rights."

42. Rawls, *A Theory of Justice*, 60–62 and 78–83.

43. To define what counts as doing a good job is obviously rather tricky. Let me offer one example: a governor of a province, if he or she has served two terms in good standing and is evaluated and given a good score by an independent committee, is considered to have done a good job.

44. There are other important institutions in a regime that can embody its meritocratic aspect. These include the executive branch, the judiciary branch, the central bank, and the military. How they embody the meritocratic aspect, how they and the legislature interact with each, and, more generally, how much meritocracy is needed to achieve the right balance for an ideal government are all important questions. Let me acknowledge them and the possibility that there can be different kinds of hybrid regimes that can address the issue of FDP but leave all these problems aside, given the limited scope of this chapter.

45. Mill, *Considerations on Representative Government*, 36.

46. Ibid., 36–55.

47. Rawls, *A Theory of Justice*, 232–233.

48. Ibid., 234.

49. To be clear, the potential for corruption in Confu-China is not the same as it is in real-world non-democratic countries. The legislators of the upper house(s) in Confu-China do not have absolute power. Their power is under the rule of law in the same way as the power of legislators

in democratic regimes are under the rule of law, and they are subject to removal by the relevant electorate. The power of the upper house(s) is also checked by that of the lower house. The danger here is that the legislators of the upper house(s) in Confu-China may be taken hostage by various private interests the same way as, or even worse than, legislators in a democracy are taken hostage by private interests, but there are plausibly workable mechanisms for mitigating the risks.

50. Rawls, *Political Liberalism*, 71.

51. See Nickel, "Are Human Rights Mainly Implemented by Intervention?" and Buchanan "Rawls's Law of Peoples: Rules for a Vanished Westphalian World." For a defense of this exclusion, see Bernstein, "A Human Right to Democracy? Legitimacy and Intervention."

52. Rawls, *A Theory of Justice*, 75–83.

53. Ibid., 60.

54. Ibid., 61.

55. Rawls, *The Law of Peoples*, 38.

56. On pp. 8 and 9 of *A Theory of Justice*, he offers a similar rationale for dealing with the problem of justice first and postponing the more pressing problem of injustice.

57. Burton Dreben, "On Rawls and Political Liberalism," 328–329. According to Dreben, there are enough problems with a coherent conception of a constitutional liberal democracy, and to argue for or against its foundation (for example, why it is better than totalitarianism) is not a worthwhile or fruitful enterprise. One can't reason with someone like Hitler, because reason has no bearing on this question for him. As Dreben suggests, perhaps the only choice when dealing with Hitler is to shoot him.

58. For an argument concerning a different kind of breakdown between the domestic case discussed in *Political Liberalism* and the international case discussed in *The Law of Peoples* and a more liberal solution of it, see Tan, "The Problem of Decent People," 88–91.

59. See, for example, Thomas Pogge, "An Egalitarian Law of Peoples" and "Do Rawls's Two Theories of Justice Fit Together?" Also see Buchanan, "Rawls's Law of Peoples: Rules for a Vanished Westphalian World," and Tan, "Liberal Toleration in Rawls's Law of Peoples" and "The Problem of Decent People."

Works Cited

Ackerman, Bruce, and James Fishkin. *Deliberation Day*. Yale University Press, 2004.

Ackerman, Bruce, and James Fishkin. "Righting the Ship of Democracy." *Legal Affairs*, January–February 2004: 34–39.

Bai, Tongdong. "A Mencian Version of Limited Democracy." *Res Publica* 14, no. 1 (2008): 19–34.

Bai, Tongdong. "The Price of Serving Meat: On Confucius's and Mencius's Views of Human and Animal Rights." *Asian Philosophy* 19, no. 1 (2009): 85–99.

Beitz, Charles R. "Rawls's Law of Peoples." *Ethics* 110, no. 4 (2000): 669–696.

Bell, Daniel. *Beyond Liberal Democracy: Political Thinking for an East Asian Context.* Princeton University Press, 2006.

Bernstein, Alyssa R. "A Human Right to Democracy? Legitimacy and Intervention." In *Rawls's Law of Peoples: A Realistic Utopia?* ed. Rex Martin and David A. Reidy. Blackwell, 2006.

Buchanan, Allen. "Rawls's Law of Peoples: Rules for a Vanished Westphalian World." *Ethics* 110, no. 4 (2000): 697–721.

Dreben, Burton. "On Rawls and Political Liberalism." In *The Cambridge Companion to Rawls*, ed. Samuel Freeman. Cambridge University Press, 2002.

Hardin, Russell. "Street-Level Epistemology and Democratic Participation." *Journal of Political Philosophy* 10, no. 2 (2002): 212–229.

Kaplan, Robert. "Was Democracy Just a Moment?" *Atlantic Monthly* 280, no. 6 (1997): 55–80.

Kristof, Nicholas D. "With a Few More Brains … ," *New York Times*, March 30, 2008.

Larmore, Charles. "The Law of Peoples, with 'The Idea of Public Reason Revisited.'" *Philosophy and Phenomenological Research* 64, no. 1 (2002): 241–243.

Martin, Rex, and David A. Reidy. "Introduction: Reading Rawls's *The Law of Peoples*." In *Rawls's Law of Peoples: A Realistic Utopia?* ed. Rex Martin and David A. Reidy. Blackwell, 2006.

Martin, Rex, and David A. Reidy, eds. *Rawls's Law of Peoples: A Realistic Utopia?* Blackwell, 2006.

Mill, John Stuart. *Considerations on Representative Government.* Liberal Arts Press, 1958.

Montesquieu, Charles de Secondat, baron de. *The Spirit of the Laws*, ed. and tr. Anne M. Cohler, Basia C. Miller, and Harold S. Stone. Cambridge University Press, 1989.

Nickel, James W. "Are Human Rights Mainly Implemented by Intervention?" In *Rawls's Law of Peoples: A Realistic Utopia?* ed. Rex Martin and David A. Reidy. Blackwell, 2006.

Ortega y Gasset, José. *The Revolt of the Masses.* Norton, 1932.

Pogge, Thomas. "Do Rawls's Two Theories of Justice Fit Together?" In *Rawls's Law of Peoples: A Realistic Utopia?* ed. Rex Martin and David A. Reidy. Blackwell, 2006.

Pogge, Thomas. "An Egalitarian Law of Peoples." *Philosophy and Public Affairs* 23, no. 3 (1994): 195–224.

Rawls, John. "The Domain of the Political and Overlapping Consensus" (1989). In *John Rawls: Collected Papers*, ed. Samuel Freeman. Harvard University Press, 1999.

Rawls, John. *John Rawls: Collected Papers*, ed. Samuel Freeman. Harvard University Press, 1999.

Rawls, John. *The Law of Peoples: with "The Idea of Public Reason Revisited."* Harvard University Press, 1999.

Rawls, John. *Political Liberalism.* Columbia University Press, 1996.

Rawls, John. *A Theory of Justice.* Harvard University Press, 1971.

Rousseau, Jean-Jacques. *The First and Second Discourses.* Tr. Roger D. Masters and Judith R. Masters. St. Martin's Press, 1989.

Rousseau, Jean-Jacques. *On the Social Contract: with Geneva Manuscript and Political Economy,* ed. Roger D. Masters, tr. Judith R. Masters. St. Martin's Press, 1978.

Tan, Kok-chor. "Liberal Toleration in Rawls's Law of Peoples." *Ethics* 108, no. 2 (1998): 276–295.

Tan, Kok-chor. "The Problem of Decent People." In *Rawls's Law of Peoples: A Realistic Utopia?* ed. Rex Martin and David A. Reidy. Blackwell, 2006.

5 Unequal Human Worth

Donald J. Munro

If an infirm close relative were to live near me, I would regularly help with household tasks, home care, transportation to a medical appointment, and so forth. Should a similarly infirm but unrelated person live in my neighborhood, I would offer to help out in some instances, but far less than for a close relation. Such help would make me feel good, and it would promote a happier community. But I do not have the time or strong motive to do more.

1 Familial Emotions—A Modern Omission

At least since the American Civil War, many patriots, politicians, and ethicists have maintained that all humans are in some sense of equal worth. The Fourteenth Amendment to the U.S. Constitution embodies the value in guaranteeing every citizen "equal protection of the laws." Advocates have defended this idea of equality in a variety of ways, sometimes as a function of different claimed sources of worth. The gradual acceptance of this position, with roots in the seventeenth century, was a departure in the West from the dominance of belief in natural inequality of worth. Inequality still had its advocates in developed countries throughout the twentieth century. However, the trend in legal and academic circles was toward affirming the idea that "all men are created equal" and the desirability of equal treatment.

In the ancient world, one of the most influential advocates of inequality was Plato, who distinguished three levels of souls: "gold," "silver," and "brass," paralleling the hierarchy of reason, spirit, and appetites. According to Plato, selective breeding would continue the flowering of golden souls.[1] Aristotle held that the majority of men were slaves by nature, because "the slave has no deliberative faculty at all."[2] The idea made its way into early Christianity via the Neo-Platonists. Saint Augustine confirmed the thesis with these words: "From heaven to earth, from the visible to the invisible, some things are good, others better than others. In this way they are unequal, so that all kinds of things might be."[3] Inequality of worth became a justification for hierarchical human institutions, religious and political. There were opponents, though with less power. The Stoic Cicero said that all men have reason as a spark of divinity in them: "This is sufficient proof that there is no difference in kind between man and man."[4]

Rumblings of a major shift away from the idea of inequality emerged in several constituencies in the Reformation. Martin Luther rejected attempts by the Church in Rome to assign different rights, powers, and privileges to people depending on whether their status was clerical or lay and their occupation "spiritual or carnal." Luther said that these distinctions were not recognized by God, for whom all souls are of equal worth—an idea that Luther claimed had emerged in early Christianity and had been lost.[5] Luther advocated equality of believers against the state or the church. But in Protestant congregations, the elders always had a claim to special worth and insight. Normally, ordinary members dared not challenge them.

Equality was taken to its logical final step by the Italian Socinians and their disciples, the Unitarians. Sixteenth-century Poland saw an increase in the numbers of Unitarians, and Unitarianism spread to Transylvania. Advocates of toleration of belief, they still accepted the need for organizational hierarchy. But their tenet of equal worth, typically based on the divine spirit's being present as reason in all persons, led to the claim that every human should be allowed to interpret the scriptures for himself. In the *Catechism of Rakau*, published in Poland in 1605, we read this:

Let each man be free to judge of religion: this is required by the New Testament and by the example of the primitive Church. Who art thou, miserable man, who would smother and extinguish in others the fire of the divine spirit which God has kindled in them?[6]

Thus, one of the early sources of equal worth to be identified was the presence of the divine spirit in all persons. Another was the claim that God loves all souls equally.

The philosophical sources of equal worth began to have their impact in the seventeenth century. Descartes said that the ability to distinguish the true from the false, or reason, "is by nature equal in all men." Rousseau argued that in the state of nature humans have no particular value status, and that only in society do they develop virtues and vices. Rousseau was an egalitarian mainly in the sense that he strongly opposed large inequalities of income and status,[7] insofar as they promote dependence on others and rob us of our freedom. He admitted that people differ in reasoning ability. The closest he came to speaking of any factual basis for equality of worth was his view that all people have a conscience, to which the weak can appeal as well as the strong.[8] And this was a significant justification for the equality among social contract members.

But it was John Locke, in *The Second Treatise of Civil Government*, whose position on equality of worth most strongly fed the form of that position that Thomas Jefferson wrote into the American Declaration of Independence. Locke wrote that in state of nature "all men by nature are equal." They are equal in "rank" in that no one has the right of power over another. Each has the right to his freedom, given by God, and only God is their Master. They have equal rights to pursue their "life, health, liberty, or possessions."[9] The most accepted source of equal human worth was God as creator and the sameness of the rights He bestowed on his human creatures. Hence the American legacy that "all men are created equal; that they are endowed by their Creator with certain inalienable rights; that among these, are life liberty, and the pursuit of happiness."

For the idea of equal worth to be influential is one thing. For it to be observed or acted upon is another. The standard attack on it, motivated by power considerations, was to challenge claims about any sameness among the "essential qualities" of being human. This was the position, reminiscent of Aristotle, of slaveholders in the United States and in Latin America, of the Nazis in Germany, and of white settlers in Australia. Claiming that aborigines were incapable of regarding land as their own native place or of nurturing their children properly, the Australian government took their "empty land" and put children of mixed blood into institutions. Not until the period 1992–2002 did the Australian courts void those policies.

It took a civil war in the United States and then the twentieth century's women's suffrage movement to effect changes, requiring equality of treatment consistent with equal worth. The Fourteenth Amendment, ratified in 1868, provided a legal form for equal treatment. The idea of equal laws had long existed in America. The Mayflower Compact of 1620, a kind of social contract of the forty-one male passengers on that ship, commits them to frame "just and equal Laws." "Equal laws" goes all the way back to a 430 BCE funeral speech in which Pericles said that "the law secures equal justice to all alike in their private disputes." I accept the fact that there is a relation between equal laws and the topic of equal worth. But in this chapter I focus more on equal worth as an ethical issue—one that is, in some ways, distinct from the ethical considerations used to evaluate laws.

I believe that one of the persistent motives to advocate equal worth has been to secure and then spread political power into a wider citizen base, beyond the Crown or landholders or other minority elites. Another reason was to have an answer to the question "Why should I be altruistic?" The value of equal worth gradually gained mainstream acceptance, as evidenced by the fact that by the twentieth century one usually did not have to give reasons for treating people the same, only for treating them differently. Handicapped people intuitively "deserve" the best parking places. So the law does not necessarily treat people the same, but it can still protect them. The law can identify the legitimate reasons for treating people differently. In private ethical choices, I will argue, our emotional bonds justify considering differences between people.

Among the recent writers who *assume* a general acceptance of the idea of equal worth is the philosopher John Rawls. In Rawls' case, all individuals are "moral persons" or have a moral personality.[10] The source of their equal worth is a fact, namely that they are rational and are capable of having a sense of justice. Rawls imagined equality as a hypothetical situation in which people who are free and rational, and who sometimes pursue their own interests, agree on how to make choices. They would agree on ruling social principles for our institutions "behind a veil of ignorance." This means that no one knows anything about his or her relative abilities, social status, or assets. The principles include "equality in the assignment of basic rights and duties." "Inequalities of wealth and authority are just only if they result in compensating benefits for everyone, and particularly for the least advantages members of society."[11] More recently, the topic of "prioritarianism," associated with Derek Parfit, gives extra weight to benefits that go to the economically poor, as compared with the more comfortable.

The utilitarian Peter Singer rejects Rawls' factual claim that all humans have moral personalities (the very young and the cognitively impaired do not have a sense of justice). But Singer does incorporate the value of impartiality into his ethics. That assumes some kind of equality of worth for those particular humans affected by a choice, action, or policy. He says that we must go beyond "I" and "you" to the universal law, "the standpoint of the impartial spectator."[12] There is no explicit claim by Singer of a factual basis for equality. The principle of equality is one of "equal consideration of interests," requiring "that we give equal weight in our moral deliberations to the like interests of all those affected by our actions."[13] We cannot have favorites. In deciding moral issues, partiality is bad. "Each [person] counts for one and none for more than one."[14] For Singer there is no special worth that comes from being a member of the human species, because chimpanzees and gorillas have personhood too. Among humans, worth varies as a function of the quality of their lives. "Life without consciousness is of no worth at all, says Singer."[15] It seems to me that, with this position, he does make factual claims about the worth of those people who have self-consciousness.

While I accept the validity and utility of holding that all people are equal under the law, I reject the claim that in private ethics or moral choices all people are of equal worth, and the claim that the interests of all persons affected in any way by my actions have equal weight in my choices. For me, that means worth is a function of perspective, of the standard one uses. I reject the theological claims about God's divine implant in our souls. In contrast, much evidence seems to support the Confucian position of unequal worth, according to which the source of worth is located in the magnitude of our emotions. And they are normally more powerful for close kin, friends, and close community than they are for people distant or unknown to us. Relationships and the reciprocal nature of the affection between the parties are objective facts. This leaves open the question of whether there is a basis for equality under the law. I will argue that there are prize-worthy traits shared by most humans, and that they are a justifiable source for judicial equality.

A moral system that works is natural in the sense that it takes account of human motives and predispositions that have their origin in biology. In theory those motives and predispositions may be explained in terms of their evolutionary function for humans or related primates. Philosophers would describe "working" as "ought should imply can," meaning that something becomes legitimate only if we *can* perform it. It ought not to put highly unreasonable demands on the subject's ordinary motives and attitudes. I will argue that utilitarianism fails to work because it refuses to allow moral choices to acknowledge the strength of emotional bonds to close family, friends, and community. Its principle of the happiness of "the greatest number" or "the greatest number of those affected by my acts" requires impartiality—that is, requires each person to count as only one. Confucian altruism also fails the workability test because its faith in the ease of natural growth from filiality to love of outsiders—conceived of as, like plant growth, dependent only on water and food—is unwarranted. One of my central conclusions in this chapter is that both the mid-imperial Neo-Confucians and the traditional Western utilitarians fail to meet the standard of a workable ethics.

2 A Challenge from Chinese Philosophy

Among the plausible insights in Chinese philosophy, there are a few that contradict traditional ethical beliefs common in Western countries. One important insight of Confucian philosophy is that kinship emotions are the first feelings to be experienced, are the root from which loving care emerges for those outside of the immediate family boundaries, and are the basis of morality. To a Westerner, a fallacy seems to appear in the Confucian inference from temporal priority to superior worth. From the earliest time, the Confucians assigned worth to family and close community members that is greater than the worth assigned to outsiders. Confucians would say, however, that the difference is not just temporal but also in magnitude of the emotional bond. Some family members count for more than one in terms of worth. This conflicts with what Singer takes as axiomatic among utilitarians and other Western ethicists: that in deciding moral issues, partiality is bad. In our judgments of events, among those affected by an action, "each [person] counts for one and none for more than one."[16]

In the Confucian classics, among the earliest and most influential textual justifications for partiality are two passages in the *Analects of Confucius* (551?–479? BCE). One, near the beginning of the current version of the text, says that "being filial toward parents and properly behaving toward elder brothers is the root of *ren* [humane treatment of others/perfected development]."[17] "Filiality" is a term that works well in English and conveys the Chinese meaning. Sometime before 200 BCE, the *Classic of Filiality* (*Xiaojing* 孝經) emerged as the lasting textual authority for the primacy of filiality. A passage in its first section asserts that "filiality is the basis of virtue and that from which all teachings come."

The second of the two passages justifying partiality describes a man whose father stole a sheep and who then testified against his father. Confucius remarked that in his own country an upright man would shield his father.[18] I assume that the bias applies mainly to the nuclear family. A similar theme can be found in Plato's *Euthyphro*. Euthyphro is going into a courthouse to prosecute his father for killing one of his servants—a violation of Greek law, which permits only kin of the dead to sue for murder. Socrates is surprised that Euthyphro would act contrary to Athenian custom, which would treat it as impious to charge one's father, ignoring one's duties to kin. The dialogue centers around the meanings of "piety" and "impiety." In the end, Socrates is not satisfied, and Euthyphro leaves.

Treating the process from basic feelings of filiality to full moral development as part of a continuous program of nurturance, the Confucians focused more on nurturing the development of virtues than on the individual knowing detailed rules. This is a matter of degree, because they favored teaching many ritual behaviors. For adults there was an obligation to nurture the young or those with immature minds, and doing so was considered a necessary part of self-completion. In English, we often use the term "to care for" where the Chinese texts speak of cultivating or nurturing. The metaphor of plant growth is present in the Chinese texts, as I will show below.

These are the parts of the Confucian thesis:

(1) People are of unequal worth, with family members having value more than outsiders.

(2) The basis for inequality endures in the mind's tendency to associate *knowledge* about the magnitude of family love and hierarchy, with certain *social emotions* (love, sympathy, shame, pride), and with *motives* (such as filiality) to act accordingly. I call this association "clustering." Pictorial metaphors, such as the plant, the sun, clear water, and the relation of ruler and ruled, are an important explanatory part of describing specific clusters.

(3) As part of the self-cultivation and nurturing processes, the presentation of models for emulation is the most efficient method. This is learning by imitation.

2.1 Family Love and Unequal Worth

The Confucian account combined the priority of family love with the belief that it is possible and desirable to extend this affection to a widening range of people. Its classical formulation is that *"Ren* is the essence of being human, and care for kin [*qin* 親] is its major expression."[19] The decrease (*shai/sha* 殺) in love for persons beyond the immediate family, and to outsiders, is objectively reflected in the different rituals observed to those groups. From this perspective, human worth varies as a function of magnitude of loving relationship. As the Neo-Confucian Cheng Yi (1033–1108) put it, "No love is greater than love (*ai* 爱) for family (*qin* 親)."[20]

Ren is both descriptive (referring to humans as beings who love their kin and can extend the sentiment to humane treatment of others) and evaluative (referring to the care for others as a proper goal for human development). The five basic sets of human relationships center around the family, with the second set often used to explain the first: prince-minister, father-son (the gender-biased symbol of the parent-child relationship), husband-wife, elder and younger brothers, and relations between friends.[21] The sincere person is able fully to develop himself, and then go on to foster the development of other people. Having done this, he can proceed to promote the development of other creatures and things.[22] So the roots of altruistic concern for others lie in the filial relationship of father and son. *Qin*, a term for "to care for/treat as kin," has the emotional content of familial love; the early etymological dictionary *Shuowen jiezi* defined *ren* as "kinship." Hence the prominence of kinship affection in love's hierarchy.

Also prominent in classical Mencian Confucianism,[23] and contrasting with the idea of unequal worth, is the belief in some common and inborn human traits and their corresponding manifestations. In the West today this would be understood as a basis for natural equality, referring to shared factual information about humans. For a Mencian, the issue is more complex. People are born with "the four minds": compassion, shame, respect, and right/wrong. Exercising them is the path to self-completion and, distantly, sagehood. Nothing is said about people having all identical potentials and so there is no basis for fundamental equal worth. As the *Analects* puts it, some people are born knowing,[24] which puts them on a higher plane from others. What the Mencian position does do is make a judgment about which are the most important traits, and those are the ones that are equally possessed, as "sprouts." Compassion is the most important trait, the essential human quality, manifest as *ren*. It is the basis for Mencius (fourth century BCE) considering human nature (*ren xing* 人性) good. It emerges in the relation between infant and caregiver, then extends to other kin, and can and should be extended beyond the family. Today in English we would also describe such love as sympathy or empathy. Its extension beyond the nuclear family we call altruism.[25]

To the early Mencian portraits of the mind, Zhu Xi (1130–1200) and his predecessors, including the aforementioned Cheng Yi, added a theory about the metaphysical origins and sustainability of that four part mind. They called it the *original mind* (*ben xin* 本心), or heavenly way (*tian dao* 天道). It is present in an individual as her *dao-mind* (*daoxin* 道心), and its content is awareness of the permanent and interrelated heavenly *li* 理 (cosmic categories/patterns/principles/coherences). To the extent that a person is clear about the *li*, her actually experienced feelings, desires, and motives (the human mind, *xin* 心) will be expressed properly or improperly. It was these Song dynasty Confucians who, from the perspective of an inborn original mind, continued the Mencian idea that anyone can be a sage. But from the perspective of how actual peoples' minds are they are unequal, because most of their minds are unclear about the *li*. Impurities (considered physical, stemming from *qi* 氣, matter/energy) in the mind often block its access to some of the *li*.

The *li* in the *dao*-mind include both descriptive and evaluative information about the interrelated classes of things known to the mind. Those mental classes mirror the same categories in the objective world. The interrelated *li* have traditionally been translated as "principles." Brook Ziporyn and Stephen Angle now describe them as "coherences,"[26] a term that nicely points to their interrelationships. They make up the content of the *dao*-mind. The *li* of most interest to some Neo-Confucians were twofold: (1) of living things and (2) of the production and reproduction of their lives, and, then, the family-centered social role relationships, plus the emotions that reinforce them. To prize the living was to care for the nurturance of living things (watering and weeding, in the case of plants; feeding, educating, and protecting, in the case of humans). To prize love of kin was to accord family love top priority, while remembering to extend caring love to the widening groups of people beyond kin. So the Mencian era cluster of emotions, cognition, and activity remains, but with the Song dynasty addition of a metaphysical theory about its source and maintenance—and a clear basis for differing degrees of actual clarity.[27]

2.2 The Interactive Cluster

Enduring support for the idea of special worth of family and close friends comes from the Confucian insight and practice that links together or clusters the emotions, cognition, and the "beginnings of action." The beginnings are similar to what in English would be called the conative events, inclinations, impulses, or motives to act. The beginnings of action may involve emotional attraction to a target plus some knowledge of that goal and its priority, and beliefs about what practices successfully lead to or obstruct achieving the goal. They coexist and mutually interact. From the time of the earliest Chinese philosophers into the twentieth century, this clustering was part of the normal description of the mind. One of the significant clusters that Confucians claimed is always accessible in the mind is the special love of kin: affection for parents and children, knowledge of the hierarchical relations involved, and the inclination to be filial.

An early and influential cluster is in the Mencian idea of the *four minds*, and their first sprouts, with which all people are born.[28] The mind of compassion *ceyin zhi xin* 惻隱之心) combines sympathy with awareness of the relationship of care-giver to recipient. The mind of shame and dislike (*xiu'e zhi xin* 羞惡之心) is an emotion associated with a sense of what is proper and improper (*yi* 義). The mind of respect (*gongjing zhi xin* 恭敬之心) is associated with awareness of hierarchy and related rules of ritualized proper conduct. The mind of right and wrong (*shifei zhi xin* 是非之心) combines the emotions of approval or disapproval with knowledge of correct and incorrect, realized as wisdom (*zhi* 智). Unlike the Greeks, for whom truth and falsity were important considerations, the Confucians were more concerned with the behavioral implications of a belief or proposition in question. What effect does adherence to it have on people? Thus, what today we would call the cognitive dimension (proper/improper, right/wrong) included knowledge of the noble and base and took hierarchy and situational specifics into account.

This human mind experiences negative feeling (shame) when a person violates what is proper. It also experiences positive pleasure when aware of what is orderly and proper (a feeling that is said to be similar to enjoying the taste of good meat) and motivates actions accordingly.[29] Along with emotion, knowing what is proper and improper is the beginning of action. The Confucians drew on the pre-philosophical belief that Heaven commands certain appropriate actions. Then they internalized the idea of command to mean that the individual mind, once knowing something to be proper, orders compliance with it.[30] This would be a "beginning of action," or something that in the West is called a conative event.

Note especially the Mencian words for the mind's sense of right and wrong: *shifei zhi xin*. The mind has a sensibility that discriminates between "correctness" and "incorrectness," a cognitive function. Yet this same phrase suggests some sort of evaluation. To *shi* something is to approve of it; to *fei* is to disapprove. These are feeling responses. This is the evaluating mind. One of the classical period's great legacies, then, was a portrait of the mind that concurrently makes cognitive distinctions and affective evaluations, which combine to motivate action.

The Mencian view of the mind, influenced by Buddhist elements such as the One Buddha Mind, became orthodox in China after the death of Zhu Xi, who had helped nurture the acceptance of his doctrines by reenergizing scholarly teaching academies and contributing to their teaching materials. In 1211 the throne published his collected commentaries on the *Four Books*—the *Analects* (*Lunyu* 論語; fifth to third centuries BCE?), *Mencius* (fourth to third century BCE), *Great Learning* (*Da Xue* 大學; fifth century BCE?), and *Doctrine of the Mean* (*Zhong Yong* 中庸; fifth century BCE?) . In 1279 the Mongol emperor decreed that the civil service examinations would require familiarity with Zhu's commentaries.

2.3 Pictorial Metaphors and Clustering

Zhu used pictorial images to explain his theories. Examples include the ruler-ruled relation to describe aspects of the mind—a bright light (such as the sun) and clear water to illustrate the mind's good content or the *li* (cosmic categories/patterns/principles/coherences), and plant growth to describe human development from childhood to maturity, or from ethical partiality to altruism. The way Zhu used the images, they performed two functions, one structural and one emotive. In *Images of Human Nature* I characterize these functions as follows:

An image structures the relations between disparate facts to which a theory applies, calling attention to certain aspects of the relationship. And, because of its familiarity within the culture, it also elicits an emotional response to those facts, thereby uncovering a value that Zhu Xi wishes to affirm. These are functions that the analyst can identify today, not ones of which Zhu Xi was necessarily aware.[31]

Metaphors and analogies play a basic structural and emotive role in Zhu's thought, structuring his idea of the relationship between certain facts, or their particular qualities, and then stimulating an emotional response to them. In no way am I suggesting that the metaphor controls the theory. The metaphors represent the way, via the body's senses, we have absorbed something concrete in our lives, such as families or light or plants, about which we may have many ideas, some abstract, not identified in the metaphor. In other words, the metaphor reveals something about how we humans think, but it does not totally limit or control how we think.

Life's Stages: The Plant Image   As early as Mencius, Confucians explained the *four minds* and their potential growth with the pictorial image of the plant, or the process from sprouts or seedlings to mature growth. The eventual qualities of knowledge and compassion, and the social emotions, perfected in the sage, all are present in the mind's seed. The clustering is revealed in the fact that the plant image conveys both descriptive information about the stages of growth, and also elicits emotional feelings in favor of helping the development, or motivation, to water and to weed the plants, or to nurture and educate the mind. The following well-known passage from Mencius is illustrative:

Take the barley for example. Sow the seeds and cover them with soil. The place is the same and the time of sowing is the same. The plants shoot up and by the summer solstice they all ripen. If there is any unevenness, it is because the soil varies and the amount of human effort devoted to tending it. Now things of the same kind are alike. Why should we have doubts when it comes to man? The sage and I are of the same kind.[32]

By mid-imperial China and the gradual rise of Zhu Xi's Neo-Confucianism, the plant metaphor remained, built into a unified cosmic structure. It explains the human mind as the repository of the life principle at the human level. It is the container of that which guides the person's development:

A disciple asked about the difference between the mind, one's nature (*xing* 性 [a.k.a., *dao*-mind]), and the feelings. Zhu Xi replied, "Cheng Yi said, 'The mind is like the seed of grain; the *li* of life in it is one's nature; the *yang* material force in bringing forth life is the feelings.'"[33]

A disciple asked, "The necessity that the seed of grain will grow is like the necessity for man to be *ren* [humane treatment of others/perfected moral development]. In this way we take growth as like *ren*. The life of the seed is the *li* of growth. So then it follows that the *li* of growth is *ren*." Zhu Xi replied, "It definitely must be this way."[34]

The growth process is present in the mind as potential, just as the life-to-be of a plant is dormant in the winter or hidden in the seed. Reference to human action requires identifying which phase one is speaking about: the dormant, hidden, tranquil, and pre-stimulus (*wei fa* 未發, or not yet released/sprouted/sprung), or the budding, revealed, active, and post-stimulus (*yi fa* 已發, or already released/sprouted/sprung). The beginnings of action were understood by analogy with the process from dormant seed to spring sprouts.

Zhu treated this theory as supporting his claim that there is no conflict between family duty and duty to public. Family duty is central in the early stages of growth. Public duty becomes possible only with maturity. Zhu chose the image of a cultivated, rather than wild, plant to explain his theory. Psychologically, it suggests the obligation to nurture. *Ren* is present at all four stages of growth (understood seasonally), but it is specific to the originating growth, or spring (*yuan* 源), the beginning of life.[35] Nurturing others is an essential part of self-completion. So the possibility of incompatibility between family and public interests disappears. Supposedly they are harmonized.

But an important question for ethics in general and Confucianism in particular is whether family and public interests really can be harmonized. Confucians emphasize the obligation to nurture, and that includes both family members and others. Nurturing family members through food, education, and love is not problematical. Confucians believe that by cultivating those caring traits, persons will go on to be altruists. This means that Confucians nurture their own social roles and then help others do the same. But this is done through education and providing the economic necessities of life. Without some attention to power politics and laws, this cannot be done. In the early 1920s, John Dewey went to China to lecture. Agreeing with many of the Chinese scholars who welcomed him, including Hu Shi, Dewey echoed their slogan "Save China through Education."[36] The trouble was that in parts of China the warlords controlled the purse strings and would not pay the teachers or fund the schools. So the nourishment process needs the backing of those in power who have the money and the will. I do not believe that the Confucians ever gave a convincing description of how to develop a person who cares for outsiders, and who can as an individual solve the dilemma of conflicting private and family obligations. Later in this chapter I will propose some ways of softening the conflict.

Aristotelian ethics reduced potentiality to mere means toward actuality or maturity. In contrast, Zhu's view is that kinship love is intrinsically valuable, though it also enhances ones ability to care for others. Note the different emphases in the following remarks:

Zhu Xi was asked if the statement that "filiality and brotherly love[37] are the root of *ren*" means the following: having served your parents and elder brothers to the utmost, you have established this root, and then you expand it to loving other people and things; thereby your loving is practiced according to *li*. Zhu Xi replied, "It is certainly so. But filiality and brotherly love are proper in themselves. It is not because you want to love people and love things that you then start with filiality and brotherly love." Ke Xue said, "Would it be like a plant having a root, then the branches and foliage can be lush?" Zhu replied, "It is so, but where there is a root, the branch and foliage will naturally be lush. It is not because of the desire to have lush foliage that you then cultivate the root."[38]

Zhu has two points here. One is that kinship love is worthy in and of itself. The other is that a person should assume that extended altruism will develop naturally out of family love, as a plant grows naturally.

Images of Clarity: the Sun, Clear Water, and Ruler-Ruled The *dao*-mind regularly interacts with the other psychological events in the mind (actual feelings, desires, and motives, or human-mind). Their relationship is explained using the metaphor of ruler and ruled, with the *dao*-mind as ruler. It is the container of all interrelated *li*. Those *li* themselves, by analogy, are self-bright or accessible to a clear mind. Zhu said that each of the moral sentiments (Mencius' four minds) innate to the mind is "like a mirror, which is originally bright."[39] He also liked to say that "clear water represents the goodness of one's nature."[40] So descriptively, the sun or clear water convey the factual information that, with education, the content of the mind is understandable or coherent, and they elicit the emotional motivation for the student to concentrate on these *li*.[41]

In China, the belief in an interactive cluster of mental events endured into the last century. At that time, the form taken by thinkers inspired by Confucianism was a fact-value fusion. Accounts of things and events should be both descriptive of their processes, and evaluative. The latter term refers to how they should be acting or developing, and how we should be acting toward them. The emotions then also play a major role in generating the judgment of approval or disapproval. The influential philosopher Xiong Shili (d. 1968) inherited the ruler-ruled metaphor. He maintained that the scope of an investigator's inquiry should be limited to the social role realm and to the innate moral sense, the ruler that resides in the "original mind" and controls all other psychological activity, including inquiry. The content of the innate sense includes the standard mid-imperial list of values: filial love as the starting point of ethics, *ren*, social hierarchy, altruism, courage, sincerity, selflessness, and the nurturing of life. One should never allow knowledge of the objective world and the controlling moral truths to be separated. They create a unified whole. However, Xiong Shili himself did not make a deep study of the methodology of inquiry.[42]

He Lin (1902–1993) translated Hegel and Spinoza, was honored by Chiang Kai-shek, and was consulted by Mao after 1949. He maintained that the knower should focus not only on facts but also on values. He said that we continually project our values on the world. The ruling mind organizes knowledge and evaluates. Thus inquiry concerns both: "The nature (*xing*) of a thing represents why a thing is the way it is [a factual matter] and also the essential factor according to which it should be as it is [a value matter]."[43]

Maoists rejected Confucian family and social role ethics in favor of one that prioritized loyalty to the Communist Party and a recognition of social class divisions. They rejected any idea of a universal innate moral sense that perpetuated the family ethic. But they inherited and continued the practice of clustering the three types of psychological events. Note the use at that time (1937–1976) of the term *renshi* 認識, which carried both the sense "to understand" and the sense "to accept." "To accept" meant to have a commitment to act in accordance with what is known and is either approved or disapproved.[44] To understand the meaning (*yi* 意) of something also meant to have a resolution or a motive (*dongji* 動機) to act.

With this combination of knowing and doing (*zhixing heyi* 知行合一) the Confucians avoided the kind of moral escapism that the naturalistic fallacy has allowed some professional ethicists in the West. Hume stated that we cannot derive an "ought" from an "is." From this idea it appears that facts, no matter the magnitude of joy or suffering to which they refer, are not relevant to our obligations. This is not the place for me to analyze critically the logical status of the Chinese legacy of the fact-value fusion. It is sufficient here for the reader to know that it is part of the reality of Chinese culture.

In the end, the important thing is that, excepting the Maoists, the value that linked psychology and ethics remained influential in China. It colored many portraits of the mind as ruler of all mental events and of the actions that follow from them. The belief in the superior worth of family and close community members endured as part of the context. Below, I demonstrate how this process was elaborated in the moral psychology of Zhu Xi.

2.4 Emulating Models

Among the ways of nurturing family love was the emulation of models of filiality, such as the legendary sage king Shun. This is an instance of what today would be called observational learning—that is, observing models in stories or in reality. The classical formulation was "teaching by example surpasses teaching by words" (*shenjiao sheng yu yanjiao* 身教勝於言教). Some models were living persons, such as a father, a teacher, an official, or a ruler. According to the *Analects*, "when those who are in high stations perform well all their duties to their relations, the people are aroused to virtue."[45] According to the Confucian text *The Great Learning* (*Da Xue* 大學; fifth century BCE?), "when the ruler, as a father, a son, and a brother is a model, then the people will imitate him."[46] Zhu Xi applauded this view that filiality practiced in the household can influence people beyond it.[47] Model officials were called parental officials (*fumu guan* 父母官). The practice of presenting models for emulation continues to the present day. Included are production models (model workers), cultural models (heroes in culture and education, such as "Excellent Teachers"), and typical models (*dianxing* 典型).

Emulating models is a way of internalizing attitudes, motives, and skills consistent with some virtue or behavior the rulers seek to be practiced. It is a way of cultivating or developing predictable action, on the path to its becoming spontaneous, as it is in sages. Many Confucians preferred this approach over emphasizing penal codes, which control through fear of punishment. Their argument was that when the policeman is not around, the old bad actions will reemerge. Model emulation internalizes motives, so they endure even if there is no enforcer around. As such, the emphasis is on practices in teaching and in the transformation of the mind through repeated proper acts, not on individuals making rational or good choices. In both Confucianism and in Chinese culture, observational learning stands out. Unfortunately, it exists in school rooms alongside excessive rote memorization of texts.

When the Western student asks how he can learn to do the right thing, the teacher is likely to answer that he should concern himself with the *choices* he makes and remember that he has a free will that makes choices possible. This position had two sources. The earlier one was the Epicurean assertion of the individual's ability to select courses of action that can maximize his personal pleasure and help him avoid pain. That assertion was directed against classical materialists such as Democritus and the founder of Greek Stoicism, Zeno, both strict determinists for whom every event was dependent on prior physical causes and so free choice was a myth. The other source was early medieval Christianity, especially the doctrines of Augustine. The problem was in locating the blame or responsibility for evil. Evil exists, but how does that square with the existence of a good, omnipotent, and omniscient God? Augustine wrote *De Libero Arbitrio Voluntatis* (On the Free Choice of the Will) to clear God of blame for evil by locating human evil in human choices. The causes of sin and evil are free will in man and angels. Human evil results from erroneous choices. God is absolved, because He could not give people free choice (a good) without simultaneously making it possible for them to err. So underlying the centrality of free will in European and American ethics are uncaused or undetermined choices, a God free from blame, the concepts of responsibility and blame that go with being a person, and a thing called "will."

By the twenty-first century, under the influence of the new cognitive neurosciences, many Western thinkers had found new evidence with which to reject the idea of free will involving uncaused choices[48]: fMRI images of the brain activity that processes choices. I agree with them. But there remains the other legacy of support for the idea of voluntary choice making, namely a justification for holding persons responsible and for blaming, punishing, or rewarding them accordingly. This justification for retaining the idea is that it is a useful part of the learning process. People may learn what unsocial conduct should not be repeated or changed.

In contrast, for Zhu Xi and his followers no entity called a "will" need be posited. The Chinese term that most often has been rendered as "will" is *zhi* 志. But it is not about regular choice making. Rather it is a commitment. A common ideal would be to become a sage. An attitudinal matter, its ideal condition is a single-minded decision to seek such goals. So it is under the individual's control for protracted periods, unlike the state of her physical endowment. It is not a matter of daily moral choices.

As for the potential for evil, evil has always existed on earth because of the material dust (*qi* 氣) that darkens the self-bright light (in the mind as the heavenly *li*) and the material obstructions (selfish desires) that hinder the correct directional movement of motives and acts. No supreme being is disgraced by evil. It is just the way things are, given the relation of the *li* to matter (*qi*). Doing the right thing and avoiding evil have less to do with assigning blame or with choices in the Confucian tradition than they do in the Western tradition. They have to do with how to use *practice* to remove the obstructions to clear knowledge, and then cultivate the spontaneity that comes from reverential concentration.[49]

For most Confucian writers, the initial way to understand practical effort was by using the plant analogy. Think of the four Mencian emotions (four minds) as sprouts. Today they would be referred to as the four moral sentiments or senses. They need nurturance in order to thrive. This involves practice in removing the weeds (certain desires) that obstruct their growth. The plant image describes eliminating the selfish desires. The individual should reduce the number of desires he craves to satisfy—specifically, those that cannot be fulfilled in accordance with rules, such as the desire to eat at the wrong time or to eat the wrong food. The process focuses on practice, not choice making. The practice involves reverential concentration and the extension of knowledge. Models serve as a teaching device.

Note that choice is not absent from Zhu's analysis. It just plays a less central role than it does in Western thought and religion. Priority goes to observing the constant and coherent moral principles (*jing* 經). Those rules are recorded in texts and objective and are thus available to officials or scholars who can publicly certify their content. For most people, they provide the guidance of authority. Only sages can understand the holistic order (*daoli* 道理) that transcends them. For most people, most of the time, the word is to obey the *jing*. This opens the gate for actual rulers and officials themselves to make the rules and to formulate acceptable model choices. They would thereby ignore other opinions, on the argument that the people's minds are unclear.

Zhu sometimes described choice as we think of it today using the metaphor of the balance scale or "scaling" (*quan* 權). People draw on their moral sense or conscience (*yi* 意) in responding to the specifics of different situations.[50] They choose actions accordingly. This is scaling or weighing what to do. Its benefit is that it allows flexible decisions. But Zhu described it also as "difficult," because it opens the door to departure from the single authoritative standard. He believed that people's minds are generally unclear. Personal judgment, being subjective, can be dangerous. An example would be the rule that requires obedience to parents in the matter of choosing a bride. If the individual considers ignoring their wishes and dares to weigh the specifics in such cases, he risks violating the *jing*. Only sages dare do that.[51] Better to start the effort by reducing selfish desires (those that are inconsistent with the constant rules), then shift to include concentration and the extension of knowledge. This includes concentration on models or exemplary persons.

Even in promoting character development, copying models was not always treated by Chinese thinkers in a way that we today would consider workable or positive. When the legendary sage Shun violated the filial injunction to seek parental approval of a marriage, his justification was that he was compelled to observe the higher priority of filiality, which was to produce offspring, and his parents would have obstructed that. Here assumptions about social class and status place limitations on who can weigh choices and when. This is similar to the limitations on democracy advocated by Aristotle and other elitists, with their claims about slaves' having no deliberative faculty.

Also on the negative side, models have been used to teach problem solving by copying models as a method of inquiry and data analysis. In pre-modern China this meant studying the texts of sages in order learn about archetypical situations they described. "When we know the mind of the sages and use that to manage our minds to the point where they are no different from that of the sage," Zhu Xi wrote, "this is what is called the transmission of the mind."[52] Some of the archetypal models were of organizations or institutions associated with utopian ages, such as portraits of land allocation or taxation. Such copying of models obstructed problem solvers from noting the differences between the classical plan and the actual present situation. However, other forms of emulation in Confucianism have had a goal consistent with how people often actually learn and continue to be successful. These involve the goal of character development or socialization. They are especially congenial to communitarian societies. Such development includes learning filiality. It is still a matter of government concern in China, when the state tries to avoid pension fund costs by shifting them to the family, where they traditionally rested.

3 Current Evidence in Support of the Confucian Positions

3.1 Partiality in Love of Family and Community

What are the known sources of human worth? One is magnitude of normal emotional bonds between an individual and the persons or groups for whom she has special emotional regard. This regard may be exhibited in her nurturing care for them, or in her use of her own resources for them, or her expectations from and duties to them. This source applies to the special worth felt by a person toward individuals in the immediate family, close friends, or community groups. A typical modern example in the case of friends is the "band of brothers" emotional bond that some in the military experience, typically in small groups that survive through mutual support. The Confucian position concerning the relation of love of kin to altruism has echoes in the views of evolutionary biologists and psychologists today. Edward O. Wilson puts it this way:

Among the traits with documented heritability, those closest to moral aptitude are empathy to the distress of others and certain processes of attachment between infants and their caregivers.[53]

Kin selection [acting beneficially on behalf of individual kin] is the natural selection of genes based on their effects on individuals carrying them plus the effects the presence of genes has on all the genetic relatives of the individuals, including parents, siblings, cousins, and others who still live and are capable either of reproducing or of affecting the reproduction of blood relatives. Kin selection is especially important in the origin of altruistic behavior.[54]

Altruism is in part an emotion. The seminal biological work on reciprocal altruism was done in 1971 by Robert Trivers, building on the 1964 work of William D. Hamilton. "The preconditions for the evolution of reciprocal altruism," Trivers states, "are similar to those for the operation of kin selection."[55]

The Neo-Confucian account of the practice of the origin and development of altruism has a plausible basis confirmed by recent findings in the sciences. This is the great strength of emotional bonds to kin. Any Western ethics that ignores these risks thereby proposes choices for individuals that are unworkable because they run contrary to our basic motivations and desires.

3.2 Clustering

David Hume was among the precursors of modern Western philosophy who rejected any isolation of the so-called mental faculties from each other. Fragmentation was a legacy of the rationalists, such as Descartes. In *A Treatise on Human Nature*, Hume wrote that reason "is, and ought only to be, the slave of the passions." In that passage, "passions" refers to love, anger, pride, envy, fear, and desire. For Hume, reason does play a role in moral choices, in looking at facts, and in noting relationships. But passions alone motivate action.[56]

Clustering was relatively absent from mainstream North American psychology until after World War II. The new change in favor of an interrelated view of the mind's activity was noted in the standard *Handbook in Social Psychology* for 1968:

Philosophers at diverse times and places have arrived at the same conclusion, that there are basically three existential stances that man can take with respect to the human condition:

knowing, feeling, and acting ... within the scientific study of attitudes, the trilogy came early and stayed late ... . The question arises of how closely the cognitive, affective, and conative components are related. If all three give approximately the same result, one should perhaps apply Occam's razor to reduce the redundant conceptual baggage ... . The results indicate that the three components are quite highly intercorrelated.[57]

By the turn of the twenty-first century, neuroscientists, using fMRI equipment and human subjects with varying kinds of brain damage, were able to identify some of the brain systems that support ethical behavior—among them the systems for memory, decision making, and creativity, which often include the cognitive brain functions and beginnings of action. For those who accept their findings, those scientific facts terminate for good the Platonic legacy that moral reasoning, or any reasoning, can occur without the emotions playing a role. This is the Plato of his dialogue *Phaedo*, not the Plato of the *Symposium*. Plato held that reasoning can and should occur in the mind all by itself, without any obstruction form the bodily and impure emotions. In the modern period, Descartes reinforced the idea that the mind has access to knowledge only if it operates apart from anything physical, making deductions from innate truths. There was no recognition that the emotions are interrelated with reasoning and can motivate study or bias its findings.

In contrast, with its long history of treating the trilogy of psychological events as interrelated, the Chinese findings warrant some depth of investigation. I will now examine that cluster briefly before discussing one of its traits: family love, which has special relevance for ethics. One consequence of clustering is that as long as the orthodox Confucian perspective was taught, that particular partial mind set (bonds to kin) would remain in most assessments of the mind. Confucians believed that the essence of being human was *ren* (humane treatment of others / perfected moral development), and its major expression is care for kin. The magnitude of love decreases as the kin relationship becomes more distant, but love also extends to non-kin.[58] From that perspective, humans are of unequal worth.

People interested in modern ethics should treat seriously the magnitude of normal emotional bonds between individual and close family, friends, and close community. This can be done while they remain mindful that there are many dysfunctional families and other non-kin relationships. Treating these bonds seriously means, first, that I accept several of the early Chinese insights about the importance of child-caregiver emotional bonds, and how they relate to altruism. Second, I believe that one of the strongest Confucian psychological positions is the relationship between the various mental events that we traditionally have called emotions, cognition, and motivation (beginnings of action). Knowing something often involves emotionally approving or disapproving of some aspect of it, which may lead to action. "When someone is willing to *act* on a moral belief," the brain scientist Michael Gazzaniga writes, "it is because the emotional part of his or her brain has become active when considering the moral question at hand."[59]

The cognitive aspect may concern the best way, based on past experience, to satisfy a desire. It may include prudential rules of conduct. The emotional signal may or may not be foremost in our awareness. According to the neuroscientist Antonio Damasio, "the emotional signal can operate entirely under the radar of consciousness. It can produce alterations in working memory, attention, and reasoning so that the decision-making process is biased toward selecting the action most likely to lead to the best possible outcome, given prior experience."[60]

In my discussion thus far, I have highlighted metaphors or images both because of their prominence in Zhu Xi's teachings and also because they illustrate so clearly the clustering of emotional and cognitive (structural) references. The plant addresses both the stages of life development and the emotional stimulus for humans to nurture (water and weed the plants). But I also do so because the study of such physical images is a recent field in cognitive linguistics. The basic work was done by George Lakoff and Mark Johnson in *Metaphors We Live By*. Its philosophical relevance to the mind-body topic and to Chinese thought has been wonderfully explored and developed by Edward Slingerland, according to whom "this idea of bodily based, concrete schemas serving as conceptual templates for our understanding of abstract, or less clearly structured, domains is the basic insight behind 'conceptual metaphor theory.'"[61] The Confucian materials, of which those by Zhu Xi are but one example, are rich sources for those interested in conceptual metaphor theory to study.

The clustering to which Gazzaniga and Damasio referred represent quite a shift from the earlier tripartite division described in that 1968 *Handbook in Social Psychology*. Before that time, it would have been unusual to think of the three types of mental activity as intercorrelated. But certain Western psychologists still open the door to a new kind of separation among them. For instance:

Two people feel strongly about an issue, their feelings come first, and their reasons are invented on the fly, to throw at each other.[62]

This may well be true in a discussion of new or unusual moral questions. But it is not true of topics about which a person has taken a stance or been taught what position is proper. When a previous topic arises again, the person's response may instantly involve emotions connected to knowledge. That may be knowledge of what in the past was the best workable choice or viewpoint to take; it may even be knowledge of reasons given in the past to justify the choice or stance. The relevant "working memory, attention, and reasoning" may have been biased by experiences, and that bias may have tilted the decision in favor of what has worked best before, as Damasio suggests in the passage quoted above.

3.3 Evidence for Imitative Learning

In the second half of the last century, American psychologists began to study what they called "observational learning," meaning learning through imitation. A leader in this pursuit was Klaus Riegel of Stanford University, editor of the journal *Human Development*.[63] In 1992, mirror neurons were discovered by a team led by the neuroscientist Giacomo Rizzolatti. These are subsets of neurons in the brains of monkeys (and perhaps humans) that react when an individual performs a certain act, or when she looks at another individual performing the same act. What remains to be found is a neural model for the acts of mirror neurons that support imitation. If found, this would support observational learning as consistent with how people naturally learn: mirror neurons enable a person to imitate the movements of others, to read their intentions, and mentally to copy their feelings and some of their thinking.

Imitation can promote fast learning and transmission of knowledge and skills within and beyond a society's borders. Empathy, often involved in altruism, may depend on neural imitation networks and those that regulate emotions, enabling us to mimic the emotions of other people. They also seem to be involved in simulation learning—that is, imagining how we would experience a situation. Chinese educators and officials have a long and successful history of using models to socialize people, either in person or by means of stories, pictures, and statues.

4 Prospects: Application of Confucian Theory

4.1 Emotions and Human Worth

As I noted at the beginning of the chapter, John Rawls supported a belief in equal worth when thinking of justice. In the West, such a belief had its roots in the claim by some European Christians that God loves all His human creations equally, or that each person has a divine spark in her soul. Modern utilitarians do not necessarily adhere to the Protestant religious claims. But the utilitarian Peter Singer is impressed that many ethicists, from Jesus ("love thy neighbor as thy self") to Continental theorists (Sartre, Habermas), "agree that an ethical principle cannot be justified in relation to any partial or sectional group."[64] Singer prizes impartiality toward all when it comes to evaluating the affect of an action on people.

I do not accept either the axiom or the idea that membership in a partial or sectional group is not relevant to an ethical principle. I believe that, from the personal standpoint of an individual's resources, care, and interests, people are of unequal worth. From that perspective, members of a person's immediate family, neighbors, some friends, and close community have greater worth than other people in the world, with special attention to the family and friends. I refer to this as *the private perspective*. In contrast, from a different standpoint, that of certain forms of the law, I believe that all people have equal worth. I call that *the public perspective*.

That some influential Western psychologists and ethicists do ignore the bonds between family members, members of bands of brothers, and friends is manifest in the unquestioned prominence of the value of impartiality in their writings. Rawls wrote that in thinking about justice we must operate under a "veil of ignorance." The biologist Marc Hauser interprets this as meaning that we should not think about anyone's personal characteristics, including relationships. In Hauser's view, these are morally irrelevant biases:

In terms of a general theory of morality, we want to exclude possible biases that may cause us to see as just situations that favor the in-group over the out-group; I use the notion of "exclude" here as a practical desideratum, acknowledging upfront that we inherited from our primate cousins (and probably before) a highly partial and biased mind-set, one designed initially to favor kin. It is this in-group bias that must be overcome if we are to advance an impartial moral theory.[65]

Hauser also writes that "our emotions are not part of the dedicated and specialized components of the moral faculty."[66]

My position, like the Chinese one, is the same as the one Antonio Damasio puts forward:

Emotion and feeling [are] not merely players in the process of reasoning, but indispensable players … . As we have argued earlier, every experience in our lives is accompanied by some degree of emotion and this is especially obvious in relation to important social and personal problems.[67]

I am shocked that a thoughtful person such as Hauser could ignore the moral relevance of our most powerful emotions, those that bind us to our kin. This applies also to Peter Singer. I conclude that in some ways their proposals for our moral choices or efforts are unworkable. To say this does not mean that I think the Confucian approach is without defect. In fact, I think the Confucians put too much faith in the supposed ease with which humane or altruistic practices can grow out of family love.

Singer would ignore those familial emotions because he believes that when a person makes an ethical judgment she should "go beyond a personal or sectional point of view" and consider of equal weight the interests of all those affected by her choice.[68] "This," he writes, "provides us with a basic principle of equality: the principle of equal consideration of interests." His justification is that facts have nothing to do with labels of inequality: "the claim to equality does not rest on the possession of intelligence, moral personality [one that has a sense of justice], rationality, or similar matters of fact."[69] In contrast, I hold that my emotional bonds to my kin often mean that their interests have more worth to me than the interests of other people. My daughter's interest in having pain removed is normally more important to me than the interests of others affected by the same natural event, such as an earthquake.[70] So long as I observe the rules that clinics are allowed to issue, I have no problem with tilting outcomes a bit in her favor. I would gather information about physicians most experienced in relevant procedures; then I would use available contacts to speed up her care and try to have the most skilled medical persons do it.

But the justification for the special worth I feel for kin is *not unequivocal*. As a function of their ages and development, it depends on their being, or learning to be, willing to show reciprocity in their own family ties, on their acting in accord with the laws that support the care of others, and, when possible, on their sharing the support offered to others by non-governmental charitable organizations. The private perspective must be balanced by the public perspective.

4.2 Limitations to the Confucian Idea of Care

There is weakness in the Confucian priority given to kinship love. It lies in how they described caring or extending that love beyond the immediate family. And this weakness reveals something for the attention of ethicists today who take the universalistic position, opposing preferential worth of family and community. Although Zhu tried to accommodate both the values of preference for family and those of public-spirited altruism, he was unable to harmonize them convincingly. In fact, his ideas of love and of "the people" often assumed that there would always be differences in socioeconomic status (possibly a form of inequality of worth) between the altruist and the recipient. Though Zhu's texts are rich in wisdom about family relations, they lack detail about how to be public-spirited. I do not believe that Zhu or his successors, up to the modern period, ever recognized how important this kind of difference is in the strength of our emotional bonds between family and public. This kind of difference forever rendered their form of altruism less theoretically and practically successful than they thought it would be.

There is a historical or social weakness in Zhu's views on public *ren* (humane treatment of others / perfected moral development); there is also a theoretical weakness. The social weakness is that Zhu's audience consisted of literati and potentially superior people (*junzi* 君子). He prepared his *Elementary Learning* (*Xiao Xue* 小學) in 1176 as an instructional guide for daily life. The low literacy rate would have restricted the size of this audience. Women would have been excluded because Zhu considered them not capable of advanced learning. Further, as was common in China and elsewhere, he thought of people in terms of standard relationships, often involving an abstraction of the family analogy. When he occasionally did discuss altruism outside the family, it was in terms of the mutual help community organization with which a person would already be connected. For example, he wrote comments on the Lü family community contract (*xiangyue* 鄉約), the purpose of which was to promote reciprocal help for moral development in the community through ceremonies, lectures, and public praise and criticism. In the *Elementary Learning* Zhu talked of showing sympathy to each other (*xiangxu* 相恤), not to people in general but to those with whom one has a formal relationship within the contract. As officials, the people with whom Zhu's class would have been concerned would often be those in the standard administrative categories into which China was then divided (communities, counties, prefectures, circuits, etc.), particularly the category for which the official was responsible or was being trained to be responsible.[71] The perspective was to relate to a group in a familiar region, occupation, lineage, or similar cohort. It was difficult to consider those who were not so related to the actor. Of course, even in the West clarity about the nature of groups and their competing interests did not begin until the emergence of the social sciences.

In addition to Zhu's positive insight into the role of the emotions in knowing, there is at least one weakness in his idea of empathic understanding. Embodiment (*ti* 體) assumes that when the individual empathizes with other humans, she can always use her own feelings as a guide, because people are similar. In fact, people have different personalities, so their motives and feelings may differ. I cannot correctly empathize with someone unless I understand her particular state of mind. It may be more difficult to empathize with people from whom I am separated by geography or by class status.

Now I turn to the serious theoretical and practical weaknesses in the mid-imperial Confucian position. Zhu's predecessor Cheng Yi, with whom Zhu agreed on the matter of the priority of family love, put it this way: "*Ren* focuses itself on love. *No love is greater than love for family* [my emphasis]. Therefore, Confucius said, 'Filial piety and fraternal love are the beginning of practicing *ren*.'"[72] As did many Confucians, Zhu condemned Buddhist teachings and practices that undercut family social role duties. They had in mind the retreat of monks and nuns to monasteries, removed from familial obligations. And they condemned practices that exempted monks from taxation and public labor service. Similarly, Zhu had criticized the classical advocate of universal love Mozi (fifth century BCE) for denying our natural familial sentiments. Mozi was said to denigrate all naturally experienced gradations of worth or preferential hierarchies in our love and care.

At the same time, Zhu and his fellow Confucians still spoke of the original "brightness" (conveying value) of human minds, and of the duty of *ren*. This introduced a kind of potential equal worth into the human condition. Practicing *ren* toward others centered on economic welfare and education. The "others" warranted it because, as Mencius noted, anyone can become a sage. Zhu Xi claimed that a knowledge of the patterns of all categories of things are innate to the mind of every human. By using the analogy of "original water" for the mind, claiming it is "good," and pointing to its penetration of every human body, Zhu was urging his audience to feel reverence for the original mind in all of us (even though it was obscured, or dirtied, in most).

Mencian claims about the four innate minds, enriched by the Buddhist idea that every person should be regarded as a potential Buddha, are the foundation for an idea of what might be called potential equal worth.[73]

From the perspective of daily life, however, most minds are sullied or obstructed to various degrees, meaning the individual needs exhaustive self-improvement and instruction by teachers to clarify or nurture that original mind. This introduced a serious obstacle to our focusing too much on the idea of our shared pure nature. The real burden is on people to "weed out" or polish or "clean away" the *unequally* possessed selfish desires that prevent growth or enlightenment, depending on the image selected. Then their acts will be more consistent with the duties revealed in the pure mind.

The theoretical weakness in Zhu Xi's position can be found in the analogy he used to interpret a compatibility between preferential affection for kin and expansive love for others. Zhu treated both values as appropriate to different stages of the human developmental or growth process. He used the plant to explain growth. *Ren* is a characteristic of the complete or mature mind. But the plant image explains it as an inevitable byproduct of self-growth. This explanation can blind the thinker to the details of public needs and how to deal with them. Zhu believed that, as with plant growth, development in the earlier stages ensures desired future progress. With those stages accomplished, the mind naturally will be "lush." So the message received from his teachings was that there is a guaranteed progressive maturity of the mind, from its four beginnings to fully developed *ren*. With the proper cultivation of the mind, success follows. In time, the plant analogy might or might not be used by Zhu's later students, but the belief in the ease of growth from the mind's fonts to the mature mind remained.

5 Alternatives and Supplements to Confucian Theory

There are modern alternatives to the Confucian belief that learning to care for family can grow into the ability to care for those outside the family. Also, there are alternatives to the need for long lists of explicit moral rules governing how we should behave toward others and for the rituals that embody them. This does not mean getting rid of customary rules of civil conduct or etiquette. Finally, there is an alternative to treating everyone impartially, or as equally worthy.

One path is Carol Gilligan's "care ethics," which emphasizes the language of care used by many women in discussing social relationships. Identifying gender differences in our thinking of care is a positive contribution. So is the position of many care ethicists that the right emotions must be cultivated to accompany our obeying laws that promote widespread care.[74] This is a point that Confucians would accept. So do I.

Another alternative is *virtue ethics*. It focuses on character traits, plus related emotions, choices, and interests. Among these traits is *ren*. Predictable care for others would be fairly reliable for a person who has cultivated that trait. The origins of virtue ethics lie in Aristotle's views of virtue (*arête*), practical wisdom on how to be nuanced in virtuous action (*phronesis*), *and* happiness or flourishing in the sense of living a virtuous life (*eudaimonia*). Two inspirations for its modern revival were Elizabeth Anscombe's 1958 article "Modern Moral Philosophy" and Philippa Foote's 2001 book *Natural Goodness*.[75] Foote held that virtues such as courage and temperance are essential to a moral life and hence are good for human life. The early advocates felt that the dominant schools in Western ethics ignored such topics as moral education, character, the emotions, and family and friendship relations. A number of Western philosophers of virtue ethics (among them Stephen Angle, Philip Ivanhoe, and Edward Slingerland) argue that Confucians were virtue ethicists, advocating the cultivation of sagely character traits, such as *ren*. Their case includes the Confucian concerns with moral education, the emotions, and family and friendship relations. Virtue ethicists believe that character traits endure over time and circumstances and are thereby dependable, and that officials should rely on them rather than on fear of penal codes.

One of my objections to virtue ethics was identified long ago: Because of its focus on cultivating character, it falls short when it comes to providing action guidance. In other words, it does not meet my workability standard. There is something to be said for Anscombe's claim that action guidance can be found in making mandates out of the moral character traits—for example, "Do what is charitable." Although I would support such calls, they lack guidance about how to deal with specific persons or events. I applaud the ever-growing numbers of laws, domestic and international, that promote health and well-being. As I will note below, I have more confidence in a law that requires a person selling a house to provide a prospective buyer with an inspector's report of the house's condition than I do in the seller's having the character trait of honesty. However, I do accept the virtue ethicists' focus on character development. It may be valuable for an individual dealing with ambiguous cases in which there are conflicts between some rules or laws and others.

My own approach is a consequentialist one, a non-traditional utilitarianism. I accept the principle that actions should be judged by their consequences, and these consequences have something to do with happiness. Like many utilitarians, I believe that happiness relates to the relative presence of joy and absence of suffering. Through these emotions, the body/mind reveals the state of its health and psychological well-being. Damasio cites "the fact that the preservation of life depends on the equilibrium of life functions and consequently on life regulation: the fact that the status of life regulation is expressed in the form of affects—joy, sorrow—and is modulated by the appetites [desires]."[76] I disagree with the traditionalists that humans should strive for "the greatest happiness of the greatest number," because that usually means counting each person affected by an act as one and no more than one. I reject the idea that the magnitude and the duration of joy and suffering can be mathematically calculated with precision.

When I use the term *well-being* I am aware of its background. It has been used with different contents by different people. When applied to the conditions for healthy societies, it may refer to climate, educational opportunities, employment figures, arts events, and available health care. My home town—Ann Arbor, Michigan—often gets high marks for these conditions, except climate. Amartya Sen uses the expression "capability approach" to refer to taking into account people's desires for such things as to live a long life, to have the money or status to buy and sell, or to be a political participant. These are useful items to bear in mind when one is studying poverty, development, and income inequality.

Whereas Westerners might refer to the well-being of a society, meaning its smooth functioning, Chinese today are concerned about the "harmonious" functioning of communities, large and small. Defining "smooth" and "harmonious" would take an entire book. To the developmental indicators just mentioned, I might add as predictors of harmony the number of conflicts within a society (in China, 74,000 mass incidents or uprisings in 2004, 87,000 in 2005), the degree of workability of existing methods of resolving conflicts, and a society's fairness in allocating resources and in applying laws. Fairness is a universal value with wide cultural variation. It begins to emerge in children around the age of 3 years, when they begin to prefer "equitable sharing" among friends. Eventually one form of fairness concerns reciprocity. These events can affect the harmony of developed societies as well as the undeveloped. I am especially concerned with fairness in the application of laws.

I do not use the term *well-being* in the sense of societal health. I use it to refer only to the psychological health of individuals (which pairs with bodily health in my standard). It is surely influenced by the societal factors, but I leave their study to others. The philosopher Martha Nussbaum, in her book *Women and Human Development*, listed ten "capabilities" that can be used to evaluate human development, including the ability to use imagination, being able to live with and for others, and having a social basis of respect.

In my case, the basis of what is objectively right and wrong is, first, our determination of the consequences of actions and policies in terms of the joy and suffering to which they lead individuals. These are consequences that are signs of health and psychological well-being. Not advocating a quantitative calculation of joy and suffering, I am content with the informal, probabilistic, educated assessments we make about what causes joy and suffering when information is available. These can be evolutionary facts. An example would be social behavior that leads to reproductive fitness or survival, as humans learn to deal with hierarchy. It can also be about proximate contributions to happiness now, such as stable families, loving relationships, and fairness. They can also be facts about what contribute to the equilibrium of life's organic and tissue functions (signals revealed in immune responses, reflexes, temperature, tissue repair, metabolism, and energy level, that are carried by electrochemical signs along nerve pathways). Other facts are matters that contribute to stress or tranquility and the satisfaction or absence of fulfillment of certain desires (neurotransmitters, such as serotonin and dopamine, and hormones, such as cortisol). Finally, I give some regard to the subjective accounts that others give about their conditions. These are various kinds of factual information, with varying levels of reliability.

Another kind of factual information is relevant to the current topic and concerns the ethical evaluation of laws. This is a product of thinking (beliefs, memory, reasoning) and of the emotions. It is the basis of my support for laws and enforcement agencies that monitor the health and well-being of people outside my range of special care. The following facts about humans are my grounds for affirming equal worth under the law. They refer to traits that we generally prize because they are known to be associated with our health and psychological well-being. The first is an awareness of joy, of a desire to experience it, and of a desire to avoid long term suffering. As Damasio has said, the body seeks to preserve itself, and joy and suffering are clues to its status in that matter. The second is the ability to express these and other feelings in language. The third is the experience of being loved by another person. Fourth, we have certain moral intuitions, such as one about fairness, and we prize its presence. Fairness has something to do with "equal sharing." As experienced, fairness is a combination of both a genetic legacy and also of culture. Culture determines the content of equal sharing, what it amounts to in a given society. It does not require exact number amounts, but it may refer to justifiable spans of resources, measured in money, animals, land, or trade goods.

There is a final trait that in itself is not good or bad but that justifies the claim that normally the previous four are shared by most people in the world. This is shared DNA (about 99 percent), although important differences among us can still exist as a result of the remaining non-similar part. So from a public perspective, the source of equal worth before the law is the shared possession by almost all humans of the four prize-worthy traits. I am comfortable arguing for equal human worth on these grounds, from this public perspective. The prominence of impartiality in Western ethics owes something to the evolution of the idea of justice, and of impartiality before the law. I have trouble with the prominence of impartiality in private ethics, not in the law.

I do differentiate between the health and well-being of different people. The health of my family and others to whom I am emotionally close count for more in judging acts or policies than the health of others. This does not mean that I do not care for the others or have no motives to aid them. Consider the consequences of treating impartiality or the equal worth of all persons as an ultimate guiding principle of human conduct. I find that it unrealistically causes people to ignore their strongly felt familial emotions. But I do believe in considering people as equal under the law, there being a factual basis for their equal worth from a different perspective than the strength of my emotional bonds. This is the most efficient way to promote the nurturing care and protection of people outside of my private sphere. I benefit from such laws too. Laws should be judged by the degree to which they promote the health and well being of people affected by them. I call this approach *two-level consequentialism.* I combine it with a proposal for the inclusion of empathy training in the schools, the content of which would be based on the similar traits that we all share (described above).

Mindful of the effort the Neo-Confucians and their successors put into dealing with the problem of *ren* rooted in family love, I finally got a handle on what had always bothered me about Western utilitarianism. It was its doctrine of "the greatest good of the greatest number." As reinterpreted by Peter Singer and others, it requires our ethical choices to consider that "each person counts for one and none for more than one" among those affected by our acts. I can agree with Singer and the others that actions should be judged by their consequences. And consequences have something to do with happiness, or with joy and suffering. But traditional utilitarianism fails the workability test because it doesn't probe the implications of the weakness that the utilitarian John S. Mill himself noted: For most individuals, the feeling of equal regard for all is "much inferior in strength to their selfish feelings."[77] Traditionalists such as Singer ignore such factual matters as the magnitude of emotions involved in kinship, close friendship, and community relations. In terms of how I deal with my own resources and care, people are of unequal worth. Those closest to me are worth more than others.

Because the magnitude of compassion people will have for those outside the family is variable and unpredictable, I deal with this by saying that *impartial laws, rules of conduct, and enforcement agencies* are required to provide protection and nurturance to those not well known to the individual choice maker. In addition to official institutions, I support non-governmental organizations and their charitable programs that have similar goals. That support may be both in individual financial gifts and in volunteer work.

When I speak of the place for laws that protect, care for, and educate the lives of people, I am referring to characteristics of the law that did not exist in imperial China. My reference is to positive law that is made by legislators elected or appointed by citizens free from illegal and coercive pressure. The dangerous sources of that pressure typically can include partisans in other branches of government, executive and judicial, and bribery from the representatives of interest groups. At the international level, international bodies are the appropriate organizations to issue similar safeguards.

There is a need for enforcement agencies to monitor the application of laws to ensure that their original intent is executed.

Although Zhu Xi charged Mozi with ignoring family-based preferences, Zhu's own universalistic theory of an equally shared, originally self-bright and pure mind posits the same danger. Part of that innate pure mind describes and requires priority for family care, and thus is in tension with altruism. It argues for a filiality-based ethical system, though it also explains altruism as an inevitable outcome, given proper nurturance. Filiality grows into care for all humans who share the self-bright, original mind. But that ultimate goal opens the door for people having to choose between violating their natural sentiment to favor their own family and community above others and being sympathetic to people they may not know, *without much guidance as to how*. Faith in ease of growth is no substitute for details on how to make the public social good a reality.

Normally, no matter what the level of nurturance one puts into the sense of love rooted in family love, it will never grow into a motivation sufficient to provide the individual with *predictable* care and resources for those beyond the family and the community. The history of human violence is one piece of evidence. The image of plant growth may turn into what a poet might describe as a plant lush with leaves and blossoms, but extended out-group altruism as an individual emotion or goal, though honorable and worthy of promotion, is unreliable in predictability and in quantity of resources to meet domestic and international needs. While recognizing the important work of private charities and non-governmental organizations in this connection, one may still argue that they lack resources to deal with the needs of so many people. This is especially true with population increasing and natural resources declining.

6 Private Choices and Public Law

I am not a law worshiper. Occasionally, some laws will appear bad to a person or a group. In such cases, according to Charles and Gregory Fried, civil disobedience may be a duty, and it may include public statements by the law breaker about reasons for her transgressions and an acceptance of legal punishments. According to the Frieds:

Some laws will be not merely imprudent or silly, but deeply wrong, contrary to the fundamental principles and interests that united the people in the first place and that transcend any specific law.[78]

One [strand of civil disobedience] professes a fundamental allegiance to the political community and its system of laws and government, but holds that if some laws are such an affront to the conscience of its citizens, it is the citizens' right and duty to disobey these laws in an attempt to change them.[79]

Note that the first citation refers to "fundamental principles" and the second to "conscience." I agree with the Frieds' positions. But never in their essay do they identify what the content of these principles is. My own position in the present chapter is to lay out what the standard should be that gives content to the terms "principles" and "conscience." For individual humans, it is the degree to which actions, policies, and laws promote their health and well-being. In addition, for societies, it is the degree to which laws also promote fairness in the application of laws and in the allocation of resources that serve the health and well-being of citizens.

But there is an important place for civil behavior—the socialized conduct usually taught in homes, schools, churches, or work organizations. We regularly mention and understand "the right thing to do" without any reference to laws or law books.

The areas in which private and public interests intersect are often ambiguous, even in real democracies. The situation is worse under totalitarian regimes, where the "public interest" may be dictated by the Party rulers. They present enduring challenges to our choices. During the era of communist dictatorships in the Soviet Union and in Eastern Europe, there was an ambiguous choice between the law and family love. This occurred when a parent was offered a chance to go abroad, but had to leave his or her family behind. One Czech woman, whose parents had already fled, said "I had no choice, but I know how difficult it has been for others, making a decision that they know will damage their children's lives and endanger family and friends." The laws permitted the government to strip the parents of citizenship while they were abroad.[80]

There are also laws at the public level with which I generally agree, but to which I would be tempted to consider exceptions at the private level. The former CEO of Random House was asked a hypothetical question : Were his children to be kidnapped, would he consider using torture (if that were in his power) to find out where they were? "If my children were kidnapped and being held hostage," he replied, "I would use anything, including torture, to find out where they were."[81] Although on the one hand I am tempted to agree with him, on the other I must also consider the societal consequences if everyone could find an exception in terms of their most powerful emotions. Would it lead to violence and chaos? I cannot come up with a clear answer. In other cases of ambiguity, I find that applying the equal-worth principle would be impractical and neglectful of my strongest emotional bonds. Further, I am helped by the customs of civil conduct that also play a role.

Suppose my parents wanted me to sell their house and give them the money for their retirement fund. I would obey any local law that required a professional building inspector to write a report on the condition of the house. I would give the report to a prospective buyer. If there were no law, I would still accept a buyer's request for such an inspection and agree to split the cost. I would disclose any defects that could potentially affect the health or well-being of the buyer's family. Minor defects I would not reveal. As I said earlier, if I were a buyer I would have more trust in laws that cover buyer protection (if they exist) than in the character of the seller.

The same holds for selling a car. I would regard superficial defects (dents, loose fenders, worn seat fabric) as matters of "buyer beware," and would not bring them up. But I would disclose any defects that could affect the safety or health of a buyer, and I would support laws that would require such disclosure.

When helping an aged parent to wait in line at a grocery checkout or at a bus stop, unless the parent were actively ill, I would be guided by the rules of civil behavior. I would not try to push to the front of the line. Normally, civil rules having to do with fairness and waiting one's turn benefit me and my parent as well as others who wait in lines. If a close and infirm relative were to live near me, I would regularly help with household tasks, transportation to a medical appointment, and so forth. Should a similarly infirm but unrelated person live in my neighborhood, I would offer to help out in some instances, but far less than for a close relation. Such help would make me feel good, and it would promote a happier community. But I do not have time or a strong motivation do more.

When it comes to laws of which I disapprove because they seem to me "imprudent or silly," I would ignore them if so doing would not adversely affect anyone's health or well-being and I could get away with it. I am still bound by my own sense of civil behavior. For example, suppose that I needed a part-time nanny for a young child. (My actual child is now 42.) If the nanny wished to be paid in cash so as to avoid the Social Security tax, and if the amount of her annual pay didn't greatly exceed the probable line above which the law requires me to fill out the forms, I would most likely accede to her wishes, pay cash, and not fill out the forms. I would still treat her with civility and generosity, because those manners of behavior endure even when I might break the law. They would not permit exploitation.

I believe that there are ways to pass on to future generations the standards I would like to see applied to evaluating policies, rules, and laws. Teaching empathy in the form of "How do you think X would feel if this event happened to her?" is effective. Decades after I am gone, my grandchildren will be able to report whether or not it worked.

Conclusion

In this chapter I have tried to show the importance of different perspectives from which humans interpret the world. For me, worth is a function of point of view. One of my distant reasons for doing so is to recapture some of the wisdom in the "Autumn Floods" chapter of *The Zhuangzi* (fourth to second century BCE):

From the point of view of the Way, things have no nobility or meanness. From the point of view of things, each regards itself as noble and other things as mean. From the point of view of common opinion, nobility and meanness are not determined by the individual himself.[82]

I am not quite as fluid about standards as the author of that chapter. But I do appreciate his praise for those who seek freedom from the limitations of having just one perspective. In its place, he wants our minds to roam over as many perspectives as possible, so those minds can respond, spontaneously or mirror-like, to a situation or to things, in a way that is appropriate to the specifics of that case. I find that doing a lot of wandering is a bit impractical, though I do enjoy imaginary trips to other ways of looking at things. I do not have the time or the emotional motivation to do more. Mostly, I would be satisfied just focusing on the points of view most relevant to our biological and moral lives, especially in terms of their consequences for our health and well-being. Humans need some standard that suggests priorities.

I reject the theological perspective, which includes claims about a God who is the source of our equal worth, by virtue of the souls implanted in us and the love She has for us. I reject the traditional utilitarian view that ultimate worth comes from being considered eligible for an equal share of the joy or happiness that comes from relevant human choices—i.e., that the agent should consider "the greatest happiness of the greatest number" and should calculate consequences such that "each person counts as one and none for more than one." I am not sure that it is possible to calculate the greatest happiness, and I see no proof that counting each person as one would produce it.

In my action choices, always trying to take into equal consideration a wide range of people is impractical and ignores the damage people suffer in being told that they should devote the care and resources that are consistent with their feelings, not to their kin, but at least in part to others they do not know. In the main Western tradition, I have found no plausible alternative sources for our worth other than the theological and utilitarian ones. Instead, the evidence I have seen supports the Confucian position of unequal worth, because the strength of our emotional ties to our immediate kin, friends, and close community is normally the strongest. Those ties to others are variable and unpredictable. This left for me the challenge of seeing if there were other sources by which I should consider people as equal in worth. I found it in the reasons for treating people as equal under the law.

Acknowledgments

A small portion of this contribution is reprinted from *Images of Human Nature: A Sung Portrait*, by Donald J. Munro, copyright 1988 Princeton University Press.

Notes

1. Plato, *Republic*, iii, 415a.

2. Aristotle, *Politics* i.13.1260a.12.

3. St. Augustine, *City of God* 11.22. See Sanford A. Lakoff, *Equality in Political Philosophy*, 16.

4. Cicero, *On the Laws*, M., quoted in George L. Abernethy, *The Idea of Equality*, 53.

5. J. Roland Pennnock and John W. Chapman, *Nomos IX:* Equality, 138.

6. John Plamenatz, *Man and Society*, volume 1, 73.

7. Rousseau, "Discourse on Inequality."

8. Ibid., 383.

9. John Locke, *Second Treatise on Civil Government*, chapter 2.6.

10. John Rawls, *A Theory of Justice*, 12.

11. Ibid., 14.

12. Peter Singer, *Practical Ethics*, 12.

13. Ibid., 21.

14. Ibid., 11.

15. Peter Singer, *Rethinking Life and Death*, 159–161.

16. Singer, *Practical Ethics*, 11.

17. *Analects*, 1.2. Unless otherwise noted, all translations are my own.

18. *Analects*, 13.18.

19. *The Four Books, Doctrine of the Mean* 20.5, and *Analects* 1.2.

20. Cheng Hao and Cheng Yi, *Er Cheng quanshu, Yishu*, 18.1b. Zhu Xi followed Cheng Yi's commentary.

21. *Doctrine of the Mean* 20.8.

22. Ibid., 22.

23. Mencian Confucianism refers to Confucian theories that are consistent with the theories of Mencius (fourth century BCE). The Neo-Confucians, including Zhu Xi, were largely Mencians.

24. *Analects*, 16.9.

25. Donald J. Munro, "Two Objects of our Affection: What We Can Learn from Zhu Xi."

26. Brook Ziporyn, *Ironies of Oneness and Difference*; Stephen Angle, *Sagehood*.

27. Closeness of relations was not the only basis for evaluating worth, though it was the primary basis. There were secondary bases, such as clarity of the mind just discussed. The morally cultivated person was of more worth than the person who failed in moral self-cultivation, and the person with more clarity from the start was worth more than the more benighted person. These secondary bases of worth do not figure into my elaboration of Confucian theory later in the chapter.

28. *Mencius*, 2A.6, 6A.

29. Ibid., 6A.7.

30. Donald J. Munro, *The Concept of Man in Early China*, 58–65.

31. Donald J. Munro, *Images of Human Nature*, 23. In my analysis of images here, I have drawn on material from chapters four and five of *Images of Human Nature*, especially pp. 121–122 on the plant image.

32. *Mencius*, tr. D. C. Lau, 6A.7, 164.

33. Zhu Xi, *Zhuzi quanshu*, 45.4b (2:1007). Hereafter cited as ZZQS. References are to *zhuan* and page in the original, followed in parentheses by volume and page in the modern edition cited.

34. Ibid., 44.10b (2:992).

35. Munro, *Images*, 122.

36. *Yong jiaoyu jiu zhongguo* 用教育救中国.

37. Brotherly love, *ti* 悌, should not be confused with brotherly love in the sense of *philia*. *Ti*, as the quoted passage goes on to imply, is hierarchically directed from younger brother to older, similar to how filiality, *xiao* 孝, is affection directed from child to parent.

38. Zhu Xi, *Zhuzi yulei*, 20.13b (2:804). Hereafter cited as ZZYL. The first set of numbers indicates the *juan* 卷, the page, and (in parentheses) the volume number of the modern edition cited and the page number in that edition.

39. ZZYL, 14.12a (1:479).

40. ZZQS, 43.25b-26a (2:980–81).

41. The image of something that is "self-bright" is consistent with the metaphor of light used in the West to describe knowing truths, ever since Plato used it to explain the transcendent Forms/Ideas. Those Platonic Ideas are understood as innate to our minds. "Idea" comes from *eidos*, related to visual perception, referring to the common look of all members of a category of things. Humans have *visions* of the Ideas. As in the parable of the cave in *The Republic*, the experience is one of being "enlightened" about which one was in the dark. In his *Meditations on First Philosophy*, Descartes refers to the "light of nature" which God gives us to see the first true principles from which all others are deduced. They occur to me with "distinctness and clearness." In the nineteenth century, the Cambridge Platonist Nathanael Culverwell explained the mind with the image of a lamp projecting light. In the words of M. H. Abrams, "'Now the *Spirit of man*

is the *Candle of the Lord*,' [Culverwell] says, for the Creator himself 'the fountain of Light,' furnished and beautified this *'lower part* of the *World* with *Intellectual Lamps*, that should shine forth to *praise* and *honour* in his Name … .'" (Abrams, *The Mirror and the Lamp*, 59) In reference to this discussion of the metaphor of light, I use material from p. 108 of my *Images of Human Nature*.

42. Donald J. Munro, *The Imperial Style of Inquiry in Twentieth-Century China*, 41–45.

43. Ibid., 48–49.

44. Ibid., 44–48.

45. *Analects*, tr. Legge, 8.2.2.

46. *Great Learning*, tr. Legge, 9.8.9.

47. Daniel K. Gardner, *Chu Hsi and the* Ta-hsueh, 110.

48. Wegner, *The Illusion of Conscious Will*.

49. Munro, *Images*, 172–175.

50. ZZQS 16.23b (1:356) and ZZYL 37.5a (3:1633). Discussed in Munro, *Images*, 177. I used material from pp. 173–175 of *Images of Human Nature* in this discussion of choice and free will.

51. ZZYL 37.7b (3:1638).

52. Zhu Xi, *Huaian xiansheng Zhu Wengong wenji*, 70.24a.

53. Edward O. Wilson, *Consilience*, 253.

54. Ibid., 169.

55. Robert L. Trivers, "The Evolution of Reciprocal Altruism," 39.

56. A. T. Nuyen, "David Hume on Reason, Passions, and Morals," 26.

57. Gardner Lindzey and Eliot Aronson, eds., *Handbook in Social Psychology*, vol. 3, 155–156.

58. *Doctrine of the Mean*, 20.5.

59. Michael S. Gazzaniga, *The Ethical Brain*, 167.

60. Antonio Damasio, *Looking for Spinoza*, 148–149. I discuss the relation between beliefs and emotions in Donald J. Munro, *Ethics in Action*, 18–20.

61. Edward Slingerland, *What Science Offers the Humanities*, 166.

62. Jonathan Haidt, *The Happiness Hypothesis*, 21.

63. He published my paper "The Chinese View of Modeling" in *Human Development*.

64. Singer, *Practical Ethics*, 11.

65. Marc D. Hauser, *Moral Minds*, 133.

66. Ibid., 53, 248–251.

67. Damasio, 145–146.

68. Singer, *Practical Ethics*, 21.

69. Ibid.

70. Ibid., 24.

71. Munro, *Images*, 14.

72. See note 20.

73. Munro, *Images* 65–66; Cheng Hao and Cheng Yi, *Er Cheng quanshu*, 25.5b.

74. *Stanford Encyclopedia of Philosophy* (http://plato.stanford.edu), s.v. Feminist Ethics.

75. Philippa Foot, *Natural Goodness*, 33.

76. Damasio, 174.

77. John Stuart Mill, *Utilitarianism* (1863), chapter 3.

78. Charles Fried and Gregory Fried, "In the Wake of War," 37.

79. Ibid.

80. Jeri Laber, *The Courage of Strangers*, 78.

81. Ibid., 78.

82. *Zhuangzi*, tr. Burton Watson, 100.

Works Cited

Abernethy, George L. *The Idea of Equality: An Anthology*. Knox, 1959.

Abrams, M. H. *The Mirror and the Lamp: Romantic Theory and the Critical Tradition*. Oxford University Press, 1953.

Angle, Stephen C. *Sagehood: The Contemporary Significance of Neo-Confucian Philosophy*. Oxford University Press, 2009.

Anscombe, Elizabeth. "Modern Moral Philosophy." *Philosophy* 33, no. 124 (1958): 1–19.

Cheng Hao 程顥 and Cheng Yi 程頤. *Er Cheng quanshu* 二程全書, *sibu beiyao* 四部備要. Shanghai: *Shangwu yinshuguan*商務印書館, 1919.

Damasio, Antonio R. *Looking for Spinoza: Joy, Sorrow, and the Feeling Brain*. Harcourt, 2003.

Foot, Philippa. *Natural Goodness*. Clarendon, 2001.

Fried, Charles, and Gregory Fried. "In the Wake of War: Judging the U.S. Government's Actions after 9/11." *Harvard Magazine*, September–October 2010, 36–42. Excerpted from *Because It Is Wrong: Torture, Privacy, and Presidential Power in the Age of Terror* (Norton, 2010).

Gardner, Daniel K. *Chu Hsi and the Ta-hsueh: Neo-Confucian Reflection on the Confucian Canon.* Council on East Asian Studies, Harvard University, 1986.

Gazzaniga, Michael S. *The Ethical Brain.* Dana, 2005.

Haidt, Jonathan. *The Happiness Hypothesis: Finding Modern Truth in Ancient Wisdom.* Basic Books, 2006.

Hauser, Marc D. *Moral Minds: How Nature Designed Our Universal Sense of Right and Wrong.* Ecco, 2006.

Laber, Jeri. *The Courage of Strangers: Coming of Age with the Human Rights Movement.* PublicAffairs, 2002.

Lakoff, George, and Mark Johnson. *Metaphors We Live By.* University of Chicago Press, 1980.

Lakoff, Sanford A. *Equality in Political Philosophy.* Harvard University Press, 1964.

Lau, D. C. *Mencius.* Penguin, 1970.

Legge, James. *The Chinese Classics,* volume 1: *Confucian Analects.* Hong Kong University Press, 1960.

Lindzey, Gardner, and Elliot Aronson, eds. *Handbook in Social Psychology.* Addison-Wesley, 1968.

Munro, Donald J. "The Chinese View of Modeling." *Human Development* 18, no. 5 (1975): 333–352.

Munro, Donald J. *The Concept of Man in Early China.* Stanford University Press, 1969.

Munro, Donald J. *Ethics in Action: Workable Guidelines for Private and Public Choices.* Chinese University of Hong Kong Press, 2008.

Munro, Donald J. *Images of Human Nature: A Sung Portrait.* Princeton University Press, 1988.

Munro, Donald J. *The Imperial Style of Inquiry in Twentieth-Century China: The Emergence of New Approaches.* Center for Chinese Studies, University of Michigan, 1996.

Munro, Donald J. "Two Objects of Our Affection: What We Can Learn from Zhu Xi." In *A Chinese Ethics for the New Century.* Chinese University of Hong Kong Press, 2005.

Nussbaum, Martha C. *Women and Human Development: The Capabilities Approach.* Cambridge University Press, 2000.

Nuyen, A. T. "David Hume on Reason, Passions, and Morals." *Human Studies* 10, no. 1 (1984): 26–45.

Pennock, J. Roland, and John W. Chapman, eds. *Equality (Nomos* IX). Atherton, 1967.

Plamenatz, John. *Man and Society: A Critical Examination of Some Important Social and Political Theories from Machiavelli to Marx.* McGraw-Hill, 1963.

Rawls, John. *A Theory of Justice.* Harvard University Press, 1971.

Singer, Peter. *Practical Ethics*, second edition. Cambridge University Press, 2005.

Singer, Peter. *Rethinking Life and Death: The Collapse of Our Traditional Ethics*. Oxford University Press, 1995.

Slingerland, Edward. *What Science Offers the Humanities: Integrating Body and Culture*. Cambridge University Press, 2008.

Sun Youzhong. "The Trans-Pacific Experience of John Dewey." *Japanese Journal of American Studies*, no. 18 (2007): 107–124.

Trivers, Robert L. "The Evolution of Reciprocal Altruism." *Quarterly Review of Biology* 46, no. 1 (1971): 35–57.

Wegner, Daniel M. *The Illusion of Conscious Will*. MIT Press, 2003.

Wilson, Edward O. *Consilience: The Unity of Knowledge*. Knopf, 1998.

Xu Shen 許慎。*Duan shi shuowen jiezi zhu* 段氏說文解字注, edited and comments by Duan Yucai 段玉裁. Taipei: *Wenhua tushu gongsi* 文化圖書公司, 1985.

Zhuangzi (Chuang tzu). *Chuang tzu: Basic Writings*. Tr. Burton Watson. Columbia University Press, 1964.

Ziporyn, Brook. *Ironies of Oneness and Difference: Coherence in Early Chinese Thought: Prolegomena to the Study of Li*. State University of New York Press, 2012.

Zhu Xi 朱熹. *Huian xiansheng Zhu Wengong wenji* 晦庵先生朱文公文集, *sibu congkan* 四部叢刊, volume 33. Shanghai: *Shangwu yinshuguan*商務印書館, 1919.

Zhu Xi 朱熹. *Zhuzi quanshu* 朱子全書. Facsimile reprint of the 1885 reprint of the 1715 ed., 2 vols. Taipei: *Guangxue she* 廣學社, 1977.

Zhu Xi 朱熹. *Zhuzi yulei* 朱子語類. Reprint, eight volumes. Taipei: *Zhengzhong shuju* 正中書局, 1962.

6 Virtue Ethics, the Rule of Law, and the Need for Self-Restriction

Stephen C. Angle

1 Introduction

It is a provocative coincidence that 1958 saw the publication of both Elizabeth Anscombe's "Modern Moral Philosophy," an essay widely seen as initiating the revival of Western philosophical interest in virtue ethics, and the "Manifesto to the World's People on Behalf of Chinese Culture," a jointly authored argument that Confucianism was still alive and had much to offer to the world. A great deal of research and debate has flowed from each of these sources over the last half-century, but so far there has been very little dialogue between modern Western virtue ethics and modern Confucianism.[1] Scholars of ancient Confucianism have begun paying considerable attention to analogs within the Western virtue-ethical tradition, and some contemporary Western virtue ethicists have begun to draw on early Confucianism, but contemporary Confucianism has been largely absent from these conversations.[1] The reasons for this absence are not hard to discover, but it is nonetheless unfortunate because one of the topics about which contemporary Confucians have debated most thoroughly—the relations among ethics, politics, and law—is among the areas about which Western virtue ethicists have had the least to say.[3] The thesis of this chapter is that anyone interested in the political philosophy that correlates with or grows out of virtue ethics has much to learn from modern Confucians, and in particular that Mou Zongsan's idea of self-restriction, suitably modified, should be central to any plausible contemporary virtue-based politics.

All Confucians recognize the importance of cultivating both "inner sagehood" (*neisheng* 內聖) and "outer kingship" (*waiwang* 外王). Most Confucian philosophers have taken these two dimensions to be intimately related, though the details of the relationship vary. After the collapse of traditional Confucian educational and political institutions at the beginning of the twentieth century, the need for and nature of a "new outer kingship"—which I will loosely render as "new politics" hereafter, because no one today is calling for a revived monarchy—became apparent. Mou Zongsan (1909–1995), the most important Confucian philosopher of the twentieth century, devoted considerable ingenuity to showing why the new politics that would be derived from Confucianism's central ethical commitments needed to be democratic. At the core of Mou's argument is the idea that individual ethical judgment must "restrict itself," thus providing a kind of independence for political and legal authority, in order for the ultimate attainment of virtue to be possible. Mou's position has been criticized from at least three directions. Some find the metaphysical basis for Mou's argument to be implausible or mysterious.[4] Others believe that Confucianism should primarily be confined to ethics, which can be shown to be compatible with democratic politics and the rule of law, to which (these authors argue) we should be committed for independent reasons.[5] A third group argues that Confucianism's new politics should not be derived from the inner needs of ethics, but rather from an updated version of past Confucian institutions; these thinkers tend to be much more critical of liberal democracy than those in either of the other two groups.[6]

Although the debates just sketched will be in the background of the present chapter, my primary interest here is less in defending Mou's position than in showing that contemporary Western virtue ethics both can and should learn from the idea of "self-restriction." The need for self-restriction emerges from two observations with which most virtue ethicists would agree: that ethical judgments are particularistic and that political and legal norms are general—that is, apply to general types of situations, perhaps within a state or perhaps universally. If one further holds that the ethical and the political/legal should each have a distinctive kind of authority, then one has to explain how these types of authority are related and what happens when they conflict. In view of the distinction between particularistic and general judgments, the need for distinctive kinds of authority seems clear. Suppose you are stopped by a police officer for speeding. You expect to be subject to a general rule rather than a situation-specific judgment, which in any event would be unmanageable. (How urgent is your errand? How skilled a driver are you? How tired? How much traffic is there? And so on.[7]) I will argue, though, that providing the needed independence for political/legal authority is actually quite difficult.[8] Accordingly, in the next section I will examine the relations found between ethics and law in two of the major sources of present-day Western virtue ethics. I will argue that for both Aristotle and Hume problems emerge when we look closely at the balance between the centrality of virtue and law's importance as a distinct source of authority. In section 3, I will present Mou's self-restriction theory in more detail; I will argue that the significance of the idea of self-restriction for politics and law can be appreciated without taking on Mou's entire metaphysical picture, and that this allows virtue ethicists to appropriate Mou's insight. In section 4, I will briefly summarize the prospects for constructive dialogue between modern Confucianism and contemporary Western virtue ethics that emerge from seeing the ways in which the heirs of Aristotle and Hume need the idea of self-restriction.

2 Aristotle and Hume

Although there is ongoing debate over the precise shape of the ethical theories of both Aristotle and Hume, there is little doubt that the two philosophers have served as major sources for contemporary virtue ethics in the West. Anscombe's inspiration, of course, was Aristotle, and Aristotle has continued to be crucial for the majority of virtue ethicists. The role of Hume (and others, including Plato, the Stoics, and Nietzsche) has also been very important both because of specific insights that Hume (and the others) have brought into contemporary discussions, and for three more programmatic reasons. First, more voices in the conversation means more dynamism, more opportunities to connect to other trends in philosophy (such as connections to empirical psychology), and thus the potential for more synthetic and robust views. Second, the more diverse debates have also made it clear that virtue ethics is still maturing and growing; it is not just a matter of fine-tuning Aristotle. Third, as virtue ethics has become more pluralistic, it has thereby opened itself to productive interactions with philosophical traditions outside the West. If "virtue ethics" just means "Aristotle," then the suggestion that Confucianism, say, is a form of virtue ethics sounds like an equation of an entire tradition of reflection with one Western philosopher. If virtue ethics itself is much broader, though, then thinking of Confucianism as further broadening and contributing to the category of virtue ethics makes more sense.

The burden of this section of the chapter is to suggest that the relation between ethics and law is both important to the various founders of Western virtue ethics—represented here by Aristotle and Hume—and yet remains something of a problem. The details of the problems depend on exactly how one understands Aristotle and Hume, so my discussion will necessarily involve some attention to interpretive disputes. I will argue that the idea of self-restriction is relevant to resolving tensions that emerge no matter what interpretation we adopt.

There is considerable scholarly consensus that Aristotle's ethical philosophy and his political philosophy are closely related to one another, and even that the *Nicomachean Ethics* and the *Politics* should be read as completing one another. Just how the individual virtue that dominates so much of the ethics is supposed to relate to the laws whose establishment is the central purpose of politics, however, is much less clear. I will sketch three views: Jiyuan Yu's, which leans toward emphasizing the ethics; Stephen Buckle's, which leans toward the laws; and Jill Frank's dialectical view. My goal is not to determine which is the best interpretation of Aristotle—though my sympathies lie with Frank—but rather to argue that on any of these three interpretations Aristotle (and thus also many present-day Aristotelians) faces a philosophical difficulty that the idea of self-restriction can help to resolve.

Jiyuan Yu's reading of Aristotle centers on the ideas of human good and virtue. He emphasizes that there is some relativity of these notions to "the historical or cultural background … that the agent internalizes in the process of habituation."[9] Still, the *ethos* of a given society is subject to improvement insofar as it does not produce excellence and flourishing (in its terms), and here the laws (or *nomoi*) have an important role to play.[10] According to Aristotle, Yu writes,

There are two kinds of laws. One is designed to curb wrongdoing through fear of punishment, and the other aims to bring about the human good and to foster a better way of life. Aristotle believes that the aim of the lawgivers should be the second kind of law, that is, to "stimulate men to virtue and urge them forward by the motive of the noble."[11]

Thus, laws can play an important role in achieving the ultimate human end. Nonetheless, laws have various limitations. They speak only in general terms, and thus can be deficient with respect to particular cases, and Aristotle also suggests that not everything can be encompassed under the law.[12] This is not to say that rule by man is automatically preferable to rule by law; under circumstances of rough equality in virtues, Aristotle prefers rule by law because of its impartiality, which helps to constrain the effects of the passions which regularly "pervert the minds of rulers."[13] If there should be one man or family who is superior to all in ethics and intellect, though, then this paragon should rule alone, relying on his own judgment, not bound by any law; he provides the law himself.[14] The picture we get from Yu, in short, rather clearly sees law as a necessary corrective in most actual situations, but seemingly always subject to limitations. Rule of law may often be the best option, but law is not an end in itself: it aims to promote virtuous, flourishing individuals and society—that is, the human good. Yu does note in passing that Aristotle at one point identifies virtue in general (that is, universal justice) with the lawful, but he glosses this by emphasizing that moral education should be the subject of our concern for law.[15]

According to Stephen Buckle, Aristotle's ethics is much less congenial to virtue ethics than has been commonly supposed. In fact, Buckle argues that Aristotle gives us a "law conception of ethics," though not exactly in the sense in which Anscombe criticizes modern moral philosophy.[16] Buckle emphasizes the connected projects of the *Nicomachean Ethics* and the *Politics*, noting that the enquiry into the good for man "finds its completion" in the latter. Insofar as virtue ethicists believe that "we should live according to virtues rather than rules or obligations," and that a "focus on character can replace … reference to acting rightly or wrongly," then they should actually find Aristotle uncongenial, because rules, obligations, and acting rightly are all important to him.[17] Some of Buckle's evidence comes from the fact that the idea of good actions seems to be conceived "independently" from the virtues of character, and instead to find its "proper home within a framework of laws."[18] Buckle also argues that the virtues of character should be understood as traits associated with the "non-rational part of the soul, and therefore the virtues of that part [are] properly directed by reason."[19] Even within the virtues of character, Buckle maintains that modern virtue ethicists have missed the significance of justice as both the most important virtue, and the one most akin to law. Buckle concludes that for Aristotle, developing in ourselves the virtues is not the whole of living well: "to live well also requires that we live according to laws, and that the best life is that in which, with others, we make and also subordinate ourselves to laws, and so fulfill our nature as political beings."[20]

Statements like "to live well also requires that we live according to laws" might admit of a weaker interpretation than Buckle intends. After all, Yu also noted the unity of the *Ethics* and the *Politics*, and also acknowledged the importance of laws, although mainly in the service of virtue. In a moment, we will consider Jill Frank's position, according to which virtues and laws are mutually constituting. For Buckle, though, law really has pride of place. He argues that for Aristotle, unlike most modern virtue ethicists, the traits or reactions of the virtuous agent are not the ultimate standard for action: "the reason why [Aristotle] affirms that 'virtue and the good person seem to be the standard' is because they are the standard *for us*, the imperfectly rational beings that we are."[21] Ethics and politics for humans are inexact because we are flawed; ultimate goodness and rightness are available only to perfectly rational beings—gods. We can only strive to be as close to the gods as possible, and that involves subordinating ourselves to laws.

Yu's reading of Aristotle leans toward the *Ethics*, and makes him a virtue ethicist. Buckle leans toward law and rejects what he understands as virtue ethics. Frank also denies that Aristotle is a "virtue theorist," which she regards as a kind of communitarian,[22] but this does not mean that she would agree with the degree of Buckle's emphasis on law. For Frank's Aristotle, impartial and general law always needs to be paired with particular, agent-specific virtue. Law and virtue, or politics and ethics, are distinct and yet mutually constituting, existing in what she calls a "dynamic harmony."[23] Ethics is not a supplement to political practice, but a central aspect of politics, for at least two reasons: legal and political judgment rely on individual virtue as well as institutional design,[24] and particular judgments of equity are needed as a corrective to laws which, in their generality, can produce injustice.[25] So law is guided by virtue, and yet law also guides and encourages the development of virtue, in turn.[26] Frank acknowledges that some of Aristotle's many statements about law can seem to conflict with some of the others, but she argues that a synthetic, dialectical interpretation is both possible and philosophically attractive. The rule of law can moderate the rule of men, while at the same time the rule of men moderates the rule of law.[27] Frank would see Buckle's interpretation as making too sharp a distinction between reason and desire, with the result that Buckle locates the idealized source of law's disciplinary power outside of those "whose unruly desires it regulates."[28] As for Yu, perhaps Frank would suggest that he underestimates the importance of distinctively legal norms, too content to conflate them with the cultural habits found in a community's *ethos*. It may be that she would be closer to agreement with Yu, though, because in the closing paragraphs of her chapter on the rule of law she writes:

> Just as virtue is composed of sedimented habits, with no precise and identifiable source, that are generated by actions and that themselves generate but do not determine activity, so too is constitution … a product of long and unvarying habit, a "way of life of a people" (*Pol.* 1295a41–b1), generated by a series of actions that have, by repetition and acquiescence, acquired the force of law.[29]

Law and virtue are distinct, but they are formed and maintained through very similar processes.

It remains to say how, on each of these accounts, problems remain that the idea of self-restriction may be able to solve. One of Mou Zongsan's worries, as we will see, is the ever-present possibility for politics to be swallowed by ethics. This happens when the powerful override laws or political norms on the basis of claims to particularistic ethical insight: for example, a Chinese emperor sees himself as a sage, and metes out punishments on the strength of his own putative understanding of ethical reality. To avoid this, Mou says, laws must have an authority that is independent from that of ethics. The routine swallowing of politics by ethics must be rendered illegitimate. It is not clear that, on Yu's interpretation, at least, Aristotle has given political or legal authority an adequately independent basis. In addition, Mou's view also explains how being restricted by law is itself a central precondition for ethical progress, and thus should not be understood as a second-best case or unfortunate compromise with reality. On this count, too, the status of law in Aristotle (on Yu's telling, at least) seems inadequate. We can refer to this as the Weak Law Problem. The story is different for Buckle's Aristotle; if we accept Buckle's interpretation, the Weak Law Problem may disappear. However, it seems to me that the idea of self-restriction may be precisely what Aristotle needs to avoid some of Buckle's conclusions. Many readers of Aristotle will find implausible Buckle's assertion that laws and obligations are prior and virtues merely derivative (call this the Priority of Law Problem), but there is no denying that Aristotle seems to want a unified account of ethics and politics. I will explain below how the idea of self-restriction allows one to maintain a strong relationship between ethics and politics while nonetheless maintaining their independence. In this way, we can have something like the role for law that Buckle's Aristotle wants, but without abandoning the virtue-ethical framework. Finally, as attractive as I find Frank's Aristotle, I believe that on her account law and virtue (especially the virtue of justice) have too strong a tendency to blend with and ultimately collapse into one another, which we can call the Distinction Problem. She recognizes that the law needs to be general and uniform[30] but places such emphasis on the role of good citizens' judgment in moderating the excesses of law[31] that the distinction between rule of law and rule of man disappears. It is true that the adjudication of law requires judgment, but this should be judgment within the framework of law, rather than ethical judgment in general. On each of these interpretations, in short, Aristotle's view of the relation between ethics and politics seems to have room for improvement. It is now time to see that the same is also true of Hume's virtue ethics.

Hume is famous for his distinction between natural and artificial virtues.[32] He argues that some virtues, of which benevolence is the best example, are the "refined and completed" forms of certain natural sentiments.[33] These virtues are not simply our innate sentiments, since the mechanism of "sympathy" plays a role in extending and completing them, but they all emerge from impulses, desires, and so on that are part of our human nature.[34] On the other hand, artificial virtues like justice (or, more precisely, honesty with respect to property[35]) have their basis in conventions that we invent because of their necessity for successful impersonal cooperation. These conventions are grounded in calculations of our self-interest. Hume emphasizes that artificial virtues are not mere conventions, however: they have become actual virtues, "durable principles of the mind" that reliably motivate us even in cases where a specific honest act will not profit us.[36] This is partly because, once such conventions are established, we naturally feel approbation toward following them. This is not a strong motivation, especially in those cases in which justice commands an action that does not conduce to our immediate benefit, so the natural feeling of approbation needs to be supplemented by the efforts of politicians, parents, and others to shape our sentiments so that justice and its ilk become robust virtues.[37]

Law comes into the picture via the very conventions that form the basis of the artificial virtues. In Rachel Cohon's words, Hume sees society as depending on adherence to "strict, exceptionless" rules of property and promising.[38] Neil McArthur explains that Hume recognizes that when the rules of conventions have what he calls "generality," they more successfully serve their function of protecting our interests. Generality means applying to everyone, applying in rigid and uniform fashion, being clear and determinate in their application, and being publically known in advance of their application.[39] This applies equally to the rules of justice and to the laws based thereon, and Hume also expects that the virtue of justice will track these strict rules.[40] The crucial reason why we must have laws in addition to the virtue of justice, then, is not because of any differences in what they instruct us to do, but rather because the virtue is not a sufficient guarantor of the rules—notwithstanding the efforts of politicians and parents to strengthen our disposition toward virtue. Indeed, Hume believes that a proper system of laws must be designed such that even if "every man be supposed a knave," society will still be preserved and people's property protected.[41]

From one perspective, there does not seem to be any concern about tensions between virtue and law on Hume's picture: since Hume believes that the virtue of justice and the laws will track one another, we apparently need not worry about particular situations in which ethical judgment might indicate that justice dictates a different result than does the law.[42] Insofar as there is any discrepancy in an actual case, Hume would have us guided by the impartial, general law; he is very cognizant of the pull on us of "the characters and circumstances of the persons" involved in any question, but argues that lest we "quickly bring disorder into the world," we must restrain our particularistic judgment by "general and inflexible principles."[43] He does allow that in emergencies like general famine or shipwreck, "the strict laws of justice are suspended … and give place to the stronger motives of necessity and self-preservation." In these circumstances, we should be guided by what "prudence can dictate, or humanity permit."[44] Still, contemporary scholar James Wallace asks, "would Hume accept the possibility … that justice might on occasion be properly tempered by mercy even though no catastrophe is threatened? This part of Hume's account is not developed."[45] We can refer to this as the Mercy Problem. What, furthermore, are we to make of the many cases in which Hume sees our benevolence rightly trumped by our sense of justice, or by the law? Is our benevolent feeling inapt, albeit unavoidable? Call this the Misleading Virtue Problem. Wallace's own suggestion is that Hume would be well-served by a recognition that our virtues, and the values that they express, should aim at harmonizing with one another; Wallace finds some version of the ancient Greek ideal of the unity of the virtues to be appealing. I am sympathetic to this move but note that the problem then resurfaces in tensions between a more unified virtue and law—call this the Competition Problem—since surely we must not abandon the idea that laws are general and exceptionless, just like Hume says. In other words, the general difficulty that self-restriction aims to solve has appeared again. As contemporary Humeans strive to work out these issues of relations among various virtues and the law, I suggest that they will find the Confucian idea of self-restriction to be fruitful.

Before moving on, there is one more aspect of Hume's account that we should consider. Recall that he believes that a good legal-political institution should be able to function even if "every man be supposed a knave." It is natural to wonder if the assumption of universal knavery might actually undermine the possibility of virtue in a society. Confucians will immediately think of *Analects* 2:3, wherein the Master says, "Lead them with government and regulate them by punishments, and the people will evade them with no sense of shame. Lead them with virtue and regulate them by ritual, and they will acquire a sense of shame and moreover, they will be orderly."[46] That is, designing a system for the regulation of knaves will encourage the knaves to do whatever is required to avoid punishment, but they will not develop a sense of shame nor more advanced forms of virtue. However, in an excellent article on Hume's goals for the design of political institutions, Baogang He shows that Hume's views are more complex than the supposition that everyone be a knave would suggest.[47] First of all, while Hume does not depend on any particular political actor being virtuous—in particular, he refuses to assume good will on the part of rulers—he does rely on the fact that honesty, sympathy, and generosity are reasonably widespread in society. He also argues that "much virtue, justice, and humanity are requisite in statesmen," as well as seeing that institutional designers themselves must have the well-being of the whole in mind.[48] Second, and relatedly, Hume recognizes the need to encourage virtue. This happens because good persons are rewarded and bad ones punished, which Baogang He refers to as a "public virtue approach" to political life, rather than a "traditional moralizing-individual approach."[49] In any event, it does not seem to be the case that Hume can simply focus on laws and other institutions, and let virtue take care of itself (another version of the Weak Virtue Problem). As we turn now to Mou Zongsan's idea of self-restriction, we will see that natural ways in which this contemporary Confucian framework can be developed will speak directly to the questions with which Hume is here grappling. Once again, Humeans today have things to learn from Confucians.

3 Mou Zongsan and Self-Restriction[50]

Traditional Confucianism conceived of the ethical and political realms as continuous and unified. Either the most virtuous should rule or, in a concession to hereditary monarchy, rulers should strive to be as virtuous as possible, and be guided by their still-more-virtuous ministers. In theory, the possession of virtue enabled the ruler to care for all in the realm; the exemplary nature of the ruler's character, especially as manifest in his concern for members of his family, was supposed to lead all in the realm toward virtue as well. To be sure, a variety of intermediary institutions evolved to enhance and spread the effects of the ruler's virtue, including bureaucrats and the system of examinations that produced them; a broad system of rituals; and a penal code designed to preserve order when all else failed. "Order" was a central goal, but it was conceived in ethical terms, and virtuous rule was understood to be both necessary and sufficient for its attainment.

At the core of Mou Zongsan's New Confucian political project is an effort to pry apart ethical and political values. Mou was worried about political systems that rely on leadership by individuals who claim to have highly developed moral insight. He had in mind the periodic, terrible excesses of both the traditional Confucian state and the modern Communist one: in both cases, leaders who believed in their own virtue sometimes sought to impose their vision of morality on the realm, with bloody consequences. Mou characterized this as politics being "swallowed" by morality.[51] To be sure, Mou was deeply committed to the importance of striving for sagehood.

Among other things, he saw laws and rights themselves as rooted in and emerging from moral struggles. Without morality, there would be no politics. Nonetheless, he recognized that "achieving sagehood is an endless process."[52] Politics (including law) must, therefore, be independent from morality, or else it, too, would be endlessly unfinished and inadequately protective. Mou thus found himself advocating a position that fell between liberal right-based theories and traditional Confucian (or Communist) good-based theories. Unlike the liberals, Mou held that moral and political value must retain a continuity, lest politics be unmoored from the underlying source of all value, in which case we would have no reason for confidence that the outcomes of our political processes were ultimately aimed at making our lives better. Unlike the Communists and earlier Confucians, though, politics and law must nonetheless stand on their own, independent of morality. In other words, Mou rejected both a direct connection between morality and politics, and a lack of connection. His alternative is an indirect connection. Political value, he says, emerges out of morality but achieves an independent status because the further development of moral value requires what he terms "self-restriction (*ziwo kanxian* 自我坎陷)."[53] I am persuaded by Mou that the concept of self-restriction is critical to a fruitful contemporary Confucian development of political philosophy, and, furthermore, that it can contribute to broader contemporary discussions of virtue-based politics. However, let me make clear from the outset that my explication of the idea of self-restriction differs in some crucial ways from Mou's. Self-restriction plays key roles in at least three different areas of Mou's philosophy. It explains how cognition of the empirical world is possible for creatures whose moral heartminds also respond to the lifeworld in a non-empirical way; it explains how and to what degree scientific norms can govern our activities, at least partly independently from morality; and it explains how laws and rights can structure our political lives without being over-ridden by individual claims to better moral insight. In each case, Mou argues that what is being "restricted" is the direct, intuitive grasping of moral reality by the moral heartmind. Understanding this latter idea, which he frequently terms "intellectual intuition," would be critical to a full account of Mou's theory of self-restriction. I believe, though, that with some re-interpretation, we can detach the idea of self-restriction from the rest of Mou's "moral metaphysics" without losing its significance for political philosophy. To be sure, self-restriction must be grounded in an account of ethical value; for present purposes, I offer the following quite general sketch of Confucian ethics in lieu of Mou's own account:

• Humans are capable of developing our attunement to and care for all aspects of our social and natural environment, which most centrally involves those people with whom we have particular relationships.

• Our care for distinct dimensions of value in our environments (e.g., family responsibilities, the well-being of strangers for whom we are responsible, and concern for our friends) must be harmonized.

• Well-lived human lives and the flourishing of our communities both depend on people successfully developing the aforementioned capacities to significant degrees.

• These capacities can be usefully explained through reference to individual virtues like humaneness and propriety, though these virtues are at least somewhat interrelated (and perhaps, depending on the specific account, ultimately just different aspects of a single capacity); and the ultimate goal of Confucian ethics is the full development of these virtues on the part of all people.

In order to concentrate on self-restriction and political philosophy, I will not defend this picture of Confucian ethics here.[54] I use Mou's specific discussion of self-restriction as my point of departure, and in fact I believe that Mou would accept virtually everything I say here about self-restriction. But we do not need to take on board all of Mou's system in order to see the value of self-restriction, and this approach opens it up to the possibility of dialogue with contemporary Aristotelians and Humeans.

Mou himself glosses "self-restriction" as meaning "self-negation (*ziwo fouding* 自我否定)" in a Hegelian sense: that is, the limitation of one thing by something else of a fundamentally distinct kind.[55] Mou draws a distinction between the functional presentations of ethical reasoning and the structural presentations of analytical reasoning. By functional presentations of ethical reasoning, he means an individual's particularist, situation-specific ethical judgments, which he sees as the core modality of Confucian ethics.[56] He understands these judgments to come from the properly cultivated moral heartmind, and in this sense to be subjective; he also puts this in terms of the individual's virtuous character.[57] The structural presentation of analytical reasoning, on the other hand, refers to general, objective rules or frameworks. With this in mind, here is Mou:

A democratic political structure is something that emerges from the conscious decisions people make in their political lives; based on this clue, we can connect it to ethical reasoning. But such political structures are objective frameworks belonging to objective practice, and thus cannot be completed by the functional presentation of ethical reason. The inner logic of the political structure itself is a manifestation of the structural presentation of reasoning; this reasoning temporarily cannot be thought of in terms of individual virtue or practical reasoning, but has shifted into analytical reasoning without ethical meaning … . But this overall political structure itself is something desired by ethical reasoning. In other words, the realization of this political structure is also the realization of a highest ethical value. This shows that in order to realize this ethical value, ethical reasoning must from within the midst of its functional presentation restrict itself (*ziwo kanxian*), step back a pace, and shift into the structural presentation of analytical reasoning. Observed from within this structural presentation of reason, politics has its independent significance, forms its own, independent realm of value, and has temporarily left ethics behind; it seemingly has no connection with ethics. From within the structural presentation, the various aspects of this political structure—like the organization of power and the definition of rights and duties—are all on par with one another, and thus can be the subjects of an independent political science. People can discuss these aspects using pure political discussion, striving to clearly establish a reasonable, impartial framework (*heli gongdao*).[58]

As we can see, for Mou that which restricts itself is a certain kind of reasoning, in favor of a different modality of reasoning. From elsewhere in Mou's writings, it is clear that the difference between ethical and analytical reasoning is more dramatic than I have been making it sound. He really has in mind two fundamentally different kinds of consciousness: an innate moral consciousness that has the ability to directly intuit the basic moral nature of the cosmos, and a cognitive, analytical consciousness that works by distinguishing subject from object.[59] One key to my appropriation of Mou is to realize that self-restriction still makes sense if we give a much less metaphysically charged interpretation of the two forms of reasoning. Mou in fact takes "the virtue of one's moral character (*renge zhong de dexing*)" to be roughly equivalent to the deliverances of one's moral heartmind; I propose simply to see ethical reasoning in terms of the perceptions and reactions of virtuous character to particular situations. This is consistent with Mou's more elaborate story, but does not require that we follow Mou in all the specifics. Furthermore, my version still provides a solid (and solidly Confucian) normative grounding for ethics, based in the general framework of Confucian ethics I sketched above.[60]

What about the reasoning that takes place within the political realm? How is this different from ethical reasoning? I accept much of what Mou says: it is reasoning in terms of different values and in keeping with general, objective rules. Rather than basing one's judgment and behavior on one's own perception of the situation, one is bound by laws and works within political processes. Among other things, this means accepting the messiness and imperfections of the political process. As he puts it succinctly in one of his lectures: if a sage wants to be a president, he must "observe the political rules."[61] Let us now take note of the first sentence from Mou's long quote: *it is important that politics emerges out of the ethical activity of individuals as they merge together in political life*, because Mou's basic picture is that a certain kind of political structure is ultimately needed as the indirect means to more complete ethical practice. Ethical reasoning "restricts itself" in order to more fully realize itself, and thereby allows for an independent realm of political value to exist. It is independent in the sense that it cannot, at least under normal circumstances, be over-ridden by an individual's claim to superior ethical insight. As Mou puts it later in the same book:

No matter how great or spiritual the attainments of one's [virtuous] character, when manifested in politics, one cannot override the relevant limits (that is, the highest principles of the political world), and in fact must devote one's august character to the realization of these limits. When one is able to successfully realize these limits, in ancient times one would be called a "sage-king"; in modern times, a "great statesperson." If one cannot, in ancient times one would be called a "hegemon," "tyrant," or "autocrat"; in modern times, a "totalitarian ruler" or "dictator."[62]

Mou ignores here the differences between ancient and modern politics; on his more considered account, even the best of ancient politics suffers from its lack of independence.

Let us take a step back. We need to understand what self-restriction is and why it is necessary. So far in this section we have made some progress toward understanding what it is, at least with respect to the relation between ethics and politics. Now let us focus on the justification of self-restriction. In summary outline, the argument is as follows. Our subjectively felt morality implicitly points toward an ideal of full, sagely virtue. Full virtue must be realized in the public, political world. Without objective structures (like laws), the public goals of full virtue are inaccessible. Since these objective structures restrict the ways in which our subjective moral feelings can be manifested, Mou concludes that the achievement of virtue requires self-restriction. Objective, public standards are thus related to inner virtue, but they are also distinct from one another. Before I unpack this argument, let me emphasize why it is important. Mou's idea, which I endorse, is not that a constitution, laws, and rights are merely *compatible* with Confucianism, but rather than these objective political structures are *required* by Confucianism if it is to realize its own goals. Mou's argument does not depend on an independent commitment to constitutional democracy, but is a critique internal to the Confucian tradition. The fact that he draws on Hegelian language does not change this fact, just as the ways in which earlier Confucians drew on Buddhist ideas does not render their critiques external to the tradition.[63]

In any event, turn now to the argument itself, albeit in a more explicit form than Mou ever provides; Mou's own statements on this subject tend to be quite elliptical, such as the long passage cited above. In order to conclude that the achievement of virtue requires self-restriction, we need the following three premises: (1) we (Confucians) are committed to seeking full virtue; (2) full virtue must be realized in the public world; and (3) the public realization of full virtue requires objective structures that are independent from claims of virtue. The first premise should be uncontroversial: the pursuit of ethical self-improvement and the criticism of those who rest content with moral mediocrity are perennial themes in Confucian writings. In the past 100 years some writers have sought to resist the second premise, arguing that Confucianism can only have a continued role in the modern world if it confines its aspirations to the development of an inner virtue that has no necessary expression or influence in the outer world. We can see something of this attitude in Yu Dan's extraordinarily popular recent book on the *Analects*, and the eminent scholar Yu Ying-shih has repeatedly made arguments to this effect.[64] However, it is absolutely central to the Confucian conception of virtue that inner states and dispositions have an outer manifestation and influence. Indeed, this is one of the real insights of the tradition that we are now beginning to see confirmed by modern psychology.[65] More certainly can be said about this premise, including its dependence on the lack of a firm distinction in the external between "private" (like family) and "public" (like political); on this score, Confucians and feminists find themselves both supporting the latter's slogan that "the personal is political." Still, it should be clear that the core of Mou's argument comes in the third premise.

The premise that the public realization of full virtue requires objective structures can itself be cashed out into three steps. First, publically realized full virtue means that everyone is also and simultaneously implicated in realizing virtue; as we read in *Analects* 12:1, "If one day he can overcome himself and turn to humaneness, the world will turn to humaneness along with him."[66] Similarly, *Analects* 12:16 says that the good person "completes the good in others"; *Analects* 4:25 tells us that "virtue is not solitary; it must have neighbors." The fundamental inter-relationship of people on which these sayings from the *Analects* are based should include all people.

Second, the attainment of virtue by others must be their individual and active achievement. As Mou explains at one point (partly using Hegelian language), actual freedom requires self-awareness, which in turn requires struggle; each person must feel that he or she is an independent individual. This is connected to the pervasive Confucian commitment to "getting it for oneself (*zi de* 自得)"; slightly later in *Analects* 12:1, the text continues: "To be humane comes from oneself; how could it come from others?"[67] Third, only when rights to exercise agency with respect to matters both large and small are guaranteed, via external political structures, can the possibility of individual, active engagement with one's own self-cultivation be assured. People need to have opportunities to take responsibility for various aspects of their world, even up to the possibility that they are most qualified to serve as the head of government. Once again, let me acknowledge that these ideas are not explicit in Mou's writings, but I take them to follow from and fill out his position. In fact, they are also partly alluded to in the 1958 "Manifesto to the World's People on behalf of Chinese Culture" that I referred to at the outset of the chapter.[68] I conclude that virtuous insight must therefore be restrained—restrict itself—by adherence to the objective structures that protect the rights of all. Only then is full virtue a possibility.

Before moving on, it is important to add that although self-restriction means that our subjective ethical feelings will much of the time willingly stand down and endorse our giving authority to general laws—even when these laws conflict with our subjective ethical judgments—it is possible for there to be exceptions to this typical stance. Legitimate self-restriction does not mean that one's full-fledged and independent ethical judgment disappears; it is simply "temporarily" suspended, as Mou puts it.[69] Therefore, one should be capable of judging when, in an extreme case, the violation of the law might be ethically justified without abandoning the general commitment to the authority of law that self-restriction demands. As John Rawls famously argued, when one willingly accepts the legal consequences of one's civil disobedience, one expresses one's continued acceptance of the rule of law and of the political authority in which it adheres.[70] If one's ethical values lead one routinely to break the law, though, then this is not civil disobedience but rather the denial that any legitimate law is actually in play.

4 Prospects for Dialogue

In earlier writings I have suggested that the idea of "rooted global philosophy" offers a fruitful way to think about the point of cross-cultural philosophical engagement.[71] Our philosophical criticism and reflection typically takes a particular tradition as its point of departure, but as we investigate the questions that a given tradition makes salient, we can still be open to stimulus and challenge from alternative traditions. This is simultaneously being rooted and global. While it is possible that new, more inclusive traditions may emerge from this process, the success of rooted global philosophy does not depend on such an outcome. For example, if an encounter with modern Confucianism leads modern neo-Aristotelians to improve the scope or power of their own theories, as seen from their perspectives, then this counts as a kind of success for philosophy.

Seen in this light, the dialogue that I have proposed in the present chapter might now proceed in any of three general directions. Most ambitiously, either Aristotelian or Humean virtue ethicists might find Mou's specific concept of self-restriction, in all of its detailed connections to intellectual intuition, cognition, and so on, to be a necessary addition or reformation to their existing theories. Of course, by myself setting aside these specific dimensions of the contents of self-restriction, I have undermined the possibility for this result. The very different metaphysical and other premises that divide Mou's full theory from those of Aristotle or Hume make this version of dialogue extremely unlikely to be fruitful. This should not lead us to conclude that there is a wide conceptual gulf separating all fully fleshed-out understandings of Confucianism from Western philosophies like those considered here; though Mou's vision of Confucianism is influential, it is also highly controversial. Alternative moments in the tradition and even alternative interpretations of the same texts on which Mou focuses may turn out to have more in common with Western orientations. But that is an argument for another day.[72]

The second and third ways in which followers of Hume or Aristotle might learn from Mou both depend on taking self-restriction in the somewhat more general sense that I have presented in this chapter. My exposition of the meaning and justification of self-restriction has drawn explicitly on Confucian texts and conceptualizations; and as I said above, while my argument for self-restriction is not exactly Mou's, it is parallel with his views, and I believe that he (and his current followers) would accept what I have said here. As for Humeans and Aristotelians, the second direction in which the dialogue could proceed is to consider whether my specific argument for the necessity of self-restriction also applies to their frameworks. Or, more loosely, perhaps the Confucian argument will inspire a roughly similar argument, albeit couched in Humean or Aristotelian terminology. Finally, the least ambitious, but still productive, way in which a dialogue could proceed is if we find ways in which an idea like self-restriction can be fruitfully inserted into Aristotle's or Hume's framework, even if it is not justified through anything like the argument discussed above. That should still count as a kind of philosophical progress that comes out of comparative dialogue.

In my discussions above of Aristotle and of Hume, I have already tentatively indicated some ways in which self-restriction may be able to figure constructively into the development of their theories. Jiyuan Yu's Aristotle faces some challenges similar to traditional Confucianism, for instance, the Weak Law Problem: inadequate protection against politics being swallowed by morality and mistakenly thinking that legal norms represent a kind of compromise with an unfortunate reality. Taking self-restriction seriously would allow us to take all that Aristotle says about law seriously and yet avoid Buckle's Priority of the Law Problem, namely that law is ultimately more central than virtue. This is welcome to anyone (like myself) who finds Buckle's reading of Aristotle unpalatable. Frank's picture can be shored up through the deployment of self-restriction to solve the Distinction Problem: it is a tool that her Aristotle can use to keep law and virtue distinct from one another, even though they are mutually constituting. For both Yu and especially Frank, finally, I see no reason why they should not endorse the central argument that I have presented for self-restriction (namely, that full virtue requires independent political/legal structures). Frank, especially, places emphasis on an inclusive, "democratic" reading of Aristotle that fits extremely well with my focus on the protection and encouragement of individuals' abilities to participate in politics.

Embracing the idea of self-restriction could also make Hume's position much stronger. The area of concern that I have identified lies in the potential conflicts among benevolence, justice, and law. Hume's basic account seems to be that barring emergencies, when benevolence and justice conflict, the latter trumps; and that since law is simply derived from the exceptionless rules of justice, there is no room for conflicts between justice and law. At the most general level, I referred to this as the Competition Problem. More specifically, there is the Misleading Virtue Problem: what to make of the regularity with which benevolence apparently leads us astray; should we still feel approbation for such an unreliable disposition? This is tied to the unrealistic and unattractive compartmentalization of virtues that Hume gives us: as I cited Taylor beginning to discuss, there are strong reasons for thinking that virtues appropriately influence one another, even if we do not want to go as far as thinking that virtue is ultimately unified.[73] In addition, while I cannot develop the argument here, there are powerful reasons (both empirical and normative) for thinking that our disposition to justice cannot be as exclusively rule-like as Hume would have us believe (this relates to, but is more general than, the Mercy Problem that I identified above). Judgments of justice or fairness need considerable contextual sensitivity in ways that publically stateable general laws cannot mimic. Depending on how many of these putative problems one finds troubling, self-restriction can ride to the rescue at one place or another. For example, a modern Humean might argue that particularistic virtue (including justice) needs to restrict itself so that we follow general laws, because only a society governed by such laws is truly conducive to the growth of virtue. This would explain away the problem of Misleading Virtue: we should not always follow benevolence because apt benevolence must regularly restrict itself. The Competition Problem is solved as well, since now we have an account of how, when, and why law trumps virtue. Self-restriction does not solve the Mercy Problem quite as cleanly, but it can be part of a solution in helping us to balance among the particularistic virtue of justice, the general rules of justice and law, and rare exceptions that call for criticism of the laws and even for civil disobedience.[74]

In keeping with the goals of this volume, the present chapter has emphasized ways in which rooted yet global Aristotelians and Humeans can benefit from an encounter with modern Confucianism. Of course, the possibilities for stimulus and challenge also operate in the other direction. For a variety of reasons, though, modern Chinese philosophers have been much more apt to take up these challenges and stimuli than have their Western peers, creating a troubling asymmetry that this chapter and this book are aimed at helping to dispel. The nature of rooted global philosophy is not to prescribe one-size-fits-all solutions but to initiate new lines of thought. Perhaps the idea of self-restriction will lead contemporary Western virtue ethicists to conclusions quite different from those that I have imagined here. This, too, should count as a kind of progress. My ultimate argument here is not for a specific, substantive conclusion, but for the fruitfulness of taking seriously philosophical challenges from China.

Acknowledgments

I am very grateful to Brian Bruya for his careful reading of an earlier version of the chapter and for his helpful suggestions.

Notes

1. Jiyuan Yu ("The 'Manifesto' of New Confucianism and the Revival of Virtue Ethics") laments this missed opportunity, though he may underestimate the degree to which key authors of the Manifesto were already committed in 1958 to an understanding of Confucianism that was not

congenial to Aristotelian virtue ethics. In treating the Manifesto as a "source," I am exaggerating somewhat: the philosophical and historical writings of its authors were already underway in 1958, so it is more a statement of joint understanding than a starting point. Still, in the years since 1958 it has had a significant influence as an independent document.

2. See, e.g., Bryan Van Norden, *Virtue Ethics and Consequentialism in Early Chinese Philosophy* and Michael Slote, "The Mandate of Empathy." I discuss the development of a virtue-ethical reading of early Confucianism in "The *Analects* and Moral Theory."

3. Three factors explain the absence of contemporary Confucianism in current conversations about virtue ethics: (1) many contemporary Chinese philosophers, following Mou Zongsan (one of the authors of the Manifesto) and others, understand Confucian ethics on a fundamentally deontological model; (2) another group of contemporary advocates of Confucianism construe it as a religious and/or cultural resource that is relevant primarily to China, rather than as a universal ethical and political philosophy; and (3) most writings of modern Confucians are only available in Chinese, making it difficult for Western philosophers to engage in a detailed fashion with specific aspects of modern Confucian philosophizing.

4. For example, Lin Anwu, *Ruxue geming lun* or Tang, *Dexing yu zhengzhi.*

5. For example, Yu Ying-Shih, "*Xiandai Ruxue de huigu yu zhanwang.*"

6. Jiang's *Zhengzhi ruxue* is a leading example. For discussion of this approach, which I call Institutional Confucianism, see Angle, *Contemporary Confucian Political Philosophy* and Fan Rui-ping, *The Renaissance of Confucianism in Contemporary China.*

7. Admittedly, an officer sometimes will decide not to write a ticket, but my sense is that this has less to do with an ethical judgment than with how successful a given driver is at charming the officer or eliciting pity.

8. This analysis applies only to virtue-ethical views that have a significant role for particularist judgment. Deontological and rule-consequentialist views, according to which our duties already take a universal form, may not face this kind of problem; after all, in "Modern Moral Philosophy" Elizabeth Anscombe criticized dominant forms of modern moral philosophy as being based on a "law conception of ethics." I set aside for another day consideration of whether act-consequentialists need self-restriction.

9. Jiyuan Yu, *The Ethics of Confucius and Aristotle*, 100.

10. As Yu notes, Aristotle says that "men in general desire the good, and not merely what their fathers had" (*Politics* 1269a3–4). Quotations from Aristotle are drawn from Aristotle, *The Complete Works of Aristotle.*

11. Jiyuan Yu, *The Ethics of Confucius and Aristotle*, 131; cf. Aristotle, *Nicomachean Ethics* 1180a6–7.

12. Yu, ibid., 138, referring to Aristotle, *Politics* 1286a10–11, 21–22, and 1287b18–19.

13. Ibid., referring to Aristotle, *Politics* 1287a29–31.

14. Ibid., referring to Aristotle, *Politics* 1288a3; the topic is clarified at *Politics* 1288a16–29.

15. Ibid., 101.

16. Buckle, "Aristotle's Republic," 568.

17. Ibid., 575.

18. Ibid., 569. Buckle writes: "To take one example: no reader of the *Nicomachean Ethics* could be in any doubt that Aristotle thinks adultery to be wicked and disgraceful. But he makes no attempt to show that its wrongness consists in its being contrary to any virtue; it is, rather, simply taken to be wrong, and the man of virtue shown to be virtuous—in part if not in whole—by the fact that he does not do dreadful things of that kind" (ibid., 569n12).

19. Ibid., 579.

20. Ibid., 576.

21. Ibid., 594.

22. Jill Frank, *A Democracy of Distinction*, 12.

23. Ibid., 50.

24. Ibid., 106.

25. Ibid., 81.

26. Ibid., 110–111.

27. Ibid., 114.

28. Ibid., 112.

29. Ibid., 136.

30. Ibid., 112.

31. Ibid., 114.

32. The account appears in his *Treatise of Human Nature*. It does not appear explicitly in his later *Enquiry Concerning the Principles of Morals*, leading some to suggest that he abandoned it. However, as pointed out by David Wiggins, the distinction "is there in the background" of the *Enquiry* ("Natural and Artificial Virtues," 135) and is explicit in Hume's still later essay "Of the Original Contract" (267). Though there are interpretive controversies surrounding Hume's views of ethics and politics, relative to the debates over Aristotle the disagreements over Hume are—at least for my present purposes—quite minor, and so they will not make an appearance in the main text.

33. Rachel Cohon, "Hume's Artificial and Natural Virtues," 259.

34. In her "Justice and the Foundations of Social Morality in Hume's *Treatise*," Jacqueline Taylor emphasizes the transformation of instinct that takes place even in the natural virtues, and

therefore suggests that other scholars have sometimes overemphasized the distinction between natural and artificial virtues.

35. Cohon, "Hume's Artificial and Natural Virtues," 260.

36. Hume, *A Treatise of Human Nature*, 575, and generally §3.1.1.

37. Cohon, "Hume's Artificial and Natural Virtues," 263; Taylor, "Justice and the Foundations of Social Morality in Hume's *Treatise*."

38. Cohon, ibid., 260.

39. Neil McArthur, *David Hume's Political Theory*, 57; see Hume, *Treatise* §3.2.6.

40. There is a certain amount of disagreement among commentators over whether Hume's legal philosophy should count as a positivist or conventionalist view or a natural law view, given that on his account laws are artificial but not arbitrary; contrast Kenneth Westphal's "From 'Convention' to 'Ethical Life'" with Neil McArthur's *David Hume's Political Theory*.

41. See Baogang He, "Knavery and Virtue in Humean Institutional Design," 543; Hume, "Of the Independency of Parliament," 118.

42. Note that "barbarous" societies ruled by the arbitrary decisions of tyrants have no laws, properly speaking, at all (McArthur, *David Hume's Political Theory*, chapter 2).

43. Hume, *Treatise*, 532.

44. Hume, "An Enquiry Concerning the Principles of Morals," 38.

45. James Wallace, "Virtues of Benevolence and Justice," 89.

46. Translation from E. Bruce Brooks and A. Taeko Brooks, *The Original Analects*, 110.

47. He, "Knavery and Virtue in Humean Institutional Design."

48. Ibid., 549.

49. Ibid., 551.

50. This section is based on material from Angle, *Contemporary Confucian Political Philosophy*, primarily in chapter 2.

51. Mou Zongsan, *Zhengdao yu zhidao*, 140. Unless otherwise noted, translations are my own.

52. Ibid., 127.

53. Mou, *Zhengdao yu zhidao*, 59. This translation of *ziwo kanxian* was first used by David Elstein; see Elstein, "Mou Zongsan's New Confucian Democracy."

54. One controversial dimension of my picture is the central role played by virtues; for extensive discussion of different approaches to these matters, see my "The *Analects* and Moral Theory."

55. Mou, *Xianxiang yu wuzishen*, 122.

56. Mou, *Zhengdao yu zhidao*, 46–48.

57. Ibid., 47.

58. Ibid., 58–59.

59. One of Mou's most controversial doctrines is that through the former consciousness, humans are capable of "intellectual intuition." For some background and discussion of these ideas, see Nganying Serina Chan, *The Thought of Mou Zongsan*; Sébastien Billioud, *Thinking Through Confucian Modernity*; and Nicholas Bunnin, "God's Knowledge and Ours."

60. There is of course more to be said about what counts as a virtuous perception or reaction, how this relates to the attunement and care that I mentioned above, how these individual reactions to particular circumstances harmonize with one another and with multiple dimensions of value, and so on. Mou offers one kind of answer, based around his idea of intellectual intuition; I offer a different answer in *Sagehood*; and other Confucian philosophers have developed still other alternatives.

61. Mou, *Zhongguo zhexue shijiu jiang*, 278.

62. Mou, *Zhengdao yu zhidao*, 128.

63. In chapter 2 of *Contemporary Confucian Political Philosophy*, I discuss at some length the question of whether Mou's "New Politics" is actually Confucian, concluding that it does count as a development of the living tradition of Confucianism.

64. See Yu Dan, *Yu Dan Lunyu xinde* and Yu Ying-shih, *"Xiandai Ruxue de huigu yu zhanwang."* I discuss Yu Ying-shih's arguments in *Sagehood*, chapter 10.

65. I summarize some of the relevant arguments and literature in "Seeing Confucian 'Active Moral Perception' in Light of Contemporary Psychology."

66. Adapted from Brooks and Brooks, *The Original Analects*, 89.

67. Theodore deBary has particularly emphasized the idea of "getting it for oneself" in his many writings on Neo-Confucianism; see, for example, *The Message of the Mind in Neo-Confucianism*.

68. See Mou et al., *"Wei Zhongguo wenhua jinggao shijie renshi xuanyan,"* 33 and, for a somewhat abbreviated English translation, Carsun Chang, "A Manifesto for a Re-appraisal of Sinology and Reconstruction of Chinese Culture," 472.

69. Mou, *Zhengdao yu zhidao*, 59.

70. John Rawls, *A Theory of Justice*.

71. Angle, *Sagehood*.

72. For an argument that Wang Yangming (1472–1529), who is one of Mou's main sources, should be understood as a kind of virtue-ethicist, see Angle, "Wang Yangming as a Virtue Ethicist." I explore several different approaches to early Confucianism in "The *Analects* and Moral Theory."

73. Hume's account is appealingly naturalistic and conforms with certain dimensions of recent research into moral psychology. But much of this research suggests that even if there are distinct emotional sources of virtue-like dispositions, there are also higher-level processes that blend and shape the basic dispositions. For some references, see Angle, "Seeing Confucian 'Active Moral Perception' in Light of Contemporary Psychology."

74. One might wonder whether, in acknowledging that ethics can sometimes override political norms, I have re-opened the Pandora's box that self-restriction was meant to keep closed. As was noted above, civil disobedience must be rare and must continue to respect the rule of law by accepting the legal consequences of one's actions; otherwise we have indeed lost our commitment to law's having an independent authority. In addition, the grounding of self-restriction in the ultimate realization of virtue for all, also gives us some guidance on when laws are problematic enough to merit civil disobedience. We must criticize laws that seriously undermine the ability of any group to achieve virtue, and if working for change within such an oppressive system proves impossible, civil disobedience may be demanded. For some related discussion, see my argument in favor of Confucian social criticism in Angle, *Contemporary Confucian Political Philosophy*, chapter 7.

Works Cited

Angle, Stephen C. "The *Analects* and Moral Theory." In *Dao Companion to the Analects*, ed. Amy Olberding. Springer, 2013.

Angle, Stephen C. *Contemporary Confucian Political Philosophy: Toward Progressive Confucianism*. Polity Press, 2012.

Angle, Stephen C. *Sagehood: The Contemporary Significance of Neo-Confucian Philosophy*. Oxford University Press, 2009.

Angle, Stephen C. "Seeing Confucian 'Active Moral Perception' in Light of Contemporary Psychology." In *The Philosophy and Psychology of Character and Happiness*, ed. Nancy Snow and Franco Trivigno. Routledge, 2014.

Angle, Stephen C. "Wang Yangming as a Virtue Ethicist." In *Dao Companion to Neo-Confucian Philosophy*, ed. John Makeham. Springer, 2010.

Anscombe, Elizabeth. "Modern Moral Philosophy." *Philosophy* 33, no. 124 (1958): 1–19.

Aristotle. *The Complete Works of Aristotle: The Revised Oxford Translation*, ed. Jonathan Barnes. Princeton University Press, 1984.

Billioud, Sébastien. *Thinking Through Confucian Modernity: A Study of Mou Zongsan's Moral Metaphysics*. Brill, 2011.

Brooks, E. Bruce, and A. Taeko Brooks. *The Original Analects: Sayings of Confucius and His Successors*. Columbia University Press, 1998.

Buckle, Stephen. "Aristotle's Republic, or Why Aristotle's Ethics Is Not Virtue Ethics." *Philosophy* 77, no. 302 (2002): 565–595.

Bunnin, Nicholas. "God's Knowledge and Ours: Kant and Mou Zongsan on Intellectual Intuition." *Journal of Chinese Philosophy* 35, no. 4 (2008): 613–624.

Chan, N. Serina. *The Thought of Mou Zongsan.* Brill, 2011.

Chang, Carsun. "A Manifesto for a Re-appraisal of Sinology and Reconstruction of Chinese Culture." In *The Development of Neo-Confucian Thought,* volume 2. Bookman Associates, 1962.

Cohon, Rachel. "Hume's Artificial and Natural Virtues." In *The Blackwell Guide to Hume's Treatise,* ed. Saul Traiger. Blackwell, 2006.

DeBary, William Theodore. *The Message of the Mind in Neo-Confucianism.* Columbia University Press, 1989.

Elstein, David. "Mou Zongsan's New Confucian Democracy." *Contemporary Political Theory* 11 (2012): 192–210.

Fan, Ruiping, ed. *The Renaissance of Confucianism in Contemporary China.* Springer, 2011.

Frank, Jill. *A Democracy of Distinction: Aristotle and the Work of Politics.* University of Chicago Press, 2005.

He, Baogang. "Knavery and Virtue in Humean Institutional Design." *Journal of Value Inquiry* 37 (2003): 543–553.

Hume, David. "An Enquiry Concerning the Principles of Morals." In *Hume's Ethical Writings: Selections from David Hume,* ed. Alasdair MacIntyre. University of Notre Dame Press, 1965.

Hume, David. "Of the Independency of Parliament." In *Essays Moral, Political, and Literary.* In *The Complete Works and Correspondence of David Hume.* InteLex, 2000.

Hume, David. "Of the Original Contract." In *Hume's Ethical Writings: Selections from David Hume,* ed. Alasdair MacIntyre. University of Notre Dame Press, 1965.

Hume, David. *A Treatise of Human Nature,* ed. P. H. Nidditch. Oxford University Press, 1978.

Jiang Qing 蒋庆. *Zhengzhi ruxue: dangdai ruxue de zhuanxiang, tezhi yu fazhan* 政治儒学: 当代儒学的转向、特质与发展. Harvard-Yenching Academic Series. Beijing: *Shenghuo dushu xin zhi sanlian shudian* 生活读书新知三联书店 2003.

Lin Anwu 林安梧. *Ruxue geming lun: houxinruxue zhexue de wenti xiangdu* 儒學革命論: 後新儒學哲學的問題向度. Taipei: *Xuesheng shuju* 學生書局, 1998.

McArthur, Neil. *David Hume's Political Theory: Law, Commerce, and the Constitution of Government.* University of Toronto Press, 2007.

Mou Zongsan 牟宗三. *Xianxiang yu wuzishen* 現象與物自身. Taipei: *Xuesheng shuju* 學生書局, 1975.

Mou Zongsan 牟宗三. *Zhongguo zhexue shijiu jiang* 中國哲學十九講. Taipei: *Xuesheng shuju* 學生書局, 1983.

Mou Zongsan 牟宗三. *Zhengdao yu zhidao* 政道與治道. Xuesheng Shuju 學生書局, 1991.

Mou Zongsan 牟宗三, Xu Fuguan 徐復觀, Zhang Junmai 張君勱, and Tang Junyi 唐君毅. "*Wei Zhongguo wenhua jinggao shijie renshi xuanyan* 为中国文化敬告世界人士宣言." In *Dangdai xinrujia* 当代新儒家, ed. Feng Zusheng 封祖盛, 1–52. Beijing: *Shenghuo dushu xin zhi sanlian shudian* 生活读书新知三联书店, 1989.

Rawls, John. *A Theory of Justice*. Harvard University Press, 1971.

Slote, Michael. "The Mandate of Empathy." *Dao* 9, no. 3 (2010): 303–07.

Tang Zhonggang 汤忠钢. *Dexing yu zhengzhi: Mou Zongsan xinrujia zhengzhi zhexue yanjiu* 德性与政治:牟宗三新儒家政治哲学研究. Beijing: *Zhongguo yanshi chubanshe* 中国言实出版社, 2008.

Taylor, Jacqueline. "Justice and the Foundations of Social Morality in Hume's Treatise." *Human Studies* 24, no. 1 (1998): 5–30.

Van Norden, Bryan W. *Virtue Ethics and Consequentialism in Early Chinese Philosophy*. Cambridge University Press, 2007.

Wallace, James D. "Virtues of Benevolence and Justice." In *Virtue Ethics and Moral Education*, ed. David Carr and Jan Steutel. Routledge, 1999.

Westphal, Kenneth R. "From 'Convention' to 'Ethical Life': Hume's Theory of Justice in Post-Kantian Perspective." *Journal of Moral Philosophy* 7, no. 1 (2010): 105–132.

Wiggins, David. "Natural and Artificial Virtues: A Vindication of Hume's Scheme." In *How Should One Live? Essays on the Virtues*, ed. Roger Crisp. Oxford University Press, 1996.

Yu Dan 于丹. *Yu Dan Lunyu xinde* 于丹《论语》心得. Beijing: *Zhonghua shuju* 中华书局, 2006.

Yu, Jiyuan. *The Ethics of Confucius and Aristotle: Mirrors of Virtue*. Routledge, 2007.

Yu, Jiyuan. "The 'Manifesto' of New Confucianism and the Revival of Virtue Ethics." Tr. Lei Yongqiang. *Frontiers of Philosophy in China* 3, no. 3 (2008): 317–334.

Yu Ying-shih 余英時. "*Xiandai Ruxue de huigu yu zhanwang* 现代儒学的回顾与展望." In *Xiandai Ruxue de huigu yu zhanwang* 现代儒学的回顾与展望. Beijing: *Shenghuo dushu xin zhi sanlian shudian* 生活读书新知三联书店, 2004.

7 Ethical Self-Commitment and Ethical Self-Indulgence

Kwong-loi Shun

1 Introduction

In this chapter, I discuss a phenomenon highlighted in Confucian thought that I refer to as *ethical self-commitment*. The purpose is to present a certain perspective on our ethical life that is distinctive of the Confucian ethical tradition, explore its implications, and draw out some of its features that might have a contemporary intelligibility and appeal. In addition, I will consider the question whether ethical self-commitment might evolve into a problematic form of ethical self-indulgence. The notion of ethical self-commitment is not intended to correspond to any specific attribute highlighted in Confucian thought. Instead, I use the notion to refer to a phenomenon that is related to the Confucian understanding of the ethical attribute *yi* 義 (propriety) as well as other attributes such as *cheng* 誠 (wholeness), *xu* 虛 (vacuity) and *jing* 靜 (stillness).[1]

In section 2, I present the historical background to the Confucian understanding of *yi*, and introduce one aspect of the notion of ethical self-commitment against this background. My discussion in that section draws on the textual studies I have conducted elsewhere.[2] In section 3, I give a more systematic account of this aspect of ethical self-commitment, relating it to phenomena highlighted in contemporary discussions of the notion of self-respect. In section 4, I consider how this aspect of self-commitment leads to a detached posture of the mind that I refer to as *reflective equanimity*. In section 5, I introduce another aspect of the notion of ethical self-commitment that has to do with a phenomenon that I refer to as *purity of the mind* and that is related to the Confucian understanding of *cheng*, *xu*, and *jing*. The discussion of *cheng*, *xu*, and *jing* again draws on textual studies I have conducted elsewhere, while my discussion of reflective equanimity and of purity in sections 4 and 5 draws on a series of earlier papers.[3]

In section 6, I introduce the notion of ethical self-indulgence, and consider the potential for ethical self-indulgence in relation to a reflective concern with one's own ethical qualities, a reflective concern that I refer to as *ethical self-regard*. I draw on contemporary discussions of the phenomenon of moral self-indulgence and of an objection to ethical views that focus on the notion of virtue, to the effect that these views are too self-centered. In section 7, I consider the potential for ethical self-indulgence specifically in relation to ethical self-commitment. In section 8, I conclude with some general observations about the Confucian position.

2 The Confucian Understanding of *Yi*

In early Confucian thought, *yi* 義 (propriety) is often mentioned along with two other attributes, *ren* 仁 (humaneness) and *li* 禮 (observance of the rites).[4] *Ren*, as one attribute among others, has to do primarily with one's concern for the interests and well-being of others. Such a concern is sometimes presented in later Confucian thought in terms of one's forming one body with others, in the sense that one is attentive and sensitive to others' well-being in the way that one is attentive and sensitive to what happens to parts of one's own body.

Li is used to refer to rules of conduct governing ceremonial behavior in recurring social contexts as well as behavior appropriate to one's social position. As an attribute of a person, it refers to a general disposition to follow such rules, with special emphasis on the attitude behind such behavior. This attitude is described in a number of ways, but what is common to these descriptions is a general attitude that involves one's focusing on and having a serious regard for others in a way that would have been appropriate to someone of higher status than oneself.[5] At the same time, one avoids having oneself at the forefront of one's thinking when interacting with others—for example, one does not unnecessarily display oneself nor seek attention and admiration.

As for *yi*, its earlier meaning had to do with a sense of honor and an absence of disgrace; it was a matter of not allowing oneself to be subject to disgraceful treatment. One's attitude toward disgrace (*ru* 辱) is referred to as *chi* 恥. *Chi* focuses on disgrace as something beneath oneself that lowers one's standing. Though often translated as "shame," *chi* differs from contemporary Western notions of shame in important respects. It can be directed toward something contemplated as well as something that has already come about. It is associated not with the thought of being seen or the urge to hide oneself, but with the thought of being tainted and the urge to cleanse oneself of what is tainting.[6] *Chi* is linked to a resolution to either remedy the disgraceful situation if it has already obtained, or to distance oneself from or pre-empt a potentially disgraceful situation if it has not yet come about.[7]

In early China, what is regarded as disgraceful is often treatment that is insulting (*wu* 侮) by public standards, such as being beaten in public, being stared in the eyes, or being treated in violation of certain accepted protocols of conduct that include *li*. Correspondingly, *chi* is associated with not just a sense of being tainted by a disgraceful situation, but also anger at the offending party and thoughts of vengeance. Early Confucians, however, advocate a transformation in what one regards as disgraceful—it should not be a matter of how others view or treat us, but a matter of our own ethical conduct. The proper object of *chi* is the ethical shortcoming in one's conduct, and *chi* is no longer linked to thoughts of vengeance. Instead, it has more to do with the resolve to distance oneself from certain situations that can be ethically tainting on oneself and to correct such situations should they arise.[8]

On the Confucian view, *yi* has to do with a resolve to distance oneself from disgraceful situations where disgrace is understood in ethical terms. It is a firm commitment to certain ethical standards, of such a kind that it can override personal interests of the most pressing kind, including one's own life. The Confucians do not deny that other conditions of life are important, but for them there is nothing more important than following the ethical path, and any other pursuit in life should be subject to the constraints of the ethical. Furthermore, it is fully within one's control to live up to the ethical standards to which one is committed, and this commitment to the ethical is independent of external influence. Someone so committed will not be led to deviate from the ethical by external influences, and this commitment itself is also something that no external force can deprive one of.

Mencius (fourth century BCE) sometimes contrasts *ren* and *yi* by saying that *ren* has to do with the human heart while *yi* has to do with the human path.[9] His point is that, while *ren* has to do with one's affective concern for others, *yi* has to do with the propriety of one's conduct. *Yi* also differs from both *ren* and *li* in another way. Unlike *ren* and *li*, *yi* involves an element of reflectivity in that it presupposes one's having a conception of certain ethical standards to which one's way of life should conform. Furthermore, one is motivated by that conception, and is firmly committed not to allow oneself to fall below such standards. For now, I will use the notion of ethical self-commitment to refer to such a commitment. Later, I will broaden the notion to include a commitment not just to acting in conformity with certain ethical standards but also to shaping one's whole person in accordance with a reflective conception of the ethical.

3 Ethical Self-Commitment and Self-Respect

The notion of ethical self-commitment relates to certain phenomena highlighted in contemporary discussions of self-respect. Without focusing too much on the different usages of the term "self-respect," it would nevertheless be useful to consider the phenomena with which its use has been associated and to situate the notion of ethical self-commitment in relation to them.

One phenomenon has to do with a favorable view of oneself by virtue of certain positive qualities one has, just as one might form a favorable view of another person based on certain positive qualities that the other person has. The phenomenon is often discussed in relation to self-esteem, though it might also provide one sense in which we may speak of self-respect—just as one can esteem or respect another person for certain qualities that the other person has, one can also esteem or respect oneself for having such qualities.[10]

Another phenomenon has to do with an ideal conception of the kind of life one lives, and a commitment not to fall below the standards that define such a way of life.[11] This phenomenon may take on different forms depending on the nature of the relevant standards. These standards might focus on what is due to oneself, and the commitment involved is a commitment not to allow oneself to be treated in violation of such standards. Or they might focus on the ethical standards that govern one's way of life, and a commitment to not fall below such standards in one's qualities and in the way one conducts oneself.

In either of these two forms, this second phenomenon differs from the first. For example, the first phenomenon can take on an excessive form because of an overly positive assessment of one's own qualities. The second phenomenon, however, is not in itself a response to an assessment of one's own qualities, and so cannot be excessive or unwarranted in this manner.[12] The first phenomenon need not, though it might, accompany the second. One might be committed to certain standards without necessarily having a favorable view of oneself by virtue of being so committed, though one might as a matter of fact have such a favorable view. That is, the second phenomenon can provide grounds for the first, but does not necessarily entail it.

That one's commitment to not fall short of certain standards might take on these two different forms is noted by various authors.[13] The early Confucian transformation of the understanding of *yi* might be regarded as a shift from a focus on one form to a focus on the other. According to the early Confucians, disgrace should be understood not in terms of the way one is treated, but in terms of our living up to certain ethical standards in our own conduct. Thus, ethical self-commitment of the kind highlighted in the Confucian understanding of *yi* is akin to the latter form that the second phenomenon takes.[14]

To elaborate further on the notion, ethical self-commitment involves in an essential way certain evaluative judgments. These judgments are not a matter of a positive view of oneself by virtue of certain qualities in oneself that one positively apprises, but a matter of subscription to certain ethical standards that one commits to upholding. Ethical self-commitment is not just a matter of evaluative judgments but also involves one's motivations in an essential way—it moves one to do or refrain from doing certain things.[15]

Now, one might be committed to abiding by certain standards because one regards the relevant standards as standards that everyone should observe, and act on the basis of such a judgment. This would be true, for example, of conscientiousness. But in ethical self-commitment, one also regards oneself as related to such standards in a special way—one regards falling below such standards as something unworthy of oneself and would respond in a way different from one's response to others' falling below similar standards.[16] Though the early Confucians transformed the understanding of *yi* to focus on one's own ethical conduct instead of the way one is treated by others, *yi* is still associated with a view of what is honorable or disgraceful, albeit understood in ethical rather than social terms.

The notion of ethical self-commitment, understood in this manner, might also characterize other ethical traditions besides the Confucian tradition. However, the way it is viewed by the Confucians takes on a distinctive form. We saw earlier that, for them, a failure to live up to the relevant standards is associated with *chi*, which differs from the notion of shame. In addition, they relate ethical self-commitment to a range of phenomena that have to do with ways in which someone so committed can transcend the external circumstances of life and thereby attain what I will refer to as a state of *reflective equanimity*.

4 Ethical Self-Commitment and Reflective Equanimity

This sense of transcendence stems from the two features of the Confucian view of ethical self-commitment mentioned earlier. This commitment is entirely within one's control and independent of external influence, and someone so committed regards upholding the relevant standards as of greater significance than any other kinds of pursuit or other external conditions of life.

Such a person maintains an independence from the way she is viewed by others. While she might desire appreciation by others and is sensitive to others' opinions as indicators of her own qualities, she will stand firm on the standards to which she is committed even if not appreciated by others. Even when looked down upon for external factors such as social status, she is little affected as she can take comfort in the realization that she has lived up to the standards to which she is committed.[17]

This sense of transcendence also extends to the way she is treated by others. The Confucians do not deny that how we are viewed or treated by others does matter. Confucius (551?–479? BCE) did lament the lack of appreciation by others, and certain kinds of treatment can of course be humiliating and hurtful even to the Confucians. The Confucian position is that, even though these things do matter, they pale in significance compared to our own ethical qualities. When we do not fare well in relation to the former, at least the latter is something we can fall back on and take consolation in.

This sense of transcendence also extends to other external circumstances of life. When presented with adverse circumstances that are either literally not within one's control or can only be altered through unethical means that one would not adopt, the person may still be affected—she may feel sorrow at the death of a beloved one, be disappointed by the lack of appreciation by others, or lament the ethical corruption of the times. But she would not be psychologically disturbed—she would not be bitter or resentful, would not devote energy to complaining about the outcome, and would not dwell on thoughts about how things could have been different nor seek to alter things by improper means. Instead, she would take contentment in the ethical in that she is immersed in the ethical and flows along with it with a sense of ease and without anxiety.[18]

To elaborate, the truly ethical person cannot be harmed by others or by external circumstances in a way that is of deepest significance to her.[19] She does attach importance to various pursuits and conditions of life other than the ethical, and so she can be affected if things do not go well. She can be frustrated if she fails in her endeavors, can feel sorrow upon the loss of a loved one, and can feel hurt at the way she has been treated by others. In these various ways, she can still be harmed. However, she is aware that what is of greatest significance—following the ethical path—is entirely within her control and cannot be affected by external influences. Thus, she cannot be harmed in the way that is of the deepest significance to her. Such harm can only be self-inflicted, as the only person who can ultimately lead her to deviate from the ethical is she herself.

In these different but connected ways, ethical self-commitment enables one to transcend the external circumstances of life. This discussion also suggests that the mind of the truly ethical person operates on two levels. On the one hand, she does care about various conditions of life, and would take appropriate action to pursue what she does care about, as well as respond to the outcomes in a way that engages her emotions and feelings. This describes the first level of operation of the mind, which comprises the more immediate responses to one's environment, responses that change with the way one relates to the environment. On the other hand, even if the outcomes go against her wishes and she responds with disappointment, frustration, pain, or sorrow, she would at the same time take on a posture that enables her to stand apart from such responses. Having done what she could within the bounds of the ethical, she would not dwell on the outcomes in a way that leads to anxiety, fear, or uncertainty. Instead, she would stay content in the awareness that what is of greatest significance to her, namely following the ethical path, remains intact. This describes the second level of operation of the mind, which involves a more detached posture toward one's environment.

For convenience, I will refer to this posture of the mind as a state of *equanimity* or, to be more exact, a state of reflective equanimity. The notion of equanimity is often associated with connotations such as calmness of mind, maintaining one's balance in the face of trying circumstances, and being unperturbed. The posture of mind we just considered involves such qualities. At the same time, it also involves a certain reflective stance: one's awareness and affirmation of the fact that one is flowing along with the ethical. Unlike the more immediate responses to one's environment, this posture is a more enduring state that is grounded in this reflective stance, and it involves a certain outlook, posture, or orientation in life, having to do with the way one views and relates to the world. Thus, this posture may be referred to as a state of reflective equanimity in that it is grounded in such a reflective stance.[20]

5 Ethical Self-Commitment and Purity of the Mind

I introduced the notion of ethical self-commitment in connection with the Confucian understanding of the ethical attribute *yi*, which focuses primarily on the ethical propriety of human conduct. But, for the Confucians, what one should devote oneself to is not just the propriety of conduct, but also shaping all aspects of one's person, including the subtlest thoughts and motivations, in an ethical direction. Whereas *yi* is used more typically in relation to human conduct, the Confucians use other terms to convey this idea of a complete ethical orientation of one's whole person.

One such term is *cheng* 誠, which refers to the complete ethical orientation of the whole person, including both her psychological activities and the way she conducts herself, as well as the congruence between the two. Another pair of terms *xu* 虛 and *jing* 靜 emphasize the absence of any psychological elements that might detract from this orientation. *Xu* emphasizes the absence of such detracting elements, while *jing* emphasizes the absence of the disturbing effects on the mind due to these detracting elements.[21]

I will refer to as the *purity of the mind* both the complete ethical orientation of the person and the absence of detracting elements and their disturbing effects.[22] This use of "purity" draws on its two connotations: that of entirety (as in the locution "this is pure orange juice") and that of the absence of contaminating elements (as in the locution "this air is pure"). Thus, although *yi* is not used to refer to a commitment to such a complete ethical orientation, the Confucians do advocate such a commitment and much of what I said about *yi* also applies to this broader commitment. For example, the Confucians believe that everyone is capable of shaping oneself in this direction, and one's doing so is of greater significance than other external conditions of life.

For this reason, from here on I will use the notion of ethical self-commitment more broadly to refer to a commitment to one's living up to a certain reflective conception of the ethical that includes not just one's conduct but also all aspects of the mind's activities, including its subtlest thoughts and motivations.[23] For the Confucians, one needs to be constantly self-reflective and self-vigilant to attain this state. One should be watchful over not just one's actions but also the subtle activities of the mind, including its minute thoughts and subtle feelings that are not externally conspicuous, and be prepared to take corrective steps if needed. At the same time, one should always be focused, alert, and in full control of one's mental attention, so that one is not vulnerable to distractions. This state of purity and the different kinds of exercise involved in managing the mind's activities are particularly highlighted in later Confucian thought.[24]

Though it might appear that this kind of reflectivity and vigilance are at work primarily in the process of self-cultivation, they should still be implicitly at work even in the state of purity. Having gone through a lifetime of moral learning and cultivation, the truly ethical person might now be able to respond appropriately to the situations she confronts without effort. But even so, this reflectivity and vigilance is still at work in that her mind is still implicitly monitoring her responses to her environment, would intervene if anything goes wrong or is about to go wrong, and would need to engage in more active and deliberate reflections if she confronts unfamiliar and challenging situations. So, the mind of the truly ethical person again operates on two levels. On the one hand, there are the immediate responses to one's environment, including not just actions but also the various aspects of the operations of the mind. On the other hand, the mind is constantly, if only implicitly, monitoring these first-level responses to ensure that they are ethically appropriate, and is ready to intervene if needed. This second-level operation of the mind ensures that all its responses are in conformity to the ethical, thereby ensuring purity of the mind.[25]

In the previous section, we also considered a two-tiered picture of the mind, where the mind's second-level operation involves the posture of reflectivity equanimity. To distinguish between these two aspects of the operation of the mind at the second level, I will refer to them as the *directive* aspect and the *detached* aspect. The *directive* aspect involves the mind's being constantly watchful over its first-level responses to ensure that they are properly directed. The *detached* aspect refers to the posture of the mind that enables the person to stand apart from his immediate responses to the environment even if things go against her wishes and even if she responds with disappointment, frustration, pain, or sorrow.

Although I have spoken of two different levels on which the mind operates, this is just a metaphorical way of describing different but still inter-connected dimensions of the mind's operations. The directive aspect of the second level of operation is clearly connected to the first level of operation, but even the detached posture of the mind is so connected. This posture enables one to stay anchored and unperturbed by one's immediate environment and one's immediate responses to that environment. But the fact that one stays unperturbed at this second level also helps to ensure that the first-level responses are appropriate and properly reflect what one regards as important. It does so not by directly intervening in the mind's activities, but by keeping the mind free from disturbing influences that might have otherwise affected its first-level responses.

The directive and detached aspects of the mind's operations are both grounded in a reflective conception of the ethical. This raises the question whether the involvement of this reflective conception might lead to a problematic redirection of one's thoughts and attention. In performing a directive function, would this reflective conception be playing a motivational role in one's responses to the environment that detracts from the value of such responses? For example, would a helping action come to be motivated by this reflective conception rather than by a direct concern for the well-being of the recipient? And suppose that I fail to help in the way I wish to, and respond with frustration and sorrow at the suffering that I failed to relieve. The detached posture of the mind involves my not being disturbed by these first-level responses, taking comfort in the fact that I have done what is ethically appropriate. But does my adopting this posture mean that I am putting more weight on my having done what is ethically appropriate than on the well-being of the intended recipient of the helping action?

Such potential misdirection of ethical attention has often been labeled moral self-indulgence, and has been highlighted in an objection to ethical views that focus on the notion of virtue, to the effect that such ethical views are too "self-centered." From here on I will refer to as *ethical self-indulgence* a problematic redirection of one's attention toward oneself in an ethical context.[26] Before considering ethical self-indulgence in relation specifically to ethical self-commitment, I will first consider it as a potential problem for ethical views that emphasize a reflective concern with one's own ethical qualities, a concern that I will refer to as *ethical self-regard*.

6 Ethical Self-Regard and Ethical Self-Indulgence

I will use the term "self-regard" to refer to any kind of concern with oneself, that is, any state of mind in which one's attention, thoughts, and motivations are directed to something related to oneself. This is the sense in which we refer to a desire whose object has to do with something related to oneself as a self-regarding desire. As for "ethical self-regard," it refers to any kind of concern that is directed to the ethical qualities of oneself, where the ethical has to do with a conception of how humans should live. For example, a concern with one's having qualities that embody this ethical conception is a form of ethical self-regard, and so is a concern that one acts in a particular situation in a manner consistent with such a conception. Ethical self-commitment, as I have introduced the notion, is one form of ethical self-regard.

Corresponding to self-regard, we may use "self-centeredness" to refer to the evolvement of self-regard into forms that place an inappropriate focus on oneself. Similarly, corresponding to the notion of ethical self-regard, we may use "ethical self-indulgence" to refer to the evolvement of ethical self-regard into forms that place an inappropriate focus on oneself. Just as ethical self-regard is a form of self-regard, ethical self-indulgence is a form of self-centeredness. Later Confucians ascribe ethical failure to self-centeredness, for which they have a specific term, *si* 私. We will not be concerned with self-centeredness as such, but only with ethical self-indulgence.

Ethical self-regard involves a reflective conception of certain qualities as ethically desirable, and one's being motivated in a way that is guided by that conception. It is a kind of reflexive concern—it presupposes one's having an ideal conception of the qualities of oneself and of one's actions, one's applying that conception to oneself, and one's being motivated by that conception.[27] Such a reflexive concern is not problematic as such, but becomes problematic when it evolves into a form that involves a misdirection of one's thoughts, attention, and concern, in a way that places an undue focus on oneself.

Such problematic evolvement can take different forms. For example, one may come to care more about one's having the relevant ethical qualities than caring about the things that one would care about by virtue of having such qualities. That is, one's image of oneself as having such qualities is more important in one's thoughts than the things that would be regarded as important by someone with such qualities.[28] When this happens, the second-order motivation to have these qualities in oneself comes to displace the first-order motivations that are part of the qualities with which that second-order motivation is concerned. Such displacement can manifest itself in different ways. One might be thinking too often about how good one is or should be, ignoring pressing other-regarding needs as a result of this excessive concern with self-improvement. Or one might be viewing oneself as being in ethical competition with others, and be filled with anxieties about one's ethical shortcomings.

Alternatively, the problematic evolvement may take the form of one's attention being too other-directed, but in a way that is still focused on oneself—one is too concerned about the ethical assessment of oneself by others. In this case, what is at work is not one's having an image of oneself as having certain qualities, but one's having an image of oneself as being seen by others as having certain qualities. In any of these forms, the problematic evolvement of ethical self-regard involves a shift of one's thoughts and attention, even though the object of one's attention might by itself appear not different from that in the unproblematic cases of a concern with one's own self-improvement.[29] This is a misdirection not just of attention but genuinely of concern, as it affects one's feelings such as what one takes pleasure in, as well as what actually gets done; in this way, it can undermine the very quality with which one is concerned.[30]

In the literature, certain lines of thought have been put forward showing how ethical self-regard might lead to such a misdirection of attention. While ethical self-regard could potentially evolve in this manner, there appears no reason to believe that it will necessarily so evolve. That is, although ethical self-indulgence might turn out to be a practical problem in certain contexts, there appears no general theoretical reason to believe that it will be a problem for any reflective concern with one's own ethical qualities.

One line of thought notes that the terms we use to describe ethically desirable qualities do not typically occur in the deliberation of the person with such qualities. These "virtue terms" are more typically third person descriptions of someone with the qualities. A reflective concern with cultivating such qualities in oneself, framed in these terms, would show that one is concerned primarily with these third person descriptions of oneself, and hence with how others view oneself.[31]

Without denying that someone concerned with these qualities might, as a matter fact, become more concerned with how she is viewed by others, there is no reason to believe that such a concern must evolve in this manner. Even if the terms describing these qualities are typically used as third person descriptions, one's concern with the qualities describable in such terms need not be a concern with one's being describable by others in a certain way. Instead, it could be a concern with one's becoming like the kind of person that one would *oneself* describe in that way. That is, the third person description is a description of others by oneself, rather than of oneself by others. And in being so concerned, the primary object of one's concern need not be the description as such, but could still be one's having certain qualities which, as it happens, can be described in this way.[32]

Other attempts to link a reflective concern with one's own ethical qualities to ethical self-indulgence can be found in recent discussions surrounding the idea of virtue ethics. For example, some have made the point that, in an ethical view that focuses on the virtues, such a reflective concern could displace a concern for the well-being or for the ethical qualities of others. Various responses to this line of thought can be found in the literature, and I will not rehearse the details here.[33] The basic point is that there is no general theoretical reason why such a reflective concern must evolve in this problematic manner. And, within Confucian thought, the emphasis on the cultivation of various ethical attributes is actually coupled with the view that the truly ethical person is someone who is also concerned for the well-being as well as ethical qualities of others.[34]

Certain other attempts to link a reflective concern with one's own ethical qualities to ethical self-indulgence invoke additional assumptions. For example, some have highlighted the potential for ethical self-indulgence if the concern for the well-being or the ethical qualities of others is viewed as somehow instrumental to the concern with one's own ethical qualities.[35] Admittedly, there can be additional assumptions invoked that would give reason to believe that a reflective concern with one's own ethical qualities will lead inevitably to ethical self-indulgence. But this is a problem not for the reflective concern as such; it is a problem only for ethical views that endorse these additional assumptions. There is no reason why the reflective concern must itself be coupled with such assumptions, such as the assumption that the good of others is instrumental to one's own good.[36]

7 Ethical Self-Commitment and Ethical Self-Indulgence

Let us turn now to ethical self-commitment, one aspect of which is built into the Confucian understanding of *yi*. The potential for ethical self-indulgence arises for *yi* in a way that it does not for other ethical attributes such as *ren* (humaneness) and *li* (observance of the rites). A person of *ren* or *li* will have appropriate concern or regard for others, but not necessarily a reflective concern for her own ethical qualities. By contrast, *yi* as such already embodies a reflective conception of certain ethical standards that one should not fall short of. Furthermore, the perspective of the *yi* person is not just that these are standards that everyone should abide by and hence that she should also abide by them. Rather, there is an added element to her perspective that relates her own honor or disgrace to these standards, and it is this element that makes *yi* particularly vulnerable to the charge of ethical self-indulgence.

The same potential worry applies to the broader notion of ethical self-commitment. Ethical self-commitment involves a reflective conception of the ethical and a commitment to live up to that conception. The ethical person would be responding in various ways to the environment, while that reflective conception would at the same time be at work on another level in the two respects described earlier, the directive and the detached. The potential worry is that the operation of this reflective conception might affect the first-level responses in a way that leads to a problematic redirection of one's thoughts and attention.

This worry can be described in terms of a potential tension in combining two points of view. From *inside* the perspective of the ethical person, one's attention is on what someone with the ethically desirable qualities would regard as important. But having a reflective conception of these qualities as ethically desirable involves an *outside* perspective from which the attention is on these qualities themselves. The concern is that taking up this outside point of view would alienate one from the inside point of view by virtue of which one is an ethical person.[37] Furthermore, if this reflective conception plays some kind of motivational role in one's psychology, it seems that one's thoughts about one's own qualities would become part of one's motives, and this smacks of a form of ethical self-indulgence.[38]

One response to this worry is to take the position that a reflective conception of the ethical is just a philosophers' conception and need not be part of the viewpoint of the ethical person.[39] However, to the extent that we do have a reflective conception of the ethical, it seems odd to insist that the ethical person should be precluded from having such a conception. Presumably, even the ethical person would at times reflect on the kind of life to lead and would have some such conception, albeit in a minimal form.[40] And it seems that the ethical person should have such a conception for at least two reasons. First, it seems desirable that people not just live the ethical life, but also regard that way of life as desirable, and actually live that way of life because of such an understanding. And second, it seems that having such a conception can actually strengthen one's commitment to that way of life, provide a backup should one's ethical dispositions weaken, and enable one to cope with new and unfamiliar circumstances of life on the basis of such a conception.[41]

But once we acknowledge that the ethical person could, and maybe should, have such a reflective conception, that conception would presumably be playing some motivational role—there would be no point in having such a reflective conception if it makes no difference to the way one lives. The key to addressing the worry about ethical self-indulgence is to distinguish between two kinds of motivational role. Drawing on a distinction I made in previous publications, a certain consideration will be playing a *directly motivating role* in case one acts because one expects one's action to bring about a desirable effect relative to that consideration, and is prepared to adjust one's action so as to bring about or maximize such effect. By contrast, it will be playing a *constraining role* if, when one acts, one is prepared to avoid courses of action that have an undesirable effect relative to that consideration or to adjust one's action to minimize such effect. For example, financial considerations will be playing a directly motivating role in a helping action if one helps with the goal of financial gain, but only a constraining role if one helps in a way that avoids excessive financial cost or minimizes such cost.

Even when a consideration plays a constraining role, it will make a difference to a person's thoughts and feelings in acting. For example, if financial considerations play a constraining role with regard to a helping action, one may have thoughts about the cost of helping and may be relieved at finding a more affordable way of helping. These aspects of a helping action are not problematic as such. But if financial considerations play a directly motivating role, they will affect the person's thoughts and feelings in a more fundamental way. They will become her main guiding thoughts in helping and will also become the main measure of success. What she will take pleasure in is financial gain as such, not just being able to help in an affordable manner. As a result, not only will the recipient of the helping action feel that his being helped is instrumental to her financial gain, but her attention will be redirected in a way that may lead her to miss certain features of the situation, resulting in her failing to help in a way that she otherwise could.

Thus, it is only when other considerations play a directly motivating role, rather than a constraining role, that the potential for a misdirection of thoughts and attention arises. Accordingly, there is no genuine tension between the inside and the outside' points of view if the reflective conception of the ethical plays only a constraining role in the psychology of the ethical person. The potential for ethical self-indulgence arises only if the reflective conception plays a directly motivating role, but nothing in what I have said so far requires it to play that role.[42]

Consider the directive aspect of the mind's operations. It involves the mind's endorsing a reflective conception of the ethical, and its being ready to intervene on the basis of that conception if anything goes wrong or is about to go wrong. This aspect of the mind's operation requires the reflective conception to play only a constraining, not directly motivating, role. A constraining role does imply that one would refrain from doing anything that deviates from that conception in the course of helping. But this is just to say that one would not act unethically in order to help, which is exactly what we would expect of the truly ethical person. When the person helps, she will be helping out of a genuine concern for the well-being of the recipient, not in order to live up to that reflective conception. And when she succeeds in helping, she will take pleasure primarily in the recipient's having been helped, not in her having been able to act ethically.

Consider now the detached posture of the mind that enables the truly ethical person to remain undisturbed despite the adverse circumstances of life. Suppose the ethically appropriate thing for her to do is to help someone in need, and though she attempts to do so, she fails to provide relief due to external hindrances. While feeling frustration and sorrow, she will not feel disturbed, taking comfort in the fact that she has done what is ethically appropriate. Would this posture show that she is putting more weight on her having acted ethically than on the well-being of others?

Now, in a sense, she does regard her following the ethical path as more important than the external conditions of life, including the well-being of others. But this is true only in the sense that she would not act unethically even if by doing so she can accomplish her goals including relieving the suffering of others. This constraining role of the reflective conception does not lead to a problematic redirection of her emotional engagement with the situation. Just as her awareness that she has acted ethically does not detract from the pleasure she feels at the recipient's having been helped when her helping action succeeds, it does not detract from her frustration and sorrow when her helping action fails. Her detached posture implies only that she stays anchored in her awareness that she has followed the ethical path and is not vulnerable to uncertainty, temptation to act unethically, or anxiety about how things could have been different. It does not mean that her frustration and sorrow are any less real or are replaced by some other kind of emotional response. They are still her dominant emotional responses, though without the disturbing effects just described.

To summarize, as long as the reflective conception of the ethical plays only a constraining role, this will not lead to an objectionable form of ethical self-indulgence. There might be moments when the ethical person would engage in conscious self-reflection, consciously thinking about her living up to this reflective conception. But this happens typically outside the immediate contexts of action and will not displace the thoughts and feelings that typically characterize the ethical person when she does act.[43]

Concluding Remarks

I began my discussion of ethical self-commitment by considering the Confucian understanding of the attribute *yi*. *Yi* differs from other ethical attributes such as *ren* and *li* in that it presupposes a reflective conception of the ethical standards to which the *yi* person is committed. Because of this difference, to describe a person as acting out of *yi* might smack of an objectionable redirection of the person's thoughts and attention in certain contexts. A person acting out of *ren* would be helping out of genuine concern for the well-being of the other party, while a person acting out of *li* would be treating someone in certain ways out of serious regard for the other party. For the person to act out of *yi* in these contexts, it seems, would be for her to act out of a concern that she herself lives up to certain standards in her actions, and this would constitute an objectionable redirection of her thoughts and attention. The focus, it seems, is too much on herself—she would be acting out of a concern that she acts in a way that is worthy of herself.[44]

There is genuine substance to this worry. To describe someone as acting out of *yi* suggests that the action is motivated by *yi* in the sense that it plays what I have referred to as a directly motivating role. In the kind of contexts just described, this does constitute a problematic redirection of the person's thoughts and attention.[45] But this is not a problem for the Confucian advocacy of *yi*, as the Confucian position is not committed to the view that, ideally, the ethical person should act out of *yi* in this sense. Instead, the ethical person whose motivations are appropriately structured would be acting out of the relevant kind of other-regarding concerns as appropriate to the situation. *Yi*, as a commitment to the relevant ethical standards, would be playing only what I have referred to as a constraining role, a role that is compatible with the action's being directly motivated by, and only by, the relevant other-regarding concerns. The person's attention would focus solely on the other party, without any conscious thoughts about her own qualities or honor, even though the commitment to the relevant standards is in the background, ready to intervene should she be tempted to deviate from such standards.

A similar point applies to ethical self-commitment as a broader notion that includes a commitment to ensuring that all aspects of one's own person, including one's subtle thoughts and motivations as well as actions, conform to the reflective ethical conception that one endorses. Just as *yi* might play a more active role when someone less than ethical is tempted to act inappropriately, ethical self-commitment in this broader sense also plays an active role when someone still falls short of that reflective conception. The person may have conscious and deliberate thoughts about how she can reshape herself in the ethical direction. This happens in the process of self-cultivation, and we often find in Confucian texts, especially in later Confucian thought, records of conversations between a master and his students in this connection. But just as *yi* plays only a constraining role in relation to the actions of the truly ethical person, ethical self-commitment in the broader sense plays only a constraining role in relation to the psychology of the truly ethical person. This role will not lead to a misdirection of her thoughts and attention, and so there is no general theoretical reason to believe that idealizing ethical self-commitment will render an ethical view vulnerable to the charge of ethical self-indulgence.

But this does not mean that ethical self-indulgence is not a genuine practical concern for such ethical views, in the sense that there is a practical risk of ethical self-commitment evolving in a problematic direction for certain individuals. On one interpretation, Mencius urges people not to be over-eager and not to be overly focused on their becoming ethical, in a way that ends up being detrimental to their own ethical development.[46] And Wang Yangming (1472–1529) also makes the point that the truly good person would not be consciously aiming at doing good; to have such conscious aims would itself detract from genuine goodness.[47] Thus, though ethical self-indulgence is not a general theoretical worry for the Confucian position, the Confucians are very much sensitive to the practical dangers of a misdirection of attention resulting from one's overly focusing on one's own ethical qualities.

Notes

1. In referring to these as "ethical attributes," I am deliberately avoiding the use of the word "virtue" as the latter is often used as a translation of *de* 德, a term that is not used to refer to some of these attributes, and to the extent that it is used to refer to some of the other attributes such as *yi*, this happens at a point later in the history of Chinese thought than the period I am focusing on.

2. Kwong-loi Shun, *Mencius and Early Chinese Thought*.

3. I provided the textual studies in "Purity in Confucian Thought," "Wholeness in Confucian Thought," and *Zhu Xi and Later Confucian Thought*. I discussed the phenomena of reflective equanimity and purity in a series of three papers: "Purity, Moral Trials, and Equanimity," "On Anger," and "On Reflective Equanimity."

4. For a more detailed discussion of these three attributes and their differences, see Shun, "Early Confucian Moral Psychology."

5. This attitude toward others is conveyed by the term *jing* 敬 as well as terms such as *gong* 恭, *jie* 戒, and *shen* 慎. It is a form of serious regard in that it involves focus of attention, dedication, attentiveness to one's manners and demeanor, caution, and being on guard against things going wrong in the way one interacts with others.

6. One example from *Mengzi* 2A:9, the context of which clearly relates to *chi*, is one's sitting on charcoal while wearing court clothes.

7. For further elaboration on *chi*, see Shun, *Mencius and Early Chinese Thought*, 58–63.

8. In a discussion of moral taint, Marina Oshana describes it as a fundamental disfigurement of the moral psyche and a compromise of the moral personality ("Moral Taint," 356). The Confucian notion of *chi* need not be associated with an ethical shortcoming that goes as deep as this, though the shortcoming is not superficial as would be suggested by the term "stain." For example, the object of *chi* can be an ethically problematic action of oneself. This shortcoming betrays flaws in one's character and so is not superficial, but such flaws can be remedied through one's own efforts and so need not constitute a major and fundamental disfigurement.

9. *Mengzi* 6A:11.

10. Gabriele Taylor speaks of self-esteem in this sense and relates self-esteem to the notion of being proud of something—one's favorable view of oneself for having a certain quality that one views positively is associated with one's feeling proud of having that quality (*Pride, Shame and Guilt*, 77–78).

11. Taylor understands self-respect in this manner, taking it to refer to a sense of one's own values (ibid., 131). She also relates self-respect to pride, in the sense of having one's pride (pp. 77–80).

12. David Sachs notes that, while we can understand the observation that someone has too much self-esteem, it would be odd to speak of someone as having too much self-respect ("How to Distinguish Self-Respect from Self-Esteem," 347–348).

13. See, for example, Colin Bird's distinction between what he calls entitlement-self-respect and standards-self-respect ("Self-Respect and the Respect of Others," 20), and Robin S. Dillon's distinction between what she calls R-self-respect and E-self-respect ("How to Lose Your Self-Respect," 126–127).

14. Bird makes a similar point in relation to the Stoic position, which he presents as subscribing to what he calls standards-self-respect rather than entitlement-self-respect. He also considers and rejects arguments to the effect that the Stoic position reflects a kind of "slave morality"—it advocates a kind of sublimated resentment that slaves feel toward their oppressors ("Self-Respect and the Respect of Others," 21–26).

15. Elizabeth Telfer makes a similar point of self-respect, noting that self-respect has a motivational, or conative, aspect ("Self Respect," 114–115).

16. The difference in the two kinds of response is conveyed by the difference between the terms *chi* 恥 and *wu* 惡 in classical Chinese, where the latter can be used of others' as well as one's own ethical shortcoming while the former can only be used of one's own ethical shortcoming. See Shun, *Mencius and Early Chinese Thought*, 58–60. Telfer also notes that, in self-respect, my relation to the standards to which I am committed is not merely that of a commitment to standards that apply to all; instead, I regard myself as dishonored or degraded if I fall short of such standards.

For this reason, she further adds that the conative aspect of self-respect is an "egoistically-tinged motive" ("Self Respect," 115–116).

17. A similar point is made by Bird in relation to the Stoic view of self-respect ("Self-Respect and the Respect of Others," 19).

18. See my discussion of the phenomena of acceptance and of contentment, conveyed through the Confucian understanding of *ming* 命 and *le* 樂, in "On Reflective Equanimity."

19. Telfer makes a similar point about how someone with self-respect has a sense of being one's own master and being in control of the situation, and cannot be overcome by adverse circumstances ("Self Respect," 117).

20. For further elaboration, see my "On Reflective Equanimity."

21. For analyses of the relevant terms, see Shun, "Purity in Confucian Thought," "Wholeness in Confucian Thought," and *Zhu Xi and Later Confucian Thought.*

22. For a discussion of the phenomenon of purity, see Shun, "Purity, Moral Trials, and Equanimity."

23. Pauline Chazan also relates a fundamental ethical commitment to the ideas of integrity and of wholeness ("Self-Esteem, Self-Respect, and Love of Self," 57).

24. See Shun, "Purity, Moral Trials, and Equanimity," for a more detailed discussion of these different kinds of exercise.

25. For further elaboration, see ibid.

26. I have used the term "ethical self-indulgence" instead of "moral self-indulgence," as the phenomenon I am discussing is broader than that usually associated with the latter term. For example, the concern with ethical self-indulgence might also arise in relation to the Daoist position, which is not usually described as a moral view. For a discussion of this broader phenomenon, which might arise for any reflective ethical view, see Shun, "Ideal Motivations and Reflective Understanding."

27. See Bernard Williams, "Utilitarianism and Moral Self-Indulgence," 46.

28. See ibid., 45.

29. For some examples of the different ways in which one's thoughts and attention might be misdirected, see pp. 112–114 of Edmund L. Pincoffs, *Quandaries and Virtues* and p. 103 of Robert M. Adams, *A Theory of Virtue.*

30. See Williams, "Utilitarianism and Moral Self-Indulgence," 47.

31. See Williams, *Ethics and the Limits of Philosophy,* 10–11.

32. See Shun, "Self and Self-Cultivation in Early Confucian Thought," 239–240.

33. See, for example, David Solomon, "Internal Objections to Virtue Ethics," 434–436.

34. See Yong Huang, "The Self-Centeredness Objection to Virtue Ethics" for a discussion of the Confucian position.

35. See, for example, Thómas Hurka, *Virtue, Vice, and Value*, 246–249.

36. For a response to Hurka, see Yong Huang, "The Self-Centeredness Objection to Virtue Ethics," 684–688. See also Christopher Toner, "The Self-Centeredness Objection to Virtue Ethics," 603–604 and 612–613, for a discussion of views that regard the good of others as derived from one's own good and those that do not subscribe to this derivation relation.

37. See Williams, *Ethics and the Limits of Philosophy*, 50–52.

38. In "Utilitarianism and Moral Self-Indulgence" (p. 49), Williams makes the suggestion that to construe integrity as a motive smacks of moral self-indulgence because this is to represent it in one's thoughts in an objectionably reflexive way, having to do with thoughts about oneself and one's own character. Some might make a similar point in relation to motivation by a reflective conception of the ethically desirable qualities.

39. See, for example, Rosalind Hursthouse, *On Virtue Ethics*, 136–139.

40. See Christopher Toner, "The Self-Centeredness Objection to Virtue Ethics," 600–601.

41. See Shun, "Ideal Motivations and Reflective Understanding," 92–93.

42. See Shun, ibid., 94–99.

43. See Robin S. Dillon, "How to Lose Your Self-Respect," 132.

44. Elizabeth Telfer describes a commitment to one's own worthy behavior as an "egoistically tinged motive" ("Self Respect," 116) and further notes that self-respect is too egoistic to be an appropriate basis for other-regarding conduct (p. 121).

45. Compare Williams' point about how it could be inappropriate to construe integrity as a motive. See Williams, "Utilitarianism and Moral Self-Indulgence," 49.

46. This is one interpretation of a certain part of *Mencius* 2A:2; see Shun, *Mencius and Early Chinese Thought*, 154–156.

47. This is one interpretation of the first sentence of Wang Yangming's Four Sentence Teaching, recorded in *Chuanxilu*, no. 315, 359–360, and this interpretation fits in with ideas in other passages. For a more detailed discussion, see Shun, "Self and Self-Cultivation in Early Confucian Thought," 107–108.

Works Cited

Adams, Robert Merrihew. *A Theory of Virtue: Excellence in Being for the Good*. Clarendon, 2006.

Bird, Colin. "Self-Respect and the Respect of Others." *European Journal of Philosophy* 18, no. 1 (2008): 17–40.

Chazan, Pauline. "Self-Esteem, Self-Respect, and Love of Self: Ways of Valuing the Self." *Philosophia* 26, no. 1–2 (1998): 41–63.

Dillon, Robin S. "How to Lose Your Self-Respect." *American Philosophical Quarterly* 29, no. 2 (1992): 125–139.

Huang, Yong. "The Self-Centeredness Objection to Virtue Ethics: Zhu Xi's Neo-Confucian Response." *American Catholic Philosophical Quarterly* 84, no. 4 (2010): 651–692.

Hurka, Thomas. *Virtue, Vice, and Value.* Oxford University Press, 2001.

Hursthouse, Rosalind. *On Virtue Ethics.* Oxford University Press, 1999.

Oshana, Marina A.L. "Moral Taint." *Metaphilosophy* 37, no. 3–4 (2006): 353–375.

Pincoffs, Edmund L. *Quandaries and Virtues: Against Reductivism in Ethics.* University Press of Kansas, 1986.

Sachs, David. "How to Distinguish Self-Respect from Self-Esteem." *Philosophy & Public Affairs* 10, no. 4 (1981): 346–360.

Shun, Kwong-loi. "Early Confucian Moral Psychology." In *Dao Companion to Classical Confucian Philosophy*, ed. Vincent Shen. Springer, 2014.

Shun, Kwong-loi. "Ideal Motivations and Reflective Understanding." *American Philosophical Quarterly* 33, no. 1 (1996): 91–104.

Shun, Kwong-loi. *Mencius and Early Chinese Thought.* Stanford University Press, 1997.

Shun, Kwong-loi. "On Anger: An Essay in Confucian Moral Psychology." In *Rethinking Zhu Xi: Emerging Patterns within the Supreme Polarity*, ed. David Jones and He Jinli. State University of New York Press, 2014, forthcoming.

Shun, Kwong-loi. "On Reflective Equanimity: A Confucian Perspective." In *Moral Cultivation and Confucian Character: Engaging Joel J. Kupperman*, ed. Li Chenyang and Ni Peimin. State University of New York Press, 2014.

Shun, Kwong-loi. "Purity in Confucian Thought: Zhu Xi on *Xu, Jing,* and *Wu.*" In *Conceptions of Virtue: East and West*, ed. Kim Chong Chong and Yuli Liu. Marshall Cavendish, 2006.

Shun, Kwong-loi. "Purity, Moral Trials, and Equanimity." *Tsing Hua Journal of Chinese Studies* New Series 40, no. 2 (2010): 245–264.

Shun, Kwong-loi. "Self and Self-Cultivation in Early Confucian Thought." In *Two Roads to Wisdom: Chinese and Analytic Philosophical Traditions*, ed. Bo Mou. Open Court, 2001.

Shun, Kwong-loi. "Wang Yangming on Self-Cultivation in the *Daxue.*" *Journal of Chinese Philosophy* 38 (supplement s1) (2011): 96–113.

Shun, Kwong-loi. "Wholeness in Confucian Thought: Zhu Xi on *Cheng, Zhong, Xin,* and *Jing.*" In *The Imperative of Understanding: Chinese Philosophy, Comparative Philosophy, and Onto-*

Hermeneutics: A Tribute Volume Dedicated to Professor Chung-ying Cheng, ed. Ng On-cho. Global Scholarly Publications, 2008.

Shun, Kwong-loi. *Zhu Xi and Later Confucian Thought* (tentative title), manuscript under revision.

Solomon, David. "Internal Objections to Virtue Ethics." *Midwest Studies in Philosophy* 13, no. 1 (1988): 428–441.

Taylor, Gabriele. *Pride, Shame and Guilt: Emotions of Self-Assessment*. Clarendon, 1985.

Telfer, Elizabeth. "Self Respect." *Philosophical Quarterly* 18, no. 71 (1968): 114–121.

Toner, Christopher. "The Self-Centeredness Objection to Virtue Ethics." *Philosophy* 81, no. 4 (2006): 595–618.

Wang Yangming 王陽明. *Chuanxilu* 傳習錄. Taipei: *Xuesheng shuju* 學生書, 1983. Passage and page numbers follow those in Chan Wing-tsit 陳榮捷, *Wang Yangming chuanxilu xiangzhu jiping* 王陽明傳習錄詳註集評 (Taipei: *Xuesheng shuju* 學生書局, 1983).

Williams, Bernard. *Ethics and the Limits of Philosophy*. Harvard University Press, 1985.

Williams, Bernard. "Utilitarianism and Moral Self-Indulgence." In *Contemporary British Philosophy: Personal Statements*, fourth series, ed. H. D. Lewis. Allen and Unwin, 1976. Reprinted in *Moral Luck: Philosophical Papers 1973–80*. Cambridge University Press, 1981.

8 Confucian Moral Sources

Owen Flanagan and Steven Geisz

1 Moral Sources in Abrahamic Traditions

It is a commonplace in the North Atlantic and Australasian academies to link a literal commitment to Abrahamic theism in any of its three main forms (Judaism, Christianity, Islam) to intolerance, irrationality, conflict, and fundamentalism-fueled fanaticism, and, in contrast, to link secularism to Enlightenment values of tolerance, rationality, diversity, and cosmopolitanism, as well as to political liberalism more broadly. It is not as if the majority of Western intellectuals think that the demise of commitment to the Abrahamic traditions would by itself produce intra- and inter-state harmony. Ethnicity, economics, and politics provide abundant sources of conflict. But there is the hope in some quarters—Richard Dawkins and Sam Harris[1] are vocal representatives of this point of view—that the elimination of commitment to the three omniscient Gods of Abraham (Yahweh, God [for Anglophones], and Allah), each of whom has a different chosen people, knows (and perhaps created) the one true set of moral norms, is fussy about creedal rectitude (Trinity or not, divinity of Jesus or not, prophetic sources, and so on), and has its own sacred authoritative texts, would reduce one source of conflict that contributes to and partly rationalizes the squelching of dissent, the oppression of minorities, and the exhibition of certain kinds of incivility and intolerance within communities, as well as colonialism, imperialism, and self-serving invasions for gain cloaked as serving "God-given" transcendent values.

On the other side is the commonplace that only religion provides strong reason to be moral, and thus that religion is the only successful source of morality ever discovered or invented.[2] Many of these defenders of religion as essential to morals claim that theism in particular provides strong and even essential foundations for morality, as well for identity-constitutive and meaning-constitutive forms of life at just the right level (abiding these norms makes you one of us) and at just the right depth (abiding these norms will make your life meaningful or "really" matter) to engender community, to bind (in-) groups to be successful cooperative units, and to prevent invasion by other groups, tribes, chiefdoms, or nation-states.[3]

This debate calls for reflection on the lessons from other traditions. What do the anthropological and comparative philosophical records teach about the necessity of theism, its varieties, and the goods (if they are goods) that stem from it, such as seriousness about norms, and about moral and political respect, tolerance, and harmony, both within large-scale communities and societies and between nation-states?

2 The Lesson of China

Some scholars think that the Chinese tradition represents the possibility proof of a successful moral community sustained without the sort of theistic or supernatural foundation—familiar from the Abrahamic traditions—that one might think necessary for a thriving, complex, and large culture.[4] The germ of this idea that the Chinese are morally serious but not particularly theistic goes back to the turn of the seventeenth century, when Matteo Ricci, a great Jesuit scholar, reached Beijing, and eventually one sees the idea of morality without religious foundations cited approvingly in the writings of Voltaire[5] and many other Enlightenment thinkers. Some think that China invented a distinctive moral code without theological foundations twice: in classical China under Confucianism, then again under communism after 1949. This would show that there are ways of being human and living in successful and harmonious communities that do not require theism (or, at least, don't require Abrahamic theism), or that do not require *much* theism. But is it true that China, and perhaps East Asia generally, provides this lesson for the contemporary world? This is our question.[6]

We focus on Confucianism. Although there have been many different strands within Confucianism over the course of its history, we will think of it broadly, following Paul Goldin's characterization of the tradition:

"Confucianism" can be usefully employed as a designation of a certain philosophical orientation. All Confucians shared a set of basic convictions: (i) human beings are born with the capacity to develop morally; (ii) moral development begins with moral self-cultivation, that is, reflection on one's own behaviour and concerted improvement where it is found lacking; (iii) by perfecting oneself in this manner, one also contributes to the project of perfecting the world; (iv) there were people in the past who perfected themselves, and then presided over an unsurpassably harmonious society—these people are called "sages" (*sheng* 聖 or *shengren* 聖人). Not all Confucians agreed about what moral self-cultivation entails, or how we should go about it, but all accepted that we can and must do it, and that it is a task of utmost urgency.[7]

This Confucian tradition is often seen as distinctively humanistic. "The distinctiveness of Confucianism as a religion," Yao Xinzhong writes, "lies in its humanistic approaches to religious matters, such as beliefs, rituals and institutions, and in its religious concerns with secular affairs, individual growth, family relationships and social harmony."[8]

The humanistic, non-theistic aspects of Confucianism are sometimes linked specifically to Confucian values that promote social harmony and to broader aspects of the

Confucian worldview that contrast with major parts of the worldviews of the Abrahamic religious traditions. For example, Li Chenyang, in a detailed discussion of Confucian conceptions of harmony, says that "the absence of a predetermined fixed order in the Confucian cosmos and the Confucian belief in the goodness of human nature[9] are among the main reasons why harmony is so central to Confucianism."[10] Li continues:

This Confucian understanding of an orderly world differs significantly from some other major world traditions. In Christianity, for example, God created the world with a purpose for each and every part of the creation … . Unlike most major world traditions, Confucianism typically does not believe in an anthropomorphic God as creator. Consequently, in the Confucian world there is no order or natural law from God. Without a pre-set fixed order, the world has to generate an order of its own.[11]

The way in which Confucianism understands the world as generating order on its own involves human beings (*ren* 人) acting in concert with both *tian* 天 (heaven) and earth (*di* 地), and although the Confucian *tian* may be best understood as a religious or spiritual source, it is neither transcendent nor capable of creating order on its own. Li writes:

Although sometimes the Confucian Heaven (天) appears to play a role that resembles the Christian God in some way, it is not a transcendent power, as the Christian God is. The Confucian Heaven is a member of the Triad of Heaven, Earth, and Humanity (天地人), and it does not have the power to impose a predetermined order on the world from without. Rather, as merely one member of the Triad the Confucian Heaven needs to achieve order through coordination with the other two members, Earth and Humanity. For Confucians, therefore, order in the world has to be achieved through harmonization.[12]

So far, these are some of the differences that begin to emerge between the structure of the Abrahamic metaphysics of morals and the Confucian grounding project: Monotheism has a transcendent, personal God who sets the moral law, and it has sacred texts with privileged interpretations, whereas Confucianism has none of the above. How then does Confucian moral grounding work?

3 The Moral Grounding Project

Like most great world traditions, Confucianism aspires to answer these two questions:

What is morality?
Why be moral?

Although Confucianism is a long and varied tradition with many sub-currents, we might fruitfully characterize its answer to the first question as follows: Morality, which is a central component of the good life for humans, involves coordinating one's way of being with *tian* 天 (heaven) or *tianming* 天命 (heaven's mandate). The first thing that strikes many Western readers about *tian* is its impersonality.[13] Despite its impersonality—or, more accurately, its *relative* impersonality—heaven has intentions and something like a will; it mandates things. In a *tian*-laden universe, there is a natural teleology, a natural trajectory, a way in which nature (the sum of all things and all processes) propels things to be and to go, a certain preferred trajectory. Sage kings are "appointed" by heaven, as if heaven has a will, and *tian* is said to protect its representatives and to punish those who offend it. But there is no supreme person, no über-Being, who creates, endorses, or doles out eternal reward or punishment for normative conformity or nonconformity.[14] Nonetheless, a life is a good one or a bad one depending upon whether or not it is aligned with *tian*. The natural and proper role of persons is to assist, not resist, this natural trajectory. Human excellence involves aligning oneself with the *dao* 道, or Way. Though it is not perfectly clear what the exact relationship is between *tian* and the Confucian *dao*, it is clear that for Confucians following the Confucian *dao* and being in accord with *tian* are, for all intents and purposes, the same thing.

One way to describe the manner in which one aligns oneself to *tian*, or with its mandate, *tianming*, is to say that it involves modeling one's behavior, one's character, and one's life on the example of the gentleperson (*junzi* 君子), who models himself upon the ancient sage kings, who in turn understood and were aligned with *dao* and *tianming*. At *Analects* (*Lunyu* 論語; fifth to third centuries BCE) 3.18, Confucius says, "How great indeed was Yao as a ruler! How majestic! Only *tian* 天 is truly great, and only Yao took it as his model."[15]

Another way to put the Confucian answer to the question "What is morality?" is as follows: Morality involves primarily the cultivation of one's character so that one has the right mental and emotional dispositions and so that one does what is right and good. In the first instance, moral cultivation involves effort on the part of the family and the wider moral community to socialize the youth in the virtues and in the practices of wisdom, ritual, and attention that will allow lifelong self-cultivation. Central to the development of good character is the development of virtues, which reliably yields good persons who do the right thing. Being virtuous and doing what is right and good is then analyzed in terms of conformity to the moral path as endorsed by *tian* or *tianming*, both conceived impersonally.

This much might make it seem as if a Confucian answer to the question "Why be moral?" is answered in a familiar way: The moral way is endorsed or, better, discovered in the ways of heaven. This sort of justification, if it is all Confucianism can provide, echoes the question from Plato's *Euthyphro*, which in the Chinese case might be something like "For what possible reasons is (are) the way(s) of heaven (conceived as displaying or endorsing, although perhaps not creating, the *dao*) taken as having any normative weight whatsoever?" One answer is that it is simply assumed that the natural trajectory of *tian* is the right direction. *Tian* just is the proper natural teleology and provides the model for intra-personal and inter-personal virtues, norms, and good action. Periods of order and harmony in the lives of Chinese people help confirm hypotheses about what *tianming* models and endorses. Some of the various patterns and trajectories that the world exemplifies are discerned as endorsed or favored by *tian*. They are the best patterns, the ways and modes of being that persons, societies, and civilizations align themselves with as they discover that these ways and modes of being produce goodness, rightness, decency, and flourishing. These ways of being human are endorsed by heaven; others are not.

But this way of thinking allows a better answer to the question "Why be moral?" to emerge. Among Confucians, insofar as there is a reason why one should be a moral person, or why one should aspire to be a *junzi*, that reason bottoms out metaphysically not simply or solely in *tian* or *tianming*, but rather in a triad that includes Earth and Humanity in addition to *tian* or *tianming*. Recall the quotation from Li above:

The Confucian Heaven is a member of the Triad of Heaven, Earth, and Humanity (天地人), and it does not have the power to impose a predetermined order on all of creation from without. Rather, as merely one member of the Triad the Confucian Heaven needs to achieve order through coordination with the other two members, Earth and Humanity. For Confucians, therefore, order in the world has to be achieved through harmonization.

Tian alone does not serve to justify or motivate normative life at the deepest level. Furthermore, in the work of Confucius himself and in that of Mencius and Xunzi, his most influential followers, there is in fact very little mention of *tian* and *tianming* serving to justify or motivate morality. Reasons to be moral are largely discussed in terms of the fact that a world populated by *junzi* is an orderly world. Being a *junzi* is productive of—in a sense even constitutive of—social order, peace, and diplomacy. One common Confucian idea is that there is something contagious about the way *junzi* think and behave and that non-*junzi*, even barbarians, will be won over and model their behavior on the *junzi*.[16] *Tian* models the harmonious order for well-developed persons, and well-developed persons model good character for less developed ones. At *Analects* 16.8, Confucius says:

Exemplary persons (*junzi* 君子) hold three things in awe: the propensities of *tian* (*tianming* 天命), persons in high station, and the words of the sages (*shengren* 聖人). Petty persons, knowing nothing of the propensities of *tian*, do not hold it in awe; they are unduly familiar with persons in high station, and ridicule the words of the sages.

The main virtues of the *junzi*, as endorsed by *tianming* and discovered over world-historical time in the interplay of heaven, earth and humanity, are the classic Five Virtues of Confucianism:

- *Ren* 仁 (benevolence, humaneness)
- *Yi* 義 (rightness or appropriateness of one's conduct and motivations)
- *Li* 禮 (respect for, and cultivated ability in adroitly performing or exemplifying, customs, rituals, mores, proper manners, etc.)
- *Zhi* 智 (discernment or wisdom)
- *Xin* 信 (trustworthiness).

Closely related—and also essential for the *junzi*—are virtues such as *xiao* 孝 (filial piety / elder respect) and *xue* 學 (being appropriately scholarly and studious).

The upshot is that Confucianism is a long-lived and morally serious tradition that, both in its earliest formulations and in many of its most influential formulations, does not postulate anything like the God of the Abrahamic religious traditions.[17] It *does* talk about things such as *tian*. The Confucian *tian* may or may not be transcendent in some sense of "transcendent" that makes it, in that one respect, analogous to the Abrahamic God(s)—that is a matter of some dispute. But *tian* clearly lacks the robust personality and other person-like characteristics of the Abrahamic God(s). Consider, for example, *Analects* 17.19, where Confucius indicates that heaven does not speak and uses that fact to justify his own reticence:

The Master said, "I think I will leave off speaking."

   "If you do not speak," Zigong replied, "how will we your followers find the proper way?"

   The Master responded, "Does *tian* 天 speak? And yet the four seasons turn and the myriad things are born and grow within it. Does *tian* speak?"[18]

In addition to the fact that *tian* lacks the robust personality of the Abrahamic God, we should also keep in mind that under no plausible analysis is *tian* thought by the Confucians to be omnipotent in the way that the Abrahamic God is thought to be. Even if heaven, earth, and humanity, taken together, are the sum of all there is, they never add up to an infinite source of anything.

Two important differences between the structure and grounding of Confucian morality and Abrahamic morality emerge:

Impersonality. Heaven is an important source of value in the relational mix—and perhaps only in that relational mix—that is the triad including earth and humanity. But heaven, despite issuing *de facto* commands, having a "preferred" trajectory and thereby in effect rewarding those who follow the *dao* and punishing those who go off it, is impersonal not personal.[19]

Spirit finitude. There are (or often are, or at least may be) person-like supernatural beings, but none of them—not even heaven itself—possess any omni-characteristics in the way that the God of Abraham does. Impersonal heaven and finite (often person-like) spirits serve as imminent grounds (in the case of *tian*), as reminders, and sometimes as enforcers of the moral order, but not as transcendent sources of it.

The *Analects* presents us with a Confucius who is not overly concerned with whether or not the spirits actually exist. See, for example, *Analects* 3.12, where Confucius says to conduct a ritual sacrifice as if the spirits were present, at least leaving open the interpretation that he either thinks there are no spirits to be present or that it does not matter whether there are such spirits, and 11.12, where Confucius responds to Zilu's question about death by deflecting it on the ground that his disciple should not worry about death until he has better understood living.[20]

The crucial point is that an ethical system with Confucian structure can be highly successful as measured by the twin standards of historical resiliency and moral seriousness. Confucianism is older than Christianity and Islam. And its official virtues, values, norms, and principles are familiar in Abrahamic moral inventories, even if their ranking is not the same—for example, abiding the rites and filial piety are prized more in Confucianism and charity more in Christianity. What seems different and worrisome, possibly downright horrifying from an Abrahamic perspective, is the lack of creedal beliefs and the lack of supreme authoritative moral sources that provide sufficient warrant for these sensible virtues, values, principles, and norms.

4 Ritual Performance and the Virtue of Tolerance

One important question is whether there are particular virtues (or vices) that are easier or harder to have if one is raised in a Confucian moral ecology rather than an Abrahamic one. And one might say that the answer is obvious: Confucians endorse and inculcate virtues such as filial piety (*xiao*) and ritual performance (*li*)—the latter often conceived by Westerners as merely etiquette—in a way that most Christians, for example, do not. But we are interested in whether there are any virtues that might better gain traction because of the existence or lack of a postulated personal and infinite theological source, not the question merely of whether each moral tradition emphasizes or makes mandatory some virtues that another tradition downplays or makes optional, and vice versa.

Tolerance (and related attitudes in its vicinity, such as, trust, respect, non-interference) at the limits, "when in Rome, do as the Romans do," and *"vive la difference,"* is an interesting virtue to consider, since many people think that Abrahamic monotheism encourages intolerance and since the Confucian emphasis on harmony and on virtues such as politeness and other forms of ritual propriety might seem naturally to promote tolerance. The question of whether Confucianism is more fertile soil for it than the Abrahamic traditions is both important and exceedingly complicated. One reason it is important is that many of us now live in places (such as New York, London, and Hong Kong) in which we are increasingly asked to tolerate people from different traditions. One reason why it is complicated is that the question itself is anachronistic. Tolerance is, by and large, a modern virtue—a child of an Enlightenment project in which there were attempts (e.g., by Kant and Mill) to preserve Christian morality without its theistic foundations, as well as increasing realization in the North Atlantic and Australasia that due to commerce and population growth people of different worldviews would somehow need to learn to get along, possibly respect, at the limit, admire each other.[21] Another reason the question is complicated is that there are many reasons besides features of morality why people tolerate one another and get along or why they fail to do so. Still the question is worth asking to see if some traditions might provide more or less fertile soil for modern virtues such as tolerance and its suite. Insofar as tolerance is associated with openness to difference and to novel practices, one might think the case for Confucian tolerance is not strong, since Confucianism is often viewed as conservative and backward looking (and this was already true when the tradition was taking form in the classical period). Indeed, the greatest critics of democratic reform in early-twentieth-century China were closely associated with Confucian culture.

One hypothesis is that the Abrahamic God, in virtue of his personhood and his infinite omni-virtues and omni-talents, is fertile psychological ground for such ideas as creedal rectitude and the closely related ideas of *heresy, the heretic, blasphemy*, and *apostasy*, all of which have their home in Abrahamic religions. Arguably, the limited roles of heaven and spirits in Confucian thinking do not encourage such ideas. Confucianism, by contrast, encourages such parallel concepts as *the confused, the misguided, the mistaken, the uncouth, barbarous*, and *the uncultivated*. Wrongdoing involves mistakes, errors, and lack of character development, and it implicates one's in-group (which bears primary responsibility for one's character). There is no word equivalent to "sin" in Confucianism, where "sin" is understood as a voluntary offense against God.[22]

If true, the hypothesis is at least a partial vindication of a Freudian hypothesis[23] to the effect that the Abrahamic religions, insofar as their God is a supremely confident ("know-it-all"), punitive ("morally righteous") father, either produce (via some complex psychosocial mechanisms) or rationalize a tendency toward intolerance, or, perhaps better, have an extra ingredient that helps explain a greater tendency of their adherents toward certain forms of intolerance.[24] Our version of the hypothesis has the advantage over Freud's of having a clear contrastive case in a large non-Abrahamic tradition (Freud's contrast cases were small shamanistic peoples) that is not theistic in the Abrahamic way(s), but which nonetheless is morally serious—something many ordinary Westerners deny can happen without the posit of God, as they understand him.

So one might ask whether Confucianism, insofar as it grounds morality in something impersonal and finite but not omnipotent (remember the triad of heaven, earth, and humanity) might have natural resources to be more tolerant than the Abrahamic traditions. Is Confucianism more fertile soil for lifestyle tolerance, moral tolerance, and religious tolerance? Might a basis for tolerance somehow be built into the internal structure or logic of Confucianism in a way that it is not built into the Abrahamic religious traditions? One reason these questions are so difficult is that even if it is true empirically that Confucians are (or have been) more tolerant of moral and religious difference than followers of Abrahamic religious traditions (and this is a big "if"), we can't know that it is the differences in moral foundations or sources that make the difference, since there are many factors that motivate people to tolerate or not tolerate—e.g., economic interests, power differentials, genuine threats of war, quirky historical contingencies, and social traditions.[25]

Confucianism emphasizes harmony (*he* 和) within families and societies and between nation-states. Although Confucian harmony is not identical to tolerance, Confucian claims about harmony and how to achieve it in difficult situations are relevant to questions about how to tolerate people, positions, and actions that are challenging to tolerate. Confucian *li* (rites, ritual, or ceremonies), so obviously central to the Confucian prescription for a good life and a harmonious society, provide a framework of soft power that shapes social interactions, softening the rough edges that would otherwise lead to interpersonal conflict and intolerance of various sorts. Confucian models of communication tend to emphasize understatement and subtlety rather than bold conversational confrontation, and this is true even in cases in which one is speaking a hard truth to power or communicating sharp displeasure with the behavior of a student.[26] This softening of speech seems likely to make tolerance more achievable, even in cases where one is taking a strong stand in favor of a commitment or a behavior that is not being exhibited by all those present.[27]

Li encompasses such things as greeting practices, dress, bodily posture, deference rules, tone of voice, diet, food etiquette, marriage and remarriage rules, funeral practices, and mourning periods. Many newcomers to the tradition find Confucians excessively fussy and moralistic about some things that non-Confucians might think are matters of etiquette—mere contingent social conventions. But here we non-Confucians have something to learn, or perhaps to see, about our own normative life. The first thing to notice is that all cultures have norms governing all these things, even if they do not highlight them as morally significant.[28] It might be, first pass, that all cultures have rites or rituals built around some such universal events as birth, coming of age, marriage, death, and, perhaps, being in relation to the divine. It may also be that it is natural, in some sense of the word "natural," to create norms where order is necessary or helpful to accomplish some task—for example, forming lines in order to accomplish the result of "first come, first served." Order is not quite harmony; but it is necessary for harmony.

In classical China, a *junzi* (gentleperson) abides the rites. He or she is *li* or has *li*, or some such. *Li* is necessary for being a good person, part of having a good character. But it is not sufficient. One also needs to be *ren* (benevolent), *yi* (appropriate), *xiao* (respectful), and so on. One might think of the relations among these virtues of character (note: calling them virtues of character does not assume that these are all, or always, straightforwardly "moral" virtues) holistically. A certain kind of attentiveness revealed in how one greets others enables and is enabled by being benevolent (*ren*) or respectful (*xiao*) to some degree. A loving and respectful family buries its members in certain ways. In China, there were sages who knew the proper rites and rituals; these exemplars modeled the virtues and performed the rites in the right ways. Ideally the rites and the right way(s) of doing the rites would spread and then eventually be maintained and sustained in their right form or forms. Of the three classical *Ru* thinkers, Xunzi is most clear that rites are necessary for individual and social flourishing. *Li* bring public order (*zhi* 治), and they work best if they function in a society-wide manner and are enforced, if necessary, by the mechanisms of state power.[29]

Now, using state power to enforce *li* does not sound very tolerant; it can be used simply to enforce one's way of doing things because one's people have the power. But by and large, among both Confucians and Mohists, state power is usually restricted to punishments for what by most anyone's lights are crimes. However, there are also abundant examples in classical Chinese philosophy of debates (we might call them trash-talking) about the right rites. In such cases, there are no threats of punishment for the wrong practices, but there is considerable confidence among different advocates that they understand the right way to do the rites, the deep rationales behind them, and so on. Consider burial practices. Confucians say to bury the dead deep in tombs that are emblematic of their lives, and to mourn for three years. Mohists say to bury them deep and respectfully and get on with it—burying a loved one with valuable mementos and then not working for three years is a waste of material and human resources. Daoists recommend an attitude of accepting the cycle of life and death, not fearing or being appalled by death, and getting on with it. Here is a famous passage from a Daoist text, *Zhuangzi*:

Zhuangzi's wife died. When Huizi went to mourn her, he found Zhuangzi squatting with his legs splayed, drumming on a tub, and singing. Huizi said, "You lived with her, brought up children, and grew old. Not to cry at her death is indeed enough already. But you even drum on a tub and sing. Isn't this going too far?!"

Zhuangzi said, "It's not so. When she first died, how could I not grieve like everyone else? But I looked into her beginnings, and originally she had no life. Not only no life, but no body. Not only no body, but no *qi* 氣 (energy-stuff). Amidst the mysterious chaos, something changed and she had *qi*. The *qi* changed and she had a body. Her body changed and she had life. Now there's been another change and she's died. These changes are to each other as the procession of the four seasons, spring and autumn, winter and summer. She was going to sleep quietly in a giant bedroom, while I in turn was wailing and weeping—I took this to show I was incompetent with respect to fate. So I stopped."[30]

This is the kind of text that makes Confucians apoplectic. But all that it shows is that normative communities feel strongly about their *li*.[31]

How could a three-way debate involving a Confucian, a Mohist, and a Daoist proceed and be resolved? It would, we know, proceed in part by each advocate bringing in considerations of what is normal, natural, and appropriate. But claims about what is natural and appropriate will invoke tradition-specific views about human nature and what makes philosophical and cultural sense, which will beg all the key questions from the point of view of the other tradition. One might appeal to the other to feel his way into the possibility of conceiving of things differently and doing things differently (e.g., greeting, funerals, marriage ceremonies, etc.). But this will almost always be an appeal to reconsider how you conceive and do your *li*, which will in part be an appeal to consider the contingency of your way of being human and the prospects for doing a life, even if not your life, in a different normatively acceptable way.

Again, Confucians express hopes that their ways will appeal even to barbarians and catch on (*Analects* 9.14). But overall across classical Chinese philosophy, not just in Confucian texts, there is a way of talking about normative life that does not defer to, or bottom out in, what sacred texts dictated by an omnipotent God, say, but rather in discussions and debates about how various sage kings—actual historical personages— thought and behaved, and about what heaven's mandate says or reveals if seen or read correctly on the basis of the ever-unfolding historical evidence about what produces generational well-being. The lengthy Confucian mourning period after the death of a parent is not warranted solely because it is endorsed by heaven, nor is the Mohist mourning period, nor is the Daoist acceptance of death. In each case, the practices are defended by deference to *tianming* and on such bases as *this is the proper mourning period to express loss*, and *this is the most efficient way to bury loved ones*, and *this is the best way to align human life with and not resist the ways in which the natural world takes away what it gifts*. These are arguments worth having, not matters over which mortal combat need arise and not matters that can be settled by some authoritative text.

Rites are seen as the key to convivial human life and serve a variety of functions:

• They help us collectively mark significant life events, reinforcing a sense of meaning to ongoing communal life.
• They encourage and reinforce emotional bonding.
• They create in-group identity and solidarity at various levels.
• They offer avenues for appropriate emotional channeling (sadness at funerals, joy at weddings, etc.)
• They promote efficiency in personal and interpersonal behavior by scripting certain practices.
• They add aesthetic value and texture to communal life.

Nearly every culture ever invented has ritual practices that perform these functions. The Confucian tradition is more attentive to and reflective on these practices and their value. The Abrahamic traditions are commonly attentive to and reflective on the manner of rituals performed by rabbis, priests, and imams inside their sacred institutions. But the Confucian emphasis of the importance of rites in social life more generally is distinctive.

One worry about rites is that they serve primarily to mark in-groups and that, despite all their gentle, interpersonally attentive, respectful, and aesthetic aspects, they thereby also mark out-groups, and that this is a familiar route to intolerance, disrespect, and conflict. Then again, if you clearly dress and behave as the kind of guy who shakes hands, and I can read that from your behavior, then even if I am a fist bumper I can use this information to greet you in the way your people—people like you—consider respectful.

To be sure, tolerance is not a categorical good. Even if I may be willing to greet and queue in the way you do out of respect (perhaps because you are an elder, or perhaps because your kind outnumber my kind around here), it is good not to be tolerant of Nazis. But tolerance is a *prima facie* good: It is better to change minds and practices by non-coercive rather than coercive means, all else equal.

"Toleration" and "tolerance" can both be used to refer to many different things. Andrew Jason Cohen argues that there is an important notion of toleration according to which toleration is not identical to indifference, to resignation in the face of something one dislikes, to a pluralism that celebrates or encourages diversity and difference, to a "strict general principle of non-interference" according to which one does not even try to use rational persuasion to change another person's beliefs or behaviors, to a kind of permissiveness driven by a kind of pessimism about the possibility of resolving differences in a satisfactory way, or to a neutrality (since "one can remain neutral between two parties by failing to tolerate either."[32]

Cohen distinguishes *toleration* from *tolerance* (although he recognizes that there is use of the terms "toleration" and "tolerance" according to which they refer to the same thing). And he suggests that it is best to use the word "toleration" to refer to the activity of tolerating and the word "tolerance" to refer to an attitude or a virtue.[33] Aside from allowing a certain kind of precision in the use of words and the application of concepts, Cohen's distinction between toleration and tolerance allows us to recognize that one can display toleration of something without thereby manifesting an attitude or virtue of tolerance. And, of course, one can tolerate (in the sense of "allow") a set of beliefs or practices without judging those beliefs or practices to be sensible, proper, or good.[34]

Although Confucianism holds harmony dear, Confucianism does not try to achieve harmony by endorsing indifference. Consider the particularly famous passage from the *Analects* in which Confucius upbraids his disciple Zigong for displaying a less-than-fully-vigorous commitment to learning the ways of the *Ru*:

Zaiwo was sleeping during the daytime. The Master said, "You cannot carve rotten wood, and cannot trowel over a wall of manure. As for Zaiwo, what is the point in upbraiding him?

The Master said further, "There was a time when, in my dealings with others, on hearing what they had to say, I believed they would live up to it. Nowadays in my dealings with others, on hearing what they have to say, I then watch what they do. It is Zaiwo that has taught me as much." (*Analects* 5.10)

Here, at *Analects* 5.10, Confucius clearly expresses his displeasure with Zaiwo, and his recorded remark about rotten wood being incapable of being carved (*xiumu bu ke diao* 朽木不可雕) remains to this day a common way in Chinese of indicating that some students are, for all intents and purposes, incapable of being taught. Confucius is by no means holding back from criticizing someone he judges to be in need of criticism, but he does it in a way that isn't entirely straightforward.[35] Although such ways of speaking were surely common in Confucius' day and were not a particular innovation of Confucianism, such indirect communication is a hallmark of the tradition that became Confucianism. While Confucius' "rotten wood" remark can be read as an example of what we might today call passive aggression or as a particularly vicious backhanded insult, it also is a famous display of what becomes a subtle, ritual-informed mode of Confucian communication that has the potential to communicate disagreement and displeasure while still allowing room for toleration. Even though Zaiwo was deemed to be rotten wood by the Master, he remained a disciple (albeit one who didn't seem to "get it," as evidenced by the additional beat-down he receives at 17.21).

Confucius, of course, can be harsh in his criticisms of violations of ritual propriety. When he sees power-hungry officials of lower status misusing the trappings of authority in order to try to boost their own social standing, he calls them out:

If the Ji clan's use of the imperial eight rows of eight dancers in the courtyard of their estate can be condoned, what cannot be? (*Analects* 3.1)

And in the *Li Ji* (*Book of Rites*), it is indicated that certain transgressions—murdering one's father, in particular—are intolerable:

With the enemy who has slain his father, one should not live under the same heaven [*tian* 天]. With the enemy who has slain his brother, one should never have his sword to seek (to deal vengeance). With the enemy who has slain his intimate friend, one should not live in the same state (without seeking to slay him).[36]

More broadly, the Confucian is not tolerant of certain kinds of challenges to Confucianism's fundamental commitments. Joseph Chan writes:

We should distinguish between ethical disagreements within the bounds of Confucian conceptions of *ren* and rites and those which violate those bounds. The first are family disputes, in which case Confucians would respect a person who exercises his ethical capacities and deliberates carefully but reaches a decision different from that of others. However, for those views which present an ethical perspective seriously at odds with the very core contents of *ren* and rites, Confucians would be inclined to reject them as unreasonable. In the face of fundamental ethical disagreements, it is unlikely that Confucians would say, "while I believe my views are correct, your views are not unreasonable either." For Confucians, when a debate comes down to ethical fundamentals, there is little room for reasonable disagreements.[37]

Thus, although Confucianism emphasizes harmony and promotes ritual propriety as a kind of social pragmatics that might smooth over some kinds of differences between people within a community, it also promotes high standards and even harsh criticism of those people within the community who purport to want to live up to those standards but fail to do so, and it also allows that there are certain kinds of ethical differences about which there can be no proper reasonable discussion.

Conclusion

Charles Taylor ends his magisterial book *Sources of the Self* with the hope that there is the God of Abraham, specifically the Christian version. His reason is that he doesn't see strong enough sources for morality otherwise. In *After Virtue*, Alasdair MacIntyre worries similarly that the Enlightenment project of reconstituting morality on secular foundations has largely failed and that we in the North Atlantic are now an unstable amalgam of skeptical, expressivist, emotivist, and nihilistic amoralists with a dangerous dose of the moral psychology of once cocky religious dogmatists.

One diagnosis is that such laments from wise and thoughtful thinkers will continue to surface among those of us—most of us in the North Atlantic and Australasia—who, by virtue of our histories, had come to expect exceedingly strong religious foundations for our forms of life. And it may even be true that we are now confused about how to get on, at one and the same time, as morally serious with high standards, while lacking absolutely firm moral foundations, while also respectful, possibly appreciative, of different ways of being human. Classical Confucianism is one example of a tradition with many centuries' worth of experience grounding a very serious moral tradition in foundations weaker than the foundations Taylor and MacIntyre hope for or think we need. Thus, classical Confucianism may be able to serve as yet another resource—another example, in addition to that provided by the Enlightenment, of a way of grounding morality without an omniscient, omnipotent, transcendent, and personal God who creates the moral law, while also showing that the emotivist, expressivist, nihilistic picture of persons and moral life is not the only alternative to that particular metaphysic of morals. A lesson, a gift, from China for us. This is a hopeful note on which to end.

Acknowledgments

We are grateful to Brian Bruya and P. J. Ivanhoe for helpful comments and criticisms.

Notes

1. See Richard Dawkins, *The God Delusion*; Sam Harris, *The End of Faith*.

2. This view is tacitly endorsed by many social scientists in the form of what is called "supernatural punishment theory," which simply states that most moralities ever invented have a supernatural system that rewards or punishes in the hereafter based on the moral quality of one's earthly life. So in the Abrahamic traditions God judges, whereas among the Indic karmic eschatologies—Hinduism, Buddhism, Jainism—the cosmos keeps track of deeds and orchestrates rebirths accordingly.

3. One problem in Plato's *Euthyphro* is this: What is the source of moral order if there are multiple gods who disagree about norms, values, and virtues, especially if no god is the final arbiter among the gods (as in polytheism)? Some think monotheism solves all problems associated with disputes among plural gods, since one God can't disagree with himself. Monotheism plus divine omniscience, omnipotence, etc., is even more powerful than monotheism alone because then the one God is unified (the "mono" part) and guaranteed to be right (the "omni-" part). A worry worth entertaining about the monotheistic solution—especially the solution that incorporates the omni-features, as do all the Abrahamic variants—is that it exacerbates normal human tendencies toward moral and political over-confidence and righteousness. In *The Essence of Christianity*, Ludwig Feuerbach offers an argument to the effect that Christianity, like all other religious traditions, does its complex work of creating community, endorsing a moral order, and explaining mystery by projecting features and needs of peoples at certain times and places. The idea of religion as projection influenced Marx and Engels and is now a major ingredient of almost all theorizing in the anthropology of religion.

4. Roger T. Ames, *Confucian Role Ethics*.

5. See, for instance, Voltaire, *Candide*.

6. Clark and Winslett ("The Evolutionary Psychology of Chinese Religion") argue that classical China was, in fact, much more theistic than many scholars, especially philosophers, typically acknowledge, and that belief in supernatural spirits that punish moral transgressions was a major element of the classical Chinese worldview. We neither accept nor deny this here. We argue that, even if there is a kind of theism that provides some of the grounding for morality in classical China, the grounding it provides is radically different from, though perhaps equally effective as, that provided by the Abrahamic theism. Roger Ames, in *Confucian Role Ethics*, offers a strong

argument that if one goes back to the pre-Confucian *Book of Changes* (*Yi Jing*) one will see a Chinese cosmology that is treated as background—as a naturalistic and a-theological common-sense metaphysics—by *Ru* (Confucian) philosophers such as Mencius.

7. Paul Goldin, *Confucianism*, 5–6.

8. Xinzhong Yao, *An Introduction to Confucianism*, 44, citing Yao, *Confucianism and Christianity*.

9. The tradition generally follows Mencius in thinking that human nature is inherently good and naturally oriented to develop morally. A notable exception was Xunzi (third century BCE), who believed that if human nature were innately good we wouldn't have to work so hard to improve ourselves.

10. Chenyang Li, "The Confucian Ideal of Harmony," 593.

11. Ibid., 593–594.

12. Ibid., 594. Philip Ivanhoe (personal communication) recommends caution here: Xunzi is the first Confucian to use these three terms; they are not used in this same way by Confucius (551?-479? BCE) or Mencius (fourth century BCE). A more nuanced interpretation than the one we offer would explore the differences among these three *Ru* thinkers in how they conceive the relational mix of heaven, earth, and world.

13. Chris Fraser, Dan Robins, and Timothy O'Leary, *Ethics in Early China*; Goldin, *Confucianism*; Donald Lopez, *Religions of China in Practice*.

14. Mozi (fl. late fifth century BCE) did believe in such a punitive heaven, but he was an opponent of Confucianism. For emphasis on heaven's literal mandate, see P. J. Ivanhoe, "Heaven as a Source for Ethical Warrant in Early Confucianism." It helps our interpretation to the degree that we can legitimately read these passages as examples of pragmatic deference to a traditional language game that involves talk of *tian* and *tianming* but is transitioning to non-literal usages of the terms *tian* and *tianming* (as when we say "God help us"), but this may be an ethnocentric and anachronistic way of reading the classical Chinese passages that talk of *tian* and *tianming*. It might be better to say that Confucian moral sources in *tian* and *tianming* involve a very powerful source that differs from the Abrahamic one mainly in that it is not personal but nonetheless has intentions, commands, and will and in that it lacks such features as transcendence, aseity, and *causa sui*-ness, and is instead immanent. Is it supernatural? It is unclear, or, again and probably better: that is a question that makes sense inside our language game(s), not theirs.

15. All translations from the *Analects* are from Ames and Rosemont, *The Analects of Confucius*.

16. Flanagan, "*Moral Contagion And Logical Persuasion in the Mozi* 墨子"; Flanagan and Hu, "Han Fei Zi's Philosophical Psychology."

17. It is worth taking stock of religiousness generally. According to a recent Pew report ("The Global Religious Landscape, 26), "More than six-in-ten (62%) of all religiously unaffiliated people [on earth] live in one country, China." The findings are that whereas 82 percent of the world's

population is religiously affiliated, more than half of the Chinese population is not, despite the fact that China has most of the world's Buddhists and most of the world's believers in folk or traditional religion as measured by Pew. One should be careful when interpreting these results, since belonging to a religion and being a theist do not align perfectly. Some religious people—for example, some Buddhists and some Unitarians—are atheists by Abrahamic standards, and some theists are unaffiliated. According to the Pew report, 7 percent of the unaffiliated Chinese adults are theists (our term for the report's "belief in God or a higher power"—one counts as a theist if one believes in God, gods, spirits, ghosts, or the Buddha), whereas a full 30 percent of unaffiliated French adults and 68 percent of unaffiliated American adults are theists by the same measurement rule (ibid., 24). It remains interesting that there is a statistically significant correlation between being religiously unaffiliated and being non-theistic, especially in East Asia, and that there is a statistically significant correlation between being religiously unaffiliated and living in East Asia. All the countries with unaffiliated populations ranging from close to 50 percent to more than 70 percent are in East Asia: South Korea (46 percent), China (52 percent), Japan (57 percent), and North Korea (71 percent) (ibid., 25) (Note that whereas China and North Korea have systematically waged communist attacks against all religions, nothing similar occurred in South Korea or Japan, so current East Asian areligiousness cannot necessarily be attributed to communist influence). Among the European countries that are thought to be most secular, the percentages of unaffiliated are 42 percent in the Netherlands, 27 percent in Sweden, 18 percent in Finland, 12 percent in Denmark, and 10 percent in Norway (ibid., 45–50). Of course, the religiously affiliated in Northern Europe include a fair number of agnostics and atheists, and some of the unaffiliated in many countries are theists. But again there is a correlation. That said, it is very tricky to count Confucians, since there is no initiation ritual in modern-day Confucianism and most people do not identify as such in terms of religious identity (see Anna Sun, *Confucianism as a World Religion*).

18. Despite what he says at 17.19 about *tian* and its lack of speech, Confucius is described at *Analects* 5.13 as reticent even to speak about *tian* itself: "Zigong said, 'We can learn from the Master's cultural refinements, but do not hear him discourse on subjects such as our "natural disposition (*xing* 性)" and "the way of *tian* (*tiandao* 天道).""" It is worth noting that Buddhism—another morally serious but non-theistic tradition in the sense of not espousing a creator God, or at least being quietist about the existence of such a God (but often chock full of finite spirits)—begins when Siddhartha Gotoma claims to have discovered a practical method to alleviate suffering and achieve virtue and wisdom, but offers only humble silence when asked theological and metaphysical questions about God, gods, and even afterlives. (See Flanagan, *The Really Hard Problem*, *The Bodhisattva's Brain*, and "The View From the East Pole.")

19. One way to think of the situation is as follows: The way or ways of heaven are discerned from among all the patterns that are realized or possible. Famines, tsunamis, and bad people are part of reality, but are not endorsed by heaven. This is discovered by sage kings as well as by lesser beings such as ordinary humans over world-historical time. Does heaven mandate the bad, destructive patterns as well as those that produce order, harmony, and goodness? No. This once again shows that heaven is not omnipotent. Heaven's mandate on this view is some set of

patterns that humans correctly see as the best ones of all the actual and possible ones. Here we have an interesting parallel between the Confucian location of moral sources of the correct *dao* and Christian natural-law philosophies (with roots in Aristotle), which see God as gifting humans with the capacities to discern in nature's best trajectories what are the right states of heart and mind, what is sinful, and so on.

20. What these passages from the *Analects* show is open to debate. Ivanhoe ("Heaven as a Source for Ethical Warrant in Early Confucianism") thinks that Confucius is not properly identified as either an agnostic or an atheist. More broadly, Clark and Winslett ("The Evolutionary Psychology of Chinese Religion") argue that classical Chinese culture, including that of early Confucianism, included widespread belief in spirits that punished moral transgressions. However, at least one of us takes very seriously a reading of these passages, and the *Analects* as a whole, that sees Confucius as more akin to an agnostic about the spirits than to a believer in their literal existence. At the very least, Confucius is not overly fussy either about what we might think of as creedal rectitude or about expressed ontological commitment to a particular theology.

21. Following this line, it might be better to refer to tolerance as a *trait* rather than a virtue, since whether it is considered a virtue or a vice depends on a background philosophical theory that includes a theory about the legitimacy of various beliefs and practices. There is a range of possibilities. One might think that tolerance is a virtue but that it depends on the content of what is tolerated. Almost no one thinks murder and rape are tolerable, so this is the default view. On this way of analyzing things, both Abrahamic moralists and Confucian moralists would think it a virtue to be tolerant about some kinds of persons and practices. Some latter-day ironists and post-modern types conceive of tolerance as a good thing but not necessarily a virtue, and think of virtue-talk as old-fashioned. Tolerance is good because it has practical advantages—we get along with each other without getting all bent out of shape about our differences, and maximizing diversity allows for interesting and creative fusions of lifestyles and life forms. (See Flanagan, "Performing Oneself.")

22. The social character of Confucian wrongdoing goes with shame, whereas the individual transgression that constitutes sin is the perfect partner of guilt.

23. Sigmund Freud, *Totem and Taboo.*

24. In disambiguating concepts such as *tolerant, conflict-prone,* and *war-like,* we would need, in addition to clearly marking differences among them, to also distinguish kinds of each. Tolerance is a complex two-place relation. One might be tolerant of other religions and/or of other sects within one's own religion but intolerant of certain kinds of economic or political organization, and vice versa. Tolerance need not be, and often isn't, symmetrical. Furthermore, tolerance is not an unambiguous good. A tolerant attitude toward the practices of a fascist state is not good. A tolerant attitude toward immigration, on the pretext that it makes for exploitable labor, is not good. Powell and Clarke ("Religious Tolerance and Intolerance") argue that tolerance requires disapproval, and that one cannot be tolerant if one is simply indifferent to a practice and way of acting. This seems too strong. One might think that practice A is better than practice B, but not disapprove of B.

25. A full discussion of Confucian resources for tolerance vs. intolerance would have to closely analyze such cases as the three suppressions of Buddhism during the first millennium CE in China and the Korean Neo-Confucian suppression of Buddhism in the second millennium. (See Wright, *Buddhism in Chinese History*, 82–85 and chapter 5; Mitchell, *Buddhism*, 202–203 and 262–264.) Were there sources internal to Confucianism that caused or at least aided and abetted these various repressions and conflicts, or were the causes of the repressions primarily economic, political, or ethnic, with religious differences serving as motivators and battle cries to coalesce each side's forces? Social scientists ask similar questions about the religious wars in Europe from 1524 to 1648, about the Crusades of the eleventh through thirteenth centuries, and even about current conflicts between Sunni and Shia Muslims. Were they really religious? In every case there is the question of whether the background moral and spiritual tradition was determining, over-determining, or inconsequential.

26. Confucius himself does not always abide the principle of the soft touch. As we discuss below, at *Analects* 5.9 Confucius likens Zaiwo to a piece of rotten wood and to a wall of manure. At 14.43 he raps Yuan Rang on the shin with his staff for sitting with his legs splayed out in a disrespectful manner while waiting for Confucius. It isn't clear whether we should say that these acts were (in context) consistent with understatement, or that Confucius loses it in these cases, or that—as is often said about Confucius—he uses different techniques to teach different students in different situations, as needed, but that overall he tends toward what we would call understatement and avoids straightforward conversational confrontation.

27. For further discussion of the social pragmatics of Confucian ritual and its contrast with conversational norms that we might think of as largely constitutive of civil society in liberal democracies, see Geisz, "Aging, Equality, and Confucian Selves."

28. An important issue is whether the domain of the moral is a well-marked social kind. In the Abrahamic traditions and in their secular descendants, it might be well demarcated, because it is exactly the zone of life on the basis of which God judges you on Judgment Day. In Confucianism, because the triad is a confluence of forces, the boundaries between the zones of etiquette, morality, aesthetics, and politics are less clearly demarcated, more blended.

29. The points made here are complex. Xunzi would have agreed that state enforcement of rites is sometimes warranted. But Confucius made an explicit distinction between *li* and *xing* 刑 (legal punitive measures), favoring the former over the latter (2:3; see also 12:19). And Mencius seemed to follow Confucius.

30. *The Complete Works of Chuang Tzu*, tr. Burton Watson, as quoted in Fraser, "Xunzi versus Zhuangzi."

31. P. J. Ivanhoe (personal communication) disagrees with our interpretation here of the debate among Confucians, Mohists, and Daoists as a debate about which *li* are the correct ones. He thinks that Mohists and Daoists reject *li*. See chapter 38 of the *Dao De Jing* for support for his interpretation.

32. Andrew Jason Cohen, "What Toleration Is," 71–75. First quoted passage, 74; second quoted passage, 75.

33. Cohen, ibid., 76–77.

34. P. J. Ivanhoe discusses a familiar liberal concept of tolerance in his defense of an alternative that he calls "ethical promiscuity" (and which he sees as similar to the "pluralistic relativism" defended by David Wong in *Natural Moralities*). Ivanhoe writes: "Tolerance is here typically understood as *the uncritical acceptance* of a range of competing and mutually irreconcilable values or forms of life. Something like this response is thought necessary in order to prevent an unjustified war among those who hold and defend competing ethical values … . Tolerance, as I have defined it here, is but one possible response to the fact of ethical pluralism, the one most characteristic and in some ways constitutive of a liberal point of view" (Ivanhoe, "Pluralism, Tolerance, and Ethical Promiscuity," 312–313; emphasis added). Although Ivanhoe does not want to defend tolerance in this liberal sense (since he thinks it doesn't do enough to embrace the possibilities provided by the fact of ethical pluralism; see ibid., 320), he does link tolerance explicitly to kinds of religious intolerance. He writes: "This [i.e., the fact that tolerance as 'uncritical acceptance of a range of competing and mutually irreconcilable values or forms of life' is seen as 'necessary in order to prevent an unjustified war'] reflects more the historical circumstances that gave rise to Western notions of tolerance—namely, religious warfare—rather than any deep conceptual fact about pluralism. Under the threat of imminent warfare or physical violence, calls for tolerance make good sense. As a matter of fact, this is when such calls almost always are heard. However, that does not mean that tolerance should be our ultimate goal. By analogy, we think it makes sense to restrain someone who is a threat to himself and others, but that is not what we want for him as an ideal life" (Ivanhoe, ibid., 312n3).

35. For a discussion of less-than-straightforward communication by Mengzi, see Geisz, "Mengzi, Strategic Language, and the Shaping of Behavior."

36. James Legge, tr., *Sacred Books of the East*; *Lî Kî, Khü Lî* 1.

37. Joseph Chan, "Confucian Attitudes Toward Ethical Pluralism, 122.

Works Cited

Ames, Roger T. *Confucian Role Ethics: A Vocabulary*. Chinese University Press, 2011.

Ames, Roger T., and Henry Rosemont Jr. *The Analects of Confucius: A Philosophical Translation*. Random House, 1998.

Chan, Joseph. "Confucian Attitudes Toward Ethical Pluralism." In *Confucian Political Ethics*, ed. Daniel A. Bell. Princeton University Press, 2008.

Clark, Kelly James, and Justin T. Winslett. "The Evolutionary Psychology of Chinese Religion: Pre-Qin High Gods as Punishers and Rewarders." *Journal of the American Academy of Religion* 79, no. 4 (2011): 928–960.

Cohen, Andrew Jason. "What Toleration Is." *Ethics* 115, no. 1 (2004): 68–95.

Dawkins, Richard. *The God Delusion*. Bantam Books, 2006.

Feuerbach, Ludwig. *The Essence of Christianity* (1841). Tr. George Eliot. Dover, 2008.

Fish, Stanley. "Mutual Respect as a Device of Exclusion." In *Deliberative Politics: Essays on Democracy and Disagreement*, ed. Stephen Macedo. Oxford University Press, 1999.

Flanagan, Owen. *The Bodhisattva's Brain: Buddhism Naturalized.* MIT Press, 2011.

Flanagan, Owen. "Moral Contagion and Logical Persuasion in the Mozi 墨子." *Journal of Chinese Philosophy* 35, no. 3 (2008): 473–491.

Flanagan, Owen. "Performing Oneself." In *The Philosophy of Creativity: New Essays*, ed. Elliot Samuel Paul and Scott Barry Kaufman. Oxford University Press, 2014, forthcoming.

Flanagan, Owen. *The Really Hard Problem: Meaning in a Material World.* MIT Press, 2007.

Flanagan, Owen. "The View from the East Pole: Buddhist and Confucian Tolerance." In *Religion, Intolerance and Conflict: A Scientific and Conceptual Investigation*, ed. Steve Clarke, Russell Powell, and Julian Savulescu. Oxford University Press, 2013.

Flanagan, Owen, and Jing Hu. "Han Fei Zi's Philosophical Psychology: Human Nature, Scarcity, and the Neo-Darwinian Consensus." *Journal of Chinese Philosophy* 38 (2) (2011): 293–316.

Fraser, Chris. "*Xunzi* versus *Zhuangzi*: Two Approaches to Death in Classical Chinese Thought." *Frontiers of Philosophy in China* 8, no. 3 (2013), 410–427. Updated preprint, May 2013: http://cjfraser.net/images//2013/07/FraserDeath-May2013.pdf.

Fraser, Chris, Dan Robins, and Timothy O'Leary, eds. *Ethics in Early China: An Anthology.* Hong Kong University Press, 2011.

Freud, Sigmund. *Totem and Taboo* (1913), tr. James Strachey. Norton, 1990.

Geisz, Steven F. "Aging, Equality, and Confucian Selves." In *Value and Values: Economics and Justice in an Age of Global Interdependence*, ed. Roger T. Ames and Peter D. Hershock. University of Hawai'i Press, forthcoming.

Geisz, Steven F. "Mengzi, Strategic Language, and the Shaping of Behavior." *Philosophy East and West* 58 (2) (2008): 190–222.

Gethin, Rupert. "Buddhist Monks, Buddhist Kings, Buddhist Violence: On the Early Buddhist Attitudes to Violence." In *Religion and Violence in South Asia: Theory and Practice*, ed. John R. Hinnells and Richard King. Routledge, 2007.

Goldin, Paul R. *Confucianism.* University of California Press, 2011.

Goleman, Daniel. *Destructive Emotions: How Can We Overcome Them? A Scientific Dialogue with the Dalai Lama.* Bantam Books, 2003.

Gutmann, Amy, and Dennis F. Thompson. *Democracy and Disagreement.* Harvard University Press, 1996.

Gutmann, Amy, and Dennis F. Thompson. *Why Deliberative Democracy?* Princeton University Press, 2004.

Harris, Sam. *The End of Faith: Religion, Terror, and The Future of Reason*. Norton, 2004.

Ivanhoe, Philip J. "Heaven as a Source for Ethical Warrant in Early Confucianism." *Dao* 6, no. 3 (2007): 211–220.

Ivanhoe, Philip J. "Moral Tradition Respect." In *Ethics in Early China*, ed. Chris Fraser, Dan Robins, and Timothy O'Leary. Hong Kong University Press, 2011.

Ivanhoe, Philip J. "Pluralism, Tolerance, and Ethical Promiscuity." *Journal of Religious Ethics* 37 (2) (2009): 311–329.

Jayatilleke, K. N. *The Buddhist Attitude to Other Religions*. Buddhist Publication Society, 1975.

Legge, James, tr. *Sacred Books of the East*, volume 28, part 4: *The Lî Kî*. Oxford University Press, 1885. (quoted from http://ctext.org/liji/qu-li-I)

Li, Chenyang. "The Confucian Ideal of Harmony." *Philosophy East and West* 56, no. 4 (2006): 583–603.

Lopez, Donald S., Jr., ed. *Religions of China in Practice*. Princeton University Press, 1996.

MacIntyre, Alasdair. *After Virtue: A Study in Moral Theory*. University of Notre Dame Press, 1981.

Mitchell, Donald W. *Buddhism: Introducing the Buddhist Experience*, second edition. Oxford University Press, 2008.

Neville, Robert Cummings. "A Comparison of Confucian and Christian Conceptions of Creativity." *Dao* 6, no. 2 (2007): 125–130.

Nisbett, Richard. *The Geography of Thought: How Asians and Westerners Think Differently ... and Why*. Free Press, 2003.

Pew Research Center. The Global Religious Landscape: A Report on the Size and Distribution of the World's Major Religious Groups as of 2010 (http://www.pewforum.org/files/2014/01/global-religion-full.pdf).

Powell, Russell, and Steve Clarke. Religious Tolerance and Intolerance: Views from Across Disciplines. (2010?) http://www.philosophy.ox.ac.uk/_data/assets/pdf_file/0013/13504/Tolerance5_background_reading.pdf.

Samsel, Peter. "The First Pillar of Islam." *Parabola* 32, no. 1 (2007): 42–49.

Sun, Anna. *Confucianism as a World Religion: Contested Histories and Contemporary Realities*. Princeton University Press, 2013.

Taylor, Charles. *Sources of the Self: The Making of Modern Identity*. Harvard University Press, 1989.

Van Norden, Bryan W. *Introduction to Classical Chinese Philosophy*. Hackett, 2011.

Van Norden, Bryan W. *Mengzi: With Selections from Traditional Commentaries*. Hackett, 2008.

Wong, David B. *Natural Moralities: A Defense of Pluralistic Relativism*. Oxford University Press, 2006.

Wright, Arthur F. *Buddhism in Chinese History*. Stanford University Press, 1959.

Yao, Xinzhong. *Confucianism and Christianity: A Comparative Study of Jen and Agape*. Sussex Academic Press, 1996.

Yao, Xinzhong. *An Introduction to Confucianism*. Cambridge University Press, 2000.

III Metaphysics and Epistemology

III Metaphysics and Epistemology

9 Senses and Values of Oneness

Philip J. Ivanhoe

In fact the whole antithesis between self and the rest of the world … disappears as soon as we have any genuine interest in persons or things outside ourselves. Through such interests a man comes to feel himself part of the stream of life, not a hard separate entity like a billiard ball, which can have no relation with other such entities except that of collision … . Such a man feels himself a citizen of the universe, enjoying freely the spectacle that it offers and the joys that it affords, untroubled by the thought of death because he feels himself not really separate from those who will come after him. It is in such profound instinctive union with the stream of life that the greatest joy is to be found.

—Bertrand Russell[1]

1 Introduction

In this chapter, I explore different ways in which people claim, or might claim, to "be one with" other parts of the world or with the universe at large, and what ethical implications might come with recognizing and living in light of such a conception of the self. In particular, I am interested in how such views about the self and its relationship with the rest of the world entail or imply various types and levels of care for other people, creatures, or things. I discuss a range of views currently being discussed among psychologists and philosophers, but my primary purpose is to describe the views of several Chinese neo-Confucian thinkers and bring them into dialogue with modern psychology and philosophy. As will be clear, I think that in order to do this I must first exert considerable care and effort in coming to understand what these neo-Confucian thinkers really thought about these topics and how the world would look when seen from the perspective of someone who took up and lived according to their kind of view. This will require me to take seriously a range of metaphysical beliefs that I describe as "heroic." I mean by this that such beliefs would be very difficult for a modern person to embrace, since they cannot be reconciled with views that are now widely accepted by science. I find these traditional metaphysical views implausible, just as I find many of Plato's views about value or Aristotle's views about human nature untenable. I would like to suggest, though, that by thinking from and through the perspective of these traditional neo-Confucians we can be led to formulate modern interpretations of their views that make significant contributions to contemporary debates about how we are related to and how we can see ourselves as related to other people, creatures, and things in the world. Describing such a conception of the self and explaining its ethical implications are the ultimate constructive aims of the chapter.

2 The Vicissitudes of Altruism

A number of philosophers and psychologists have sought to understand our capacity to care for others and the ways in which we might improve and strengthen whatever abilities we have in this regard. David Hume and Adam Smith offered different but related accounts of "sympathy" and the ways in which sympathy functions to develop and strengthen other-regarding desires and behavior. For quite some time, modern philosophers, biologists, and psychologists have tended to doubt the possibility of genuine psychological altruism—self-consciously choosing to benefit others and not oneself at one's own expense—but recent work in all three fields has reestablished not only the possibility but also apparently the fact of such altruism. Thomas Nagel attempted to defend one version of this claim: that human beings can freely and rationally choose to act in consideration of the interests of others without having any ulterior, prudential motives.[2] Developing a parallel between agent-relative and agent-neutral reasons for acting, Nagel argued there is an objective moral requirement on all rational agents to behave altruistically. Biologists have always recognized biological altruism, defined simply in terms of behavior: one organism acting in ways that benefit others at its own expense. Seen in terms of evolutionary biology, altruism is behavior that decreases the fitness of one organism while increasing the fitness of others.[3] Psychological altruism was regarded as impossible, since it was thought to be inconsistent with natural selection, but recently Elliot Sober and David Sloan Wilson have shown that such altruism is fully consistent with natural selection when selection is viewed in terms of groups rather than individual organisms.[4] Their work has overturned years of opposition to the very idea of psychological altruism and has reinvigorated inquiry into the nature of altruism and into all its expressions and forms. Additional momentum and interest has come from experimental psychologists; the most developed and influential line of inquiry in this field is known as "the empathy-altruism hypothesis."[5] Those who defend the empathy-altruism hypothesis claim that empathy with others can lead to caring for and working to increase their welfare, even at the expense of the agent. Among other consequences, this research has helped to foster a revival of sentimentalist virtue ethics in the tradition of Hume and Smith. Since "sympathy," or more properly empathy, plays a central role in sentimentalist-virtue-ethical conceptions of the virtues, the findings of psychologists who do research on the empathy-altruism hypothesis has provided considerable support for such theories.[6] Prominent among the exponents of such new versions of sentimentalism is Michael Slote, whose work draws on contemporary psychological studies such as those of C. Daniel Batson and Martin L. Hoffman.[7] Stephen C. Angle relates Hoffman's views to neo-Confucians such as Wang Yangming, paying particular attention to moral development and education.[8] In section 4, I will discuss the empathy-altruism hypothesis, both its psychological formulation and philosophical use, and will contrast this view with an alternative account of other-directed feeling and behavior, what I will call the "oneness hypothesis."[9] To set the stage for this comparison, I will offer a general discussion of the concept of oneness and a rough survey of Chinese views about oneness.

3 Oneness and Chinese Philosophy

Even a concept as apparently simple as "oneness" can be complex: it turns out there is more than *one* way to be one.[10] The strongest sense in which two or more things can be one is by the relation of numerical identity: Clark Kent and Superman are one in this way. Some who defend environmental concern based on interpretations of the Gaia hypothesis rely on an only slightly less robust sense of oneness—something we might refer to as the "nature is a blended whole" hypothesis—when they insist that each and every part of the world is inextricably intertwined and passes in and out of one another.[11] Two or more things can also be one by being parts of a single organic body, as my arm is one with the rest of me. This idea often is confused with the idea of being part of a single ecosystem. In the latter case, though, the relationship between part and whole is not as direct or crucial as in the former. Removing important members of an ecosystem may *alter* the system, but rarely will it lead to its collapse or directly and immediately affect all the other parts; cutting off a person's arm or head will have more immediate and dire results. A fifth way to be one with others is as a member of some tradition, institution, team, club, or group. Those who identify themselves as members of such associations, to varying degrees, take the interests of other members in the group as their own. They share a sense of solidarity, of being one with others, at least in regard to certain activities and on certain occasions. One finds examples of all these different senses of oneness in the course of Chinese history and exploring the different ways this concept has played out over time is a most worthy project to undertake. Here, though, I will not attempt an adequate survey of conceptions of oneness in Chinese history; I aim only to present a number of examples in order to help prepare for and frame my discussion of distinctively neo-Confucian conceptions of oneness.

In early texts such as the *Yi Jing* (which was created by many hands over the course of the first millennium BCE) there is a clear and persistent metaphysical motif that describes the world as condensing out of inchoate, primordial *qi* 氣. Roughly, the idea is that the universe began as a vast undifferentiated reservoir of *qi*, and that over time it began to fracture, shift, eddy, and gather into discrete layers or zones, differing in clarity, purity, density, movement, and other characteristics. These regions of different quality *qi* eventually gave rise to distinct types of *qi*: clear, turbid, light, heavy, active, inactive, and so on. This primal soup continued to stir and began to form regular patterns, discernible as vague images (*xiang* 象), which served as the basis of more distinct and stable shapes (*xing* 形). Individual things (*qi* 器) gradually precipitated out of this ongoing process, and the world came into being. The important point for our purposes is that all the things in the universe—the starry heavens above and the most modest mote of dust below—arose out of *qi*. In these respects, the things of the universe are one in a deep and distinctive sense.

Daoists took up these ideas and gave them a different spin by emphasizing how everything we see and make use of in the world comes from an original state of nothing (*wu* 無), by which they tended to mean not a state of absolute "nothingness" but "no-things-ness": a stage in which there were no discrete and individuated entities. According to the *Dao De Jing*, "the world and all its creatures arise from what is there; what is there arises from what is not there" (*tian xia wan wu sheng yu you; you sheng yu wu* 天下萬物生於有; 有生於無).[12] This was also a prominent theme in the writings of Wei Dynasty thinkers such as Wang Bi (226–249) and He Yan (d. 249), who understood and appreciated Daoist thought but insisted that Kongzi (Confucius; 551?-479? BCE) was superior to Laozi (sixth to fourth century BCE?) because only the former really understood how everything arose from primordial nothing (*ben wu* 本無) and is unified by that common origin. In their thought we see clearly the connection between the metaphysical unity of the world and an ethical imperative to care for everything in the world: because of our primordial connection with every aspect of the world, we are fundamentally one with all things and should care for them as more distant extensions of ourselves.

A similar and related view about the world as a unified system or spreading web of *li* 理 (principles/patterns) emerged around the same time and expressed another sense of oneness, something close to being part of an ecosystem.[13] On this view, the phenomena of the world constitute an interconnected system, like the system of roads in a country or like the various parts of a living organism such as a tree. The latter idea was captured and deployed by terms such as "root" (*ben* 本) and "branch tip" (*mo* 末), which convey not only the fact that different parts of the whole are organically connected or "one" but also the fact that some parts (the roots), though hidden from view, are still integral to the system, that each part has its distinctive place and role, and that some parts are more fundamental or important than others. The metaphor of root and branch invites one to examine or investigate the things of the world in order to understand and appreciate its unified structure, starting from the accessible and obvious (branch tips) and tracing one's way back along the complex web of intertwined patterns to arrive at the hidden, fundamental "root" of things. Such ideas were taken up by neo-Confucians and shaped their thinking. Drawing upon a term found in the *Great Learning*, neo-Confucians developed different conceptions of how to carry out the "investigation of things" (*ge wu* 格物), but for them the world and its underlying *li* had changed under the broad and profound influence of Buddhism.

I will not rehearse the complex story of Buddhism's influence on neo-Confucian philosophy, which I have argued for in previous publications, but I will describe some of the most important results of this interaction.[14] Under the influence of Buddhist metaphysical beliefs, neo-Confucians developed a more robust and dramatic sense of oneness as a kind of identity between self and world. Rather than seeing the world as an interconnected system or web of *li*, they believed that each and every thing in the world contained within itself all the *li* in the universe. This idea, which we might identify as "all in each," came most directly from certain teachings within Huayan Buddhism (established in the sixth century CE). One can see this idea illustrated in many Buddhist temples around the world by displays in which the figure of the Buddha—representing our original nature and containing all the *li* in the universe—is placed within a circle of mutually reflecting mirrors. The effect is that the image of the Buddha is projected and appears everywhere, with the pattern repeated in infinitely expanding repetitions.[15] Wherever one looks, one finds the perfect image of the Buddha. The lesson is that all things possess pure and perfect Buddha-nature. In neo-Confucian terms, each thing contains within a shared original nature (*ben xing* 本性), which consists of all the *li* of the world. Individual things and types of things are what they are not because of a difference in their original natures or stock of *li* but because their endowment of *qi* allows only certain *li* to manifest themselves. Humans are unique among creatures because the *li* of their heart-minds provide them with access to all the *li* in the universe. Nevertheless, they must refine the *qi* that blocks the *li* within to the point where the *li* of their heart-minds can shine forth and illuminate the things they encounter or imagine, resulting in proper understanding and appreciation. These ideas all are clearly expressed in the following passage from Zhu Xi:

Someone asked, "Since the physical endowment of *qi* can be more or less dull and impure, is the [original] nature endowed by heaven sometimes complete and sometimes partial?"

[Zhu Xi] said, "There is never a difference of complete or partial. It is like the light of the sun or moon. If you are in an open field, then you see it all. If you are inside a thatched hut, some of the light is blocked, and so you see some of it but not all of it. Dullness and impurity occur only because of *qi* being dull and impure. As a result, there will naturally be some [*li*] that are blocked, as if [in the example of light being blocked] one was inside a thatched hut. Nevertheless, in the case of human beings, the blockage can be penetrated.

Birds and beasts all have this same nature; the only problem is they are constrained by their physical forms. From birth they are severely blocked and cut off and have no way to penetrate the blockage. If we consider the benevolence of tigers and wolves [which they show toward their young], the way otters perform sacrifices [by washing and apparently arranging their food], the dutifulness of bees and ants [who attend to their respective roles in the hive or colony], we see that they are able to penetrate through [their physical endowments] in these various ways—like a sliver of light shining through a crack [in the thatch]. If we consider apes, their physical shape is similar to human beings and so they are the most intelligent among the other animals. The only thing they cannot do is talk."[16]

Given this general picture, neo-Confucians have not only a more metaphysically robust sense of oneness but also a new and strong justification for universal care: our shared *li* supply a deep connection with other people, creatures, and things.[17] Along with this came an explanation for *why* people are emotionally affected not only by the suffering of other people but also by the suffering of non-human animals, the harming of plants, and even the wanton destruction of inanimate objects. Such phenomena are familiar to all human beings, even though the explanation for *why* people tend to feel this way is not at all obvious or straightforward. Neo-Confucians had a ready explanation. For example, Zhou Dunyi (1017–1073) famously refused to cut the grass growing in front of his window, saying, "I regard it in the same way as I regard myself." Zhang Zai (1020–1077) expressed the same sentiment when he heard the braying of a donkey.[18] Like other neo-Confucians, these men felt a profound sense of oneness not only with other human beings but with the entire universe. The self was, in some deep sense, not only connected or intermingled with other people, creatures, and things but coextensive with the universe. One of the most influential and moving expressions of this ideal is Zhang Zai's "Western Inscription" (*Xi Ming* 西銘):

Qian is my father, *Kun* my mother and even an insignificant creature such as I have a place within their midst.[19] And so, what fills the universe is my body; what directs the universe is my nature. All people are my brothers and sisters; all things my companions. The emperor is the eldest son of my father and mother; the great ministers are his stewards.

Respect the aged, as this is the way *to treat the elderly as elders should be treated*; love those who are orphaned and weak, as this is the way *to treat the young as youths should be treated*.[20] The sage is the harmonious power of Heaven and earth; the worthy its refined expression. Those who are weary, infirm, crippled or sick, those who are without brothers, children, wives, or husbands—all these are my brothers, who are suffering distress and misfortune and have nowhere to turn.[21]

Wang Yangming (1472–1529) takes up this set of beliefs and general point of view giving special emphasis to the metaphor of being one body with heaven, earth, and the myriad creatures (*tian di wan wu wei yi ti* 天地萬物為一體). Wang deploys this image (not original with him) in new and powerful ways, urging us to feel the connection between ourselves and the rest of the world in the way we feel the connection among the various parts of our bodies[22]:

Great people regard Heaven, earth, and the myriad creatures as their own bodies. They look upon the world as one family and China as one person within it. Those who, because of the space between their own bodies and other physical forms, regard themselves as separate from [Heaven, earth, and the myriad creatures] are petty persons. The ability great people have to form one body with Heaven, earth, and the myriad creatures is not something they intentionally strive to do; the benevolence of their heart-minds is originally like this. How could it be that only the heart-minds of great people are one with Heaven, earth, and the myriad creatures? Even the heart-minds of petty people are like this. It is only the way in which such people look at things that makes them petty. This is why, when they see a child [about to] fall into a well, they cannot avoid having a sense of alarm and concern for the child.[23] This is because their benevolence forms one body with the child. Someone might object that this response is because the child belongs to the same species. But when they hear the anguished cries or see the frightened appearance of birds or beasts, they cannot avoid a sense of being unable to bear it.[24] This is because their benevolence forms one body with birds and beasts. Someone might object that this response is because birds and beasts are sentient creatures. But when they see grass or trees uprooted and torn apart, they cannot avoid feeling a sense of sympathy and distress. This is because their benevolence forms one body with grass and trees. Someone might object that this response is because grass and trees have life and vitality. But when they see tiles and stones broken and destroyed, they cannot avoid feeling a sense of concern and regret. This is because their benevolence forms one body with tiles and stones.[25]

This imagery readily lent itself to another aspect of the neo-Confucian view: neo-Confucians don't lose the self in or wholly merge the self with the world; they maintain the hierarchy of concern characteristic of Confucians in every age. Wang uses the world-as-body metaphor to emphasize our visceral connection with the world; at the same time, he explains that the various parts of one's own body display a natural hierarchy of concern: we instinctively use our hands and feet to protect our eyes, not because we do not value our hands and feet, but because we spontaneously recognize and follow a natural order. "According to the *li* of the Way," says Wang, "there naturally is a hierarchy of importance" (*wei shi dao li zi you hou bo* 惟是道理自有厚薄).[26] Thus, while we are one with every aspect of the universe, there is a hierarchy of concern, a core and a periphery to the universal self, modeled on the natural hierarchy among the parts of our physical bodies.[27] From the perspective of *li*, our oneness with the world is complete and universal and expresses a particular structure and order; from the perspective of our physical embodiment, this unity gets manifested in our being "one body" with the world.

4 Empathy, Altruism, and Oneness

The most widespread and influential contemporary view about how we can feel a connection with and develop concern for other people involves various conceptions of empathy.[28] Hume and Smith offer examples of such a view, though, as was noted above, they employ the term "sympathy" and use it more broadly than the sense of empathy on which I am relying. In psychology, this view finds its clearest representative in what is known as the empathy-altruism hypothesis; roughly, this is the idea that our feelings of empathy encourage and sustain selfless or altruistic feelings and behavior. Regardless of the particular conception of empathy one chooses or whether one finds this idea in philosophy or psychology, such views about our care for others share several features; I would like to highlight three such features, as these provide helpful ways of comparing the empathy-altruism hypothesis and the oneness hypothesis.

The first feature of the empathy-altruism hypothesis I want to draw attention to is that it is based on *general features of human psychology*. That is to say, the foundation for our connection with others is psychological rather than metaphysical in nature, not simply the ability to feel as another feels but to do so out of concern for the other. Properly speaking, the view involves a claim about a psychological capacity for *empathic concern*.[29] The second feature is that those who rely on empathic concern as their explanation for other-regarding care tend to begin from *how individual agents feel and respond to other individuals*, often others who are suffering in one way or another.[30] Hume asks us to imagine how we would respond to someone intentionally and for no reason stepping on another man's gouty toes.[31] This is important because it tends to interpret the issue of care exclusively in terms of the psychological bond between two people. It seems dubious to believe that we can fully empathize with most non-human animals, and we cannot empathize at all with plants or inanimate objects under this description; even in the case of intimate non-human animals it is not clear how successfully we can empathize with them, as opposed to simply projecting human feelings and concerns onto them.[32] The third and final feature of the empathy-altruism hypothesis concerns the issue of altruism. Advocates of empathy argue that it is *the path to selfless or altruistic behavior*. When I feel as another feels and am concerned with the other's welfare, I become interested in and more willing to behave in ways that benefit the other, even at my own expense. Empathy leads to altruism: my ability to feel as others do leads me to a greater willingness to risk or sacrifice my welfare for theirs.

Several contemporary psychologists have argued that a sense of oneness and *not* empathic concern is what motivates people to help others.[33] Such research relies on the idea that most often people feel *and act* in a benevolent manner not because they experience more *empathic concern* for another, but "because they feel more *at one with* the other—that is, because they perceive more of themselves in the other."[34] On such a view, our concern for others is not purely selfless or altruistic, because it is grounded in what I will call an *expanded view of the self*. In addition to a growing number of experimental results, this view is supported by notions like "inclusive fitness" in evolutionary theory. Here, the sense of oneness is more palpable and related to shared genetic inheritance. Contemporary research on mirror neurons can also be understood as providing support for the primacy of oneness. While our understanding of mirror neurons is still in its infancy, they appear to play a direct and important role in our ability and tendency to imitate or mimic the behavior of others. Such imitation or mimicry plays a vital role in empathy and our more general capacities to simulate and understand others.[35] While the *process* by which mirror neurons enable us to feel what others feel functions more like empathy than oneness, the fact that we *have* this shared capacity to engage in automatic, unconscious simulation points to a deeper, preexisting oneness among people in something like the way our greater tendency to empathize with kin depends on perceived genetic relatedness. It is only because we are one in the sense of having such innate mechanisms that we are able to feel with and understand each other as well as we do.[36] A sense of oneness, though, is not limited to shared genes or mirror neurons; we can feel one with others in many different ways; for example, we can identify with ideas, beliefs, images, symbols, and practices transmitted and inherited across generations just as strongly. In both these cases, a modern, non-metaphysical interpretation of Wang Yangming's idea of shared *li* readily lends itself as a general way to explain what we share.[37]

Wang's way of looking at the phenomenon of oneness takes us considerably beyond the work of contemporary philosophers and psychologists who tend to focus exclusively on the possibility of genuine concern for the suffering of other *human beings*. Recall that Wang thought we are one not only with other people, but also with other animals, plants, and even inanimate objects. There is every reason to think that we in fact can and to some extent already do feel a sense of oneness with many of these and that such a sense is essential for getting us to act on behalf of these other creatures and things. For example, it is quite plausible to maintain that we need to believe and feel we are one with Nature in order to sustain anything resembling an adequate commitment to protecting Nature. Such a belief and sensibility need not in any way conflict with science or be irrational or mystical. Quite the contrary, a *denial* of our intimate connection to the natural world, properly understood, and our linked common future is clearly contrary to our best scientific understanding, irrational, and a dire threat to human welfare as well as many other forms of life on earth.[38] Wang's kind of view suggests that one of the most powerful bases of our concern for other people, creatures, plants, and things is an *enlarged sense of self*; at least in a number of cases, for example in the cases of inclusive fitness and our general, evolutionary interrelationship with Nature, this is more than just a stance on the world, it reflects important facts about *how we actually are* related to things in the world that we hold dear.

One challenge to such a view is that it seems to deny the possibility of altruism, for it appears to say that when we act in the interest of other people, creatures, plants, and things, we really are simply helping ourselves.[39] Altruism requires that our acts be *selfless* but to some extent oneness includes the other within the self; albeit a new and expanded sense of oneself. This is a complex and subtle issue, which I will not attempt to settle definitively here. I do, though, want to suggest that some have sought to settle it too quickly. For example, Cialdini et al. claim that "when the distinction between self and other is undermined, the traditional dichotomy between selfishness and selflessness loses its meaning."[40] I am not so sure about this. If we could not *in any way* distinguish between self and other, the notions of excessive self-centeredness and selflessness would indeed lose meaning. That, though, is not what modern psychologists such as Cialdini or neo-Confucians such as Wang Yangming have argued for. They have described an expanded sense of self and identified varying types and degrees of "interpersonal unity."[41] For example, while Wang insists that underneath it all there are shared *li*, he does not dissolve the self into the world; *qi* preserves the world of physical things and a hierarchy of concern even for the sage. What the proposed, modern conception of oneness brings with it is a greater sense of harmony between self and world and the need to *rethink* the meaning of notions like selfishness and selflessness.

Conclusion

In conclusion, I would like to compare the oneness hypothesis to the empathy-altruism hypothesis in regard to each of the three features of the empathy-altruism hypothesis mentioned in section 4. My aim is to show not only how the former differs from the latter but also how it offers different and in some cases greater resources for handling certain ethical problems. The first feature I noted was that the empathy-altruism hypothesis is based on *general features of human psychology* and not metaphysical claims about the self or the world. At first this seems to be a great advantage, and it surely is a great advantage if by "metaphysical claims" we mean the heroic metaphysics of people like Wang Yangming. However, if instead we understand metaphysics in very low-flying terms, as a general view about the nature of the world, then we can see an important contrast between the oneness hypothesis and the empathy-altruism hypothesis. The former insists that moral theory must rely significantly on how things are in the world and not just, or even primarily, on how human psychology disposes us to be. Such a view recognizes human psychology as an important *part of the story*, but the story is larger and more complex; it's about the world as much as the mind; it concerns genes, mirror neurons, and much more.[42] For example, the story told by the oneness hypothesis involves the evolutionary history of human beings and their intimate and enduring contact with the natural world. It includes the long histories of different cultures and their various effects on the lives of human beings. These and many other facts about the world contribute as much as human psychology to what and how we value. The fact that human beings have had such a long and complex history with Nature explains why we feel certain ways about features of the natural world. The more we understand this history and our actual relationship with the natural world, the greater the likelihood that our appreciation for the value of Nature will deepen.[43] In a similar way, the histories of human cultures contribute in unique ways to what and how we value. Being parts of different, complex traditions is something distinctively human and often of immense value, and this value only emerges in our reflective understanding of actual cultures and traditions. Human values are not just discovered by the study of human psychology, they are forged and crafted in the course of our complex biological and cultural histories. The oneness hypothesis offers us a way not available to the empathy-altruism hypothesis to see why we care about and for so many of these things. We are moved by aspects of Nature because in a fairly direct and intricate way *we are one* with it; we are committed to and admire various cultures and traditions because *these are parts of* individual lives and the common heritage of humanity.

The second feature I discussed is that those who rely on empathic concern as their explanation for other-regarding care tend to begin from *how individual agents feel and respond to other individuals*. This point highlights the degree to which the empathy-altruism hypothesis is based and focuses attention on interpersonal responsiveness. This differs from the oneness hypothesis in several ways. For one thing, the latter view foregrounds the larger wholes of which individual people, creatures, and things are parts; in this respect it tends to valorize the greater, common good and invite the individual to fit into and find a place within the larger whole—e.g., Zhang Zai's "Western Inscription." In other words, the oneness hypothesis is more holistic and communal; the empathy-altruism hypothesis is more individualistic. In certain respects, evolutionary theory favors the oneness hypothesis as having priority over empathy and altruism. As was noted earlier, psychological altruism developed out of *group* not *individual* fitness. The common good of groups offers the explanatory foundation not only for the evolution of altruism but also its primary value.[44] Another difference is that the empathy-altruism hypothesis is restricted almost exclusively to feelings *between human beings*. It can, with varying degrees of success, accommodate relationships between humans and non-human animals, but even on this score there are the challenges and difficulties noted above. The rest of the living and non-living natural world is left completely out of the picture, as are all human artifacts. We cannot *empathize* with these parts of the world for the simple reason that they are insentient and unfeeling; empathic concern is not a possibility. And yet, it is clear that we care, often deeply, about these parts of the world. The oneness hypothesis also readily accommodates our ability to care for larger groups, entities, or collections; we can feel one with large numbers of individuals (such as all human beings, all sentient creatures, or all living things), with larger systems (such as ecosystems or the planet Earth), and with sets or collections of things (such as expressionist paintings or a particular architectural style).[45] The oneness hypothesis has the advantage of offering us a ready way to understand and develop our feelings for these aspects of our lives.

The third feature of the empathy-altruism hypothesis is the claim that empathy is *the path to selfless or altruistic behavior*. The oneness hypothesis does not aim at and is widely understood as undermining the possibility of altruism because it describes our apparently selfless, other-regarding actions as in some sense aimed at our own good. As was noted above, the denial of pure altruism blurs but does not completely collapse the distinction between self- and other-interest. Some seem to think that if I act out of a sense of oneness, my actions not only aren't altruistic but are in fact selfish. But unless we mean by "oneness" something like identity, this stronger claim does not follow. Selfish actions place excessive or even exclusive weight on one's narrow self-interest and neglect the welfare of others. Acting out of an enlarged sense of the self clearly takes the welfare of others seriously and can even give them priority over one's narrow self-interest. A person acting out of such an enlarged sense of self not only can act for another but can do so *for the other's sake*. What I can't do from the perspective of the enlarged sense of self is act *exclusively* for the sake of another. Outside of religious contexts (for example, Christianity, in which *agape* expresses a distinctive theological value), it is not immediately evident why this latter kind of selfless, pure altruism is such a wonderful thing. As a regular and general perspective on the world, it may strike one as more pathological than fine: living *only* for others is not a particularly appealing ideal.[46] At the very least, this kind of view has the potential to generate new and distinctive ethical problems.[47]

Take, for example, my desire to benefit my children. I regard myself as one with my children in the sense of seeing their good as my own. When I benefit them, I seek to act *for their sake*, but in doing so I further my own good as well. Most times, when I do things for them, I don't think about how much I am sacrificing; quite the contrary, I enjoy helping them flourish. I realize and embrace the idea that in order to achieve their happiness I must pay careful attention to what they want and be on guard not to simply project my own desires and aspirations onto them. Nel Noddings has shown how central such concern for the one cared for must be in genuine cases of caring.[48] This already shows that seeing my children as parts of my life does not entail merging or dissolving myself completely in them (or them in me). I would sacrifice my personal welfare and even my life in order to protect my children; some might insist this shows I am prepared to act "selflessly" on their behalf, but I disagree and find such claims in some respects self-congratulatory and pretentious.

An excessive emphasis on self-sacrifice distorts the true nature of caring. For example, my wife and I are happy to devote considerable sums of money to educate our children, but our aim has never been to spend ("sacrifice") our money but to educate our children. If some anonymous benefactor offered to pay the rest of our son's future tuitions with no strings attached, my wife and I would not object; we would be delighted to accept. We would not feel that we were being *deprived* of the opportunity to sacrifice for our child. Our aim is to see him get a good education and flourish. If we were to insist on using our own money to pay the tuition so that we could enjoy reflecting on what remarkably self-sacrificing parents we are, this would show our real concern is not our child's welfare but some self-centered desire to feel good about ourselves.[49] This is one kind of problem neo-Confucians worried about; such cases show that at least sometimes caring is not about avoiding selfishness, understood as being overly concerned with one's narrow personal welfare, but more about an avoidance of being self-centered in one's life and relationships.[50]

Being self-centered overlaps with but is different from our normal conception of being selfish. Being selfish means to give excessive or exclusive weight to one's own narrow interests over and against the interests of others; being self-centered means to take the self as the center of one's thoughts about the world.[51] It is a general point of view and seems to involve both a *metaphysical* claim and an *evaluative* claim. This clearly is how neo-Confucians regarded self-centeredness; to take the self as the center of the world involves cutting oneself off from a world with which one *really is* intimately connected—like denying the connection between one's arm and the rest of one's body—and, by alienating oneself from the world, becoming *unfeeling* toward it.

Adopting the perspective of a concern with self-centeredness alters the way we look at many cases of caring. Imagine a woman who by nature acts with great generosity and kindness but who thinks of her attitude and actions as expressions of *her* remarkable compassion toward the world. Neo-Confucians such as Wang Yangming would fault her for having the wrong view not only about herself but about her relationship with the world. Of course, many Western ethicists would also tend to think there is something wrong with her view. Kantians would say her kindness has no moral worth because she acts out of her nature and not the moral law. Most virtue ethicists would think she is not virtuous because she thinks too much about how nice she is and not enough about the needs of others; the proper focus of her attention is the latter not the former. Most people, if encouraged to think about it a bit, would worry about the moral value of her attitude (though not what she *does*). She seems overly full of herself, and this familiar yet uncommonly wise expression implies that the problem largely lies in her self-conception. The early Confucian Mengzi (Mencius; fourth century BCE) would say she is *acting* benevolently but not acting out of benevolence. Wang would agree but would diagnose her problem as having a wrong view of herself and her relationship with the people, creatures, and things of the world. Her view is too self-centered; it is also selfish, but only in an indirect and rather unusual sense.

Taking neo-Confucian thinkers as my primary inspiration, I have developed and presented a notion of oneness as an alternative way of thinking about how and why we come to care for other people, creatures, and things and have drawn certain contrasts between this view and the empathy-altruism hypothesis. I have argued that the oneness hypothesis offers some significant advantages over the empathy-altruism hypothesis; it allows us to account for a much greater range of human concern and avoid the problems empathy poses in regard to our care for non-human animals. I do not, though, intend to imply that the oneness hypothesis offers an exclusively better account of human caring than those that rely on empathic concern. In many cases, empathy and oneness are related, complementary, and mutually supporting. On the one hand, regarding others as parts of one's life tends to lead one to develop greater empathy with them (though here we are on firm ground only when we talk about other human beings). On the other hand, those toward whom we have empathic concern tend to come to be regarded as parts of our lives: we feel varying degrees of oneness with them. Sometimes empathizing may precede a sense of oneness; other times a sense of oneness gives rise to feelings of empathy. There is a logical connection but no fixed and necessary ordering. Other factors can come into play as well. For example, often our practices or routines establish connections with other people, creatures, or things that are the basis for a sense of oneness or give rise to empathy. We can engage in such practices or routines before having either a sense of oneness or feelings of empathy, but there is a natural relationship among these. Contemporary psychological research on imitation and mimicry shows not only how important these are for empathy and mutual understanding but also how they regularly occur without intention or conscious awareness.[52] Rituals and other kinds of routinized behavior can be understood as intentional policies that tap into this deeper, hard-wired feature of human nature. Oneness or empathy can, of course, and almost always does result in us taking up practices and routines that express and reinforce our sense of oneness or feelings of empathy. There is a natural relationship among these three features of human life but no absolute sequential ordering or necessary connection.[53] Such issues warrant much more systematic study by both philosophers and psychologists. What I hope to have contributed is the idea that oneness should be a central concern for anyone interested in how and why we care for many of the things we do.

Acknowledgments

Thanks to David W. Tien for many conversations on oneness and Wang Yangming and for comments on an earlier draft of this chapter. Thanks also to Daniel A. Bell, Brian Bruya, Erin M. Cline, Michael R. Slater, Justin Tiwald, Bryan W. Van Norden, and Christian Wenzel for helpful comments and suggestions on earlier drafts of this chapter. Thanks also to JeeLoo Liu for organizing a panel at the East Coast APA in December of 2010, at which I was invited to present this paper, and to the Templeton Foundation for its generous support of this event.

Notes

1. Bertrand Russell, *The Conquest of Happiness*, 191.

2. Thomas Nagel, *The Possibility of Altruism*.

3. Which organism or group receives or loses benefit and what type of fitness is gained or lost are complex issues and depend on the precise definition of "altruism" one employs. For a careful analysis of this issue, see Benjamin Kerr, Peter Godfrey-Smith, and Marcus W. Feldman, "What is Altruism?"

4. Elliot Sober and David Sloan Wilson, *Unto Others*.

5. The earliest work on this theory was done by C. Daniel Batson. For example, see his, "Prosocial motivation" and *The Altruism Question*. This theory has also been well defended against egoistic alternatives. For example, see, C. Daniel Batson, Janine. L. Dyck, J. Randall Brandt, Judy G. Batson, Anne L. Powell, M. Rosalie McMaster, and Cari Griffitt, "Five Studies Testing Two New Egoistic Alternatives to the Empathy-Altruism Hypothesis." Martin L. Hoffman has made influential contributions to this movement and especially in regard to the methods of cultivating empathy. See his, *Empathy and Moral Development*.

6. Sympathy and empathy overlap in sense and use. Given our purposes, we will focus on empathy, which entails not only feeling *for* another but feeling *as* another feels. I can have sympathy for others who are not themselves aware of their situation and hence who have not experienced any feelings for me to share. For a careful and revealing analysis of these issues, see Stephen Darwall, "Empathy, Sympathy, Care."

7. See Michael Slote, *The Ethics of Care and Empathy* (13–15) and *Moral Sentimentalism* (13–25).

8. See Stephen Angle, *Sagehood*.

9. As I argue in section 5, the notions of empathy and oneness are not mutually exclusive, though they are distinct and offer different perspectives on other-regarding care.

10. I offer an analysis of different senses of oneness in regard to notions of anthropocentrism in "Early Confucianism and Environmental Ethics."

11. See, for example, the work of Joanna Macy, quoted in Lawrence E. Joseph, *Gaia*, 243. The Gaia hypothesis takes many forms; its original formulation, by James Lovelock, focused on the ways in which the earth is a self-regulating system and in this respect can be understood as a single living organism.

12. All translations from the Chinese are mine unless otherwise noted.

13. For a most informative survey of the notion of *li* in the history of Chinese thought, see Wing-tsit Chan, "The Evolution of the Neo-Confucian Concept *Li* as Principle." See also the numerous entries under "pattern" in the index of John Makeham, *Transmitters and Creators: Chinese Commentators and Commentaries on the* Analects.

14. See, for example, Ivanhoe, *Confucian Moral Self Cultivation*; *Ethics in the Confucian Tradition*; *Readings from the Lu-Wang School of Neo-Confucianism*; and "Virtue Ethics and the Chinese Confucian Tradition."

15. For those devoted to *gongfu* movies, this common Buddhist teaching device is the inspiration for the famous "hall of mirrors" fight scene in Bruce Lee's classic movie, *Enter the Dragon*.

16. *Yu zuan Zhuzi quan shu* 御纂朱子全書, 42.29a,b.

17. Neo-Confucian thinkers described a lack of feeling for the welfare of people, creatures, and things as being "numb" (*buren* 不仁) to the world. This allowed them to play on the term *buren* which, in their age, had the ethical sense of "lacking benevolence" *and* the medical sense of "paralysis." One who was "unfeeling" toward the things of the world was like a person with a paralyzed limb. In both cases, they failed to see and appreciate an underlying connection between themselves and something else. For a more thorough discussion of this idea, see Ivanhoe, *Ethics in the Confucian Tradition* (27–29) and "Virtue Ethics and the Confucian Tradition."

18. Both of these stories are recorded in the same passage in chapter three of *Henan Cheng shi yi shu* 河南程氏遺書.

19. *Qian* 乾 is the first hexagram in the *Yi Jing*; it represents heaven and the *yang* force. *Kun* 坤 is the second hexagram; it represents earth and the *yin* force.

20. The italicized phrases are from *Mengzi* 孟子 (*Mencius*) 1A7.

21. Zhang Zai, *Zhangzi quan shu* 張子全書, 79–82 (1.1b–7a).

22. The somatic aspects of many forms of empathy, both cognitive and affective, offers a way one might reinterpret Wang's claims about being "one body," at least with other sentient creatures. For this idea, see Jeanne C. Watson and Leslie S. Greenberg, "Empathic Resonance," 129.

23. Wang here is paraphrasing the example of the child and well from *Mengzi* 2A6.

24. *Mengzi* 1A7 offers the example of King Xuan being "unable to bear" the anguished cries and frightened appearance of an ox being led to slaughter and goes on to infer a general aversion to seeing any animal suffer.

25. See Ivanhoe, *Readings from the Lu-Wang School of Neo-Confucianism*, 160–162.

26. This line and the analogy of the use of the hands and feet are found in section 276 of Wang's *A Record for Practice* (*Chuan Xi Lu* 傳習錄; Ivanhoe, *Readings from the Lu-Wang School*). For a translation of the entire passage, see Wang Yangming (tr. Wing-tsit Chan), *Instructions for Practical Living*, 222–223.

27. In comments on an earlier draft, David W. Tien pointed out to me that the hierarchy described here, which is typical among neo-Confucians, is more subjective in nature: positions in the hierarchy are relative to their relationship to the subject. One also finds within traditional Chinese thought a more objective hierarchy in which the sage-king occupies a more prominent position than the commoner. Both of these are distinct from a Christian hierarchy, laid out in 1 Corinthians 12:12–28, which also is illustrated by using the metaphor of the body and its

various parts. In the biblical example, the positions are relative to an objective hierarchy set by God. These constitute three different senses of "hierarchy within oneness."

28. Earlier, I sketched the particular sense of empathy I use in this paper, but the term has a varied history and is defined and employed differently in contemporary writings. For a helpful survey and analysis, see C. Daniel Batson, "These Things Called Empathy."

29. Such a capacity is actually an active human tendency to empathize with others, as seen in the phenomenon of psychological contagion observed in very young children. In this respect, the modern psychological evidence offers some support to Mengzi's claims about moral "sprouts" and Wang Yangming's claims about "pure knowing." For Mengzi's and Wang's ideas, see Ivanhoe, *Confucian Moral Self Cultivation*.

30. As thinkers such as Hume make clear, one can have empathic concern for the joy of others, but as ethicists tend to be most interested in getting people not to act badly, the primary examples of empathy involve relieving the distress or suffering of others. Psychological studies of empathy almost all focus exclusively on the relief of perceived distress or suffering on the part of human beings.

31. David Hume, *An Inquiry Concerning the Principles of Morals*, 53. I have argued that Mengzi's examples of empathic care are much more complicated. See note 23 to my "Virtue Ethics and the Chinese Confucian Tradition."

32. Richard Holton and Rae Langton express considerable skepticism about how well we can simulate animal states of mind and therefore how exclusively or strongly we should rely on empathy in moral theory. See their "Empathy and Animal Ethics." For a brief response to their concerns, see Slote, *The Ethics of Care and Empathy*, 125–126.

33. See, for example, Robert B. Cialdini, Stephanie L. Brown, Brian P. Lewis, Carol Luce, and Steven L. Neuberg, "Reinterpreting the Empathy-Altruism Relationship." This is an especially important contribution because it is one of the earliest clear statements of this view and because the authors note the connection this view has with East Asian societies. For a groundbreaking study that explicitly relates the psychological literature to the philosophy of Wang Yangming, see David W. Tien, "Oneness and Self-Centeredness in the Moral Psychology of Wang Yangming."

34. Cialdini et al., "Reinterpreting the Empathy-Altruism Relationship," 483. The current literature often describes other-regarding feelings as either empathy or oneness, but, as I will argue below, there is no good reason to draw a sharp line here or to regard these as mutually exclusive.

35. On mirror neurons, see Jennifer H. Pfeifer and Claus Lamm, "'Mirror, Mirror, in My Mind'"; on imitation, see Rick B. van Baaren, Jean Decety, Ap Dijksterhuis, Andries van der Leji, and Matthijs L. van Leeuwen, "Being Imitated: Consequences of Nonconsciously Showing Empathy."

36. A significant volume of research links abnormal mirror neuron functioning with autism; this implies those who lack this shared mechanism for imitation suffer an at times severe deficit in regard to an ability to empathize and thereby are cut off from a normal sense of human community. See Pfeifer and Lamm, "'Mirror, Mirror, in My Mind,'" 190–191.

37. Lawrence Blum, in his "Particularity and Responsiveness," defends a similar view, arguing that human beings begin life with a strong sense of oneness with particular others and that this "sense of connection, on which sympathy is founded" (317) is a fundamental part of a child's sense of self.

38. I have defended a version of this claim in "Freud and the Dao."

39. Ensuring that human beings do at times act selflessly or altruistically is a central concern of C. Daniel Batson's defense of the "empathy-altruism hypothesis." For example, see his "Prosocial Motivation."

40. Cialdini et al., "Reinterpreting the Empathy-Altruism Relationship," 491. This is a much stronger claim than that one made by Bertrand Russell in the epigraph of this chapter.

41. Cialdini et al., "Reinterpreting the Empathy-Altruism Relationship," 490.

42. This feature of the oneness hypothesis makes it more clearly an example of moral realism.

43. This view is powerfully advanced and defended in Edward O. Wilson's book *Biophilia*. I develop and relate this view to other thinkers, East and West, in "Freud and the Dao."

44. I do not intend to claim or believe that oneness explains *all* that is valuable about altruism or caring for others. As I note below, in reference to the work of Nel Noddings and Michael Slote, caring often requires us to understand and appreciate the particular, individual preferences and aspirations of others. The common good does not exhaust the good of caring and can even mask certain important goods that mature forms of empathy reveal.

45. Thanks to Justin Tiwald for pointing out this virtue of the oneness hypothesis.

46. For a revealing exploration of how altruism can go wrong, see Barbara Oakley, Ariel Knafo, Guruprasad Madhavan, and David Sloan Wilson, eds., *Pathological Altruism*.

47. In this respect, the oneness hypothesis has certain formal similarities with Nietzsche's criticisms of compassion and his call to "revalue" this value. For a clear and insightful account of Nietzsche's ethical philosophy, which analyzes his concerns with virtues like compassion, see Brian Leiter, *Nietzsche on Morality*. Thanks to Michael Slater for encouraging me to note this comparison.

48. See Nel Noddings, *Caring*. Michael Slote has developed this insight into a robust account of how sentimentalism supports respect and autonomy. See his *The Ethics of Care and Empathy*, 55–66 and *Moral Sentimentalism*, 107–139.

49. Such a desire could take many forms. The example I have offered has the desire connected to a hedonic end, but it could just be a desire to sacrifice or to uphold an ideal of parental obligation.

50. One can try to understand the case I have proposed in terms of selfishness. For example, one might say that such parents are selfishly concerned about their moral reputations and not properly concerned about their child's education. This, though, is not the way we normally think about selfishness. A more conventional conception of selfishness might suggest the parents are

selfish in wanting to secure for themselves excessive or exclusive claim to being *caring parents*, thereby denying due recognition to other parents. There is nothing, though, in the view I have described that would entail or imply such an attitude. Self-centered parents could welcome other parents having a similarly self-centered view about themselves and *their* children; it would not affect them in the least. This suggests strongly that understanding the problem in terms of self-centeredness is more intuitive and revealing. I thank Christian Wenzel for comments on this issue.

51. In therapeutic settings, empathic concern for others often is described in terms of "de-centering" the self: a process of moving people from the "default mode" of egocentricity. This seems to support the idea that the goal is weakening self-centeredness—a view about the self and its relationship with the world—rather than working to eliminate selfishness—an attitude about the relative importance of one's needs and desires. For "de-centering," see Watson and Greenberg, "Empathic Resonance," 131.

52. For an informative analysis of imitation, see van Baaren et al., "Being Imitated."

53. There is a parallel here with moral cultivation in general. For example, the practice of rituals, which figure prominently in all forms of Confucianism, often precedes feeling or understanding in the process of cultivating ethical dispositions; in some cases, practice or feeling is largely constitutive of understanding. As Brad Wilburn argues in "Moral Self-Improvement," these three, practice, feeling, and understanding, take turns and cooperate in the development of virtue and in the larger project of forming and defining a way of life.

Works Cited

Angle, Stephen. *Sagehood: The Contemporary Significance of Neo-Confucian Philosophy*. Oxford University Press, 2009.

Batson, C. Daniel. *The Altruism Question: Toward a Social-Psychological Answer*. Erlbaum, 1991.

Batson, C. Daniel. "Prosocial Motivation: Is It Ever Truly Altruistic?" In *Advances in Experimental Social Psychology*, volume 20, ed. Leonard Berkowitz. Academic Press, 1987.

Batson, C. Daniel. "These Things Called Empathy: Eight Related but Distinct Phenomena." In *The Social Neuroscience of Empathy*, ed. Jean Decety and William Ickes. MIT Press, 2009.

Batson, C. Daniel, Janine L. Dyck, J. Randall Brandt, Judy G. Batson, Anne L. Powell, M. Rosalie McMaster, and Cari Griffitt. "Five Studies Testing Two New Egoistic Alternatives to the Empathy-Altruism Hypothesis." *Journal of Personality and Social Psychology* 55, no. 1 (1988): 52–77.

Blum, Lawrence. "Particularity and Responsiveness." In *The Emergence of Morality in Young Children*, ed. Jerome Kagan and Sharon Lamb. University of Chicago Press, 1987.

Chan, Wing-tsit. "The Evolution of the Neo-Confucian Concept Li as Principle." *Tsing Hua Journal of Chinese Studies* 4, no. 2 (1964): 123–149.

Cheng Hao 程顥 and Cheng Yi 程頤. *Henan Cheng shi yi shu* 河南程氏遺書. Taipei: *Taiwan shangwu yinshuguan* 台灣商務印書館, 1978.

Cialdini, Robert B., Stephanie L. Brown, Brian P. Lewis, Carol Luce, and Steven L. Neuberg. "Reinterpreting the Empathy-Altruism Relationship: When One into One Equals Oneness." *Journal of Personality and Social Psychology* 73, no. 3 (1997): 481–494.

Darwall, Stephen. "Empathy, Sympathy, Care." *Philosophical Studies* 89 (1998): 261–282.

Hoffman, Martin L. *Empathy and Moral Development: Implications for Caring and Justice.* Reprint: Cambridge University Press, 2007.

Holton, Richard, and Rae Langton. "Empathy and Animal Ethics." In *Singer and His Critics*, ed. Dale Jamieson. Blackwell, 1999.

Hume, David. *An Inquiry Concerning the Principles of Morals*, ed. Charles W. Hendel. Bobbs-Merrill, 1957.

Ivanhoe, Philip J. *Confucian Moral Self Cultivation*, second edition. Hackett, 2000.

Ivanhoe, Philip J. "Early Confucianism and Environmental Ethics." In *Confucianism and Ecology: The Interrelation of Heaven, Earth, and Humans*, ed. Mary Evelyn Tucker and John Berthrong. Harvard University Press, 1998.

Ivanhoe, Philip J. *Ethics in the Confucian Tradition: The Thought of Mengzi and Wang Yangming*, second edition. Hackett, 2002.

Ivanhoe, Philip J. "Freud and the Dao." In *The Reception and Rendition of Freud in China*, ed. Tao Jiang and Philip J. Ivanhoe. Routledge, 2012.

Ivanhoe, Philip J. *Readings from the Lu-Wang School of Neo-Confucianism*. Hackett, 2009.

Ivanhoe, Philip J. "Virtue Ethics and the Chinese Confucian Tradition." In *Cambridge Companion to Virtue Ethics*, ed. Daniel C. Russell. Cambridge University Press, 2013.

Joseph, Lawrence E. *Gaia: The Growth of an Idea.* St. Martin's Press, 1990.

Kerr, Benjamin, Peter Godfrey-Smith, and Marcus W. Feldman. "What Is Altruism?" *Trends in Ecology and Evolution* 19, no. 3 (2004): 135–140.

Leiter, Brian. *Routledge Philosophy Guidebook to Nietzsche on Morality.* Routledge, 2002.

Makeham, John. *Transmitters and Creators: Chinese Commentators and Commentaries on the Analects.* Harvard University Press, 2003.

Nagel, Thomas. *The Possibility of Altruism.* Princeton University Press, 1979.

Noddings, Nel. *Caring: A Feminine Approach to Ethics and Moral Education.* University of California Press, 1984.

Oakley, Barbara, Ariel Knafo, Guruprasad Madhavan, and David Sloan Wilson, eds. *Pathological Altruism.* Oxford University Press, 2012.

Pfeifer, Jennifer H., and Mirella Dapretto. "'Mirror, Mirror in My Mind': Empathy, Interpersonal Competence, and the Mirror Neuron System." In *The Social Neuroscience of Empathy*, ed. Jean Decety and William Ickes. MIT Press, 2009.

Russell, Bertrand. *The Conquest of Happiness*. Reprint. Routledge, 1995.

Slote, Michael. *The Ethics of Care and Empathy*. Routledge, 2007.

Slote, Michael. *Moral Sentimentalism*. Oxford University Press, 2010.

Sober, Elliott, and David Sloan Wilson. *Unto Others: The Evolution and Psychology of Unselfish Behavior*. Harvard University Press, 1998.

Tien, David W. "Oneness and Self-Centeredness in the Moral Psychology of Wang Yangming." *Journal of Religious Ethics* 40, no. 1 (2012): 52–71.

van Baaren, Rick B., Jean Decety, Ap Dijksterhuis, Andries van der Leij, and Matthijs L. van Leeuwen. "Being Imitated: Consequences of Nonconsciously Showing Empathy." In *The Social Neuroscience of Empathy*, ed. Jean Decety and William Ickes. MIT Press, 2009.

Wang, Yangming. *Instructions for Practical Living and other Neo-Confucian Writings*, tr. Wing-tsit Chan. Columbia University Press, 1963.

Watson, Jeanne C., and Leslie S. Greenberg. "Empathic Resonance: A Neuroscience Perspective." In *The Social Neuroscience of Empathy*, ed. Jean Decety and William Ickes. MIT Press, 2009.

Wilburn, Brad. "Moral Self-Improvement." In *Moral Cultivation: Essays on the Development of Character and Virtue*, ed. Brad K. Wilburn. Lexington Books, 2007.

Wilson, Edward O. *Biophilia*. Harvard University Press, 1984.

Zhang Zai 張載. *Zhangzi quan shu* 張子全書. *Si ku quan shu* 四庫全書, volume 697. Shanghai: *Shanghai guji chubanshe* 上海古籍出版社, 1987.

Zhu Xi 朱熹. *Yu zuan Zhuzi quan shu* 御纂朱子全書. *Si ku quan shu* 四庫全書, volume 721. Shanghai: *Shanghai guji chubanshe* 上海古籍出版社, 1987.

10 What Does the Law of Non-Contradiction Tell Us, If Anything? Paradox, Parameterization, and Truth in Tiantai Buddhism

Brook Ziporyn

1 The Problem of Contradictions in Mahayana Texts

This chapter will present arguments derived from the Tiantai school of Chinese Buddhism that attempt to show that the law of non-contradiction (henceforth LNC) is incoherent in the absence of an essentialist ontology, and sketch out some of the alternate notions of truth that Tiantai puts in the place of that founded on the absolutization of that alleged law.

The LNC has long seemed to many philosophers an unavoidable starting point for all philosophical inquiry, and when explicitly formulated, even one of the few literally indubitable or *a priori* truths upon which all rational people can agree. A bit of a splash has been made in recent years, however, by philosophers (among them Graham Priest) who have called into question the applicability of LNC for all truth claims.[1] Priest has also turned his attention to Buddhist thought in this connection, and has collaborated with the Buddhist scholars Jay Garfield and Yasuo Deguchi to attempt an interpretation of the very common occurrence of seemingly paradoxical propositions in Mahayana Buddhist literature. This is the question at issue, for example, in Deguchi, Garfield, and Priest's stimulating essay "The Way of the Dialetheist: Contradictions in Buddhism." The premise for this exposition is the traditional Indo-Tibetan Buddhist Madhyamaka Two Truths theory, which rests on a sharp separation of what it calls *Conventional Truth* and *Ultimate Truth*.

Conventional Truth in Madhyamaka consists of (1) ordinary non-theorized speech and logic as it is practiced consistently within a speech community (for example, the commonsensical ideas of "cause" and "effect," of "self" and "other," of "good" and "bad" and so on), (2) early Buddhist doctrine and terminology (for example, the doctrines of non-self, impermanence, suffering, Nirvana, the Four Noble Truths, etc.), and (3) the *rejection* in later Buddhist doctrine and terminology of the literal truth of those very same early Buddhist doctrines and terminologies (for example, the declaration that because of Emptiness, there is really no such real entity denoted by either non-self *or* self, and likewise no impermanence, no suffering, no Nirvana, no Four

Noble Truths). Ultimate Truth, in contrast, is the transconceptual correlative, or real referent, of the negations in category 3 above: some sort of experience of actual liberation, which transcends the applicability even of these negating statements. The contradictions in category 3 are mere means to get beyond all statements, including themselves.

Note that this theory makes for a very limited range of Conventional Truth. The everyday concepts of ordinary speech, when consistent, are permitted, but metaphysical theories claiming to unpack these concepts into a fully worked-out and universally applicable theory are not even included as Conventional Truths. This allows for a few contradictions among levels, but each level is itself understood to be strictly self-consistent. Also, some views are excluded: although the everyday concepts of ordinary speech, when consistent, are permitted, metaphysical theories claiming to unpack these concepts into a fully worked-out and universally applicable theory (e.g., to deduce from the everyday usefulness or even indispensability of the concept of causality that causality is a necessary and absolute aspect of reality, thus producing a theory of a first cause; or alternately, to deduce from the necessity of a state prior to every existent state that the universe is beginningless, and thus to deny the possibility of a first cause) are not even included as Conventional Truths; all such theories that claim absolute validity (e.g., to deduce from the everyday usefulness or even indispensability of the concept of causality that causality is a necessary and absolute aspect of reality, thus producing a theory of a first cause; or alternately, to deduce from the necessity of a state prior to every existent state that the universe is beginningless, and thus to deny the possibility of a first cause) are understood as just plain errors because Ultimate Truth is construed as some kind of realization, not a proposition. The same goes for eccentric, idiolectic speech, poetry, paradoxes, mad ravings and so on: all excluded. "The world has a beginning," "the world has no beginning" are both false, as are "the world is ultimately made of matter," "the world is ultimately made of spirit," "the world consists of two substances, spirit and matter" and so on. "2 + 2 = 5," "water causes fire to boil," and "a cup is an elephant" are also false. "2 + 2 = 4," "Heat causes water to boil," "I have desires which cause suffering," and "I don't exist [as an ultimate substance], so I have no desires," "there are no desires [as ultimate substances] and no end to desire" are all conventionally true. Ultimate Truth is some kind of realization of the last proposition, to which that proposition is stipulatively non-adequate.

With this background in mind, Deguchi, Garfield, and Priest (henceforth DGP) consider several possible interpretations of the paradoxical assertions commonly found in Mahayana Buddhist texts, statements of the kind included in category 3 above. One possible interpretation is that they might be metaphors, not meant to be taken literally. Alternatively, they might be meant only as *upāyas* (skillful means) which are not themselves ultimately true, but serve a therapeutic function to undermine attachments.[2] A third possible interpretation is that these statements are themselves meant to be taken as true, but true in a sense that is rationally incomprehensible, beyond conceptualization, thus also tending toward a form of irrationalist mysticism. These three possibilities are, according to DGP (based on their understanding of the Madhyamika "Two Truths" doctrine), the default interpretive stances of Indo-Tibetan Buddhist traditions. On this reading, and consistent with the Madhyamika position described above, all verbal propositions fall *at best* into Conventional Truth; no such propositions, contradictory or otherwise, are Ultimately True.

The structure here follows the parable of the raft in early Buddhism,[3] which compares Buddhism itself, including all its doctrines and practices, to a raft which is meant to be used to cross a river, but to be abandoned when the opposite shore is reached. The other shore is the end of suffering, Buddhism's practical soteriological goal. The raft is to be clung to and followed only for a time, and its sole justification lies in its ability to make itself obsolete, to lead to its own abandonment. A good raft is a raft that leads beyond itself, which succeeds in making itself no longer necessary. This stipulation strictly delimits the sense of what it will mean to call statements true within the context of Buddhist doctrine. Buddhism is, in this vision, a hundred per cent *pragmatic* in its approach to truth. The question of what kinds of statements may count as *legitimate* is the only standard of truth in this Buddhism, and this is thoroughly determined by the overriding soteriological aims of the entire Buddhist tradition. Every statement and every practice are justified *solely* in terms of their utility for the goal of *diminishing suffering*.

That means that both Buddhist epistemology and Buddhist ethics are thoroughgoingly pragmatic: what is *true* at the conventional level is what is conducive to ending suffering, and what is *good* is action that is conducive to ending suffering. What helps one get across the river is good, is useful, is valid, is to be clung to for the duration of one's journey. What is on the other shore is neither true nor untrue, neither good nor bad; all such terms pertain only to the intermediate realm of what is relevant for the goal of ending suffering—and of course this means mainly Buddhist doctrines and practices.

Still following DGP's account of the default "Indo-Tibetan interpretation of the Two-Truths theory, this side (the near shore of pre-enlightenment) is the realm where it is meaningful to speak of good and bad or true and false, and in which one is pragmatically faced with a choice between them. True is different from false, as clinging to the raft is different from sinking. But this has nothing to do with contradiction; it has to do with utility in the goal of ending suffering, which is accomplished by ending attachment to desire and definitive views about reality.[4] Conventional Truth is a raft that functions well only if it leads beyond itself; all propositions are good propositions to the extent that they lead to the end of all propositions. And a proposition's being "good" in this sense is the only meaningful way in which it can be called true.

Deguchi, Garfield, and Priest offer an alternative interpretation of how to understand the contradictions in category 3. They argue that at least some of the contradictions in Mahayana literature are meant to be (1) rationally comprehensible and (2) descriptions of facts, and thus true statements. Specifically, they are to be understood in terms of self-inclusion paradoxes, which deal with self-referential totalities (e.g., the liar's paradox, Russell's paradox, etc.). Priest has argued that even though they are paradoxical, they are nonetheless logically permissible.[5] In Mahayana Buddhism, these would include the common appearance of claims that "the essence of all things is essencelessness," "the only truth is that there is no truth," "it is accurate to describe reality as beyond description," and so on. These statements are read by DGP as sharing the structure of Russell's Paradox ("the set of all sets that do not include themselves does not include itself") or the liar's paradox ("all statements made by me are false," or, in simplified form, "this statement is false"). Priest has argued that in spite of their self-contradiction, these statements are nonetheless literally true, and the same goes for the isomorphic claims in Mahayana literature. Their paradox derives from the specification of a totality that includes the specification itself, where the specification involves a self-negation. "The nature of all things is to be devoid of any nature"—this statement is, according to DGP, rationally comprehensible, logically consistent, and literally true. Derivatively, "a cup is not a cup" is also literally true, since the true essence of a cup is essencelessness. However, this is as far as the implications go; the spread of paradoxicality does not extend beyond this relatively small number of propositions involving self-referential totalities. Others must be chalked up to mere heuristics, *upāyas*, and metaphors. Hence, statements like "a cup is an elephant" are, at best, merely conventionally true—which for Priest and his co-authors, as for the Indo-Tibetan traditions generally, means, in the final analysis, not actually true.

The DGP solution to the self-inclusion paradoxes in Mahayana texts is a step in the right direction if we are to overcome the limits of Indo-Tibetan Buddhist thought, which tend to mirror the assumptions of traditional Indo-European logics. However, they leave the remaining contradictions in place. If we are to take these seriously and take seriously the challenges posed by Chinese Buddhism, in particular the Tiantai Buddhist view, in which such statements as "a cup is an elephant" are also claimed to be rationally comprehensible, logically consistent, and literally true, then we must go a step further. In this chapter, I will draw from Tiantai Buddhism (founded by Zhiyi 智顗, 538–597 CE), where it is claimed that there is no need to divide the contradictory claims into the different interpretive categories (e.g., therapeutically refutable conventional truths, non-literal metaphors, rational and literal truths). Rather, these interpretive paths can be construed as distinct modalities that *converge* in a truth-preserving way. To get there, we must invoke a specifically Tiantai understanding of the roles of *upāya* in Buddhism and the possible definitions of "truth," one of which, in sharp contrast to the Indo-Tibetan sources of DGP's Buddhological stance, develops out of the very specific Chinese approach to these questions, rooted in earlier Chinese traditions. Here, if we may extend the metaphor, the raft is still only a good raft if it leads beyond itself—but what it finds on the other shore is not the end of all rafts but a raft factory, as it were, which comes to include the production of even the original raft: the other shore is the skill to create and use an infinity of rafts at will, and to move smoothly from any one to any other. This will, however, require an expansion of the implications of the DGP claims to which DGP themselves would perhaps not be friendly, and which cast new light on the question of meaning and application of the LNC. I believe these expanded implications are desirable both ethically and philosophically, and will also enable us to answer the question of how apparent *reductio ad absurdum* arguments can be understood as having any force in spite of the acceptance of self-contradiction as a characteristic of true statements, which DGP themselves admit is for them an unresolved problem point.[6]

2 The Chinese Background of the Tiantai Position

The Tiantai position is highly unorthodox in Buddhism, proposing a "Three Truths" position unknown in India and Tibet. It is a uniquely Chinese contribution to Buddhist epistemology and metaphysics. In particular, Tiantai inherits and expands on the epistemological ideas of the ancient Daoist philosopher Zhuangzi (fourth century BCE). Zhuangzi offers his own version of the paradoxes of totality and self-inclusion (concerning "existence" and "speech" generally), based on an analysis of indexical language and the dyadic holism of meaning it implies. Very briefly, Zhuangzi holds that to specify anything is to pick it out of a whole and designate it as a "this." But "this" is an indexical term whose meaning changes in accordance with what is indicated when it is uttered, and further, this change is guaranteed to occur due to the immanent structure of this act of picking out a "this" itself. For a "this" is picked out in contrast to a "that," but because these terms are indexical, the "that" is also a "this" in its own right, which requires the original "this" to serve as its "that." Hence every "this" necessarily must also be "that." And this applies to even the largest and most all-encompassing categories: "being" is a "this" which requires the contrasted being of a non-this, a "non-being," which as itself a new "this" and thus a new standard of what is to count as "being," simultaneously posits the original "being" as rather a kind of non-being. "Meaningfulness" is a "this" which requires the copresence of a non-this, a meaninglessness, which as itself a new "this" requires that the original "meaningfulness" now to count in contrast as a meaninglessness.

It is this sort of approach, rather than that applying only to self-referential totalities, that establishes the inevitability of the paradox. If the whole is paradoxical, all of its parts are seen to be paradoxical. But more, there is a totality of "this and non-this" that applies directly for any specific determination just as it does for that of the totality. Every determination without exception involves a self-referential totality paradox. The premise here is a kind of holism that presupposes from the beginning that the identities of individual things are wholly dependent on their context, i.e., are indexical, as Zhuangzi argues earlier in this same chapter. But it is not just that this makes them ultimately dependent on "the whole," i.e., the totality of all possible contexts, such that if the whole is unmoored, every individual component is likewise unmoored. It is true that for Zhuangzi, if "Being as a whole" and "stateability as such" are incapable of non-paradoxical articulation, the same must apply to every individual proposition about any being and any predicate. But this is because every "this/not-this" is itself a paradoxical and self-referential totality. That is, the self-referential paradoxes are *necessary and inevitable*, pertaining not only to certain peculiar self-negating types of propositions ("This statement is false," etc.), but by necessity pertaining to any proposition at all, due to the very structure of what a proposition is, i.e., the necessary involvement of both self-negation and dependence on a self-including totality that pertains to every proposition qua proposition. The conditions of "self-negation" and "self-reference" and "reference to a self-including totality" thus pertain to all statements as such. This allows Zhuangzi to move from these totality paradoxes directly to the "anything goes" unraveling of *all* propositions (the old man is young, the tip of a hair is large, the mountain is small, and all things are born together with me).[7]

3 The Tiantai Approach to Contradiction

The Tiantai approach, in accordance with this tradition, adds two new ideas to the traditional Two Truths. The first is the idea of a third perspective, which lies neither at one extreme nor the other; it is neither an affirmation nor a negation of how things appear within a particular conventional framework. This perspective is simultaneously a "neither/nor" and a "both/and" judgment on what had previously been opposed as Conventional and Ultimate Truth (and thus as means and ends). This is the Third Truth, which in Tiantai is called the "Mean" (or "Middle" or "Center"; *zhong* 中). The second idea, following from the first, is that "all possible phenomena are derivable from, converge into, and are always discoverable within" something.[8] This something into which all things converge is at first understood as the determination of being the "Mean" alone (i.e., the character of being central, centrality as such, which here means the non-mutual-exclusivity of being provisionally posited as a specific finite determination and the negation and transcendence of that same determination). But finally it is understood to be in *all three* of the determinations (Emptiness, Provisional Positing, and the Mean), and indeed in all determinations without exception. This is the derivation of the idea of mutual penetration and interfusion, the idea that all possible entities interpervade, that is so distinctive to the Tiantai school.[9] The Mean is said to denote "the identity" between Conventional Truth and Ultimate Truth—the idea that they are synonyms, that "Conventional" and "Empty" (i.e., "Ultimate" Truth) are alternate words for one and the same meaning. But this is a peculiar type of "sameness," and we cannot understand in what sense this sameness implies "all possible entities are derivable from, converge into, and are discoverable in" the Mean, the second of the new ideas in Tiantai Three Truths theory, unless we understand in just what sense these two are "the same." This peculiar mode of sameness is explained in the Tiantai doctrine of "opening the provisional to reveal the real (*kai quan xian shi* 開權顯實)." This is a way of further specifying the relation between Conventional and Ultimate Truth, illustrating the way in which the two extremes are not only synonymous, but also irrevocably opposed, and indeed identical only by means of their opposition. Provisional Truth is the antecedent, the premise, and indeed in a distinctive sense the *cause* of Ultimate Truth, but only because it is the strict exclusion of Ultimate Truth.

The clearest way to explain this structure is to compare it to the contrasting relation between the set up and the punch line of a joke. Here is a suitably silly example.

Setup: It takes money to make money.

Punch line: Because you have to copy it really exactly.

Let's talk about that structure. When I said, "It takes money to make money," it seemed to be, and was likely to be interpreted as, a serious remark, a real piece of information, perhaps about investment strategies or the like. It had the quality of seriousness, of factuality, of non-ironic information. There is nothing funny about that statement. But when the punch line comes, retrospectively, that set up *is* funny. That set up is funny because it has been recontextualized by the pun on the word "make," which is made to have more than one identity when put into a new context.

The interesting thing here, most closely relevant to relation of identity between Conventional and Ultimate in the Tiantai Three Truths, is that it is precisely by *not* being funny that the setup was funny. In other words, if it were already funny, if you didn't take it seriously for at least a moment, the contrast between the two different meanings of this thing could never have clashed in the way that is necessary to make the laughter, to create the actual effect of humorousness. We have a setup which is serious and a punch line which is funny, but when you look back at the setup from the vantage point of having heard the punch line, *that setup is also funny*. After all, we don't say that just the punch line is funny. We say the whole joke is funny. The set up is funny, however, in the very strange mode of "not being funny yet." It is only funny because it wasn't funny. This is the sense in which the Third Truth, the Mean, reveals the "identity" between Provisional Positing and Emptiness. Provisional Positing *is* Emptiness only inasmuch as it is the very opposite of Emptiness, the temporary exclusion of Emptiness. It is by being Non-Empty (i.e., something in particular) that it is Emptiness (i.e., devoid of any unambiguous or unconditionally definite essence). Its Emptiness is present *as* Provisional Positing, and as any particular provisional posit, just as humor is present in the deadpan setup *as* seriousness. This same form of "identity"—really neither identity nor difference, or both identity and difference— then applies at the meta-level between the Mean itself and the other Two Truths: they "are" the Mean precisely because they are not the Mean, because they are the two opposed extremes.

What is important here is to preserve *both* the contrast between the two *and* their ultimate identity in sharing the quality of humorousness that belongs to every atom of the joke considered as a whole, once the punch line has been revealed. The setup is serious, while the punch line is funny. The humorousness of the punch line depends on the seriousness of the setup, and on the contrast and difference between the two. However, once the punch line has occurred, it is also the case that the setup is, retrospectively, funny. This also means that the original contrast between the two is both preserved and annulled: neither humorousness nor seriousness means the same thing after the punch line dawns, for their original meanings depended on the mutually exclusive nature of their defining contrast. Is the setup serious or funny? It is both: it is funny *as* serious, and serious *as* funny. Is the punch line serious or funny? It is both, but in an interestingly different way. It is obviously funny, but is it also serious? Yes. Why? Because now that the setup has occurred, both "funny" and "serious" have changed in meaning. Originally, we thought that "funny" meant "what I laugh at when I hear it" or something like that, and "serious" meant "what I am in earnest about" or something similar. But now we see that "funny" can also mean "what I take to be serious, what I am *not* laughing about, what I am earnestly considering, or crying over, or bewailing even." But this means also that the meaning of "serious" has changed as well: it can mean "what can turn out to be either funny or serious." The whole of the funny joke does possess this quality of being-able-to-turn-out-either-funny-or-serious, and thus the joke as a whole is now seen to be "serious," just as the whole joke has turned out to be "funny."

So both "funny" and "serious" now both mean "funny-and-serious, what can appear as both funny and serious." Each is now a center that subsumes the other; they are intersubsumptive. As a consequence, the old pragmatic standard of truth is applied more liberally here: all claims, statements and positions are true in the sense that all *can*, if properly recontextualized, lead to liberation—which is to say, to their own self-overcoming. Conversely, none will lead to liberation if not properly contextualized.

Emptiness (*kong* 空) and Provisional Positing (*jia* 假) (Ultimate and Conventional Truth) are "identical," and this identity between them is what the Third Truth, the Mean, is. This also entails the claim that Conventional and Ultimate are here viewed as intersubsumptive, each instantiating the other: on the one hand, "Emptiness" is a merely Provisional Truth, since it is, like every other determinate view, a concept, a word, something which succeeds in having an effect and thus necessarily negates other things, which is thus finite and thus conditional, and hence only locally coherent. Hence Emptiness is Conventional, *kong* is *jia*. But *jia* is also *kong*: that means, *not only* that all provisional posits are themselves empty, but *also* that what Provisional Positing per se is is what emptiness is per se: that what emptiness really is is to provisionally posit. For an entity to be empty, then, means not only for it to have no essence or fixed identity, but also for it to produce, and further indeed to always already have, infinite essences and identities. It is in this way that the Zhuangzian version of the self-inclusion totality paradoxes come to bear fruit in the Tiantai system. Any of the three modes is itself the whole truth, and each *separately* accounts for all of reality. All things are Provisional Positing, including Emptiness and the Mean. All things are Emptiness, including Provisional Positing and the Mean. All things are the Mean, including Emptiness and Provisional Positing. All propositions are reducible to Conventional Truths. All propositions are reducible to Emptiness. All are reducible to the identity between the two, which is itself the only "object" apprehended in these two alternate ways.

Thus in the Tiantai "Three Truths" theory, in contrast to the Two Truths model, instead of concluding that every particular view and proposition and thing is ultimately false, we conclude that all is, ultimately, true, but in a very specific sense. Tiantai abolishes the Madhyamaka hierarchy between the Two Truths, as well as the category of plain falsehood. The contents of Conventional Truth are now expanded to include every possible locally coherent proposition without exception—whatever can in any possible circumstance serve as a "raft," i.e., applying the same criterion as we saw in Indo-Tibetan Two Truths theory, anything that serves to overcome attachments, including the attachment to itself. Anything that leads beyond itself, like a raft, is a Conventional Truth. But propositions are only capable of having a specifiable meaning if they exclude something. To exclude something is to be finite. To be finite is to be conditional. To be conditional is to be self-canceling, since any specification of its essence necessarily includes what its essence excludes: by assenting to its existence, you are also assenting to the existence of what excludes it. To be is to be finite, and to be finite is to necessarily require the existence of what is beyond itself. To posit any finite thing is to posit a beyond to that finite thing. Hence, the positing of any finite thing is a way of indicating the copresence also of a beyond to that finite thing. Hence, all propositions are Conventional Truths, but the contents of Conventional Truth are precisely the contents of Ultimate Truth, for the latter signifies only the simultaneous positing and negating of all Conventional Truths, the infinitely productive "raft factory" to which every raft leads. Each possible view is a truth, and in each case in the three distinct senses specified by the Three Truths.

4 The Logic of Contradiction

Thus Tiantai, following the Chinese traditions outlined above, claims that contextualism, plus the holism thus entailed, plus the self-inclusion totality paradoxes, equals potentially infinite meanings for every meaning-candidate and potentially infinite essences for every essence-candidate. Since "infinite" here will entail both opposites in any pair of opposites, the results of this will fly in the face of the law of non-contradiction generally. Following DGP, for the traditional Indo-Tibetan reading of the Two Truths, the LNC gives no true ontological information at all, as it applies only to the Conventional Level and there is no true ontological information to give on that level: only Ultimate Truth is "real" truth. For Tiantai, the LNC also gives no ontological information except that expressed in Spinoza's dictum: determination is negation. It means simply that *whatever is determinate is also conditional* (basic Buddhism, in other words). Put otherwise, the LNC, in the absence of an essentialist, or substance ontology, means only that *for any condition that can be imagined, there is necessarily some other condition that is capable of excluding (negating, destroying) it, by definition.* And this, lo and behold, says exactly the same thing that the *denial* of the LNC says: anything determinate necessarily entails the thinkability of its own negation, the possibility of being negated by some conceivable other, which is as inseparable from and constitutive of its being-what-it-is as anything else attributed to its essence. Here we have the shortest version to the Tiantai Three Truths: the LNC (X is X) and the anti-LNC (X is always *also* constitutively non-X) turn out to be synonyms. Provisional Positing (*jia*) is precisely Emptiness (*kong*), and this identity between them is the Mean (*zhong*). The Three Truths thus express the idea that the self-inclusion/self-negation totality paradox applies to the LNC itself.

This has large implications for our understanding of LNC. The law of non-contradiction is given by Aristotle in three forms, according to the accepted doxa: the ontological form, the logical form, and the psychological form. The "ontological version" (*Metaphysics* IV 3 1005b19–23) concerns what predicates can belong to the same subject. "It is impossible for the same thing at the same time both to be-in and not to be-in the same thing in the same respect."[10] The logical version (*Metaphysics* IV 3 1011b13–14) concerns two contradictory propositions: they cannot both be true at once. The psychological version (*Metaphysics* IV 3 1005b23–25) concerns two beliefs: one cannot believe both of two contradictory claims at once. The latter two versions are dependent on the first version; if the first version were false, the other two would also be false. We can thus expand on the meaning of the logical version, bringing out its fuller meaning, by restating it as follows: "the same proposition cannot be true and false *in the same sense.*"

But we should see an enormous red flag in Aristotle's formulation: it is the words translated "at the same time" and "in the same respect," and in our expanded logical version, "in the same sense." With these words, the entire principle is exposed as a world-historical instance of gerrymandering hand-waving.

What is a "respect"? A "respect in which something is asserted" is, perhaps, a set of relations, or a context, specified by a particular point of view that determines the items that are to be considered of relevance in this instance, abstracting one aspect or part of the item in question and addressing that alone, in separation from the other aspects or parts of that very same thing. How do we determine which relations and how many of them get to count as a single "respect"? Answer: only those relations and contexts which render a non-contradictory set of predicates count as a single respect. Therefore, "in the same respect" is a circular condition. I allow only as much into a "respect" as can turn out to be non-contradictory. Whatever leads to a contradiction I simply relegate to another "respect." The same can be said, *mutatis mutandis*, for what it means to say something is true "in one sense" and untrue "in another sense," or even, more searchingly, is true "at one time" and is untrue "at another time." How long is one "time"? Unless moments are dimensionless simples, which I take to be impossible, the duration of a "time" must be variable, and the same problems about their definition applies: however much time can include a set of events that are non-contradictory in whatever sense is under examination will be what counts as a single time in that case. The law of non-contradiction is true only in the same way that the "law" that there are twelve inches to a foot is true. Whatever exceeds twelve inches is considered part of the next foot. Metaphysicians are badly mistaken when they think that it tells us something deep about reality; we should be no more amazed to find it always true than we are amazed to find that, no matter where we might search throughout the cosmos, however many billions of light-years away, we always find that every foot of space has exactly twelve inches in it, no more and no less. It tells me nothing about the world, other than the conditionality of anything determinate (i.e., that there are always more inches than twelve available for counting).

The law of non-contradiction does not tell me that the world, or any actual entity in the world, or any truth about the world, is non-contradictory. It just tells me that wherever I can describe two contrary characteristics as coexistent in some composite, I will describe that coexistence as a non-contradictory complexity of a single entity, and whenever the elements in a composite entity fail to coexist, due to a conflict between them, I will simply define the elements as no longer belonging to a single entity. We might say, in Kantian terms, that it is Transcendental, in fact that it is an analytic *a priori* judgment. That it must be so of all our propositions proves something about the nature of (certain of) our mental operations only.[11] Since all Mahayana Buddhists agree that there are no simples, and that "entities" are not a natural kind, that the boundaries that serve to determine what counts as "this entity" as opposed to "that entity" are not final ontological facts about the world that can only be correctly identified in one way, the LNC must be seen to be strictly circular for these Buddhists. Whatever exists is composite—i.e., in some sense or other contradictory, both "this" and "something other than this." The sense in which this composite is not contradictory is a description of the coexistence of these differences and the judgment (not uniquely warranted) that these are in fact parts of a single entity rather than two or more entities.

Is it an accident that a single proposition allows of many "senses"? That each thing can be described in more ways than one? That propositions admit of more than one "sense" in which they can be understood? Or is it a constitutive condition of there being any meaning at all that there is always *more than one* respect? To establish the latter, which is the Tiantai claim, we need to show that the presence of any single respect necessarily implies the presence of another respect—that seeing something in a particular way entails the ability to also see it in *other* ways, that viewing something within some given set of parameters necessarily implies the possibility of other, excluded, parameters, that one context always implies other contexts. And this can be established, I claim, purely on the basis of considering what constitutes a respect— namely, a context.

To specify a respect or sense in which something is meant is to allow some among all possible contextualizing factors to enter the consideration of this thing, to serve as the relevant context, while excluding others. Hence it necessarily comes with the simultaneous presence of other alternate contexts. That the act of excluding a context from consideration is necessary means that it is possible also not to exclude it, and indeed that one is already considering it in the act of excluding it. "O" is the letter that follows "N" in the context of the alphabet, and thus in the sense that it can form a part of this series, but in the sense that this same sign can be viewed in the context of the series of all integers it is also the sign for zero. The fact that either of these contexts is one context among many, not the sum of all contexts, means that the application of either always involves the possibility of the other. But more searchingly, even "the whole," the putatively unique sum of all contexts, is a *selective* context in that it has to be chosen as the relevant context in any given case in preference to some other possible context (i.e., any partial context), and it is only to that extent that it is meaningful at all, i.e., to the extent that it excludes something, that it specifies something. To say, "I view this in relation to the whole universe" is to neglect to view it in the way it might appear in light of the changed priorities and effectivities that all the items in its local context would bring to it, even if those same items, otherwise contextualized, would also appear in the larger context of the whole.

Further, the whole is itself unstable, unspecifiable in non-paradoxical terms, as the DGP paradoxes establish. In Tiantai terms, this is argued in the following way: identities must be specifiable to be meaningful. To be specifiable is to be contrasted to something, to be the case sometimes and in some case but not in all. Determination is negation; to be determinate is to be non-all. The all, therefore, cannot be determinate—even as "the all." If the largest context is thus incapable of maintaining any single identity which is true *simpliciter* rather than "in some contexts, in some sense," then the same will be true for every other proposition. Every claim implies a relation to the whole, to the unconditional, but the unconditional is definitionally devoid of any fixed identity. That is, we cannot, in Kantian fashion, claim something like the following:

We can say nothing about the unconditional, or about the universe as such, but we can at least say that heat causes water to boil—i.e., make local claims about conditional facts.

"Heat causes water to boil" actually entails the claim that "the universe is such that heat causes water to boil." If no fact can be established about the universe, in the sense of the whole beyond which nothing exists and thus as the unconditional, we cannot say "the universe is such that heat causes water to boil," and thus cannot say "heat causes water to boil" as if it were truth *simpliciter*. It is true, but it, like every other possible proposition, is only true "in some sense, in some respects."

The other argument used by Aristotle and his admirers in support of LNC is an even more disgraceful bit of desperate hand-waving. LNC is admitted to be indemonstrable, because circular: any attempt to demonstrate it assumes it in advance. But then, lo and behold, this circularity, which in all other cases is used as an argument *against* the validity of a claim, is used as an argument for its absolute certainty. First there is some name-calling and threats against those who deny it: they are uneducated, they are fools, they are not worth our time. Then there is the suggestion that it is an axiom which must be accepted on faith, like the axioms of mathematics—gosh, you can't prove everything! For it is claimed that the law of non-contradiction is assumed in argument, and that no discussion can proceed without assuming it.[12] But even if this were true, it would amount to no more than saying that when certain north American contractors buy and sell lumber by the foot, they are also assuming twelve inches to the foot, and otherwise no business could be done. That doesn't mean that a foot *must* have twelve inches. Other people—poets, politicians, madmen, non-logicians—talk contradictorily at times, and their talk proceeds and has effects in the world just as much as do the discussions of those who, temporarily and in some contexts, decide to adhere to the law of non-contradiction.

So Tiantai has no problem accepting the argument that for someone to argue for a position at all, and therefore to be involved in the conversation, presupposes that he believes there is a difference between his opponent accepting his view and not accepting it. For Tiantai does accept that *in a sense* there is a difference—precisely the sense that is relevant in the act of disagreeing. Our point is that this constitutively involves the presence of at least one more sense or respect, a sense which must really differ from the first sense, a sense in which, therefore, there is no such difference.

Sometimes it is claimed that the behavior of people proves that they do accept the law of non-contradiction. The care I take when I cross the street seems to mean that I accept that there is a real difference between being hit by a car and not being hit by a car. But this is not denied by the denier of the law of non-contradiction. All that is denied is that this cannot coexist with a simultaneous belief that there is no relevant difference between the two. If I want X and also don't want X, my behavior may sometimes, under some conditions (random or non-random) display my desire for X. The claim is simply that this is not the whole story about what I desire. It is far from implausible to say, for example, that I both desire to die and desire to avoid death. This is where the metaphysical version of the LNC comes in: its defender will say "I desire to die in one respect—or at some times—and I desire not to die in other respects, or at other times." So again, the psychological version of the LNC depends on the ontological version, and its feasibility depends entirely on what is defined as a "respect" and as a "time." I claim that these are defined with reference to contradiction itself, and so the entire principle collapses into meaningless gerrymandering. This of course rests on the claim that any other attempt to specify what constitutes a "time" and a "respect" in isolation of an explicit appeal to non-contradictoriness will, when closely examined, reveal that it presupposes a prior acceptance of non-contradiction in the definitions of each proposed criterion.

In Buddhist terms, we may say simply that "respects" or "senses" or "contexts" do not have self-natures. They have no single unambiguous, true-in-all-contexts boundaries that define contexts as having just this set of characteristics and no others. We may see here why it is that Buddhist thinkers in particular have an insight into the non-ultimacy of the LNC: the claim that "a thing cannot contradict itself" is entirely dependent on how we define a "thing," where we draw the boundaries between "this" and "something else," how much of the total swath of experience is separated off as one thing as opposed to another. That is, we usually define "this thing" as simply "as many bits of information as can be experienced consistently and as not contradicting each other; where the contradictions start, we ipso facto consider a new thing to have begun." "Same thing" in Aristotle's definition is as problematic as "same respect" and "same time," and for the same[13] reason. "Real entity" and "LNC" are two alternate descriptions of the same idea: a real entity is just defined as whatever accords with the LNC. The Buddhist rejection of any fixed and unambiguous boundaries for any single entity entails also a rejection of the LNC. Contexts must themselves be contextualized to be the contexts they are. Contextual accounts of truths necessitate holism, and holism has no non-arbitrary stopping point. The most comprehensive holism is self-undermining, as the self-reference and self-inclusion paradoxes show. Conventional Truth cannot be kept safe from the ravages of Ultimate Truth, i.e., the fact that the latter negates the truth of every Conventional Truth. The contexts which warrant Conventional Truths are infected by the undermining of them that we see initially in the universal Ultimate Truths. But not to worry: all this means is that there are infinite Conventional Truths, infinite Ultimate Truths, and, thus, infinite paradoxes.

The Tiantai claim is that parameterization is intrinsic to the simple act of making *two* statements, even two non-contradictory statements, about "the same" thing. To play with a very old Chinese example, if I have a white horse before me, and I say "it is white" and also "it is a horse," the sense in which it is white is not the sense in which it is a horse. What makes it true that it is white is not what makes it true that it is a horse. In one sense it is a horse, in one sense it is white. "Horse" is the answer to one kind of question about it, while "white" is the answer to another. It is in the context of someone's concern with color that it is correctly (usefully, successfully) called white. It is in the context of someone's concern with animal taxonomy (say) that is it correctly (usefully, successfully) called horse.

So it cannot be that "there is an absolute truth," and "there is no absolute truth"[14] are meant "in the same way," for no two statements can ever be meant in "the same" way, if "same" is meant to signify something radically distinct from "different." The point is that a statement always brings with it its own way of being true, its own parameters, and parameterizing is literally unavoidable.

What prevents logical chaos, and the arbitrary changing of reference, is thus purely *pragmatic* and *social*. Consider the claim, "It is raining in Singapore right now" and the counterclaim, "It is not raining in Singapore right now." By LNC, these two claims form a contradiction and are thus not permitted in the same narrow time span. Now consider three potential resolutions of this contradiction permitted under the discussion above, progressively less trivial. (1) The most trivial sense in which the contradiction is permissible is by focusing on two distinct senses of "Singapore." It is raining in one part of Singapore but not in another part. (2) It is only slightly less trivial to say, in traditional Buddhist terms, that in one sense, *there is no rain falling anywhere* in Singapore, and that in another sense, this is not true (i.e., in a sense there is *no such thing* as rain: in the Buddhist "no-essence" sense). In this same sense, there is or is not such a self-identical thing as "Singapore": the space designated on the map is called, conventionally, Singapore, but in another sense this is just a name—all that is there is really soil and buildings and people and molecules and energy, etc.[15] (3) What Tiantai adds to this rather trivial set of considerations is that the same can apply to other metaphorical applications, providing other senses that are equally valid, and for exactly the same reason: it is not just that X exists in one sense and does not exist in another sense, but that X is in a sense an example of Y and Z and G and L. Singapore "is" Athens (e.g., in an op-ed defending its policies against the claim that "Singapore is the Sparta of modern city-states."). The DMV in Cleveland Ohio "is" Singapore (consistently applying stringent fines for petty offenses—much more so, let's suppose, than the DMV in other cities: it is the Singapore of civic DMVs). Perhaps Singapore "is," in some linguistic, social, or soteriological contexts, Athens, or the dog park, or Michael Jackson, or a new kind of fat-free yogurt. These statements seem strange to us because we are used to drawing a strict separation between this usage, which might be called "metaphorical," or regarded as a shorthand for an analogical claim ("Singapore is in some ways analogous to Sparta"), and another, "literal," meaning of "is." But under Tiantai premises this distinction cannot be maintained. The "is" here refers to a certain kind of relationship within particular contexts, as for example when one says, when explaining to someone who fails to see the face of the man in the moon, "That crater *is* the eye, that ridge *is* the nose." In all cases, the "is" is conditional upon a context: *to the extent* that there is a face here, it is that crater that is the eye. The claim here is that there is really no other kind of meaning for the word "is." For there is an implicit ontological essentialism embedded in the literal application of the copula: the form of a judgment implies that X is Y, however broadly construed, and not not-Y, *simpliciter*, or that in our final ontology we can subsume and categorize in a single consistent way which will allow us to apply a flat either-or "is" or "is not" *somewhere* along the line. X and Y must be at once both distinguishable from and identifiable with one another to make "X is Y" at all meaningful. Even if they are simply "two different names for the same thing," in the absence of a prior presupposition that our ways of naming and our modes of experience are somehow ontologically distinct from the rest of reality, which would be circular here, "X is Y" can only mean "X has some necessary connection to Y, and the two can be juxtaposed in thought in a mutually significant way, i.e., in a way that causes us to view them otherwise than we might have outside of this conjunction," and this will apply to any two terms in the Tiantai universe.[16]

Even the self-referential totality paradoxes are, thus, parameterized; the issue is whether the parameters are (1) ultimately separable and (2) hierarchical. Tiantai says no to both. "In one sense" there is an essence, "in another sense" there is no essence, and so *mutatis mutandis*. But the Tiantai view may be restated as the claim that reality itself is parameterized. The attempt to separate these parameters into neat and perfectly determinate, self-contained units, with no overlap, *is* primal ignorance: the attempt to stipulate a self-nature, which is to stipulate unequivocal definiteness, the being of X as opposed to non-X, which requires a coherent account of what a boundary is, which is, according to the Tiantai understanding of Nāgārjuna (ca. 150–250 CE), impossible. And that means that the available contexts, and the available respects in which valid descriptions of any given item can be made, cannot be non-arbitrarily limited. Because there are unlimited senses in which something can be so, there are unlimited truths. Because these senses are inseparable, however, each truth leads beyond itself to other truths—and this, on the Tiantai view, is what alone makes any of them qualify as a "truth."

We may conclude from this that the question "what is true and what is false" is a not very interesting and not very important question. Instead of asking of any given proposition "Is it true or false?" we stipulate as a trivial matter of course that it is both true and false, neither true nor false—every proposition is in some sense true and in some sense false, in some contexts true and in some contexts false, under some parameters true and under some parameters false. These are rhetorical matters having to do with how we wish to, and can get others to agree to, describe other descriptions. But this gets us nowhere interesting and is of little significance. Rather, we should be asking, "*In what way* is it true and in what way is it false? In what contexts true and in what contexts false? To what speakers true and to what speakers false? In how many contexts true and in how many contexts false? How often true and how often false? With what algorithm of probability true and with what algorithm of probability false? When true and when false? To what degree true and to what degree false? To what end true and to what end false?" So the issue is not *whether* or not the paradoxes are parameterized, but *in what way* they are so, and with what consequences.

It is important to note here that this means that Tiantai rejects the bivalence of truth not only about external facts in the world, but also about one's own beliefs, and indeed rejects the very claim that there is a simple, consistent, univocal fact-of-the-matter about one's own beliefs. One's own thoughts are no more transparent to oneself nor ontologically unambiguous than anything else; there is always more to them than one can see at any one time. But the concept of the Three Truths in Tiantai explicitly foregrounds the necessity of *some* determinate appearance at all times: it must always seem one way rather than another (Provisional Positing), and yet *thereby* entail the ambiguity (Emptiness) and intersubsumption (the Mean) of that appearance and its concomitant claims of truth with all other possible appearances and claims. "All things are true" never appears as a global truth—it appears only *as* some other local truth, or, when stated as a putatively global claim, ipso facto is functioning as a merely local truth (the assertion that this is true *rather than* something else). We *must* always believe that we believe something in particular as opposed to something else; *only* in this way can our simultaneous embrace of all beliefs occur.

The same goes for our embrace of a *purpose*, which is indeed the real starting point of Tiantai theoretical elaborations, as it is the central claim of the root text of the school, the *Lotus Sutra* (no later than 200 CE).[17] There must always be the subjective embrace of *a* purpose, but it is precisely by means of this purpose and the ignorance it entails that *other purposes* are actually accomplished. We cannot for an instant be without some choice, some purpose; but purposes are means by which something other than what they envision are accomplished. No purpose gets what it wants—but in thus failing, they succeed in bringing about other ends. This is strictly parallel to the case of truth, as we should expect on this pragmatic conflation of value and truth. All statements are true because they are specific truth claims that fail, that contradict themselves and self-destruct. All purposes are endorsed because they necessarily aim for a specific goal, attaining one thing *rather than* another, and fail to attain it, thereby leading beyond themselves. Here we can see the Tiantai response to Priest's final ditch attempt to argue against what he calls "trivialism" (the claim that all contradictions are true) in favor of a limited dialetheism from the phenomenology of choice.[18] Given the specific Tiantai notion of truth and purpose, the inevitability of the subjective sense of choice and purposive action, far from being an objection, is the *sine qua non* of the Tiantai species of "trivialism."

In other words, we may say that Tiantai accepts a contextualist view of truth, but adds to this a rejection of the possibility of bivalent truths about what constitutes a "context." Contexts too are devoid of intrinsic nature. It is incoherent to speak of any statement belonging simply to one set of contexts and not others. Contextualism entails holism, because each context must itself be contextualized before it can be assigned the character of being "this context and no other." This means that it is impossible to non-arbitrarily limit the horizon of relevant contexts pertaining to any candidate for a truth claim. All statements are in all contexts. All contexts can themselves be recontextualized into other contexts, thus changing the manner in which they are able to disambiguate that which they contextualize. In the simplest instance, this can be thought of temporally, as it is in the original *Lotus Sutra* elaborations from which the Tiantai position is partially derived: the identity of A in context C is changed when C is itself retrospectively recontextualized by E. The lines dividing contexts are not natural kinds "existing" *simpliciter* in the world.

Tiantai thus claims that all beliefs, including its own, are never true *simpliciter*, but are always true in a certain sense, which is the only sense in which anything is ever coherently true. This is its version of the liar's paradox. But in response to the question, "OK, so there are no non-parameterized truths *simpliciter*, truth is pragmatic, truth is expressivist, truth is self-cancelling—is *that* true?" Tiantai can simply answer, "Yes, but it is true, but not *simpliciter*; it is pragmatically true, it is true in a sense, it is true under certain parameters, it is true in that it expresses a viewpoint, it is true in that it is self-canceling." The questioning might continue: "Is it true that there is a viewpoint it expresses? Is it true that it self-cancels? Is it true that expression takes place? Is it true that there are parameters?" Tiantai will again answer, "Yes, but … ." Tiantai holds that it is "yes, but … " all the way down. Indeed, it is quite all right to say that there is an absolute truth (the "yes" part), and Tiantai even holds that this is inescapable as the framework for any specific statement. But there is always also a "but … " part. The Tiantai position, expressed so much more elegantly in the Three Truths, has always been that *every* statement is at once an absolute truth *simpliciter*, *and* that every statement is not an absolute truth, *and* that these are in fact merely alternate ways of stating the same fact.

Tiantai thus vehemently denies that its position leads to "epistemological anarchism," with which it has sometimes been charged. Propositions are still true or false unproblematically with respect to any alleged particular contexts, i.e., to the extent that the presuppositions of the framing of the question can seem for awhile to be itself contextualized by certain shared assumptions. It's just that "the extent to which" this is true is always limited and revisable; indeed, this revisability is entailed in the very act of contextualizing. The controls are exactly the same as they are in the more monolithic contextualism of pre-Tiantai Conventional Truth. $2 + 2 = 4$ is true in certain contexts (probably 99.9999 per cent of all possible contexts), in that it is useful in communicating, and in making calculations for building stuff in some precincts of the universe at least, which are crucial for communicating liberating attachment-neutralizers. Its truth is dependent upon prior acceptance by large communities of sentient beings with whom one wishes to communicate, and with those "beings" sentient and insentient in that precinct of the universe that behave accordingly. The only difference is that we do not assume that all sentient beings think in the same ways, or share in the same convictions and desires, nor do we see any reason for imposing a normative value on which particular kinds of conventions they use, since these conventions are themselves all non-Ultimate Truths and justified solely in terms of their shared efficacy within communities. If there are subcultures that for whatever reason see $2 + 2 = 5$, rather than just saying they are insane or trying to first convince them that $2 + 2 = 4$, a good bodhisattva will find a way in which it can be construed as provisionally true (i.e., attachment-undermining) and to communicate liberating truths in terms of the premise that $2 + 2 = 5$ (including, of course, showing the senses in which that claim is false, just as they would for $2 + 2 = 4$). There is no reason to assume in advance whether there do or do not exist such weird communities. The only other difference is the way in which these alternate systems of Conventional Truth, alternate "respects" or "senses" in which something might be asserted, are related. They are fuzzy edged, a complete separation between them cannot be coherently constructed any more than can any other two putatively separate entities: they are inseparable from one another, they collapse into one another, they entail and reduce to one another, they are aspects of the Truth of the Mean, which is simply the free and unobstructed convertibility between all possible Conventional Truths.[19]

We can see that this embrace of paradox as truth does *not* entail the end of all adjudication in argument. On the contrary, we can continue to use *reductio ad absurdum* arguments to point out contradictions inherent in propositions under discussion, and thereby refute those propositions. On the Tiantai account, however, to show the self-destruction of an opponent's view on its own premises is to show that it is a good raft: this is exactly what it's supposed to do. It is a Conventional Truth which leads beyond itself by destroying itself: this is precisely what makes it an Ultimate Truth, and also an instantiation of the Mean, the absolute. Its refutation is a way of showing that it too is an *upāya*, and hence is the Ultimate Truth. To refute it is to set it to work as an attachment-underminer, continuing the process it has laudably started and allowing it to go on to do all the truth-work of which it is capable.

For Tiantai, "Conventional Truth" means *anything that* can *be conducive to the elimination of suffering—which is clinging, attachment, desire and fixed views of objectivity*. Not "will" or "must," but "can." For no idea, not even *Emptiness, always* conduces thereto. It is situational, and this is the *sole* criterion and meaning of truth. Now given this definition, anything and everything is a Conventional Truth: anything *can*, under the right conditions, dislodge an attachment and lead to reduced suffering. Nothing always does so, but everything without exception, in the right context, can do so. Everything without exception is therefore a Conventional Truth. But Conventional Truth, as we just saw, is in Tiantai not merely a means to Ultimate Truth, but is Ultimate Truth itself. Ultimate Truth is just the coexistence and maximally skillful application of any and all Conventional Truths. Since everything is Conventional Truth, everything is Ultimate Truth. But they are Ultimate Truth *because* of their interpenetration and mutual non-obstruction, because what would be mutually exclusive if taken as "truths" in the sense of "corresponding to how things really are, *simpliciter*, independently of any other factors including experiencers of them as such" are now seen to be true in the sense of "conducive to liberation from suffering sometimes." This renders their coexistence not only possible, but *necessary* for Ultimate Truth. Ultimate Truth *is* the copresence of what would, on the naive realist "objective" definition of truth, be contradictory, the *interchangeability* of the two apparently contradictory forms of Conventional Truth.

I conclude then that the question about whether the contradictory statements in Mahayana literature are meant to be true statements or are meant merely as therapeutic *upâya* to undermine attachments while making no claims about reality is, from a Tiantai point of view, infelicitously constructed. For these two alternatives are synonymous. Truth *means* nothing but "undermining attachments," and Conventional Truths *are* Ultimate Truths. Put otherwise, therapeutic measures are our only descriptions of "how the world is." For truth in Tiantai is always truth about delusion, for it is only delusion that provides *any* determinate content to experience. Enlightened experience ("truth") is *also* full of content and differentiations, but only because it builds upon and reconfigures a priorly existing delusion and delusion-derived determinacies and differentiations, which are its sole raw material—*not* some reality-as-it-is untouched by any (deluded) consciousness. Every determination is inherently contradictory, but it is this very contradiction, and its self-destruction, that establishes its reality.

Here we can begin to see the unique Tiantai contribution to our understanding of the LNC. For looked at this way, we can assert that in a sense the LNC is just another name for the Three Truths themselves, which thus serve to disclose the actual ontological information which the LNC provides—quite in opposition to its initial appearance of prohibiting paradox. All three of the Tiantai Three Truths refer to the same fact: conditionality itself, dependent co-arising (*pratītyasamutpāda, yuanqi* 緣起). This is simply the fact that all identifiable characteristics are finite, hence constitutively have an outside, i.e., are necessarily co-present at all times with an outside, are conditioned by what they exclude, and thereby include in their essence precisely what they exclude. Provisional Positing (*jia*) means conditionality. This means that the conditions must always be qualitatively distinguishable from the conditioned: the presence of an X must be accompanied by some non-X, whether as antecedent cause or as qualitatively distinct components or as surrounding contrasting otherness. The LNC is one way of describing this fact, which is the only real information it gives in the absence of a substance ontology: any putative determination can only be established if there exist along with it, constitutively to it, other possible determinations that will necessarily somewhere and sometime undermine this coherence (which the LNC thus simply designates as belonging not to this entity but to other entities). Provisional Positing means that anything that can be pointed out is finite, and thus that it can be contradicted and negated by something else.

Emptiness (*kong*) also means conditionality: it means that every local coherence is globally incoherent, that it is thus and so in some manners of speaking but not in others. The non-X conditions that are necessary for X to exist are themselves conditional. This conditionality, however, cannot mean the arising of a single effect from a single cause, for this would make the effect a mere aspect or expression of the cause, always arising when the cause arises, and thus not arising at all except when the cause arises. This would push the conditionality back to the cause rather than the effect, but the same consideration would apply there, and so on *ad infinitum*. Hence no cause acting alone can produce an effect, and hence no entity has any definite essence: it is not thus and so solely due to itself, but only thus and so with the help of certain other, but not all other, entities. For if it arose due to all other entities, these entities would have to form a consistent non-paradoxical totality, and thus would count as a single entity. It has a definite character only within some arbitrarily limited horizon of relevance. Whatever it appears to be is posited only provisionally, and since this applies to any essence-candidate, all determinations are only provisional posits, indicating no mutually exclusive essences. Whatever is so is so merely "in a manner of speaking." All claims are implicitly parameterized.[20] There are always further parameters. If all parameters (senses, respects, times) were taken into account at once, and all applications and aspects brought to bear, the original coherence would vanish into ambiguity. The *denial* of the LNC is a way of expressing this fact, which is the only real information it gives: this coherence is not unconditional, it always necessarily arises with other contrary coherences that exclude and negate it, which, because this is *necessary* to its determination, thus belong as much or as little to its alleged essence as anything that may be claimed to be constitutively internal to it. The essence must be "self-contradictory" to be there at all.

The Mean (*zhong*) also means conditionality: it means that Provisional Positing and Emptiness are alternate statements of the same fact, which is conditionality, which at once both affirms and denies the LNC. The LNC is thus itself parameterized: it is true in one sense, and untrue in another sense. What the Mean signifies is that these two senses are mutually entailing.

Tiantai offers two versions of the Mean: the Exclusive Mean, and the Non-Exclusive Mean (*budanzhong* 不但中). The above specification applies only to the Exclusive Mean, the Mean considered above and beyond the two extremes of Provisional Positing and Emptiness, as the identity between them which is a third fact in addition to the two facts which it identifies with one another. But the Non-Exclusive Mean, which sees an identity between not only the two extremes, but between each extreme and the third fact which is the identity between the two extremes, also means conditionality: the arising of any coherence is the arising of every other coherence, as any attempt to limit it to a finite set of determinations will fail: any totality, if determinate, will imply a further totality beyond it. Any coherence plus its constitutive context is a new X, which requires, and thus in the same way again "is," a further context, and so *ad infinitum*. Every globally incoherent local coherence subsumes all other local coherences—which in turn subsume it, for the same reason. Every subsuming is thus an intersubsumption. Each entity is readable as every other entity, as part of every other entity, and as the whole that subsumes all other entities as its parts. Each entity is identifiable, ontologically ambiguous, and all-pervaded as all-pervading. Each entity is a raft that leads beyond itself, but what it reaches in going beyond itself is always only another raft which leads back to it and to all other rafts, all other entities, such that each raft is the interpenetration of all rafts, and no raft ever leads beyond itself.

The Tiantai view then is not mere dialetheism, "the view that some contradictions are true," as Deguchi, Garfield, and Priest put it.[21] It claims that *all* statements, claims, experiences and entities are (implicitly) contradictions, and that *therefore* they are *all true*. Tiantai's procedure is to show the way in which all these propositions contradict themselves, and thus are all true—i.e., are all disclosures of one another, enablers of the free flow of propositions leading beyond themselves to each other, where each encompasses all the others thereby (the process of "opening the provisional to reveal the real"). It does this for the LNC as well: the LNC is just a clumsy, inexplicit way of asserting the Three Truths. As such, the LNC is also self-contradictory, and when fully explored shown to be identical to its opposite—and therefore, in the Tiantai sense, it is true.

It would be unsurprising if many readers were reluctant to embrace conclusions as extreme and at variance with commonsensical intuitions as those advanced in classical

Tiantai Buddhism. I hope I have shown, however, that the motivations for this reluctance are not necessarily purely logical ones. In any case, if the LNC is indefensible in the absence of an essentialist ontology, as I've tried to demonstrate, then some alternative to that ontology, even if it is not the Tiantai alternative, must be advanced by those unwilling to commit to essentialism. It is hoped that this chapter will provide a stimulus for further attempts to do so.

Notes

1. See Graham Priest, "What's So Bad About Contradictions."

2. This undermining of attachments is deemed to be the main task for Buddhist soteriological procedures. In this case, the goal would be to undermine attachments to non-contradictory propositions, mistakenly taken to be a privileged and literal disclosure of ontological information in discursive form, which Mahayana Buddhism, on this reading, considers impossible.

3. *Alagaddupama Sutta*, Majjhima Nikaya 22.

4. It should be noted, as well, that the endeavor to end suffering is itself something one may choose to embark upon or not; Buddhism is good and true only to the extent that the liberation from suffering is one's goal. It may be that all goals can be (not "must be") reduced to this goal—all human activity can be seen (not "must be seen") as various attempts to reduce suffering in one way or another. But this is different from asserting that something that is useful for this goal is true or good outside of the context of having adopted this goal explicitly.

5. See Graham Priest, *In Contradiction*.

6. See Yasuo Deguchi, Jay Garfield, and Graham Priest, "The Way of the Dialetheist."

7. Zhuangzi, chapter 2. See Ziporyn, *Zhuangzi*, 15, where we see Zhuangzi proceed directly from the paradoxes of being-and-non-being (and of beginning and not-yet-beginning, of saying and not-saying, of being-similar and being-dissimilar—analogs of the DGP self-reference and self-inclusion paradoxes) to these paradoxes concerning individual finite propositions: "Nothing in the world is larger than the tip of a hair in autumn, and Mt. Tai is small. No one lives longer than a dead child, and old Pengzu died an early death. Heaven and earth are born together with me, and the ten thousand things and I are one." (For an analysis of the argument underlying this progression in Zhuangzi's thought, see my "Zhuangzi as Philosopher.") This move is partially motivated by Zhuangzi's perspectivism, which strongly inclines toward relativism. It is reasonable to assume that the Tiantai concern with *upāya* as a central concern in epistemology, with the relation between various points of view, as having something to do with this precedent—as well as with the Confucian tradition of "teaching according to capacity (*yin cai shi jiao* 因材施教)" as an essential characteristic of the sage, often exemplified in the *Analects* by Confucius himself, rooted in an ontology that sees intersubjective sociality as the paradigmatic and always ultimate category of philosophical theory.

8. Zhiyi, *Miao fa lianhuajing xuan yi* 妙法蓮華經玄義, in Takakusu Junjirō, Watanabe Kaigyoku et al., *Taishō shinshû Daizōkyō* [T] 33.702c.

9. A superficially similar idea of interpenetration is developed in the Huayan school, but on different premises and with different consequences.

10. Aristotle, *Metaphysics* (tr. Lawson-Tancred), 88. In more traditional language: the same attribute cannot at the same time belong and not belong to the same subject and in the same respect. In either case, the references to "respect" and "time" are ineradicable from the principle.

11. Unlike Kant, however, but like Schelling and Hegel, Tiantai will reject that this is thus the *only* way in which we are capable of thinking—on the contrary, this very consideration itself is an instance of the contrary; our ability to think both the LNC and its automatic application *and* the presence of something *to which* it is being applied is already an experience of stepping beyond the LNC and *experiencing* its non-ultimacy. For the mere fact of thinking of an alternative is already a demonstration of the non-ultimacy, the negotiable character, of any particular way of thinking.

12. Versions of both of these moves are already apparent in Aristotle, *Metaphysics* IV:4.

13. And this applies to this "same" as well.

14. Or "The statement 'this statement is false' is true" and "The statement 'this statement is false' is false."

15. However, our soteriologically conditioned social and pragmatic concerns allow us to apply the appropriate context for any particular speech act. No logical Armageddon ensues. What constitutes linguistic competence here is not always using these terms in the same sense, but being able to switch seamlessly from one context, and one sense, to another.

16. But even more directly, if the "this sentence is true" simply *means* "this speech-act can be conducive to overcoming attachments, including the attachment to itself," then "Singapore is frozen yogurt," full stop, and "Singapore is sort of like the frozen yogurt of modern city-states" are in exactly the same boat: if either one is capable of making one sentient thing experience any aspect of the world *differently*, seeing things in another light, providing a new angle of insight, this is ipso facto an overcoming of an attachment to, limitation by, whatever way that sentient being was previously experiencing that aspect of the world. The mere empowerment of a new way of seeing—even if it will quickly be overruled by alternate considerations—already qualifies any of these statements—whether in the "is" or in the "is like" form—as truth. The range of applicability of any of these statements would then be in the hands of any bodhisattva to determine according to its *costs* in terms of other attachments: if it removes a small attachment but thereby creates other, larger ones, compassion will seek to avoid it in that context.

17. Most explicitly, in Sariputra's claim, "We attained it without seeking it (*bu qiu zi de* 不求自得)" in the third chapter of the *Lotus Sutra* (T9.16b; for the English version, cf. Gene Reeves, *The Lotus Sutra*, 142.). Note that he does not and cannot in context be saying "We attained it without seeking *anything*." Rather, it is attained as a by-product of seeking *something else*: the status of Bodhisattvahood is attained by practicing the Śrāvaka (non-Bodhisattva, "Small Vehicle") path,

which even explicitly entails the *denial* of the goal of Bodhisattvahood. But this is the basic structure of all the Lotus parables—burning house, lost son, treasure trove. In each case, it is by desiring X, and explicitly not seeking Y, that Y is actually attained. This is meant as a metaphor for the relation between two competing Buddhist schools in the context of the Sutra. Tiantai extrapolates its general metaphysical principles from this structure: *some* purpose—i.e., some desire—is always operative, but that desire always leads to results and desiderata other than the ones it explicitly envisions, including those it explicitly denies. Compare the Schelling-Hegel notion of the "cunning of Reason."

18. See Graham Priest, "Could Everything Be True?" Priest explicitly references the Transcendental Deduction of the categories of cognition in Kant's First Critique in appealing to the phenomenological inevitability of free choice, although this topic is the centerpiece of Kant's Second Critique and of Fichte's elaborations thereof (and thence arguably of Sartre, whom Priest also invokes here). In either case, the point is the Transcendental character of the either-or in action (in "practical reason," to use Kant's term). But this is just a further application of the LNC, which in our view, as in Kant's, is itself Transcendental: our minds our constructed such that we cannot fail to apply the LNC. Our rejoinder to Priest here is analogous to the Schelling-Hegel rejoinder to Kant: the fact that we cannot fail to apply the LNC in all cases not only forbids us to regard this as evidence that it is applicable to extra-mental reality, as in Kant, but also shows exactly why it does not exhaust even our own mental operations and thus cannot be an absolute law even of *phenomena* as experienced by ourselves—for the simple reason that, in becoming aware of the fact that the LNC is unavoidable and restricted to our subjectivity, we have thereby implicitly passed beyond it and entertained the idea of an alternative. That we are able to think of the LNC as applicable only to phenomena and not to noumena already shows that we are able to experience *phenomenally* the non-application of the LNC. For our *thinking this thought* is also a part of our experience. In the present case, noticing the circularity of our own necessary and compulsory application of the LNC—that is dependent on our way of dividing up objects, and yet that this way of dividing up objects is dependent on our demand for the LNC—is the thought of stepping beyond the LNC in our own experience. Our experience includes *both* the (necessary) application of the LNC and its abrogation.

19. Here we see the Tiantai response to another of Priest's dialetheist arguments against trivialism: the claim that, at least if we accept a contrastive account of meaning, trivialism entails "the meaninglessness of public language" (Priest, "Could Everything Be True?" 192). But this claim presupposes that the "meaning" in public speech requires *complete identity* of meaning of words for all users in order to be intelligible or useful, which Tiantai emphatically denies. On the contrary, neither the sense nor the reference of a word can be completely identical in any two uses, and that *only* thus does speech succeed in communicating. The idea of X associated with a word "X" must be partially the same and partially different for there to be any reason for one person to make a claim about X to another; they must be understanding it in a minimally different sense for there to be any point to the demand for an adjustment in the other's claims about the identity, implications, entailments or factual relations of X. There must be enough difference to *motivate* the claim, but also enough sameness to make the claim *possible*. Needless to say, it is impossible to ever assign clear-cut boundaries to just what parts are "the same" or

"different" in any case: the entire relation will prove to be *ultimately* incoherent, as we have been arguing. But it does so *only* by means of its appearing to be initially, locally, provisionally coherent. Priest's claim also seems to assume the existence of a single coherent "public" with a synordinate set of understandings of all parts of its speech, or at least the possibility of strictly continent separations between different speech-communities, which is also rejected by basic Tiantai Three Truths doctrine. While Priest ultimately denies that this approach provides a decisive refutation of trivialism, he does so on other grounds, admitting that a trivialist might accept this conclusion and *therefore cease to assert anything*. But in the Tiantai case, this step is obviously by no means warranted.

20. This means that every coherence is a local coherence: it remains coherent as such and such only within a limited horizon of relevance (i.e., taking into account some but not all of the possible manners of speaking, which are by definition not limitable to any finite set). That is, its legibility depends on the fixing of a certain scale, frame or focal orientation; its identity as this precise thing depends phenomenally on restricting the ways in which it is viewed, or the number of other factors which are viewed in tandem with it.

21. Deguchi, Garfield, and Priest, "The Way of the Dialetheist," 401.

Works Cited

Aristotle. *Metaphysics*, tr. Hugh Lawson-Tancred. Penguin, 1998.

Deguchi, Yasuo, Jay Garfield, and Graham Priest. "The Way of the Dialetheist: Contradictions in Buddhism." *Philosophy East and West* 58, no. 3 (2008): 395–402.

Priest, Graham. "Could Everything Be True?" *Australasian Journal of Philosophy* 78, no. 2 (2000): 189–195.

Priest, Graham. *In Contradiction: A Study of the Transconsistent*. Martinus Nijhoff, 1987.

Priest, Graham. "What's So Bad about Contradictions?" In *The Law of Non-Contradiction: New Philosophical Essays*, ed. Graham Priest, J.C. Beall, and Bradley Armour-Garb. Oxford University Press, 2007.

Reeves, Gene. *The Lotus Sutra: A Contemporary Translation of a Buddhist Classic*. Wisdom Publications, 2008.

Takakusu Junjirō, Watanabe Kaigyoku, et al. *Taishō shinshū Daizōkyō* 大正新脩大蔵経. 100 volumes. Tokyo: *Taishō issaikyō kankōkai*, 1924–1934.

Ziporyn, Brook. "Zhuangzi as Philosopher," supplement to *Zhuangzi: The Essential Writings with Selections from Traditional Commentaries*. http://www.hackettpublishing.com/zhuangziphil.

Ziporyn, Brook. *Zhuangzi: The Essential Writings with Selections from Traditional Commentaries*. Hackett, 2009.

11 Knowing-How and Knowing-To

Stephen Hetherington and Karyn L. Lai

1 Western Epistemology: Some Conceptual Preliminaries

Gilbert Ryle's account of knowing-how in the 1940s presented a challenge to mainstream Western philosophers who prioritized conceptually the possession of knowledge-that—prioritizing it over all other forms of knowledge.[1] Ryle questioned that picture's applicability to knowledge-that and knowledge-how in particular. He spoke of the "intellectualist legend."[2] This was the assumption that, necessarily, all actions manifesting knowledge-how are accompanied by thoughts that guide them. These accompanying thoughts would be knowledge-that. So intellectualism was conceiving of knowledge-that as essentially involved in knowing how to carry out a particular task. But putting into effect some knowledge-how, Ryle argued, is one activity, not two:

> When I do something intelligently, i.e., thinking what I am doing, I am doing one thing and not two. My performance has a special procedure or manner, not special antecedent.[3]

A focus on *doing*—on performance as constitutive of knowledge—is one aspect of Chinese philosophy that we discuss in this chapter. Ryle's thesis extends further: he contends not only that knowledge-that's presence is insufficient for constituting whatever is knowing-at-all in knowing-how, but that knowing-how is basic in a range of ways, not least in ordinary life, where "we are much more concerned with people's competences than with their cognitive repertoires, with the operations than with the truths that they learn."[4]

Ryle's account of knowing-how is, however, unclear: knowing-how is a "higher-grade disposition";[5] it is also associated with a range of terms such as "abilities and propensities" and "capacities, skills, habits, liabilities and bents."[6] In discussion of how we might concede that a person knows how, Ryle—in this case using the example of shooting—suggests that "there is no one signal of a man's knowing how to shoot, but a modest assemblage of heterogeneous performances generally suffices to establish beyond reasonable doubt whether he knows how to shoot or not."[7] At the level of ordinary common-sense attributions of know-how, Ryle seems correct. However, conceptually there is something more to the "assemblage of heterogeneous performances" that, in Ryle's account, are loosely associated with knowing-how. And our aim in this chapter is to discuss one element of that "something more."

That element will concern *how* a person's knowing-how becomes manifest in action—specifically, the role of knowing-*to* in putting knowing-how into effect, into action.[8] And such epistemology could profit, we will find, from attending to some pertinent Chinese philosophy. Some Chinese philosophical texts discuss matters in a manner that emphasizes knowing-to, as an accompaniment to their talking of knowing-how. Their discussions were not markedly conceptual, being more focused on applications of knowing-how. Nevertheless, we may regard their focus as an encouraging datum with which to complement any conceptual investigation of knowing-to and its epistemological significance.

In anticipation of the data we will soon present, then, here is how we may begin fashioning a concept of knowing-to. Think of someone who knows how, for example, to choose the right words for calming a group of agitated or angry people. Imagine her being confronted by just such a group. Part of her knowing how to calm them is, we assume, her having the ability to do so. But how does this ability lead to her acting in a way that manifests or expresses it? As indicated earlier, such a result would be what Ryle called an intelligent action. An action is intelligent in his sense precisely *by* manifesting or expressing some knowledge-how. To cook a healthy and tasty meal, for instance, is to act intelligently in Ryle's sense of manifesting the knowledge-how to perform that sort of action. One is putting *into* action the ability which, we are supposing, is one's knowledge-how.

Again, though, *how* does that transition occur? By what means does the knowledge-how to perform a general sort of action become manifested in a particular action? The knowing-how is itself more or less general. So, we may view the following as a crucial question about the process of manifesting or expressing the knowledge-how: What *particular knowledge*, if any, is added to the knowing-how so as to produce the particular intelligent action?[9] Intellectualism's answer is that some knowledge-*that* is needed—and that this is sufficient for rendering the particular action intelligent (in the sense of being some sort of manifestation of a way of knowing). Ryle famously argued against that answer. And our related suggestion is that knowing-*to* is also needed as a further ingredient. Knowledge-that, even if present, is not enough to *spark* or *activate* the knowledge-how into action on the given occasion. And knowledge-that is not *itself* active.[10] It is *inert* in the relevant sense. All of this is why knowledge-*to* is needed.

Thus (to return to our example), whenever someone has an ability to calm dangerous crowds, such as by saying word W at just the right time and in just the right way, then even on an occasion when it would be appropriate for her to put into effect that ability she might fail to do it. And although there are a few possible reasons for this failure, one of them could be her lacking at that crucial moment the knowledge *to* calm the particular crowd in front of her by uttering W aptly. She could still know how to accomplish that general sort of outcome, without—at the vital moment— knowing *to* do it right then and there. How might this failure occur? Perhaps she has overlooked at that moment a subtle indicator of the *need* for her to act swiftly and calmingly in that W-saying special way of which, in general, she is so capable.[11] And this combination has resulted—as surely *as if* she did not know how in general to calm crowds—in her not performing the action of calming this particular crowd by giving voice to W in the appropriate way at the appropriate time. She was capable of doing so; she knew in general how to do so. But in fact, at the relevant moment, she did not know *to* do so. She did not know then and there to say W as was needed.[12]

Of course, if that sort of failure to implement a given kind of knowledge-how happened *too* often in pertinent circumstances, we may well begin denying that the person really does know how to perform the given kind of action. Still, we need not reach for that denial on the first occasion of non-implementation, maybe not even on the second such occasion. This would depend upon contextual factors. In any case, in general we have the conceptual license to allow that a given kind of knowledge-how is *fallible*—hence that at least *some* failures to act in a way manifesting that knowledge-how remain compatible with nonetheless knowing how to perform actions of that kind. Epistemologists often concede that knowledge- *that* is a fallible form of knowledge. Even more readily available, it seems, is a conception of knowledge-*how* as a fallible form of knowledge. After all, remember that for argument's sake we are conceiving of each case of knowledge-how as an ability. And it is clear that in general abilities can be fallible. How many of your own many abilities are *not* fallible? Exactly so. And in each case although an ability's being fallible is an imperfection in it, such imperfections are part of the usual *reality* of having abilities.

We will reinforce that intuitive thought by explaining briefly what such fallibility within some knowledge-how would involve. Here is one simple way of possibly articulating the nature of fallible knowing-how:

An instance of knowing-how to do X is fallible, just in case it is possible for that knowledge-how not to be manifested or expressed even when circumstances are apt (and all else is equal). And *when* the knowledge-how to do X is not being manifested or expressed, the following state of affairs would obtain:

One does not do X, even while knowing how to do X and not being disinclined to do X, and even while the particular circumstances are apt for doing X, maybe even while one knows that they are.

For instance, one would not calm a particular crowd by saying W in the needed way, even while knowing in general how to do so and while not being disinclined to do so, and even while the particular circumstances are apt for doing so, maybe even while one knows that they are.

That formulation is supported by being sufficiently analogous to how fallibility could well be described (at any rate in a first approximation) for knowledge-that:

An instance of knowledge-that—some case of knowledge that *p*—is fallible, just in case it was possible for the same true belief that *p* not to arise, even given the same means and motivations for arising (even deliberatively and responsibly so) from the same evidence.[13]

So there is an independent *prima facie* case for allowing knowing-how, like knowing-that, to be fallible. Within each, some indeterminate amount of non-success is conceptually allowed. And the explanatory point we are adding here is that, at least sometimes, the non-success can eventuate *because* appropriate knowing-to is absent. How often can that happen? Even if knowing how to perform a given kind of action need not always be accompanied by knowing to perform it on a particular apt occasion, the knowledge-how had better be *mostly* accompanied by such knowing-to whenever this would be apt. Otherwise, the knowledge-how will be unable to mostly be *manifested* when this would be apt. Certainly in practice, therefore (this being the domain of such manifestations), when we attribute to someone a particular form of knowledge-how on the basis of her acting thus-and-so (acting in a way exemplifying that knowledge-how) we are crediting her likewise with associated knowledge-to. For this, we are suggesting, is the extra epistemic element *whereby* the knowledge-how is exemplified in the specific action.

But some might direct this objection against our suggestion:

One's knowing to say W precisely when confronted by a particular group of agitated people is simply one's *being able to manifest or express on that occasion* one's knowledge-how to calm crowds by saying W suitably. Hence, the knowing-to is thereby itself knowing-*how*. Indeed, it could even be *part* of that same knowing-how-to-calm-crowds-by-saying-W. It could be so, such as by being the knowledge *how to manifest or express the other* parts of that knowing-how-to-calm-crowds-by-saying-W. In that case, we are mistaken in regarding knowing-to as conceptually *distinct* from knowing-how—as a different *way* of knowing from knowing-how.

No. That objection's first two claims are false. (1) The knowing-to in question is not simply one's *being able* to manifest or express on the given occasion one's knowing how to calm a crowd by saying W, for example. The knowing-to is not mere ability. Whatever it is exactly (and we are not offering a full account of it), it is not merely that. In general, there is a constitutive gap between having an *ability* to do X and knowing *to do* X here and now. The ability need not result in action (even with all else being equal); whereas knowing-to must do so (all else being equal). (2) Even *if* (contrary to what (1) has claimed just now) one's knowing to calm this crowd by saying W is one's being able to manifest or express on this occasion one's knowing how to calm this crowd by saying W, it need not itself be knowing-how.[14] This is because, even then, it need not be a *general* ability to manifest or express the knowing-how. Instead, this knowing-to is endemic to *a particular here-and-now*. Correlatively, it should be understood along these lines:

If a person knows how to calm agitated crowds by saying W, she must also—if that sort of action is to be performed intelligently by her on a particular occasion, manifesting or expressing that knowledge-how—have the knowledge to calm this specific crowd *right here and now*, at the vital moment in the vital location. (Otherwise, that general knowledge-how of hers remains latent, unexpressed in this particular circumstance where and when it should be manifested or expressed.) That knowledge-to only ever arises, though, within a given context—a particular "right here and now"—for which the intelligent action in question is apt. And the important point is that this knowledge-to is not quite knowledge-how. It is knowledge to act—but *only specifically here and now*. It is thereby knowledge *to* do, *here and now*, what one knows *how* to do more generally, in some range of circumstances relevantly *akin* to this particular circumstance here and now.

Accordingly, we find a *prima facie* place in the epistemological story for talk of knowing-to. We see that knowing-to is contextually constituted and perhaps contextually fleeting. These features do not clash with its being a kind of knowledge.[15] Schematically, we may express this example as follows:[16]

Sally knows how to calm angry or agitated crowds.

On a specific occasion O, there is an agitated crowd.

Sally utters W.

The crowd calms down.

> Know-how: Sally has the general ability to calm crowds by uttering W on each relevant occasion.
> Know-to: On the particular occasion O, Sally knew to utter W so as to calm that crowd.

Again, the knowing-to has a central success component (namely, the action in question being performed) that is akin to the success component in knowledge-that (the true belief's arising). And the knowing-to's central success component properly includes its arising only in contexts where an associated knowing-how *can* be manifested or expressed intelligently. This is like a true belief's arising only in apt contexts if it is to be knowledge.[17] Hopefully, these contexts include ones where the knowing-how can be useful in practice. In what follows, that potential usefulness will be clear in the examples discussed.

2 Knowing in the *Lüshi Chunqiu*

For the purposes of our discussion, we have selected a text, the *Lüshi Chunqiu* 呂氏春秋 (*Master Lü's Spring and Autumn Annals*), written around 239 BCE,[18] for two primary reasons.

First, the *Lüshi Chunqiu* emphasizes the ability of the ruler to handle a range of tasks associated with government. Most important among these was the selection of capable officials, and the ability to put their talents to good use. This was a concern shared by many thinkers of the Warring States period (475–221 BCE). To use officials effectively in one's government was referred to in some of the texts of the time as *zhi ren* 知人, often translated as "to know men."[19] The meaning of the term *zhi* roughly corresponds to knowledge, understanding, insight, and their cognates. In the Warring States texts, two key characters denoting knowledge overlap in meaning: *zhi* 智, meaning *wisdom, skill*,[20] or *intelligence*; and *zhi* 知, meaning *to know, to understand, be aware of, be acquainted with*, or *to appreciate*.[21] While the former is the nominal form of the term and hence more closely approximates to the term "knowledge," both were used interchangeably during the period in question. This is indicative of the lack of a distinction between knowing-that and knowing-how.[22] Yet a majority of discussions in the texts emphasize *manifest* knowledge, therefore giving the impression that its primary epistemological interest is in knowing-how.[23] The *Lüshi Chunqiu*'s conception of *zhi* falls in line with this pattern of usage, but we can also detect in some of its passages a sense of knowing-to.

Second, the text is by far the most systematic and comprehensive text of its time, aiming to present "a total cosmological scheme, intertwining the world of man with the course of Heaven and the sequences of the seasons on Earth."[24] Each topic in the text, specified in the chapter titles, is elaborated on by the use of two or three examples. This structure not only lends itself to analysis, it seems that its references to knowing may be interpreted as statements of general knowing-how, accompanied with specific examples of knowing-to.

Before we proceed to that in the following sections, we examine a passage in the text that captures its sense of knowing. The passage also helps us to demonstrate the way in which knowing-how is expressed in some of the discussions in Chinese philosophy of the period. In this particular example, the text makes a distinction between a person's knowing the notion of *shi* 士 (an official) and knowing to *apply* it in particular situations. The passage considers what it means to *know* officials (*zhi shi* 知士).[25] The *Lüshi Chunqiu* 16/8.2 states:

As a general rule, confusion arises when name and form do not match. A ruler, though unworthy, may seem to employ the worthy, heed the good, and do what is proper. The problem is that those he calls "worthy" are nothing more than foolish, those he calls "good" are nothing more than wicked, and what he calls "proper" is utterly unreasonable and contradictory. This is an example of form and name being different in reality, and of word and actuality referring to different things. ... King Min of Qi was an example of this. [He knew to speak of *shi* (*zhi shuo shi* 知說士), but he did not know how to appropriately deem *shi* (*bu zhi suo wei shi* 不知所謂士).] Thus, when Yin Wen asked the king to explain himself, he was unable to respond.[26]

King Min has a problem, in that he calls and deems "worthy" those who are unworthy. To *wei* 謂 (call), is not merely to carry out the performative of naming a *shi* but also to evaluate each *shi*'s capacities accurately. The term *wei* may refer to both the act of calling and the judgment that underlies the act. This very possibly draws on a text, the *Mozi* (late fifth century BCE), associated with a group of thinkers dubbed the Mohists.[27] A passage in the *Mozi* articulates the gap between knowing the terms in language and applying them.[28] It discusses the case of the terms "white" and "black," whereby it concludes that a blind person does not know black and white not because they do not know their definitions but because they cannot *select* them from among black and white objects.[29] The upshot of this passage is that simply *saying* what black and white are does not constitute knowledge of black and white. To be able to select (*qu* 取) black objects or white ones is a necessary condition of knowing (the terms) black and white.

That King Min was not able to *select* the right *shi*—he deems "worthy" those who are foolish—constitutes his not knowing how to select (capable) officials. In similar vein to Ryle's suggestion that knowing-how is basic, King Min's *not* knowing how to select officials—rather than his ability to speak about them (evidence of knowing *that* they are such and such)—is basic in knowing officials. This passage prioritizes knowing-how over knowing-that, although it articulates the contrast between the two not in the terms typical in Western epistemology, where practical knowledge is contrasted with conceptual knowledge. Although it is not clear that the early Chinese thinkers recognized the *idea* of conceptual knowledge, as such, this does not prevent them from expressing the view that simply to *say* X is different from correctly using the name X. This indicates that to know X *is* the ability to put knowing-how into effect.

To further illustrate our point, there is an example in the text of how the Lord of Jingguo had such ability.[30] In the chapter titled "Knowing *Shi* (*zhi shi* 知士)" (9/3.2; tr. Lai), the Lord of Jingguo is known to have a reputation for knowing *shi*; this means that he has an accurate understanding of their capacities and dispositions. The passage presents an account of how he demonstrated this capacity in relation to Ji Maobian 劑貌辨. Many spoke against Ji Maobian, but the Lord of Jingguo maintained a close relationship with him. The passage recounts how Ji Maobian remained loyal to the Lord of Jingguo, sacrificing much for the Lord. Ji Maobian took measures to defend the Lord of Jingguo, on pain of death. Ji Maobian sought an audience with King Xuan (宣王), who was extremely displeased with the Lord of Jingguo. Ji Maobian explicitly expresses his loyalty to the Lord of Jingguo: "My purpose is not to seek to have my life spared. I beg you, you must let me go."[31] That Ji Maobian's loyalty was demonstrated subsequent to the Lord of Jingguo's sustained support proves that the Lord made the right decision about Ji Maobian. This in turn holds up the text's assertion about the Lord's knowing *shi*. In the conclusion of this detailed account, the Lord of Jingguo is commended for his knowledge of Ji Maobian: "At this time, the Lord of Jingguo could properly be said to have the ability to [know] others on his own."[32]

How the conclusion is drawn in this passage is significant to our discussion of knowing-to in two ways. First, the conclusion explicitly recognizes the *moment* of the Lord of Jingguo's ability to *zhi ren*: "at this time (*dang shi shi* 當是時)." This emphasizes a particular feature of knowing-to, *timeliness*, which we discuss in greater detail in section 4. Second, the judgment about the Lord of Jingguo's capability is announced in the phrase "could properly be said to (*ke wei* 可謂)." In other words, the Lord of Jingguo may correctly be deemed "*zhi ren*" because he was able to manifest *zhi ren* in relation to Ji Maobian. This attribution of knowledge is demonstrated by a specific example, suggesting that the text is not concerned to describe ability in general terms—it implicitly acknowledges that there are different types of know-how in some of its chapter titles—but to provide details of successful manifestation of knowledge in particular situations. In the case of the Lord of Jingguo:

The Lord of Jingguo has the ability accurately to know people.

Ji Maobian was slandered.

On this occasion, the Lord of Jingguo stood by Ji Maobian, ignoring the widespread slander.

Ji Maobian proved to be deeply loyal to the Lord of Jingguo, sacrificing much for the Lord.

> Know-how: Has the general ability accurately to know people.
> Know-to: On the specific occasion when Ji Maobian was slandered, the Lord of Jingguo knew to stand by him.

The following section notes how, in a number of the text's discussions, various individuals are said to "zhi"—to have knowledge—on the basis of particular measures they have taken, in response to specific circumstances. We suggest that these attributions of knowledge assume a particular conception of knowledge, namely, knowing-to.

3 Attributions of Knowledge in the *Lüshi Chunqiu*

There are seven other occurrences in the text that have a similar logical structure to the Lord of Jingguo passage.[33] Each mentions a particular instance where a person successfully manifests an ability in a particular activity. On the basis of each particular instance, the text judges that the person should be deemed to have knowledge of the relevant kind. Can knowledge be so fleeting, so as to vary from one situation to the next? In note 15 we suggested that this is possible for knowing-to, at any rate. It seems that one successful instance of knowing-to helps to substantiate the claim that a particular person, X, knew Y. Here, we discuss two such instances in detail.

In the first, the State of Wey (衛) was deemed to know (how to effectively use) the capacities of the officials. Wey had shrewdly sent ten *shi* to the State of Zhao (趙), and they advised Viscount Jian of Zhao (趙簡子) not to attack Wey. The conclusion upholds the actions of Wey, noting that "It may be said that Wey understood to employ men (*wei ke wei zhi yong ren yi* 衛可謂知用人矣)."[34] Hence,

Wey knew how to effectively use the capacities of officials.

Viscount Jian of Zhao was planning to attack Wey.

Wey sent ten *shi* to convince Viscount Jian of the immorality of attacking a weaker state.

Viscount Jian heeded their advice and did not wage war.

> Knowing-how: Has the general ability to employ *shi*.
> Knowing-to: On the particular occasion when Viscount Jian of Zhao thought of waging war, Wey knew to send ten *shi* to counsel Viscount Jian against the attack.

In the second occurrence, Duke Huan (*huan gong* 桓公) is said to know how to confer rewards. In this passage, Bao Shu 鮑叔 had persisted in his recommendation of Guan Zhong 管仲 for prime minister even when the latter was in prison. When he was appointed Prime Minister, Guan Zhong more than adequately proved himself; "everything he initiated ended in success."[35] To reward these men, Duke Huan first rewarded Bao Shu, who suggested the appointment of Guan Zhong, rather than simply reward Guan Zhong, the capable official. The conclusion is drawn that "it may be said of Duke Huan that he knew to distribute rewards *huan gong ke wei zhi xing shang yi* 桓公可謂知行賞矣.[36] Hence,

Duke Huan has the ability to distribute rewards (appropriately).

Bao Shu recommended Guan Zhong for Prime Minister.

Duke Huan acted on Bao Shu's advice.

Guan Zhong proved to be a highly successful Prime Minister.

Duke Huan gave the first reward to Bao Shu as Guan Zhong was appointed on Bao Shu's recommendation.

> Know-how: Has the general ability to distribute rewards appropriately.
> Know-to: On the particular occasion, Duke Huan knew to give the first reward to Bao Shu in recognition that he was the person who had initiated the appointment.

The syntax of the conclusions in these passages is "Person X *may properly be regarded as (called)* knowing Y" (X *ke wei zhi* 可謂知 Y). The construction "X *ke wei zhi* 可謂知 Y *yi* 矣" is reasonably widespread in the text and hence we take it that the argument structure in these passages expresses a kind of knowledge that cannot simply be assimilated to know-how,[37] for the latter does not typically vary from one instance to the next. For example, we do not speak, from one case to the next, in the following way:

Samantha knew how (or had the ability) to cook on Monday, Tuesday and Friday. But because she burnt the food on Wednesday and served undercooked chicken on Thursday, she therefore did not know how to cook (or lacked the ability) on Wednesday and Thursday.

In the *Lüshi Chunqiu*, the view of knowledge implicit in the passages with the construction "X *ke wei zhi* Y *yi*," is a particular *type* of knowing, whereby a single occasion in which a person appropriately deals with or responds to the situation at hand is deemed to have *sufficiently* demonstrated knowledge. Additionally, in these passages, the focus is on the person's manifest knowledge in particular circumstances. It is not about whether a person *knows how to X* because to say that suggests that, up to a point, a person knows how to X, but on some occasion *may fail to manifest X*. To say that a person *knows to X* is to say that such knowledge is or has been manifest in a particular situation. These manifestations of knowing—knowing-to—are partly constitutive of knowing-how's being exemplified and therefore not reducible to knowledge-how. Manifestations of knowing-to are irreducibly contextual and timely; which explains our description of it as "knowing to act in the moment." In the following section, we discuss four features of knowing-to that are explicitly discussed in the *Lüshi Chunqiu*.

4 Knowing-To in the *Lüshi Chunqiu*

A number of the *Lüshi Chunqiu*'s chapter titles and discussions deal specifically with aspects of knowing to act in the moment. Although these passages do not always refer to or contain the term *zhi*, some of them are no less important than those that do, in revealing the text's epistemological assumptions. It is clear from some of the discussions that there is a concern in the text about how knowledge (knowing-to) is manifest. The question we consider is, "What kinds of considerations might apply in the realization of knowing-how in specific circumstances?" The *Lüshi Chunqiu*'s discussions cover a number of these, including the anticipation of outcomes, acting in a timely manner, attentiveness to relevant contextual cues, and understanding what is weighty. We discuss each of these in turn.

4.1 Anticipating Outcomes

Chapter 16/6, "Scrutiny of the Subtle (*cha wei* 察微)," commends Confucius on his ability to focus on subtle aspects of situations which in turn contributes to his knowledge in the anticipation of outcomes. In this account, Confucius was deemed capable of "realizing what the end result would be from the very beginning, because his ability to perceive future developments [*hua* 化] was far-reaching."[38]

In 23/3.1–2, *hua* is used in a construction directly involving knowledge. To *zhi hua* 知化 is not to know *about* transformation but rather to know to incorporate potential changes into one's decisions. The passage that elaborates on *zhi hua* states:

As a general principle, the value of the intellect [*zhi* 智] lies in being able to *predict how things will change* [*zhi hua* 知化]. Foolish rulers possess no such ability. Before change comes; they are unaware of it; and when change has already occurred, they may recognize after the fact that it has happened. But this is exactly the same as their not having recognized it at all … .[39] [emphasis added]

Knoblock and Riegel's translation of *zhi* in this passage as a verb, "to predict," is appropriately sensitive to the coupling of *zhi* and *hua* in this passage. *Zhi hua* refers to the ability to anticipate potential changes. The passage also highlights two possible scenarios in which a ruler is said to lack an ability to anticipate change.

In contrast, returning to the previous passage that ascribes such knowledge to Confucius, two specific examples are given of Confucius' ability. We suggest that these two examples demonstrate Confucius' knowing to anticipate outcomes with respect to two of his followers:

According to the laws of Lu, if a native of Lu was a servant or concubine to another feudal lord and could be purchased out of bondage, the purchase price would be recompensed from the Lu state treasury. The disciple Zigong 子貢 purchased a Lu native from a feudal lord: but when he returned from his mission, Zigong refused the payment of recompense from the treasury.[40]

Confucius remarked that Zigong's decision not to receive recompense was erroneous. It was fueled by Zigong's zealousness in not accepting undue payments, seeing *all* undue payments as potentially morally corrupt. However, in this case, "obtaining money for such a purpose does not damage moral conduct; but if the price is not recompensed, no one will ever again purchase the freedom of others."[41] In brief, Zigong did not appreciate the negative consequences of his staunch commitment to be morally upright. In the same schematic representation used earlier:

Zigong purchased a Lu native from a feudal lord.

(In all cases) if a native of Lu could be purchased out of bondage, the purchase price would be recompensed from the Lu state treasury.

Zigong refused such recompense.

Confucius anticipated that Zigong's refusal would have the effect of dissuading others in the future from purchasing the freedom of other slaves (as the recompense would no longer seem guaranteed).

> Know-how: Has the general ability to anticipate outcomes.
> Know-to: On the particular occasion, Confucius disagreed with Zigong's actions, knowing to anticipate that they would produce undesirable consequences.

In the second case in the same passage, another follower, Zilu 子路, rescued someone who was drowning. Zilu was rewarded with an ox, which he accepted.[42] In this case, Confucius agreed with Zilu's actions, suggesting that this would encourage others to engage in similar acts of assistance for people in need. Accordingly,

Zilu saved a drowning person.

Zilu was offered an ox as a reward.

Zilu accepted the reward.

Confucius anticipated that the possibility of reward would motivate people to help others in need.

> Know-how: Has the general ability to anticipate outcomes.
> Know-to: On the particular occasion, Confucius agreed with Zilu's actions, knowing to anticipate that they would produce desirable consequences.

The point of this passage is not to focus on the specific actions of the two followers but rather to focus on Confucius' capacity to explain and enlighten the correctness of their decision *in light of* anticipated outcomes. What the potential changes are in each situation will vary according to circumstantial factors, among other things, as demonstrated in the two cases. Indeed, when we reflect on some of the cases of knowing-to discussed previously—of Wey sending officials to counsel Viscount Jian against war, and of Duke Huan rewarding Bao Shu first—we see that these involve to some degree the anticipation of outcomes. In summary, a person's ability to "know change" cannot fully be explained with respect to know-how as a general ability, as to know change is necessarily manifest in specific situations.

4.2 Timeliness

In *Lüshi Chunqiu* 20/6.1, the distinctiveness of a ruler's conduct and responsibilities is expressed partly in terms of his timely actions and measures:

The conduct of a ruler is different from that of people who wear the clothes of commoners. When the circumstances are not advantageous and the time not beneficial ([*shi bu li*] 時不利), a ruler must serve his opponents in order to survive. He holds in his hands the fate of his people. To hold in one's hands the fate of the people is a heavy responsibility, and so he cannot permit himself to do as he pleases.[43]

The passage highlights that an important characteristic of a good ruler is knowing to act in a timely fashion. Clearly, considerations of timeliness must be made in context. In this passage, when the ruler decided to serve his opponents, he takes on what he would not normally do, even though it is *at this point in time* an appropriate response. Timeliness is a major factor in a ruler's success in putting into effect the range of initiatives and measures associated with government as, for instance, in implementing or reforming regulations, instituting agricultural and military ventures, and negotiating his relationships.[44] Two chapters in the text deal explicitly with the term *shi* 時 (time): "Awaiting the Right Time (*xu shi* 胥時)" and "Examining the Season" (*shen shi* 審時; 26/6).[45] Another chapter, titled "On 'Encountering' and 'Coinciding' (*yu he* 遇合),"[46] discusses the centrality of timing to opportunity: if timing does not fit on one occasion then a person needs to wait for another that does: "Opportunity (*yu* 遇), in general, is a matter of fitting (*he* 合). If one does not fit (*he* 合) with the times (*shi* 時), one must wait to fit, and only afterward can things be done."[47]

James Sellman's meticulous investigation of timing in the *Lüshi Chunqiu* covers a range of realms—environmental, historical-political, and interpersonal—and the importance of the ruler's timely, effective integration of matters across these realms in his government. What is *timely* will vary according to the relevant time frames of particular activities and their contexts: in swerving one's car to avoid an accident, the time frame is a question of seconds, while the question of when to present a reward may be relative to the recipient's opportunities to manifest his abilities. The passage above recognizes that the measure of appropriate timing is that of *fit* (*he* 合). According to this analysis, all of our examples above of successful manifestations of knowing-to require timely execution: for example, rewarding Bao Shu for Guan Zhong's successes could have been premature, had Guan Zhong's capacities not been fully demonstrated—or it could have been belated. Sellman highlights another passage in the *Lüshi Chunqiu* that recognizes the momentariness and particularity of opportunities: "The fitting opportunity is never constant, and giving advice is a matter of occasion too."[48] This statement clearly expresses the importance of attentiveness to timeliness, especially in light of its situationality. This is a key characteristic of knowing to act in the moment.

4.3 Context

A passage in the chapter titled "On Being Appropriate to the Circumstances" (*dang wu* 當務) best exemplifies the importance of sensitivity to context:

Discriminations [*bian* 辨] that do not correspond to proper assessments, keeping faith [*xin* 信] where it does not conform to reason, being brave [*yong* 勇] where it will not agree with one's moral duty, making laws [*fa* 法] that are inappropriate to the circumstances—all these are like the dazed man who rides a fast-galloping horse or the madman who wields the Ganjiang sword of Wu. The four must be regarded as the most disruptive things in the world.[49]

In this passage, each of the four terms (prominent in the debates of the Warring States period) is tempered with reference to their respective contexts of realization. This move draws attention to contextual factors that affect judgment, decision, and action. On this account, knowing to act appropriately in light of particular contextual factors is not merely knowing-how or knowing-that. For example, it is not simply that a person knows how to keep faith except when it does not agree with her moral duty. Nor is it just that a person understands the limits of keeping faith and the notion of moral duty. Rather, it is knowing *in context* that one's moral duty will be challenged in light of one's keeping faith, and responding *within that context* in a way that moral duty is not compromised. The epistemological picture underlying such sensitivity to context is the conception of knowing-to: knowledge that is meaningful only when appropriately, correctly, or successfully manifested in specific contexts.

These contextual factors do not simply refer to the physical environment. They capture a deeper, thicker, sense of the situational context that may involve knowledge of others who are involved in the situation including, where relevant, their personal characteristics and dispositions. For example, in order for Wey to send ten *shi* to persuade Viscount Jian that it was immoral for a large state to attack a small state, Wey would have had a sense that moral argument has persuasive power as far as Viscount Jian is concerned. Had Viscount Jian been an unconscionable warrior, Wey could have lost the ten officials. Such awareness of context is not to be taken lightly.

4.4 Understanding Weightiness

As a corollary to knowing in context, it is important also to know the weight, and relative weight, of matters. This idea is expressed in one of its passages in terms of "knowing the unimportant and the important" (*zhi qing zhong* 知輕重; lit.: to know the light and the heavy).[50] In this passage, Master Hua (*zi huazi* 子華子) presented sound advice to the Marquis of Han 韓. The two states, Han and Wei 魏, were disputing over territory. Master Hua counsels the Marquis of Han to abandon the fight as he had much to lose (i.e., the entire state) for want of the disputed territory. The passage suggests that Master Hua knew the relative weight of wins and losses in the territorial wars, concluding: "It may properly be said of Master Hua that he [knew the unimportant and the important]. Because he knew this, his assessments were never in error."[51]

We have also seen how the Lord of Jingguo was praised for his ability to understand people. He considered his own judgment more weighty than the views of many others, who were mumbling against and slandering Ji Maobian. This could be a profoundly foolish act and it could, we imagine, lead to disastrous consequences in certain situations. Clearly, to ignore the views of many is not a universalizable rule. But, in this passage, the Lord of Jingguo's judgment was proven correct, hence corroborating the claim that he knew people (*zhi ren*).

In the passage on Duke Huan's ability to distribute rewards appropriately, it is again in part a case of appreciating what is weighty. Duke Huan looks not to reward

Guan Zhong in the first instance, but the person, Bao Shu, who recommended Guan Zhong. In commending Duke Huan's ability, the text notes that he knew in that situation to reward the initiator of this course of action; the word used to describe the initiator, *ben* 本, also has the meaning of "root" and was commonly used to refer to what is fundamental.

In this section, we have demonstrated the ways in which some of the *Lüshi Chunqiu*'s examples address elements of knowing-to. The discussions on anticipating outcomes, acting in a timely manner, sensitivity to context, and understanding weightiness, express the importance of manifest knowledge. For example, if a person fails successfully to manifest their know-how of a certain activity, it may be because they have failed to anticipate outcomes, or to understand the relevance of a particular aspect of a situation, and so on. But what exactly are these aspects, and are they necessary or sufficient for knowledge-to? Apart from timeliness,[52] seemingly none of them is either necessary or sufficient. Given the nature of knowing-to, some of them will be pertinent, even critical, in some, but not all, cases. For instance, sensitivity to contextual cues may not be as relevant as, for example, when one is preparing a typical family dinner.

Furthermore, these four aspects of knowing-to we have identified in the *Lüshi Chunqiu* do not jointly constitute an exhaustive list. There may be others, such as sensitivity to facial gestures and other bodily cues, or appreciation of the nuances of verbal communication, or of language more generally. It is not our aim here to present an exhaustive list of facets of knowing-to; in fact, we doubt that this is possible for reasons stated above. Nevertheless, these aspects have an important role to play in our understanding of knowing-how and of the relationship between knowing-how and knowing-to. Where a person's ability in a particular type of activity fails on a specific occasion, it may well be due to a lack of attentiveness to one or more relevant aspects of knowing-to. In other words, *some* failures to manifest know-how are failures or absences of knowing-to. On the other hand, each failure of knowing-to of a particular activity does not, on its own, constitute a lack or absence of ability or know-how. Over the longer term, however, patterns of successes and failures of knowing-to in a particular type of activity are indicative of a person's ability in undertaking that activity. Should Samantha consistently undercook chicken, or should Sally often fail to calm particular crowds, we might conclude that they do not know how to carry out these respective kinds of activity. Such details expand our understanding of knowing-how's being manifested, courtesy in part of repeated instances of knowing-to.

Conclusion

Western epistemology tends to be developed as an autonomously conceptual project of theory-building. When data are sought, often the quest begins and ends with apparently shared intuitions, particularly ones claimed to reflect present language-use. Here, we have expanded the relevant domain of such searches, both culturally and temporally. Specifically, can contemporary Western epistemology welcome data from some comparatively ancient Chinese philosophy? We believe so, as this chapter demonstrates.

Thus, we have offered some specific suggestions for one respect in which an enriched conception of knowing could be gained. Our main piece of advice is this: Do not forget the constitutive importance of knowing-*to*. Any epistemological discussion of knowledge can thereby be a discussion of so much *more* than has generally been the case within Western epistemology. To talk about some specific knowledge, we suggest, is to talk about any or all of the following: a specific content that is known; a state of a person—the knowing-that—in which she actually or potentially contemplates that content; an ability of that person—the knowing-how—to act in some or all of the ways (asserting, questioning, replying, explaining, building, appointing, etc.) that are relevantly related to that content and that state; *and* the person's proceeding to act in such a way, on a particular occasion, as to manifest that ability in one or another way. This sort of action is what we have highlighted. *It* is knowing-to. And it is vital if knowledge—a content; some contemplation; an ability to act—is ever to be put into *effect*, so to make an actual difference in someone's life of action. This has been made manifest in the passages we have discussed from the *Lüshi Chunqiu*.

Acknowledgment

We appreciate Brian Bruya's excellent comments on drafts of this chapter.

Notes

1. Gilbert Ryle, *The Concept of Mind*, chapter 2 ("Knowing How and Knowing That").

2. Ibid., 29.

3. Ibid., 32.

4. Ibid., 28.

5. Ibid., 44, 46.

6. Ibid., 45. Are dispositions conceptually distinct from abilities? And is one of these two categories—dispositions, abilities—more conceptually apt than the other for understanding knowledge? Alan White argues so (*The Nature of Knowledge*, 111–121). Perhaps the most important difference, for our purposes, is that an ability might admit of a wider *range* of strengths than a disposition does. (This will be important later in our chapter.) On whether abilities as such are conceptually apt for understanding knowledge, see Jeremy Fantl, "Knowing-How and Knowing-

That"; Stephen Hetherington, *How to Know* (chapter 2); Ephraim Glick, "Abilities and Know-How Attributions."

7. Ryle, *The Concept of Mind*, 46.

8. Our thanks here to Phillip Staines, who first suggested to one of us the possible philosophical significance of attending to the nature of knowledge-to.

9. We include "if any" in case whatever is added plays a merely causal role, not an epistemic one. Our hypothesis will be that knowing-to is epistemically explanatory (and that others, too, have realized this, at least implicitly).

10. There is recent epistemological discussion of whether knowledge(-that) is *normatively* linked to action (e.g., Timothy Williamson, *Knowledge and Its Limits*, chapter 11; John Hawthorne and Jason Stanley, "Knowledge and Action"; Jeremy Fantl and Matthew McGrath, *Knowledge in an Uncertain World*). But our claim will be *constitutive*, adverting to the actual presence within action of some knowledge(-to).

11. Potential objection: "Must her overlooking this need have been constituted by her lacking some knowledge-*that*—such as her not knowing at the crucial moment that the circumstance is one where her saying W would be effective in calming the crowd?" If so, we must accept (contrary to what Ryle argued) that the intellectualist is right in thinking that knowledge-that is required within any intelligent action—that is, required even for guiding the action to fruition. Ryle considered this form of intellectualist objection ("Knowing How and Knowing That, 215–216). Once more, though, even *if* knowledge-that is always involved in explaining such a circumstance (and whether it was Ryle's battle, more so than it is ours), our point is that knowing-to is *also* needed in one's moving from having some general knowledge-how to one's performing a particular action expressing that knowledge-how. This is so, even *if* knowledge-that is part of what one would be implementing in bringing about the intelligent action. We expand upon this point below. (And we acknowledge that sometimes "He knows to do X" is a report of knowledge-that— only analogously, however, to the way in which "He knows how to do X" can be used to mean "He knows how it is that X is to be done." Just as the latter sense of "knows how" is not the relevant one for understanding the Rylean sense of knowledge-how, neither is the sense of "knows to" that we acknowledged just above. The sense of "knows to" on which we are focusing is inherently and always linked to "knows how." Only accidentally and sometimes, we suspect, does it involve "knows that.").

12. Potential objection: "Suppose that saying W is a somewhat complex action. Then would the person's knowing at a particular time to say W require her to know at that time to do various further actions—sub-actions, in effect—before she could know to do W? Would our understanding her as knowing to do W require us to embark on a vicious infinite regress—needing to understand more and more actions endlessly, even to understand just one? Would there be knowing to know to know to … to do each specific sub-action? That would be impossible." No, the conceptual requirements are not *so* demanding. There could be further knowing-to involved in performing each sub-action, *so long as* each of these is itself an intelligent action. But even this would not entail that, for each of those sub-actions, there are still further

intelligent actions—more and more knowing-to, unto infinitude. Knowing to say W could have an internal structure, whereby it comprises conceptually, even if not practically, separable cases of knowing-to, without each of these *also* having an internal structure involving further cases of knowing-to.

13. For more on epistemic fallibilism, see Hetherington, "Knowing Failably" and "Fallibilism"; Trent Dougherty, "Fallibilism."

14. We have assumed that knowledge-how is always an ability—not that all abilities are cases of knowledge-how.

15. Potential objection: "Yet how *could* knowledge be like that—contextually constituted, contextually fleeting, so immediate in its content and so transient in its existence?" This is a larger issue. But a few comments will be useful. First, the knowledge is so transient in its existence partly *because* it is so immediate in its content. Second, suppose that someone knows for quite some years how to calm a crowd by saying W. Suppose that during those years, although she is faced on ten occasions with an upset group of people, on only eight of those ten times does she know *to* act in the way encompassed by her general knowledge-how to achieve the desired calming effect. (And so on those eight occasions the person *does* act accordingly: she utters W.) Do those eight occasions also share a *general* knowledge-to—one that is apt for *all* such circumstances? Not on our approach. Rather, each instance of knowledge-to is unique and passing. All that is general is the knowledge-how. (So—if we are counting—the person would throughout those years have one case of knowing *how* in general to calm a crowd by saying W, along with, as it transpires, eight specific cases of knowing-*to*-act-at-an-apt-time-and-place-for-implementing-that-general-knowing-how. Granted, people sometimes make claims like "He generally knew/knows to do X when he needed/needs to do it." But that is not a report of *general* knowing-to. It is a general report, or even prediction, of *particular* instances of knowing-to.) Finally, what of those two occasions when the person *failed* to know to act aptly, thereby failing to apply the general knowledge-how to calm a crowd? Could she nevertheless retain the knowledge-how to act aptly, even on such occasions of not implementing it? Yes, but *fallibly* so. Those two occasions are themselves a manifestation or expression *of* the fallibility that is part of the knowledge-how.

16. This way of representing the example is one we will use several times in the chapter. Its aim is to clarify the differences and links between knowing-how and knowing-to, rather than to provide analytical definitions. Again, our overall aim is to make a *prima facie* case even for *using*—as against reductively defining—a concept of knowing-to within epistemological discussions. (This is why the entries for "know-to," here and later in the chapter, will use the phrase "knew to").

17. It is worth noting that some epistemologists regard knowing *as* a matter of a true belief's arising by manifesting a pertinent cognitive ability. See, for example, Ernest Sosa, *Knowing Full Well* and John Turri, "Manifest Failure."

18. The text bears the name of Lü Buwei 呂不韋, Prime Minister of the Qin 秦 state from 250 to 235 BCE, who commissioned it. The text comprises three sections, the "Almanacs" (*ji* 紀), the

"Examinations" (*lan* 覽), and the "Discourses" (*lun* 論). Although scholarly opinion generally agrees that the text was completed before Qin unification (221 BCE), there is some uncertainty on the date of the completion of the text and whether its "Examinations" and "Discourses" sections (the second and third sections) post-date the text's "Postface" (*xuyi* 序意), which follows the "Almanac" section. In light of this and other factors, John Knoblock and Jeffrey Riegel suggest that the extant text is incomplete with respect to the design that Lü originally had in mind for the book (see a discussion in their translation, *The Annals of Lü Buwei*, 32). Unless otherwise noted, the translations and chaptering convention of the *Lüshi Chunqiu* used here (for both Chinese and English text) are from Knoblock and Riegel, *The Annals of Lü Buwei*.

19. See, for example, Simon Leys, *The Analects of Confucius*, 12.22 (59). Also see *Analects* 20.3.

20. In Lisa Raphals' examination of metic intelligence, where she dwells on the semantic range of *zhi*, she notes that it has "a wide variety of meanings from *wisdom*, *knowledge*, and *intelligence* to *skill*, *craft*, *cleverness* or *cunning*" (*Knowing Words*, 7).

21. Ibid., 16.

22. In her comparison of knowledge in the Chinese and Greek philosophical traditions, Raphals suggests that *zhi* in the Confucian tradition involves *both* knowing-how and knowing-that (ibid.). Although Raphals does not specifically refer to the phrases "knowing-how" and "knowing-that," she states that "Confucian knowledge concerns both ideas and modes of action" (ibid., 33). Here, Raphals integrates knowing how and knowing that in the life of the accomplished person in Confucianism. This challenges an important assertion of the intellectualist debate that reduces knowing-how to knowing-that. For an influential recent version of that form of intellectualism, see Stanley and Williamson, "Knowing How."

23. Chad Hansen states that in Confucian philosophy *zhi* 知 denotes knowing-how rather than knowing-that: "Knowledge is knowledge of *dao*, knowledge of what to do. ... *Zhi*[knowing] [*sic*] is more akin to skill than to information processing. We should understand *zhi*[know] as *know-how* or *know-to* rather than *know-that*. To *zhi*[know] *dao* is to know (how) to perform it properly" (*A Daoist Theory of Chinese Thought*, 85–86). Here, Hansen refers to knowing-how and knowing-to interchangeably. In our view, the conflation of these two types of knowing can conceal important differences between the two, resulting in a conceptual incompleteness also present in Ryle's discussion. What we wish to demonstrate in this chapter is that the classification of epistemology in Chinese philosophy in terms of knowing-how does not do justice to the discussions in some of the texts.

24. Knoblock and Riegel, *The Annals of Lü Buwei*, 42. The text is unique in that its discussions transcend doctrinal boundaries, borrowing extensively from other texts belonging to a range of traditions including the Confucian (*rujia* 儒家), Mohist (*mojia* 墨家), Daoist (*daojia* 道家), and Legalist (*fajia* 法家). It has therefore been classified as having a mixed character (*zajia* 雜家), as if to suggest it was a miscellany (Knoblock and Riegel, ibid., 43). Yet the discussions are neither unwieldy nor unsystematic as the text reads as a unified whole, "representing previously distinct positions" (ibid.). The text considers a wide range of topics including beliefs and

customs, administration of government, moral cultivation, technical knowledge, agriculture, and music.

25. The terms *jun* 君 and *shi* 士 are fairly similar, meaning *official*, although we may take it that *shi* is the more general term, with *jun* used frequently by the Confucians to refer to an official with moral standing. Stephen Angle notes that in one passage in the *Xunzi* (third to second? century BCE), there are stages of progression from *shi* 士 to *jun* 君 to *sheng* 聖 (a sage) (*Sagehood*, 21).

26. Knoblock and Riegel, *The Annals of Lü Buwei*, 401 (passage in brackets translated by Karyn Lai).

27. The *Mozi* is noted for its explicit attention to issues concerning language (*yan* 言) and its action-guiding nature (Lai, *Introduction to Chinese Philosophy*, 136–139). King Min was conversing with Yin Wen (fl. 350–285 BCE), a Mohist thinker (see also Chang, *The Rise of the Chinese Empire*, 116). Knoblock and Riegel emphasize the Mohist connection of this passage: "When the early Mohist Yin Wen claims that those who do not fight when insulted are not disgraced and that the king should reward such individuals with official appointment, King Min of Qi is too weak-minded to respond. According to this chapter, the success of Yin Wen's argument signals the demise of the grand old state of Qi and calls for a Rectification of Names (the chapter's title) in the state" (*The Annals of Lü Buwei*, 372–373).

28. *Mozi*, "*Gui yi* 貴義," 47, 83 (lines 23–26).

29. The passage reads as follows: "A blind person says, 'That which is bright is white. That which is dark is black.' Even those who are clear-sighted cannot change this. But if we mixed black and white [objects], and asked the blind to select them, they are not able to know. Hence the basis on which I say, 'The blind do not know white and black' does not lie in their definition but in selection" (*Mozi*, "*Gui yi* 貴義," tr. Lai). Although classical Chinese does not have a single term or phrase that captures the idea of a "concept," it is implied in this passage that whoever only grasps the definitions (*ming* 名) of "black" and "white" does not *know* (*zhi* 知) them. This example clearly prioritizes knowing-how over knowing-that.

30. Knoblock and Riegel, *The Annals of Lü Buwei*, 9/3.2, 214–215.

31. Knoblock and Riegel, ibid., 9/3.2, 214.

32. Ibid., 215 (passage in brackets translated by Lai).

33. These can be located in ibid., as follows: (1) 13/2.3, 285–286, (2) 15/6.4, 361–362, (3) 19/6.4, 497–499, (4) 20/3.4, 520–521, (5) 21/4.3, 558–559, (6) 25/4.6, 636–637, (7) 25/5.3, 637–639.

34. Tr. Lai; see ibid., 21/3.2, 554–555. The characters in the phrase *zhi yong ren* 知用人 may be read literally as "know employ people." Translation into English requires the insertion of a qualifier for *zhi* (know). Interestingly, in a grammatically correct English construction, that qualifier tells us the *type* of knowledge required in employing people (e.g., *knows that* or *knows how to*). The use of the phrase in this passage rules out *knowing-that* and what comes most readily to mind then, for most speakers of English, is *knowing-how*: Wey knew how to employ men.

(Refer to Knoblock and Riegel's rendering.) However, the Chinese phrase *zhi yong ren* does not preclude its translation as "knew to employ men." Lai's translation here aims to capture the situational focus of the type of knowledge alluded to in the passage.

35. Ibid., 24/2.2, 610.

36. Tr. Lai; see ibid., 24/2.2, 609–610. The point made in note 34 applies also to this translation—compare Knoblock and Riegel's rendering.

37. It might be objected that these instances of such reasoning reflect hasty generalizations in attributing knowledge to a person on the basis of one successful or effective execution of a task. We argue, contrary to this objection, that there are passages in the text that warn against generalizations. For example, in chapter 25/2, lacquer and copper are used as examples to demonstrate how their properties manifest differently under different conditions (ibid., 25/2.1, 627). The passage cautions against generalizing from single cases. Although it may be pointed out that this passage merely reflects the views of a particular thinker in a composite text, we demonstrate in the following section that the attentiveness to context and timeliness—which is indicative of some resistance against generalizations—is present in many of the text's discussions.

38. Ibid., 16/6.2, 394.

39. Ibid., 23/3.1, 593.

40. Ibid., 16/6.2, 394.

41. Ibid.

42. Ibid.

43. Ibid., 531; see also 14/3.3, 313.

44. Cf. James Sellman, *Timing and Rulership in Master Lü's Spring and Autumn Annals*, 133–139.

45. Knoblock and Riegel, *Annals*, 14/3 and 26/6 respectively.

46. Ibid., 14/7.

47. *Lüshi Chunqiu* 14/7.1; tr. Sellman, *Timing and Rulership*, 140.

48. *Lüshi Chunqiu* 14/7.3; tr. Sellman, ibid., 141.

49. Knoblock and Riegel, *Annals*, 11/4.1, 250.

50. *Lüshi Chunqiu*, 21/4.3; tr. Lai.

51. Knoblock and Riegel, *Annals*, 21/4.3, 558 (passage in brackets translated by Lai).

52. Why do we make this exception? See section 1 on knowing-to's inherent here-and-now directedness. What we have seen in the subsequent sections is that this directedness may be understood more rather than less broadly—encompassing time periods of varying durations, as a given context demands. Each of these periods is nonetheless a *now*, for the purpose of knowing-to here and now within a particular context.

Works Cited

Angle, Stephen C. *Sagehood: The Contemporary Significance of Neo-Confucian Philosophy*. Oxford University Press, 2009.

Chang, Chun-shu. *The Rise of the Chinese Empire*, volume 1: *Nation, State, and Imperialism in Early China, ca. 1600 B.C.–A.D. 8*. University of Michigan Press, 2007.

Chinese Text Project. Lüshi Chunqiu 呂氏春秋. http://ctext.org/lv-shi-chun-qiu.

Dougherty, Trent. "Fallibilism." In *The Routledge Companion to Epistemology*, ed. Sven Bernecker and Duncan Pritchard. Routledge, 2011.

Fantl, Jeremy. "Knowing-How and Knowing-That." *Philosophy Compass* 3, no. 3 (2008): 451–470.

Fantl, Jeremy, and Matthew McGrath. *Knowledge in an Uncertain World*. Oxford University Press, 2009.

Glick, Ephraim. "Abilities and Know-How Attributions." In *Knowledge Ascriptions*, ed. Jessica Brown and Mikkel Gerken. Oxford University Press, 2012.

Hansen, Chad. *A Daoist Theory of Chinese Thought: A Philosophical Interpretation*. Oxford University Press, 1992.

Hawthorne, John, and Jason Stanley. "Knowledge and Action." *Journal of Philosophy* 105, no. 10 (2008): 571–590.

Hetherington, Stephen. "Fallibilism." Internet Encyclopedia of Philosophy. 2005: http://www .iep.utm.edu/f/fallibil.htm.

Hetherington, Stephen. *How to Know: A Practicalist Conception of Knowledge*. Wiley-Blackwell, 2011.

Hetherington, Stephen. "Knowing Failably." *Journal of Philosophy* 96, no. 11 (1999): 565–587.

Hetherington, Stephen, and Karyn Lai. "Practising to Know: Practicalism and Confucian Philosophy." *Philosophy* 87, no. 3 (2012): 375–393.

Knoblock, John, and Jeffrey Riegel. *The Annals of Lü Buwei*. Stanford University Press, 2000.

Lai, Karyn L. *Introduction to Chinese Philosophy*. Cambridge University Press, 2008.

Leys, Simon. *The Analects of Confucius*. Norton, 1997.

Mozi Yinde 墨子引得, ed. Ye Hong. Harvard-Yenching Institute Sinological Index Series, Supplement no. 21. Harvard University Press, 1956.

Raphals, Lisa. *Knowing Words: Wisdom and Cunning in the Classical Traditions of China and Greece*. Cornell University Press, 1992.

Ryle, Gilbert. *The Concept of Mind*. Hutchinson, 1949.

Ryle, Gilbert. "Knowing How and Knowing That" (1946). In *Collected Papers*, volume 2. Hutchinson, 1971.

Sellman, James D. *Timing and Rulership in Master Lü's Spring and Autumn Annals (Lüshi Chunqiu)*. State University of New York Press, 2002.

Sosa, Ernest. *Knowing Full Well*. Princeton University Press, 2011.

Stanley, Jason, and Timothy Williamson. "Knowing How." *Journal of Philosophy* 98, no. 8 (2001): 411–444.

Turri, John. "Manifest Failure: The Gettier Problem Solved." *Philosophers' Imprint* 11, no. 8 (2011): 1–11.

White, Alan R. *The Nature of Knowledge*. Rowman & Littlefield, 1982.

12 Quine's Naturalized Epistemology and Zhuangzi's Daoist Naturalism: How Their Constructive Engagement Is Possible

Bo Mou

In this chapter I aim to examine how it is possible for Zhuangzi's Daoist naturalism to constructively engage W. V. Quine's naturalized epistemology to jointly contribute to our understanding and treatment of specific epistemological issues in a broad naturalist framework. My strategy has two parts. In section 1, I will consider whether they can be got to talk to each other and whether some apparent differences are merely verbal disagreements or substantial ones. In so doing, I will identify and specify the structures of these two seemingly competing types of naturalism along with some of their joint concerns, especially in view of their metaphysical foundations and underlying methodological strategies. In section 2, I will examine how Quine's naturalized epistemology can be constructively engaged by Zhuangzi's naturalist approach and how they can thus jointly contribute to two philosophically interesting components of epistemology in a broad setting: (1) naturalism and normativity, and (2) the relationship of philosophical inquiry to science and scientific methodology.

The central treatment in the chapter is interpretative, in two connections: (a) the characterizations of the structures of Quine's and Zhuangzi's versions of naturalism are given in terms of an interpretative framework, and (b) what are called respectively "Quine's naturalized epistemology" and "Zhuangzi's Daoist naturalism" are not restricted to describing the literal senses of Quine's and Zhuangzi's relevant texts alone but also include due elaborations of their texts and certain relevant ideas of their allies, elaborations which either expand on some of their basic positions or articulate points that are essentially shared between them.

One question that emerges immediately is "Why is Quine's naturalized epistemology chosen, instead of some other, as Quine's approach is quite extreme among a cluster of views often collectively labeled 'naturalized epistemology'?"[1] There are three reasons for this: (a) Quine's naturalized epistemology is the most influential among variants of naturalized epistemology in contemporary epistemology, and his celebrated essay "Epistemology Naturalized" is one of the most thought-provoking writings in the literature on naturalized epistemology in contemporary philosophy. (b) Methodologically speaking, Quine's view is quite representative among many contemporary analytic philosophers in the trend of (scientific) naturalism in metaphysical and epistemological studies.[2] (c) There are two significant issues in Quine's account concerning the relationship between naturalism and normativity on one hand and the transcendental character of a naturalist approach on the other, to which Zhuangzi's resources can contribute.

The exploration of the structure of naturalism, in general, and that of Zhuangzi's Daoist naturalism, specifically, are not intended to be exhaustive so as to cover their moral and socio-political dimensions; rather the discussion focuses on their closely related metaphysical, methodological, and epistemological dimensions. My discussion of Quine's case is also not intended to be comprehensive: I will focus on two philosophically interesting points in Quine's naturalized epistemology that also bring out some tensions within Quine's account, and I will show how these tensions can be resolved by engagement with Zhuangzi's view.

One significant conception in the foregoing characterization of the approach taken in this work is that of "constructive engagement," a central strategic goal and methodology of comparative philosophy. Briefly, the constructive engagement strategy is to explore how, by way of reflective criticism (including self-criticism) and argumentation, distinct approaches from different philosophical traditions (whether distinguished culturally or by style and orientation) can learn from each other and jointly contribute to the contemporary development of philosophy on a range of issues or topics, which can be jointly approached through appropriate philosophical interpretation and/or from a broader philosophical vantage point.[3] The constructive engagement strategic goal and methodology can be manifested and implemented in various distinct ways, with distinct emphases and at different levels, and sensitive to the needs and purposes of specific research projects, instead of being restricted to one fixed pattern or merely one level. Indeed, an ideal situation would be that engaging parties, like conversation partners on the same occasion, directly talk with each other and learn from each other at each of the involved levels of engagement while addressing various distinct aspects of their subject of joint concern.

However, more often engaging parties learn from each other and make joint contributions through their respective constructive effects or roles. They enhance our understandings and treatments of distinct aspects of an issue of joint concern, sometimes at different levels of engagement (say, the methodological-guiding-principle level, the methodological-perspective level, or the methodological-instrument level—terminology to be explained below). For example, sensitive to the purposes and needs of a project, one can effectively start with a contemporary figure's account of an issue and then focus on exploring how some ancient thinker's view can engage the former at one or more levels in treating some aspect of that issue; at the same time, one can also address the contemporary figure's contribution at another level in treating some other aspect of the issue—one can thus have both parties *jointly* contribute to *a more promising new account in a broader framework* that *integrally includes reasonable and eligible elements from both sides.* In this way, although one does not explicitly or primarily talk about how the ancient side can learn from the contemporary side (or how the contemporary side can engage the ancient side), both sides actually engage and learn from each other at a deep level through their joint contributions to the new account or broader framework. This is one kind of "constructive-engagement" treatment, which the current project is undertaking: I aim to examine how it is possible for Zhuangzi's Daoist naturalism to constructively engage Quine's naturalized epistemology at certain levels and in treating some specific epistemological issues (while also implicitly addressing Quine's contributions in some other connections); in so doing, I explore how they can jointly contribute to a more complete account of epistemology in a broader naturalist framework (thus both sides engage and learn from each other), instead of within Quine's own framework.

1 A General Account of Two Types of Naturalism

In this section, I intend to characterize the relevant structures of Quine's and Zhuangzi's distinct kinds of naturalism. I will do this by introducing conceptual and explanatory resources that can be used to identify and specify what is at issue and in which dimensions the two philosophers can constructively engage each other. In presenting these resources, in order to save space, I assume that the reader already has a working knowledge of the basic ideas of Lao-Zhuang classical Daoism[4] and the basic contents of Quine's naturalized epistemology; and thus I do not give a comprehensive presentation of their various views but only highlight their relevant points for the purpose of my inquiry.

1.1 Some Preliminary Resources

To fulfill the above strategy, I must introduce some explanatory resources, conceptual distinctions, and the relevant part of a meta-methodological framework in order to analyze and clarify the methodological structures of the two philosophers' naturalist accounts. As the details of these resources have been elaborated previously,[5] my introduction to them here is brief.

The term "method" or "methodological approach" means a variety of ways that respond to *how* to approach an object of study. There are three distinct but related ways in which one can approach an object of study, which together constitute three distinct dimensions of a methodological approach as a whole.

(1) A *methodological perspective* is a way of approaching an object of study[6] and is intended to point to or focus on a certain aspect of the object and capture or explain that aspect in terms of the characteristics of that aspect, together with the minimal

metaphysical commitment that there is that aspect of the object. There are two important distinctions concerning methodological perspectives. First, there is the distinction
between *eligible* and *ineligible* methodological perspectives. An eligible methodological
perspective points to and captures a certain aspect that is really possessed by the object,
while an ineligible one does otherwise. Second, there is the distinction between a
methodological-perspective simplex and a methodological-perspective complex. A
simplex is a single discernible methodological perspective, and a complex is either
a combination of simplexes ("multiple perspective complex") or an association of
one perspective (simplex) with a certain methodological guiding principle ("guiding-
principle-associated perspective complex"). By "perspective" below I mean a methodological perspective simplex unless otherwise indicated.

(2) A *methodological instrument* is a way in which to implement, or give tools to realize,
a certain methodological perspective. Methodological instruments are largely neutral
in the sense that they can serve to implement different methodological perspectives,
though there is still the distinction between more and less effective methodological
instruments in regard to a given methodological perspective.

(3) A *methodological guiding principle* regulates and guides a certain methodological
perspective (or perspectives) in regard to an object of study. Presupposed by the agent,
it implicitly guides and regulates how the perspective should be evaluated and used
and contributes to the establishment of its desiderata (especially, the purpose and
focus that it is to serve). There are *adequate* and *inadequate* methodological guiding
principles. Primarily, in looking at the relation between the agent's current perspective
in treating an object of study and other eligible perspectives (if any), a methodological
guiding principle is considered adequate (in regard to recognizing perspective eligibility) when it allows in other eligible perspectives to complement the application of the
current perspective and thus has the agent realize that these eligible perspectives do
separately capture distinct aspects of the object and thus can jointly make complementary contributions to capturing the way the object is. It is considered inadequate
if otherwise.[7]

On the one hand, the merit, status, and function of a methodological perspective
per se can be evaluated independently of certain methodological guiding principles
that the agent might presuppose in her actual application of the perspective, and
taking a certain methodological perspective as a working perspective (this reflective
practice per se) implies neither that one loses sight of other genuine aspects of the
object nor that one ignores or rejects other eligible perspectives in one's background
thinking. On the other hand, it does matter whether one's taking a certain methodological perspective is regulated by an adequate or inadequate guiding principle,
especially for the sake of constructive engagement of seemingly competing approaches,
for an inadequate guiding principle will close out certain eligible perspectives.

The following "method house" metaphor illustrates the relevant points. Suppose that a person intends to approach her destination, say, a house (the object of study), which has several entrances—say, a front door, side door, and upper story window (various aspects of the object of study)—and several paths, each of which is difficult to discern. If a path really leads to an entrance of the house, the path is called an *eligible* one. She chooses a path (methodological perspective) to approach the house, believing that the path leads to an entrance (say, the front door). In order to proceed on the difficult to discern path, she wields a certain tool (a methodological instrument) to clear her path—say, a machete if the path is overgrown with brambles or a snow shovel if the path is heavily covered with snow. She also has a certain idea in her mind (methodological guiding principle) that explains why she takes that path, instead of another, and guides her to the house. Such a guiding idea can be adequate or inadequate. For example, if the guiding idea allows her to recognize that other eligible paths are compatible with her current path (that is, they all lead to the house), then her guiding idea is adequate; in contrast, if she fails to recognize this and thus understands her current path as exclusively eligible (the only path leading to the house), then her guiding idea is inadequate—even though her current path is, itself, eligible.

1.2 Naturalism, Quine's Naturalism, and the Contemporary "Liberal" Challenge

The term "naturalism" is supposed here to cover a wide range of theoretic or reflective accounts which, in contrast to supernaturalism, share one central ontological thesis: nothing exists beyond nature—i.e., the natural world (including human society), which is not created by nor does it include or imply supernatural entities (such as gods, spirits, etc.).[8] This central ontological thesis is underlain by a general methodological approach, the structure of which deserves a refined characterization.

Using the methodological resources introduced above, the structure of the methodology of naturalism can be characterized in the following way. Its methodological perspectives seek to capture aspects really possessed by nature (call them "nature-aspect-capturing perspectives"). Its methodological instruments serve as tools or means by which to implement nature-aspect-capturing perspectives. What really distinguishes naturalism from non-naturalist approaches lies in the former's following a methodological guiding principle concerning the legitimacy of perspectives: only nature-aspect-capturing perspectives are eligible and legitimate; no methodological perspectives (together with their associated substantial explanations) should be accepted as legitimate whose statements can in any way contradict the laws or principles of nature. However, whether an *ad hoc* version of naturalism's foregoing methodological guiding principle is *adequately* implemented would depend on whether it has a correct/true understanding of the identity of nature, for various types of naturalism have distinct understandings of the identity of nature (and of the identity of the laws/principles of nature) and thus different understandings of the full meaning of the term "nature." Such a kind of adequacy condition for a methodological guiding principle can be called an "external" one, while there are also various "internal" adequacy conditions. For example, given a certain identity of nature, whether an *ad hoc* version of naturalism's methodological guiding principle would be *adequate* would depend on whether it allowed for all available eligible perspectives on nature.

Scientific naturalism is one type of naturalism, maintaining that ontology should be shaped by the (natural) sciences alone, in principle because the (natural) sciences are said to be able to account for reality in all its aspects and carve nature at its joints, in contrast to other characterizations of the world. Quine's naturalism is a strong version of scientific naturalism, and since science is (at least in principle) the only legitimate source of knowledge, philosophy has to take a scientific form. The point is highlighted by Quine's dictum: "Philosophy of science is philosophy enough."[9]

The methodological approach of Quine's scientific naturalism can be characterized, using the interpretive resources above, in the following way. Its methodological perspective is to capture *physical* aspects and causal laws really possessed by nature (call this a "physical-aspect-capturing perspective"). It is understood that these physical and causal aspects of nature can be accessed only by the natural sciences. The methodological instruments are those methods that serve as tools or means by which to implement physical-aspect-capturing perspectives, i.e., a variety of scientific (instrumental) methods. The methodological guiding principle is: the only eligible perspectives are physical-aspect-capturing perspectives—no methodological perspectives (together with their associated substantial explanations) should be accepted whose statements can in any way contradict the principles and laws of physical nature.

With this methodological approach, Quine's naturalized epistemology looks at epistemology as "a chapter of psychology"[10] in treating how a cognitive agent (as a physical human subject) knows the four-dimensional physical world. "It studies a natural phenomenon, viz., a physical human subject"[11]; "it sees natural science as an inquiry into reality, fallible and corrigible but not answerable to any supra-scientific tribunal, and not in need of any justification beyond observation and the hypothetico-deductive method."[12] In so saying, Quine shares a widely held assumption by many in contemporary analytic philosophy to the effect that natural science carves nature at its joints, a central point in treating the status of science, standard first-order logic, and ontological realism.

It is no wonder that, for Quine, ontology should be shaped by the natural sciences alone (as a chapter of physics); in principle, the natural sciences can account for reality in all its aspects. Quine identifies naturalism as the fifth (and the last) milestone of empiricism: "abandonment of the goal of a first philosophy prior to natural science."[13]

As a challenge to scientific naturalism, what is usually called *liberal naturalism* has emerged in contemporary (analytic) philosophy. Liberal naturalism covers a wide range of accounts between scientific naturalism and supernaturalism which largely result from critical reflections on scientific naturalism especially after the middle of the twentieth century.[14] Its methodological approach, again in terms of the resources introduced above, can be characterized in the following way. As far as its methodological-perspective dimension is concerned, it is intended to capture, in addition to physical aspects of nature, some non-physical (but also non-supernatural) aspects of nature that really exist and that science cannot fully explain or explain away. It methodological-instrument dimension takes various instrumental methods that implement non-physical-aspect-capturing perspectives as well as those scientific methods that implement physical-aspect-capturing perspectives. Its methodological guiding principle takes the (eligible) scientific-oriented perspectives and the (eligible) non-scientific-oriented perspectives to serve different purposes and be (at least) compatible. Whether an *ad hoc* version of liberal naturalism's methodological guiding principle would be completely adequate would depend on whether it has a correct understanding of the identities of nature and of the laws and principles of nature. In this way, the ontological position of liberal naturalism is this: some nonscientific and non-supernatural entities or some non-physical aspects of nature may exist that science or the scientific method cannot fully explain or explain away, even in principle. For example, what naturally exists can include what John McDowell calls "second nature," as he characterizes it in the following passage:

The naturalism of second nature [conceptual capacities such as understanding and spontaneity (p. 87)] that I have been describing is precisely a shape for our thinking that would leave even the last dualism not seeming to call for constructive philosophy. The bare idea of *Bildung* ensures that the autonomy of meaning is not inhuman, and that should eliminate the tendency to be spooked by the very idea of norms or demands of reason. This leaves no genuine questions about norms, apart from those we address in reflective thinking about specific norms, an activity that is not particularly philosophical. There is no need for constructive philosophy, directed at the very idea of norms of reason, or the structure within which meaning comes into view, from the standpoint of the naturalism that threatens to disenchant nature ... . We need not connect this natural history to nature as the realm of law any more tightly than by simply affirming our right to the notion of second nature. [15]

It is my opinion, based on positions like McDowell's, that a bridge can be built between liberal naturalism as a position in the West and classical Daoist naturalism in the East. Given a characterization of the structure of classical Daoist naturalism (see below), we can begin to capture in which connections and at which levels relevant resources in classical Daoism can contribute to the current debate between liberal naturalism and scientific naturalism and to related contemporary epistemological issues and concerns.

1.3 The Structure of Zhuangzi's Naturalism: Metaphysical Foundation and Methodological Strategy

As explained above, naturalism consists primarily of an ontological or metaphysical position together with its underlying methodological attitude; its epistemological dimension needs to be understood and captured eventually in terms of these two things. In view of the foregoing general structure of naturalism, and with consideration that the focus of the subsequent discussion is on how Zhuangzi's epistemological approach can constructively engage Quine's on two philosophically interesting fronts, I first present the structure of Zhuangzi's Daoist naturalism in regard to its metaphysical foundation and underlying methodological attitude; I then explore how the epistemological dimension of Zhuangzi's Daoist naturalism can contribute to relevant discussions in contemporary philosophy via four cases.[16] It should be noted that the metaphysical foundation of classical Daoism (the *dao* 道) and its basic *naturalist* methodological attitude are most thoroughly articulated in the *Dao De Jing* 道德經 (sixth to fourth centuries BCE?), the basic ideas of which are essentially shared by Zhuangzi (fourth century BCE) as presented in the Inner Chapters of the *Zhuangzi* 莊子 (fourth to second centuries BCE).[17] Because of this dual sourcing, I refer, as was noted above, also to "Lao-Zhuang" naturalism when addressing the metaphysical and methodological dimensions of Zhuangzi's Daoist naturalism.[18]

The Lao-Zhuang naturalist account of the world takes it that the world where we live, nature (designated mainly by the term *ziran* 自然 in the *Dao De Jing* and the term *tian* 天 in the *Zhuangzi*),[19] is a "thick," multiple-dimensional nature (instead of a mere four-dimensional physical nature) that is not limited to four physical dimensions but also includes moral, aesthetic, literary, and other non-physical dimensions (at least in the human-society part of nature), and which is not limited to ready-made "first" nature but also embraces "second nature" (in McDowell's sense above; including the spontaneous "moral" trait that a moral agent might obtain through long-term deliberate moral cultivation). Further, the *dao*, as the fundamental unifying power/way of nature and as the origin of nature that is inherent in nature rather than transcendent in any supernatural entities,[20] manifests itself through a variety of local ways and particular concrete things (objects and events) in nature, which are understood as individualized *daos* or *de* 德.[21] It is in these senses that the *dao* consists in and of nature.[22]

Daoists seek ultimately to capture the *dao* (the way things in nature are) and manifest the *dao* in all dimensions of their lives, and we may call this comprehensive attempt a *dao*-pursuing methodology, which is highlighted in such key passages in the classical Daoist texts as these:

The human being models him/herself upon earth; earth models itself upon heaven; heaven models itself upon the *dao*; the *dao* models itself upon what is natural (*dao fa ziran* 道法自然)[23]

Capturing things in the light of nature (*zhao zhi yu tian* 照之於天)[24]

Relying on natural patterns ... and following the way things are (*yi hu tian li ... yin qi guran* 依乎天理 ... 因其固然)"[25]

The methodological approach of Lao-Zhuang naturalism can be characterized in terms of the previously introduced resources as follows. As far as its variety of methodological perspectives is concerned, they include any eligible perspectives that point to and capture various aspects of nature, including its physical and non-physical aspects;[26] whichever is taken as one's current working perspective will be sensitive to one's current purpose and focus. Its variety of methodological instruments consist of means by which to effectively implement various eligible "nature-aspect-capturing" perspectives while also avoiding using them in an excessive way—this would be the instrumental dimension of *wuwei* 無為 whose central idea can be highlighted in the dictum "don't do those things that are against *being natural*" (something excessive—beyond the natural limitation or not naturally needed).

As far as its methodological guiding principle is concerned, the crucial point to be made is that there is a concern for "transcending" limited, finite, and local perspectives. We can highlight several further relevant points here (more will be said in subsection 2.3) with regard to how the Daoist methodological guiding principle "transcends" various eligible but finite perspectives: (a) it is sensitive to context; (b) it treats differing eligible perspectives as complementary and aims at realizing their limits and connections from a higher point of view[27]; and (c) it aims at guiding them in harmonious balance, avoiding over-employing them in an excessive way (another dimension of the manifestation of *wuwei*).[28] The foregoing methodological guiding principle constitutes the core of Zhuangzi's naturalism, and in view of its "transcendental" character, it may be most appropriate to refer to it as "transcendental" naturalism.[29]

2 Engaging Quine via Zhuangzi

In this section, using resources from the previous section, I examine how Quine's naturalized epistemology and Zhuangzi's Daoist naturalism can constructively engage each other on two philosophically interesting fronts concerning epistemology in a broad setting: (1) naturalism and normativity and (2) the relationship of philosophical inquiry to science and the scientific method. In subsection 2.1, I identify grounds and norms in Quine's approach that are also common to other types of naturalism and explain how Quine's approach can contribute in this connection. In subsection 2.2, I identify and explain how two philosophically interesting points in Quine's account might also bring about some tensions at certain levels within Quine's account; but I would render these tensions also constructively promising for the sake of the philosophical engagement between his views and Zhuangzi's naturalism. In subsection 2.3, I discuss how Zhuangzi's Daoist naturalism can constructively engage Quine's line and contribute to our treatment of the issues addressed by Quine in his naturalized epistemology. In this way, some morals and lessons will be drawn from this comparative engagement in regard to what should be expected in treating some (if not all) epistemological issues and concerns as addressed in contemporary philosophy.

2.1 Naturalism and Normativity

When some scholars challenged Quine by saying that his naturalized epistemology would be purely descriptive,[30] Quine disagreed and listed a number of norms involved in his account.[31]

There are two basic norms shared by Quine's naturalism and Daoist naturalism and which thus provide two bases on which the two can constructively engage each other. I call these two norms the "same-nature norm" and "the truth-pursuit norm." (Quine explicitly identifies and addresses one of the two norms, i.e., the truth-pursuit norm; however, some of his remarks on it need clarification and due explanation from a comparative point of view.)

The same-nature norm can be got at by observing that both Quine and Zhuangzi talk about the same natural world in which we live instead of something else. How is it possible for them to talk about the same nature but have such distinct understandings of it? A double-reference account of reference can provide a reasonable explanation;[32] the basic point relevant to the current subject does not need any elaborate theoretic resources for understanding, but resorts instead to our pre-theoretic "common-sense" understanding. As such, each of the two types of naturalism under examination here makes a distinct double reference (semantic-whole reference and context-perspective reference): as far as the semantic-whole reference is concerned, the two types talk *about* the *minimally same* thing as their minimally common *semantic reference* to the extent that it is this natural environment around us which is not created by any supernatural entity (such as a god or spirit) but which is shared by us (including Quine and Laozi/Zhuangzi) and in which we live. As far as the context-perspective reference is concerned, Quine and Lao-Zhuang focus respectively on distinct aspects of nature via distinct perspectives that are (whether or not the advocates themselves realize) sensitive to distinct contextual purposes and focuses. The term "nature" ("natural world") and its Chinese counterpart(s) under their respective uses thus have their *distinct double-referential meanings*. What seem to be different meanings of their uses of "nature" ("natural world") and its Chinese counterpart(s) lies basically in their distinct context-perspective references, which constitute distinct dimensions of the meaning of the term "nature" (or its Chinese counterpart) in their uses. In this way, we can see that the disagreement between the two types of naturalism is merely verbal on the one hand (they both point to the minimally same semantic reference) but also substantial on the other (their context-perspective references are quite distinct).

The truth-pursuit norm can be got at by observing that the two types of naturalism both have a "transcendental" character when taking pursuing (non-epistemic and non-linguistic) truth as a strategic goal (and thus a regulatory norm) of their inquiries into nature.[33] It is well known that Quine says that truth is immanent to our theory of the world.[34] However, this is just one dimension of Quine's whole account of truth. Quine also stresses the "transcendental" character in a certain sense.[35] To understand and capture Quine's point, let me cite two relevant passages in Quine's writings related to his naturalized epistemology, adding emphasis as indicated by underscores:

The relation between the meager input and the torrential output [of the human subject as construed from the standpoint of empirical psychology] is a relation that we are prompted to study for somewhat the same reasons that always prompted epistemology: namely, in order to see how evidence relates to theory, and <u>in what ways one's theory of nature transcends any available evidence</u>.[36]

Truth *off* the hierarchy [of truth predicates relative to different rungs of the ladder of language], absolute truth, would indeed be *transcendent*; bringing it down into scientific theory of the world engenders paradox. So naturalism has no place for that [kind of concept of absolute transcendent truth].

Still, our concept of truth strains at its naturalistic moorings in another way. We naturalists say that science is the highest path to truth, but still we do not say that everything on which scientists agree is true. Nor do we say that something that was true became false when scientists changed their minds. What we say is that they and we *thought* it was true, but it wasn't. We have scientists pursuing truth, not decreeing it. Truth thus stands forth as an ideal of pure reason, in Kant's apt phrase, and <u>transcendent indeed</u> … .

C. S. Peirce tried to naturalize truth by identifying it with the limit that scientific progress approaches. This depends on optimistic assumptions, but if we reconstrue it as mere metaphor it does epitomize the scientists' persistent give and take of conjecture and refutation. <u>Truth as goal remains the established usage of the term, and I acquiesce in it as just a vivid metaphor</u> for our continued adjustment of our world picture to our neural intake. <u>Metaphor is perhaps a handy category in which to accommodate transcendental concepts</u>, from a naturalist point of view.[37]

What is the point here? Is there any genuine tension between Quine's serious talk of the *transcendental* character of truth *indeed* and his talk of the transcendental character of truth as *just a vivid metaphor* when he elaborates his naturalist position, especially in view of his naturalized epistemology? As I see it, first, the transcendental character of Quine's naturalism lies in the *transcendental* dimension of non-linguistic truth (i.e., capturing the way things are), which is highlighted by Quine in terms of the point that "truth should hinge on reality, not language."[38] This means that non-linguistic truth has the characteristic of being *cross-linguistic* (i.e., its cross-linguistic transcendental dimension), even though its linguistic presentation (or its linguistic-manifestation dimension) is immanent in language in which our theory of the world is expressed, instead of being transcendent or beyond language (that is, it can be expressed and evaluated only in and through language). In this sense, and to this extent, non-linguistic truth is both cross-linguistic transcendental with respect to language and immanent in (instead of beyond) language.

Second, Quine's statements are consistent in view of the following two distinctions: one is the distinction between *truth nature* (i.e., the nature of non-linguistic truth, capturing the way things are, which is independent of what we believe to be true and is thus non-epistemic) and *truth means* (i.e., the epistemic criterion or means by which we arrive at beliefs—which are truths), and the other is that between (non-epistemic) truth pursuit as a strategic goal (regulatory norm) and (epistemic) truth pursuit as a tactical goal (justificatory norm).[39] When Quine talks about the transcendental character of truth, he points to the nature of non-linguistic and non-epistemic truth, the pursuit of which constitutes a strategic goal as a regulatory norm in the (naturalist) epistemological enterprise; in contrast, when Quine talks about the immanent character of truth, he not only points to the aforementioned linguistic presentations of non-linguistic truth that are immanently relative to a variety of languages but also addresses truth pursuit (as justificatory norm) as well as truth means, both of which are (at least arguably) immanently associated with our epistemic theories. Note what Quine says above about metaphor being "a handy category in which to accommodate transcendental concepts from a naturalist point of view." By "transcendental concepts," he means non-epistemic notions of non-linguistic truth (nature); and by "naturalist point of view," he means the epistemic point of view of naturalized epistemology. In this latter context, it may pay to recall the title of the article in question ("Naturalism; or, Living within One's Means") and the opening statement of its abstract: "*Naturalism* holds that there is no higher *access to truth* than empirically testable hypotheses" (emphasis added).

It is arguably correct to say that, essentially following Tarski's line concerning the metaphysical dimension of the philosophical concern with truth via his semantic conception of truth,[40] Quine's account of truth can substantially enhance our understanding and treatment of the immanent and transcendental characteristics of truth-pursuit[41] as a strategic goal and norm in a naturalist approach to the enterprise of epistemology. To sum up, on the one hand, Quine emphasizes the transcendental character of non-linguistic truth whose nature consists in (the truth bearer's) capturing the way things are, which fundamentally underlies the truth-pursuit norm in the naturalist epistemological enterprise; on the other hand, he also emphasizes the immanent character of truth in view of its linguistic-presentation immanence and its truth-means and truths-pursuit immanence in the aforementioned senses.

2.2 Philosophical Inquiry and Science / Scientific Method: Tensions and Promising Directions in Quine's Account

The reason why in the previous section I address the (transcendental) truth-pursuit norm in Quine's own account is this. If my understanding of his position is correct, this norm would bring about a tension in his naturalized epistemology regarding his dictum of "science as the highest path to truth." In view of those non-physical aspects that nature genuinely possesses, his dictum would compromise his truth-pursuit norm as interpreted in the previous section. However, this tension can positively prompt a due modification of the scope of the dictum in a constructive direction when put in combination with some of his methodological considerations (part of his methodological guiding principles) in treating modal logic.

Whether or not Quine's position on writing off modal logic is tenable, one methodological point that Quine made in his evaluation of quantified modal logic is especially interesting and I think correct (to some extent):

The notion of knowing or believing who or what someone or something is, is utterly dependent on context. Sometimes, when we ask who someone is, we see the face and want the name; sometimes the reverse. Sometimes we want to know his role in the community. Of itself the notion is empty ... . The ... notions of ... vivid designator and rigid designator are similarly dependent on context and empty otherwise. The same is true of the whole quantified modal logic of necessity ... . The very notion of necessity makes sense to me only relative to context. Typically it is applied to what is assumed in an inquiry, as against what has yet to transpire.[42]

My question is this: can Quine apply the same methodological point to looking at the role of scientific method in the following two related connections? First, would the notion of knowing what nature is be also "utterly dependent on context"? For instance, wouldn't it be taking "nature" out of context to stipulate *a priori* that it is limited only to physical aspects? Second, would the very notion of the role of scientific method per se be also "utterly dependent on context"? In other words, should science or scientific method be indiscriminately out of context as "the highest path to truth"?[43]

To illustrate the point, let me raise a question, following the spirit of the above passage but replacing key terms with terminology from the "method house" metaphor (introduced at the end of subsection 1.1): Can we say that "sometimes, when we ask what the *house* [say, nature] is, we see the *front door* [say, the four-dimensional physical aspect] and want the name [say, the theory of the physical aspect of nature, which is supposed to be achieved from the physical-aspect-capturing methodological perspective to be implemented by means of its associated scientific instrumental methods]; sometimes the reverse [say, we start with the theory but not the empirical evidence of the physical aspect to project how the physical nature goes]. Sometimes we want to know the *side door* [say, the moral dimension of human society as part of nature, which is supposed to be achieved from some moral-aspect-capturing perspective] ... "?

Indeed, following his own methodological point in treating modal logic, Quine would be expected to say that science is the highest path to truth *only* regarding the physical aspect of nature and that the physical aspects of nature, as understood through science, do not exhaust *all genuine aspects* of nature. However, this brings out another tension within Quine's account. As mentioned at the outset, I would render this tension in Quine's account representative among many contemporary analytic philosophers in the trend of (scientific) naturalism in metaphysical and epistemological studies to the following extent: on the one hand, their strategic goals include the pursuit of truth concerning nature or the natural world, which intrinsically requires them to pay due attention to various genuine aspects of nature; on the other hand, they take it that the only eligible perspectives are physical-aspect-capturing perspectives—no methodological perspectives (together with their associated substantial explanations) should be accepted whose truth can in any way contradict the principles and laws of physical nature.

To constructively resolve the tension, Quine's naturalized epistemology per se is in need of a revised constraint on its applicability scope and of joint efforts from some friendly approaches, and cannot be taken as an exclusive and complete naturalist account of how an epistemic agent is to know nature.

2.3 Zhuangzi's Contributions

To see how Zhuangzi's naturalist approach can constructively engage Quine's line and contribute to our treatment of the issues addressed by Quine in his naturalized epistemology, let me start with Zhuangzi's general methodological guiding principle and then his particular treatments of four cases relevant to concerns in contemporary epistemology.

One of the most philosophically interesting messages in chapter 2 of the *Zhuangzi, Qi Wu Lun* 齊物論 (*On The Equality of Things*), is the following:

Everything has its *that* aspect and its *this* aspect. One cannot see the *this* aspect of a thing if one looks at the thing from the perspective of the *that* aspect; one can know the *this* aspect if one comes to know the thing from the perspective of the *this* aspect. Therefore one can say that the *that* and the *this* come from each other … . Thus, the sage is not limited to looking merely at the *this* or *that* aspect [from the finite point of view] but captures [all the aspects of] the thing in the light of nature. The *this* is also the *that*, and the *that* is also the *this*.... When the *this* aspect and the *that* aspect cease to be viewed as opposite, it is called "the pivot of taking a *dao* point of view" *dao shu* 道樞; one's capturing the pivot is like one's standing at the center around which all things revolve in endless change: one can deal with endless change from the *dao* point of view … . Therefore it is said that the best way to look at things is in the light [of nature].[44]

Zhuangzi's viewpoint here can be understood as a kind of *objective perspectivism* that constitutes his basic methodological guiding principle in treating various reflective issues.[45] For, instead of "any perspective goes," Zhuangzi bases relevance and eligibility of a perspective (given an object of study) upon whether it points to some aspect that is really or objectively possessed by the object of study. There are two strategic points that are closely related. First, each thing has its various aspects, and one can take a finite perspective (as a working perspective) to look at one aspect to which the finite perspective points: one can look at its *this* aspect, from a *this*-aspect-concerned perspective, and see it as a *this*, and one can also look at its *that* aspect, from a *that*-aspect-concerned perspective, and see it as a *that*. Although from each limited perspective, other perspectives may appear incompatible, the basic metaphysical foundation is this: various aspects, the *this* aspect and the *that* aspect, ontologically depend on each other; various (eligible) perspectives, the *this*-aspect-concerned perspective and the *that*-aspect-concerned perspective, thus complement each other. Second, for the purpose of looking at the connection of various aspects of a thing and/or of having a comprehensive understanding of the thing, Zhuangzi also encourages us to look at things from a *higher* and broader point of view which *transcends* various finite points of view; in this way, those different aspects cease to be viewed as opposite or incompatible but complementary. With the understanding of these two strategic methodological points of Zhuangzi's objective perspectivism, one can effectively understand Zhuangzi's substantial approaches to various issues (in metaphysics, epistemology, philosophy of language, etc.). Zhuangzi's basic methodological strategy can best be labeled (in his own term) a "*dao-shu-qi-wu* 道樞齊物 (*dao* pivot that equalizes things)" strategy and can best be understood as constituting the guiding-principle core of his "transcendental" naturalism.

In the following subsections, I explain how, under the guidance and through the implementation of the foregoing *dao-shu-qi-wu* strategic guiding principle, Zhuangzi addresses four issues that are either currently discussed in contemporary epistemology or currently less addressed but reflectively very worthy of contemporary development in epistemological studies: (1) how one part of the world can be epistemologically related to other parts, (2) the relationship between the true epistemic agent (*zhen ren* 真人) and true knowledge (*zhen zhi* 真知); (3) the status and nature of various organs contributing to the knowing process, and (4) the epistemic status of dreaming experience. (My accounts below are more or less schematic for the sake of the purposes here, and each of them deserves a more detailed elaboration, which is to be undertaken in future writings.)

Epistemological World Relations: The "*Dao*-Nature" Vantage Point of the *Dao-Shu-Qi-Wu* Strategy In contemporary English-speaking philosophy, among various approaches to naturalizing epistemology, one dominant orientation in treating the basic epistemological issue of how one part of the world can be epistemologically related to other parts (as highlighted in Quine's approach), is to reduce the phenomena in question to the empirical findings of the natural sciences and scientific treatment. In contrast, one immediate implication and implementation of Zhuangzi's foregoing general methodological strategy in treating this basic epistemological issue is this: Zhuangzi would categorically reject such a reductionist approach that indiscriminately reduces the phenomena in question to the empirical findings of the natural sciences. His basic strategic insight with associated points (contributing to his general "methodological guiding principle") are clear: first, the scientifically oriented perspective is only one finite and local perspective, pointing to and capturing only the aspect(s) of an object of study that can be subjected to scientific treatment; second, being sensitive to one's purpose and focus, one can not only legitimately but also *must* take a finite and local perspective (such as a scientific perspective) in its own terms; however, third, in so doing, one must also simultaneously "transcend" finite and local perspectives and have a higher and broader vantage point to achieve a more comprehensive and holistic understanding of various aspects of the object. Zhuangzi's basic strategic insight on the issue is more or less echoed by some contemporary philosophers; for example, Bernard Williams employs contemporary resources to capture essentially the same insight on the issue in more explicit terms as follows:

Naturalism is a general outlook which, in relation to human beings, is traditionally, if very vaguely, expressed in the idea that they are "part of nature" … . Trying to find something that is not trivial, we may say that what naturalism recognizes are just those things recognized by the natural sciences … . So naturalism gets tied to the project of physicalistic reductionism … . We should get away from the preoccupation with reductionism. It cannot be that the concerns of those who have wanted to understand human beings, in their ethical as in other aspects, as parts of nature, are essentially bound up with the prospects for the Encyclopedia of Unified Science … . Questions about naturalism … are questions not about reduction but about explanation … . The questions concern what we are prepared to regard, at each level, as an explanation. Moreover, we have no reason to think that what is to count as an explanation, from bits of nature describable only in terms of physics to human beings and their cultures, is at each level the same kind of thing. The question for naturalism is always: can we explain, by some appropriate and relevant criteria of explanation, the phenomenon in question in terms of the rest of nature?[46]

Of course, Zhuangzi did not use the Chinese counterparts (if there are any) of the same conceptual resources and did not use jargon such as "reduction," "physicalist," and "science," yet his conclusions bear an important resemblance. As I see it, Zhuangzi's insight is implemented in a distinct way and can contribute to our understanding and treatment of the issue in two connections, which are related respectively to the two strategic points of his general *dao-shu-qi-wu* methodological guiding principle. First, Zhuangzi actually takes a two-tiered approach to implementing the foregoing insight: on the one hand, Zhuangzi's approach would reject reducing all epistemic facts to empirical findings and empirical knowledge in the natural sciences ("one cannot see the *this* aspect of one thing if one looks at the thing from the perspective of the *that* aspect"); on the other hand, unlike Williams' genealogical treatment which is intended to explain human epistemic facts in terms of "the rest" of nature, such as human history and culture via ethnology,[47] Zhuangzi would allow each perspective to be explained in its own terms ("one can know the *this* aspect if one comes to know the thing from the perspective of the *this* aspect"); to this extent, a scientific perspective per se can still be maintained and explained in its own terms when its associated goal (and the current focus) is to carry out a scientific exploration of the empirically available aspect(s) of an object of study. Second, while rendering one's finite and local perspective eligible or even indispensable in one's pursuit, Zhuangzi's approach encourages one to simultaneously make efforts to take a higher, unifying "*dao*-nature" vantage point, which is intended to "transcend" the limits of various finite local perspectives and achieve a more comprehensive understanding of the thing under examination at a higher "pivot" level, although such a "*dao*-nature" vantage point is neither something that one can be born with nor something that one can achieve once and for all but is in need of one's long-term cultivation of wisdom while being sensitive to the changing world with its "yet-to-be-known" aspects (and thus to newly projected eligible perspectives).[48] Indeed, Zhuangzi would even take Williams' genealogical treatment to be another finite perspective (or a finite multiple perspective complex in achieving a certain degree of unification), for Zhuangzi would also render as local, partial, and finite the relevant human history and culture achieved via ethnology insofar as such a genealogical perspective has yet to (or cannot) see its own limits, and insofar as a higher and broader "*dao*-nature" vantage point is essentially an open-ended vision that is intended to do justice to all relevant eligible perspectives including both the scientifically oriented perspective and other finite perspectives that are not explained in ethnological terms of human history and culture. At this moment, it is important to note that Zhuangzi's point lies in encouraging one to simultaneously *both* take a certain relevant *finite* perspective explained in its own terms, being sensitive to one's current purpose and focus, *and* seek a *unifying "dao-nature"* vantage point at a higher level. On the one hand, in order to fulfill the current purpose and with the focus on one aspect of an object of study, we need to adopt an eligible finite perspective, but on the other hand, in order not to be trapped in that perspective but to have a more comprehensive understanding while seeing the limit of the finite perspective, we must also keep our eye on a wider, non-exclusive vision that is open to other relevant perspectives, which may not at present even be available.

Such a unifying "*dao*-nature" vantage point is also implemented and illustrated prominently by Zhuangzi's treatments of several other related epistemological issues, some of which are explored in the three subsections that follow.

True Agency: The Subject of the *Dao-Shu-Qi-Wu* Strategy

Zhuangzi's account of a true agent and true knowledge, as suggested in chapter 6 *Da Zong Shi* (大宗師) and as understood in the whole context of the *Zhuangzi*, is not only epistemologically interesting and significant, but it also contributes to the across-the-board philosophical issue of truth.[49] Although it can be treated as a Daoist account of virtue epistemology, I rather consider it to be a more comprehensive and holistic account of what it is to (fully) know things (or "know full well," to borrow a phrase from Ernest Sosa's recent book on the issue),[50] because, according to Zhuangzi, the identity and epistemic power of the true epistemic agent do not lie merely in her intellectual virtues/faculties but also include her cultivated capacity to capture the *dao* and its resulting wisdom in guiding her to fully know things. In the following, I first give an interpretative elaboration of Zhuangzi's account, and then I explain how Zhuangzi's view can constructively engage the Quinean account in this connection.

In the following, to enable the reader to have a close look at Zhuangzi's original narrative account of the true agent and true knowledge, I first provide several of the most relevant passages from chapter 6 with some explanatory paraphrases (in braces); then I give an interpretation of Zhuangzi's relevant points in the context of classical Lao-Zhuang Daoism, especially in view of Zhuangzi's general methodological strategy as a way of treating various issues as characterized above. Now let us take a close look at how Zhuangzi makes his point in the text.

The one who knows what *tian* 天 [heaven as nature] does and what the human does has reached the utmost. The one who knows what *tian* does lives with *tian*. The person who knows what the human does uses the knowledge of what one knows to support the knowledge of what one does not know, and one thus completes one's natural [*tian*] span of life without dying young half way {completely following the *dao* without failing half way}. This is knowledge in its greatness. However, there is one difficulty. Knowledge must have what it waits for {as its objective basis} and may then be made applicable, and what it waits for is changeable. How can I know that what I call "*tian*" is not really the human, and what I call "the human" is not really *tian*? {The key to overcoming this difficulty is that} one needs to first become a true agent [*zhen ren* 真人] and then have true knowledge [*zhen zhi* 真知] {which would be sensitive to what is changeable}.

What is meant by a "true agent"? The true agent in ancient times did not reject {but was sensitive to} what is little, did not brag about achievements, and did not scheme things [against being natural]. A man like this would not regret it when missing something and would not be complacent when making achievements. A man like this would not feel frightened when climbing high places, would not feel soaked when entering the water, and would not feel hot when going through fire {he would not be restricted by apparent limits but would transcend them with his vision}. Such is the knowledge by which one can climb all the way up on the course of the *dao*.

The true agent in ancient times ... regarded knowledge as a product of time ... . To regard knowledge as a product of time means that he needs to respond to situations and changes as if he could not keep from doing so ... . The person who is called a true agent renders *tian* and the human in accord instead of one overcoming the other.

Assume that the English term "true" is used in line with our pre-theoretic understanding of truth. It does not appear immediately plausible to talk here about a *true* agent or translate *"zhen ren"* as "true agent." For we usually consider the bearer of truth to be such mental things as thoughts and beliefs or their linguistic expressions (sentences or statements).[51] However, considering that the truth (a true understanding of nature) as conceived in our pre-theoretic understanding of truth consists in (the truth bearer) capturing the way things are, it should be neither implausible nor odd to talk about the *true* agent. For it does make sense to say that the subject (or even the primary subject in a certain sense, to be explained below) of *capturing the way things are* is the human epistemic agent, or the thinking creature, instead of some non-thinking thing. It is arguably right then that, in the context of the *Zhuangzi*, Zhuangzi relates *true knowledge* with the *true agent* and uses *"zhen"* in both cases along the same line with the basic pre-theoretic "capturing the way things are" understanding of truth (the way *tian*, the human, etc. are). For *dao* pursuing is the fundamental mission of a *zhen ren*, whether she is spontaneously or reflectively fulfilling this mission; and *dao* pursuing is simply the Daoist version of truth pursuit, i.e., capturing the way things are.

At this point, one further question emerges: given that it does make sense to interpret Zhuangzi's talk about *zhen ren* into talk about a *true* (epistemic) agent in this context, is there any serious reflective need or any theoretic significance to highlight this conception as Zhuangzi does? Or is this just a kind of innocent and insignificant rhetorical locution? It is arguably correct to say that there is a significant connection in which Zhuangzi's account can make a significant contribution to a holist understanding and treatment of the epistemological issues under discussion.

One crucial claim of Zhuangzi's account in regard to the relation between the true agent and true knowledge is this: "one needs to first become a true agent (*zhen ren*) and then have true knowledge (*zhen zhi*)." The point of Zhuangzi's claim and its significance need to be placed both in the textual context and in view of his whole thought.

The passages around the claim show how Zhuangzi addresses some related epistemological issues in the context of the whole text.[52] First, the object of knowledge is changeable; true (or, strictly speaking, *holistically* true) knowledge of the object thus needs to be regarded as a product of time in accordance with the change of the object; but it is the human subject, instead of the fixed beliefs and their linguistic expression as the definite and stable result of a previous knowing process which can be directly sensitive and respond to situations and change. Second, it is the human epistemic agent's (inter-subjective) epistemic capacities and powers (i.e., her intellectual virtues/faculties, in contemporary terms) that provide a reliable knowing process to aptly respond to situations and a changing environment and thus contribute to producing (holistically true) knowledge. Third, and more significant, Zhuangzi makes the point of how to achieve knowledge that is comprehensive and holistic (say, a unified knowledge of both *tian* and the human, a coordinated knowledge of various aspects of the object). It is the human subject who can be armed with adequate guiding insights and wisdom, which can result from her *dao*-pursuing cultivation and even go beyond those intellectual faculties that are normally possessed by the human epistemic agent in an inter-subjective way, and who can thus autonomously and creatively transcend the limitations of piecemeal individual beliefs and their linguistic expressions and unify her various individual beliefs into a holistic, comprehensive and coordinated understanding of the way things are.[53] Thus, the true agent can overcome epistemological difficulties that cannot be overcome by looking at piecemeal individual beliefs and their linguistic expressions.

In this sense, to this extent, and for the sake of achieving (holistically) true knowledge that captures various aspects of the changing world in a holistic way, one needs to first become a true agent who proceeds with adequate guiding insights as well as intellectual virtue and can thus be sensitive and respond to situations, change, and complexity (or the changing, dynamic, and becoming aspect of the thing as the object of knowledge) and autonomously and creatively transcend the limitations of piecemeal individual beliefs. In this way, through his conception of the true agent and his account of the relation between the true agent and true knowledge, Zhuangzi actually captures and highlights the dynamic layers and holistic dimension of the truth pursuit involved in epistemology, instead of the stable layer and piecemeal individual dimension alone.[54] Zhuangzi's view thus enlarges and enriches the across-the-board concept of truth as correspondence (with reality) and our understanding of how it is for the epistemic agent to have comprehensive and holistic knowledge of the natural world (including the human being itself) through his account of the true agent and true knowledge.

At this point, how Zhuangzi's account of the true epistemic agent and true knowledge can constructively engage Quine's approach becomes clear. First, as various relevant natural "human" dimensions of the true epistemic agent cannot be fully explained in terms of the natural sciences (even if partial explanation is possible), any Quinean reductionist treatment of the identity and characteristic features of the true epistemic agent would be fundamentally flawed. Second, however, a scientific perspective that points to and captures a (relatively) definite and stable "true knowledge," which can be individually delivered via beliefs and linguistic expressions, can be not only compatible with but can be constructively coordinated into a holistic account of a true epistemic agent and true knowledge, as Zhuangzi's way endeavors to show. Third, Zhuangzi's account provides us with a promising direction and partial resources for a holistic naturalist account of what it is to fully know things.

A Variety of Organs Contributing to Knowing Processes: Joint Play and "Equal" Status Viewed from the *Dao-Shu-Qi-Wu* Strategy   Zhuangzi's view on the status and function of a variety of organs contributing to knowing processes can also constructively engage Quine's naturalist approach in this regard. Let me first cite a passage from chapter 2 of the *Zhuangzi* that explicitly makes relevant points:

The hundred bones, the nine external cavities, and the six internal organs are all in my body as a complete whole; which part shall I love best? Should I love all of them to the same extent or with some preference? Shall I treat them all as servants alike? Isn't it that they then would not govern each other? Or shall I let them serve respectively as governor and as servant by turn? Isn't it that there is no [exclusive] genuine governor who [permanently] controls the others?

Zhuangzi's insight here has significant epistemological implications which can be highlighted in terms of two basic points. First, there are a variety of distinct aspects of an object of study (and/or of the world as a whole) that are both knowable and worthwhile knowing, and such knowledge is acquired through a variety of distinct knowing-contributing organs.[55] This is in contrast to a view that would assume that there is an "exclusive" aspect of the object of study that is taken as the only aspect worthy of being known and that such knowledge is acquired via a single eligible kind of knowing-contributing organ(s) as the "exclusive" primary know-contributing organ(s).[56] There are various (kinds of) eligible human organs that contribute to the knowing process,[57] and each of them (along with its associated perspective-access capacity) has its distinct role to play in their joint contributions to a comprehensive knowing power of the human agent in regard to an object of study and thus to a complete account of the object of study. Zhuangzi's point here would not be at odds with, but compatible with, the central role played by the brain as the common (physiological) ground and the final channel (for knowledge products via the brain) for any knowing process—in this sense and to this extent, the brain can be viewed as *the* (only) knowing organ (as generally understood by many cognitive scientists), instead of merely an organ that contributes to the knowing process. The point is that, given the brain as the common physiological basis for any knowing process, and given a variety of knowledge (say, practical knowledge as well as propositional knowledge), there are distinct organs of the human agent that contribute to the knowing process and which play distinct roles and jointly contribute to a comprehensive understanding of various aspects of various objects of study.

Second, if the first point is still a more or less common-sense way to capture a pretheoretic observation of the roles of distinct organs that contribute to the knowing process, what is philosophically interesting and insightful lies in Zhuangzi's evaluative characterization of the epistemic status of such knowing-contributing organs and their relationship: the epistemic status of each is rendered *eventually equal*; (notwithstanding the brain as *the knowing organ* and the common physiological basis of the knowing process and its results,) there is no *absolutely* superior knowing-contributing organ that can serve as the exclusive and permanent "governor" of the knowing process but only temporarily becomes "governor" in regard to a certain perspective access, depending on context and being sensitive to the purpose and focus in knowledge pursuit. Zhuangzi's insight here has its "transcendental" character, so to speak, in the following three connections, which implement the "transcendental" vision of his "transcendental" naturalism. (a) It transcends the view that considers the inter-subjective rational mind as the only eligible knowing organ. (b) Furthermore, it also transcends the traditional Western debate between empiricism and rationalism, concerning whether sense experience or non-sensory reason (or unaided inter-subjective rationality), should be taken as the primary source of knowledge, or whether the senses or the mind should be taken as the permanent "governor" *par excellence* of the knowledge acquisition process. Instead of taking either side, Zhuangzi's position essentially agrees to neither of their guiding principles that privilege either the sense-experience-producing organs (the senses) or the non-sensory-producing organ (the rational mind). (c) Generally speaking, given the brain as the common physiological basis, and depending on one's purpose and focus, one can "transcend," or shift from, one's primary reliance on one specific human organ in the knowing process in regard to one kind of knowledge to a primary reliance on some other specific organ(s) contributing to the knowing process in regard to another kind of knowledge.[58]

It should be noted that Zhuangzi's approach is sometimes presented as this or that kind of skepticism[59]; nevertheless, the point of Zhuangzi's "skeptical" position (if it can be called that) may be illustrated by his treatment of the nature and roles of the various organs contributing to the knowing process. It is clear that Zhuangzi does not deny the possibility of knowledge of the natural world but puts into doubt absoluteness and one-sidedness in the following senses. First, knowing and not-knowing are relative to the organs of the knowing agent that contribute to the knowing process: as illustrated by those examples given in note 55, knowing via one knowing-contributing organ does not amount to knowing via some other knowing-contributing organ; Zhuangzi thus brings into doubt whether the agent who knows via one knowing-contributing organ or one exclusive set of celebrated knowing-contributing organs (say, the organ of inter-subjective rationality plus the organs of our five senses, through which one sets out to employ scientific methods) does not know things whose knowing requires resorting to some other knowing-contributing organ(s). Second, knowing and not-knowing are relative to a certain aspect of the object of study accessible by certain organs: knowing *this* aspect of the object (say, the physical aspect) primarily via *this* knowing-contributing organ does not amount to knowing *that* aspect (say, some non-physical aspect) primarily via *that* knowing-contributing organ[60]; Zhuangzi thus brings into doubt whether the agent who knows *this* aspect primarily via *this* knowing-contributing organ also knows *that* aspect primarily via *that* knowing-contributing organ. Zhuangzi's point is not that the epistemic agent has to be trapped in one or another local and finite perspective which can be most effectively processed only through one or another knowing-contributing organ without the prospect of achieving a (more) comprehensive knowledge and a holistic understanding of the natural world around us. Rather, his point is this: such a comprehensive knowledge results from all eligible knowing-contributing organs' joint play in their due roles; it is up to the true (epistemic) agent who can achieve such a holistic understanding through her cultivated knowing power in the *dao*-pursuit to "transcend" the limits of various local knowing-contributing organs (on the common physiological basis of the brain as *the knowing organ*) and of various finite perspectives and adequately coordinate them in joint play from the "*dao*-nature" vantage point.[61]

Zhuangzi's overall target is not just to recognize the limits of perspectival knowledge and of various local knowing-contributing organs but to offer a path to overcome those limits. Although our first intuition may be to take this in a mystical way, the foregoing account demonstrates a more down-to-earth understanding in line with Zhuangzi's general naturalism and is an exemplification of his *dao-shu-qi-wu* methodological strategy.

The Dream of the Butterfly: Epistemic Perspectives Unified in the *Dao-Shu-Qi-Wu* **Metaphysical Outlook**   Zhuangzi's "transcendental" naturalism also provides a metaphysical foundation for understanding and resolving Zhuangzi's classic epistemological dilemma, the dream of the butterfly:

Once upon a time, Zhuang Zhou [Zhuangzi] dreamt of himself becoming a butterfly, a lively butterfly; he thus felt so complacent that he forgot himself to be Zhuang Zhou. All of sudden, Zhuang Zhou woke up realizing that he was Zhuang Zhou; but this surprised and bewildered him: he was thus not sure whether it was Zhuang Zhou who was dreaming of himself becoming a butterfly or whether it was the butterfly who dreamt of itself becoming Zhuang Zhou. There must be some distinction between Zhuang Zhou and the butterfly. This is what is meant by "all [distinct] things being unified into one [*wu hua* 物化]."[62]

The points of Zhuangzi's dreaming argument need to be captured in the context of the whole inner chapters. First, in contrast to Descartes' dreaming argument,[63] the dreamer's epistemological dilemma of Zhuang Zhou dreaming himself as a butterfly or the butterfly dreaming itself as Zhuang Zhou cannot be eventually based either on the human being's own daytime case as the ultimate criterion or on the finite perspective of the dreamer like Zhuang Zhou (as a human knowing/epistemic agent). Second, the dreamer's two alternative finite perspectives have equal epistemic status and are equally unresolvable within the dreamer's own sight. Third, the epistemological dilemma needs to be understood and resolved in a broader metaphysical outlook (held by Zhuangzi as the dreaming story teller) that "transcends" the dreamer's own two alternative (finite) perspectives: this higher and broader metaphysical outlook enables one to capture the distinctions between all distinct things (including Zhuang Zhou and the butterfly) and their unifying connections (*wu hua*).[64] It should be noted regarding this final point that Zhuangzi is not alleging that there are no distinctions or demarcation lines among things (there are, though some are transient), nor is he indiscriminately claiming that all things just "transform" or simply change into each other in form, appearance, or structure (though some do), nor is he maintaining that it is (epistemologically) impossible to have a higher "*dao*-nature" vantage point from which one can transcend the dreamer's own alternative finite perspectives to adequately identify the distinctions and unification among all things; rather, one major point in the passage is that it is exactly from this "*dao*-nature" vantage point that all things are *unified into one* but without losing their own (relatively) distinctive identities.

From the above four case analyses, one can see that while Quine treats his naturalism as the limit and epistemic means of epistemology, Zhuangzi proposes a "transcendental" naturalism to open up our vision for the epistemic enterprise through providing various implementations and manifestations of his fundamental *dao-shu-qi-wu* strategic guiding principle in treating the foregoing issues in epistemology, which are presented as a broader metaphysical outlook, a higher vantage point of methodology or a more comprehensive *dao*-pursuit goal guidance. One can further see that the scientific-oriented perspective in Quine's approach can be not only compatible with but complementary to other non-scientific perspectives in a broader naturalist framework as suggested by Zhuangzi's naturalism. The trick lies partially in having Quine's own science-oriented perspective be guided by, instead of having it bring about a tension at odds with, a thorough implementation of his own "transcendental" truth-pursuing norm and his methodological point regarding context-sensitivity (as illustrated in his evaluation of quantified modal logic), which are more or less kindred in spirit with the *dao*-pursuit goal and the "transcendental-perspectivism" methodological point of Zhuangzi's "transcendental" naturalism. Indeed, Quine's science-oriented perspective together with its associated rich resources can *thus* constructively contribute to a more comprehensive epistemic account in a broader naturalist outlook; to this extent, surely, Zhuangzi, or the Zhuangzi-style naturalist approach, can also learn substantially from Quine's resources that can be reasonably included in such a more comprehensive naturalist account.

Conclusion

In sum, what this chapter is intended to contribute to the relevant discussion in contemporary philosophy lies in two connections. First, via introduced conceptual and explanatory resources, I have endeavored to identify and specify the structures of the two types of naturalism under examination, what is at issue between them, and in which aspects they can constructively engage each other. Second, with the foregoing understanding of the structures of the two types of naturalist accounts and what is at issue, I have endeavored to primarily explain how Zhuangzi's Daoist naturalism can constructively engage Quine's naturalized epistemology on the two fronts concerning epistemology in a broad setting (i.e., that of naturalism and normativity, and that of the relationship of philosophical inquiry to science/scientific method) and in treating some specific epistemological issues; in so doing, some reasonable parts of Quine's resources have been also constructively evaluated. In this way, I have explored how Zhuangzi's Daoist naturalism and Quine's naturalized epistemology can jointly contribute to a more complete epistemological account in a broader naturalist account.

Acknowledgments

I am grateful to the following colleagues for their helpful comments and suggestions on earlier versions of this chapter: Brian Bruya, Linhe Han, Xiaofei Tu, and Anand Vaidya—especially Bruya and Vaidya, who have given helpful detailed comments on various points and made constructive suggestions. I am grateful to Gilbert Harman and Ernie Lepore for their stimulating and meticulous talks and discussions on Quine's thoughts, from which I learned a lot, at the NEH 2011 Summer Seminar on "20th Century American Philosophy: Quine and Davidson" (Princeton University) during which an early draft of this chapter was worked out. My thanks also go to the audiences who raised questions and made helpful comments when earlier versions of this chapter were presented at a group session of the aforementioned NEH 2011 Summer Seminar, at a colloquium held in 2011 at Peking University's Institute of Foreign Philosophy, and at the ISCWP session at the Pacific Division 2012 meeting of the American Philosophical Association in Seattle.

Notes

1. For a clear summary introduction to a cluster of views labeled "naturalized epistemology," see *Stanford Encyclopedia of Philosophy*, s.v. "Naturalized Epistemology" (by Richard Feldman). For a recent discussion of Quine's naturalized epistemology in contrast to another major approach to naturalizing epistemology in contemporary philosophy, see Ram Neta's explanation of Alvin Goldman's account, in "Quine, Goldman and Two Ways of Naturalizing Epistemology."

2. It is arguably correct to say that all of the major post-Quine approaches to naturalizing epistemology essentially share one central point of Quine's approach, namely, that epistemology must be in contact with the findings of empirical science. See, for example, Goldman, *Epistemology and Cognition;* Christopher Cherniak, *Minimal Rationality;* Jonathan Weinberg, Shaun Nichols, and Stephen Stitch, "Normativity and Epistemic Intuitions"; Hilary Kornblith, *Knowledge and Its Place in Nature.*

3. For a systematic elaboration and explanation of the constructive-engagement strategy of comparative philosophy, see Bo Mou, "On Constructive-Engagement Strategy of Comparative Philosophy." For the results of several recent collective projects that explicitly take the constructive-engagement strategy and effectively illustrate various ways of implementing the strategy through exploring the constructive engagement between Davidson's philosophy and Chinese philosophy, that between Searle's philosophy and Chinese philosophy, and that between analytic and "Continental" approaches in philosophy, see, respectively, Mou (ed.), *Davidson's Philosophy and Chinese Philosophy*; Mou (ed.), *Searle's Philosophy and Chinese Philosophy: Constructive Engagement*; Mou and Tieszen (eds.), *Constructive Engagement of Analytic and Continental Approaches in Philosophy*. The strategy has been also effectively channeled by the journal *Comparative Philosophy: An International Journal of Constructive Engagement of Distinct Approaches toward World Philosophy* (http://www.comparativephilosophy.org).

4. In keeping with standard practice, I use the phrase "Lao-Zhuang classical Daoism" to refer to points that are essentially shared, or can be complementarily possessed, in the two classical Daoist texts *Dao De Jing* and *Zhuangzi* which provide the metaphysical and methodological foundations for Zhuangzi's naturalist approach to specific epistemological issues. For more on their shared and distinct characteristics in various connections, see A. C. Graham, *Disputers of the Tao*.

5. See Mou, "An Analysis of the Structure of Philosophical Methodology." For a more complete account of the aforementioned meta-methodological framework (especially the part explaining a set of adequacy conditions for methodological guiding principles), see Mou, "On Constructive-Engagement Strategy of Comparative Philosophy" and "Constructive Engagement of Analytic and Continental Approaches Beyond the Western Tradition."

6. The identity of a (genuine) object of study in philosophy is understood broadly: as a naturally produced object in physical reality, a constructed object in social reality, a "linguistic" object (such as a word), an abstract object in philosophical theory, or an "issue" object in philosophy (such as the philosophical issue of truth with its distinct but related dimensions), referentially accessible and critically communicable among participants in philosophical dialogue.

7. This adequacy condition may be called the "the perspective-eligibility-recognizing condition." There are other adequacy conditions in view of some other connections, as explored in Mou, "On Constructive-Engagement Strategy of Comparative Philosophy."

8. Many contemporary philosophers in the analytic tradition tend to characterize this general label in terms of scientific naturalism. For example, Timothy Williamson describes naturalism in this way: "Many contemporary philosophers describe themselves as naturalists. They mean that they believe something like this: there is only the natural world, and the best way to find out about it is by the scientific method" ("What Is Naturalism?"). Williamson resists this description, himself, primarily because of the vagueness of "the scientific method"; he prefers the less vague term "the scientific spirit," which merely emphasizes scientific virtues like curiosity, honesty, accuracy, precision, rigor, etc.

9. Quine, *The Ways of Paradox*, 149.

10. Quine, "Epistemology Naturalized," 82.

11. Ibid.

12. Quine, *Theories and Things*, 72.

13. Ibid., 67.

14. See a recent edited anthology by Mario De Caro and David Macarthur (*Naturalism and Normativity*), which presents an engaging variety of forms of liberal naturalism in contemporary philosophy.

15. John McDowell, *Mind and World*, 94–95.

16. Others have also given accounts of Zhuangzi's naturalism. See, e.g., Paul Kjellberg's characterization in view of its relationship with what is labeled "Zhuangzi's skepticism" ("Sextus Empiricus, Zhuangzi, and Xunzi on 'Why Be Skeptical?'" 8–21).

17. The text *Zhuangzi* consists of 33 chapters which are usually divided into three parts: (1) the Inner Chapters (1–7), whose author is considered to be the historical figure Zhuangzi; (2) the Outer Chapters (8–22); and (3) the miscellaneous chapters (23–33). The authors of the chapters in the second and third parts are considered to be Zhuangzi's later followers.

18. If ignoring both historical setting and philosophical-tradition associations, one might be tempted to take Daoist naturalism as one form of liberal naturalism in view of apparent similarities. However, that would conflate some significant things that perhaps ought not be conflated. Historically speaking, Daoist naturalism did not, of course result from critical reflection on scientific naturalism in the twentieth century; and theoretically speaking, instead of one competing approach within the analytic tradition, Daoist naturalism developed as a distinct major philosophical tradition with its own style, orientation, and rich cultural associations.

19. For this author's account of the historical development of the concept of *tian* in classical Chinese philosophy, see Mou, *Chinese Philosophy A-Z*, s.v. "tian 天," 145–147.

20. In the *Zhuangzi*, there is the repeated mention of "*shen* 神." Though the character in contemporary Chinese is sometimes used to indicate supernatural entities, like gods or deities, the term in the *Zhuangzi* is not used to mean anything supernatural: typically, it is used to indicate a state of mind of the human being, such as in "*qi shen ning* 其神凝 (his mind concentrating)" (chapter 1) and "*chen yi shen yu … er shen yu xing* 臣以神遇 … 而神欲行 (I follow my mind's maneuver [in moving around my knife] … my mind still proceeds)" (chapter 3), or describe something or someone remarkable, extraordinary, or nearly miraculous, such as in "*shen ren* 神人 (the extraordinary person)" (chapter 1).

21. Construing *de* in the broad sense of the term as the manifested *dao* through particular concrete things in contrast to its narrow sense as human moral virtue.

22. For further elaboration of the nature and status of the *dao* as characterized in the *Dao De Jing*, see Mou, "Eternal *Dao*, Constant Names, and Language Engagement."

23. *Dao De Jing*, chapter 25.

24. Ibid., chapter 2.

25. *Zhuangzi*, chapter 3.

26. It is philosophically interesting to ask what count as non-physical aspects of nature respectively for Daoist naturalism and for liberal naturalism, and thus whether the set of non-physical aspects in Daoist naturalism is the same as that in liberal naturalism. A trivial answer to the former question is this: both would take as non-physical aspects all the aspects of nature that are not physical; this answer cannot bring about a substantial answer to the latter question, as what is really at issue is what counts as nature or what is the identity condition for the non-physical aspects of nature. To my knowledge, no thinkers in Daoist naturalism or in liberal naturalism have ever provided, or intended to provide, a precise set of sufficient and necessary conditions for what counts as nature (and thus what counts as a non-physical aspect of nature), except for some overall insights, general descriptions, and narrative accounts that would contribute eventually to our pre-theoretic intuitive understanding in this regard. However, this does not compromise the intelligibility of the very notion of non-physical aspects of nature.

27. See especially chapter 2 of the *Zhuangzi*.

28. See especially chapter 77 of the *Dao-De-Jing*.

29. Although the term "transcendental" is often metaphysically loaded in its usage in the history of philosophy, and one might thus expect it to be replaced by another appropriate term that has less historical baggage, I prefer, or feel the need, to retain it here, for three reasons. First, the term seems to most readily capture the three aspects of the Daoist methodological guiding principle, as just described. Second, although, alternatively, Zhuangzi's methodological guiding principle can be characterized using its own distinctive conceptual resources (e.g., I use "*dao-shu-qi-wu* 道樞齊物" in subsection 2.3), in the context of this constructive-engagement, I exploit the term "transcend" in a line of argument below to demonstrate a "transcendental" character that is shared between Zhuangzi and Quine. Third, in general, to avoid any unexpected connection of a term with associated baggage in its usage history, one can clarify in what sense the term is used in the current context, while keeping other usages to a minimally shared, philosophically innocent meaning, which is what I do here. The notion of "transcendence" is arguably what most significantly distinguishes Zhuangzi's Daoist naturalism from other types of naturalism and will be explored further below.

30. One representative and influential criticism of Quine's naturalized epistemology in this connection is made by Jaegwon Kim in "What Is 'Naturalized Epistemology'?" It should be noted, however, that although it is correct for Kim to point out that the concept of truth per se is not a specifically epistemic notion but a "semantical-metaphysical" one (p. 383), the concept of truth pursuit, which Quine categorically maintains as part of his enterprise, is essentially a normative epistemic one.

31. Quine, "Naturalism; or, Living within One's Means," 258–261.

32. See Mou, "A Double-Reference Account: Gongsun Long's 'White-Horse-Not-Horse' Thesis," in which the main points of the double-reference account are characterized in order to test its explanatory force in treating the seemingly paradoxical "white-horse-not-horse" thesis in classical Chinese philosophy. In the article, the distinction between semantic-whole reference and

context-perspective reference addressed here was presented in less accurate terms as the distinction between "semantic reference and pragmatic reference."

33. For a detailed discussion of the relationship between truth pursuit and *dao* pursuit, see Mou, "Truth Pursuit and *Dao* Pursuit," and relevant discussions in Mou, *Substantive Perspectivism*, chapter 5.

34. See, e.g., Quine, *Theories and Things*, 21–22.

35. Various philosophers have presented their own explanations of Quine's view in this regard. For example, from the point of view of the philosophy of language, Gilbert Harman makes general points concerning the distinction between transcendental notions and immanent notions, which are repeated here to help shed light on Quine's view: "(1) transcendent notions apply to languages in general, perhaps 'sentence,' 'word,', etc.; (2) immanent notions make sense only for a particular language; (3) there is both an immanent notion of truth and a transcendent notion; (4) the immanent notion of reference in my language can be explained via disquotation: 'rabbits' refers to rabbits; this cannot be applied to other languages; (5) the transcendent notion can be explained in terms of translation: t in L refers to x if and only if the translation of t in L into my language (immanently) refers to x" (Harman, "Seminar Notes on Quine"). Ernest Lepore has also explained the distinction basically from the point of view of the philosophy of language (Lepore, "Seminar Notes on Quine"). My discussion below tries to explain Quine's point here also in view of the case of epistemology via the two distinctions to be addressed.

36. Quine, "Epistemology Naturalized," 83.

37. Quine, "Naturalism; or, Living within One's Means," 261.

38. *Philosophy of Logic*, 10.

39. The former distinction is not new and has been widely recognized. The basic idea involved in the latter distinction should not be new, though (to my knowledge) it had yet to be formulated into an explicit distinction before my detailed discussion of it in Mou, *Substantive Perspectivism*, 111–117.

40. Tarski, "The Concept of Truth in Formalized Languages" and "The Semantic Conception of Truth and the Foundations of Semantics." For a detailed discussion of the relationship between Quine's account of truth and Tarski's account, see Mou, "Tarski, Quine, and 'Disquotation' Schema (T)," and also see relevant sections in Mou, *Substantive Perspectivism*, chapters 2 and 3.

41. The Daoist equivalent of Quine's truth-pursuit is *dao*-pursuit.

42. Quine, "Intensions Revisited," 121.

43. For a recent article on an analytic approach to science from a broader vantage point, see Richard Tieszen, "Analytic and Continental Philosophy, Science, and Global Philosophy."

44. All translations from the *Zhuangzi* are mine.

45. For a detailed examination of the nature of Zhuangzi's perspectivism, see Mou, "Searle, Zhuangzi, and Transcendental Perspectivism."

46. Williams, *Truth and Truthfulness*, 22–23.

47. See Williams, ibid., chapter 2 ("Genealogy").

48. This topic of how to understand the identity of such a *"dao-*nature" vantage point in view of the nature and status of distinct objects of study and how to foster and enhance it deserves a separate article. Suffice it to say that it is not something odd or mysterious or totally out of touch with people's own reflective practice. I think we all have had the experience of stepping out of a limited perspective to get a broader view. Here I appeal to the readers' pre-theoretic understanding of this sense of a "broader view," of its identity and characteristic features, while pondering their own reflective practice.

49. I have given an elaboration of how Zhuangzi's account of the true agent and true knowledge can contribute to the truth-pursuing-agent dimension of the philosophical concern with truth in Mou, *Substantive Perspectivism* (section 5.3). What is given here is a further elaboration of its epistemological relevance and significance.

50. It is well known that Ernest Sosa is one of the earlier advocates of virtue epistemology in contemporary analytic epistemology (see, for example, Sosa, *Knowledge in Perspective: Collected Essays in Epistemology*). In his recent book *Knowing Full Well*, Sosa incorporates his previous points on virtue epistemology into a more comprehensive account of what it is to "know full well."

51. This may be why some translators avoid translating the term *"zhen"* in *"zhen ren"* as "true" and instead choose alternative locutions, such as "authentic" or "genuine."

52. For the sake of focusing on the purpose here and due to space constraints, let me put aside the partially technical but reflectively interesting issue of how to translate/interpret the Chinese term *"zhi* 知*,"* a counterpart to the English "knowledge/knowing," without compromising Zhuangzi's basic points here. Suffice it to say that *zhi* involves more than just the acquisition of a conceptual representation that corresponds with reality, and further implies the dynamic process of knowing as well as the achievement of a more comprehensive understanding that allows for effective action in the world.

53. One can further evaluate the need of the conception of the true agent in view of such reflectively interesting questions as whether or not there is something *as a whole* that is beyond what piecemeal individual beliefs or statements can tell us but that can still be captured by the human agent and whether or not there are things that *at least currently* cannot be descriptively captured by any particular predication expressions but that can be understood and captured by the human agent and only generally covered by "the way the things are."

54. In chapter 8 of *The Value of Knowledge and the Pursuit of Understanding*, Jonathan Kvanvig emphasizes the value of (a more complete) understanding that is achieved in a holistic way in contrast to knowledge that can be achieved piecemeal. Kvanvig's point is kindred in spirit with that of Zhuangzi's account of the truth-pursuing agent.

55. An organ that contributes to the knowing process ('knowing-contributing organ' for short) is to be distinguished from a knowing organ per se: the former means any organ of the human agent that can directly or indirectly contribute to the process of forming knowledge, while the

latter means the human cognitive organ that directly (or in a direct physiological way) processes information with the end product being knowledge. Clearly, any knowing organ is also a knowing-contributing organ, while the reverse does not necessarily hold. The term "organ" is used here in a broad sense: it can be a distinct part of the human body (like an ear or the heart) or a distinct "functional" part of the brain (or mind) that performs distinct "organ" functions which contribute to the knowing process (on the common physiological basis of the brain), such as the non-sensory inter-subjective-rationality-producing "organ" that achieves knowledge, the morality-appreciating "organ" (typically associated with the "organ" of 心 (heart-mind) in classical Chinese philosophy) that achieves knowledge of human morality, and the beauty-appreciating "organ" that achieves knowledge of aesthetic aspects of things.

56. Such as the senses or the mind, which are claimed to be the exclusive primary knowing-contributing organ(s) by the two sides in the traditional Western debate between empiricism and rationalism.

57. Surely what Zhuangzi refers to as "the hundred bones," "the nine external cavities," and "the six internal organs" are neither exhaustive nor limited to organs that contribute to the knowing process as understood in a narrow or straightforward sense. However, the context bears out an epistemological construal. First, while the hundred bones of the human agent are not usually considered to contribute to the human knowing process, it is not unreasonable to maintain that they contribute to the human agent's practice via the human body and thus her practical knowledge, though in an indirect way. Second, organs that contribute to the knowing process for empirical knowledge are among the referents of "the nine external cavities" which include a pair of ear cavities for the sense of sound, a pair of eye cavities for the sense of sight, a pair of nose cavities for the sense of smell, and the mouth-tongue cavity for the sense of taste. Third, *liu zang* 六藏 (臟) (six internal organs) in the Chinese original traditionally refers to the human heart, liver, spleen, lungs, kidneys, and stomach and does not include as a referent either the brain or any abstract "organ" that might carry out a process that contributes to knowledge (such as non-sensory reason, inter-subjective rationality, or mathematical calculation, etc.); nevertheless, the heart was traditionally understood to be the seat of emotion and reflection.

58. For one example, one relies primarily on one's non-sensory inter-subjective-rationality-producing "organ" to learn and achieve mathematical knowledge, while one relies primarily on one's five senses (as knowing-contributing organs) to learn and achieve empirical knowledge. For another example, one relies primarily on the foregoing two sorts of organs to build up and formulate scientific theoretic knowledge. In contrast, a distinct set of "organs" primarily contributes to the process of producing a certain sort of practical knowledge (say, the knowledge of how to ride a bicycle). *In so doing*, one "transcends" or shifts from one's primary reliance on one specific knowing-contributing organ (or set of organs) to reliance on some other(s).

59. See, e.g., several chapters in Paul Kjellberg and Philip J. Ivanhoe (eds.), *Essays on Skepticism, Relativism, and Ethics in the Zhuangzi*. Kjellberg writes: "Zhuangzi and Sextus use similar types of arguments … inducing uncertainty … . This suggests a different vision of the whole text [the *Zhuangzi*] not as providing solutions but rather as asking questions leading to uncertainty" ("Sextus Empiricus, Zhuangzi, and Xunzi on 'Why Be Skeptical?'" 9–10).

60. Just consider as an example the simple case of a person as an object of knowledge: this hypothetical person possesses a normal variety of aspects—a physical aspect (as a physical object), a moral aspect (as a moral agent), an aesthetic aspect (as an object of beauty appreciation), etc. Having knowledge of the physical aspect of the person primarily via one's five senses (plus, perhaps, a more sophisticated understanding through the study of physics via one's non-sensory inter-subjective-rationality-producing "organ" in addition to rudimentary empirical observations) amounts neither to one having knowledge of the moral aspect of the person (which would occur primarily via one's morality-appreciating "organ(s)" involving one's own innate moral sensibility along with what has been morally cultivated), nor to one having knowledge of the aesthetic aspect of the person (which would occur primarily via one's beauty-appreciating "organ(s)" which might result from one's aesthetic cultivation). Although we currently have yet to fully understand how these "organs" upon which one's knowledge of the moral, aesthetic, and other non-physical aspects of a person primarily relies are related to the physiological (dimension of the) brain, one thing is certain: they are neither the same as the organs of the senses and the non-sensory inter-subjective-rationality-producing organ (upon which scientific knowledge primarily relies), nor can they be exhausted by the latter.

61. What is said in this paragraph with regard to knowing can also be said with regard to not knowing, and vice versa.

62. A traditional translation of *"wu hua 物化"* is "transformation of things." In my opinion, such a translation in the context of the *Zhuangzi* (especially here) can be misleading: one might mistake Zhuangzi's point here to mean that things just transform into each other without demarcation lines among them. This is not Zhuangzi's point here. Zhuangzi does not categorically deny distinctions among things; rather, his point is that all things are *unified into one* but without losing their own (relatively) distinctive identities.

63. For a recent clear introduction to the debate on Descartes' dreaming argument in contemporary philosophy, see Jack Crumley, *An Introduction to Epistemology*.

64. For other interpretations of Zhuangzi's dream passage, see Allinson, "The Myth of Comparative Philosophy or the Comparative Philosophy Malgré Lui"; Lisa Raphals, "Skeptical Strategies in the *Zhuangzi* and *Theaetetus*"; Kelly Clark and Liu Zongkun, "The Polished Mirror."

Works Cited

Allinson, Robert E. "The Myth of Comparative Philosophy or the Comparative Philosophy Malgré Lui." In *Two Roads to Wisdom? Chinese and Analytic Philosophical Traditions*, ed. Bo Mou. Open Court, 2001.

Cherniak, Christopher. *Minimal Rationality*. MIT Press, 1986.

Clark, Kelly James, and Liu Zongkun. "The Polished Mirror: Reflections on Natural Knowledge of the Way in Zhuangzi and Alvin Plantinga." In *Chinese Philosophy in an Era of Globalization*, ed. Robin Wang. State University of New York Press, 2004.

Crumley, Jack S. *An Introduction to Epistemology*, second edition. Broadview, 2009.

De Caro, Mario, and David Macarthur, eds. *Naturalism and Normativity*. Harvard University Press, 2010.

Goldman, Alvin. I. *Epistemology and Cognition*. Harvard University Press, 1986.

Graham, A. C. *Disputers of the Tao: Philosophical Argument in Ancient China*. Open Court, 1989.

Harman, Gilbert. "Seminar Notes on Quine." Talk delivered at NEH 2011 Summer Seminar "20th Century American Philosophy: Quine and Davidson," Princeton University.

Kim, Jaegwon. "What Is 'Naturalized Epistemology?'" *Philosophical Perspectives* 2 (1988): 381–405.

Kjellberg, Paul. "Sextus Empiricus, Zhuangzi, and Xunzi on 'Why Be Skeptical?'" In *Essays on Skepticism, Relativism, and Ethics in the Zhuangzi*, ed. Paul Kjellberg and Philip J. Ivanhoe. State University of New York Press, 1996.

Kjellberg, Paul, and Philip J. Ivanhoe, eds. *Essays on Skepticism, Relativism, and Ethics in the Zhuangzi*. State University of New York Press, 1996.

Kornblith, Hilary. *Knowledge and Its Place in Nature*. Clarendon, 2002.

Kvanvig, Jonathan L. *The Value of Knowledge and the Pursuit of Understanding*. Cambridge University Press, 2003.

Lepore, Ernie. "Seminar Notes on Quine." Talk delivered at NEH 2011 Summer Seminar "20th Century American Philosophy: Quine and Davidson," Princeton University.

McDowell, John. *Mind and World*. Harvard University Press, 1994.

Mou, Bo. "An Analysis of the Structure of Philosophical Methodology in View of Comparative Philosophy." In *Two Roads to Wisdom? Chinese and Analytic Philosophical Traditions*, ed. Bo Mou. Open Court, 2001.

Mou, Bo. *Chinese Philosophy A–Z*, revised edition. Edinburgh University Press, 2010.

Mou, Bo. "Constructive Engagement of Analytic and Continental Approaches Beyond the Western Tradition." In *Constructive Engagement of Analytic and Continental Approaches in Philosophy from the Vantage Point of Comparative Philosophy*, ed. Bo Mou and Richard Tieszen. Brill, 2013.

Mou, Bo, ed. *Davidson's Philosophy and Chinese Philosophy: Constructive Engagement*. Brill, 2006.

Mou, Bo. "A Double-Reference Account: Gongsun Long's 'White-Horse-Not-Horse' Thesis." *Journal of Chinese Philosophy* 34, no. 4 (2007): 493–513.

Mou, Bo. "Eternal *Dao*, Constant Name, and Language Engagement: On the Opening Message of the *Dao-De-Jing*." In *Comparative Approaches to Chinese Philosophy*, ed. Bo Mou. Ashgate, 2003.

Mou, Bo. "On Constructive-Engagement Strategy of Comparative Philosophy: A Journal Theme Introduction." *Comparative Philosophy* 1, no. 1 (2010): 1–32.

Mou, Bo, ed. *Searle's Philosophy and Chinese Philosophy: Constructive Engagement*. Brill, 2008.

Mou, Bo. "Searle, Zhuangzi, and Transcendental Perspectivism." In *Searle's Philosophy and Chinese Philosophy: Constructive Engagement*, ed. Mou Bo. Brill, 2008.

Mou, Bo. *Substantive Perspectivism: An Essay on Philosophical Concern with Truth*. Springer, 2009.

Mou, Bo. "Tarski, Quine, and 'Disquotation' Schema (T)." *Southern Journal of Philosophy* 38, no. 1 (2000): 119–144.

Mou, Bo. "Truth Pursuit and *Dao* Pursuit: From Davidson's Approach to Classical Daoist Approach in View of the Thesis of Truth as Strategic Normative Goal." In *Davidson's Philosophy and Chinese Philosophy: Constructive Engagement*, ed. Bo Mou. Brill, 2006.

Mou, Bo, and Richard Tieszen, eds. *Constructive Engagement of Analytic and Continental Approaches in Philosophy from the Vantage Point of Comparative Philosophy*. Brill, 2013.

Neta, Ram. "Quine, Goldman, and Two Ways of Naturalizing Epistemology." In *Epistemology: The Key Thinkers*, ed. Stephen Hetherington. Continuum, 2012.

Quine, W. V. "Epistemology Naturalized." In *Ontological Relativity and Other Essays*. Columbia University Press, 1969.

Quine, W. V. "Intensions Revisited." *Midwest Studies in Philosophy* 2, no. 1 (1977): 5–11.

Quine, W. V. "Naturalism; or, Living within One's Means." *Dialectica* 49, no. 2–4 (1995): 251–263.

Quine, W. V. *Philosophy of Logic*. Prentice-Hall, 1970.

Quine, W. V. *Theories and Things*. Harvard University Press, 1981.

Quine, W. V. *The Ways of Paradox: And Other Essays*. Random House, 1966.

Raphals, Lisa. "Skeptical Strategies in the *Zhuangzi* and *Theaetetus*." In *Essays on Skepticism, Relativism and Ethics in the Zhuangzi*, ed. Paul Kjellberg and Philip J. Ivanhoe. State University of New York Press, 1996.

Sosa, Ernest. *Knowing Full Well*. Princeton University Press, 2011.

Sosa, Ernest. *Knowledge in Perspective: Selected Essays in Epistemology*. Cambridge University Press, 1991.

Sosa, Ernest. "Reliabilism and Intellectual Virtue." In *Knowledge in Perspective: Collected Essays in Epistemology*. Cambridge University Press, 1991.

Tarski, Alfred. "The Concept of Truth in Formalized Languages." In *Logic, Semantics, Metamathematics: Papers from 1923 to 1938*, second edition, tr. J. H. Woodger. Hackett, 1983.

Tarski, Alfred. "The Semantic Conception of Truth and the Foundations of Semantics." In *The Philosophy of Language*, sixth edition, ed. A. P. Martinich and David Sosa. Oxford University Press, 2013.

Tieszen, Richard. "Analytic and Continental Philosophy, Science, and Global Philosophy." *Comparative Philosophy*, 2, no. 2 (2011). http://www.comparativephilosophy.org/index.php/ComparativePhilosophy/article/view/100/94.

Weinberg, Jonathan M., Shaun Nichols, and Stephen Stitch. "Normativity and Epistemic Intuitions." *Philosophical Topics* 29, no. 1–2 (2001): 429–460.

Williams, Bernard. *Truth and Truthfulness: An Essay in Genealogy*. Princeton University Press, 2002.

Williamson, Timothy. "What Is Naturalism?" *New York Times*, September 4, 2011.

13   Action without Agency and Natural Human Action: Resolving a Double Paradox

Brian Bruya

Harry Frankfurt introduced an understanding of action defined in part by a notion of guidance:

An explication of the nature of action must deal with two distinct problems. One is to explain the notion of guided behavior. The other is to specify when the guidance of behavior is attributable to an agent and not simply, as when a person's pupils dilate because the light fades, to some local process going on within the agent's body. The first problem concerns the conditions under which behavior is purposive, while the second concerns the conditions under which purposive behavior is intentional.[1]

In considering this problem, David Velleman adverts to the idea of effortless action in Zhuangzi (fourth century BCE) along with Mihaly Csikszentmihalyi's psychological construct of flow to conclude that

Actors in flow have … achieved a higher wantonness [Frankfurt's term]. They act wantonly in the sense that they have dispensed with self-regulation. But they have dispensed with self-regulation only because it has been so effective as to render itself unnecessary. And their capacity for self-regulation remains in reserve in case it is needed. Hence, their wantonness is also a consummate example of agency.[2]

In the end, Velleman says that there is no contradiction in the fact that a person can simultaneously be a wanton (characterized by a "mindless indifference to the enterprise of evaluating his own desires and motives"[3]) and a human agent in the normal philosophical sense of the term. And yet, surely, there is. Velleman himself says:

Lacking a human essence, in the *Zhuangzi*'s sense, must entail lacking that "concern with our own motives" that makes us "care about what we are."[4] It therefore entails lacking what Frankfurt identifies as the source of human agency.[5]

According to Velleman, the resolution of this paradox of agency without agency lies in Frankfurt's notion of guidance—wantonness is not entirely wanton because it is still under the guidance of the agent. But there is still no explanation of how an agent can be present as guide while also being absent as agent. Without a more robust explanation, *agency without agency* as part of a solution to the basic question "What is action?" comes frightfully close to question begging.

Velleman notes a deeper problem in passing:

When a human being "finds flow" in the exercise of a skill, does he instantiate agency, as Frankfurt conceives it, or does he instantiate wantonness instead? Or is this case, rather, a challenge to the categories of agent and wanton altogether?[6]

This question seems to be more to the point. Perhaps we (Frankfurt, Velleman, and most holders of theories of action that fit the traditional framing of the issue) have a conception of agency that does not fit all the facts of human action.[7] As Velleman notices, Csikszentmihalyi's concept of flow presents a good opportunity to reassess what notions of agency and action really amount to. As a way of exploiting this opportunity, I will shift focus slightly. Discussions of human agency inevitably begin with the human side of the problem, asking: what is human action and what is its relationship to other motion in nature? This question, while not necessarily presupposing that human action is of a different order from natural motion, begins with a distance between the two. In what follows, I will begin, instead, from a key concept of motion in nature and try to understand how that can function as a model for human action. The project will presuppose that humans are fundamentally of a piece with nature and so aim to place human action in a framework of natural motion, and from there explain what sets some kinds of motion apart, as distinct, as action rather than motion *simpliciter*.

1 The Problem

There are two sources of the paradox of natural human action, but the basic idea is this: human action must be natural insofar as human beings are part of the natural order, and yet, a persistent philosophical distinction between the human realm and the natural realm rules out *natural human action* in principle by mutually exclusive definitions of "the natural" and "the human."

1.1 Version 1: Aesthetic Appreciation

An enduring question in aesthetics is how to account for the different experiences one has when appreciating an aesthetic object with natural origins vs. an aesthetic object made by the hands of a human artisan or artist.

It is often pointed out that when appreciating an artifact such as that shown in figure 13.1, we consider such things as the usage of particular materials for particular ends in creating the artifact; techniques employed by the artist to create specific effects; how the work of art fits into the history of art, into the contemporary intellectual milieu, and into the own artist's body of work; and what the intentions of the

Figure 13.1
Leonardo da Vinci, *Mona Lisa*.

Figure 13.2

artist may have been in creating the work. By contrast, none of these questions is available in appreciating the scenery in figure 13.2 (*in situ*, not as a photograph). Observing a vista in nature, it is not part of one's experience of appreciation to inquire into techniques, materials, lineages, or intentions. The distinction comes clearer if one attempts to appreciate the two rocks in figures 13.3 and 13.4.

We can begin by appreciating their luster and try the feel of the texture, but to go further, we must wonder at their genesis, at whether they were carved and worked by human hands or whether they were fashioned from the forces of nature. The answer would put each in a very different light with respect to its alternative. For instance, one feels a certain astonishment to realize that the rock in figure 13.4 could come to be entirely by the forces of nature. And upon learning that figure 13.3 is a Brancusi (*Sculpture for the Blind*), a naive feeling of wonder gives way to an intellectual curiosity about such things as how this piece fits into Brancusi's larger oeuvre and what meaning he could have been trying to convey.

The upshot of the distinction between appreciating objects as natural vs. appreciating them as artificial is that a mutually exclusive dichotomy forms, separating the human from the natural. The exact contours of this dichotomy come clear when we look at how current philosophers of aesthetics handle it:

The aesthetic appreciation of nature … is identical with the aesthetic appreciation not of that which is nature, but of nature *as nature and not as art (or artifact)*.[8]

Figure 13.3
Copyright 2014 Artists Rights Society (ARS), New York/ADAGP, Paris.

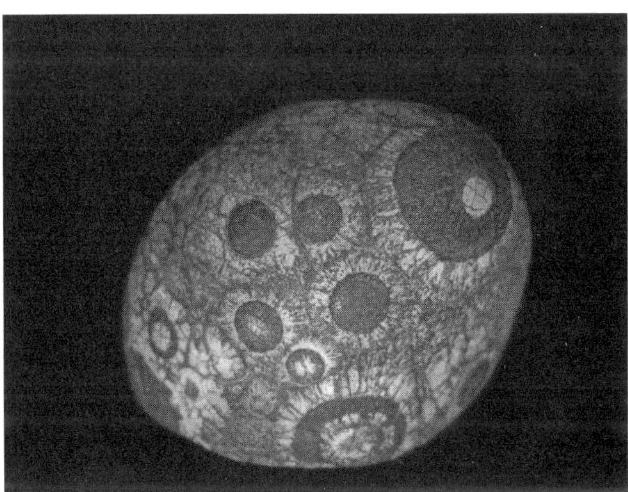

Figure 13.4
Copyright 2014 Nebula Stone.

Natural objects ... lack a human maker.[9]

Aesthetic experience of nature always demands our realizing that nature itself is a nonartistic object, not designed by any artist for our admiration, not framed or put on a pedestal—all this is much of the secret of nature's aesthetic power, construct though we may the aesthetic categories through which such nature is experienced.[10]

In analyzing the issue of aesthetic appreciation with respect to nature vs. art, philosophers have defined the human and the natural in contrast to each other. As a result, the unity of the human and the natural in this domain becomes a theoretical impossibility. To speak of *natural human action* as an object of aesthetic appreciation (as in dance) would be a contradiction in terms.

1.2 Version 2: Philosophy of Action

In the philosophy of action, something similar happens. From the time of Aristotle, it has been of paramount importance in ethics to be able to ascribe responsibility to others for their actions. Book III of the *Nicomachean Ethics* begins as follows:

Since virtue is to do with feelings and actions, and since voluntary feelings and actions are praised and blamed, while the involuntary ones are pardoned and occasionally even pitied, presumably anyone considering virtue must determine the limits of the voluntary and the involuntary.[11]

As Aristotle says, responsibility ascription depends on determining whether an action is voluntary or involuntary. Aristotle defines the involuntary as "things that happen by force or through ignorance" and says "what is forced is what has an external first principle, such that the agent or the person acted upon contributes nothing to it."[12] Of the person who acts voluntarily, he says "the first principle of moving the limbs that serve as instruments lies in him."[13] There is more to be said of what exactly counts as human action for Aristotle, which I discuss elsewhere,[14] but the difference comes down to drawing a bright line around the rational adult human. Sarah Broadie offers this comment on the passage quoted just above:

"In him" may mean, "in him as a rational or potentially rational individual." Cf. 3, 1112a32–3, where man and nature (which includes human biological nature) are contrasted as distinct types of cause.[15]

I take this interpretation to be correct. While natural movement in Aristotle is marked by necessity and chance, human action, for which one may be held responsible, is marked by rational deliberate choice.[16]

With this distinction, it is not an exaggeration to say that Aristotle determines the framework for much of the entire Western tradition of philosophy of action. For both the human and the natural, atomism prevails—the human as a discrete essence initiating action, and natural objects as discrete entities banging into each other.[17]

In later philosophers, the concept of the human essence becomes further refined with reference to the will and terminates as a vanishing point of agency outside of the natural laws that determine the movement of everything else.[18] And so, human action is conceived as that which is not natural, and natural movement is everything but human action. Again, *natural human action* becomes a theoretical impossibility.

The paradox with which aesthetic appreciation and the philosophy of action leave us cannot be easily resolved without either eliminating the very useful human/nature distinction or ruling out "natural" as a possible descriptor of human action. This chapter takes a third route, which is to reconsider human action from a core feature of natural motion, namely, *self-organization*. This concept, often employed in the sciences but absent in discussions of human action, allows for a new distinction in the concept of the human self that will do the work of the old human/nature distinction while still allowing for human action that can be categorized as natural. A second, related, concept will be introduced, as well—the *plural self*. In Frankfurt and Velleman's notion of action and guidance, the agent is allowed different levels ("orders") of reflection, but, following Aristotle, the agent, itself, is understood as irreducibly singular, or monadic.[19] A self conceived as plurally self-organized, in contrast, allows for both unity and disassociation.[20]

To draw these distinct lines of exploration more clearly together, in what follows I take the two paradoxes above—the paradox of agency without agency announced by Velleman and the paradox of the impossibility of natural human action explained in this section—to be essentially the same problem. In fact, just seeing them as the same problem points to a plausible resolution of both paradoxes: for a human being to act naturally involves surrendering a sense of agency—it is *action without agency*. But how to build a theory that makes sense of such a thing without relying on paradoxical locutions? That is the purpose of what follows.

2 Self-Organization and Natural Action

The enduring problem in philosophy of action has been reconciling the subjective feeling of freedom with the objective nomology of natural regularity. Natural nomology is commonly understood as significantly deterministic, taking a more or less clockwork view of the universe as a model for natural motion, and human subjectivity is commonly the starting point for explorations of the difference between what humans do in acting and the motion that happens in the rest of the universe. Classical efficient causality predominates as a fundamental presupposition for explanations of natural motion. The problems and paradoxes that result from this approach require no rehearsal here, as they still populate the pages of journals and monographs. This chapter takes a different approach. Rather than beginning with human subjectivity, we shall begin with an exploration of a fundamental kind of natural motion known as *self-organization.*

Self-organization is a well-entrenched working concept in the sciences.[21] The earliest reference that I can find goes back to 1906 in a French article on the nature of chemical reactions.[22] The concept gained some theoretical traction in the 1950s, the 1960s, and the 1970s, largely in the fields of biology, chemistry, and cybernetics. Major works include John von Neumann's *Theory of Self-Reproducing Automata,* Manfred Eigen's "Self-Organization of Matter and the Evolution of Biological Macromolecules," and Ilya Prigogine's *Self-Organization in Non-Equilibrium Systems.* From the many discussions of self-organization in the literature, one can extract a minimal working definition that is appropriate for the issue under discussion: self-organization refers to *any event in which multiple entities interact to create order among themselves without external direction.* A contradistinction is often made with the second law of thermodynamics, in which isolated systems are described as necessarily tending toward disorder. Examples of self-organization are found all around us and include galaxies, clouds, cells, crystals, leaves, animal populations, wind, and so on. Wherever there is an appearance of order in nature, we generally have an instance of self-organization. Examples of exclusions would be such things as the dung ball of a dung beetle and the striations on driftwood, which are created by significant input from external forces.[23]

From this distinction among good and bad examples of self-organization, it becomes evident that "self" in the term "self-organization" plays a dual role. It refers not only to the newly formed entity composed of the original multiple entities (the boundaries of a self-organized system are the boundaries of a self), but it also refers to the process in which the event occurs absent an external directing force (to *self*-organize is to organize *of one's own accord,* without significant external direction).[24] In the former role, it is nominal; and in the latter role, it is adverbial, describing a process or an activity. There are similar instances of an adverbial "self" in English—for example, in the terms "self-govern," "self-propel," "self-generate," "self-fertilize," "self-sustain," and "self-replicate." Each of these terms denotes a process or activity by which multiple entities cooperate as a single entity in the execution of that activity or process, without external direction. This grammatical distinction is important because of the contrast it provides with another adverbial usage of "self." In examples such as, "self-enrich," "self-doubt," or "self-immolate," we see something quite different. While "self" still functions in an adverbial role, we no longer see multiple entities cooperating and instead see a single entity directing action toward itself: the self as subject doubts the self as object; the self as subject enriches the self as object; the self as subject immolates the self as object. From these two senses of the adverbial "self," it becomes clear that two distinguishable phenomena in the world are being described. The first is what may be called a *plural self,* in which the elements that make up an entity act through mutual cooperation as a unified entity, without a sense of a single directing force, internally or externally. The second may be called a *monadic self*, in which there *is* a sense of a single, internal, directing force, which is a subject in a world of objects. The distinction can be made explicit as follows:

Plural self: structure is complex; motive impetus is internal, multiply sourced, and interactive
Monadic self: structure is simple; motive impetus is internal, singly sourced, and directive

It is probably evident by now that the monadic self is exemplified in phenomenal consciousness, where the questions of the philosophy of action generally begin—for example, "What am I doing *mentally* that makes *my* action different from what occurs in nature?" However, for present purposes we want to begin in nature, not in the human being. The plural self, then, is our potential source of action in nature.

In order to make the leap from self-organization in nature to self-organization in the human, we may extend the plural/monadic distinction from the natural to the human by positing a further instrumental distinction. From the notion of the plural self, we may posit the *c-self*—any self-organizing complex in the natural world. This will include all natural systems, including the human being. They are characterized by their persistence over time, and they can give rise to a phenomenal self. The phenomenal self (φ-*self* for short) is an exemplification of the monadic self described above. It is found in human beings and some other animals, is characterized by intermittence (e.g., it vanishes during sleep), and is rooted in a c-self.[25]

Having made the above distinctions, not only in terminology but also among phenomena instrumentally denoted by the terminology, we can return to one of the paradoxes that prompted this line of thought. The paradox was the theoretical impossibility of natural human action despite the fact that human beings are inescapably natural creatures. By beginning with motion in nature via the common phenomenon of self-organization, we have arrived at a taxonomic hierarchy. The c-self is the basis of all motion arising from self-organized systems. Out of the c-self, a phenomenal self may arise, which is the source of what is generally understood as human action. By virtue of this taxonomic hierarchy, the human being is situated within the realm of natural motion, and so without a strict dichotomy separating the human from the natural, we have an avenue for the possibility of human action that is also natural. But we cannot stop here and conclude that all human action is natural because that would eliminate the useful distinction between the natural and the artificial. Instead, we must define the natural and the artificial without reference to the human. To do so, we must reconcile the notion of action with the notion of the plural self.

The φ-self as defined above was an example of the monadic self, which was characterized as having a simple structure and a motive impetus that is internal, singly sourced, and directive. We see in this description a traditional (Aristotelian) characterization of human action—motion that arises from a single, directive, internal source. Going forward, we shall use this understanding to stipulate that action arising from the φ-self is *artifice*. In contrast, we shall stipulate *natural behavior* as any behavior arising from a self-organized system by dint of that self-organization. I must appeal to the reader's own intuitions as to whether these stipulations are allowable within the normal parameters of the terms "nature" and "artifice." I submit that they are. Now, notice that there is an important gap between artifice and nature—we have not aligned the human being, or human action, with either side. Though we may reflexively align the human and human action with artifice and the φ-self, I will demonstrate below that this does not have to be the case—we can also align the human and human action with nature and the c-self.

The first step in aligning human action with nature is to acknowledge the following. Because the φ-self is subject to intermittence (e.g., in sleep) and decrements (e.g., inebriation) and because the human being does not necessarily cease moving during these episodes, any overt behavior during such episodes cannot be entirely attributed to the φ-self and so must be attributed, at least partially, to the c-self. Therefore, if we can identify human c-self behavior that is demonstrably and uncontroversially characterizable as action, absent significant contribution from the φ-self, then we will have resolved the double paradox above. We will have found action without agency, and we will have identified *natural human action*.

3 Three Candidates for C-Self Natural Action

In virtually all lines of action theory in which a definition of action is sought to explain how human action is distinct from other kinds of motion, an intimate relationship is either stated or implied among action, volition (or something like it, e.g., intention, purpose, guidance, etc.), and the sense of the self as the seat of volition (or something like volition). We can understand this relationship as a three way mutual entailment with volition as the middle term. There is *action* (or potential action) just in case there is *volition*, and there is volition just in case there is a *phenomenal sense of self* as the seat of volition. Lacking a phenomenal sense of self, there is no seat of volition, no sense that there is an agent choosing to perform an action. Without a sense of volition, behavior is not distinguishable as action. Action depends on agency, and agency is reducible to volition (or something like it) plus a sense of a self. This formula holds even for theories that eschew overt mention of volition, such as Frankfurt's and Audi's[26] theories of guidance. Action under these theories presupposes a *sense of agency* as the guiding force, whether one invokes the term "volition" or not.

It is this relationship of mutual entailment in the dominant theories of action that sets the dividing line between action and other motion at the boundary of the human.

In what follows, we shall see that action can persist in the human sphere even after this entailment has been broken, giving us a way to free the concept of action from the exclusively human and paving the way for action that is both human and natural.

Under what conditions can human behavior persist absent a phenomenal sense of self? In what follows, I shall describe three candidates, progressively approaching a case that is demonstrably and uncontroversially a case of action but absent the φ-self, absent a sense of subjective agency. As c-self action, it will belong to the natural sphere, though performed by humans, and thus qualify as natural human action.

Before continuing, we must first be clear that even though the φ-self is commonly conceived in action theory as an indivisible monad, and even though it is felt in experience to be indivisibly monadic, it is actually divisible. It is a unity composed of numerous phenomenal components, such as thoughts, feelings, desires, goals, memories, self-consciousness, a sense of effort, hopes, skills, etc. In a normal phenomenal state one can reflect on the magnitude of each of these in what James and others have called the specious present. In a diminished phenomenal state, one or more are no longer accessible to such reflection. For instance, in amnesia, one's long-term memory is no longer accessible. One still has a unified sense of self as agency, but it is a diminished sense, and when that sense diminishes to the point that one's actions can no longer be attributed to it, we have crossed over into c-self behavior.

In the following three subsections, I offer examples in which the phenomenal self is compromised. In each, I make a case for how one could argue that it is a bona fide case of c-self behavior. As the examples progress, the behavior increasingly resembles action, until we find a genuine case not just of c-self behavior but of c-self action.

3.1 Sleepwalking

Sleepwalking is a classic case of human behavior with a diminished φ-self. Although physiologically asleep,[27] a sleepwalker can get up and carry out a wide range of purposeful activities, including talking, writing, cooking, driving, and sex.[28] In normal phenomenal experience, all such activities would qualify as actions, as they entail both volition at some level and a sense of self underlying the volition. In the case of sleepwalking (sleep-activity), when the φ-self has blinked away, the situation is no longer so clear cut.

EEG activity during sleepwalking shows a "dissociation between mental and motor arousal."[29] A brain scan study during sleepwalking showed that

The decreased regional cerebral blood flow in the frontoparietal cortices found during sleepwalking is consistent with the view of sleepwalking as a dissociated state consisting of motor arousal and persisting mind sleep. This deactivation of prefrontal cortices during normal sleep and sleepwalking also explains the lack of self-related awareness, insight, and recall that characterise both conditions.[30]

In sleepwalking, clearly the movement is happening at the level of the c-self. Clearly, there is neither volition nor a sense of a phenomenal self guiding the behavior, and without them, no sign of genuine action, which is not surprising because behavior performed while asleep is generally at a quite low level of competence. Indeed, sleepwalking is as close as humans get to what philosophers of mind call zombie-like behavior. So, although we cannot take sleepwalking as a case of natural human action, we can identify it as a case in which the c-self is guiding behavior that has a semblance of normalcy while the φ-self has been diminished to the point of irrelevance. What if it were possible for the c-self to guide behavior while the φ-self had been diminished to the point of irrelevance *and* it looked for all intents and purposes like action? Let us consider two further cases.

3.2 Hypnosis

In hypnosis, we have another example of behavior under a diminished φ-self. Rather than canvassing the many manifestations of this phenomenon, I will focus on one particular study that highlights its relevance. Amir Raz and Natasha Campbell hypnotized subjects and ran them through the Stroop task.[31] Under normal circumstances, when one performs the Stroop task, one's ability to read will interact with one's ability to identify color such that when one is asked to identify the color of a word that is printed in color, one's reaction time slows if the color differs from the meaning of the word (interference effect) and increases if the two are the same (facilitation effect). Raz and Campbell hypnotized subjects and implanted a post-hypnotic suggestion that temporarily stripped them of their ability to read. Performing the Stroop task under hypnotic suggestion, some subjects accomplished something never before accomplished—they were able to perform the identification task absent an interference effect—there was no lag in their reaction times when the meaning of a word and the color of the word conflicted.

In the theoretical terminology introduced above, subjects in Raz and Campbell's study performed a task with a diminished φ-self—they had lost the skill of reading, a core phenomenal trait of contemporary adult humans—and yet performed better than when in a normal phenomenal state. In this case, one cannot say that what occurred was not action, especially when the performance was improved over normal performance.[32] While it may appear that the action occurred entirely under the influence of the φ-self rather than the c-self, a close reading of the study shows that while the interference effect was stifled, the facilitation effect was not.[33] And so the skill of reading must have still been functioning at the sub-phenomenal level, at the level of the c-self.[34] Here is a case in which one could claim to have not had the experience of reading, and yet the experimental results demonstrate that reading was in fact taking place in cooperation with the goal to perform well on the task. As such, we can see that a subject was performing the *action* of reading absent phenomenal awareness or a sense of volition (or the like). Thus, we have our first clear case of action without agency, of action that qualifies as both human (performed by a human being) and natural (the result of a self-organized system's goal-directed behavior).

One may object and claim just as adamantly that this is *not* action, exactly because the three-part biconditional relationship was broken—if the person's phenomenal experience was one of non-reading, with no prior intention of reading, then we cannot attribute the reading to her. But isn't it the case that in any complex action, there are many things we are doing that are beneath awareness? Here, as she performed the Stroop task, she read to improve performance—just as a person walking bobs beneath awareness in order to conserve momentum and increase efficiency.[35] In this controversy, we have moved from the ontology of action generally to a mereological problem—which parts of action count as action per se? Rather than try to resolve it, let us move on to a more definitive example.

3.3 Autotelic Experience

It is easy to dismiss cases of sleepwalking and hypnosis as so far removed from normal life that although they may be interesting boundary cases, they do not have a bearing on the central features of action theory. What we need is a case that is at once in the realm of normal human behavior and meets the conditions for c-self action explained above. Aside from hypnosis and sleepwalking, there are many varieties of diminished φ states: inebriation, dizziness, dreaming, adrenaline rushes, daydreaming, schizophrenia, etc. But all of these are, again, far enough removed from normal phenomenal experience that any behavior resulting from them would not necessarily qualify as genuine action. There is one kind of experience, however, in which (1) there is a diminished φ-self which (2) is an important part of normal human experience and which (3) results in genuine action. It is the one that Velleman brings up in relation to the *Zhuangzi*, known through its technical term, *autotelicity*, and more broadly as *flow*.

The circumstances and features of autotelicity have been detailed in many different publications.[36] For the purposes here, we will concern ourselves with the following characteristics of autotelic experience:

- altered sense of time
- high level of concentration
- confidence and comfort in meeting each new high challenge
- absence of felt effort
- absence of self-consciousness

Autotelicity occurs when one's level of skill comports with an activity's level of challenge such that one's attention is fully engaged in the activity. This is the notion of high concentration. It is importantly distinct from highly habituated but "mindless" behavior in which one is capable of carrying out a skilled activity while one's mind is elsewhere—for instance, driving while not noticing the passage of landmarks.

Autotelicity is also marked by two significant negative[37] features that set it off as a diminishment of the φ-self, namely, an absence of felt effort and an absence of self-consciousness. In typical phenomenal experience, one has a clear sense of one's being participant in intersubjective activity with the understanding that one's thoughts and actions, as well as the thoughts and actions of others in response, have some normative valence for oneself. In other words, a core feature of the φ-self is self-consciousness.[38] In autotelic experience, this core feature of the φ-self vanishes. Also gone in autotelicity is a sense of effort—a sense that one is expending energy, that one is *trying*. Movements flow without a sense that one is actively executing them.

Although the language used to describe autotelicity can sometimes come off as mystical, the experience itself is shown to be quite common across populations and across a wide variety of activities. There is no question but that it is a part of normal human experience. In fact, the achievements made in autotelic experience, like the hypnosis example above, regularly exceed non-autotelic levels of achievement.[39] Because of its normalcy and because of its high level of achievement (in contrast to that of sleepwalking), we cannot easily dismiss autotelic experience as occurring outside the realm of human action.

It is helpful to look at actual descriptions of autotelic experience from normal subjects in order to get a clear sense of the phenomenal characteristics. The following quotations are from rock-climbers and are representative of autotelicity generally:

You don't feel like you're doing something as a conscious being; you're adapting to the rock and becoming part of it.[40]

You're so involved in what you're doing [that] you aren't thinking about yourself as separate from the immediate activity.[41]

Somehow the right thing is done without you ever thinking about it or doing anything at all … . It just happens. And yet you're more concentrated.[42]

The right decisions are made, but not rationally. Your mind is shut down and your body just goes.[43]

Taken together, these descriptions give us a kind of behavior that involves skill, that is conscious, and that is performed at a high level, and yet it lacks any sense of volition or effort, and even lacks a clear subjective sense of an individuated self.[44] In other words, the normal sense of a phenomenal self as the seat of action has blinked out. As a result, we must ascribe such behavior to the c-self. We have, then, found a third example of c-self behavior, and this example, unlike the examples of sleepwalking and hypnotism is difficult to gainsay as being something other than action. Surely, examples of rock-climbing, classical piano performance, basketball playing, jazz singing, stage acting, dancing, etc. that may occur as autotelic experience count as action. To be sure, the three-part biconditional relationship of action has been severed, placing the normally understood ontological status of such action in doubt, but would one deny ascription on this basis? If a tennis player wins a match experienced autotelically, would we want to deny her the winning trophy?

Autotelicity provides us with a case in which (1) we can have action without agency and (2) under the definitions used above we can identify a kind of human action that can also be called natural.

Conclusion

Discussions of action and agency often entail an appeal to ethics—we need to be able to attribute action to an individual in order to ascribe responsibility. As I pointed out in section 1, this was a central part of Aristotle's project. Contemporary philosophers make a similar move—using potential for responsibility ascription as a gauge of genuine action.[45] In fact, it is often difficult to separate the ethical desideratum from the ontological. Would we be satisfied if a general account of action did not entail some sense of responsibility or if a general account of responsibility had nothing to say about agency? Not likely.

Because the notion of action is part of a language game that includes an important place for related ethical concepts such as responsibility, it makes sense that they be defined and understood in terms of each other. I started out this chapter with an appeal to aesthetic appreciation as a basis for understanding the human/nature distinction. Bringing aesthetics into the ontological question of action and agency was not a category mistake. Just as the linguistic categories of action and agency are connected in a socially constructed semantic web with those of credit and blame, so they are also connected with categories of aesthetic worth—though this connection has rarely been explored in the philosophical literature.[46] When we see human behavior performed at an extremely high level, such as in artistic performance, say in dance or jazz trumpet playing, it is part of our language use that even if the trumpeter after a virtuoso performance disclaims credit, saying something like "the trumpet was playing itself," we will still proclaim the greatness of the performance and of the trumpeter who performed it.

In the case of autotelic experience, the entailment among action, volition, and the φ-self breaks down. In the face of a severely diminished φ-self, we must attribute an instance of behavior to the c-self, to the level of a naturally functioning self-organized system. Under the dominant onto-ethical theories of action, the activities of a self-organized system, a c-self, do not rise to the level of action. Autotelic experience acts as a counterexample to these dominant theories, giving us human action that cannot be attributed to a φ-self and so must belong to a c-self, to the level of a naturally functioning self-organized system. And so, as the behavior is human and qualifies as action, and as it stands on the side of nature in contradistinction to the phenomenal, it is a clear example of natural human action.

From the evidence above, we must draw two conclusions: that the dominant ways of distinguishing the natural and the human as two distinct and mutually exclusive categories in theories of action and aesthetics is mistaken, and that the line separating the natural from the artificial lies not at the boundary of the human but rather at the boundary of the phenomenal self.

We can now return to Velleman's question that precipitated this inquiry:

When a human being "finds flow" in the exercise of a skill, does he instantiate agency, as Frankfurt conceives it, or does he instantiate wantonness instead? Or is this case, rather, a challenge to the categories of agent and wanton altogether?

And we can return to the conclusion that ends his article:

Actors in flow have thus achieved a higher wantonness. They act wantonly in the sense that they have dispensed with self-regulation. But they have dispensed with self-regulation only because it has been so effective as to render itself unnecessary. And their capacity for self-regulation remains in reserve in case it is needed. Hence, their wantonness is also a consummate example of agency.

In Velleman's attempt to preserve Frankfurt's paradigm of action under guidance, he suggests that action involves an agent guiding movements even if only passively. It is the conscious guidance that allows for both agency and action. We see, however, that in autotelicity, or flow, guidance is not tantamount to agency and occurs at the level of the c-self, not at the level of the agent in any normal sense of phenomenal agency. There is agency only if you believe that action necessarily entails it. What Velleman misses is that in autotelicity there is no immediate sense of the phenomenal self, and so, although there is action, there is no agent as such. In this way, Velleman is correct that flow (along with Zhuangzi's ideas informing his discussion) is indeed a challenge to the prevailing categories of action and agency.

In closing, let us entertain possible objections.

The Artistic Elephant Objection To suggest that we cannot draw a bright line around the human being in defining the natural and the artificial implies that there are other creatures that can act with artifice, which sounds absurd.

Yes, intuitively, this sounds absurd. But recall for a moment the recent push to bestow personhood on non-human animals. Peter Singer, at the forefront of the movement, employs criteria such as autonomy, rationality, and, interestingly, self-consciousness in distinguishing personhood.[47] I suggested above that self-consciousness is the hallmark of the phenomenal self, which is the driving force behind artifice. If these avant-garde ethicists are correct, then we can ascribe artifice to animals. You may be envisioning the ridiculous image of a daubing elephant wearing a French beret as an exemplar of animal artifice, but there are other examples of animals executing creations in their environments that bear the hallmarks of artifice, perhaps even of creativity. The first example that comes to mind is the bowerbird of Indonesia and Australia, some species of which build not only large complex bowers to attract mates but even surrounding gardens.[48] Certain species of cichlid fish do something similar in the sand.[49]

The philosopher Xunzi (third century BCE), who has long discussions on nature and artifice, posited that cultural forms constitute artifice, and although he precluded animals at the time as creators of artifice, there is now abundant evidence of non-human animal culture.

Thus, the objection stands; this theory does imply artifice in animals, but it turns out to not lead to a reductio.[50]

The Autopilot Objection Autotelicity is simply an example of what is commonly called being on autopilot—automatic, highly habituated activity that unfolds of its own accord. There is nothing creative or special about it, and it doesn't deserve to be placed on a pedestal, even if it results in high achievement.

There are two things going on in this objection: an objective claim and a subjective claim. The objective claim is that autotelicity and automaticity are the same. This claim is false. Autotelicity involves automaticity, but it also involves a high level of concentration in an activity that is absent in pure automaticity. As I pointed in the example of driving in subsection 3.3, when one is "on autopilot" one's attention is somewhere else other than on the activity at hand. In autotelicity, one is completely absorbed in the details of the activity while paradoxically being unselfconscious of the overt control of one's actions.

And yet this objection cannot be dismissed quite so easily. Joshua Ackerman and John Bargh claim that the essential components of autotelic experience lie within the boundaries of automaticity as they define it and that attention to one's actions in flow is essentially that of a spectator, with no conscious control over one's actions.[51] If this is true—that the behavior of basic knitting that can be done while one's attention is directed elsewhere is no different from knitting a complex design that requires full attention but which is experienced effortlessly—then all instances of autotelicity would, indeed, be cases of working "on autopilot." This claim has certain advantages (e.g., theoretical parsimony), and Ackerman and Bargh offer plausible evidence. However, if the agent's attention is a spectator's in the same way that another person's is, then when either of them turn their attention away, the same thing should happen. And yet it is obvious that the two cases would have very different results. If a spectator stops paying attention to a knitter who is the midst of a complex knitting task that requires high concentration, the knitting would continue. But if the knitter turned her attention away, the task would falter and the knitting end. The same goes for all instances of autotelicity. Attention in autotelicity is constitutive of the experience, not superfluous.

The second part of this objection, the subjective claim, is that high achievement under autotelicity merits no special consideration. This is partially true in that action that occurs autotelically is not necessarily exceptional in relation to similar such actions. A poor golfer can have a great game that is experienced autotelically, perhaps achieving a personal best, and yet still come in behind an average score of an average golfer. But isn't there something normatively distinct about the first golfer's experience——a cause for celebration? In fact, Csikszentmihalyi's research shows flow experiences to be the highlights of people's lives generally.[52]

The Inebriation Objection If behavior in autotelic experience counts as natural action, then so does behavior under the influence of alcohol, where the c-self is guiding movement under a diminished φ-self—this seems counterintuitive.

Zhuangzi tells the story of a drunk carriage passenger who falls off a fast-moving conveyance and because of his inebriated state suffers no injury.[53] The message of the story is that if inebriation can protect oneself, then imagine what being in accord with nature can do. The parallel between inebriation and autotelicity is apt exactly because of the diminishment of the φ-self. My view is that to the extent that inebriation inhibits self-consciousness without impairing motor activity or attention, it can, indeed, deserve an ascription of naturalness. One problem is the meaning of "natural," itself, and the question of what kind of normative valence it carries. This will be considered further in the next objection.

The Natural Murderer Objection One can imagine a serial killer who, in the process of torturing, killing, and disposing of a victim, performs all tasks in rapt autotelicity. Does your theory allow for natural murder?

The theory of autotelicity certainly allows for autotelic murder. Although autotelic experience, as was noted above, is often understood as adding value to life, outside of individual phenomenal experience it is ethically neutral. It can be put to good ends and ill. But what of the term "natural?" I have to admit that I want this theory to allow for a great jazz piano performance, experienced autotelically, to be better *because* it is more natural. I have not come forward and made that claim, however, nor am I currently prepared to do so. I will concede, however, that a "natural" murderer is probably a "better" murderer, by whatever reasonable standards of murdering one might want to put forward—efficient, resists detection, etc.

For many decades now, philosophy teachers have cautioned students away from the naturalistic fallacy, which is often taken to be a warning that whatever is natural is not necessarily good by dint of being natural. I think that warning applies here, as well, at least in terms of ethics. Aesthetically, however, I think the case is still open.

However macabre it might be, it is worth considering whether a natural murderer, under the definition of "natural" given above, is more aesthetically accomplished than a less natural one. Aesthetic appreciation is traditionally understood as necessarily providing pleasure, but there is a circle of philosophers who have recently been exploring the aesthetics of disgust, and their considerations may be relevant to this question.[54] I leave the question open.

The Determinist Objection Strict determinism is the law of the universe, and all forms of self-organization fall within it, despite specious claims of the violation of the second law of thermodynamics to the contrary. Hence, there is no point in making a fine distinction by saying that human behavior is a form of self-organization. It is still determined, and so the compatibilist's goal that you set out at the beginning has not been met.

This chapter does not present an argument for compatibilism. The reference to compatibilism was a reference to the standard way of doing philosophy of action. This chapter is intended to offer a different approach.

It is worth noting in this context that the Chinese tradition is absent an overt concept of metaphysical freedom. I think the basic reason for this absence is the concomitant absence of any claim to strict determinism or fatalism. Human behavior in the Chinese tradition has always been understood to fall under the same general patterns as nature's own regularity, and that has been sufficient for the Chinese.

I am not convinced that strict determinism really is the law of the universe, and when I have posed the question to physicists in casual conversation, I have received a polarized set of answers: "Of course it is" and "Of course it isn't." I won't advert to quantum indeterminism or books like the *Tao of Physics* or common notions of randomness and stochasticity. It is enough that the matter is not nearly so settled as some philosophers of action seem to take it to be. For this reason, I think that compatibilists have jumped the gun—reconciling free will with determinism before either of them have received sufficient empirical support.[55]

But suppose determinism is true and that self-organization is vulnerable to it. It isn't clear to me that my basic thesis would suffer under a deterministic regime, as I am not positing an overtly non-deterministic theory. The purpose in laying out the notion of self-organization was not to place it in contradistinction to determinism as such but to offer a narrower nomological scope. If determinism is the law of the universe and is natural and that natural law applies to humans, then all human behavior must be determined. That move does not address the issues raised above. One horn of the paradox of natural human action is that human action must be in some way natural. To note that it is also deterministic along with all of natural motion does not move the issue forward. The problem, as I am construing it, is how to distinguish natural human action from natural motion on one side and from artifice (non-natural action) on the other. Placing human behavior in the context of self-organization, because it helps explain natural motion while allowing for non-self-organized motion,[56] sets the stage for the possibility of just such a distinction. Absent the explanatory power of self-organization, it is difficult to build a theory of non-agentive behavior that allows for genuine action. Many theories of subconscious behavior, unconscious behavior, and automatic behavior inevitably devalue it and almost by definition remove it from consideration, not of contributing to genuine human action, but of standing on its own as genuine human action. By beginning with self-organization, one avoids this pitfall.

I have rehearsed the basic problem of action. Traditionally in the West, the problem is how to reconcile the internal feeling of freedom with the external appearance of determinism. But is that the only way to construe philosophical issues around human action? The Chinese have viewed natural action as an ideal mode of human conduct and so have built theories around optimization of action. This chapter has attempted to bring a Chinese view of action optimization that is ethical[57]/aesthetic on the surface but which has metaphysical undercurrents[58] into conversation with a Western view of reconciliation between action and motion that is metaphysical on the surface but which has powerful ethical undercurrents. As I show, the embedded axiological concerns of both views allow for a bridge to unify them in a theory of human action with minimal ontological commitments.

Acknowledgments

Thanks to the many listeners and commenters at venues where different iterations and aspects of this chapter have been presented: Grand Valley State University, the University of Michigan, Oakland University, the University of New Mexico, National Taiwan University, and Nanyang Technological University. Thanks especially to the coordinators of those talks. Thanks also to Artists Rights Society for permission to reproduce a photo of Brancusi's *Sculpture for the Blind* and to Ron and Karen Nurnberg for permission to use a photo of one of their Chocolate Galaxy specimens.

Notes

1. Harry G. Frankfurt, "The Problem of Action," 159.

2. J. David Velleman, "The Way of the Wanton," 188.

3. Velleman, ibid., 171.

4. Harry G. Frankfurt, *The Importance of What We Care About*, 163.

5. Velleman, *The Way of the Wanton*, 186.

6. Velleman, ibid., p.187.

7. In an empirically grounded and persuasive article, Michael Brownstein argues that prominent philosophers who have engaged the subject of flow (Railton, Annas, Velleman) plainly get the phenomenology wrong, incorrectly imputing a clear knowledge of "what" and "why" to subjects in flow. See Brownstein, "Rationalizing Flow."

8. Malcolm Budd, "The Aesthetic Appreciation of Nature," 208.

9. Emily Brady, "Imagination and the Aesthetic Appreciation of Nature," 139.

10. Holmes Rolston III, "Aesthetic Experience in Forests," 160. It is interesting to note that Kant uses very similar language to these three philosophers when defining "art": "A product of fine art must be recognized to be art and not nature" (*Critique of Judgment*, §45, 306.30). Nature can work through a genius and be visible in art, but art, for Kant, still bears a Platonic defect, as it is an imitation. Even Kant's description of a genius is reminiscent of Plato in the sense that Kant's genius is like someone possessed, who is at a loss to explain the artist's own work of art. So for Kant, it still seems that there cannot be a true union of the natural and the human.

11. Aristotle (tr. Roger Crisp), *Nicomachean Ethics*, 1109b, 37.

12. Ibid., 1110a, 37.

13. Ibid., 1110a, 37–38.

14. Brian Bruya, "The Rehabilitation of Spontaneity."

15. Aristotle (tr. Christopher Rowe and Sarah Broadie), *Nicomachean Ethics*, 312.

16. In "The Rehabilitation of Spontaneity," I consider a passage in Aristotle's *Physics* that offers a contradictory account and suggests a distinct but unexplored way of looking at the human/nature distinction.

17. This is not to say that this is Aristotle's theory in its entirety, just two representative elements that are relevant here.

18. Although Aristotle's human/nature distinction remains the dominant view of human agency throughout the Western tradition, other philosophers have occasionally attempted to unify the human and the natural. For an examination of some of these views, see Bruya, "The Rehabilitation of Spontaneity."

19. I use the word "monadic" to mean *single and indivisible*.

20. The idea of a multi-modal individual has, of course, been around for some time (from Plato's tripartite soul to current cognitive science), but the background notion of monadic agency with respect to the concept of action is remarkably resilient, and is evident in theories that appeal to levels of reflection, rather than to competing modes, to resolve such problems as akratic action. Here, I explore the big-picture theory of action from a multi-modal perspective, ignoring detailed neuroscientific models. For a perspective that discusses the kind of action discussed here but from a detailed scientific perspective, see Bruya, *Effortless Attention*.

21. There are thousands upon thousands of articles in the scientific literature that contain "self-organization" in the title or list it as a keyword. For instance, on May 17, 2013, Thomson Reuters' Web of Science database listed 14,618 such articles.

22. E. Solvay, "On the Organisation and the Possibility of Self-Organisation of the Chemical Reaction. The idea of self-organization, itself, goes back much further, of course. Kant has a treatment of it in the Third *Critique* that is consistent with the description here. He says of natural self-organization that, "the parts of the thing combine of themselves into the unity of a whole by being reciprocally cause and effect of their form" [§65, 373.10], in contrast to the making of a watch, in which "the producing cause of the watch and its form is not contained in the nature of this material but lies outside the watch" [§65, 374.15]. Even further back, the Stoics viewed the universe as a self-regulating organism, albeit one that had motion with law-like regularity—except for the human *hegemonikon*, which alone was capable of violating the laws of nature.

23. I don't mean to suggest that the concept of self-organization (and of order, for that matter) is without ambiguity. The purpose of this chapter is to explore and explain instrumentally useful concepts with regard to the human/nature distinction and the action/motion distinction, not to discover the truth of what action is, in fact, once and for all. For a perceptive discussion of self-organizing systems and order—one that disproves the very existence of self-organizing systems—see H. von Foerster, "On Self-Organizing Systems and Their Environments."

24. Energy and catalysts are not here construed as directing forces.

25. Thomas Metzinger makes a similar but much more nuanced distinction in *Being No One*. He describes three theoretical entities—a phenomenal self-model, a phenomenal model of intentionality relation, and a transparent global model of the world—that combine to give us a "minimal concept of *subjective* consciousness," or a sense of *self as subject* (411). He refers to the underlying system as characterized by self-organization, which, under the right conditions, manifests a self as subject: "if an organism operates under a phenomenally transparent self-model, then I possesses a *phenomenal self*' (563).

26. Robert Audi, *Action, Intention, and Reason.*

27. American Academy of Sleep Medicine, *The International Classification of Sleep Disorders, Revised*, 146–147.

28. For a complete description, see Claudio Bassetti, "Sleepwalking (Somnambulism)."

29. Claudio Bassetti, Silvano Vella, Filippo Donati, Peter Wielepp, and Bruno Weder, "SPECT during sleepwalking," 484, citing R. J. Broughton, "Sleep Disorders: Disorders of Arousal?"

30. Bassetti et al., 485.

31. Amir Raz and Natasha. K. Campbell, "Can Suggestion Obviate Reading?"

32. I refer here and elsewhere in the chapter to a judgment of the competence or aesthetic quality of movement in support of its being categorized as an action. This is an intuitive move. If one cannot fall back on the canonical criteria for determining action, and if one wishes to

allow a sufficiently broad scope to capture what intuitively counts as action, then one must rely on plausible criteria. I am suggesting that high competence is, if not a sufficient criterion, then at least a potential marker for action—an indication that what is occurring may be something more than bare involuntary movement.

33. Raz and Campbell report (ibid.) that the Stroop facilitation effect vanishes under suggestion for highly suggestive individuals (HSIs) (which is true by the technical definition, comparing it to the neutral trials), but there was still some facilitation. According to Raz and Campbell's results, the difference in reaction time (RT) between the congruent and incongruent trials for HSIs is statistically significant. Furthermore, in this and another study (Amir Raz, Jin Fan, and Michael I. Posner, "Hypnotic Suggestion Reduces Conflict in the Human Brain,"), the RT for HSIs in congruent trials dropped under suggestion, dramatically so in "Hypnotic Suggestion." These two sets of results indicate that there is still a significant amount of reading going on.

34. What is the difference between this kind of sub-phenomenal reading and something like balancing while riding a bicycle, which also occurs beneath awareness? The difference is one of access. While riding a bicycle, one can bring one's vestibular system at least partially into awareness—to the extent that one can sincerely acknowledge, "Yes, I am balancing," and be aware of some parts of the body—hips, arms—involved in the process. For Raz and Campbell's subjects, the entire process of reading was beyond the reach of awareness.

35. Massaad, Firas, Lejeune, and Detrembleur, "The Up and Down Bobbing of Human Walking: A Compromise Between Muscle Work and Efficiency."

36. See, for example, Mihaly Csikszentmihalyi, *Beyond Boredom and Anxiety* and Brian Bruya, ed., *Effortless Attention.*

37. "Negative" in the sense of being absent, not in a normative sense.

38. For a more precise definition of "self-consciousness," see Bruya, "What Is Self-Consciousness?"

39. In addition to Csikszentmihalyi's *"Beyond Boredom and Anxiety,"* see also *Flow* and *Finding Flow.*

40. Csikszentmihalyi, *Beyond Boredom and Anxiety*, 86.

41. Ibid.

42. Ibid., 87.

43. Ibid.

44. It is interesting to ask whether autotelicity would satisfy Metzinger's criteria for a subjectless self. "To my knowledge," he writes, "there is only one other phenomenal state class [other than Cotard's syndrome] in which speakers sometimes consistently refer to themselves without using the pronoun 'I,' namely, during prolonged mystical or spiritual experiences" (*Being No One*, 459). He calls this phenomenon, as mentioned in the Introduction to this volume, "system consciousness" (566). For a more detailed description, see p. 460 of *Being No One.*

45. See, for example, Harry Frankfurt, "Alternate Possibilities and Moral Responsibility." The basic sides of the argument for and against ascriptivism can be found in H. L. A. Hart, "The Ascription of Responsibility and Rights" and in George Pitcher, "Hart on Action and Responsibility." Andrew Sneddon explores the question in depth in *Actions and Responsibility*, concluding, as did Hart, that action is irreducibly social.

46. I consider some of these rare instances in "The Rehabilitation of Spontaneity."

47. Peter Singer, *Practical Ethics*. His understanding of self-consciousness appears to be one of simple self-awareness—a lower bar than in my understanding of self-consciousness.

48. See Jared Diamond, "Animal Art: Variation in Bower Decorating Style among Male Bower-birds *Amblyornis inornatus*"; Albert C. Uy, "Say It With Bowers."

49. Kenneth McKaye, Svata M. Louda, and Jay R. Stauffer, "Bower Size and Male Reproductive Success in a Cichlid Fish Lek"; Thomas D. Kocher, "Adaptive Evolution and Explosive Speciation."

50. The anthropologist Robert Aunger defines the term "artifice" in a way that makes room for non-human animals: "the enduring forms or structures created by animals through niche constructive behaviour primarily to be used in a way that increases their biological fitness" ("What's Special about Human Technology?" 117, n. 1).

51. Joshua M. Ackerman and John A. Bargh, "Two to Tango."

52. These studies are documented in *Flow* and *Finding Flow*.

53. *Zhuangzi*, chapter 19.

54. See, for example, Carolyn Korsmeyer, *Savoring Disgust*.

55. An informative but difficult book on the topic of the scientific status of determinism is *A Primer on Determinism* by John Earman. A more readable version of the theory, for the non-scientist, is Mark Wilson's review "Critical Notice: John Earman's *A Primer on Determinism*."

56. "Non-self-organized motion" refers to the normal way of understanding human agency, employing my terminology.

57. I have not discussed the ethical side. Confucius (551? BCE – 479? BCE) took effortless action to the be height of human ethical conduct. See Edward Slingerland, *Effortless Action*.

58. I have not discussed the metaphysical undercurrents. This is a reference to the Chinese *qi* 氣 cosmology. One explanation can be found in Philip J. Ivanhoe's chapter in this volume.

Works Cited

Ackerman, Joshua M., and John A. Bargh. "Two to Tango: Automatic Social Coordination and the Role of Effort." In *Effortless Attention: A New Perspective in the Cognitive Science of Attention and Action*, ed. Brian Bruya. MIT Press, 2010.

American Academy of Sleep Medicine. *The International Classification of Sleep Disorders, Revised: Diagnostic and Coding Manual.* American Academy of Sleep Medicine, 2001.

Aristotle. *Nicomachean Ethics*, tr. Roger Crisp. Cambridge University Press, 2000.

Aristotle. *Nicomachean Ethics*, tr. Christopher Rowe and Sarah Broadie. Oxford University Press, 2002.

Audi, Robert. *Action, Intention, and Reason.* Cornell University Press, 1993.

Aunger, Robert. "What's Special about Human Technology?" *Cambridge Journal of Economics* 34, no. 1 (2010): 115–123.

Bassetti, Claudio. "Sleepwalking (Somnabulism): Dissociation Between 'Body Sleep' and 'Mind Sleep.'" In *The Neurology of Consciousness: Cognitive Neuroscience and Neuropathology*, ed. Steven Laureys and Guilio Tononi. Elsevier, 2009.

Bassetti, Claudio, Silvano Vella, Filippo Donati, Peter Wielepp, and Bruno Weder. "SPECT During Sleepwalking." *Lancet* 356, no. 9228 (2000): 484–485.

Brady, Emily. "Imagination and the Aesthetic Appreciation of Nature." *Journal of Aesthetics and Art Criticism* 56, no. 2 (1998): 139–147.

Broughton, R. J. "Sleep Disorders: Disorders of Arousal?" *Science* 159 (1968): 1070–1078.

Brownstein, Michael. "Rationalizing Flow: Agency in Skilled Unreflective Action." *Philosophical Studies* 168, no. 2 (2014): 545–568.

Bruya, Brian, ed. *Effortless Attention: A New Perspective in the Cognitive Science of Attention and Action.* MIT Press, 2010.

Bruya, Brian. "The Rehabilitation of Spontaneity: A New Approach in Philosophy of Action." *Philosophy East and West* 60, no. 2 (2010): 207–250.

Bruya, Brian. "What Is Self-Consciousness?" In *Labirinti della mente: Visioni del mondo*, ed. Grazia Marchianò. Società bibliografica toscana, 2012.

Budd, Malcolm. "The Aesthetic Appreciation of Nature." *British Journal of Aesthetics* 36, no. 3 (1996): 207–222.

Csikszentmihalyi, Mihaly. *Beyond Boredom and Anxiety.* Jossey-Bass, 1975.

Csikszentmihalyi, Mihaly. *Finding Flow: The Psychology of Engagement with Everyday Life.* Basic Books, 1998.

Csikszentmihalyi, Mihaly. *Flow: The Psychology of Optimal Experience.* Harper Perennial, 2008.

Diamond, Jared. "Animal Art: Variation in Bower Decorating Style among Male Bowerbirds *Amblyornis inornatus*." *Proceedings of the National Academy of Sciences* 83 (1986): 3042–3046.

Earman, John. *A Primer on Determinism.* Springer, 1986.

Frankfurt, Harry G. "Alternate Possibilities and Moral Responsibility." *Journal of Philosophy* 66, no. 23 (1969): 829–839.

Frankfurt, Harry G. *The Importance of What We Care About: Philosophical Essays*. Cambridge University Press, 1988.

Frankfurt, Harry G. "The Problem of Action." *American Philosophical Quarterly* 15, no. 2 (1978): 157–162.

Hart, H. L. A. "The Ascription of Responsibility and Rights." *Proceedings of the Aristotelian Society* 49 (1948–49): 171–194.

Ivanhoe, Philip J. "Senses and Values of Oneness." In *The Philosophical Challenge from China*, ed. Brian Bruya. MIT Press, 2015.

Kant, Immanuel. *The Critique of Judgment*. Tr. James Creed Meredith. Oxford University Press, 1952.

Kocher, Thomas D. "Adaptive Evolution and Explosive Speciation." *Nature Reviews Genetics* 5 (2004): 288–298.

Korsmeyer, Carolyn. *Savoring Disgust: The Foul and the Fair in Aesthetics*. Oxford University Press, 2011.

Massaad, Firas, Thierry M. Lejeune, and Christine Detrembleur. "The Up and Down of Human Walking: A Compromise between Muscle Work and Efficiency." *Journal of Physiology* 582 (2007): 789–799.

McKaye, Kenneth, Svata M. Louda, and Jay R. Stauffer Jr. "Bower Size and Male Reproductive Success in a Cichlid Fish Lek." *American Naturalist* 135, no. 5 (1990): 597–613.

Pitcher, George. "Hart on Action and Responsibility." *Philosophical Review* 69, no. 2 (1960): 226–235.

Raz, Amir, Jin Fan, and Michael I. Posner. "Hypnotic Suggestion Reduces Conflict in the Human Brain." *Proceedings of the National Academy of Sciences* 102, no. 28 (2005): 9978–9983.

Raz, Amir, and Natasha K. J. Campbell. "Can Suggestion Obviate Reading? Supplementing Primary Stroop Evidence with Exploratory Negative Priming Analyses." *Consciousness and Cognition* 20, no. 2 (2011): 312–320.

Rolston, Holmes, III. "Aesthetic Experience in Forests." *Journal of Aesthetics and Art Criticism* 56, no. 2 (1998): 157–166.

Singer, Peter. *Practical Ethics*, third edition. Cambridge University Press, 2011.

Slingerland, Edward. *Effortless Action: Wu-Wei as Conceptual Metaphor and Spiritual Ideal in Early China*. Oxford University Press, 2007.

Sneddon, Andrew. *Action and Responsibility*. Springer, 2006.

Solvay, E. "On the Organisation and the Possibility of Self-Organisation of the Chemical Reaction." *Comptes Rendus des Seances de la Société de Biologie et de ses Filiales* 58 (1906): 785–787.

Uy, Albert C. "Say It with Bowers." *Natural History*, 111, no. 2 (2002): 76–83.

Velleman, J. David. "The Way of the Wanton." In *Practical Identity and Narrative Agency*, ed. Catriona Mackenzie and Kim Atkins. Routledge, 2008.

von Foerster, H. "On Self-Organizing Systems and Their Environments." In *Understanding Understanding: Essays on Cybernetics and Cognition.* Springer, 2003.

Wilson, Mark. "Critical Notice: John Earman's *A Primer on Determinism*." *Philosophy of Science* 56, no. 3 (1989): 502–532.

Contributors

Stephen C. Angle   received his BA from Yale University in East Asian studies and his PhD in philosophy from the University of Michigan. Since 1994 he has taught at Wesleyan University, where he is now professor of philosophy. In March of 2010, at the University of Michigan, he presented the inaugural Tang Junyi Lecture, some aspects of which find their way into his article in the present volume. In the summer of 2008, with Michael Slote, he co-directed a National Endowment for the Humanities Summer Seminar on "Traditions into Dialogue: Confucianism and Contemporary Virtue Ethics," which also lies behind his chapter in this volume. He is a recipient of a Fulbright Research Grant, a Millicent C. McIntosh Fellowship, a Chiang Ching-Kuo Postdoctoral Research Fellowship, and the Binswanger Prize for Excellence in Teaching, and is a past president of the International Society for Comparative Study of Chinese and Western Philosophy. He is the author of *Human Rights and Chinese Thought: A Cross-Cultural Inquiry* (Cambridge University Press, 2002), *Sagehood: The Contemporary Significance of Neo-Confucian Philosophy* (Oxford University Press, 2009), and *Contemporary Confucian Political Philosophy: Toward Progressive Confucianism* (Polity, 2012), a co-editor and co-translator, with Marina Svensson, of *The Chinese Human Rights Reader* (M. E. Sharpe, 2001), and a co-editor, with Michael Slote, of *Virtue Ethics and Confucianism* (Routledge, 2013).

Tongdong Bai 白彤东   is Dongfang Chair Professor in the School of Philosophy at Fudan University. He holds a bachelor's degree in nuclear physics and a master's degree in philosophy of science from Peking University and a doctoral degree in philosophy from Boston University. He was tenured associate professor at Xavier University in Cincinnati before moving to Fudan University. His research interests include Chinese philosophy and political philosophy, especially the comparative and present-day relevance of classical Chinese political philosophy. He has published numerous articles in Chinese journals and a monograph titled 旧邦新命——古今中西参照下的古典儒家政治哲学 (*A New Mission of an Old State: The Comparative and Contemporary Relevance of Classical Confucian Political Philosophy* (Peking University

Press, 2009). A revised version of the latter in English is under review for its presentation in the English speaking world. He has also published *China: The Political Philosophy of the Middle Kingdom* (Zed Books, 2012), an introduction to traditional Chinese political philosophy that presents it from a comparative perspective and demonstrates its present-day relevance. At Fudan, he launched an MA program and a program for visiting students in Chinese philosophy, with courses taught in English. That program has proved to be the most successful of its kind—in terms of the number and quality of the students—in China.

Brian Bruya is associate professor of philosophy at Eastern Michigan University and center associate at the University of Michigan's Center for Chinese Studies. His work focuses on bringing insights from Chinese philosophy into contemporary action theory, with implications for metaphysical theories of action, the cognitive science of action and attention, as well as the fields of aesthetics, ethics, and education. A recipient of several research awards at Eastern Michigan University, he has been a Templeton Senior Fellow in Positive Psychology at the University of Pennsylvania, a Tang Junyi Visiting Scholar at the University of Michigan, and a Fulbright Scholar at National Taiwan University. His representative works are the edited volume *Effortless Attention: A New Perspective in the Cognitive Science of Attention and Action* (MIT Press, 2010) and "The Rehabilitation of Spontaneity" (in *Philosophy East and West*, 2010).

Owen Flanagan is James B. Duke Professor of Philosophy at Duke University. He works in philosophy of mind, ethics, moral psychology, and cross-cultural philosophy. Among his influential publications are *The Bodhisattva's Brain: Buddhism Naturalized* (MIT Press, 2011), *The Really Hard Problem: Meaning in a Material World* (MIT Press, 2007), *Consciousness Reconsidered* (MIT Press, 1992), and *Varieties of Moral Personality: Ethics and Psychological Realism* (Harvard University Press, 1991). He has published articles on Mozi and Han Fei in the *Journal of Chinese Philosophy*. In 2014, he gave the 78th Aquinas Lecture at Marquette University (published by Marquette University Press in 2014 under the title *Moral Sprouts and Moral Teleologies: 21st Century Moral Psychology Meets Classical Chinese Philosophy*).

Steven Geisz is associate professor of philosophy and chair of the Department of Philosophy and Religion at the University of Tampa. He has published papers on classical Chinese philosophy, philosophy of mind, and political philosophy. His current research focuses on body practices such as qigong and haṭha yoga that purport to have ties to various Chinese and Indian philosophical and religious traditions, examining the ways in which these practices—either in their historical forms or in their contemporary popular manifestations—can be seen as embodied philosophies. He is a certified full instructor in the Healing Tao qigong system of Mantak Chia and a student in the Qigong Research & Practice Center teacher-training program of Ken Cohen, as well as a 200-hour Registered Yoga Teacher (200-RYT), having trained at the

Kripalu Center for Yoga & Health in Stockbridge, Massachusetts. He holds a BA in biological sciences and philosophy from the University of Maryland Baltimore County and a PhD in philosophy from Duke University.

Stephen Hetherington is professor of philosophy at the University of New South Wales. He was educated at the universities of Sydney, Oxford, and Pittsburgh. He has written seven books, including *Good Knowledge, Bad Knowledge* (Oxford University Press, 2001), *Self-Knowledge* (Broadview, 2007), *Yes, But How Do you Know?* (Broadview, 2009), and *How To Know* (Wiley-Blackwell, 2011), and has edited four books, including *Epistemology Futures* (Oxford University Press, 2006) and *Epistemology: The Key Thinkers* (Continuum, 2012). The author of more than seventy papers (published or forthcoming) on metaphysics and on epistemology, he is a Fellow of the Australian Academy of the Humanities and he is editor-in-chief of the *Australasian Journal of Philosophy*.

Philip J. Ivanhoe (PhD, Stanford University) is Chair Professor of East Asian and Comparative Philosophy and Religion at City University of Hong Kong, where he also serves as director of the Center for East Asian and Comparative Philosophy and the Laboratory on Korean Philosophy in Comparative Perspectives. He specializes in the history of East Asian philosophy and religion and their potential for contemporary ethics. Among his published monographs are *Confucian Moral Self Cultivation* (Hackett, 2000), *Ethics in the Confucian Tradition* (Hackett, 2002), and *Confucian Reflections* (Routledge, 2013). He also has published many articles and book chapters, including "Human Nature and Moral Understanding in Xunzi" (*International Philosophical Quarterly*), "Nature, Awe, and the Sublime," (*Midwest Studies in Philosophy*), and "Was Zhuangzi a Relativist?" in *Essays on Skepticism, Relativism and Ethics in the Zhuangzi* (SUNY Press, 1996), and a number of translations, including *The Daodejing of Laozi* (Hackett, 2003), *The Essays and Letters of Zhang Xuecheng* (Stanford University Press, 2009), and *Master Sun's Art of War* (Hackett, 2011). His numerous edited volumes include *Readings in Classical Chinese Philosophy* (with Bryan Van Norden; Hackett, 2005), *Working Virtue: Virtue Ethics and Contemporary Moral Problems* (with Rebecca Walker; Oxford University Press, 2007), and *Readings in the Lu-Wang School of Neo-Confucianism* (Hackett, 2009).

Karyn L. Lai is associate professor of philosophy at the University of New South Wales. Her primary research is in pre-Qin Confucian and Daoist philosophies. Her work is often of a comparative nature, drawing insights from Chinese philosophies to address issues in moral philosophy, environmental ethics, reasoning, argumentation, and epistemology. She is currently working on epistemology in the Confucian *Analects*, proposing that a particular conception of knowing—"knowing to"—is better suited to capturing the *Analects'* emphasis on exemplary lives in actual contexts. Her investigations may prompt a reconsideration of knowing-how in epistemology in Western philosophy. She intends to extend these investigations to other traditions in pre-Qin philosophy, especially to Daoism. She is the author of *Learning from Chinese Philosophies* (Ashgate, 2006), *Introduction to Chinese Philosophy* (Cambridge University Press, 2008), and numerous articles in scholarly journals. She is editor of *Philosophy Compass* (Chinese Comparative Philosophy Section), associate editor of the *Australasian Journal of Philosophy*, co-editor of the *Stanford Encyclopedia of Philosophy* (Chinese philosophy section), and assistant editor of *Sophia: International Journal of Philosophy and Traditions*.

Bo Mou 牟博 is professor of philosophy and former director (2007-2013) of the Center for Comparative Philosophy at San Jose State University. A former president (2002–2005) of the International Society for Comparative Studies of Chinese and Western Philosophy, he serves as editor in chief of the journal *Comparative Philosophy*. After receiving a B.S. degree in mathematics, he obtained an MA in philosophy at the Graduate School of the Chinese Academy of Social Sciences and an MA and a PhD at the University of Rochester. He has published in analytic philosophy and in Chinese and comparative philosophy, addressing issues in philosophy of language, metaphysics, epistemology, philosophical methodology, and ethics. He is the author of the monographs *Substantive Perspectivism* (Springer, 2009) and *Chinese Philosophy A–Z* (Edinburgh University Press, 2009). His articles on Tarski and Quine have been published in *Synthese* and in the *Southern Journal of Philosophy*. He has edited several volumes in comparative philosophy, including *Comparative Approaches to Chinese Philosophy* (Ashgate, 2003), *Davidson's Philosophy and Chinese Philosophy* (Brill, 2006), *Searle's Philosophy and Chinese Philosophy* (Brill, 2008), and *History of Chinese Philosophy* (Routledge, 2009). He is editor and primary translator of 真理、意義與方法:戴維森哲學文選 (*Truth, Meaning and Method: Selections from Donald Davidson*; Commercial Press, 2008).

Donald J. Munro   is professor emeritus of philosophy and of Chinese at the University of Michigan. When he retired, in 1996, he was chair of the Department of Asian Languages and Cultures. He received an A.B. in philosophy from Harvard University and a PhD in Chinese and Japanese (with work in philosophy) from Columbia University. As a graduate student, he studied with Aisin Gioro Yu in Taiwan and with Tang Junyi in Hong Kong. He is the author of an influential trilogy on the concept of human nature throughout the history of Chinese philosophy: *The Concept of Man in Early China* (Stanford University Press, 1969), *The Concept of Man in Contemporary China* (University of Michigan Press, 1977), and *Images of Human Nature: A Sung Portrait* (Princeton University Press, 1988). Since his retirement, as a member of faculty seminars in culture and cognition, evolutionary psychology, and group dynamics at the University of Michigan's Psychology Department, he has developed a basic familiarity with the new cognitive sciences that have relevance to Chinese and Western ethics. In 2006, as the Tang Junyi Visiting Professor at the Chinese University of Hong Kong, he taught and lectured on this topic. In 2008, he published *Ethics in Action: Workable Guidelines for Public and Private Choices* (Chinese University Press).

Hagop Sarkissian conducts research at the intersection of cognitive science, ethics, and classical Chinese philosophy. He uses insights from the cognitive and behavioral sciences to explore questions concerning moral psychology, moral agency, and the status of morality and to consider how culture may shape cognition in these domains. In addition to drawing from the empirical sciences, he also uses the tools of experimental psychology. He has authored or co-authored papers published in *Philosophical Studies*, in *Philosopher's Imprint*, in *Mind and Language*, in *Annual Review of Psychology*, in *Philosophy Compass*, in *Review of Philosophy and Psychology*, in *History of Philosophy Quarterly*, in the *Journal of Chinese Philosophy*, and in *Moral Psychology*, volume I: *The Evolution of Morality: Adaptations and Innateness* (MIT Press, 2007). He co-edited (with Jennifer Cole Wright) *Advances in Experimental Moral Psychology* (Bloomsbury, 2014). His works have been translated into Chinese and Korean. Currently he is working on a book-length treatment of the moral psychology of Confucius and its relevance for contemporary normative ethics. He spent the fall of 2006 as a visiting scholar at the Research Centre for Chinese Philosophy and Culture at the Chinese University of Hong Kong, and the fall of 2012 as a visiting scholar at the Center for Human Evolution, Cognition, and Culture at the University of British Columbia. He holds a BA in philosophy and East Asian studies and an MA in East Asian studies from the University of Toronto, and a PhD in philosophy from Duke University. He teaches at Baruch College of the City University of New York.

Bongrae Seok is associate professor of philosophy at Alvernia University. He received his BA from Seoul National University (South Korea) and his MA and PhD from the University of Arizona, where he studied philosophy and cognitive science. As a postdoctoral research fellow in the Neural Systems, Memory, and Aging program at the University of Arizona, he conducted research on the functional specialization of the dorsolateral prefrontal cortex. His primary research interests lie in philosophy of mind, cognitive science, Asian comparative philosophy, and moral psychology. He has published books and articles on cognitive modularity, cultural psychology, Confucian moral psychology, moral nativism, and moral reasoning. His book on cognitive peculiarities of the human mind, *Logic and Psycho-Logic* (Seo Kwang Sa, 2003), was selected as one of the recommended academic books of 2004 by South Korea's Ministry of Culture, Sports, and Tourism. His recent book *Embodied Moral Psychology and Confucian Philosophy* (Lexington, 2013) analyzes Confucian moral philosophy from the perspectives of embodied emotion, social cognition, and moral intuition. His current work focuses on several interdisciplinary and comparative topics (including embodied and affective moral intuition, relational categorization and taxonomic reasoning, and cultural psychology of rationality and probabilistic reasoning) that bring the ancient wisdom of Asian philosophy to the forefront of cognitive science.

Kwong-loi Shun 信廣來 has been a professor of philosophy and an academic administrator at the University of California at Berkeley, the University of Toronto, and the Chinese University of Hong Kong. He has now returned to teaching at UC Berkeley, and is currently working a multi-volume project on Confucian ethics. The first volume, *Mencius and Early Chinese Thought*, was published by Stanford University Press in 1997. A manuscript of the second volume, *Zhu Xi and Later Confucian Thought*, is under revision, and the third volume, *From Philology to Philosophy*, is close to completion. The fourth volume, *On Self and Self Transformation*, will discuss a central theme in Confucian moral psychology, and the fifth volume, *A Study in Confucian Ethics*, will provide a primarily philosophical discussion of Confucian ethics.

David B. Wong is the Susan Fox Beischer and George D. Beischer Professor of Philosophy at Duke University. He has written two books in contemporary ethical theory that incorporate Chinese philosophy: *Moral Relativity* (University of California Press, 1984) and *Natural Moralities: A Defense of Pluralistic Relativism* (Oxford University Press, 2006). He has co-edited *Confucian Ethics: A Comparative Study of Self, Autonomy and Community* (Cambridge University Press, 2004). His published articles include "Coping with Moral Conflict and Ambiguity" (*Ethics*, 1992), "Moral Reasons: Internal and External" (*Philosophy and Phenomenological Research*, 2006), "Zhuangzi and the Obsession with Being Right" (*History of Philosophy Quarterly*, 2005), and "Is There a Distinction between Reason and Emotion in Mencius?" (*Philosophy East and West*, 1991). His other publications include *"Naturalizing Ethics"* (with Owen Flanagan and Hagop Sarkissian), in *Moral Psychology*, volume 1: *The Evolution of Morality: Adaptations and Innateness* (MIT Press, 2007), and "How Are Moral Conversions Possible?" in *In Search of Goodness* (Chicago University Press, 2011).

Brook A. Ziporyn is a scholar of ancient and medieval Chinese religion and philosophy. He received his BA in East Asian Languages and Civilizations from the University of Chicago, and his PhD from the University of Michigan. Before joining the faculty of the Divinity School at the University of Chicago, he taught Chinese philosophy and religion at the University of Michigan, at Northwestern University, at Harvard University, and at the National University of Singapore. He is the author of six published books: *Evil and/or/as the Good: Omnicentrism, Intersubjectivity, and Value Paradox in Tiantai Buddhist Thought* (Harvard University Press, 2000), *The Penumbra Unbound: The Neo-Taoist Philosophy of Guo Xiang* (SUNY Press, 2003), *Being and Ambiguity: Philosophical Experiments with Tiantai Buddhism* (Open Court, 2004), *Zhuangzi: The Essential Writings with Selections from Traditional Commentaries* (Hackett,

2009), *Ironies of Oneness and Difference: Coherence in Early Chinese Thought; Prolegomena to the Study of Li* (SUNY Press, 2012), and *Beyond Oneness and Difference: Li and Coherence in Chinese Buddhist Thought and its Antecedents* (SUNY Press, 2013). He is currently working on a cross-cultural inquiry into the themes of death, time and perception (tentatively titled *Against Being Here Now*) and on a book-length exposition of atheism as a form of religious and mystical experience in the intellectual histories of Europe, India, and China.

Index

Citations of notes followed by brackets refer the reader back to the text for which there is an endnote. For example, 91n77[82] refers to a citation in note 77 on page 91 addressing a relevant passage on page 82. Page numbers in *italic* followed by *f*, such as *74f3.1*, refer to figures.

Abrahamic monotheism. *See also* Christianity; Islam
 heaven of distinguished from *tian*, xxvii, 207, 210, 220n14
 intolerance associated with, xxi, 205–206, 211–213
 moral law traced to, 205–207, 219nn2,3, 219–220n6, 223n28
Ackerman, Bruce, 106, 116n28
Ackerman, Joshua M., 355–356
action. *See also* autotelicity; *dao-shu-qi-wu*
 in Aristotle, 344–345, 353
 and flow (or autotelicity), 339, 340, 351–356
 and guidance, 339–340, 345, 348, 354
 and knowledge, 80
 natural human. *See* natural human action
 new perspective from the Chinese philosophical traditions and, xxiv, 358
 without agency, xxiii, xxiv, 339–340, 344–345, 353
 in Zhuangzi, 339, 351, 354, 356
aesthetics and aesthetic value
 aesthetic appreciation, 340–345, 353, 357
 beauty-appreciating "organ(s)," 334n60
 and Lao-Zhuang naturalism, 310, 332–333n55, 358

natural origins vs. artifice, 340, 342, 344–345, 353–354, 359n10
 and *qi*, 362n58[358]
 of ritual behavior, 215–216, 223n28
agency
 and action, 348, 353–354
 and Frankfurt's paradigm of action under guidance, 339–340, 354
 moral agency, xxi, 68
 and natural laws, 344–345
 political agency, 111, 172
 sense of agency/volition, 347–349, 349–352, 353–354
 true. *See* epistemology
 without agency, 339, 340, 345
altruism. *See also* oneness hypothesis
 and caring. *See* care ethics
 Confucian, 125, 142, 149
 and empathy, 127, 140
 empathy-altruism hypothesis, xxii, 232–233, 238, 240–242, 244
 and oneness, xxii, 238–242, 244
 and partiality, 129
 psychological, 232, 241
 and *qin* (love of kin), 127, 132, 137, 138